MAKING MALA

MALAITA IN SOLOMON ISLANDS,
1870s–1930s

MAKING MALA

MALAITA IN SOLOMON ISLANDS, 1870s–1930s

CLIVE MOORE

PRESS

PACIFIC SERIES

Published by ANU Press
The Australian National University
Acton ACT 2601, Australia
Email: anupress@anu.edu.au
This title is also available online at press.anu.edu.au

National Library of Australia Cataloguing-in-Publication entry

Creator: Moore, Clive, 1951- author.

Title: Making Mala : Malaita in Solomon Islands, 1870s-1930s / Clive Moore.

ISBN: 9781760460976 (paperback) 9781760460983 (ebook)

Subjects: Malaita Province (Solomon Islands)--History.
Malaita Province (Solomon Islands)--Social life and customs.
Malaita Province (Solomon Islands)--Civilization.

All rights reserved. No part of this publication may be reproduced, stored in a retrieval system or transmitted in any form or by any means, electronic, mechanical, photocopying or otherwise, without the prior permission of the publisher.

Cover design and layout by ANU Press. Front cover image: The chief's brother at Bulalaha, southwest Malaita. Photograph by John Beattie, 1906.

This edition © 2017 ANU Press

Contents

List of Illustrations vii

List of Tables xvii

Acknowledgements xix

Abbreviations xxiii

A Note on Spelling Malaitan Words xxv

Introduction: Malaitan Tropes 1

1. Malaita in Recent Centuries 39
2. Trade and Labour 83
3. Malaitan Christians Overseas, 1880s–1910s 139
4. The Melanesian Mission, 1877–1909 183
5. Abu`ofa and the Exodus from Queensland, 1894–1908 231
6. From QKM to SSEM, 1904–09 261
7. Qaibala: Establishing `Aoke Station, 1909–14 301
8. Labour, the Malayta Company and Catholicism 335
9. Koburu: William Bell, 1915–27 363
10. Making Mala into Malaita, 1927–42 405

Conclusion: Tropes, *Kastom* and the Modern Solomon Islands 449

Bibliography 461

Index 521

List of Illustrations

Figures

Figure Introduction 1: High Commissioner Sir Robert Stanley at the inauguration of the first Malaita Council in 1952 19

Figure Introduction 2: Salana Ga`a, the first President of the first Malaita Council, and some of its members in 1952 20

Figure Introduction 3: Two of the Malaita Eagles, with weapons 26

Figure Introduction 4: Destroying Dodo Creek Agricultural Station in 2000 26

Figure Introduction 5: Honiara's Chinatown burning during the riots in April 2006 27

Figure Introduction 6: Ishmael Idumaoma Itea (*circa* 1904–2005) at Sango, Fataleka, 1988. 30

Figure Introduction 7: Noel Fatnowna (1929–91) and Rex Ringi Angofia in Honiara in 1988. 30

Figure Introduction 8: Three east Fataleka leaders in the Bubuileli Council House, 1976. 31

Figure 1.1: Malaitan plank-built ocean-going canoe from Langalanga Lagoon 49

Figure 1.2: Malaitan women and children in dugout canoes near one of the artificial islands, possibly in Lau Lagoon 50

Figure 1.3: Maasupa Village, Maro`umasike (Takataka or Deep Bay), east `Are`are, 1970s. 52

Figure 1.4: Langalanga women using hand drills to make holes in the process of making *akwala`afi* shell wealth in 1933 57

vii

Figure 1.5: Langalanga women grinding shells to make *akwala`afi* during a 1998 demonstration of shell wealth manufacture for tourists on Gwaelaga Island 58

Figure 1.6: Lobotalau rolls up his *bata* after a mortuary feast for the death of Na`oni`au at `Ai`eda in east Kwaio in August 1996 ... 58

Figure 1.7: Porpoise hunting at Bita`ama, north Malaita, early 1960s. 60

Figure 1.8: Gwali Asi of Sulufou artificial island was an important bigman in Lau Lagoon early in the twentieth century 61

Figure 1.9: A large hamlet in central Kwaio, inland from Sinalagu, in `Oloburi Harbour's watershed. Two men's houses sit at the upper reaches 62

Figure 1.10: A well-built hamlet at `Ai`eda, inland from Sinalagu in Kwaio, at 853 metres (2,800 feet) above sea level 68

Figure 1.11: `Are`are woman wearing traditional jewellery and smoking a pipe, 1969 69

Figure 1.12: `Are`are woman and child, 1969 70

Figure 1.13: Bush women at Roas Bay, south Malaita, 1906. 72

Figure 1.14: Sacrificial altar at Ferasubua Island in Lau Lagoon, 1906 77

Figure 2.1: Christie Fatnowna with the model ship made by Jack Marau 84

Figure 2.2: John Renton managed to get this piece of wood with its message on both sides to the *Bobtail Nag* in August 1875. 95

Figure 2.3: An illustration of the *Peri* survivors being picked up by HMS *Basilisk* off the coast of Queensland in early 1872 ... 104

Figure 2.4: Recruiting at Maanakwai in north Malaita 108

Figure 2.5: Malaita men in the 1920s at the age typical of labour recruits 108

Figure 2.6: This photograph from Bundaberg in 1889 is of the *Helena*, a 126-ton schooner, which made 40 voyages from 1882–99, and the *May*, a 237-ton schooner, which made 15 voyages from 1888–94 114

LIST OF ILLUSTRATIONS

Figure 2.7: There are no known photographs of accommodations below decks. On the early voyages it would have been much more basic. This sketch is by William Wawn, who was a captain in the labour trade from 1875 to 1894. It probably depicts one of his 1880s ships 117

Figure 2.8: Men from Guadalcanal and Malaita on Foulden plantation at Mackay, Queensland, in the 1870s 118

Figure 2.9: At Mackay, Hugh Hossack owned one of the larger 'Kanaka stores', shops that catered predominantly to Islanders. They bought their trade boxes and their contents there, and were allowed to store their possessions there. The photograph shows how central Islanders were to Hossack's trade, and his relationship with them 122

Figure 2.10: This photograph, of a Malaitan canoe in Fiji, presumably manufactured and decorated there, is one of the most remarkable from the overseas plantations. The image, from a collection by A.M. Brodziack & Co., was probably taken in the 1880s. The canoe is in Walu Bay, an old local shipping area and Solomon Islander settlement 137

Figure 2.11: Malaitans at Innisfail in north Queensland early in the 1900s. The slit-drum and the bows and arrows would have been made in Queensland 138

Figure 3.1: Queensland Kanaka Mission baptism by full emersion, Johnstone River, Geraldton (Innisfail), 1906 146

Figure 3.2: Students at Mary Robinson's Anglican Selwyn Mission when it operated from Marian in the Pioneer Valley west of Mackay. The photograph dates from the 1890s when William Wawn visited 154

Figure 3.3: Many mission photographs are of groups of men, though women and children also attended services and classes. This group is at the Selwyn Mission in 1905. 156

Figure 3.4: The congregation at St Marys Church at Pioneer, outside Mackay, in the early 1900s. 157

Figure 3.5: One of the Islanders' grass-roofed churches in north Queensland, possibly the one at Cordelia Mount 158

ix

Figure 3.6: The Churches of Christ Mission Hall in the Isis,
with John Thompson's house alongside 167

Figure 3.7: Rev. McIntyre with his Sunday school class,
Presbyterian Mission at Walkerston 168

Figure 3.8: This photograph is thought to be of the Methodist
mission to Islanders in Fiji 174

Figure 3.9: Kwailiu Fatnowna and his wife Orrani and family
at Mackay in 1906, not long before his death. 181

Figure 4.1: St Andrew's College, Kohimarama, Auckland,
New Zealand. A small number of Malaitan students were
there between 1862 and 1867. 198

Figure 4.2: The Melanesian Mission school at Uru,
east Malaita, 1906 200

Figure 4.3: Clement Marau and Joseph Wate`ae`pule
in about 1890 205

Figure 4.4: The new church built at Fiu, 1904 212

Figure 4.5: A food storage house at `Adagege Island,
Kwaisulia's stronghold in Lau Lagoon, 1906. 220

Figure 4.6: Rev. Arthur Hopkins's mission house at Ngorefou,
Lau Lagoon, 1906 222

Figures 4.7–8: Outside and inside the mission palisade
at Ngorefou, 1906 222

Figure 4.9: St Barnabas College staff and students,
Norfolk Island, 1906 227

Figure 4.10: Interior of the St Barnabas College dining room,
Norfolk Island 228

Figure 5.1: Peter Abu`ofa in middle age 233

Figure 5.2: Men and youths of `Adagege, Kwaisulia's island,
Lau Lagoon, 1906 235

Figure 5.3: The final decision to close the Queensland Kanaka
Mission and reestablish it as the South Sea Evangelical Mission
was made at this religious convention at Katoomba,
New South Wales, in 1904. 244

LIST OF ILLUSTRATIONS

Figure 5.4: The 12-ton lugger-style *Daphne*, which Florence Young brought with her in 1904. The ship served as the main means of transport for the QKM until the *Evangel* arrived in 1907. 245

Figure 5.5: Florence Young, superintendent of the Queensland Kanaka Mission and the driving force of the South Sea Evangelical Mission until the mid-1920s 246

Figure 5.6: Mrs L.D. Eustace, holding classes at 'Yungaba', the Immigration Depot at Kangaroo Point, Brisbane, 1906 . . . 251

Figure 5.7: Malaitans on the beach just after returned labourers have been landed with their boxes of trade goods, northwest Malaita, 1907. Similar scenes occurred thousands of times between the 1870s and the 1930s. 255

Figure 5.8: A scene of labourers returning to east Kwaio, probably at the site of the present-day SSEC Gounaabusu Village at the southern end of Sinalagu Harbour 258

Figure 6.1: SSEM mission staff and children in the 1910s 263

Figure 6.2: Senior teachers at Baunani in the 1910s 264

Figure 6.3: The SSEM church and school at 'Oloburi, east Malaita . . 268

Figure 6.4: *Evangel*, the first of many SSEM ships of this name. It was built for the mission in Sydney in 1906 and arrived in the Solomons the next year 268

Figure 6.5: Northcote Deck at a river baptism at Maanakwai in north Malaita. 270

Figure 6.6: Much of the religious teaching employed a roll of illustrated Bible stories. Here Northcote Deck and his staff carry a roll as they go ashore to preach at Fouia in Lau Lagoon 274

Figure 6.7: The newly constructed SSEM mission house at Onepusu, west Malaita, probably in 1905 276

Figure 6.8: Malu'u mission house, north Malaita, probably in the 1910s. 278

Figure 6.9: Feriasi SSEM mission station on the mainland opposite Kwai and Ngongosila, east Malaita. 282

Figure 6.10: The SSEM mission station on Ngongosila Island, east Malaita 284

Figure 6.11: Street scene in the women's quarters on Ferasubua Island, Lau Lagoon, 1906. 287

Figure 7.1: The residency, the Malaita resident magistrate's (later the district officer's) house, and the office built for Thomas Edge-Partington in 1910 316

Figure 7.2: The police commander's house at 'Aoke, built for Frederick M. Campbell in 1912. 319

Figure 7.3: Malaita's first protectorate official, Resident Magistrate Thomas Edge-Partington, with the Armed Constabulary 324

Figure 7.4: Men from an inland village around 1910 325

Figure 7.5: Mary Edge-Partington in the living room of the resident magistrate's house, 'Aoke, 1913 or 1914. 331

Figure 7.6: 'Aoke police barracks and tennis court, pre-1915 332

Figure 7.7: 'Aoke hospital in about 1914 333

Figure 8.1: On board a recruiting vessel in about 1914. 339

Figure 8.2: The river mouth at Baunani, showing the young coconut palms on the Malayta Company plantation 346

Figure 8.3: SSEM teachers at Manaba, part of the Malayta Company plantation 349

Figure 8.4: The Baunani labour line accommodation sometime before 1914 351

Figure 8.5: Arisimae, the most feared *ramo* in 'Are'are 357

Figure 8.6: Two brothers, Donatien and Jean Coicaud, served as Catholic priests on Malaita. This is Donatien and one of his congregation, probably from the late 1910s at Buma 358

Figure 9.1: William Bell with his police 364

Figure 9.2: William Bell on patrol by canoe 367

Figure 9.3: Three of William Bell's police 369

Figure 9.4: In 1921 the protectorate provided the Malaita administration with its own patrol vessel, the *Auki*. 379

LIST OF ILLUSTRATIONS

Figure 9.5: An elderly Peter Abu`ofa in a SSEM group photograph with his rival Shem Irofa`alu (later a key Maasina Rule leader), among others, probably from the 1920s. 386

Figure 9.6: A game of cricket at `Aoke during William Bell's years as district officer 394

Figure 9.7: Waterfront view of Onepusu, the SSEM headquarters, in the late 1920s or 1930s 400

Figure 9.8: School boys drilling at the SSEM Onepusu School, 1922 403

Figure 10.1: A member of the 'Whiskey Army' expedition, possibly one of the crew from HMS *Adelaide* sent from Australia to support the 1927 government expedition to east Kwaio. The Malaitan man is from Kwaio. 409

Figure 10.2: Feeding the labourers and police who accompanied the punitive expedition to east Kwaio, 1927. 411

Figure 10.3: Lining up to pay taxes at Maro`umasike (Takataka or Deep Bay), southeastern `Are`are, about 1936. A policeman stands on the right. 417

Figure 10.4: Hospital of the Epiphany at Fauaabu, northwest Malaita in the 1930s 420

Figure 10.5: Qaibaita leper colony, the first in Solomon Islands, was established in 1929 as an outstation of the Hospital of the Epiphany at Fauaabu. In the 1930s it was moved closer, to a new site overlooking the hospital 421

Figure 10.6: Patients at the Hospital of the Epiphany at Fauaabu . . . 422

Figure 10.7: Training a young boy as a dresser (an orderly) at the Hospital of the Epiphany at Fauaabu 422

Figure 10.8: SSEM girls' school at Onepusu, with Mr and Mrs Cronau and son, and Miss Dring 425

Figure 10.9: This dance was performed at the Hospital of the Epiphany at Fauaabu in the early 1930s. 444

Figure 10.10: Peter Abu`ofa in old age working on carving a slit drum. By the time Abu`ofa died in 1937 he had become alienated from the SSEM, which he helped found 446

Maps

Map 1: Solomon Islands. 1

Map 2: Malaitan topography, passages, bays and place names. 40

Map 3: Called Greater Bukida by some archaeologists, one long island once stretched from Buka to Isabel, with Guadalcanal almost joined to it, but never Malaita, which was within easy reach but required a sea crossing. 44

Map 4: Malaita languages and dialects. Guala`ala`a is the language of Kwai and Ngongosila, and is also used for trade along the east coast 47

Map 5: East Fataleka migration patterns from Bina to Fokanakafo Bay, according to oral testimony in the 1970s 65

Map 6: The Malaitan 'eight isles' world and the extent of the trading area for Malaitan shell valuables. 75

Map 7: Shipping routes between eastern Australia and Asia in the eighteenth and nineteenth centuries. 88

Map 8: Sketch of Port Adam from the visit of HMS *Havannah* in 1850 98

Map 9: Typical recruiting voyages around Malaita, 1881–95 115

Map 10: Typical recruiting voyages around Malaita, 1897–1900 . . . 116

Map 11: Sugarcane growing areas in Queensland and New South Wales 141

Map 12: Early Melanesian Mission bases, 1877–1909 202

Map 13: Major SSEM and Malayta Company plantation bases on Malaita 262

Map 14: Major foreign bases on Malaita, 1910 315

Map 15: The 24 kilometres of Malayta Company land claims along the west coast of Malaita in 1920 347

Map 16: Major settlements around Malaita, 1930s. 412

Map 17: By the mid-1920s, the SSEM had spread throughout Malaita and Makira, with other bases on Guadalcanal, the Russell Islands and Rennell and Bellona Islands 426

LIST OF ILLUSTRATIONS

Plan

Plan 1: Gender divisions in Malaitan houses, villages and canoes, and garden design 71

Graphs

Graph 1: Migration of Pacific Islanders to Queensland, 1863–1905, showing total migration, and numbers from Solomon Islands and from Malaita Island. The black section indicates Malaitan recruiting... 113

Graph 2: Migration of Pacific Islanders to Queensland, 1863–1904, showing ships' voyages that visited Malaita Island 113

Graph 3: BSIP annual labour statistics, 1924–39 416

List of Tables

Table 1: Solomon Islander indentured labourers in Queensland
and Fiji, 1870–1911 102

Table 2: Estimate of major Pacific Islander populations
in Queensland, 1891 and 1901 143

Table 3: Malaitans baptised overseas before 1910 177

Table 4: Major QKM and SSEM bases and schools,
Malaita Island, 1895–1906 270

Table 5: Internal labour trade in Solomon Islands, 1913–40 336

Table 6: Labour employed in Solomon Islands, 31 March 1911 338

Table 7: BSIP annual labour statistics, 1924–39 415

Acknowledgements

This book has had an overly long gestation. Some of the research materials go back 40 years to my doctoral thesis begun in 1977. Based in Brisbane onwards from 1987, I was able to visit Honiara for a week or two a year, slowly burrowing into the British Solomon Islands Protectorate Archives in the National Archives of Solomon Islands. Since the archive had no photocopy machine, I began by handwriting notes and then graduated to a laptop. Progress changed when I arrived one year with a portable photocopy machine, and again when I had access to a photocopy machine belonging to the Leung family at Acor (The Bookshop). On two occasions I was able to stay with Hudson, Hadley and Andrew Leung, for which I thank them greatly. They have remained long-term friends. Eventually, I received an Australian Research Council Discovery Grant for the project and in 2005 was able to employ Karlyn Tekalu as a research assistant for several weeks; using two digital cameras we took 35,000 digital images and revolutionised the rate of progress. Through all of this I was aided by many staff at the archives and I am grateful for their interest and assistance.

I have also used the Queensland State Archives, the National Archives of Australia, the Western Pacific Archives at the University of Auckland, the Mitchell Library of the New South Wales State Library, the John Oxley Library of the Queensland State Library and the library of the University of Queensland. I thank all of their staff. Work in archives and libraries has been an essential part of the research process, but so too have been Solomon Islanders, particularly the people of Malaita. Since 1975, I have been a friend of the Fatnowna family in Mackay, particularly Noel and Minnie Fatnowna and Charles and Kay Fatnowna and their families. Through Noel, I was introduced to Ishmael Itea and Charles Luiramo, brothers from Fataleka in east Malaita. Incredibly fortunate to have met them, I was adopted into the Rakwane extended family and have friendships crossing three generations. Without them, this study would have been impossible. In Honiara, my thanks go to extensions of the Rakwane descent group: Ella and John Ru`ugwata Kaliuae, Caroline and John Maetia Kaliuae, David and Enta Kaliuae, Rex Ringi Angofia, Fred Talo, and Betty and Harry Masae and their families. Trish Dallu was always there to give me wise advice. More recently, the Toa`tee family has befriended me and Henry Billy has taught me a great deal about Malaitans. I was also honoured to become friends with Sir Peter and Lady Margaret Kenilorea and their family and to assist Sir Peter with his autobiography.

I have dealt with four Christian denominations on Malaita, and here several individuals have eased my path. Bishop Terry Brown has assisted with advice on the history of the Anglican Melanesian Mission. During the time it took me to complete this book, his Pacific section of Project Canterbury was created, providing extended knowledge of the documentation of the Diocese of Melanesia. He also facilitated my access to photographs held by his church. I would like to thank Patricia and Stuart Braga for their kindness and cooperation in talking to me about the Young and Deck families. The papers of Norman Deck, documenting the South Sea Evangelical Mission in Solomon Islands, were lent to the Pacific Manuscript Bureau by Patricia Braga; they were microfilmed (PMB 1253) in August 2005 and then transferred to the National Library of Australia. Mrs Braga also transferred a fine series of Norman and Northcote Deck's Solomon Islands photographs. I am indebted to her for giving me access to private copies of these photographs, a number of which are reproduced in this book. John Roughan provided an understanding of Catholicism on Malaita. His son Paul and his wife Karlyn have continued the family friendship. Early on, Dennis Steley helped me develop my knowledge of Seventh-day Adventism. I met him in my first week in Honiara in 1976. Many of the Mackay Solomon Islanders are Seventh-day Adventists and through them I learnt to understand the church.

Several Malaita anthropologists have assisted me: Ian Hogbin, Roger Keesing, Pierre Maranda, Daniel de Coppet, Pei-yi Guo, Ian Frazer and, in particular, Ben Burt and David Akin. Ben Burt has prepared a range of books on the Kwara`ae and most recently has produced a pictorial history of Malaita (2015) that will serve as a model for similar studies in the Pacific. Ben has been supportive and enabled access to many images held by the British Museum. David Akin has been a colleague and a friend for many years, generous with his editorial skills, his detailed knowledge of Malaita and his critical insight. Recently, he pointed out an instance of my failure to see beyond missionary rhetoric. If I am allowed to mangle metaphors, I thank him for untangling my foot from the collective missionary mouth. He is equally as sharp in his ability to cut through the rhetoric of various district officers.

Making Mala does not stand alone and is supported by the considerable body of literature on Malaita and Malaitans, and more generally on Solomon Islands and the Pacific. This book has benefited enormously from earlier publications, and not only those focused on Malaita. I would like to acknowledge Judith Bennett's *Wealth of the Solomons* (1987), the only historical study of the protectorate as a whole. Based on meticulous research, her book provides necessary wider context and analysis. David Akin, an anthropologist whose skills include archival research, has provided new depths of understanding of Malaitan history in his *Colonialism, Maasina Rule, and the Origins of Malaitan Kastom* (2013). Akin tracks over some of the same period as *Making Mala*, although his focus and perspective—Maasina Rule—is quite different. Twenty years ago, Ben Burt, also an anthropologist, published *Tradition and Christianity* (1994) based on his Kwara`ae research, a fine-grained account of Malaitan Christianity and its relationship to local culture, which has aided my analysis. As well, all scholars of Solomon Islands are beholden to Sally Edridge for her *Solomon Islands Bibliography to 1980* (1985) and to Graeme Golden for his painstaking *The Early European Settlers in the Solomon Islands* (1993). Other useful books are referred to in the text, footnotes and bibliography.

I have used images and photographs drawn by, taken by, or collected by David Akin, William Amherst, John Beattie, Patricia Braga, the British Museum, Terry Brown, Ben Burt, Charles Templeton Crocker, Jock Cromar, John Northcote Deck, Norman Cathcart Deck, the Diocese of Melanesia, Thomas Edge-Partington, Lloyd Francis, Walter Gibbins, Pei-yi Guo, Alison Griffiths, Walter Ivens, James Cook University, Roger Keesing, Robert Lever, Thomas McMahon, W. T. Mann, Peter O'Sullivan, Queensland Museum, Douglas Rannie, L. M. Raucaz, George Rose, Max Quanchi, the State Library of Queensland, James Tedder, John Todd, Philip Vigors, William Wawn, Geoff Willmot, Florence Young and Hugo Zemp. I have permission to use the images, or they are beyond copyright, or I have been unable to trace the original creator. The maps and graphs are either my own work or were created in 1980 by the cartography section of the Geography Department of James Cook University, or by

Robert Cribb or Vincent Verheyen. Vincent also restored some of the photographs and images. My thanks to all of those who have assisted in strengthening the visual side of *Making Mala*.

The Australian Research Council provided me with a Discovery Grant (2005–08). Although I have been slow, they got a bargain: this book (the subject of the grant), the *Solomon Islands Historical Encyclopaedia*, the foundations for editing the Kenilorea autobiography, and two more monographs, on Tulagi and Honiara, now in their final stages. Augmenting Karlyn Tekalu's research work in Honiara, in Brisbane Tony Yeates worked as a research assistant, turning Pacific Manuscript Bureau microfilms back into paper form, a task that has sustained my research ever since. I also want to thank for continued support my colleagues at the University of Queensland, particularly those in the School of Historical and Philosophical Inquiry. Max Quanchi and Brij Lal have been important colleagues and friends over the many years of this project. As ever, my thanks go to Serena Bagley and Judy King for their cheerful assistance whenever my computer got the better of me.

Lastly, I thank Stewart Firth and ANU Press for making this publication possible, and David Akin for his assistance with copyediting.

Clive Moore
Brisbane
December 2016

Abbreviations

A/DO	Acting District Officer
A/RC	Acting Resident Commissioner
AWW	Allen W. Walsh
BC	*Brisbane Courier*
BSIP	British Solomon Islands Protectorate
BSIP AR	*British Solomon Islands Protectorate Annual Report*
CC	Commander-in-Chief
CMW	Charles Morris Woodford
CNFB	Charles N.F. Bengough
CO	Colonial Office
CRMW	Charles R. M. Workman
CS	Colonial Secretary
DO	District Officer
FJB	Frederic J. Barnett
FNA	Francis Noel Ashley
G	Governor
GA	Government Agent
GEDS	George E.D. Sandars
HC	High Commissioner
IA	Immigration Agent
IFM	Isatabu Freedom Movement
IL	Inspector of Labourers
JCB	Jack C. Barley
MEF	Malaita Eagle Force
MM	The *Mackay Mercury* and *South Kennedy Advertiser*

xxiii

MV	Motor Vessel	
NAA	National Archives of Australia	
NIV	*'Not in Vain', What God hath Wrought Amongst South Sea Islanders*. Report of the Queensland Kanaka Mission and the South Sea Evangelical Mission	
NMP	Native Medical Practitioner	
NSW	New South Wales	
OPMM	*Occasional Papers of the Melanesian Mission*	
PMB	Pacific Manuscripts Bureau	
PNG	Papua New Guinea	
QKM	Queensland Kanaka Mission	
Qld	Queensland	
QSA	Queensland State Archives	
QVP	*Queensland Votes and Proceedings*	
RAMSI	Regional Assistance Mission to Solomon Islands	
RC	Resident Commissioner	
RM	Resident Magistrate	
RNAS	Royal Navy Australia Station	
RNZAF	Royal New Zealand Air Force	
RRK	Richard R. Kane	
SCL	*The Southern Cross Log*, journal of the Melanesian Mission	
SDA	Seventh-day Adventist	
SG	Secretary to Government	
SINA	Solomon Islands National Archives	
SSC	Secretary of State for the Colonies	
SSEC	South Sea Evangelical Church	
SSEM	South Sea Evangelical Mission	
TWE-P	Thomas W. Edge-Partington	
US CSD	Under Secretary, Chief Secretary's Department	
WF	William (Wilfred) Fowler	
WFMC	Warren Frederick Martin Clemens	
WPHC	Western Pacific High Commission or Western Pacific High Commissioner	
WRB	William R. Bell	

A Note on Spelling Malaitan Words

I should say at the outset that I am linguistically ill-equipped to write a book about an island with a dozen distinct languages. Ten years ago, as part of preparations for the *Solomon Islands Historical Encyclopaedia, 1893–1978*, and for this book, I began to try to develop a set of standard spellings for Solomon Islands words. It was far from the first attempt, and it is a perpetual challenge. Useful gazetteers of geographic terms exist from colonial times, although they tend not to use glottal stops and indicate sounds in different ways, for example by doubling letters, turning a 'b' into an 'mb', turning a 'd' into 'nd', or using a 'q' to begin a word that today would begin with a 'kw'. I soon realised that there was no standard way, and even anthropologists and linguists have sometimes changed their recording methods. A prime example is the name of Malaita's northern language group: I chose to use To`aba`ita, although it is also written as To`ambaita or Toabaita or To`abaita.

Deciding to try to spell words phonetically as they were used in particular language areas, I contacted several Malaitan academics, foreign anthropologists and linguists who had lived and worked in the various Malaitan-language areas, asking their advice on local variations. The word 'Malaita' is a problem in itself: strictly speaking it should be Mala. There are academics who insist on using the Mala`ita form, but I regard that battle as long lost. 'Malaita' is now too well established to consider anything else. The word that has caused me the most heartache is the name of the provincial headquarters: is it `Aoke or Auki? The modern usage is Auki, but the name comes from nearby `Aoke Island in Langalanga Lagoon, and anyway, the site of `Aoke/Auki was originally called Rarasu. I have held out for `Aoke. I have standardised some things, for instance, the spelling of *fataabu, aofia* and *ramo*, three main leadership roles. I doubt that any reader would put up with me using *ramo, namo* and *lamo*, all standard versions of the same word in different Malaitan languages.

My anthropologist colleague David Akin suggests that two things are crucial: (a) being consistent in how you spell a particular name; and (b) consistency in orthography. His advice, which I have taken, is that if I write 'bina' (which is pronounced with an initial 'm' sound, like all 'b's' in Malaitan languages), I should not then write Mbasikana, or Maana'omba somewhere else. Likewise, 'd' does not need an 'n' written in front of it because all 'd' sounds automatically have an 'n' sound in front of them. To write 'nd' (or 'mb') is simply to add an unnecessary letter. Solomon Islanders are aware of this sound, although outsiders may be more comfortable with the 'nd' or 'mb' rendering.

Another basic rule Akin suggested is that a glottal stop can never be next to a consonant, either before or after, since such sounds do not occur in Malaitan languages. That is, the glottal stop is itself a consonant and consonants are always separated by vowels. (When one sees English consonant pairs such as 'kw', 'gw', 'mw' or 'ng' in the rendering of Malaitan words, they represent single consonant sounds in Malaitan languages.) Many of the misspellings of words with glottal stops in them (including leaving initial glottal stops out) happened because Europeans could not hear glottal stops (particularly initial ones) and so left them out or sometimes just stuck them in willy-nilly. They taught Solomon Islanders the same mistaken spellings. Some Solomon Islanders use no glottal stops in their texts, and many others miswrite glottal stops because they have never been taught how to write them properly, even if they are otherwise literate. Sometimes they insert them where they do not belong in an effort to make up for glottal stops that Europeans have always left out. Solomon Islanders and foreigners alike often add glottal stops in between what is really a long vowel: they turn the word 'laalaa' into 'la'ala'a' because these seem good places to put glottal stops. The Solomon Islands educational system in the past placed little value on local languages, and people were simply trying to find their way on their own. Sadly, the same applies today. The glottal stops are difficult and sometimes subtle. Nonetheless, they can make a big difference in meanings. For example, in most Malaitan languages *uru* means a harbour (and also means to wade, as in water). Uru is now the name of a harbour in east Kwaio, but '*uru* pronounced with an initial glottal stop in the local language there means 'vagina'. Akin tells me that a timeless source of jokes remains when national radio service messages tell people they will be picked up by a canoe at 'Vagina Harbour'.

A NOTE ON SPELLING MALAITAN WORDS

The following is Akin's short pronunciation guide to Malaitan and Solomon Islands Pijin words (slightly modified from Akin 2013a, xvii):

> **a** pronounced as in 'mama'; **b** pronounced mb, as in 'timber'; **d** pronounced nd, as in 'candy'; **e** pronounced as in 'egg'; **g** pronounced ng as in 'mango'; **i** is pronounced like e in 'me'; **o** pronounced as in 'go'; and **u** pronounced as in 'true'.
>
> A glottal stop (`) is a consonant and treated as the last letter of the alphabet. In an index, words with glottal stops at their beginning come last. Doubled vowels are pronounced as lengthened and accented (e.g., Maasina Rule).
>
> Many Malaitan names have English origins—Dio (Joe), Falage (Frank), Biri (Billy), Tome or Tomu (Tom), Sale (Charlie) etc. These can be spelt phonetically by Malaitan pronunciations. These personal names vary by area (following consonant and other language shifts). If a person adopted a particular spelling, that is followed here.

I have attempted to standardise geographic terms, but largely I have left personal names as I found them, with a few exceptions where the spelling has wandered too far. Like Akin, if a Malaitan adopted a certain spelling of their personal name, even if it is phonetically incorrect, then that is the spelling I use. Jonathan Fifi`i is a good example. In Kwaio, his surname should be Fifii`i, but he never spelt it that way.

For some personal and place names we only have spellings used by government officers in documents, which are often wrong or inconsistent. I have been able to correct many but not all of these, and no doubt some remain misspelled. Quotations maintain original spellings. Solomon Islands Pijin pronunciations vary on Malaita and in the Solomons, typically by local language conventions. Thus there are no universally 'correct' phonetic spellings of Pijin English words, and I generally follow pronunciations I am most familiar with, from central Malaita.

Introduction: Malaitan Tropes

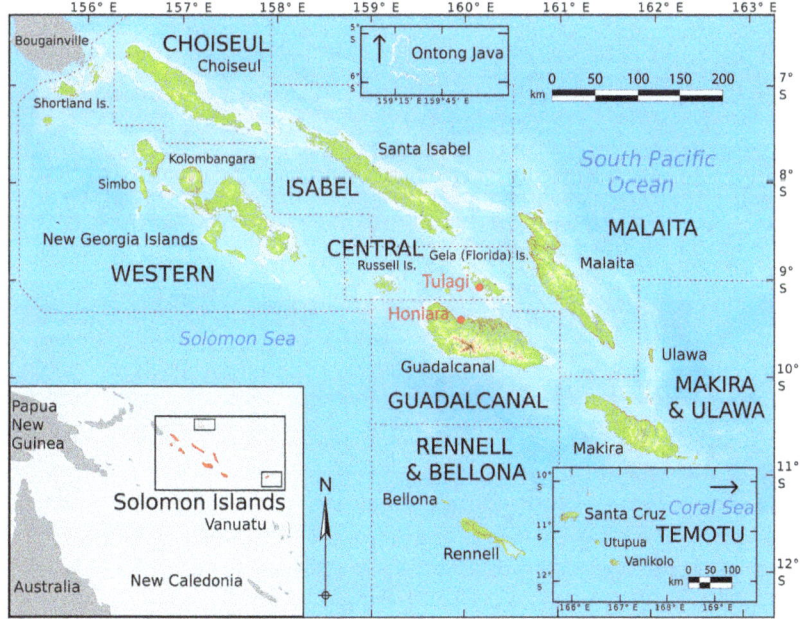

Map 1: Solomon Islands.
Source: Courtesy of Vincent Verheyen.

This is Malaita, of evil fame. A hundred miles long and twenty-five across, the island is one vast forest, which, clothing the sides of a thousand hills, rises to far off mountains. Through this dim jungle there swarms a hidden people, naked, silent, desperate, treacherous too, and venomous, who, under cover of the forest darkness, kill and are killed, and feast on human flesh. And from the bag slung around the neck of many a warrior, as he glides along the trail, hangs a fragment of human flesh, a bone, a talisman, a trophy of some dark murder.

—Northcote Deck, South Sea Evangelical Mission, 1910[1]

---

1 PMB 1290, Woodford Papers Reel 1, Bundle 3, 9/19, The Daily ?, 24 ? 1910 (the cutting details are incomplete).

> My grandfather ate better men than are in this room.
>
> —Noel Fatnowna, grandson of Kwailiu and Orrani from Fataleka, Malaita, speaking in Queensland in the 1970s to an Australian Seventh-day Adventist group

Mala

Making Mala has several meanings. Mala is the old name for Malaita Island, including both the main island and the smaller island on the south side of Maramasike Passage. Mala was used in the north, with similar language and dialect variations further south. Some early sources use Mara, Maratta, Marahatta, or Malanta as the standard name for Mala. Small Malaita was also known as Malamwaimwei (*mwaimwei* means small in the language of Small Malaita) and sometimes as Maramasike (*masike* also means small) or even Sa`a (an area on the east coast of Small Malaita, and the name of the language spoken there). All of these names can be found on maps. The passage between the two Malas is known as Maramasike Passage, or Raroi su`u (inside the passage), or Su`urado (dark passage) in the languages of the south. People from Small Malaita also called the main island Malapaina or Mwalapaine (large Mala).[2]

Mala was first recorded as 'Malaita' or 'Malayta' by Spanish explorers in 1568, which may have been because of a misunderstanding. When the Spaniards pointed to the island on the horizon and asked what it was called, the people of neighbouring Isabel Island are thought to have said 'Mala ita': that is Mala over there.[3] Gallego, from Mendaña's 1568 expedition, called it Isla de Ramos (Island of Palms) because they first sighted it on Palm Sunday morning, although this name was never used; unlike the Spanish 'Santa Ysabel', which survives in Isabel Island, or San Cristobal, now better known as Makira. Mala's people were known in Pijin English as 'Man Maratta' when they worked on nineteenth-century sugar plantations in Queensland. In Solomon Islands Pijin, Malaita is still sometimes known as Mala or Mara.

---

2   My thanks to Apollos Kalialaha for his assistance with the Small Malaita details, Nov 2015.
3   Amherst and Thomson 1967 [1901], 1, xxix, Narrative of Gallego, 1, 25; Woodford 1926, 482; Ivens 1927, 22–23.

There are a dozen different Malaitan-language groups, which interacted with each other while identifying primarily with their local regions and cultural mores. There are linguistic similarities, particularly grammatically, although people living in the south generally could not understand the languages of those in the north, or vice-versa. However, the diversity is not as great as once thought, and there is some degree of mutual intelligibility, particularly in the northern languages as far south as Fataleka. Some of the differences are due to word taboos and word plays, in which Malaitans delight. Trading languages are also used: Guala`ala`a, the language native to Kwai and Ngongosila islands, was used as a central east coast trading language, and the northern Lau kin and linguistic connections to Walade on east Small Malaita were exploited, allowing Lau language to be used far away from its origins in the north.

Interisland associations could be as important as intraisland ones: South Malaitans had much in common with people from Ulawa and Makira, Langalanga Lagoon people traded with Guadalcanal and Gela (Florida), many southwest Malaitans, mainly the `Are`are, were allied and related to the people of Marau Sound on Guadalcanal, which is probably best described as a Malaitan colony. North Malaitans always had strong links to Isabel Island. However, from the point of view of outsiders such as labour recruiters, missionaries and government officials, Malaitans were one people living on one island, bound by geography and cultural similarities. Government recruiting registers and mission baptism records gathered the people together as Marattas or Malaitans and recorded their names and the bays and passages (gaps in the reefs and lagoons) from which they enlisted. Malaitans first became united on these voyages to overseas plantations, where their similarities were far greater than their differences relative to the inhabitants of the 70 other Near Oceanic islands involved in the labour trade.

Pijin English learnt in Queensland became the *lingua franca* of Solomon Islands, accompanied by literacy among some. The new language helped create what became a rudimentary national consciousness.[4] A truly united Malaita would not emerge until just after the Second World War (here also referred to as the Pacific War), when Malaitans, dissatisfied with their lives under British rule, at a time when the war had seriously disrupted colonial administration, created the Maasina Rule movement.

---

4   Jourdan 1995.

Regional loyalties and interisland links were also important to this movement. Chapter 1 attempts to describe Mala as it existed before exposure to outside forces began to create one Malaita. The remaining chapters cover the development of Malaita through until the Pacific War and Maasina Rule.

Most Solomon Islanders are 'Melanesians', a term still used widely as a geographic descriptor for the group of island peoples spread from Timor and New Guinea in the west to Manus in the northeast and south to Vanuatu, New Caledonia and Fiji on the eastern fringe of the Solomon and Coral Seas.[5] The inhabitants of what is now often called Near Oceania share a mixed heritage, descended from the original migrants who travelled east and south out of New Guinea 30,000 years ago, but more so from Austronesian migrants from a few thousand years ago, with direct connections to the Southeast Asian Archipelago, southern China and Taiwan. Malaita sits in the middle of the Solomon Archipelago, a double-chain of islands below the Bismarck Archipelago east of New Guinea. The modern Solomon Islands nation starts in the north at the Shortland Islands, and the New Georgia Group and Choiseul where the double-chain begins. Buka and Bougainville, the northern single-file end of the archipelago, became part of German New Guinea in 1886 and remain part of Papua New Guinea, although they are now recognised as forming an autonomous region. The modern Solomon Islands nation also includes the smaller and more isolated Santa Cruz, Reef and Duff Groups, which are south of the main chain and closer to Vanuatu, as well as several Polynesian outliers, most on the outer east rim, and also Rennell and Bellona to the southwest.[6] In the 1950s, the British resettled Micronesians from the Gilbert Islands (today's Kiribati) into the protectorate, and they are now well incorporated into the nation, making Solomon Islands one of the most ethnically diverse parts of the Pacific Islands.

---

5   The division of the Pacific Islands into three zones called Melanesia (black islands), Polynesia (many islands) and Micronesia (small islands) is usually credited to the French explorer Dumont d'Urville in the late 1830s. Largely based on geography, with some basis in linguistic and cultural affinities, it is also partly derived from Eurocentric stereotypes of race. Melanesia is the least accurate of the three terms, given the diversity and time-depth of the habitation in these islands. Now discredited in some academic circles (and replaced by Near Oceania), Melanesia is still used by the people within that diverse region and by many writers. Douglas 1979; 2014; Thomas 1989; Green 1991; Green and Cresswell 1976.
6   Kirch 1984.

Malaitan Tropes

This Introduction discusses common Malaitan tropes—a literary allusion or stereotype, a commonly recurring rhetorical device—from the past and the present. First, there is the trope of 'Melanesianism'. I and other Pacific historians have been chastised by Tracey Banivanua-Mar for absorbing undigested attitudes from nineteenth-century sources; she suggests that we legitimate the 'Melanesian savages and cannibals' trope by accepting Melanesia and Melanesian as current terms. Banivanua-Mar suggests that themes of 'Islanders' natural tendency towards unbridled revenge, murderous brutality, and violent irrationality … communicated through metonymic references that are more subtle and enduring'[7] are perpetuated through this old trope. While I plead not guilty and hope this book exonerates me, there is a lesson for all historians to not get so close to their sources that they can no longer see clearly or analyse the evidence in a modern light. I also use Near Oceania as an alternative term to Melanesia, while noting that inhabitants of the region have few issues with the old term and at a political level have now appropriated the word 'Melanesia' as their own. Surely the real test of its usefulness is whether the term is accepted and still used by the inhabitants themselves? It has been indigenised by the people to whom it was first applied in the nineteenth century. As Vanuatu's first Prime Minister Hon. Rev. Walter Lini once said, 'Melanesia is not a concept but a reality'.[8]

My list of Malaitan tropes (which have been used by outsiders and also absorbed by some Malaitans) includes several types, and in some cases they contain elements of truth. First, there is the consequence of a continually large population, which means Malaitans numerically dominate the central Solomons, and have for at least 150 years, possibly for 500. Then there is their allegedly 'pushy' nature and their use of violence and compensation payments as problem-solving mechanisms, both historically and today. There is some truth in this, but much of this is a consequence of historical circumstances. Malaitans have also been accused of being head-hunters, which is untrue,[9] of being cannibals, which has some limited, archaic

---

7   Banivanua-Mar 2007, 16, see also 14–19, 22–26.
8   'Maritime boundary negotiations between Vanuatu and Solomon Islands successfully completed after 32 years', *Vanuatu Daily Post*, 21 Nov 2015. Many Melanesians believe that they have cultural elements in common, and modern regional ideologies such as Bernard Narokobi's 'Melanesian Way' and organisations such as the Melanesian Spearhead Group within the Pacific Forum and the Anglican Church of the Province of Melanesia are strengthening this contemporary, regional identity. See Kabutaulaka 2015 for a recent analysis.
9   Aswani 2000; Lawrence 2014, 54–61.

truth, and of practicing infanticide (see Chapter 6). Malaitans were also slow to embrace Christianity relative to other parts of Near Oceania, and they preserve aspects of customary behaviour that sit uncomfortably with other Solomon Islanders. This includes nonrecognition of the potential of women to take a leading role in the modern nation. Although this failing is more widespread than just on Malaita, it misreads the role of women in traditional Solomon societies and points up a masculinisation that has taken place, fuelled by 150 years of reshaping of Solomon cultures. During these years, Malaitans have been the main participants in the Solomons' diaspora, which today allows them to dominate urban areas, and they always seem to be involved in social movements, discontent and urban disturbances.[10] Malaitans are to Solomon Islands what Highlanders are to contemporary Papua New Guinea, though for different reasons. They are depicted as proud, dynamic and industrious, willing to migrate to better themselves, easy to anger, and likely to demand compensation for alleged wrongs. Oddly, they are also depicted as conservative and clinging to old ways. Hopefully, this book will dissuade readers from the latter stereotype.

Cannibalism features in the two quotations at the beginning of this chapter, although Noel Fatnowna was trying to inject a little humour into a rather dry church meeting—he certainly got their attention. The other description was written by Northcote Deck, a pioneer missionary with the South Sea Evangelical Mission (SSEM), recounting his March 1910 walk across Malaita from the east Kwara'ae coast near Ngongosila Island to Bina Harbour in west Kwaio, accompanied by four Malaitans. He was writing to impress possible donors to the SSEM, and might be forgiven a little hyperbole, although not his total excess. His references to cannibalism (repeated elsewhere)[11] are exaggerated: there was no institutionalised cannibalism on Malaita of the sort found on some other Near Oceanic islands, although it did occur occasionally, usually with the corpse of someone killed for incest or some other heinous offence. It was a gesture of absolute contempt.[12] Banivanua-Mar argues that accusations of cannibalism on the colonial frontier transmitted 'racialized relations

---

10   Disturbances in Honiara in 1989 and 1996 caused the government to pay compensation for disputes between Malaitans, Bellonese and Reef Islanders. Akin 1999b, 57–58. Ma'asina Forum, the only enduring large-scale political pressure group in Solomon Islands in recent years, is dominated by Malaitans and plays on Maasina Rule in its title.
11   SINA, BSIP 18/II 1, John Northcote Deck, evidence to Lands Commission, 22 Jan 1912, 94.
12   Keesing wrote a pun-filled article (1973) about how to divide up a body for eating in Kwara'ae based on kinship status. See also Hopkins 1928, 201–04; Guidieri 1972; Beaver 2002.

of power between colonized and colonizer' and was used to disempower the former,[13] and Deck was indeed using his supposed knowledge of Malaitans to assert Christian and colonial authority.

The trophy bags Deck mentions, called *wa`ifirua* in the Kwaio language of central Malaita, did exist. They were hung on a string around the neck, hanging down the back, and decorated with woven rings that were trophies of pig theft (almost a sport for young men), cone shell rings for secret murders, and tiny bags representing shell wealth thefts. Along with these *wa`ifirua*, men sometimes wore beautiful pearl-inlaid batons on cords around their necks, often with a stone, typically a pyrite nodule, plaited to one end. These batons are called *fou`atoleeleo* or *founisulesikwanga* in Kwaio and *hauanoreereo* or *wariihau* in `Are`are, and they were carried while collecting shell wealth and pig bounties awarded for killings.[14] Deck did not understand what he was seeing. David Akin provided an explanation of these bounty-hunters for a recent exhibition held at the Musée du quai Branly in Paris:

> Until the later 1920s, when a Malaitan was murdered, his or her relatives could announce a bounty of shell money and pigs to be paid for a revenge killing. They might specify a victim, but sometimes killing anyone from the murderer's group would suffice, expressing the view that a person's relatives or allies can be held collectively liable for their misdeeds. From the 1870s into the 1920s, various Malaitans posted open bounties for any white-person's death or the taking of a ship, to avenge European killings, kidnappings, or other abuses. Although Europeans saw bounties as displaying Malaitan brutality, they were a crucial levelling mechanism since they allowed militarily weak groups to use wealth gained through production and exchange to defend against groups with more fighters or guns—bounties assured a rough balance between martial and economic power, and integrated them. But they could also lead to murders of innocents, including women and children. *Lamo* was the Kwaio term for men who killed for bounties, and important fighters generally; `Are`are call them *namo*. In the more hierarchical societies of the far south, *namo* could hold formal positions as a chief's executioners.[15]

---

13 Banivanua-Mar 2010, 281.
14 They were most important for ceremonially claiming bounties paid for killings, called *sikwa* in Kwaio, *siwa* further south and *fo`oa* in northern languages. The sixteenth-century Spanish visitors thought that these contained gold, part of the reason for linking the islands to King Solomon. Coppet 1977. My thanks to David Akin for help with the explanation of the objects Deck described. See also Akin 2015.
15 This book uses *ramo*, the north Malaitan equivalent of *lamo* and *namo*. Akin 2013a, 354 n 80; 2013b, 228.

Although Deck's imagination was working overtime, his attitude is fairly typical of early Europeans describing Malaita and its inhabitants. Deck at least does not accuse Malaitans of head-hunting, but two books published in 1988 and 2003 do so erroneously in their titles and texts.[16] Europeans registered a sense of menace and danger, and singled out Malaita from other Solomon Islands as a place where outsiders had to take care of their safety. (As I point out in the Conclusion, some outsiders still do.) Deck was not alone in his extreme characterisation of Malaitans. Labour recruiters seldom relaxed while at Malaita and often reported that they kept their revolvers loaded and ready. More than on other islands, ships often tried to keep Malaitans from coming aboard, and if they did, kept constant guard. The only ones always welcome were a few bigmen who acted as passage masters (the men who controlled labour recruiting at bays and passages), such as Kwaisulia in Lau Lagoon, but even they were never fully trusted.[17] John Gaggin from Fiji, who visited Malaita in the 1890s, claimed that recruiting ships carried small canons, and sacks of broken glass tied high in the masts ready to scatter across the deck at the first sign of trouble, to hinder barefoot attackers. (I know of no collaboration for this and it may be an exaggeration.) Gaggin added, 'Every white kept his Winchester, Martini, and revolver loaded in his bunk, day and night' while at Malaita.[18] Jock Cromar, a recruiter in the 1880s and later a trader in the Solomons, provided a standard view:

> This island had an evil reputation, and was one which many recruiters avoided. The Malaita natives had attacked many vessels, killed their crews, and then looted and burned the ships. The objective of the New Hebrideans was the possession of rifles from the recruiting boats, and they rarely attacked the ships themselves, but the Malaitamen were not satisfied unless they had looted the whole ship and burned it.[19]

However, Cromar contradicts himself on the next page of his book, describing a peaceful scene in Langalanga Lagoon in 1884:

> As soon as we dropped anchor the *Madeline* was surrounded by canoes large and small, containing men, women, and children. The men and lads soon hopped on board, leaving the women in the canoes all crying out for tobacco. It was now time for our luncheon, and we had some difficulty

---

16   Holthouse 1988; Randell 2003, 82–86, 124–27, 131, 249. These are both based on the life of Jack Renton, a castaway from the 1860s and early 1870s, mentioned in Chapter 2.
17   Wawn 1973 [1893], 415, 417; Corris 1973a; Keesing 1992b.
18   Gaggin 1900, 179–80; Wawn 1973, 415.
19   Cromar 1935, 135.

in keeping sufficient deck space clear of natives to allow us to proceed with it. Some of them however took to the rigging and sat like crows in the ship's yards … Presently one of them dived into the water from the yardarm, entering it feet first. This was the beginning of an aquatic display in which most of them joined enthusiastically, and in a very little time there was a constant stream of natives swarming up the rigging to the yards, and plunging thence into the water.[20]

The labour trade could be violent and the violence was on both sides, and there can be no doubt that there were dangers for outsiders visiting Malaita, especially in certain places. Nevertheless, the negative pictures of Malaitans painted by Deck, Gaggin and Cromar reveal more about their own ignorance, bigotry and personal agendas than any understanding of the inhabitants of the island or its contact history.[21] Over the almost 450 years since Mendaña's expedition landed on Malaita, and the over 160 years since crew from Captain John Erskine's HMS *Havannah* landed there in 1850 (see Chapter 2), visitors have left us descriptions of the island and its people. Malaitan savagery and aggression has been a constant trope, more so than for any other Solomon Island. Today, Malaitans still get a 'bad press', usually from outsiders (both other Solomon Islanders and foreigners) who unthinkingly condemn the inhabitants of the island as somehow more conservative, difficult, obstreperous and aggressive than other Solomon Islanders. They seem to say that all Malaitans share a more truculent manner of behaviour. Forgotten are two Malaitan prime ministers and many bishops, priests, pastors, nuns and teachers, and other Malaitan men and women in business, politics and the public service and the churches who have been and remain national leaders, as well as the many thousands of others who are simply good citizens.

One of the more focused Malaitan tropes concerns aggression during the nineteenth century by the people of the central east coast. Chapter 7 describes several labour trade ship massacres that occurred along a few kilometres of the Kwara'ae and Kwaio coast. A glance at Judith Bennett's 1987 book's appendix on violent conflicts between Solomon Islanders and Europeans *circa* 1860–90 is a sobering extension and corrective.[22] Attacks occurred throughout the archipelago, and these large-scale Malaitan attacks occurred mostly during a concentrated period in the 1880s. Many early attacks relate to reprisals for European transgressions,

---

20 *Ibid.*, 136.
21 See, for instance, Knibbs 1929, 188–89; Boutilier 1979.
22 Bennett 1987, 390–96.

although eventually leaders realised that facilitating economic interaction with Europeans was more rewarding. During these same decades, the people of New Georgia in the northwest were by far the most 'dangerous' of all Solomon Islanders, feared as head-hunters and slavers throughout the north and centre of the archipelago. Isabel Island was attacked by New Georgia warriors in war canoes, and Isabel's Gao and Bugotu people, in turn, attacked areas of their own island and also north Malaita.[23] Today, both Solomon Islanders and outsiders accept this past ferocity with little comment, as an historical curiosity, while Malaitans remain feared, with a reputation for violence. During much of the time that Western Solomons and Isabel war canoes were marauding far and wide, most Malaitans stayed at home minding their own business, although there was also internecine violence on Malaita. The violence in both the northwest Solomons and Malaita was exacerbated by access to European technologies, but only in the western islands did it develop into regular interisland violence.

People also refer knowingly to the 1927 massacre of District Officer William Bell and his tax-collecting party by people from east Kwaio (see chapters 9 and 10), and to the Kwaio claim, decades later, for compensation for a government punitive attack that followed Bell's death.[24] Although the attack on Bell was horrific, it is the British response that deserves the most condemnation. The reputation of the Kwaio remains tarnished because of another trope: a considerable number of villagers in the central mountains have maintained their pre-Christian religion based around ancestor worship. It is as if there was something shameful in preserving customs and religion from the past. What goes unstated is that accepting Christianity goes arm-in-arm with accepting the modern economy and government, and brings major changes to cultural norms. Preservation of ancestral religious practices is often assumed to be widespread rather than an anomaly on modern Malaita. Most Kwaio are indistinguishable from other Solomon Islanders: they attend the same churches and work in urban areas. Furthermore, as David Akin has described, Kwaio ancestral religion itself has changed tremendously through the years, and can only be understood today, not as an anachronism, but as a contemporary and dynamic belief system. East Kwaio also has been slow to change in other ways, partly because a lack of roads there has kept the people very isolated—an issue relating to economic development, not culture. It is

---

23   McKinnon 1975; Ivens 1930, 185–86; Richards 2012, 9–60; Aswani 2000.
24   Akin 1999b, 41.

also worth mentioning that two anthropologists have worked in east Kwaio, Roger Keesing and David Akin. Keesing was the most prolific of all Malaita-based anthropologists and Akin has published influential work and most recently a substantial book that, although covering all of Malaita, has a strong knowledge base from east Kwaio. Both Keesing (who died in 1993) and Akin have also published on Malaita as a whole. Although it was never their intention, and it is unfair to criticise Keesing, or to group Akin with Keesing, their extensive English-language publications on the Kwaio have inadvertently made Kwaio belief systems dominant in anthropological literature. If Malaita is referenced, it is often through Keesing's celebratory writing on Kwaio difference. Likewise, perhaps academics (me included) and other writers have, through sheer productivity, inadvertently preserved some of the tropes about Malaita. Malaitans feature frequently in any descriptions of Solomon Islanders.

Even Maasina Rule, the protonationalist movement that rocked the British Solomon Islands Protectorate (BSIP) after the Pacific War and into the early 1950s, has unfairly been interpreted as a negative trope. Malaitans were at the centre of Maasina Rule and deserve to be proud of their pacifist success against the might of the British Empire. Historical circumstances positioned Malaita as central to this political development, but it was not the first such movement. People from other islands initiated the Fallowes movement (sometimes called 'Chair and Rule' in the literature) of the late 1930s, which began in Isabel and spread to the Gela Group, where some leading Malaitans became involved. Other islands, such as Makira and parts of Guadalcanal, participated in Maasina Rule, but hold little place in the largely Malaita-centric literature. The Moro movement on Guadalcanal, which flourished between the 1950s and 1980s, had many qualities similar to Maasina Rule: self-help, economic development and advocacy of regional independence.[25] As with these other protonationalist movements, the clever and well-organised Maasina Rule was, sometimes out of ignorance and sometimes through political design, glossed by the movement's opponents as simply a cargo cult, as if disturbing the colonial power's right of dominance was wrong and irrational. Some younger Solomon Islanders still misunderstand the movement this way, although in recent years many have been revising their views.[26]

---

25 Moore 2013c entry.
26 See Akin 2013a, 290–99, for some complexities of cargo ideas during Maasina Rule.

The second, third and fifth chapters discuss Malaitans as labourers overseas, and the reputation they developed as good workers who were nonetheless aggressive and unpredictable. Later chapters pursue this same reputation on plantations within the protectorate: they were hard-working, dour 'rough diamonds', easily angered and not to be trifled with. In the 1970s, Judith Bennett conducted a series of interviews with Malaitan and other labourers. Reading through these personal work histories, as well as Bennett's 1993 chapter on resistance, and considering my own interviews and research in Queensland, it seems that Malaitans may have realised their reputation and made a virtue of it, partly to protect themselves from outsiders, both other Solomon Islanders and the plantation bosses who belittled them, yelled at them and physically mistreated them, yet also feared them.[27] Perhaps this trope can be understood partly as a Malaitan protection mechanism. That said, I would argue that although there is some truth in this behavioural categorisation, it is the result of historical processes and not any inherent ahistorical 'Malaitanism'. On overseas plantations in the 1890s and 1900s in Queensland and continuing until the mid-1910s in Fiji, and then for the several decades on protectorate plantations, Malaitan numbers were so large that they had the upper hand. What Bennett suggests for the protectorate was also true for Malaitans in Queensland: they played on their aggressive side, to an extent that an 80-year-old Australian South Sea Islander friend of mine still believes that Malaitans can never be trusted. That is what her mother told her.

Allied to this is the trope of supermasculinity explained by Michael Scott, an anthropologist working on neighbouring Makira. Scott suggests that nineteenth- and twentieth-century 'labour and mission discourses … tended to masculinize Malaitans as strong, warlike and competitive and to feminise other island-specific populations as small, weak, timid, and indolent …'.[28] He also suggests that more recent academic and journalistic representations have contributed to this gender imaging and have been 'double-voiced' by Solomon Islanders. As well, Malaitan social organisation and land tenure increasingly are depicted by Malaitans themselves as patrilineal and patriarchal, when actually they are far more complex. Anthropologists have expended a great deal of ink and paper showing this complexity. Because of the large size of the Malaitan population and their spread to the nation's capital of Honiara and throughout other provinces, matrilineal spaces are being appropriated. This trope feminises Makira,

---

27 Bennett 1981b; 1993.
28 Scott 2012, 134.

Guadalcanal, Isabel and the Western Solomons against the increasingly masculine Malaita. The trope ignores female power on Malaita, which has in the past been expressed through female ancestral power and can be articulated in land rights through cognate descent links. In many ways, Malaitan female power remains strong. As explained in Chapter 1, Malaitan women's power can negate male power and is treated with great respect. Still, if Scott's analysis is correct, and if Malaitan numbers continue to outstrip those from all other Solomon Island provinces, then contemporary Malaitan masculine dominance can only increase, just as male power is increasing in land systems throughout the country where women's rights have been stripped away by colonial and postcolonial reinterpretations.

Understanding Malaita

What will become clear in the following chapters is that, since the 1870s, Malaitans, due to their numbers and lack of other options, have been a primary source of plantation and other manual labour, and there has been very little commercial development on their own island. Resident traders and planters in the Solomons had minimal incentive to try to create bases on Malaita, and the only large plantation enterprise ever established there was an expensive failure. The economic pickings elsewhere in the archipelago were richer. All of this has shaped Malaitans.[29]

Malaitans developed a reputation for being difficult, despite the fact that tens of thousands of them worked as indentured labourers overseas between the 1870s and 1910s, and kept the protectorate's copra plantations and the Guadalcanal plains agricultural developments operating during the twentieth century. Labour traders had a maximum impact on Malaita, almost more than anywhere else in Near Oceania. Christian missionaries also had considerable impact, and a large part of this book's argument is that historians and some anthropologists have been misled about the size of this. Few missionaries ever appreciated that they were dealing with Malaitan cosmologies and sets of religious and philosophical beliefs that were highly complex and adaptable. The protectorate government first concentrated on direct rule through district officers (DOs) and their police to achieve pacification then, onward from the 1920s, moved toward indirect rule using local agents. Even the best of these foreign

---

29 Moore 2007.

officials never really understood Malaitan cultures and this contributed to serious errors in judgement. They also tried to systematise what were diverse cultures into a single administrative unit. Some missionaries learnt local languages but no DO ever became fluent in any Malaitan language.[30] Each foreign group attempted to comprehend Malaitans, but with little success, and they frequently exhibited fear of them.

While the traders, missionaries and government officers who ventured to Malaita in the nineteenth century depicted a savage scene, at the same time they realised that the island and its inhabitants were unusual, even within the diversity of the Pacific, and they all admired Malaitan industriousness. We know that Malaita has been heavily populated for hundreds of years: the people lived both deep in the mountains and on artificial islands in the lagoons. Introduced diseases probably caused a decline in the population during the period of 'first contact' with outsiders, although not to the same extent as on many other Pacific Islands. Their sheer numbers—probably exceeding 100,000 in the mid-nineteenth century—made Malaitans important and dominant.

Europeans had little appreciation of the complexity of Malaitan cultures and were often condescending and racist. Even the best intentioned foreign residents had a limited ability to understand what they observed on the island. A good corrective example of this is the descriptions of the complexity of Malaitan religion and culture provided by Malaitan scholars John Naitoro and David Gegeo. This is not to take anything away from anthropologists, who have described Malaitan religions, nor to deny that anthropologists have influenced Malaitan scholars, but there is an 'indigeneity' in both Naitoro's and Gegeo's writing that to me is informative and passionate.

Malaitans were undoubtedly puzzled and troubled by the European encroachment and felt powerless to combat it. Malaitan cultures were robust and complex, and although they varied greatly from one end of the island to the other, Malaitans had physical and social characteristics that made them recognisable to other Solomon Islanders and to foreigners. Even though I argue that the many cultural groups only became politically unified in modern times, there was always a core culture that linked them together, and all the chapters will tease this out. In all of this we must bear in mind that Malaitans, like other Solomon Islanders, have proven

---

30 Akin 2013a, passim, and particularly 5–6, 54–55, 67–68, 70, 357–58 n 16, 361 n 53, 362 n 59, 363 n 60.

extraordinarily flexible and able to adapt their belief systems to suit new circumstances, contradicting yet another common accusatory trope that their perspectives are rigid and unchanging.

The Pacific War and Maasina Rule

Making Mala is not about the Pacific War or Maasina Rule, but both events are part of the modern context and need to be understood as background. The war arrived in the protectorate in the first half of 1942: evacuations began in December 1941, with the government's headquarters at Tulagi finally abandoned to the Japanese in April and into May 1942. I have included a short summary of the effects the war had on Malaita in the Conclusion. Thousands of Solomon Islander males joined the British Solomon Islands Defence Force and the Solomon Islands Labour Corps, and just as on the prewar plantations, the majority were from Malaita. Their wartime experiences were crucial to the development of Maasina Rule, but so too were changes that took place between the 1870s and 1930s. The war was over relatively quickly in the Solomons, but it had a profound impact on the protectorate. After the fairly small-scale mission, government and plantation presence before 1942, the sheer quantities of war machinery and troops that suddenly arrived was beyond comprehension. Until then, most foreigners had been British or Australian or Chinese. Suddenly, hundreds of thousands of Japanese, Americans, New Zealanders, Fijians and Tongans arrived and fought pitched battles on many islands, in the skies and on the seas. The British had ruled with 'smoke and mirrors' bolstered by a seemingly indomitable sense of their own racial and cultural superiority. The loss of face was immense when most foreigners (except some of the Chinese community) were quickly and in an undignified manner evacuated from the islands. Solomon Islanders needed no Western education to understand that the British were in trouble in a way that had never previously seemed possible.[31]

Maasina Rule began in `Are`are in southern Malaita in early 1944, at a time when many Malaitan males were working in the wartime Labour Corps on Guadalcanal and Gela. Maasina means 'his brother' or 'his sibling' or even 'his friend'. This is not the place for a detailed history of Maasina

---

31   Refer to this book's Conclusion, which briefly examines the coming of the war and its effect on Malaita and Malaitans. Also see Horton 1970; Lord 1977; Laracy 1974; 1988a; Laracy and White 1988; Akin 2013a, 132–63; and Moore 2013c entry on the Second World War.

Rule, so richly documented by Hugh Laracy in *Pacific Protest: The Maasina Rule Movement, Solomon Islands, 1944–1952* (1983), and written about with ethnographic and historical precision by David Akin in *Colonialism, Maasina Rule, and the Origins of Malaitan Kastom* (2013).[32] In retrospect, Maasina Rule was an astonishing development: people of diverse and once divided societies on several islands came together to confront the might of British colonialism. Reading Akin's account, upon which I have drawn extensively below, left me pondering how it had all been possible on an island with no history of unity.

The leaders spread messages espousing Malaitan unity and independence. Maasina Rule advocated improvements in gardening, concentration into larger, better organised villages, and, later, noncooperation with the government and missionary groups. These teachings were coupled at some stages with hopes for American liberation and millenarian ideas, although this aspect of Maasina Rule was often exaggerated by officials, and later by anthropologists and historians influenced by government accounts. Between 1944 and 1946, Maasina Rule spread to all areas of Malaita and to neighbouring islands, particularly Makira and parts of Guadalcanal, and dominated the political scene in the central Solomons into 1952. It was peaceful, indigenous protonationalism grounded in a desire for self-government and self-determination. Although the hopes of many followers for American intervention and independence from Britain were unrealistic, Maasina Rule did strain the government almost to the breaking point at a time when it was still weak after the war. No other single island people in the Pacific managed to confront the British so effectively. Several factors made Maasina Rule possible. One was shared experiences within the exploitative indentured labour system. Others were the influence of Christianity, Pijin English and literacy, and several decades of ineffectual colonial administration that, while introducing policing and taxation, provided virtually no social services. As well, there was the cataclysm caused by the Pacific War and dashed expectations that change would follow it. The British were intent on reestablishing their old regime, whereas Solomon Islanders expected something new. The wartime experience was a catalyst for resentments that had been growing for decades, particularly in the 1920s when wages were reduced and taxation

---

32   There is a large literature on Maasina Rule. The best source is the bibliography in Akin 2013a. Also see Laracy 1983; Keesing 1978b.

was introduced, and they were exacerbated during the Great Depression when Malaitans suffered from the crash of the plantation economy, their main source for money and goods.

The basic message of Maasina Rule was that Malaitans and others had the right to control their own affairs and the movement instituted various measures to form indigenous-run governments on the islands involved. Maasina Rule on Malaita elected 'head chiefs' presiding over large areas, which had never been a characteristic of Malaitan leadership except in the far south. The movement combined customary leadership expertise with the knowledge of the new, more literate generation. Of the 10 original head chiefs, five belonged to the SSEM, which was used as a web of contacts, as were other mission structures to varying degrees. Initially strongest in 'Are'are in the south, by late 1945 the movement was well on its way to becoming an alternative government across Malaita, and in 1946, by one estimate, 95 per cent of Malaitans were adherents. Movement followers refused to labour away from the island; Malaitans had dominated the prewar plantation labour force (over 60 per cent of workers) and the strike distressed a government anxious to get the war-devastated economy back on its feet. Malaitans also collected and codified *kastom*, much in the way that the British officials had instructed them to codify 'custom' before and just after the war for use in nascent native courts. *Kastom* was, however, more indigenous, and quite different from 'custom'—it including many new and novel concepts and practices upon which Malaitans would base social reform, and forbade many older practices. *Kastom* was the foundation of Maasina Rule's political ideology, and Maasina Rule courts employed *kastom* codes to mediate, arbitrate and in some cases adjudicate disputes free from government interference.

The British reaction was initially conciliatory, then harsh and, finally, realising that Malaitans, and movement adherents on neighbouring islands, were united and implacably opposed to allowing the old regime to return, conciliatory once more. Huge meetings were held, such as the 6,000–7,000 Malaitans who met with the district commissioner (the island's senior colonial official) at 'Aoke in June 1947. Two months after that meeting, the BSIP Government arrested the major Maasina Rule chiefs on charges of conspiring to overthrow the government and holding illegal courts. The head chiefs were each sentenced to six years at hard labour. Malaitans responded with a massive campaign of civil disobedience, refusing to pay a reimposed capitation (head) tax, submit to a census, or cooperate in any other way. Most villages erected small fences to differentiate between *kastom* and British jurisdictions, and a few built stockades (an old Malaitan defence strategy) to keep out government officers and police. A series of government operations between 1948 and 1952 employed mostly Western Solomons police to arrest thousands of Malaitans and Makirans. Most of them lined up peacefully to be taken to prison. This suppression did little to quell the resistance and greatly heightened resentment. The British hurriedly created prison camps, which overflowed but required no fences because the prisoners did not try to escape. Reading the government archives it is clear that officials were at a loss to know how to resolve the situation. Their response for several years was simply to increase suppression.

In early 1950, a new resident commissioner (the senior administrator of the protectorate) took a more conciliatory approach. He released the head chiefs and promised Malaitans an island-wide council with half its members elected by Malaitans, an offer that the movement declined as inadequate. Resistance continued, although Malaitans stopped lining up for prison and instead fled police, and many moved inland. Though small numbers were recruited for shorter-term labour contracts, and some submitted to census and paid the tax in order to avoid further imprisonment, noncooperation remained the main strategy. The government found itself despised and hamstrung, unable to reassert any real control or pursue plans for the future.

Malaitans were remarkably efficient in communicating a united view and arguing their case. Multiple copies of information letters were circulated widely on the island, using literacy to advantage. Malaitans demanded locally run courts and councils, and a single island-wide council with a Malaitan leader. In response, officials from the protectorate and the Western Pacific High Commission (WPHC) insisted that only if all Malaitans paid tax and submitted to the census would arrests stop and a Malaitan be chosen to sit on the protectorate's Advisory Council (although they planned to appoint a loyalist headman).[33] Once more, Malaitans refused. In 1952, a new district commissioner, recognising that suppression had failed, that many Malaitan grievances were legitimate, and that rapprochement was necessary, worked to break the deadlock. His softer approach, which had at best mixed success among the now bitter and suspicious population, was later bolstered by newly appointed

---

33 Moore 2013c entry. A headman was a government-appointed indigenous official.

High Commissioner Sir Robert Stanley, who arrived in Honiara in late 1952 when the WPHC shifted its base to there from Suva. Stanley met with movement leaders in `Aoke, with the ground for cooperation already tilled by the district commissioner's work. Stanley granted Malaitans most of what they had demanded. The most important agreement was for the formation of a Malaita-wide council that would have a Malaitan president, represent fully all the people and take considerable responsibility for managing the island's affairs. In 1978, I had the honour to spend a day with Salana Ga`a (aka Maega`asia), the Malaita Council's first president. Small of stature, this wonderful old man lived in a rambling house outside `Aoke. I remember that he prayed for my wayward soul.

Figure Introduction 1: High Commissioner Sir Robert Stanley at the inauguration of the first Malaita Council in 1952.
The interpreter on the right of the table is Frederick Aubarua Osifelo (1928–2001), later Sir Frederick, Speaker of the Legislative Assembly.
Source: Walter Gibbons Collection.

Figure Introduction 2: Salana Ga'a, the first President of the first Malaita Council, and some of its members in 1952.
Source: James Tedder Collection.

Malaitans also asked for a government school. In response, the first permanent government school in the protectorate, 'Aoke Experimental School (often called Aligegeo School), was established outside 'Aoke, shambolically from 1948 to 1951 and permanently in 1952, renamed King George VI School. In 1958, it was expanded to include secondary students and in 1963 was moved to Honiara as a secondary school.[34]

Most of the members of the first Malaita Council in 1953 were former resistance leaders (only eight of its 41 members were government appointees, some of them also former resistance leaders). Maasina Rule achieved many of its aims, although some others had been naïve. Although it cannot be credited with having led to Solomon Islands independence in 1978, the movement was instrumental in bringing about changes in attitudes and institutions that speeded the process toward that end. Maasina Rule certainly restored many people's faith in their own abilities to control and direct their islands.

---

34   Moore 2013c entry; Kenilorea 2008, 47–93.

INTRODUCTION

I have described Maasina Rule in some detail because it was a remarkable development when compared against any other resistance to colonial rule in the Pacific or elsewhere in the British Empire. One cannot discuss the decades leading up to Maasina Rule without signalling what was to come. Also, it was a peaceful protest movement, a strong counter to the trope of Malaitan violence. As I read Akin's account, questions continued to swirl in my mind. How had a people divided by many languages, with no overriding political unity, managed to unite and challenge British authority so effectively? Rather reluctantly, I abandoned one easy answer—Malaitan uniqueness—and challenged my earlier acceptance of this argument. Malaitans are not unique among Pacific peoples, although they are apt to claim that they are, and in the 1970s and 1980s I had absorbed part of this view through long association. Along the way, I also became more aware of debates among anthropologists during the 1980s about the formation of *kastom*, and of course Akin's more recent assessment of Malaitan *kastom*. But neither was it just historical circumstances. There are elements of culture and history involved.

As an historian, I lean towards explanations based on historical circumstances. In the early 1870s, Malaitans began to participate in the labour trade outside the Solomons. Then, once overseas work was closed to them, onward from the 1900s and 1910s, Malaitans became the most important plantation labour force within the protectorate. Some Malaitans absorbed Christianity while working away from their island (see Chapter 3) and also at home, although until the 1930s and 1940s the majority continued to follow their ancestral religions (though the growing and sometimes aggressive Christian presence also changed ancestral religious practices). Malaitans had British control imposed on them in a rudimentary way onward from 1909, although not until the mid-1920s did a substantial administrative hold develop, and even then it was limited largely to coastal areas. The 1930s reinforced the earlier pattern, but only edged forward, drawing Malaita into the protectorate.

Malaita of the 1940s was very different from Malaita of the 1870s. In the 1870s, Malaitans were divided most basically into two distinct groups. The vast majority lived in small inland communities—really just related hamlets—and practised subsistence horticulture. A small minority lived around the coast or on artificial islands in the three lagoons, along the shores of Maramasike Passage or on the few natural offshore islands. They utilised mostly marine resources and either traded with the inland people for other foods or had small agricultural holdings on the coast opposite their mainly lagoon-bound islands. Malaitans were subdivided by a dozen languages, all with the same linguistic base and mainly in east–west 'belts' that stretched across the island. Their material culture, leadership, gender, and religious systems all shared similarities. All were involved regularly in internecine fighting and a nonspecialist warrior class operated, largely as bounty-hunters. In the 1870s, outsiders had made no inroads on Malaita as they had already on many other Solomon Islands. While the traditional justice system was sometimes violent, it tapped into a social and cosmological equilibrium and, against coarse European impressions, was not notably irrational.

Malaita in the 1940s was still divided between inland and coastal peoples. The 'belts' of languages remained, which the British attempted to turn into administrative units. The coast was by then peppered with mission villages, which Anglican Bishop Cecil Wilson called 'beacons all along the shores'.[35] These new villages were large and drew many (but by no means all) of the mountain people into a Christian lifestyle down to the coast, which put pressure on ownership and control of coastal land and complicated the old inland–coastal population and cultural divisions. The Christian denominations, which were highly competitive, also introduced new forms of religious authority. Over several decades, Malaitan males became dominant participants first in the intercolonial and then in the Solomon Islands internal labour trades. On returning home, they diluted old authority structures and altered the nature and control of wealth. Outsiders, in the shape of labour recruiters and missionaries, became regular visitors and residents around the coast. After trying to combat or ignore the encroachment of the British protectorate government, by the 1930s Malaitans had largely accepted that peace was preferable to internecine fighting and the days of the violent bounty-hunters were over. Some rudimentary government services had been introduced. The idea of modern Malaita was already established.

This book is about the making of Mala into modern Malaita, first and foremost by its indigenous inhabitants, but also by the British and Australians. The book is set within a wider context of modern Malaita, as

---

35 Wilson 1932, 207.

its people continuously reinvent themselves within the Solomon Islands nation and beyond. *Making Mala* is an analysis of the dynamic processes that have shaped Malaitans and Solomon Islanders.

Making Mala attempts to comprehend the tropes and changes of the past. These also provide partial explanations of what happened in the 1990s when simmering tensions overflowed and brought the nation so low. The book is positioned between my *Kanaka* (1985) and *Happy Isles in Crisis* (2004). By looking back at the history behind the problems that developed in the 1990s, we can readily discern the consequences of the spread of Malaita's large population and of poorly balanced colonial economic development policies. Malaita Island, with around 35 per cent of the Solomon Islands population, and always the major source of labour, was left internally underdeveloped, a result of flawed planning by both the colonial and postindependence governments.[36] This economic inequality was at the base of the lengthy and aggressive dispute that led to the arrival in July 2003 of the Pacific Forum-initiated Regional Assistance Mission to Solomon Islands (RAMSI). Sadly, little has been done to rectify this inequality.

The 'Tension Years', 1998–2003

Just as Maasina Rule required discussion here, so too we must outline the 'Tension Years' of civil unrest. As I have said, Malaita Province's population has always been the largest in the modern Solomon Islands and their numbers make them dominant at home and also in Honiara. They have also spread significantly through all the country's provinces, mainly through marriage and also in the workforce. In recent decades, Malaitans have been involved in several disturbances in Honiara. This is not surprising given that Malaitans have always been proportionally dominant in the city's population. Then, during 'the Tension', a Malaitan militia in cahoots with the police overthrew Prime Minister Bartholomew Ulufa'alu, a Malaitan, and ruled the streets of Honiara for some years. But what provoked this situation? Were Malaitans just being difficult, as some commentators appeared to believe?

---

36   Moore 2007.

It needs to be said that some of the people and political leaders of Guadalcanal, including Ezekiel Alebua, a former prime minister (1986–89) and then premier of Guadalcanal Province, were guilty of deliberately exacerbating an already volatile situation. They may have been motivated by legitimate complaints, but they were playing with fire. What is often forgotten is that the militia, the Malaita Eagle Force (MEF), was formed to defend Malaitans in Honiara from the unlawful, violent excesses of a minority of the people of Guadalcanal. Though the Tension Years added to the trope that Malaitans were difficult people, they were initially provoked to defend their rights as citizens. In the end, though, these unhappy years brought no credit to either side.[37] It is notable that during these years most other provincial governments threatened secession, but never Malaita Province, a positive sign perhaps of belonging to the nation?[38]

Malaitans are long-term circular labour migrants and many have permanently settled on other islands. Guadalcanal people, quite correctly, objected to the encroachment onto their traditional lands by Honiara's urban sprawl and the lack of adequate recompense for the large oil palm plantations begun in the 1970s on extensive plains outside Honiara. The Guale (people of Guadalcanal) were also uneasy about environmental factors related to the new Gold Ridge mine that began production, briefly, in 1998, and their limited economic remuneration from the mine.[39] Many Guale also felt that Malaitans, the dominant immigrant group, disrespected their customary ways. After two decades of souring relations, some Guale political leaders encouraged the formation of a militia called the Isatabu Freedom Movement (IFM), which forced the expulsion of around 20,000 of their fellow citizens—overwhelmingly Malaitans—from Honiara and its surrounds. Thousands of other Solomon Islanders also evacuated their families and possessions from Honiara and returned to their home islands for the duration of the Tension. Many Malaitans acknowledge that if one lives as a guest on the land of another and is asked to leave, the honourable thing to do is to depart, which they did. This is their cultural reaction to being 'strangers', immigrants on another island. On the other hand, the Guale militants knew full well that they

---

37 Moore 2004a; Fraenkel 2004.
38 The only region of the Solomon Islands that ever came close to actual secession was Western Province in the late 1970s. Premdas, Steeves and Larmour 1984.
39 Nanau 2014. These fears have been proved correct; the mine is now closed and has done significant environmental damage.

had also insulted Malaitans and physically harmed thousands of them, and that this would eventually require customary compensation or would lead to retaliation. Here, the trope of ascribed Malaitan characteristics cuts in. I can remember giving an interview on the BBC World Service as the evacuation was occurring. When asked what would happen, based on my long knowledge of Malaitans, immediately I said that there would be large-scale retaliation. The Guale knew this better than I did, and still, utterly frustrated at losing control of the urban and most developed areas of their island, militants among them pushed 20,000 of their fellow citizens off Guadalcanal.

Alebua's behaviour was misguided; he thought he could make political mileage for himself and still control his people. He underestimated the Malaitans, who formed a rival militia to safeguard the remaining population of Honiara, which became a Malaitan-dominated enclave. The MEF combined with Malaitans in the police to take control and, six months later, staged a June 2000 coup that removed Prime Minister Ulufa`alu.

The years 1998 to 2003 were a time of turmoil as rival militias from the two islands skirmished, the parliamentary system was disrupted, and Malaitan militants patrolled Honiara. Law and order, the economy, and many other central government functions collapsed, amid calls from three prime ministers (Ulufa`alu, Sogavare and Kemakeza) for outside intervention. The saving grace was that more than 85 per cent of Solomon Islanders lived on customary land and continued to maintain themselves through subsistence agriculture and fishing. Urban law and order broke down, education and health suffered, and the export economy plummeted. The MEF and the IFM bullied and coerced in Honiara and elsewhere on Guadalcanal and in parts of Malaita, but rural life throughout much of the country continued relatively unaffected. Guadalcanal had its own internal refugees and its rural people lost access to markets in Honiara, while Malaita bulged at the seams as resources were stretched to accommodate refugees.

Figure Introduction 3: Two of the Malaita Eagles, with weapons.
Source: Clive Moore Collection.

Figure Introduction 4: Destroying Dodo Creek Agricultural Station in 2000.
Source: Clive Moore Collection.

INTRODUCTION

The country was badly scarred by the Tension and the scar covers a wound on the body of the nation that has yet to heal. RAMSI arrived in mid-2003 and quickly removed weapons and attempted to reform lapsed governance practices. Disaster struck again in 2006 when a parliamentary vote elevated a new prime minister many considered to be corrupt: Snyder Rini was forced to flee from the parliament and resigned within days. Rioters burnt down most of Chinatown, a major hotel and other shops after the police side of RAMSI mishandled the volatile situation.[40] Malaitans were involved, but the most ferocious street fighting came not from them but from Santa Cruz Islands people, famed for their accuracy with slingshots. Although some Malaitan leaders inflamed the riots they were not carried out primarily by Malaitans.[41] Nevertheless, the riots did not improve the reputation of Malaitans.

Figure Introduction 5: Honiara's Chinatown burning during the riots in April 2006.
Source: Clive Moore Collection.

---

40   Dinnen and Firth 2008; Braithwaite, Dinnen, Allen, Braithwaite and Charlesworth 2010.
41   Moore 2008a; 2014; Braithwaite, Dinnen, Allen, Braithwaite and Charlesworth 2010; O'Callaghan 2013.

The 2012 Truth and Reconciliation Commission Report, based on evidence collected between 2009 and 2011, recorded in great depth the animosities and tragedies that occurred during the Tension Years. These involved connections between the neighbouring peoples of Guadalcanal and Malaita and people's deep-seated discontents with central government planning. Solomon Islanders have indigenous means of healing conflicts that involve reconciliation and compensation processes, though they are by no means always successful. These apply established social mechanisms to normalise relations, and sometimes mechanisms of ancestral power. They pursue political and social ends, such as the restoration of social equilibrium. Today, compensation has been extended into the complex arena of national politics and often incorporates large dollar payments where once customary wealth was used. Compensation now usually also involves Christian prayer and forgiveness. That said, the societies involved remain tied to traditional lands where ancestral shrines remain, deserted perhaps, but largely intact and potent. These *tabu* (sacred) sites are preserved as part of heritage, often treated with reverence, and serve as important evidence of the land boundaries of descent groups. On Malaita, some mountain populations have never taken up Christianity and still practise their ancestral religion and conduct sacrifices in their shrines. Because of this complexity, any national reconciliation process must involve a combination of modern and ancient cultural forces that together can bring about healing.

My Relationship with Malaitans since the 1970s

The British Solomon Islands Protectorate was never an Australian territory, yet its proximity to Australia had created steady ties. I have argued elsewhere that the Coral Sea was treated by Queensland as if it were its own lake, with Solomon Islands on its eastern shore.[42] Key historical links are the Queensland labour trade; Christian missions, particularly the Queensland Kanaka Mission (QKM) and later the South Sea Evangelical Mission (SSEM) and then the South Sea Evangelical Church (SSEC), now the third-largest denomination in Solomon Islands; and the effect of the mass deportation of Solomon Islanders in the early

---

42   Moore 1997.

1900s due to the White Australia Policy. During the early twentieth century, the protectorate, rather like Australian Papua and the New Guinea Mandated Territory, became a job-hunting ground for young Australian men like William Bell, the most important Malaita district officer before the Pacific War. Australian companies such as Burns Philp & Co. and W. H. Carpenter & Co. controlled many of the plantations and maritime transport routes. Brisbane, Sydney, Port Moresby, Samarai and Rabaul became the marine and later air links to Solomon Islands. The Coastwatchers during the Pacific War reported to military authorities in Australia, and although connections waned starting in the 1950s, once the Tension began in the 1990s Australia became intimately involved, funding and controlling RAMSI starting in 2003. Today, the independent nation of Solomon Islands has far closer connections to Australia than to distant Great Britain. As well, the largest Solomon Islands community outside of the nation lives in the Pioneer Valley at Mackay in Queensland, sister city to Honiara.

I first visited Malaita in 1976 at the invitation of Ishmael Idumaoma Itea, then the most important leader in east Fataleka, a language area in the central north of the island. I was 25 years old, fresh from an honours degree and a tutorship in the history department at James Cook University, and innocent and ignorant about Solomon Islands society.[43] During 1974–75, I had become involved in a project to collect oral testimony from the descendants of Pacific Islanders who had migrated to Queensland as indentured labourers in the final four decades of the nineteenth century. Most of my oral testimony research was carried out in Mackay, where I was born, and also in the Burdekin district.[44] As a child, I attended school with Islanders, although I never had reason to differentiate Malaitans from other descendants of immigrant Islanders, today known as Australian South Sea Islanders. Then, having developed an academic interest in the history of the sugar industry and its workforce, and starting to collect oral testimonies, I became friendly with Noel Fatnowna (1929–91), the leading Malaitan in the Mackay district, and through him met Ishmael Itea (*circa* 1904–2005) who was visiting his Queensland family.[45]

---

43 Moore 2004b.
44 Moore 1979.
45 Moore 2013c, entries for Fatnowna and Itea.

Figure Introduction 6: Ishmael Idumaoma Itea (*circa* 1904–2005) at Sango, Fataleka, 1988.
Source: Clive Moore Collection.

Figure Introduction 7: Noel Fatnowna (1929–91) and Rex Ringi Angofia in Honiara in 1988.
Source: Clive Moore Collection.

Figure Introduction 8: Three east Fataleka leaders in the Bubuileli Council House, 1976.
(L to R): Salekana (holding betel nut spatula and beating time), Elu`u (with typical Malaitan woven bag) and Ishmael Itea (singing and beating time).
Source: Clive Moore Collection.

These were fortuitous relationships. The two men—one a Solomon Islander and the other an Australian—embodied qualities of leadership on Malaita. Noel was entrepreneurial and gregarious, a caring leader in his community, hobbled by his upbringing as the grandson of immigrant sugarcane labourers, which had limited his education, although he had become a senior officer in the Queensland Ambulance Service (1950–91) and then Queensland Government Commissioner for Pacific Islanders (1976–84). In 1989, Noel, assisted by anthropologist Roger Keesing, published *Fragments of a Lost Heritage*, by far the best book on Australian South Sea Islanders by a descendant.[46] Even though a third-generation Australian, he was a classic Malaitan bigman and political leader. Ishmael, from the Rakwane descent group in east Fataleka, was also a consummate leader, a statesman amongst his people, a religious leader both in their ancestral religion and Christianity, and a government leader through his roles as district headman (1949–75), member of the Malaita Council (1964–67), and elected paramount chief (1987–97). He too had little formal education, having taught himself to read and write, but he

---

46 Moore 1994–95.

combined the qualities of a Malaitan chief (*aofia*) and traditional priest (*fataabu*). I was lucky to have met them both in the 1970s, when they were at the height of their powers, since they were my passports into the Australian South Sea Islander community and Malaitan and Solomon Islands society.[47] I was also befriended by the younger Rakwane generation, the children of Itea and his brother Charles Luiramo, and their cousins, such as Rex Ringi Angofia and Fred Talo, and these have proved enduring relationships. I am proud to be adopted into the Rakwane descent group.

I researched and wrote 'Kanaka Maratta: A History of Melanesian Mackay' based on documentary and oral sources, first as a doctoral thesis submitted in 1981 and published, much altered (with Maratta removed from the title) as a monograph in 1985. *Making Mala* is a long overdue sequel to *Kanaka*. However, while the initial chapters necessarily discuss Malaitan sojourns on overseas plantations, my focus here will be on events on Malaita.

My connections with Solomon Islands always remained strong, although I also lived in and published on New Guinea, providing me with a wider Pacific perspective, and I have written about Australia, again widening my regional outlook and continuing my earlier research on the Pacific diaspora. A regular visitor to Honiara and Malaita, I have also managed to travel widely in the beautiful archipelago. Between 1998 and 2003, the Tension brought the nation, independent since 1978, close to the status of a failed state. I followed this upheaval almost day-to-day and in 2004 published my account of the events. The Tension was not primarily based on ethnicity, although it clearly had ethnic aspects. It was caused mainly by inequality in economic development and opportunity, for which the British administration and all postindependence governments must take the blame. Another recurrent trope relates to Malaitan development: Malaitans are said to be too concerned with stopping land alienation to allow development on their island. There is some truth in this—in recent years, Gwaunaru'u Airfield near 'Aoke, Malaita's main airfield, was closed due to land disputes (it reopened in May 2016). Nevertheless, even acknowledging that development is always difficult where customary land tenure survives, it has occurred elsewhere in the world and it should not be beyond the whit of a national government to keep air services viable in the most populous province and create crucial economic development opportunities.

---

47   Moore 2004b.

Soon after the Tension, between 2006 and 2008, I assisted Sir Peter Kenilorea, the nation's first prime minister, to publish his autobiography, *Tell It as It Is* (2008). Sir Peter, who died in 2016, was born in 1943 in 'Are'are in the southern part of Malaita. This collaboration gave me a chance to widen my knowledge of Malaita and to study the last 70 years of Solomon Islands history in detail, particularly the administration and politics of the nation. Currently I am involved in three more historical projects: *Solomon Islands Historical Encyclopaedia, 1893–1978*, published as a website in 2013, and monographs about urban social space on Tulagi and in Honiara. They too have prepared me for this study of the precolonial and early colonial years on Malaita and their wider context.

Since the 1970s, I have been talking to Malaitans about their history and have combed through archives and other written sources to enable me to write a history of Malaita. Initially, I considered writing about Malaita onwards from 1893, when the British protectorate over the Solomon Islands was proclaimed, until independence in 1978. Then the Tension intervened and I began to try to answer puzzles in my own mind. I knew from my 1970s research that Malaitans were a force to be reckoned with during the plantation days in Queensland and Fiji. After the Pacific War and into the 1950s Malaitans created Maasina Rule, which disturbed the British attempt to reintroduce their prewar administration. Malaitans also dominated Honiara and the economic development of Guadalcanal plains, and whenever there was an urban flashpoint Malaitans always seemed to be involved. During the tense period in the 1990s and 2000s, Malaitans were central to the dispute. Had they always been one of the most obstreperous peoples in the Pacific? Just because they lived on one island, should they really be considered to be one people? Were they different from other Solomon Islanders? These are the questions that went through my mind.

Making Mala

The argument in *Making Mala* concentrates on the 1870s to 1930s and suggests that four major elements combined disparate Mala societies into one Malaita. Malaita has an extensive anthropological literature, although much of it now dates to an earlier era, when anthropology was fixated on what were portrayed as traditional and unchanging societies. This literature does not ignore labour, Christianity and government, but equally does not usually make these themes central in the way that *Making Mala* does.

While not underplaying Peter Corris's classic *Passage, Port and Plantation*, or my own earlier writing on labour, I argue that the importance of the involvement of Malaita's menfolk in indentured labour over this 70-year period has been underestimated, as has the absence of any successful commercial development of the island. The important role of Christian missions, before there was any government presence, has also been underappreciated. This is not to ignore Ian Hogbin's early writing, Ben Burt's excellent 1994 monograph and his associated work, or Akin's writing on Christianity during Maasina Rule.[48] Nevertheless, the ethnographic historiography of Malaita does not concentrate on Christianity in the way Debra McDougall's and Christine Dureau's writings on the Western Solomons do, or Geoffrey White's and Michael Scott's writings on Isabel and Makira.[49] There are general histories of the Catholic and Anglican missions in Solomon Islands by Hugh Laracy, Claire O'Brien and David Hilliard, and of Seventh-day Adventism by Dennis Steley, but there are no detailed Malaita-wide studies of the beginnings of Christianity there.[50] Malaitans also experienced three decades of direct forceful rule by district officers, tempered before the Pacific War by a decade of half-hearted indirect rule. Only Akin's *Colonialism, Maasina Rule, and the Origins of Malaitan Kastom* provides a detailed coverage of the early years of protectorate administration and the missions on the island. The fourth element I focus on is the flexibility of Malaitans. Although often depicted as conservative and incapable of accepting change, they were in fact eminently practical when it came to change. This theme begins to be explained at the end of Chapter 2 and is carried throughout the remainder of the book.

The power of the feared head-hunters from the Western Solomons and Isabel collapsed quickly in a few years once the government established a base at Gizo in 1899 and the Shortlands in 1907. Malaitan resistance took longer for the colonial government to quell—over 20 years—and even then Malaitan success with Maasina Rule in the 1940s showed that they were united, determined, flexible, unbowed and politically

---

48 Hogbin 1939; Burt 1994; Akin 2013a. See also Keesing 1967; 1989; Guo 2009.
49 McDougall 2004; 2013; Dureau 1994; Scott 2012; 2013; White 1991; 2013.
50 Laracy 1976; Hilliard 1978; Steley 1983; 1989; O'Brien 1995.

astute. Their pacifist methods showed just how adaptable they could be. These themes will be teased out in *Making Mala* and I reach conclusions that may surprise. The combination of highlighting the importance of participation in overseas labour and Christianity (chapters 2 and 3) with detailed accounts of the establishment of the missions on Malaita (chapters 4 to 6) and the effect of labour (chapters 2, 5 and throughout) and government (chapters 7 to 10) creates a united argument. The third through the sixth chapters concentrate on the Anglican's Melanesian Mission, the QKM and the SSEM, and also contain an extensive analysis of the nature of Malaitan Christianity before and after the arrival of the protectorate government. Onwards from Chapter 7, the focus shifts to the government and Malaitan reactions to both its strictures and benefits, with religion incorporated into the analysis. The context of the aforementioned Malaitan tropes is also explored. The Conclusion draws the argument together.

The first chapter attempts to depict Malaita before outside influences, searching for the elements that enabled the people of Malaita to develop one shared culture. It seems reasonable to regard Pacific Islanders living on one island as one people, but Pacific migrations over thousands of years created diversity with hundreds of languages and small, fairly distinctive social units throughout the islands. One question here is how much did nineteenth-century Malaitans regard themselves as one people, distinct from those on neighbouring islands with local area identities tied to language areas? Many aspects of life are similar or interconnect all across Malaita—material culture, cosmology, religion, languages, music, dances and other customs—yet Malaitans never regarded themselves as one people. Although there is now a single Malaitan identity, in 1870 there was extreme regionalism and in some parts of the island links with neighbouring islands were stronger than the unity of living on the same island. There was no sense of overall 'government' or political unity. The argument presented in *Making Mala* is that much of this came together onwards from the 1870s and that the process was substantially complete by the 1930s. The Pacific War intervened, although its direct effect on Malaita was fairly minor, other than allowing breathing space from having to obey the British rulers. However, the war did expose Malaitan men to new labour and military situations that were crucial to enabling what followed. Based on newly unified Malaitan society and wartime experiences, they were able to build Maasina Rule, a formidable political movement that restored pride in the ability of the people to stand against foreign colonisation. The success of Maasina Rule was a basic building block in Solomon Islands nationalism.

Making Mala has contemporary relevance today in the modern nation. The book is an exploration of the unification process that created one Malaitan people, the largest island population in Solomon Islands. It is a study of the building blocks of Pacific nationalism and has relevance far beyond Solomon Islands because many indigenous peoples have faced similar issues.

Despite political and administrative advances, the lack of economic development and therefore opportunity on Malaita, and its consequences, were becoming increasingly clear decades ago. Along with this came the rapid path to national independence during the 1960s and 1970s when future economic and political patterns were established.[51] After independence in 1978, and particularly onwards from the late 1980s, the government of Solomon Islands was unable to steer a course free of corruption and personal greed, a result of which was poor national planning. Long-established patterns—of Malaitans relying on working away from Malaita and no realistic plans for economic development on Malaita—continued to be reinforced. Finally, the Tension Years arrived. Malaitans felt that they were left with no option other than to safeguard their own people and their rights as citizens. I am not blind to the faults of Malaitan aggression and 'masculinity', although as I will explain, these are largely tropes and not an assured reality. The pacifism of Maasina Rule is clear evidence of Malaitans' adaptability. Development choices made by Resident Commissioner Charles Woodford in the 1890s and 1900s and by planners in the 1940s are still being played out. Malaitans became a perennial labour pool for the rest of the protectorate and eventually became the major urban population in Honiara. It could have been otherwise.

Making Mala argues that elements had come together by the 1930s to create a new Malaita that was capable of united action. Malaita's dominant characteristics were no longer disparate language groups, clans and descent group clusters; Malaitans had developed an ability to act as one political entity. No one could have anticipated the enormous disruption caused by the Pacific War, which drew off labour and exposed Malaitans once more

---

51   Moore 2013b.

to new ways of thinking. The war altered the circumstances sufficiently for already imbedded cultural shifts to play out through Maasina Rule. The result was that a newly unified Malaita was able to create a successful passive resistance movement capable of forcing the British to negotiate, largely on Malaitan terms. No other single Pacific island ever accomplished this level of manipulation and control of the British. Essentially, this was all possible because the central elements of modern Malaita were 'made' by the 1920s and 1930s, and they have emerged as an ever-stronger force over the subsequent decades up to the present. We need to examine in detail the years between the 1870s and the 1930s to understand how this occurred.

The results have significant implications for development planning in the 2010s for Malaita Province, Honiara, Guadalcanal and the entire nation. There is a lesson here for planners in the Solomon Islands Government and those attached to external aid donors. They need to understand and accept historical changes and allow for them in development planning. If the argument put forward is correct—that events over 150 years have created modern Malaita—planners and politicians need to take note. If they do not, they should expect to fail.

1

Malaita in Recent Centuries

> The hill men move quickly, with a bouncing, springy walk, moving from the hips, while the shore men have a slower movement, a glide, the whole body being carried along with an easy grace. The shore men are slimmer in build, and their stature is a little taller than that of the hill men.
>
> The women of both shore and hill are much shorter than the men, but the average woman of the hills is lighter built than her sister of the shore. I have seen Lau women who were so powerfully built that one could speak of them as being enormous.
>
> —Rev. Walter Ivens, *The Island Builders of the Pacific* (1930)[1]

Today, Malaita Island still has only a limited road system consisting of one major road in the north to Lau Lagoon, a second across the central mountains to Atori on the east coast, and a third down the west coast to Su`u. There are also small feeder roads, but no substantial government roads in west Kwaio or `Are`are or on Small Malaita, leaving much of the south with no modern transport network except coastal shipping. There is, however, an extensive network of walking tracks that has been there as long as the people themselves, which, along with canoes, were always the communication network. This chapter attempts to depict old Malaita, the differences between Malaitans who lived inland and those who dwelled along the coast, the complex wealth manufacturing and trading systems that bound Malaitans to neighbouring islands, descent group territories, patterns of leadership and gender divisions. We need to understand what

---

1   Ivens 1930, 31.

Malaitans were like when they first came into contact with Europeans, as preparation for understanding changes that occurred between the 1870s and the 1930s.

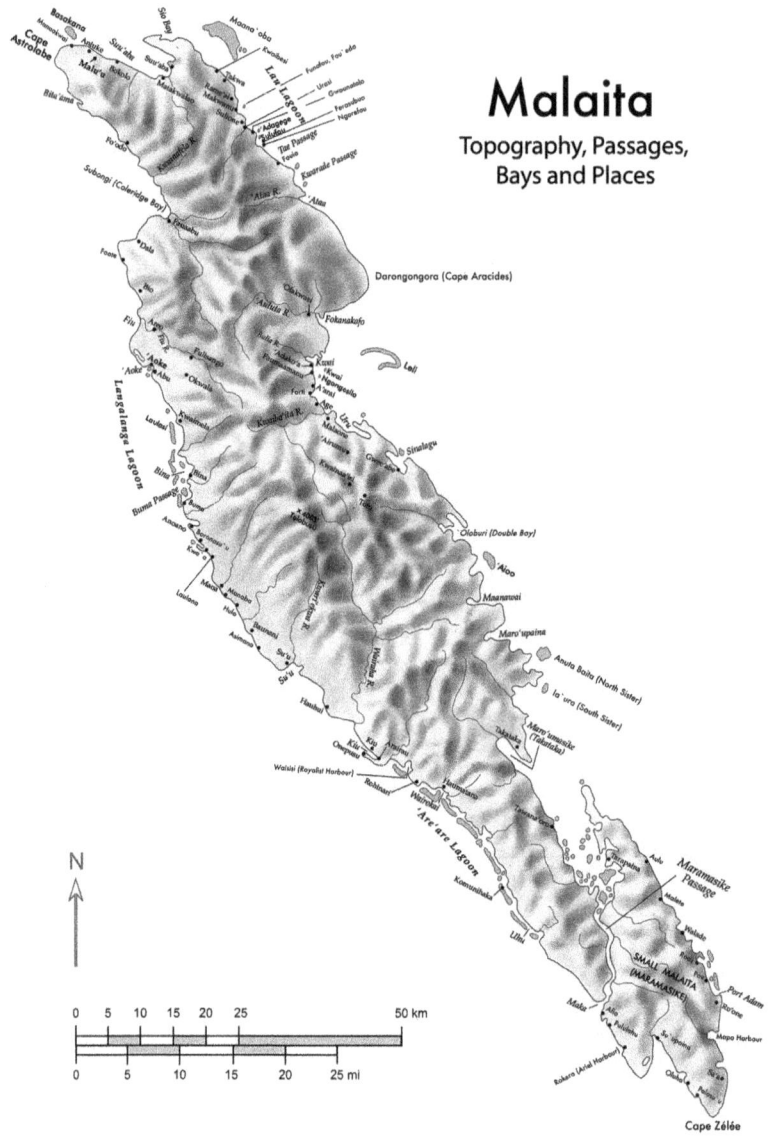

Map 2: Malaitan topography, passages, bays and place names.
Source: Courtesy of Vincent Verheyen.

1. MALAITA IN RECENT CENTURIES

Geography

Map 1 (Introduction) shows the position of Solomon Islands within the Pacific Ocean. Map 2 shows the main topographic features on Malaita and the major settlements, mainly around the coast. There are also hundreds of villages scattered throughout the inland areas, although the last century has seen a substantial shift to settlements around the coast.

Malaita is an elongated continental island with a high central spine. The island covers 4,307 square kilometres spread over a land mass 190 kilometres long and 10 to 40 kilometres wide. Its rugged central mountains commonly rise to 1,000 metres. The highest point is Mt Tolobusu in Kwaio at 1,220 metres (4,003 feet). In the north, the central ridge rises to 975 metres (3,200 feet). The interior is dissected by razor backed ridges and deep valleys that make travelling even short distances an ordeal for most outsiders. I have only been to the central mountains once, in the 1970s when I was in my 20s. I was part of a group of 12 going to sacred Fataleka ancestral shrines that had been closed for many decades. The oldest person in the party was 80 and he puffed along in 10th position, I was a slower 11th and there was always a 12th to make sure I did not fall over. The ridges we traversed were about a metre wide at the top and descended steeply for 300 metres on either side. Occasionally a fallen tree allowed a magnificent view, and rotting trees along the path had to be treaded upon with care since they disintegrated under your feet. Nevertheless, it was one of the most awesome experiences in my life.

The only substantial flat area on Malaita is around the `Aluta River basin on the central east coast, where since 1976 I have lived, cumulatively, for upwards of a year. Malaita is actually two islands separated by the narrow, winding Maramasike Passage, which is no wider than a large river at its western end and then spreads out to become a sheltered, mangrove-shrouded waterway meandering east. The central mountains combine volcanic ridges with limestone-rich karst lands, and are flanked by hilly plateaux, hills and narrow coastal terraces interspersed with valleys and swamps. Most of the coastline is made up of low terraces broken by river valleys, and on the east side high karst plateaus extend to the coast, with often precipitous descents. There are extensive shallow lagoons bound by outer reefs along the northeast (Lau), central west (Langalanga) and southwest (`Are`are) coasts, and Maramasike Passage forms another sheltered haven from harsh seas. The lagoons and the mangroves swarm with fish. Some sections of the lagoons are lake-like in appearance, while others are long narrow fringing strips, replete with passages to the open sea and patches bare at low tide. There are also small fringing islands and artificial islands. Adjoining areas of the coast, once also part of lagoons, are often swampy, and mangroves abound.

Malaita is a high tropical island with little variation in temperature and humidity throughout the year; the island has a maritime climate with two seasons based on prevailing winds. Daytime temperatures range from 20°C to 33°C. From March to November the trade winds blow from the southeast, making canoe or sailing boat travel along exposed coasts difficult. Around December the winds reverse to come from the northwest until February. This is also the cyclone season, and several travel south through the Coral Sea each year, occasionally devastating islands. Cyclones cause floods and landslides and the force of the winds can cut 10-kilometre-wide tracks through an island, stripping off all vegetation, destroying all building materials and causing famine. Cyclonic damage must always have been one catalyst for migrations. The northwest winds also bring squalls that rake along the exposed east coast. Rainfall is always heavy, although lighter on the coast than in the central mountains; 3,750 mm a year is common on the western coastal plain, while the eastern coast can receive in excess of 7,500 mm annually. The northwest season is slightly drier than when the southeast winds blow. Thousands of rain-fed streams and rivers drain the interior mountains, some navigable by small craft and canoes for several kilometres inland from their tidal reaches. Malaita Province, created in 1978 out of the old Malaita District, also includes small Maana`oba and Basakana islands off the northeast of the main island, Da`i (Gower) Island halfway to Isabel Island, many islets in the lagoons and several contiguous small islands. Remote Ontong Java and Sikaiana atolls are also part of the province, for administrative convenience rather than any strong historic relationship with Malaita.[2]

Malaita is a beautiful tropical island, from its lagoons and reefs to its high peaks and the gushing, ice-cold rivers that pour down to the coast. The island has good soils and one can imagine the delight of the first settlers in having found such a gem. However, when they first arrived, the Solomon Archipelago looked very different from today.

---

2   Great Britain Government 1974b, 3, 4–11.

First Settlement

Modern extended-family descent groups trace their ancestry back as far as 25 to 30 generations.[3] Malaitans are therefore surprised when confronted with archaeological and genetic evidence that suggests they have lived on the island for at least 10,000 years and possibly longer. Telescoping of generations has occurred, and thousands of years have been condensed into mythical ancestral categories. The 'real' direct lines of ancestors probably only have reasonable veracity for about 10 generations, typical of exact human memory and oral transmission worldwide.

The scientific proof of this long occupation comes from genetic studies in the Kwaio area[4] and archaeological evidence gathered north of Malaita in the 1980s, on Manus, New Britain and New Ireland in the Bismarck Archipelago, and from Buka, where human occupation dates back 29,000 years. During the geological Pleistocene Era—from 1 million years until about 16,000 years ago—sea levels were 60 to 100 metres lower, which made island hopping from the northern islands all the way to the eastern tip of Makira much easier. Today's Solomon Islands were once joined as one island from Buka down to Isabel and the Gela (Florida) Group. Guadalcanal was close but always separated by a deep sea trench (see Map 3).[5] Malaita was also separate but accessible by raft or canoe. Little archaeological work has been done on the island and we can only conjecture that settlement may date back tens of thousands of years.

We know that about 5,000 to 4,000 years ago 'Austronesians' travelled in canoes from the north, originally out of southern China and Taiwan and down through the Southeast Asian Archipelago. They found the earlier Papuan (or non-Austronesian) language speakers already established in the archipelagos off eastern New Guinea. We do not know if these earlier inhabitants had ventured to Malaita, but given the time-depth they could have, since their descendants live nearby on Savo and the Russell Islands. Today's Malaitan languages are all part of the Malayo-Polynesian Southeast Solomonic (Austronesian) group. The Austronesians carried with them domesticated pigs, dogs and chickens, as well as a range of nut trees and other domesticated plants. Their distinctive dentate-stamped pottery tradition known as 'Lapita' may have evolved further when they

---

3   Burt and Kwa'ioloa 2001, 10–16.
4   Friedlaender 1987; Froehlich 1987.
5   Spriggs 1997, 23–42. Skylark Passage (now Iron Bottom Sound) is deep and has always separated Gela from Guadalcanal.

'loitered' for 1,000 years in the Bismarck Archipelago. Although Lapita pottery has been found on Buka and in the New Georgia Group in the north, and south of Malaita in the Santa Cruz and Reef islands, and pottery without the Lapita dentate stamp (probably post-Lapita) has been found on Bellona, New Georgia and Isabel islands, there is no evidence that pottery was ever manufactured on Malaita.[6] These early settlers were agriculturalists who also relied on marine resources and the fauna, plus wild plant foods and cultivation, and a set of strategies that enabled them to utilise and occupy the heavily forested island.[7] Today, in times of crisis when gardens fail, Malaitans still rely on these wild plants, particularly wild taro and yams, and indigenous fauna still supplement domesticated animals and birds.[8]

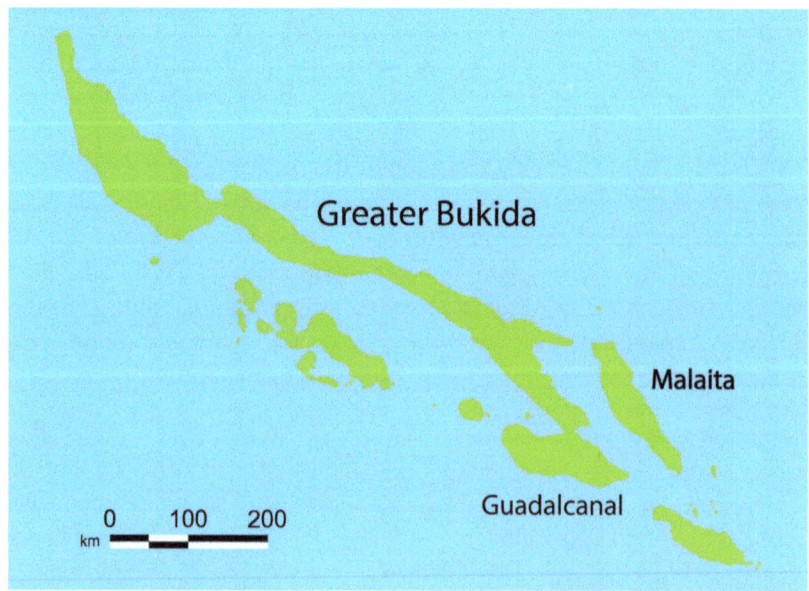

Map 3: Called Greater Bukida by some archaeologists, one long island once stretched from Buka to Isabel, with Guadalcanal almost joined to it, but never Malaita, which was within easy reach but required a sea crossing.
Source: Based on a map by Peter Sheppard, University of Auckland, redrawn by Vincent Verheyen.

6   Spriggs 1995, 113; Summerhayes 2006–07; Summerhayes and Scales 2005.
7   Moore 2003, 34–41; Spriggs 1995, 113; Bedford and Sand 2007; Bedford and Spriggs 2008; Anderson and O'Connor 2008.
8   Mayr 1931.

1. MALAITA IN RECENT CENTURIES

These early migrants arrived in small numbers and adapted to their new environment. Probably around 1,000 years ago, Austronesian societies became less involved in long-distance migrations and were more sedentary, leading to development of smaller dialect chains and fixed settlements in various localities. Political ideology became more localised and territory-based and inland economic resources were incorporated into indigenous economies as horticulture became more important to support a growing population.⁹ Malaria probably always acted as a limiter on population expansion. The *Plasmodium vivax* parasite only requires around 100 humans to maintain the disease and would have become a population limiter soon after the migrants arrived. The disease itself, and related birth spacing—suggested to have been around four to five years, necessary for the physical and psychological wellbeing of mothers—slowed population increases.¹⁰ If we assume an initial few canoe loads of humans, and perhaps some later similar migrations both from the north and south, the population buildup on Malaita would have been very slow. Initially, Malaitans would have lived in small colonies around the coast, each increasingly localised. Malaria is not transmitted at higher elevations, however, and so was not as important a population limiter as on some other islands because eventually the great majority of Malaitans lived in high inland areas.

Once we discount the longer-term accuracy of Malaitan genealogies, there is little to guide us between the first arrivals and recent centuries. The work of geographer Patrick Nun provides a few Pacific-wide clues. There was a climatic 'medieval' warm period from AD 700 to 1250, a time of plenty when long-distance voyaging still flourished. This was followed by rapid cooling and increased precipitation *circa* AD 1250 to 1350, which would have caused a food crisis for coastal inhabitants and societal tensions. There was an even cooler period from AD 1350 to 1800 when there was higher climate variability and a food crisis, further exacerbating tensions and disruptions. Finally, post-AD 1800 a warmer period with reduced climate variability allowed societies to recover, although people's interactions with foreigners have obscured much of

---

9   I have been guided by Takuya Nagaoka's conclusions from Nusa Roviana in the New Georgia Group (2011, 296).
10 Groube 1993; Spriggs 1997, 39–40.

this recent change. If we follow the scenario sketched here, in recent centuries Malaita was home to prosperous societies capable of supporting substantial populations, most of them inland.[11]

The first, fleeting contact with Europeans began in the sixteenth century, although there was no substantial interaction until the nineteenth century. All of the early European accounts describe people living in ways not dissimilar to today, with a clear division between people who lived a maritime existence and a larger group living in the mountainous interior.

Malaitan Languages and Territories

For readers to fully understand what follows, I must introduce contemporary Malaitan languages and dialects, as depicted in Map 4, and their political and social dimensions. When talking to Malaitans, conversations inevitably contextualise individuals within their language affiliations or descent group territories. Most Malaitans know their 'generations', land rights and any relationships with Malaitans from other areas of the island, but readers should not assume that the 'shape' of modern language areas dates back unchanged to some mythical first settlement thousands of years ago. Language areas developed through initial isolation of settlements in various parts of the island and have been continuously reshaped in more recent times. The colonial government used language zones as they understood them as administrative divisions and at times falsely separated groups, sometimes using a river as a marker of the divide. This is the origin of the east coast Fataleka–Kwara`ae border, which follows the `Aluta River at Fokanakafo Bay. The reality is more complex.

There are Malaitan words that describe the two main residential groups: *to`aitolo*, inland people, and *to`aiasi*, peoples of the coast and lagoons, particularly the artificial islands in the lagoons. Because the spelling of these words differs throughout the island, I have used the equivalent English words instead.

---

11   Nunn 2007; Nunn. Hunter-Anderson, Carson, Thomas, Ulm and Rowland 2007.

1. MALAITA IN RECENT CENTURIES

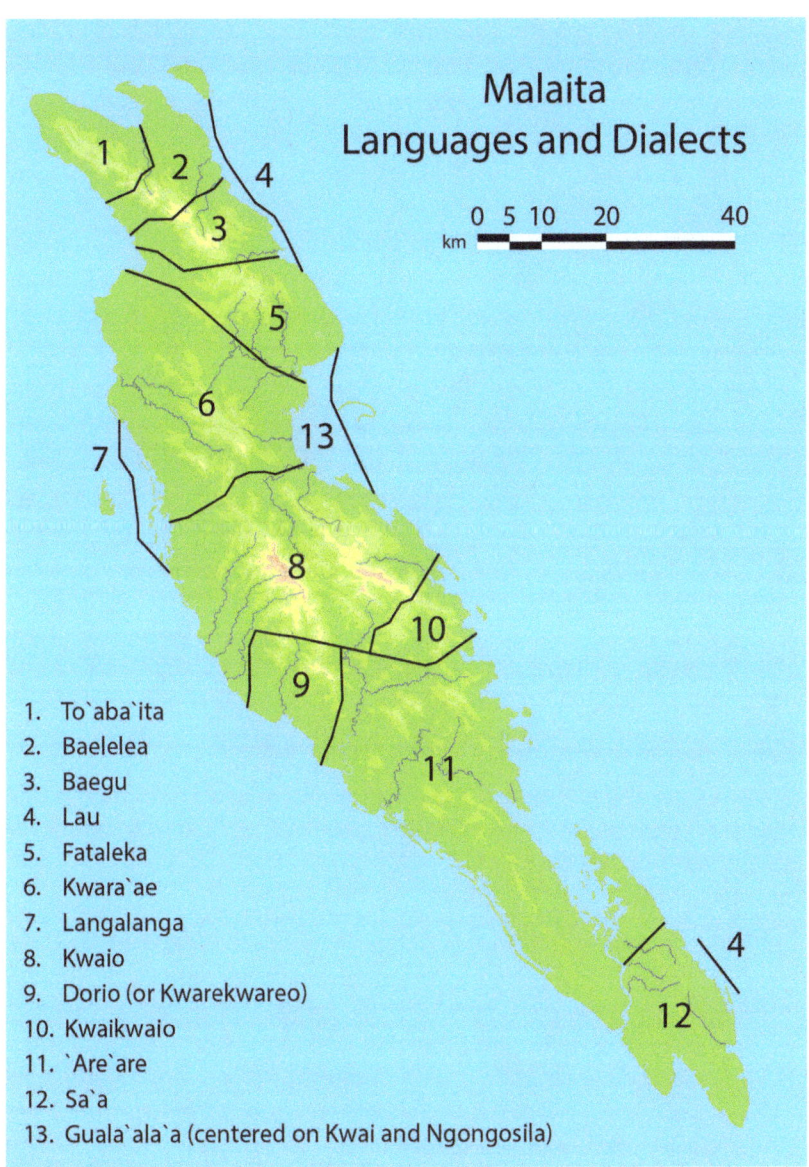

Map 4: Malaita languages and dialects. Guala`ala`a is the language of Kwai and Ngongosila, and is also used for trade along the east coast.
Source: Courtesy of Vincent Verheyen.

Again, the vast majority of Malaitans were inland people, although today many of the inland descent groups, or some members, have left their mountain domains to live in coastal villages, making the divisions less clear than in the past. Anglican missionary Walter Ivens, who lived on or was a constant visitor to Small Malaita between 1895 and 1909, noted that there were virtually no villages on the coast, other than those on artificial islands in the lagoons and transitory populations on the few small offshore islands such as `Aioo, Anuta Baita and Ia`ura on the east coast.[12] The coastal people were the first to come into contact with outsiders and they subsequently became the intermediaries in dealings between inland peoples and foreigners. Despite the divisions in places of residence, coastal people were and are closely related to their inland neighbours by kinship, language and exchange systems and regular trade, although, because of their coastal position, their ancestors include more castaways and migrant groups. The people who lived on the artificial islands in the lagoons moved offshore for greater security and access to fishing and to escape malaria-carrying mosquitoes.[13] Some had migrated around the coast or from other islands to escape feuds, sorcery, disease or famine. Landless, they built their own islands in the lagoons. Others are descendants of trading partners from neighbouring islands such as Isabel, Makira, Guadalcanal and Gela.

Reports from the nineteenth and early twentieth centuries indicate little trust and limited interaction between the inland and coastal people. The latter saw themselves as more sophisticated than their inland 'country cousins', who in turn believed that they were morally superior to the more 'wayward' coastal people. The crowded artificial islands were a unique environment laboriously constructed in the lagoons, where their inhabitants survived by trading resources of the ocean and the lagoons for the agricultural and other products of the inland people.[14] The time-depth of the lagoon settlements is quite short, probably around 600 years, and, based on genealogies, the Lau precede the peoples of Langalanga and `Are`are lagoons.[15] The open sea abounds with fish, particularly bonito, tuna and mackerel. The lagoons and reefs provide smaller fish, crayfish, crabs, shellfish and *bêche-de-mer*. Fruits from the *Bruguiera* mangrove are processed to make a delectable food called *koa*, and molluscs and bivalves

---

12   Ivens 1930, 21.
13   Parsonson 1966; 1968; Chowning 1968.
14   Ross 1970; 1976; 1977; 1978b; Akimichi 1978; Cooper 1970; 1971; 1972.
15   Maranda 2001, 97; 2008; Guo 2003.

are standard fare. Porpoises are still caught seasonally, both for food and for their teeth, which are a recognised currency throughout the island. Hawksbill turtles were once plentiful, as were estuarine and saltwater crocodiles.

Canoes of all sizes—from tiny dugouts for children to ocean-going war canoes 20 metres long and capable of holding over 30 men—were the common vehicles of the coastal people, just as in other areas of Solomon Islands. The large canoes were made from planks shaped with adzes and smoothed with hard stones, and laced on the edge with dry creeper fibre, all squeezed into shape by an external frame, the pressure balanced by the internal ribs made from curved mangrove roots and benches wedged across at intervals. The lacing was gradually tightened and the joints caulked with cement made from puttynut flesh that dries hard. The smaller canoes are dugouts, but these can also be as long as 9 metres.[16]

Figure 1.1: Malaitan plank-built ocean-going canoe from Langalanga Lagoon.
Source: Ivens 1930, 224.

---

16   Hopkins 1904, 7.

Figure 1.2: Malaitan women and children in dugout canoes near one of the artificial islands, possibly in Lau Lagoon.
Source: Cromar 1935.

Most people who did not live in the lagoons did not use canoes regularly, although some 'Are'are people did, as their lands bordered lagoons on the west coast and were cut through by Maramasike Passage. To'aba'ita people used outrigger and dugout canoes to traverse the sheltered Suu'aba Bay in the far north.[17] The inland people met regularly but guardedly with the coastal people on market days at specified places along the shore. On borders between language groups there was always a blurring of differences, and intermarriage created a maze of kinship links. For instance, the Rakwane people from the mountains of east Fataleka are closely related by marriage to the coastal people at 'Ataa (and therefore the rest of Lau) and people at Walade on Small Malaita, and also the Baegu, who they claim are partly an out-movement from Fataleka descent groups. The Rakwane and other Fataleka people also have Kwaio and Kwara'ae connections. Similar links occurred all over Malaita.[18]

---

17 Ivens 1930, 29; Coombe 1911, 289; Woodford 1909.
18 Anthropologist Remo Guidieri (1972; 1975a; 1975b; 1976; 1980) worked in Fataleka in the 1970s.

1. MALAITA IN RECENT CENTURIES

In 1904, there were around 20 artificial islands in lagoons along the northeast coast, spread between ʻAtaa at the south of Lau Lagoon and Suuʻaba Bay in Toʻabaʻita. Some were as big as half an acre (0.2 hectare). The average artificial island had a population of around 200. When the number of inhabitants became too great then new houses were built on stilts off the edge. If overcrowding continued, a new island was constructed. Shrines for ancestral worship were located on the artificial islands and worship continued in much the same way it did on land.

Coastal people traded their produce with the inland people at beach markets every three or four days, and although there was intermarriage, for the most part they kept themselves separate. The inland people lived in the central mountains or if nearer the shore then high up on coastal mountain slopes. They possessed large territories containing central shrines for ancestral worship and were related each to the other by descent from founding ancestors. Most mountain people could not swim and few felt at home in water environments. Their settlements were always small—four or five houses, usually on ridges. Neighbouring hamlets were really chains of extended families. The hamlet pattern was probably adopted to safeguard against attacks while remaining in easy communication distance, but the small settlements also meant that endemic diseases, such as respiratory problems including tuberculosis, and also leprosy (Hansen's disease), could be better isolated. This same residential pattern may have mitigated the impact of new diseases carried back by participants in the overseas labour trade. There was always movement: new families moved to new areas; and when there were outbreaks of diseases, infected hamlets were deserted. Great natural disasters such as cyclones, floods and earthquakes could also cause migrations.

As horticulturalists, Solomon Islanders used shifting cultivation methods to farm swamp and dry taro, varieties of yams (mainly one known as *pana*), recently introduced sweet potatoes or *kumara* (*Ipomoea batatas*), bananas, sugarcane and many varieties of green vegetables, particularly *Hibiscus manihot*.[19] The men cleared patches of primary or secondary forest, and women then planted root crops on the land over one to three years, before

---

19   *Colocasia esculenta* is the main variety; it cannot be stored and must be eaten within three days of picking. It is usually cooked in, or roasted on, hot stones. *Cyrtosperma chamissonis* (swamp taro) is used mainly in puddings, or as raw grated slices, leaf-wrapped and baked in a stone oven. There are also other varieties: *Alocasia macrorrhiza* and *A. Amorphophallus*, which are used in times of crop failure. Yams (*Dioscorea alata*) and pana (*D. esculenta*) are cultivated in recently forested loam, and are cooked in similar style to taro. They store well for up to five months. Tedder 1973.

gardens sites were left to regenerate for up to 25 years. The cycle could be shorter—10 to 20 years, dependent on soil fertility and population pressures—and tree crops remained in use over decades. Taro and yam cultivation involved rituals at planting, weeding and harvest times. Taro, in particular, requires specific soil types and frequently moved garden plots, which necessitates control over large areas and suits smaller, less permanent settlements. The labour input was efficient but this method of cultivation needed large land areas—around 3.75 hectares for each person over an average lifetime.[20]

Figure 1.3: Maasupa Village, Maro`umasike (Takataka or Deep Bay), east `Are`are, 1970s.
Source: Photograph by Daniel de Coppet, 1973, Hugo Zemp Collection.

Villagers also raised pigs for ceremonies and exchange, although overall pork was never a large part of diets. Pigs needed large areas of land, and either the gardens had to be fenced to keep them out or enclosures were built to protect crops and house the animals. The lagoon people kept pigs penned up on their artificial islands. The inland people were primarily vegetarians, consuming root crops, green vegetables and nuts in large amounts to provide sufficient bulk and obtain enough protein, keeping their pigs for consumption at ceremonies and feasts.[21]

---

20   Bennett 1987, 10.
21   Insects are an important source of protein for inland children.

Wild foods, particularly yams, taro and small animals such as possums, bats, flying foxes, arboreal rats, feral pigs, birds (particularly *Ducula* pigeons and hornbills) and insects supplemented swidden horticulture. People lived off these for short periods if there was a famine due to a cyclone or some other traumatic event. Travellers needed no more than a fire-stick and weapons at their side, relying on wild food for sustenance and building rough shelters in the bush. Through trade, both inland and coastal peoples shared the exploitation of useful cultivated trees, including coconuts, and two species of protein-rich *ngali* (*Canarium*) nuts,[22] a favourite seasonal staple, mixed with taro to make puddings. The nuts from betel palms provided a stimulant and recreational drug, and the pith of sago palms was used as food for pigs and as food for humans in emergencies, while the leaves were used as thatch for houses. Breadfruit was also cultivated.

The size of Malaita's population before contact with the outside world is unknown, although there is enough evidence to say that the island was heavily populated.[23] However, the Malaitan habit of moving residence every few years, and sometimes returning to old village sites, may have skewed the statistics. Foreigner observers equated abandoned sites as signs of population decline, although they only had easy access to the coast and seldom ventured inland. Their estimates are all from long after first contact with the outside world, which we know on other islands introduced new diseases that reduced population levels. The first full government census in 1931 calculated a total of 41,052 Malaitans, as well as another 5,000 either working or domiciled in other parts of the protectorate. There is reason to believe that the census was not an accurate count of the inhabitants of the central mountains. A 5,000 to 10,000 discrepancy would be believable, taking the real population to around 50,000.[24] Descriptions left by the Mendaña expedition of 1568 suggest that Guadalcanal was more heavily populated than Malaita, although the Spanish records are contradictory, and they never went inland.[25] The presence of irrigated taro pond-fields and 'plantation scale' *Canarium* growing/processing in the Visale area on Guadalcanal suggests a substantial population existed about 1,200 to 1,000 years before the present, which presumably traded with surrounding islands. The British

---

22   *Canarium indicum* and the 'wild' *C. salomonense*.
23   Boutilier 1979, 45.
24   McArthur 1961, 9; SINA, BSIP 14/62, DO Malaita to SG, 6 June 1931.
25   Spriggs 1997, 223–36.

records of the last 100 years show that Guadalcanal carried less than half the population of its eastern neighbour, Malaita.[26] It is unclear exactly what caused the changes that led to population decline on Guadalcanal while Malaita maintained or perhaps increased its population.[27] Daniel de Coppet and Matthew Spriggs both suggest that depopulation may have begun with diseases introduced by the Spanish, although it is difficult to be sure that oral testimony gathered in the twentieth century is accurate that far back.[28]

Perhaps it is because Malaita was spared most of the predatory raids by head-hunters from the north during the second half of the nineteenth century, and may also have escaped disease epidemics that depopulated islands in closer contact with whalers and traders in the first half of the century. It may also be that men returning from work as indentured labourers in the 1870s did introduce new disease and that a level of immunity had developed by the 1890s, allowing the population to increase again. In more recent times, Malaita and Bougainville have been the most populous of the Solomon Islands. Bougainville is larger than Malaita; although proportional to its geographic size, Malaita seems always to have been more heavily populated. Recent estimates of the precontact population of Vanuatu suggest that its islands (now with a population half that of the Solomons) might once have been home to 700,000.[29] The precontact population of Solomon Islands, recorded as 94,066 on 1931, may once have been in excess of 200,000 and possibly twice or even three times that level. A precontact number of 500,000, close to the present-day population level of 625,000, is entirely plausible and may still be far too low an estimate. Malaita could easily have had a precontact population in excess of 100,000. Demographic issues are addressed throughout this book with conclusions presented in Chapter 10.

---

26   Amherst and Thomson 1967 [1901] (Guadalcanal) 40, 90, 175–76, 177, 292, 309 (Malaita) 25, 45, 90, 177, 345.
27   Roe 1992. I am indebted to David Roe for discussion of his research on Guadalcanal. Great Britain Government 1974a, 1–4; Solomon Islands Government, Ministry of Provincial Government 2001a (Guadalcanal), 4; Amherst and Thomson 1967 [1901], 177, 181.
28   Coppet 1977; Spriggs 1997, 234.
29   Matthew Spriggs conjectures that Vanuatu could once have carried a larger population than Solomon Islands, given its constantly renewing volcanic soils, lower rainfall and lower levels of malaria, plus evidence of major centres of taro irrigation on south Aneityum, northwest Santo and central and south Pentecost and Maewo. The precontact population of Solomon Islands was probably in excess of 200,000 and possibly twice or even three times that level. A figure of 600,000, close to the present-day population level, is entirely plausible. SINA, BSIP 14/40, RM TWE-P to RC CMW, 30 Mar 1911; Huffman 2012; conversation with Matthew Spriggs, The Australian National University, Nov 2012.

Wealth and Trade

Malaita was known throughout the archipelago for its manufacture of wealth items. Before the introduction of European manufactured goods, Malaitan trade was central to the archipelago's economy. Solomon Islanders use many traditional forms of wealth, made from shells, porpoise and dog teeth, feathers and stone, used for compensation and payments in bride exchanges and mortuary feasts. None of these wealth systems equate exactly with European currency. Each island had its own 'valuables', with rarer forms regarded as sacred and kept only by chiefs and priests.[30] Government officers learnt to calculate the modern value of tradition wealth and sometimes these items were used to pay fines or taxes, or as good behaviour bonds.

Interisland and intraisland exchange and trade networks allowed raw materials and manufactured goods and foods to circulate. Just as Malaitan cosmology connected the 'eight isles' (see below), trade was also networked with Ulawa, Uki (also Uki ni masi), Three Sisters and Makira in the east, and Guadalcanal, Gela, Savo, Russell (also known as Cape Marsh) and Isabel islands in the west and north. Aside from these interisland links, the inland and coastal people traded regularly with each other at the weekly markets and on other occasions. There was a regular trade in adze blades and shells for manufactured wealth items, ornaments and shell-cutting tools, foods such as taro and *Canarium* nuts, and exchanges of women through marriage.[31]

Malaita had several types of currency valuables: strings of porpoise teeth and shell valuables, largely produced and controlled by the coastal people, and flying-fox and dogs' teeth, which are available all over the island. Shell and other body ornaments and special sacred weapons extended the varieties of Malaitan wealth items. Shell and teeth wealth is used for marriage exchanges or other ceremonial occasions and in compensation

---

30   Burt and Bolton 2014.
31   Five areas of the Solomon Islands are well known for the manufacture of shell valuables: several parts of Malaita; at Houniho on Makira; at Talise on Guadalcanal's south coast; on Choiseul; and the Roviana and Marovo lagoons on New Georgia, where arm rings are manufactured from fossilised clam shells. Ross 1970; Green 1976, 13; Bennett 1987, 14; Moore 2013c entry for 'Material Culture: Forms of Wealth'.

payments, and can be used as apparel to indicate wealth and dignity.[32] Shell valuables were circulated, used in transactions to create, perpetuate and repair social relationships. Marriages necessitated large exchanges of valuables and food, as did mortuary payments, rewards for services, and compensations for wrongs. As in most Near Oceanic societies, circulation was a more important means for social advancement than was accumulation.

The main form of shell valuables, *bata*, was (and still is) laboriously manufactured by clans in Langalanga Lagoon on the west coast. *Bata* was traded through intermediaries over long distances north as far as Bougainville, New Britain and Manus in Papua New Guinea, and south to the Banks Group in Vanuatu.[33] *Bata* consists of polished sections of red, white and black bivalve mollusc shells interspersed with small beads made from seeds (*fulu* and *kekete*) strung onto pandanus fibre strings of various lengths. The usual form is ten-strings wide and a fathom (1.82 metres or 6 feet) long, separated by wooden or turtle-shell bars and decorated with colourful tassels of *kekete* seeds and, now, pieces of red cloth. In the Langalanga language it is called *akwala`afi*, but this wealth item is more usually known as *tafuli`ae* (the Kwara`ae word).[34] Smaller pieces were used for lesser transactions and all *bata* could carry magical properties. The *fulu* and *kekete* seeds came from riverine plants, and were usually obtained from the nearby mainland. The most essential and high-value shells, the red *romu*, were found on the reef face about 10 fathoms down. They came mainly from Langalanga, around Tarapaina in Maramasike Passage, Suu`aba Bay and Maana`oba Island in To`aba`ita, Lau Lagoon and Boli Passage, Gela. Another shell, the white *kakadu*, also came from reefs but not from the same depth and was usually purchased from Tarapaina or Boli. The third essential shell, *kurila*, is black, much larger (8 millimetres in diameter) and collected in Langalanga Lagoon or from north Malaita.

Based on observations back to those of Woodford in the early 1900s, Matthew Cooper described seven forms of Langalanga shell valuables. They vary through colour, the size of the shell beads, the level of finish and the number of strings. Although no longer used for day-to-day purchases, since modern drills were introduced *bata* have become almost

---
32   Guo 2004; 2006.
33   Bennett 1987, 267 notes that in the 1930s Langalanga shell wealth was being traded to the Shortlands and Bougainville. See also Connell 1977.
34   My thanks to Pei-yi Guo for her advice on these terms, Taiwan, January 2015.

ubiquitous in Solomon Islands, essential for bridewealth payments and other ceremonies. Today, short strings are also sold as fashionable necklaces throughout the Western Pacific. The processing—cutting, drilling and polishing—is complex, involved the whole community and was incorporated into religious practices. Elaborate rituals accompanied the diving for shells (for instance, to insure against shark attack), and collection was done in limited seasons to conserve supply. Most of the process was women's work, although males did the diving, the long-distance trading and the final polishing. Before modern tools, one *tafuli`ae* is estimated to have taken one woman one month to produce, providing some idea of its relative value. Polygamous households made the division of labour possible, although it is unlikely that women were ever totally dedicated to making *bata*, since they shared household duties.[35]

Figure 1.4: Langalanga women using hand drills to make holes in the process of making *akwala`afi* shell wealth in 1933.
Source: Temple Crocker Expedition.

---

35 Guo 2014; Kwa`ioloa 2014; Deck 1934; Woodford 1908; Bartle 1952; Cooper 1971; Connell 1977.

Figure 1.5: Langalanga women grinding shells to make *akwala`afi* during a 1998 demonstration of shell wealth manufacture for tourists on Gwaelaga Island.

Source: Pei-yi Guo Collection, 1998.

Figure 1.6: Lobotalau rolls up his *bata* after a mortuary feast for the death of Na`oni`au at `Ai`eda in east Kwaio in August 1996.

Source: Photograph by David Akin.

The Kwaio and `Are`are manufacture other predominantly white forms of *bata* (which the Kwaio call *kofu*), some of which are longer than *tafuli`ae*. The Lau Lagoon people also have their own, similar forms of shell wealth. The To`aba`ita, Baelelea, Baegu, Fataleka and Kwara`ae seem to have relied on trading with their neighbours for their supplies.[36] However, all Malaitan-language groups used short *bata* strings for compensation, for which they often purchased the raw materials from Langalanga. Malaitan shell valuables reached neighbouring Guadalcanal via the `Are`are colony at Marau Sound, although Guadalcanal also had its own form of shell wealth.[37]

Valuable items often mix together shell beads and teeth. Porpoises were hunted mainly from around Fauaabu on the northwest coast, Bita`ama and Basakana in the north, Uru in east Kwaio and at Walade on Small Malaita, and there were also porpoise drives in other areas such as Langalanga and Lau Lagoons. People on neighbouring Makira also hunted porpoise for meat and used their teeth for valuables and decoration.[38] There are eight extant species of porpoises, which are actually small, toothed whales and closely related to oceanic dolphins. The teeth were obtained in annual drives that collectively killed thousands of the animals. One or two hundred and sometimes up to 600 porpoises could be killed in one drive, with around 150 usable teeth collected from each animal. The old hunting method continues to be used in some places: stones are hit together underwater to drive the animals to shore (upsetting their soundwave reception), where they bury their heads in the sand or mud, easy targets for people waiting to club them to death. Their teeth are extracted and strung together as currency and ornamentation. In the past, ancestral and later Christian religious rituals accompanied the drives.[39]

---

36 Hogbin 1939, 48–50, 61–63; Ross 1973, 88–91; Burt 1994, 39–40; Akin 1999a.
37 Gege 2014.
38 *BSIP News Sheet*, 15 June 1971; Cromar 1935, 204.
39 *BSIP News Sheet*, 31 Aug 1968; Dawbin 1966; PMB 1290, Woodford Papers, Reel 2, Bundle 15, 10/31/1–3 and 4/32/1, F. J. Barnett, 'Notes and Photographs on Porpoise Catching at Auki, Malaita', Nov 1909.

Figure 1.7: Porpoise hunting at Bita'ama, north Malaita, early 1960s.
Source: John Todd Collection, British Museum.

Porpoise, flying-fox, possum and dog teeth also were worn as necklaces and collars and were used as currencies. Indigenous dogs were supplemented from the nineteenth century onward with imported dogs. Human teeth were worn in a similar fashion, attached as a fringe to red shell bead bandoleer-style chest ornaments, called `umaaru in Kwaio, or as necklaces, called kolee`uma in Kwaio. However, these ornaments generally had ancestral heirloom significance and so were not circulated in exchange.

On Malaita, exchanges around the coast and beyond were accomplished by the lagoon and artificial island-dwellers, providing them with some control over their inland neighbours, although some of the wealth items were available all over the island. Dog teeth were also used as currency in the Eastern Solomons and on Guadalcanal. In 1896, Marau Sound trader Oscar Svensen estimated that one-quarter of a million dog teeth had passed through his hands since he began trading in the Eastern Solomons and on Guadalcanal in 1890. In the nineteenth century, a trade developed in dogs from Australia and hundreds were imported for their teeth.[40]

---

40   Bathgate 1993, 56; Bennett 1981a; Laracy 2013, 116.

Figure 1.8: Gwali Asi of Sulufou artificial island was an important bigman in Lau Lagoon early in the twentieth century.

Wearing porpoise teeth as befits his status, he suffered from blindness. Missionary Walter Ivens said that this was a common condition caused from glare on the water, though Gwali Asi may also have had cataracts.

Source: Ivens 1930, frontispiece.

As will be discussed in the next chapter, the importance of this wealth item trade was disturbed when the Western Solomons and Makira achieved earlier access to European manufactured items (usually called 'trade goods') than did Malaita. The New Georgia and Isabel head-hunters further disrupted trading patterns to the north of Malaita.

Territory and Leadership

Control of wealth was in the hands of leading men in descent groups or larger clusters of descent groups, each with its land and sometimes also sea territories. Describing Malaitan societal and territorial divisions requires I slip between past and present tense. Some characteristics remain the same—in inland areas, particularly in Kwaio, there has been less change—while other areas have now altered considerably. Some of the Kwaio and other, smaller remnants in `Are`are, Kwara`ae, Fataleka and Baegu have never adopted Christianity and prefer to maintain worship of their ancestors. For them, these descriptions require the present tense, but for most Malaitans the description is of the past, although territorial allegiances have survived and old gender divisions have been partly enforced.

Figure 1.9: A large hamlet in central Kwaio, inland from Sinalagu, in `Oloburi Harbour's watershed. Two men's houses sit at the upper reaches.

Source: Photograph by David Akin, 1996.

Land on Malaita remains divided into nested, named territories that vary in size, with each territory related to surrounding territories by an ordered relationship through descent from founding ancestors. Up until the late nineteenth century, when outside influences began to alter residential patterns, Malaitans lived in kin-based groups, each related to the other by descent from primary ancestors in an established hierarchy. Each territory contains sacred ancestral shrines where sacrifice of pigs took place. In Fataleka, the shrines were ranked depending on the precedence and importance of the ancestors buried there, although this is not the case in Kwaio (though Kwaio do have primary shrines and secondary, satellite shrines). In prayers and sacrificial ceremonies, priests must recite long lists of ancestors, whereas in today's Christian communities these lists are often written down to use as proof of heritage and claims in land courts. Even for Christian Malaitans, ancestors remain central to life. The ancestors differ in power and importance; some are from the mythical past, while others are more recent, from a century or more ago. The spirits of dead parents, grandparents and even siblings may receive sacrificial pigs. In major sacrifices, a Kwaio priest gives pigs not just to the shrine's apical ancestor (or ancestress), but also to the entire line of priestly spirits who sacrificed there before him, through which the group's connection to the founding ancestor has been maintained. Access to power is through this ancestral hierarchy. In a non-Christian community, everyone understands the power of the spirit world, but only specialist priests have the right to perform rituals to intercede directly with the more important *akalo* (ancestral spirits) and possess the secret knowledge, such as spells, to do so properly. Many people in a given community, including some women, have a deep understanding of their ancestors, and sometimes of the rituals involved. The rituals are performed by groups of men led by the priests.

One of the primary assets of any descent group is their land, which for coastal and lagoon-dwellers extends to their reefs and marine resources. Anthropologist Daniel de Coppet wrote of the views on land of Aliki Nono`oohimae Eerehau, the great twentieth-century `Are`are leader. Nono`oohimae explained that it was not that the people owned the land, but rather that the land owned the people:

> Land is not only part of the genealogical origin of each living person, land is also intimately related to each succeeding generation, to each male or female descendant, including those living today… Land is clearly not simply soil, but rather an entity fused with the ancestors, under whose joint authority the living are placed.[41]

Inland descent group territories average 80 to 120 hectares, while coastal territories may include a fringe of the coast, real and artificial islands and surrounding reefs and fishing areas. A shrine was the conceptual centre of the territory, but often outer boundaries are less defined, each merging into its neighbour, marked by natural features such as rivers and rocky outcrops. Shrines also existed on artificial islands, where spatial divisions mirrored those on land. Descent group territories all have names, which apply both to the land and to the people entitled to live there. Land and maritime rights are communal, not individual, shared by all in the corporate group who can trace a line of descent from the putative founding ancestor of the territory. Individuals have ties with numerous descent group territories. Map 5, depicting east Fataleka, shows a migration pattern that is similar elsewhere. Inland clans always claim to be descended from central shrines in the mountains, though there must have been a migration to the centre before the descent to the coast.

Land is more than a physical asset. When Malaitans look at their land they also see the dimension of time: the past exists in the present. To use Roger Keesing's description of the Kwaio:

> The ancestors are not simply remembered; they are ever present. It is they who confer the stream of spiritual energy without which humans cannot succeed, and infuse the efforts of their descendants with power (*mana*) as pigs consecrated in their names root around Kwaio settlements. The ancestors also zealously watch over their descendants to be sure that a rigid and complex set of taboos are carefully observed. Violation brings down ancestral punishment, manifest in sickness, death or misfortune, and only sacrifice of pigs can cleanse the violation and restore the balance of good living.[42]

---

41 Coppet 1985, 81.
42 Keesing 1975, 33.

1. MALAITA IN RECENT CENTURIES

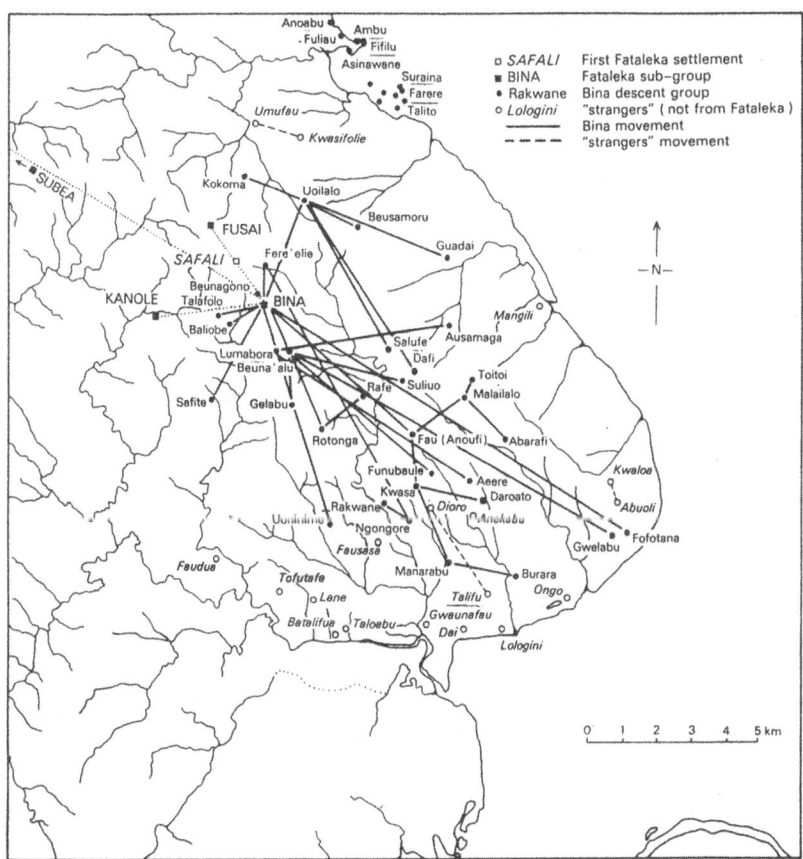

Map 5: East Fataleka migration patterns from Bina to Fokanakafo Bay, according to oral testimony in the 1970s.
Source: Moore 1981a, 34.

Malaitans can inherit land through cognate descent links to founding ancestors traced through combinations of male and female forebears. All people who can demonstrate such links have some rights to live and cultivate within a territory, but there is a patrilineal bias that gives primary rights to those descended only through male links. Those related to a piece of land through cognatic or matrilineal ties need formal permission from primary owners to use it. Sometimes people with secondary rights, because of long-term residence on the land, and linked to the primary ownership lineages through intermarriage, can become primary residents with the equivalent of primary rights. This occurs particularly where the direct descendants of the original land owners have died out or are weak politically. Before Christianity and modern systems of government,

65

control of land rested with male primary landowners and was perpetuated through the priestly sacrifices in shrines. Senior male descendants controlled sacrifices to ancestors and the distribution of primary and usufructuary rights to land. Not everyone possesses deep genealogical knowledge, and experts are brought in to testify in land disputes.[43]

Exercising one's rights to belong to a descent group is the basis for residential mobility within and between language areas. Individuals may live in several places in a lifetime or even in two simultaneously. Swidden horticulture and the impermanence of leaf, wood and bamboo houses enable this flexibility and mobility. These rights carried responsibilities to propitiate and carry on reciprocal relationships with ancestral spirits. Malaitans do not divide their lives neatly into secular and religious activities. Individuals are part of descent groups within territories that are the physical focus of their cosmological outlook. The descent groups conduct religious festivals (particular mortuary feasts), make sacrifices and share word, food and many other taboos enforced by their shared ancestors,[44] to whom they also dedicate their gardens and fishing grounds. Ancestors empower the group in all their undertakings, or withhold their power when they are displeased. In the past, descent group alliances changed as these groups accumulated, controlled or lost wealth, arranged feasts and marriages, and interacted with other kin units in warfare, politics and exchange. *Mamana*, the Malaitan version of *mana* (power), resided in leading individuals and descent groups, but could ebb and flow dependent on ability, hard work and ancestral support.

Traditional leadership on Malaita has both secular and religious aspects. Formal positions of power vary but exhibit some central characteristics. Leadership positions in the past were held by influential adult males and generally there was a triumvirate of power best translated in English as priest, chief, and warrior or bounty-hunter.[45] Using terms from Kwara`ae (the largest language group), the *fataabu* (*tabu*-speakers or priests) represented their descent group in communications with ancestors and other nonhuman spirits. They tended their group's shrines and offered sacrifices aimed to achieve social and cosmological stability and success.

---

43 In east Fataleka, for example, 'strangers' intermarried with the founding families and began to claim primary rights to land. These were people taken in as refugees in times of war, particularly during the final decades of the nineteenth century, when guns procured through the labour trade were used in regional power struggles.
44 Keesing and Fifi`i 1969.
45 Keesing 1985a; 1997.

They were custodians of knowledge and respected as a conduit to the spirit world. Women, however, could also play a similar role. In Kwara'ae, according to Ben Burt, there are rare examples of women who became priests (*fataabu keni*), usually the wives of male priests, who were responsible for 'women spirits' (*akalo keni*). David Akin also provides details of Kwaio women with special relationships with ancestors and ancestresses maintained through shrines of their own.[46] The next leadership role is the *aofia* (chief) who sometimes also held hereditary status and maintained social and political cohesion. He encouraged exchange relations and trade with neighbouring descent groups and aggregated and redistributed wealth items. The bigman/chief position required distribution of surpluses, achieved by manipulation of descent group resources, generosity and persuasion.[47] The third position was that of *ramo*, the warrior, war-leader, bounty-hunter and assassin. These warriors could be aggressive, often unpredictable and did not necessarily follow orders, although they too were part of maintaining social and cosmological balance. While the chiefs could also be warriors/bounty-hunters, the priests, due to the spiritual delicacy of their position, usually abstained from killing (though they might have been *ramo* when younger, before taking on the priesthood).[48]

Political groupings are usually small, with leaders responsible for only around 200 people, although there is considerable regional variation in patterns of leadership. Northern leadership is usually described as achieved in classic Melanesian bigman mode. However, Pierre Maranda described 'aristocrats' in Lau and a chiefly system,[49] and in Fataleka and Kwara'ae there are some leaders of high importance. In the centre of Malaita, taking the Kwaio as an example, leadership is much smaller in scale and descent groups are more autonomous, although they are linked by worship and descent from founding ancestors, and exchange relations.[50] South of the Kwaio, the people of southern 'Are'are have developed a more rigid and hereditary political system, qualities even more pronounced on

---

46   Burt 1994, 58; Akin 2003.
47   Keesing 1968.
48   *Ibid.*, 66–76; 1982d, 11; Hogbin 1939, 61–81. The spelling of these words varies between language areas. In this book, priest, chief and warrior/bounty-hunter, or *fataabu*, *aofia* and *ramo*, have been used, and *akalo* is used for ancestors. 'Bigman' is used as a generic term when the exact descriptor is not needed or is unclear. Keesing (1978a) provides the portrait of a classic Kwaio bigman via the autobiography of 'Elota.
49   Information from Pierre Maranda, Quebec, 10 Sept 2007.
50   Keesing 1967; 1978a; 1982c, 78–79.

Small Malaita.[51] Other variations occur among the coastal people as each group has made distinctive economic adaptations and specialisations to suit their marine environments. The Lau and Langalanga have a more rigid descent system and observe strict polarisation of the sexes, exacerbated by the small spaces they inhabit on the artificial islands.[52]

Figure 1.10: A well-built hamlet at `Ai`eda, inland from Sinalagu in Kwaio, at 853 metres (2,800 feet) above sea level.

Clearings are scraped clean for aesthetic and sanitary reasons, and also to demarcate hamlet boundaries beyond which some ancestral taboos are relaxed or ignored. Sturdy fences keep out unwelcome, roaming pigs.

Source: Photograph by David Akin, 2004.

The warrior/bounty-hunter category was the most standard, existing all over Malaita. Roger Keesing, an anthropologist who studied the Kwaio, suggested that because earlier academic writing on Malaitan leadership was produced after the government stopped fighting, there was a tendency to underplay the importance of the role of the warrior. This argument seems to be supported by the clashes between the warriors and various early district officers, some of which took years to resolve.[53] Leaders also had to avenge deaths and slights to their descent groups, through

---

51 Coppet and Zemp 1978; Codrington 1891, 48–51; Ivens 1927, 109–29, 242; Coppet 1965, l–5.
52 Cooper 1970, 57, 86–88, 120, 142; Ivens 1930, 84–92, 149; Ross 1978a; 1978b; 1978c, 12–14; 1973, 188–91; Russell 1950, 6.
53 Keesing 1968; 1982c; 1985a; 1997.

mobilising the *ramo* in the role of hired assassins. Akin argues that the availability of bounty-hunters allowed equalisation between different sized descent groups, since superiority in numbers did not necessarily mean dominance.[54]

Gender Divisions

Figure 1.11: `Are`are woman wearing traditional jewellery and smoking a pipe, 1969.
Source: Hugo Zemp Collection, 1969.

---

54 Akin 2015.

Learning to be Malaitan begins at birth in the safety, security and intimacy of the immediate family. Very soon, a child realises that they are part of an extended family and that there are no divisions between parents, siblings and the wider family circle. Hamlets are close together and children may wander between them, conscious of belonging to a wider group, aware of relationships with the living and the ancestors who are all around. Coastal children feel at home in the water, and use canoes at a remarkably young age. Education includes proper behaviour, mutual help, maintaining harmony and avoiding displays of anger. Learning is gendered with clearly demarcated male and female roles. Beyond the hamlet or artificial island are strangers, enemies and sorcerers, to be negotiated with care, but also relationships to be cultivated.

Figure 1.12: `Are`are woman and child, 1969.
Source: Hugo Zemp Collection, 1969.

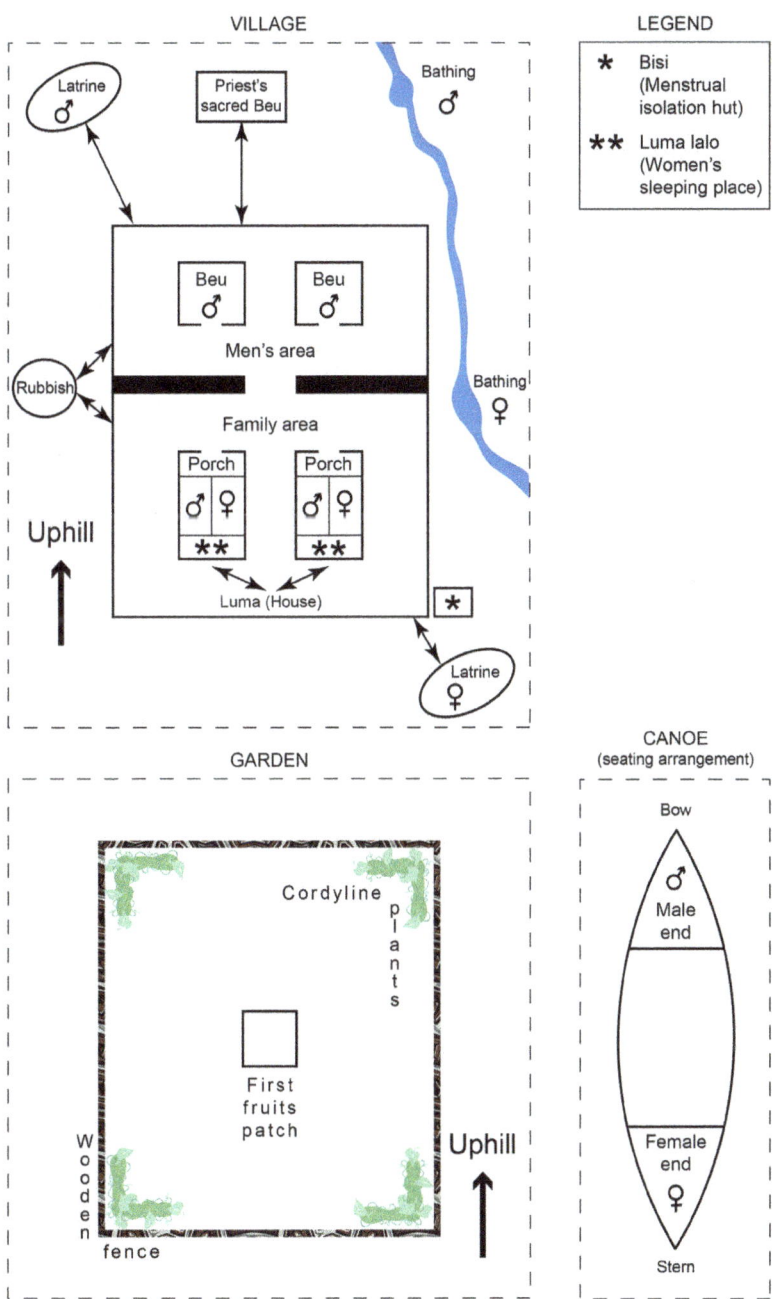

Plan 1: Gender divisions in Malaitan houses, villages and canoes, and garden design.
Source: Based on Ross 1973, 84, 179, redrawn by Vincent Verheyen.

Figure 1.13: Bush women at Roas Bay, south Malaita, 1906.
Source: Beattie Collection, 505.

Women seldom appear to feature at all in the formal power structure and men will say that they control and speak for women. It is true that women often needed the permission of fathers and husbands before they undertook any important activity. However, social and residential spaces on Malaita were strictly divided between males and females, and power and balance in society cannot be measured solely by designated male political and religious positions. Male–female balances permeate Malaitan cosmology and society and it could be argued that women in some contexts possess superior power, given the fear of and respect for women's power at a metaphysical level. The deeply imbedded gender balance is indicated by the symmetry in many aspects of Malaitan society, where music structurally mirrors society,[55] myths encapsulate gender patterns, and gardens, houses and villages are structured to duplicate metaphysical beliefs.[56]

---

55 Zemp 1971; 1972; 1981; 1996.
56 Keesing 1985b; 1987; Schreiner 1977; Maranda 1970; 1974; Maranda and Maranda 1970; Akin 2003.

Houses, canoes and villages were designed so that their shapes and uses were conducive to the ordering of male–female relationships (see Plan 1). Separated men's and women's areas were walled off—literally or symbolically—to ensure that transgression could not occur inadvertently, and men carried special amulets to ward off danger or could quickly access more powerful neutralising agents. Traditionally, when men and women walked through the bush, men went first, and when climbing hills men walked in front so that their heads remained higher than the women's pelvic areas. Non-Christians still follow these principles, and many Malaitan men, even in modern Honiara, will never walk across a woman's legs or under a woman, or under clothes line on which women's clothing is dried. In Lau, depending on the tides, the lagoon switches between 'male' and 'female': during high tides it belongs to men who fish and on low tides the lagoon belongs to women who collect shellfish. Men and women in the past usually went naked, but after marriage, women wore a pubic apron to signify the importance of their reproduction. Traditionally, menstruation and birth were considered highly dangerous to the rest of the community. On such occasions the women lived apart in a *bisi* (a seclusion area), relying on separate gardens and food preparation for sustenance. The power behind female 'pollution' in reproduction, the nurturing of children, women's wealth, and specific female roles in the economy, is clearly a balancing counterweight to male power. In Lau, for example, the lineage and residence rules are structured to consolidate male authority over women, although women have also developed their own strategies to control marriage patterns so that several women from the same clan will marry into another, creating strength through sisterhood. Women's power is not weak: it is potent and can at times neutralise even the most powerful male power.[57]

Malaitans had much stronger controls over sexual activity than, for instance, on neighbouring Makira, where nineteenth-century whalers and traders were able to avail themselves of sexual favours from young women.[58] The strict Malaitan sexual codes were probably one reason Europeans made few contacts with the island during the nineteenth century. There is no formal male initiation on Malaita, and homosexuality is not prominent, although it does, of course, exist, and situational homosexuality seems to have been widespread on colonial plantations.[59]

---

57   Maranda 2001, 98–99, 104–06; Burt 1994, 61–64; Akin 2003; 2004.
58   Bennett 1987, 29–30.
59   *Ibid.*, 174, 182; Moore 2010–12, 12, 36–37.

The Centrality of Religion

Despite regional differences, Malaita has a united cosmology. In some areas, a central characteristic revolves around the number eight. Along with its multiples, eight was the greatest force in Malaitan cosmology, numerology, mathematics, music and dance, everyday thinking and speech, and geographic knowledge. In legends, Malaitans often complete actions eight times, have eight sons, eight genealogical lines or eight territories. In music, the minimal structure is made of a series of two pairs of segments played twice ($4 \times 2 = 8$) to which is added the final formula, making nine units. The extra musical unit locks the others together and assures the totality of the eight segments. Eight represents the greatest force, complete totality: even numbers indicate movement, and uneven numbers motionless states.[60] The 'eight isles' concept, called *Waru Marau* in `Are`are, has been described by Daniel de Coppet and John Naitoro. The known `Are`are world was called the 'eight isles': four in the east (Ulawa, Uki, Three Sisters and Makira); and four in the west (Guadalcanal, Gela, Russell and Isabel). Malaita is the ninth part of this universe, bringing totality to the world, assuring stability and plenty. Malaitans also knew of other nearby islands, such as Ontong Java and Sikaiana (Polynesian outlier atolls to the northeast). Occasionally, outrigger canoes from these islands drift ashore on east Malaita, and one Lau clan traces its origins to Ontong Java.[61] Islands to the north of Isabel were also known, although less intimately than the 'eight isles' world. Similar regional connections exist in the northwest Solomons, although the people there are more routinely interisland in their everyday connections than are Malaitans.[62]

---

60 Daniel de Coppet, personal communication, Paris, 2 Apr 1980; Coppet 1978, 111–26. Similar 'eight' imagery is used in Kwara`ae (Burt and Kwa`ioloa 2001, 10) and in Fataleka, Baegu and Kwaio.
61 Kirch 1984.
62 Hviding 2014, 77–78.

1. MALAITA IN RECENT CENTURIES

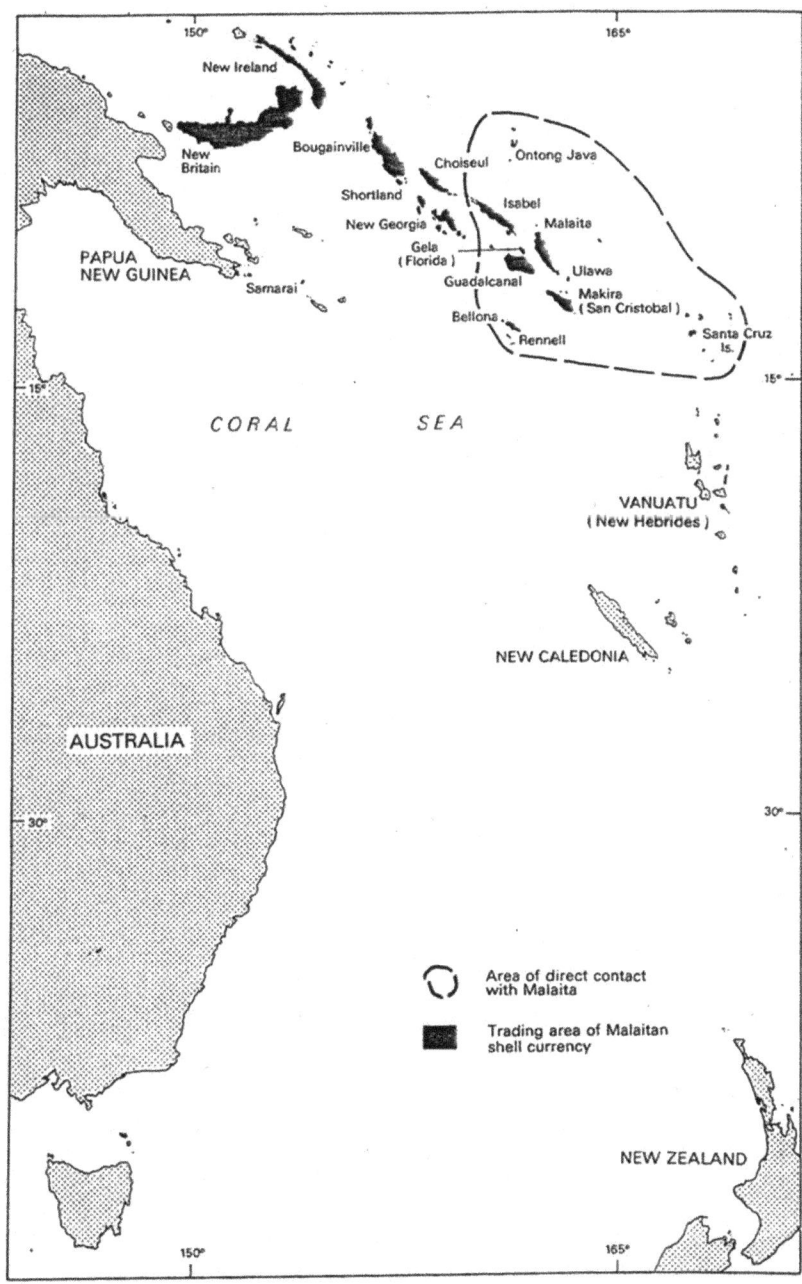

Map 6: The Malaitan 'eight isles' world and the extent of the trading area for Malaitan shell valuables.
Source: Moore 1981a, 45.

Gao in southern Isabel Island has always been the main supply area of `ainigao, the black ebony wood north Malaitans used for certain weapons, and trading and raiding voyages have linked north Malaita and Gao over many centuries in the same way that `Are`are and Small Malaita link to Makira, Ulawa and Guadalcanal. East Fataleka legend records that long ago many north Malaitan descent groups joined forces to attack the Gao people and avenge killings committed in the Falae district of Malaita. Malaitans in the north were in regular contact with Isabel Island: missionary Walter Ivens was told of major Gao attacks on north Malaita, which he dated to the 1850s or 1860s.[63] In the 1870s and 1880s, Gao people made regular visits to Malaita, bartering their canoes and other commodities for Malaitan shell and porpoise teeth valuables. They raided along the north Malaita coast, just as they in turn were raided by people from New Georgia to their west.[64] Malaitans also traded, intermarried with and raided the inhabitants of the surrounding islands. There was steady canoe traffic from west Malaita to the Gela Group, and to Guadalcanal, especially to the `Are`are colony at Marau. Raiding between Makira and Small Malaita has a long history. In 1905, a leader from Malaita's west coast is said to have refused to join an Anglican mission school until he could avenge the deaths on Makira of 40 of his descent group. In the same year, `Ataa men from the southern end of Lau Lagoon joined raids on Makira, presumably linked to their kin at Walade on Small Malaita, and they were also raiding areas of Small Malaita. `Are`are people today still make claims to land on Makira and Uki and maintain kin relationships with people on both islands.[65]

---

63   Ivens 1930, 186.
64   Ishmael Itea and Charles Luiramo, personal communications, Fataleka, 10 Oct 1976; Ross 1973, 109; Russell 1950, 11; Cromar 1935, 153–54, 241; Marwick 1935, 37.
65   Wilson, 'The Bishop's Visitation, 1905', Mar 1906, 5; 'Annual Report of the Melanesian Mission', Wilson, 'S. E. Mala', *SCL*, Apr 1906, 9, 38; Kenilorea 2008, 190–91.

Figure 1.14: Sacrificial altar at Ferasubua Island in Lau Lagoon, 1906.
Source: Beattie Collection, 522.

Religion was all-pervasive, based on spirit-beings and worship of ancestors, and pan-Pacific concepts like *mana* and *tabu* (*mamana* and *abu* in some Malaitan languages). ʻAreʻare people, for instance, believe that their first ancestors came into an already functioning world with three elements: land, sea and sky. Their religious ideology, which can be extrapolated to indicate wider Malaitan patterns, divides into two concepts: *waratoʻo* (to hit and create at the same time) and *rioanimae* (common ancestor).[66] John Naitoro described his people's physical, social and cultural world as based on these two concepts. The theory behind *waratoʻo* is that it has the power to do both good and evil and was responsible for the formation of the sea, land, air, stars and the spirit world. Naitoro described this as the basis of religious reasoning and the way social and cultural norms were legitimated:

> *Waratoo* [sic] also refers to the 'spontaneous' power or energy vested in the 'uttered' sounds of the words associated with the spirits. The belief was that humans could, when in possession of this potent power, carry out actions, by simply 'willing' things or events to occur spontaneously. There were conditions to being able to realise this power, the most important of which was complete surrender and obedience to the will of the spirits through respect for the ancestors.[67]

---

66 Coppet 1985, 80.
67 Naitoro 1993, 28–29.

This power could exert force on either physical or spiritual reality, merely by uttering words, and the key to legitimation was the concept of a common ancestor, *ri`oanimae*, possessing the power of the word and 'central to the social organisation and religious ritual'.[68] *Ri`oanimae* was at the head of a group of living descendants and was the ultimate guardian of the land of these descendants. Naitoro went on to describe the essence of *warato`o* as singular, but the common ancestors, as multiple and diverse:

> Thus, there was not one common ancestor for all `Are`are, but many, the number corresponding to the number of family groups or sub-clans in society at any given time. Because of the large number this meant that there was wide variation in social and cultural norms among different family groups associated with them.[69]

These differences were displayed through different totems, such as crocodiles, sharks and eagles, used by different subclans (*arata*), but common ancestry was the basis of the land tenure system and the allocation of physical resources.

Relationships with ancestors varied from one family to another. Malaitans believed that all good fortune or illness and misfortune had a cause and attempted to placate and manipulate the spirit world to their own benefit. Sorcery was practised, and even today unexpected illness or death is often attributed to malevolent magic. Sorcery fears could act as a limiter on overexploitation by individuals and was thus a levelling social mechanism, ensuring that people cooperated with their kin and neighbouring social units.

David Gegeo, from the Kwara`ae region, has written extensively about Malaitan epistemology, emphasising the importance of *gwaumauri`anga* or 'life and well-being', which covers spiritual, psychological and physical needs.[70] The Kwara`ae strive to achieve *gwaumauri`anga*, the 'good life'. Gegeo describes the changes that have occurred over the last century, from *tua lalifu`anga* (living in rootedness) and *tua `inoto`a`anga* (living in dignity) to *tua malafaka`anga* (literally, living in imitation of ways brought by ships, or pseudo-Westernisation). *Falafala* (*kastom*) has

---

68 *Ibid.*, 29.
69 *Ibid.*, 30.
70 Gegeo 2001; 1998, Gegeo and Watson-Gegeo 1996; 2002; Ouou 1980.

been modernised, but it does not necessarily bring *gwaumauri`anga*. He lists nine key cultural characteristics to create a good life, in essence not so different from the biblical Ten Commandments:

> *alafe`anga* 'kin love, kindness', *aroaro'anga* 'peace, peacefulness', *babato`o`anga* 'stability', *enoeno`anga* 'humility', *fangale`a`anga* 'sharing', *kwaigwale`e`anga* 'welcoming, comforting, hospitality', *kwaima`anga* 'love, kindness, eros', *kwaisare`e`anga* 'giving without expectation of return', and *mamana`anga* 'truth, honesty and sacred power'.[71]

As a central philosophy, *gwaumauri`anga* refers to the ideal state of *ali`afu`anga* (total completeness), where *mauri`a* (life) and *mauri`anga* (the process of living) lead to the nine qualities listed above. Gegeo says that to achieve *gwaumauri`anga* spiritual, psychological and physical needs must be met.

> Why is *gwaumauri`anga* so fundamental to Kwara`ae society? The Kwara`ae argue that a person who achieves the state of *gwaumauri`anga* is a *ngwane ali`afu* 'a complete person' and *ngwae lalifu* 'a rooted person'. A person who has achieved the state of *ali`afu`anga* 'completeness'; and *lalifu`anga* 'rootedness' is said to live in or embrace the Kwara`ae nine key cultural values mentioned. Such a person shows *fu`usi`inoto`a`anga* 'respect', is *fu`usiiinoto`oa* 'respected' by others, and is said to live in *manata fauto`o`anga* 'contentment'. In principle, then, a *gwaumauri* person is someone who is the ultimate Kwara`ae *gwaunga`i* 'important, respected, dignified, revered person or elder' who has achieved *gwaunga`i`anga* 'headness'.[72]

Respect for the living and the dead cannot be separated, and there is a strong belief in life after death. The spirits of the dead in southern Malaita go to Malapa Island (the place of the dead) in Marau Sound, where they mingle with the dead of the local Guadalcanal people. From Kwaio northward the spirits of the dead are said to go first to Gaomae (Ramos) Island halfway between Malaita and Isabel, before settling on Maumolu Naunitu Island close to the southern end of Isabel.[73] These resting places are an indication of the ancient connections between the peoples of these areas.

---

71   Gegeo 2000, 73.
72   *Ibid.*, 74.
73   Ishmael Itea, personal communication, Fataleka, 2 Oct 1976.

Roger Keesing described their 'categories of religious thought, and their expression in the arrangement of settlements and the patterning of everyday social relations and ritual' as having 'a coherent, global, and elegant structure'.[74] Kwaio symbolic schemes have meanings in everyday life and experiences. The main academic scholars of Malaita—Hogbin, Frazer, Maranda, Ross, Guidieri, de Coppet, Naitoro, Gegeo, Burt, Cooper, Guo, Keesing, and Akin—all tell us a great deal about Malaitan religious and cultural systems. There are also points of similarity regarding how Malaitans have conceptualised Christianity, but early missionaries failed to fully recognise the complexity of Malaitan culture and the relationships between wellbeing and ancestral worship. Today's Malaitan pastors, however, exploit these similarities to advantage.

Indications are that early traders and government officers understood very little about Malaitan cultures. Even the approximate boundaries of the different language divisions seem to have eluded them. David Akin's *Colonialism, Maasina Rule, and the Origins of Malaitan Kastom* shows clearly how ignorant most district officers and their deputies were concerning Malaitan culture, and how often their seemingly carefully justified decisions were hamfisted attempts to induce change that aggravated and frustrated Malaitans. Sometimes, these local officials had to deal with quite bizarre instructions from bosses in Tulagi or Suva who had no inkling of Malaitan realities, and while some tried to mitigate the impacts of such policies, they had no choice but to follow orders. Some of the early missionaries, particularly those that stayed for long periods—for instance, Ivens, Hopkins, and the Coicaud brothers—were in a position to observe Malaitan culture more closely and better understood their surroundings, but even they sometimes made blinkered interpretations.

There are clearly similarities between all Malaitan societies. Although some readers may interpret this as one basic Malaitan culture that overrides the variations, contemporary Malaitans will always point out local variations in behaviours, which usually relate to the language areas where they hold their primary identity. In the past, people always identified primarily with their specific region, not the whole island. There were always long-distance links, particularly where there had been migrations—the `Ataa (southern Lau Lagoon) links with Walade in east Small Malaita is classic. However, it is undeniable that authority in the south is far more hereditary

---

74 Keesing 1982d, 4.

and chiefly than in the north, and there were always great differences between language groups and between the inland peoples and those on artificial islands in the lagoons. Malaitans saw themselves split into a dozen or more cultures, with nested identities within those, and it is the circumstances of the unification that occurred between the 1870s and 1930s that interests us here.

Modern Malaita

Malaita Province of today is not the same as Mala of the past. Not only has Malaita changed over the last 150 years, but based on administrative convenience, not cultural histories, Sikaiana and Ontong Java (Polynesian chiefly societies on isolated atolls with limited natural resources) are now incorporated into the province. Early twentieth-century interpretations of language boundaries became administrative divisions and then national political boundaries. Most modern Malaitans have moved their settlements toward the coast and regrouped into large villages, lured by Christianity, health clinics, schools, government services, roads and cash crops marketing. Male and female roles have changed, and circular labour migration created new power hierarchies and cultural motivations. Having said this, there are core Malaitan characteristics that are easily recognised in the modern Solomon Islands. Over the last 100 years of colonial and postcolonial activity, some of these have become more consolidated than they ever were in the nineteenth century. And, as described in the Introduction, there remain many tropes about Malaita and Malaitans. Malaitans are often physically large relative to other Solomon Islanders, and they exhibit concomitant physical strength; they are famously hard workers. Many maintain respect for gender taboos and ancestral power, at a time when Solomon Islanders from some other islands have disregarded these for decades. Although Malaitans are often wrongly stereotyped as unusually violent and aggressive, it is fair to say that many have a characteristically bombastic disposition that, when angered, is better not crossed. As this chapter has attempted to demonstrate, there are many variations of Malaitan lifestyles, and while some of the behaviours described belong only to the past, a surprising number are still evident today: more fully in a few places, such as with Kwaio who still follow their ancestral religion, and partially in many other areas including urban communities.

Early visiting Europeans, many from Britain or Australia, arrived with a belief in the superiority of their own cultures, exhibited through technology and Christianity. They had little interest in understanding the complexity and richness of island life and typically related to Malaitans only on a superficial level. As Judith Bennett so nicely put it:

> When the white men came in numbers to the Solomon Islands, they little understood the religious values of the Melanesians and so flouted them, through either ignorance or, more often, disregard. Europeans touched or even carried away sacred objects such as offerings at ancestral shrines, bathed in spirit-haunted streams, walked alone at night, and, again and again, broke taboos that Solomon Islanders believed would bring sickness and death in their wake. Sorcerers could vent their magical fury on the white man and see scant result. Not only were the white men able to survive sorcery, but they were able to defeat great warriors who had called on the support of their own ancestors. Consequently, Solomon Islanders began to doubt the wisdom of generations.[75]

The chapters that follow trace changes that occurred in the late nineteenth and early twentieth centuries.

---

75 Bennett 1987, 115.

2
Trade and Labour

> Through the labour traffic I suppose no island has been so much affected by contact with the white man. Change is going on so rapidly that it is very difficult to write of things as they are; what is true to-day may be very different to-morrow.
>
> —Rev. Arthur Hopkins, *Southern Cross Log*, 1908[1]

This chapter begins with an outline of the first Malaitan contacts with outsiders from beyond the Pacific and then examines labour migration up until 1914. Malaita provided more indentured labourers in the external Melanesian labour trade than any other island in Solomon Islands or Vanuatu (the New Hebrides). Malaitans travelled to Queensland and Fiji on 14,447 indenture contracts between 1870 and 1911 (Table 1), out of a total of 24,865 contracts for all Solomon Islands, equalling 58 per cent. Malaitans also took part in the internal protectorate labour trade starting between the 1900s and 1910s. Accurate statistics for this internal trade begin in 1913, and from that year through 1940, 36,596 labour contracts were issued to Malaitans, 67.6 per cent of the 54,110 total (Table 7, Chapter 10). The total number of Malaitan labour contracts (including those before 1913) would be higher by a few thousand.

---

1   Hopkins, 'Mala and Its People', *SCL*, June 1908, 9.

Figure 2.1: Christie Fatnowna with the model ship made by Jack Marau.

Marau, a Guadalcanal man at Mackay, made this ship, modelled on the labour trade vessel that brought him to Australia.

He is thought to have been from the Malaitan colony at Marau Sound on Guadalcanal. At Mackay he married a Malaitan woman and always lived with the Malaitans. In his final years, he lived with Norman and Hazel Fatnowna; they inherited the model when he died. It was photographed in 1988, with Norman's brother Christie.

Source: Clive Moore Collection.

2. TRADE AND LABOUR

The chapter explores the external labour trade (beyond the Solomon Archipelago) and argues that these experiences were at the base of all changes that occurred on the island before the Pacific War. The internal labour trade will be discussed in subsequent chapters. Along with the other two changes I highlight—the arrival of Christianity and government—participation in external wage labour was instrumental in providing unity through Pijin English, the acquisition of trade goods, the ability to work with groups beyond one language area and initial contact with Christianity and literacy. The labour trade created a new level of sophistication and understanding of the world beyond Malaita. The size of Malaita's population made this large labour movement feasible, although it was driven by a lack of economic opportunity on the island, two points still valid today. The Malaitan diaspora within Solomon Islands remains larger than that of any other island group and influences many contemporary issues in the modern nation. The fourth element in the transformation of Malaitan societies, which becomes clear at the end of this chapter, is Malaitans' ability to change creatively. Malaitans have always displayed great flexibility and practicality in adjusting to changing circumstances. Without this ability they could never have survived and flourished as they have.

Similar to most Pacific peoples, Malaitan contact with the world outside the archipelago began with occasional visits by ships along their coast. Slowly, these increased as European explorers, naval expeditions, whalers and traders passed through. Early contact was seldom onshore, since most visitors felt safer trading from their ships to surrounding canoes. Malaitans, with no idea of what was to come, were curious and wanted to possess the strange items offered. The first time any Malaitan was able to communicate with a foreigner was in the 1820s, and then again in the 1860s and early 1870s, when castaways lived in the lagoons. Until then, communications were by miming and offering items in barter trade.

Participation in plantation labour led to the earliest large-scale introduction of foreign manufactured items and the beginnings of the adoption of new ideas and technologies. The effect of the outside world was slower to leave its mark on Malaita than in the Western Solomons, Makira and some Polynesian Outliers, where whalers and traders made an earlier impact. However, once Malaitans became the main Solomon Islands labour force on overseas plantations and farms in Queensland and Fiji, and to a lesser extent in Samoa and New Caledonia, and then in the twentieth century within the protectorate, the impact on the island was extreme.

The sheer size of the Malaitan involvement in the circular labour trade—58 per cent of all Solomon Islands labourers working in Queensland and Fiji (1870–1911) and around 68 per cent within the protectorate before the Pacific War—indicates the importance of the movement of Malaitans, predominantly males, away from their island. I argue that there must have been significant depopulation once new diseases were introduced, but there is no way to be sure of the precontact population size, other than that it was substantial. The trade in labour meant that the majority of the island's young adult males began leaving for several years and usually returned with new material possessions, which altered their standing in their communities. This chapter contends that Malaitan culture had already irreversibly changed before any European lived permanently on the island in the 1890s, able to observe local behaviour or know the size of the population. If we take introduced languages as an example—pijin versions of English and Fijian—thousands of Malaitans already spoke or understood these languages to varying degrees in the 1890s, and many had achieved rudimentary literacy. The quantity of European goods and chattels introduced brought about huge changes both in technology and in the ownership and control of resources.

Much of the literature on Malaita comes from anthropologists who have seldom taken historical documentation into account. Ian Hogbin in the 1930s is the early anomaly, and then more recently Ian Frazer, Ben Burt and David Akin have successfully straddled anthropology and history. Most others, partly because of their training and the earlier foci of the discipline, chose to ignore, or underestimated, the impacts of early outside influences on Malaita. A similar pattern exists elsewhere in the Solomons and in Near Oceania generally. There were early studies, such as geographer Richard Bedford's *New Hebridean Mobility* (1973), or historian Judith Bennett's MA thesis 'Cross-Cultural Influences on Village Relocation on the Weather Coast of Guadalcanal, Solomon Islands, c. 1870–1953' (1974), which show that wider analysis has been possible for 40 years, although in the main ethnographic history was not pursued. Aside from Peter Corris's excellent *Passage, Port and Plantation* (1973), which dealt with Solomon Islands labourers in Fiji and Queensland, all of the major labour trade historical studies are Queensland-based and share a reverse fault to the anthropological writing: they are largely document-based and display little understanding of anthropology. Only my *Kanaka: A History of Melanesian Mackay* (1985) concentrated on one island (Malaita) and only Corris and I (and Bennett for her *Wealth of the Solomons* (1987)) spent time interviewing Malaitans in the islands. Of the work published by historians on the overseas labour trade, only Patricia Mercer's *White Australia Defied: Pacific Islander Settlement in North Queensland* (1995) and my *Kanaka* (1985) draw from large bases of oral testimony. Hopefully, the way forward will be for historians, geographers and anthropologists to work in a multidisciplinary manner.

First Contact with the Outside World

Malaitans first experienced foreigners from outside the Pacific Islands in 1568 when a Spanish expedition led by Alvaro de Mendaña y Neyra visited Malaita. On Palm Sunday, 11 April, the Spaniards sighted Malaita from neighbouring Isabel Island. Later, a brigantine left the other ships at Port Cruz (now Honiara) on Guadalcanal and set off southeast, coasting past elongated Rua Sura Island and on to Marau Sound, a Malaitan colony on Guadalcanal. The ship crossed Indispensable Strait and reached Malaita on 25 May, entered `Are`are Lagoon at Uhu Passage, then sailed along the coast and anchored at Rokera (Ariel Harbour), which they named Port Ascension. The visitors also landed at the large Su`upaina Bay, a short distance from Cape Zélée, the southern-most point of Small Malaita. Attacked at Uhu by 25 canoes, the Spanish returned fire with their arquebuses, killing and wounding some of the attackers. At Ariel Harbour they were met by a crowd of 200, although there was no close interaction, and at Su`upaina once more there was an altercation dispersed with gunfire. Like many of these early exploratory visits to Pacific islands, two aspects stand out: the defensive violence of the visitors and lingering after-effects, such as disease. Anthropologist Daniel de Coppet believed that a memory of the visit lingered into the twentieth century, recounted because of an epidemic disease that spread from the contact, although the oral history is hazy and this could have followed later European visits instead.[2]

---

2   Amherst and Thomson 1967 [1901], xxxviii–xli, 140–42, 176–77, 204–05, 280–85, 339–51; Coppet 1977; Spriggs 1997, 234.

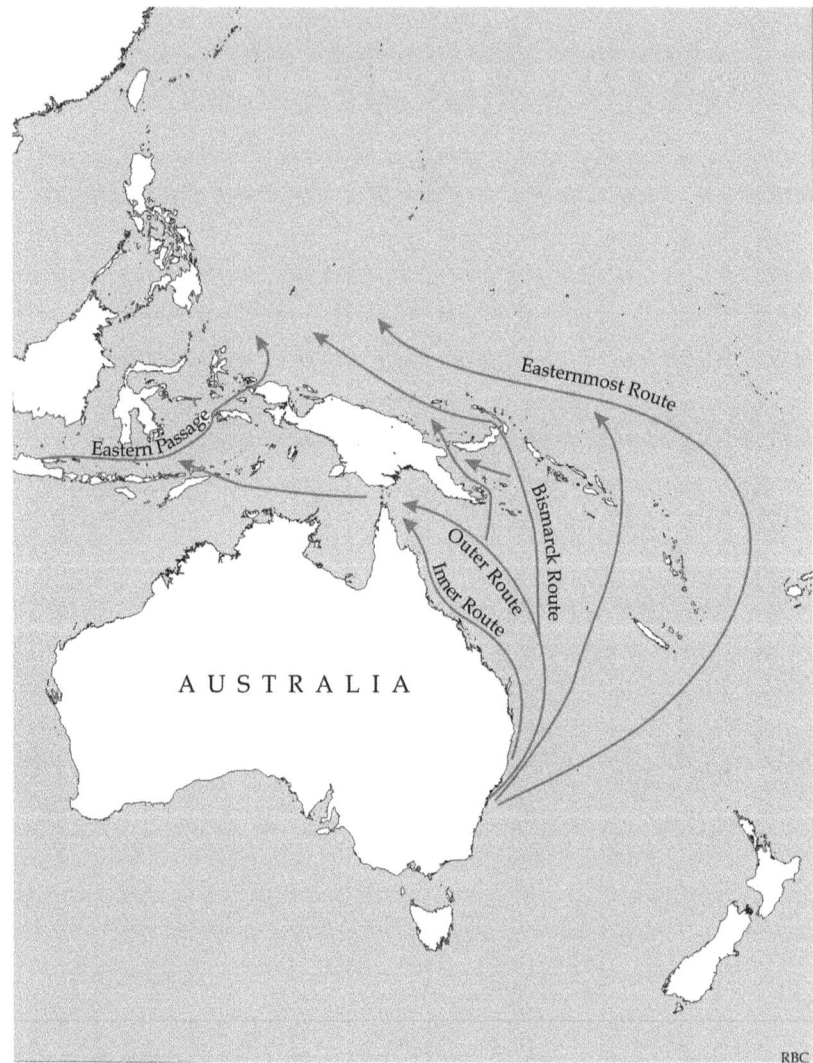

Map 7: Shipping routes between eastern Australia and Asia in the eighteenth and nineteenth centuries.
Source: Moore 2003, 105; courtesy of Robert Cribb.

After the Spanish visit, the Solomon Islands disappeared again from European view, hidden by the vagaries of poor navigational science until a further round of exploration in the eighteenth century. Malaitans made occasional contact with Europeans, such as the occupants of a canoe seized near small Da`i Island off the northwest end of Malaita in 1767 by Philip Carteret on HMS *Swallow*. Two years later, Jean-François-Marie de Surville, on board *St Jean-Baptiste*, passed east of Malaita, keeping well out to sea. The next contacts were probably a quarter century later when, in 1790, Lieutenant Ball, sailing from New South Wales, travelled north along the east coast of Malaita, and two years later when *Recherche* and *Espérance*, commanded by Bruny D'Entrecasteaux, sailed close by Small Malaita, searching for the ill-fated Pérouse expedition. Another French explorer, Dumont d'Urville, also left his mark on Malaita when he sailed along the southwest coast in 1838, naming the southern and northern ends of the island Cape Zélée and Cape Astrolabe after his ships.[3]

Once the British settled at Sydney, New South Wales, in 1788, merchant vessels began to use routes to Asia just east of the Solomon Archipelago, passing by Malaita, or travelled through Indispensable Strait on Malaita's west side.[4] While actual landings were rare, the ships must have been visible and the regular canoe traffic between Malaita, Guadalcanal, Gela, Ulawa, Makira and Isabel would have come into some sort of contact with these foreigners.

Whaling

Malaitans were never central to the substantial whaling industry that developed in the archipelago between the 1820s and the 1860s. With the Atlantic whaling ground in decline, whalers began to ply their trade in the archipelago and around similar islands off east New Guinea. The fleet was bolstered by the addition of some of the vessels used to transport convicts to New South Wales.[5] Whaling vessels began to sail close to Malaita onwards from 1800, and by the 1820s there is evidence of some limited direct contacts between their crews and Malaitans.[6]

Whaling and associated trading altered power balances among Solomon Islanders. Ships from southern Pacific ports began to sail north to the Solomons and New Guinea from May to November, while others sailed south out of Micronesia during the rest of the year. Whalers were bound by the migratory habits of whales—they usually take the same paths in their annual movements north and south through the Pacific—and by

---

3   Woodford 1909, 506; Spate 1988, 95–98, 116–19; Duyker 2014, 393.
4   D'Entrecasteaux 2001, Map 4, 89; Spate 1988, 92–94; *BSIP AR*, 1971, 113.
5   Moore 2003, 104–09.
6   Bennett 1987, 30–31, 350–55.

the availability of suitable sheltered anchorages to enable replenishment of supplies of food, water and timber, without aggressive interactions with the local people. Simbo (Eddystone), Mono (Treasury) Island just south of Bougainville, Makira, small Santa Ana and Santa Catalina islands, and Sikaiana Atoll became early favourite haunts of whalers while they pursued their prey nearby. A subsidiary trade in pearl-shell and turtle-shell increased in the 1860s, supplemented by *bêche-de-mer* (which required beach processing) north of Malaita around New Georgia, Kolombangara and Simbo.[7] Whalers restocked their supplies close to whaling grounds, wherever there were safe anchorages and friendly people, and where possible they avoided the inner coastlines of the Solomon Archipelago— the shores of New Georgia Sound and Indispensable Strait—which were not properly surveyed until the 1860s and 1870s.

The islands that the whalers chose benefited enormously from the barter that developed, and the new material possessions it brought increased their power.[8] The vast lagoons in the northwest Solomon Islands, with their many reefs and islets, made them a good centre for trade and refreshment of ships' supplies. Although east Malaita has some excellent harbours, as well as Lau Lagoon and Maramasike Passage, there is a similarity to Guadalcanal's Weather Coast in that much of the coast is exposed. Coupled with a lack of barter items, this made Malaita unattractive for regular visits. We know that the *Alfred*, under its master Edwin Cattlin, landed on Malaita in 1827 (see below) and was also in the vicinity between October 1828 and April 1829. Cattlin returned to Malaitan waters again on the *Australian* between December 1831 and February 1832.[9] Other whalers presumably followed a similar pattern, but they left no records. The whalers, and later labour recruiters, traded large quantities of hoop iron and steel tools such as axes into the archipelago. These made swidden horticulture less laborious and freed up men for more extensive, almost imperialist extensions of warfare. While interisland raiding had been slowly increasing in range and amount for around 300 years,[10] the large numbers of steel axes traded into the northwest Solomon Islands were used to extend existing trade for turtle-shell, and for head-hunting and

---

7   Moore 2003, 117–22; Bennett 1987, 24–44.
8   Gray 1999.
9   Richards 2012, 17.
10 Woodford 1922; Aswani 2000, 53.

slave-raiding activities. Missionary Walter Ivens recounted the effect of the new weaponry on the efficiency of these raids beginning in the 1850s and 1860s:

> The presence of English ships in the Solomons in these two decades, and the distribution by them of iron tomahawks, gave great impetus to the head-hunting. These tomahawk-heads were mounted on a long handle by the Rovoiana people, and received the name *kilakila* (stone axe). The use of them spread as far south as Sa`a and Ulawa, and the name 'kilakila' went along with it … Later on head-hunting raids were made on Maana oba village on the island of Ngwalulu, on Malu`u in Suu, on Fokanakafo near Uru, and on Langalanga.[11]

On many islands the raids forced coastal groups to move inland for protection. By the 1880s, these raids had depopulated considerable areas of New Georgia, Isabel, Choiseul, the Gela Group and the west coast of Guadalcanal. While areas of Isabel were stripped of population by New Georgia raiders, Gao and Bugotu people from Isabel also participated; it was never a one-way movement out of New Georgia. As Ivens indicates, occasionally these raids reached the north and central coast of Malaita, usually through Isabel intermediaries. Malaitans suggest that their bowmen and their parrying skills with large shields were more than a match for the close-combat long-handled steel axes wielded by the men from the northwest islands. These raids must have had some impact, but there is no hint that they caused large-scale depopulation.[12]

Royal Navy Australia Station (RNAS) statistics show that Malaitans were trading with Europeans during the late 1870s, although they must have been very frustrated that they were unable to obtain large amounts of iron and tools and weapons, the equal of the supplies flowing into neighbouring Makira and the Western Solomons.[13] As described in Chapter 1, Malaita had been at the centre of an indigenous trade network based on shell and teeth valuables, then, over a couple of decades, the power focus shifted. This was the first large-scale contact with the outside world and a bonanza for those who participated. Judith Bennett's research provides an outline of the level of contact: she found records from around 150 whaling ships

---

11 Ivens 1930, 186.
12 McKinnon 1975; Chapman and Pirie 1974, 215–17; Codrington 1891, 305, 345; Fox 1958, 179–81, 189; Aswani 2000. The raiders had the advantage of steel axes but these were only superior in close fighting. They only used small shields, which were easy for Malaitan bowmen to get around.
13 RNAS, Yearly Estimates of the Solomons Trade, including New Britain, New Ireland and the Admiralty Islands, Captain Purvis, 30 Sept 1879, 15.

visiting the Solomons between 1800 and 1890. The peak of Solomons whaling was in the 1840s and 1850s, and then began to wane in the 1860s when many American ships were recalled due to the Civil War, and as whale oil became less essential for industry because of easier access to petroleum oil, and technical advances in processing copra for oil.[14]

Most of these early contacts took place at sea rather than on shore, and whalers usually chose the smaller islands where there was less chance of large-scale attacks. Initially, the Islanders paddled out to the ships to exchange their food stuffs for hoop iron, glass, knives, fish-hooks, cloth and tobacco. However, over several decades as the whaling trade continued, whalers became more familiar with some ports and local leaders, felt comfortable enough to spend time on land, and trade items became more sophisticated.[15] Wood, water, fruit and vegetables, artefacts, shells, and turtle-shell were traded for iron, steel, guns, tobacco and glass. 'Slaves' (women and children captured in indigenous raids) were also used to provide sexual services.

Apart from prestige value, access to iron and steel reduced male gardening and canoe-building workloads considerably, while increasing the size of gardens, which allowed more pigs to be fed, and more time invested in ceremonies and warfare.[16] The influx of iron and steel caused communities near whaling ports to prosper and long-established trade linkages began to change. Malaitan shell and porpoise-teeth currencies had for generations been important trade items linking Malaita to the surrounding islands. Earlier, ʼAreʼare and Small Malaita had dominant links with Makira, but then onwards from the 1840s Makira began to gain the upper hand since Malaitans had nothing of value to barter with whalers and traders. Bennett's research suggests that between 1850 and 1870, on average three whaling ships a year visited Makira Harbour, each staying a few days.[17] Malaita's lagoons were numerous but not commodious, and the warlike reputation of Malaitan men made Europeans wary. Strict Malaitan sexual codes meant that women were not available to satisfy the lusts of the crews.[18] Aside from contacts with a few castaways and the occasional passing trading or whaling

---

14   Bennett 1987, 360–65; Townsend 1935.
15   Bennett 1987, 29–30; Gray 1999.
16   Salisbury 1962a, 110, 220; 1962b; Townsend 1969; Godelier 1986.
17   Bennett 1987, 28–29.
18   *Ibid.*, 29–30 provides examples of Makira professional prostitutes (*urao*) and unmarried women, as well as slave women on other islands, providing sexual services to Europeans. This was a variation of traditional practices in which women were exchanged to cement alliances.

ship, Malaitans remained outside the early nineteenth-century spread of European influence into the Pacific.[19] They were mostly unable to obtain the European manufactured items that were becoming common elsewhere unless they traded for them at surrounding islands.

This changed quickly once the indentured labour trade to Queensland and Fiji began in the 1870s and Malaitans became avid participants. It is true that there was kidnapping and illegality at the beginning, but taken over the full period, from the 1870s to the 1910s, Malaitan participation in the external labour trade was largely voluntary. They had at last found a commodity to trade: fit young male bodies. They were motivated primarily by their desire for iron and steel tools, and obtaining guns, first unreliable muzzle-loaders and then, increasingly, more powerful and accurate breech-loading rifles. These were put to use to defend and advance the interests of descent groups in the jockeying for regional dominance on Malaita, and as a defence against marauding raiders from further north. Tobacco was another large import. This restored Malaitans' dominance among Solomon Island societies and their interactions with others added to the tropes of Malaitan violence and unpredictability.

Castaways

Once European ships began frequenting the Pacific Islands, one side-product was deserters and castaways—men who survived wrecks, were downloaded from ships, or chose to remain in indigenous communities they had visited on voyages. Their effect on host island communities has long been debated.[20] Bennett notes that between the 1850s and the 1870s some 30 deserters from whaling ships lived on Makira, giving the people there a level of early familiarity with outsiders that did not exist on Malaita.[21] There are only a few references to shipwrecked mariners surviving on Malaita for a few years. Peter Corris mentions a 'Lascar' supposed to be the only survivor from an English brig captured by Malaitans in the 1820s. Fourteen Englishmen and six other 'Lascars' perished, and the sole survivor was rescued in the late 1820s.[22]

---

19   Corris 1973b, 6–23; Bennett 1987, 21–44; Moore 1985, 33–36.
20   Maude 1968, 134–77; Campbell 1998; Bargatzky 1980.
21   Bennett 1987, 29–30, 41.
22   'Lascar' usually means a sailor from the Indian subcontinent. Corris 1973b, 12; Smith 1844, 203–06; Bennett 1987, 29–31.

Another early European resident on Malaita, John Matthews, known as Doorey, was second officer on the whaler *Alfred* out of Sydney, which reached Malaita in December 1827. The ship was attacked and several crew members were killed, and Matthews lived on Malaita for an unknown number of years.[23] In *Pageant of the Pacific*, Rhodes recorded that in September 1831 Captain Harwood of the whaler *Hashemy* was trading at Malaita when he received a message written on a piece of bamboo. Mathews warned that the people were about to attack the ship, however, the message was undated and Harwood decided that it was old. Matthews was not located.[24]

The next outsider to reside on Malaita seems to have been John (Jack) Renton, a Scottish seaman and the only survivor among five deserters from the American guano ship *Renard* in 1868. He and his companions drifted almost 2,000 kilometres in one of the *Renard*'s boats before landing at Maana`oba Island off the northeast coast of Malaita. His four companions were killed and Renton was taken to Kabbou, a Lau Lagoon bigman on Sulufou artificial island, where Renton lived from 1868 until 1875. It was during this period that labour recruiting vessels out of Queensland and Fiji initially ventured to Malaita, the first arriving in late 1870 and early 1871. In August of 1875 Renton was rescued by the crew of one of these, the Queensland ship *Bobtail Nag*.

Renton learnt the Lau language and participated in life on the lagoon for eight years, and there are indications that he developed close relationships, yet the account he left us is disappointingly shallow. He returned to Malaita as an interpreter on a recruiting ship in late 1875 with gifts for his adopted family, but he never visited the island again and died in 1878.[25] One thing Renton helped to bring about was the rise of Kwaisulia, the leading Lau passage master (the 'in-between' men who controlled the interface between the labour recruiters and potential labourers) from the 1880s until the 1900s, described later in this chapter.

---

23   Forster 1975, 97; Bennett 1987, 30–31.
24   Rhodes 1937, 253 (no source is given); Bennett 1987, 350 records the *Alfred* in 1828–29, but not the *Hashemy*.
25   Moore 1985, 35–36. Renton subsequently was employed as a Queensland government agent who accompanied recruiting ships on their voyages, until he was killed in 1878 at Aoba Island in the New Hebrides while aboard the *Mystery*. His account of his life on Malaita and the logs of his voyages were published in Marwick 1935. Also see the novels by Holthouse (1988) and Randell (2003).

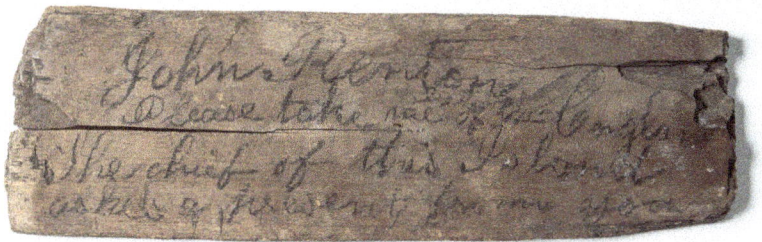

Figure 2.2: John Renton managed to get this piece of wood with its message on both sides to the *Bobtail Nag* in August 1875: 'John Renton. Please take me off to England. The chief of this island asks a present from you. Won of the ship's crew come on shore that I can speak with him. Shipwrecked on this island about 5 years ago'.
Source: Queensland Museum.

Strangely, a new Malaitan trope appeared in relation to Renton in 1988, when the Queensland-based historical sensationalist author Hector Holthouse published a book on Renton's adventures titled *White Headhunter*, with a subtitle trumpeting *The Extraordinary True Story of a White Man's Life among the Headhunters of the Solomon Islands*. This was followed by a 2003 novel of similar subject by Nigel Randell, *The White Headhunter*. While the titles might have been useful to sell books, they are poor descriptions of the people of Lau Lagoon, who were not headhunters like those of New Georgia or Isabel. It would seem that the Renton story is already compelling enough to sell books without embellishment, but these authors nevertheless added to the Malaitan tropes.

Through Lau's links to Small Malaita, Renton may have heard that another group of castaways arrived on Small Malaita's eastern coast at Port Adam on 1 June 1873. The barque *Plato* out of Newcastle, New South Wales, was wrecked near New Caledonia on 10 May; the crew sailed north in small boats, heading for Makira, but they overshot their target. Nine of them were killed the next day, and only John Collins was kept alive. He was rescued by HMS *Renard* and transferred to HMS *Dido*, which had been tasked with returning men kidnapped by the *Nukulau* (see below). Both ships proceeded to Port Adam, where they found the America schooner *Hallie Jack* trading, and captured three of the murderers.[26]

---

26   *Queenslander*, 15 Nov 1872.

Royal Australia Naval Station

This capture was legal because in 1817 the supreme courts of New South Wales and Van Diemen's Land (Tasmania) were given authority to try serious crimes committed in the Pacific Islands. Beginning in 1821, the British Navy annually detached a ship from the East Indies fleet to patrol the Pacific. In 1843, the *British Foreign Jurisdiction Act* extended British law to cover subjects beyond British territory, utilising concepts of 'sovereignty' and 'protectorate' to enable Britain to establish a system of jurisprudence in consular courts without the costs of formal annexation. This was applied in the Pacific, and once the British Royal Navy's Australia Station (RNAS) began operations out of Sydney in 1859, Malaita came within the jurisdiction of its ships.

One early visit was from Captain Erskine on HMS *Havannah*, which patrolled waters surrounding the island in 1850. The ship called at Port Adam between 21 and 24 September, edging her way into the uncharted bay. Two descriptions of the visit have survived. The villagers gathered to watch the strange craft approach:

> A canoe or two came off to within 60 or 80 yards of the vessel, the natives holding up cocoanuts, and throwing themselves down in their canoes, at the same time striking their breasts to represent being killed, and calling out Matè-matè (which I believe means to kill)—No offer would induce them to come alongside.[27]

The next Malaitan reaction was to evacuate 30 women and children in a large canoe. A boat was lowered from the ship and a pantomime developed with up to 14 canoes venturing out and suddenly turning back, the men clearly terrified but curious. When the next day dawned, canoes ventured out to the ship to trade and a party from the *Havannah* went ashore. There were 20 houses in a village on one of the islands just offshore, and the crew began to trade: the most sought-after items were red cloth, tomahawks, knives and bottles. Activity was heard in the village on the nights of the 22nd and 23rd, but when the crew again visited on the 24th the village was empty.

---

27 Vigors 1850, 202. The word may have been '*matai*', which in Lau (also used at Walade) means 'to be ill'. The same word seems to have been used elsewhere in the Solomons in a similar way in 1565 to discourage the Mendaña expedition. It may refer to diseases brought by foreign ships. Amherst and Thomson 1967 [1901], see section 'Narrative of Gallego', 31.

There was contact on land, and local etiquette displayed when a leader at the village noticed that Lieutenant Pym was lame and asking him to be seated. The crew felt that this was not the villagers' first contact with Europeans and that perhaps whalers had visited, with unfavourable results. Philip Vigors described the men as naked except for cane hoops around their waists, shell, nut and human teeth necklaces, and shell armlets worn just above the elbow. They also wore cane bands on their ankles and on their upper arms, and their hair was cut short, although 'some few had clotted wisps of a reddish colour and nearly 10 inches in length'.[28] Charles Moore noted that the points and the inner cartilage of the men's noses were perforated with a piece of bone inserted across the nose and pearl-shell nose plates attached, facing up the nose.[29] Each house was walled with cane and had two rooms, one open at the sea end and the other closed with a door. The floors were also of cane, covered with mats. Their weapons were clubs, 1.5-metre bows, arrows and 2.7-metre spears. There were canoes and finely made fishing nets up to 55 metres long with shells for floats. One item from the visit is now in the British Museum: a pattern-strap armband in the style of south Malaita or Makira. It includes two blue glass beads that must have come from an earlier visiting ship. Since more ships had visited Makira, the beads were probably traded in from there.[30]

Settlement of Australia and New Zealand increased the British Pacific presence. After the passage of Queensland's *Polynesian Labourers Act* in 1868, and Britain's *Pacific Islanders' Protection Act* in 1872, the British Navy began to traverse the Solomon Archipelago more regularly. An 1875 revision of the latter created the position of high commissioner with jurisdiction over all British subjects in the Western Pacific, and this was followed in 1877 by an Order-in-Council that established the Western Pacific High Commission (WPHC). Fiji became a Crown colony in 1874 and from 1877 until 1952 its governor was also the high commissioner.[31] The first attempt to apply British law to Malaitans came in 1873–74, when the three Malaitans were captured by HMS *Dido* for the murder of crew members of the barque *Plato* (mentioned above), to be tried in the Supreme Court of New South Wales. One of them died on the

---

28   Vigors 1850, 209.
29   Moore 1850.
30   Burt 2015, 14.
31   Bach 1983; 1986. In 1952, the WPHC headquarters was moved to Honiara and the position of BSIP resident commissioner was incorporated into that of high commissioner.

Dido's voyage, poisoned from eating stick tobacco, possibly a suicide. The legalities of the case relied on the murdered men being in the ship's longboat, and therefore under British Admiralty jurisdiction, but because the boat was aground on Malaita, the men had to be released and sent home.[32]

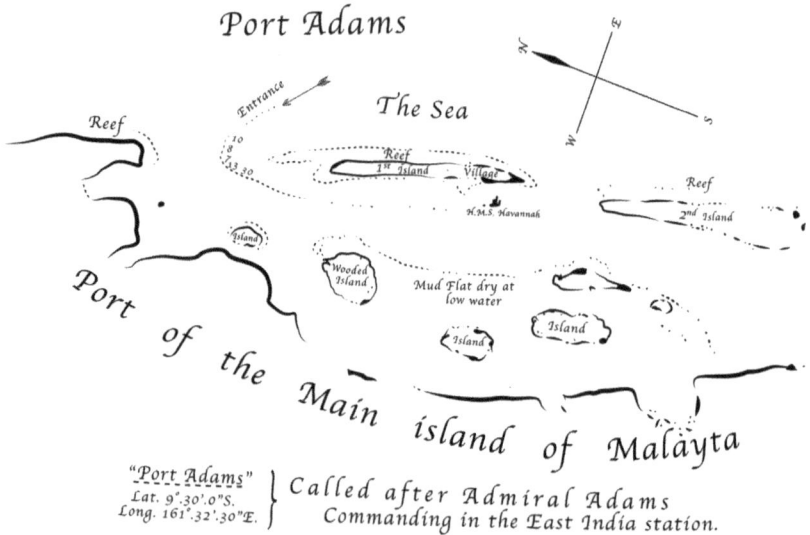

Map 8: Sketch of Port Adam from the visit of HMS *Havannah* in 1850.
Source: Vigors 1850, 201; redrawn by Vincent Verheyen.

The earliest WPHC deputy commissioners were often captains of RNAS ships on patrol through the islands. Then the high commissioner appointed Hugh H. Romilly in 1883 as the first deputy commissioner specifically for Melanesia, with a brief to regulate the excesses of the Fiji and Queensland labour trades. Soon Malaita began to be visited regularly by RNAS ships and the WPHC began trying to regulate the labour trades.[33]

Malaitan Labour Migration, 1870–1914

Jack Renton's years of residence in Lau bridged the period when change was beginning. The earliest known labour kidnapping in the Solomons occurred in 1857 when 14 men were taken to Réunion in the Indian

---

32 Scarr 1967a, 38, 305 n 5.
33 Romilly 1893; Moore 2003, 133–35.

Ocean, never to return.[34] When the first British labour trade schooners began sailing around the coasts of Malaita in the early 1870s, the people had had little contact with the world beyond the surrounding islands. Malaitans, like other Pacific Islanders, participated in the labour trade for a variety of reasons: while some were kidnapped in the early years, in the longer run their primary reason for going abroad was that circular labour migration was the only way for them to obtain the European trade goods beginning to circulate throughout the islands.

There are two distinct periods of movement of people to work outside Malaita. The first began in 1870–71 and continued for about 10 years: it often involved violence and coercion, but even in these years there are cases, such as the men who knew Renton, in which the circumstances are more complex and involved a degree of voluntarism. The second phase was circular migration, when the movement of labour became more regular, albeit still with great complexity: there were skirmishes, attacks and disputes along with regulation on both sides. Although there was still occasional kidnapping during the second phase, it involved bigmen and passage masters who aided and abetted the recruiters for their own gain, and the continuing circulation and return of labourers to their villages. The violent kidnapping days of the 1860s (in the New Hebrides and Loyalty Islands) and 1870s tainted the whole labour trade and left an impression, played on by detractors and early generations of historians, that the whole process was based on illegality.

What motivated participation from Malaitans and other Solomon Islanders, New Hebrideans and New Guineans is one of the least understood aspects of the labour trade. There are also issues about the legitimacy of the whole process. Is it correct to distinguish only between what was legal and illegal under British law? Today, Australian descendants of these labourers certainly do not see it this way and regard themselves as the descendants of kidnapped slaves. In earlier writing, I introduced the term 'cultural kidnapping' to describe the entire exploitative process. During over 40 years of research into this subject I have tried to distinguish between what was clearly kidnapping and what was voluntarism, although there is a large grey area in between, and I can discern aspects of slavery and trickery that linger in the British, French and German Pacific colonies, regardless of legal abolition. It was not de jure slavery, but in many ways

---

34   Shineberg 1984.

aspects of the Pacific labour trade were de facto slavery.³⁵ That said, along with other labour trade historians, I distinguish between contemporary emotional and political statements based on often dubious oral testimony with no basis in documentary evidence, and the overwhelming evidence of Islander agency in the process, gained from several types of sources and thoroughly researched since the 1960s.³⁶

As John Taylor notes in his study of north Pentecost, 'The degree to which Melanesians chose to enlist does not undermine the reality of European exploitation, both on the beaches and passages of Island Melanesia and on the plantations themselves'.³⁷ The explanation involves both physical and 'cultural kidnapping', with the latter term describing the process by which young Melanesians continued to be lured with cheap but desirable trade goods for many decades after physical kidnapping ended, along with their lack of understanding of the legal aspects of indenture agreements. The process proved irresistibly attractive to many youths and young men, particularly on Malaita. Even the missionaries became resigned to the labour traffic. The Anglican Melanesian Mission's *Southern Cross Log* for August 1897 provided an honest assessment:

> Little boys listened eagerly to tales of the wonders to be seen in the white man's land, and talk among themselves of the coming day when they shall make their venture, just as little white boys weave romances of the wondrous exploits that they are going to perform when they are grown up. As soon as, or even before they reach the legal age (for a Melanesian's real age is a very uncertain quantity), they are off at the first opportunity, with a delicious spice of adventure to flavour the start, as they slip off in the recruiting boat, a company of choice spirits, and 'snatch a fearful joy' by eluding their parents, guardians and teachers. The parents are supposed to be compensated by a present of various articles to the value of £2 for each boy, but practically the whole of this, or the equivalent in native money, is forfeit as a fine to the local chief for allowing their boys to go.³⁸

---

35   Allain and Bales 2012.
36   Moore 1985, 47–48; 2015b; Moore and Mercer 1993.
37   Taylor, 2008, 55.
38   'The Labour Traffic in Florida', *SCL*, Aug 1897, 9.

Although the Melanesian Mission decried the labour trade, the process by which that mission collected youths as students, first in Auckland and later on Norfolk Island (discussed in Chapter 3), was strikingly similar. As Taylor suggests, Islanders' perceptions of the labour trade and the 'mission trade' were 'more ambivalently fraught, displaying a mixture of both division and complexity'.[39]

There is also an overlap between colonial labour venues. We know that some individuals worked in several colonies or returned on multiple occasions to one colony, or worked overseas and on several contracts within the protectorate. This means that our statistical emphasis can only be on the number of contracts, and we cannot equate those with the number of individuals who recruited. Beginning in 1871 and continuing until 1904, there are records of 9,298 Malaitan recruits bound by indenture contracts to work in Queensland, 14.7 per cent of the total circular migration of Pacific Islanders to that colony. Between 1870 and 1911, 5,149 contracts similarly bound Malaitans to work in Fiji, 19 per cent of the total number of indentured Islanders who went there, and 62.6 per cent of those who went there from the Solomons.[40] A few hundred worked in Samoa and New Caledonia.[41] The level of Malaitan participation in the internal labour trade is even larger and no other island in the Solomons or Vanuatu comes anywhere near this level of participation in either the external or internal labour trades. Overwhelmingly, they were young males aged between 16 and 35 years. Only 3 to 4 per cent of the Malaitan labourers in Queensland and Fiji were female.[42] When plantations were established within the protectorate, Malaitan males continued to dominate the workforce. Their nearest rivals were from Guadalcanal (15.3 per cent).

---

39 Taylor 2008, 56.
40 I have excluded Bougainville and Buka from these figures.
41 Corris 1973b, 150; Munro 1990; Shineberg 1999; Meleisea 1980.
42 This is based on my reading of Price with Baker 1976, Siegel 1985 and Bedford 1973, which indicate that the Malaitan pattern is not duplicated in Vanuatu.

Table 1: Solomon Islander indentured labourers in Queensland and Fiji, 1870–1911.

Province	1870–87			1888–1911			1870–1911	
	Queensland	Fiji	Total	Queensland	Fiji	Total	Total	Percent
Central	971	81	1,052	1,575	9	1,594	2,646	10.64
Choiseul	58	27	85	0	0	0	85	0.34
Guadalcanal	1,575	892	2,467	2,613	322	2,935	5,402	21.72
Isabel	92	90	182	116	31	147	329	1.32
Makira	509	563	1,072	520	97	617	1,689	6.79
Malaita	2,216	2,727	4,943	7,082	2,422	9,504	14,447	58.10
Rennell & Bellona	65	4	69	0	0	0	69	0.27
Temotu	26	2	28	6	0	6	34	0.13
Western	130	34	164	0	0	0	164	0.65
TOTAL	5,642	4,420	10,062	11,912	2,881	14,803	24,865	

Source: Price with Baker 1976; Siegel 1985; Corris, 1973b, 149. The Fiji statistics are not considered fully accurate until after 1876.

The labour trade was also shaped by the imposition of and changes to international borders. For instance, in the archipelagos off east New Guinea in the early 1880s, there was a resurgence of the earlier kidnapping phase by Queensland's recruiters, followed by the proclamation of a British protectorate over southeast New Guinea in 1884. This ended the Queensland labour trade around east New Guinea and recruiters refocused on the Solomons and the New Hebrides. At the same time as the British annexation, Germany declared a *Schutzgebiet* (a mercantile territory) over northeast New Guinea. Between 1886 and 1899, this was extended into the northwest Solomon Islands: the Shortlands, Choiseul and Isabel (but not the New Georgia Group or Mono Island) were incorporated into German territory. This German move restricted British Queensland and Fiji recruiting ships to the New Georgia Group (from which very few recruits came since they had other ways to get trade goods) and the central Solomon Islands, with a concentration on Malaita and Guadalcanal. The Santa Cruz Islands and other outlying islands, including Rennell and Bellona, were not added to the BSIP until 1898 and 1899, as part of German and British negotiations over what became German and American Samoa, Tonga and other colonial territories. Although some small-scale recruiting continued across colonial borders, these territorial claims largely controlled the nationality of recruiters. Malaita became central to the British labour trade to Queensland and Fiji.[43]

The early decades of the labour trade—a moving labour frontier that preyed on an untapped labour reserve—involved considerable kidnapping and deception. Historians agree that during the first 10 years of recruiting at any Pacific island, the predominant methods were likely to involve illegality. A visit by the *Nukulau* recruiting out of Fiji in 1871 is symbolic of the very worst excesses in the early labour trade. The *Nukulau* kidnapped along the Malaitan east coast, at Isabel and in the northwest Solomons, before returning to Fiji with 89 captives. Sixty men were transhipped onto the *Peri* to go to a plantation on Taviniu Island, but a mutiny occurred, the crew was killed and, horribly, the vessel drifted 2,900 kilometres across the Pacific to Queensland, where it was found by HMS *Basilisk* in early 1872. Thirteen of the Malaitans survived by eating about 30 of the others. Eleven were returned to Malaita on HMS *Dido* in 1873.[44]

---

43 Moore 2003, 149–52.
44 Burt 2002; *Queenslander*, 15 Nov 1873; *Australasian Sketcher*, 29 Nov 1873.

Figure 2.3: An illustration of the *Peri* survivors being picked up by HMS *Basilisk* off the coast of Queensland in early 1872.
Source: *Illustrated Monthly Herald*, 3 Feb 1872.

The British labour trade reached its lowest point in 1871, the year Anglican Bishop John Patteson was killed on Nukapu Atoll in the Reef Islands, seemingly in retaliation for labour trade kidnapping.[45] The voyage of the *Nukulau* was not the only early voyage to involve illegality. Two voyages (1871–72) by the *Carl* out of Fiji became infamous for kidnappings at many islands and a massacre that took place on board.[46] Also in 1871, the *Helen* under Captain H. McKenzie was recruiting for New Caledonia around Sa`a on Small Malaita. At least five Ulawa men swam ashore from the ship at Sa`a, having been taken against their wills. The *Helen* used the typical kidnapping method of luring canoes out to the ship and then smashing them and forcing their occupants on board.[47] Some Malaitans

---

45 Kolshus and Hovdhaugen 2010.
46 Moore 1992; Brewster 1937, 231–37; Carter 1999; Banivanua-Mar 2007, 20–22, 29–34.
47 Shineberg 1999, 28–29.

2. TRADE AND LABOUR

who were kidnapped managed to return home within a few years, rich in European goods. Ben Burt gives an early 1870s example. Misuta and others from Kwakwaru in east Kwara`ae were kidnapped from a canoe while bonito fishing near Leli Atoll. Their families, presuming they were dead, sacrificed pigs to their ancestors, but then Misuta returned after a term as a labourer, stayed a short time and then reenlisted of his own free will.[48] Other men kidnapped in the 1870s did not return to Malaita until 30 years later, such as Amasia and Lau`a, who came back with Fijian wives and culture and were involved in spreading Christianity.[49]

Despite the excesses in the early years, over the decades between 1870 and 1911 Malaitans became willing participants, just as they were when the internal protectorate labour trade began in the 1900s. The process became a rite of passage for young men and a regular source of trade goods for their families, and later provided a way to pay taxes imposed by the government. The motivations for enlistment and the characteristics of the work remained much the same from the late 1870s until the early 1930s.[50] However, in my writing on the labour trade since the 1970s, I have felt uneasy about this simple division between legal and illegal recruiting, based largely on European definitions and classifications. This is why I introduced 'cultural kidnapping' as a term to communicate how the whole labour trade was exploitative for its duration, preying on Pacific Islanders who had different values systems from the Europeans who convinced them to agree to indenture contracts they could not understand. While it is true that many chose to participate, it was never an equal bargain and, as I noted earlier, their descendants in Australia today keenly press the argument that the process was akin to slavery.[51]

Taylor argues correctly that the motivation for men and women to leave their islands was not just to obtain material possessions such as iron, steel, guns and tobacco.

> I would further suggest that in travelling to the destinations offered by the labor recruiters, people from north Pentecost and elsewhere equally sought intellectual and spiritual cargo, cultural capital, and a more intimate knowledge of the encroaching Western culture.[52]

---

48 Burt 1994, 87.
49 *Ibid.*, 88–89.
50 Moore 1985, 23–46; Corris 1973b, 24–44.
51 Moore 2015b.
52 Taylor 2008, 56.

The same applies to Malaita and other islands. Having mixed with people from other island groups on plantations and farms, and after interactions with Indigenous Australians, Malaitans brought home new words, languages, plants, material culture, social habits, dances, songs, spiritual dimensions, and partners. Malaitans also carried back various Fijian practices, for instance kava drinking (which continued until the 1930s in west Kwara`ae), a style of outrigger canoe, and new food plants and magics. Ben Burt mentions that the Kwara`ae also brought back sweet potatoes, 'red tapioca', 'short bananas' and 'big red chickens', expanding their diet. David Akin, with experience in neighbouring Kwaio, mentions new varieties of taro and yams, bananas, sugarcane and sweet potatoes, plus pineapples and papaya and ornamental plants and trees, all introduced through the labour trade.[53]

As well, inadvertently, the indenture process both suited established gender and age roles in Malaitan society, and stretched existing roles. The recruiters wanted strong young males. Women were not generally available to be recruited, and the small numbers who left the island usually did so as partners of men. Because of Malaitan beliefs related to pollution during menstruation and birth, it was always problematic to have women cooped up with men for months on small, crowded recruiting ships, or later on the plantations and farms.

Malaitans did not practise male initiation of the sort that occurred in many Near Oceanic societies, and this allowed unmarried teenage and young adult men to travel more freely. Not yet fully functional members of their communities, they were adventurous and often keen to escape the rigidity of village life. They could advance themselves by spending several years in Queensland, Fiji, Samoa, New Caledonia or, starting in the 1900s, on plantations within the Solomons; returning with a box of foreign trade goods, they could distribute them for social credit within their communities. The circular nature of the labour trade tapped into existing patterns of residential mobility and customary mechanisms of compensatory religious sacrifices to ancestors. This made it possible for Malaitans to travel, yet remain safely within their cosmologies and religions. Mortality rates were high, particularly in the first six to 12 months of new contracts in the external labour trade, when recruits were exposed

---

53   Burt 1994, 100, 112, 147; Akin 2013a, 17.

to potent new diseases.⁵⁴ But for them the benefits outweighed the risks. Malaitans used the labour trade as their way to gain the coveted products of European technology, and thereby transformed Malaitan society.

Because of Near Oceanic cultural characteristics, the labour trade did not lead to capital accumulation, although it did enhance agricultural development. Recruits converted most of their cash into overpriced manufactured goods, since there was no need for cash until head taxes were introduced in the Solomons in the early 1920s. These European goods—tobacco, iron and steel items, glass, cloth, guns and so forth— were consumables that boosted individual and collective prestige, but (except for steel axes) did not last long. Very few of these early trade items have survived in the islands: there are a few antique axe heads and Snider rifles still extant, as well as some porcelain armbands and glass beads of European and Asian manufacture. Examples of these still exist in shrine areas and as heirlooms on Malaita, and in museums.⁵⁵

With steel tools, male tasks such as garden-clearing and boat- and house-building were accomplished more quickly, releasing men for other tasks. The new tools made forest clearing for gardens up to four times faster. If we can extrapolate from Salisbury's research on New Britain in the 1950s, and Townsend's research in the Sepik and Godelier's work with the Baruya, both in the 1960s, the introduction of metal tools enabled an increase in the size of gardens. Men's time was freed up, which was then invested in warfare, ritual and exchange, while women's garden and pig-rearing work increased. Steel axes also enabled men to work alone in forest clearing, as opposed to the team work necessary for clearing using stone axes and fire. Larger gardens meant more pigs could be fed, which presumably increased the size of mortuary and other feasts. The new technology revolutionised shell wealth manufacture, which may have inflated brideprices. Steel tools increased gender inequality and, along with the firearms introduced at the same time, caused other large-scale changes.⁵⁶

---

54   Shlomowitz 1987; 1990a; 1990b.
55   Gesner 1991; Beck 2009. Peter Sheppard from the University of Auckland has noted that ceramic armbands are occasionally found in shrine areas in the Western Solomons. Since there was little participation in labour migration from this area, these armbands would have been introduced by traders and whalers. Oceanic Anthropology Discussion Group (www.asao.org/asao-listserv.html, accessed 11 Oct 2007).
56   Salisbury 1962a, 110, 220; 1962b; Townsend 1969; Godelier 1986. I have benefited from discussions with David Akin on this topic.

Figure 2.4: Recruiting at Maanakwai in north Malaita.
The sketch by William Wawn, a labour trade captain, shows a typical Malaitan recruiting scene. Two boats were always used, one staying off shore to guard the boat on shore.
Source: Wawn 1893, frontispiece.

Figure 2.5: Malaita men in the 1920s at the age typical of labour recruits.
Source: Coombe 1911, 268.

Plantation Culture: Malaitans and Foreigners

In the 1980s, Roger Keesing used the term 'plantation culture' to describe the elaborate social codes evolved between all groups on the ships and on the plantations and farms.[57] Others have used the term 'contact culture' with a similar meaning.[58] It may well be that the *wantok* ('one talk', or sharing a language) concept began in Queensland and Fiji where men from one language area, or neighbouring areas on one island, or from one island, came to regard each other as friends, even when they were not close kin. The same applied to labourers working within the protectorate in the twentieth century. The term may also come from sharing a single voyage. Alan Lindley, who lived in Solomon Islands between 1952 and 1969, remembers old men saying 'you me two fella one scoon', meaning that they both travelled on the same schooner to the plantations, an explanation of brotherhood beyond kinship.[59]

In Queensland, Malaitans worked initially in the sugarcane, pastoral and maritime industries, and could be found anywhere from cattle stations in the Gulf of Carpentaria to the pearl and *bêche-de-mer* industries of Torres Strait, and in the sugar industry along the Queensland coast and into northern New South Wales.[60] The sugar industry absorbed the vast majority, but even there the nature of their employment altered over time. From the late 1870s, government regulations began to restrict the Islander labourers to unskilled work in tropical agriculture, and 1892 legislation excluded them from work in sugar mills, leaving them as field labourers. Around the same time, the industry also began to be transformed from an initial plantation base (large farms with their own mills) to a central milling system where associations of growers owned their own mills (with the help of government finance). In the 1890s and 1900s, Malaitans in Queensland were more likely to be working in small groups for farmers than within large labour forces on plantations. And there were always anomalies; photographs exist of teenagers working as house servants, proof that restrictions to field labour did not always apply.[61]

---

57   Keesing 1986b.
58   Schwartz 1962.
59   Alan Lindley, Adelaide, notes provided to the author, 2013.
60   Census of Queensland, 1891, *QVP* 1892, 3, 1, 391; 1901, 2, 956.
61   Moore 2008b.

Early Malaitan labourers in Fiji worked on cotton plantations, although most their experience was of sugarcane plantations and later (1890s onwards) on coconut plantations. The small numbers who made their way to Samoa worked on copra plantations, and the few in New Caledonia were involved in different kinds of unskilled labour—working on cattle stations, coffee and sugarcane plantations, and mixed farms, as boats' crews and in other types of transport.[62]

Malaitans did not work overseas only with other Solomon Islanders; in all of these colonies they worked in mixed groups that included other Pacific Islanders and Asians. In comparison with the next largest Pacific groups,[63] Malaitans were usually of outstanding importance.[64] They became still more prominent when recruiting of New Hebrideans began to decrease in the early 1890s; by 1894, Solomon Islanders permanently outnumbered the others and Malaitans were always at least half of them.[65] In Fiji, Solomon Islanders made up some 30 per cent (8,228) of the Islander workforce before 1911. New Hebrideans were the majority (14,198), along with a few thousand from the eastern New Guinea archipelagos and the Gilbert and Ellice islands, but the much larger group came from Asia, overwhelmingly from India (60,965).[66] In comparison with the next largest Pacific Islands groups,[67] the 5,149 Malaitan contract labourers were extremely dominant, even more so than in Queensland.[68] In the German colony of Samoa, the numbers are more difficult to ascertain. The German Solomon Islands extended south to Isabel Island until the end of the nineteenth century, and Germans were still able to recruit within the British Solomon Islands until 1914. However, most of Samoa's workforce came from the archipelagos off New Guinea, and Malaitans remained a small minority. The New Caledonia statistics and dates are also not firm, but a few hundred Malaitans and other Solomon Islanders worked alongside a few hundred Indians, 33,000 Javanese and around 10,000 to 13,000 labourers from the New Hebrides.[69]

---

62 Corris 1973b; Meleisea 1980; Shineberg 1999.
63 Epi (5,084), Tana (4,241), Guadalcanal (4,188) and Ambrim (3,464).
64 Moore 1985, 6. These figures are deceptive as they count indenture contracts not individuals. There were 62,000 contracts, but probably only about 50,000 individuals since many enlisted more than once.
65 *Ibid.*, 328.
66 Lal 1983.
67 Santo (1,820), Malakula (1,699), Tana (1,176), Guadalcanal (1,214), and Isabel (1,211).
68 Siegel 1985, 48–49.
69 Munro 1990.

Their British, French and German employers were imbued with European racial stereotypes common in the second half of the nineteenth century; these mixed ideas about a 'Great Chain of Being' with newer Darwinian concepts. Europeans placed themselves on the top of the scale, with some variations in the rankings of other races. Melanesians were placed near the bottom, just above Indigenous Australians, with local variations, such as in Fiji, where the indigenous people were judged superior to New Guineans, Solomon Islanders and New Hebrideans. A generation before the Pacific labour trade began, Britain had accepted slavery as normal (it was outlawed in the 1830s) and slavery had only been abolished in the United States a few years before the first Solomon Islanders were taken from their islands to work on plantations. Slavery continued to be legal in some other European jurisdictions until late in the nineteenth century. Thinking resembling the racial justification for slavery was used to justify entrapment of Pacific Islanders, and even more liberal Europeans regarded the Islanders as 'niggers' and 'savages' who could be exploited brutally.

How much Malaitans understood the contempt with which they were viewed is difficult to discern. Three things are clear. First, Europeans were almost uniformly frightened of what they regarded as a Malaitan propensity for violence, whether against recruiters working Malaita or on the plantations and farms in the colonies and the protectorate. As Ben Burt notes, 'Malaitan military strength was undiminished and indeed enhanced by the labour trade …'.[70] Second, Malaitans seldom acknowledged the supposed superiority of Europeans or other racial and ethnic groups of labourers. In fact, often they seem to have felt superior themselves, and failed to absorb the message that they should know their lowly place in the European race-class hierarchy.[71] In the Introduction, I suggested that they in fact played on the fear that others had of their inclination toward violence. The third point is that before the Second World War, Malaitan men had already worked with men (and some women) of many ethnicities and races for over 70 years. Much is made of the effect of Solomon Islanders meeting Black Americans during the 1940s, and although this was clearly influential in shaping thinking that led to Maasina Rule, it was not a totally new phenomenon.[72]

---

70 Quotation from Burt 1994, 103; see also Moore 1993.
71 Price with Baker 1976; Munro 1990.
72 Akin 2013a, 139–40. The Black Americans were different in that they appeared not to suffer the indignities of shared poverty that would have been the case with nineteenth-century contacts. Many Black Americans were comparatively well-educated and politically savvy, and able to articulate hopes for a future free of oppression.

The Recruiting Pattern

Malaita dominated the labour trade in the 1890s and 1900s, with the majority of Queensland and Fiji voyages visiting the island. The graphs below are from the Queensland labour trade; no similar detailed research findings exist for the Fijian labour trade, although the pattern would have been similar. My research from the 1970s suggests that the largest number of labourers travelling to Queensland (and presumably also Fiji) came from east Small Malaita (Walade and Sa`a), east Kwaio and Kwara`ae, Lau and Langalanga lagoons and Suu`aba Bay in To`aba`ita in the far north.[73]

Ships often spent between one and several weeks around Malaita. Most were dependent on sails, which shaped some of the contact patterns. Bays and passages that were difficult to access were often overlooked, or could only be entered by the ships' small boats. Captains and recruiters also had favourite areas, where they were friendly with a local passage master, or had recruited large numbers in the past, or where they knew there were large populations.

Recruiting vessels circled the island, loitering at favourite passages where passage masters mustered the men and received substantial rewards. Even though labour enlistment became something of a rite of passage for young men, recruiting was dangerous, with the chance of attack and ambush always present, even in the 1900s and 1910s. When recruiting vessels arrived they usually set off a charge of dynamite to let inland people know that recruiting was occurring. The hulls of the Queensland vessels were painted white with a black streak at least 15 centimetres wide on both sides just below the covering-board and, while recruiting, they had a 46-centimetre black ball hauled up the main mast as a clear signal to those watching from shore. The ships' whaleboats were painted red and worked in pairs, one going ashore and the other covering from several metres out, ready to shoot if necessary. The Fiji vessels used different colours. Bargaining took place on the shore. 'New chums'—those who had never before left their islands—were hired at the base rate: £6 for Queensland and £3 for Fiji. There was also always a beach bonus as a present for the recruits' relatives on shore, an equivalent to a customary exchange gift. Experienced recruits were able to bargain for a higher annual wage and in later years cannier labour recruits asked that their beach bonuses be given

---

73 This is illustrated by Map 7 in Moore 1985.

to themselves in cash for their own use. This could cause problems since their families often felt that no exchange bargain had been struck and they sometimes extracted revenge on the next labour trade ship that called in.[74]

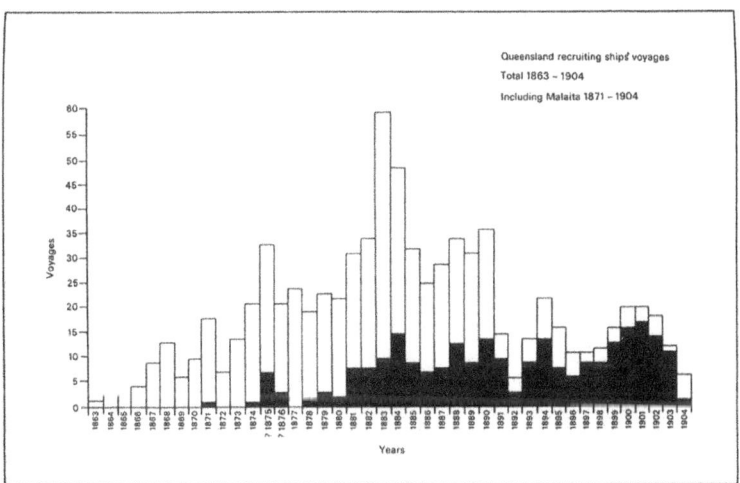

Graph 1: Migration of Pacific Islanders to Queensland, 1863–1905, showing total migration, and numbers from Solomon Islands and from Malaita Island. The black section indicates Malaitan recruiting.
Source: Moore 1981a, 65.

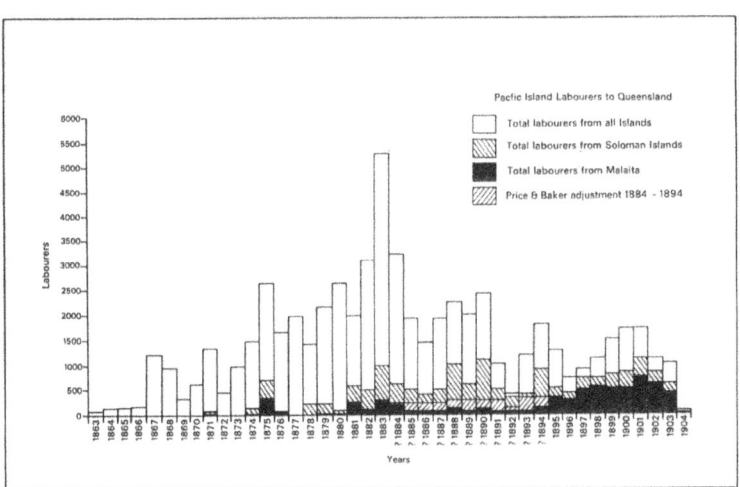

Graph 2: Migration of Pacific Islanders to Queensland, 1863–1904, showing ships' voyages that visited Malaita Island.
Source: Moore 1981a, 66.

---

74 Shineberg 1999, 18.

Figure 2.6: This photograph from Bundaberg in 1889 is of the *Helena*, a 126-ton schooner, which made 40 voyages from 1882–99, and the *May*, a 237-ton schooner, which made 15 voyages from 1888–94.

Labour trade ships were usually two- and three-masted schooners, brigs and barquentines ranging from 100 to 300 tons. Both of these ships visited Malaita many times. One of the voyages in Map 9 is by the *Helena* in 1893.

Source: State Library of Queensland, neg. 2245.

Maps 9 and 10, based on eight Queensland voyages between 1881 and 1900, are typical of many dozens of voyages from that colony and from Fiji. Some ships sailed up just one coast and stopped at a couple of passages. Others spent several weeks working around the island, calling at some passages more than once.

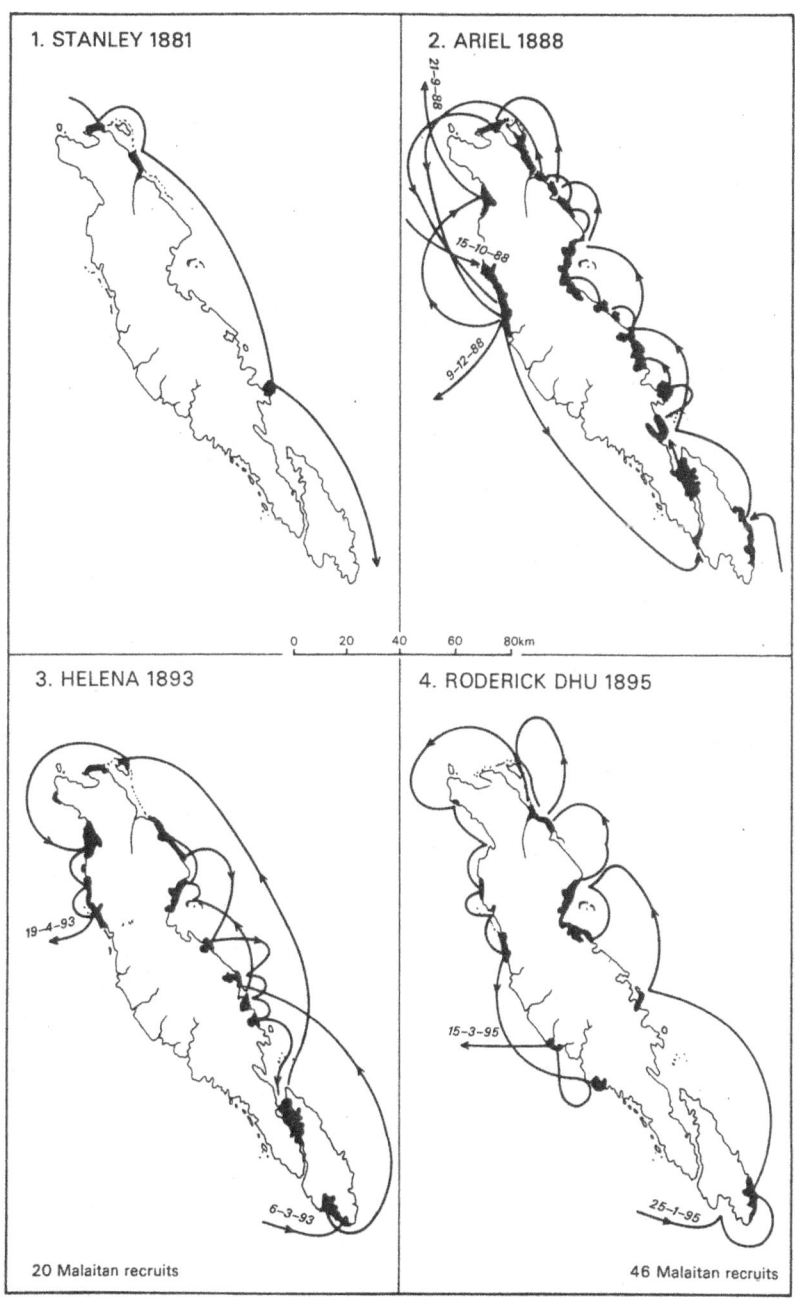

Map 9: Typical recruiting voyages around Malaita, 1881–95.
Source: Moore 1981a, 155.

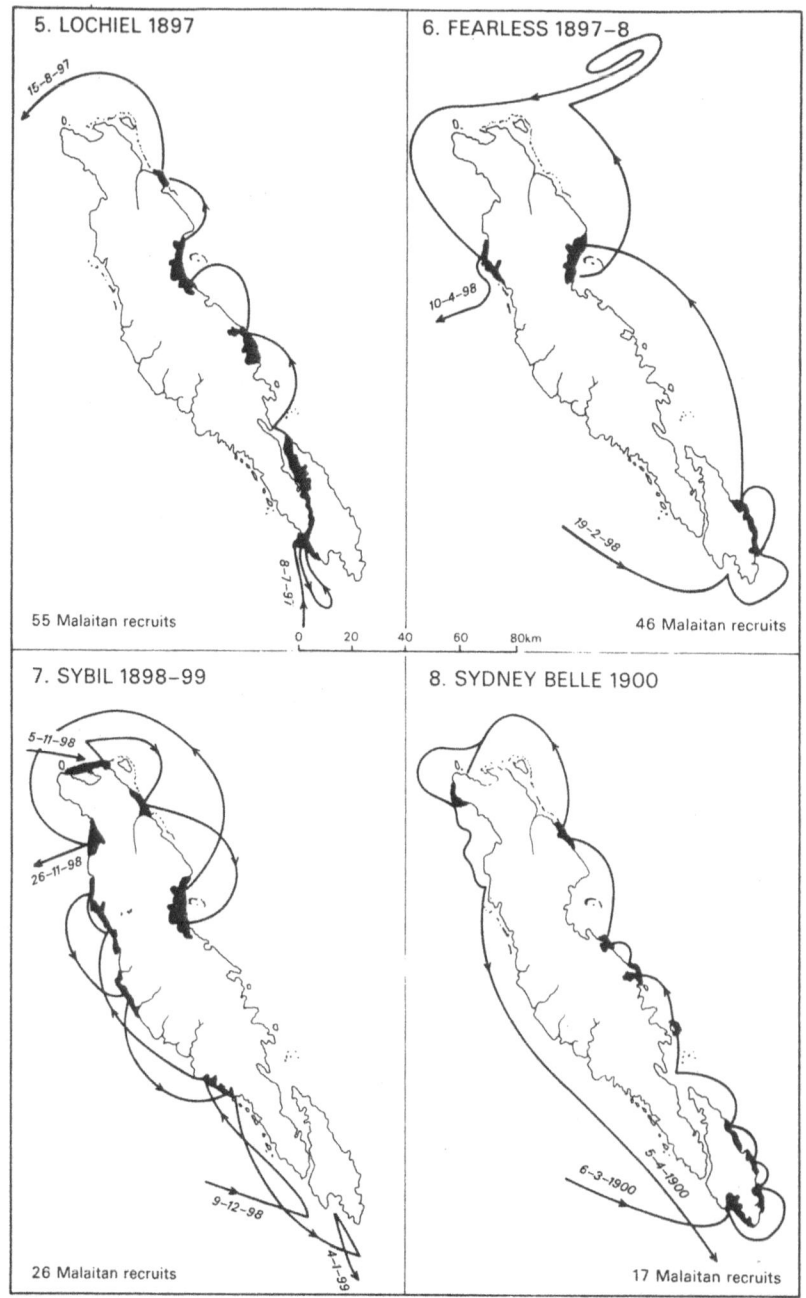

Map 10: Typical recruiting voyages around Malaita, 1897–1900.
Source: Moore 1981a, 156.

The captains and recruiters knew the local passage masters, gave them presents and arranged for inland recruits to come down to the coast at a prearranged time. There was a high level of collaboration. The passage masters are too often left out of the equation; certainly the bulk of the recruiting could not have been accomplished without their cooperation.

Figure 2.7: There are no known photographs of accommodations below decks. On the early voyages it would have been much more basic.
This sketch is by William Wawn, who was a captain in the labour trade from 1875 to 1894. It probably depicts one of his 1880s ships.
Source: Wawn 1893, 4.

Several points need to be stressed at this stage with bearing on my argument that what made Malaita different was primarily its people's large-scale participation in the labour trade. First, the overseas plantation experience was very cosmopolitan. Malaitans learnt to work with other Pacific Islanders, Asians and Europeans. While most preferred to spend their after-work time with their own *wantoks* or at least other Solomon Islanders from surrounding islands, Malaitans were exposed to many different cultures and ethnicities: British, French, German, Indian, Singhalese (Sri Lankan), Chinese, Japanese, Javanese, New Hebridean, Micronesian, Polynesian, Fijian, Samoan, New Caledonian and Indigenous Australians. Second, the experience of young Malaitan males as labourers working outside of their island changed their place within power structures when they returned home. Although returning labourers were obligated to distribute their new wealth for the communal good, they also achieved a more important position in society than their brothers who stayed at home. A third important element, the introduction of new diseases brought home by returning labourers, will be discussed later.

Figure 2.8: Men from Guadalcanal and Malaita on Foulden plantation at Mackay, Queensland, in the 1870s.
Source: Amherst and Thomson 1901, frontispiece.

Away from home, these men were freer than they had ever been before, even though they were indentured labourers bound by fairly draconian legislation, both the *Masters & Servants Acts*—which were applied also to other labourers, including Europeans and Asians—and legislation designed specifically to govern the working lives of the Islanders. Most of them settled down fairly quickly once they had adjusted to the new experiences of regimented work within specific time frames, the strangeness of industrial and agricultural machinery and implements, new animals and assertive overseers, and urban life and a colder climate. They operated socially in the new environment in ways that European colonists seldom understood. Most Europeans cared little for the Islanders so long as they worked hard and stayed out of trouble. Although Islanders socialised and preferred to live in language and island groups, and obeyed local community leaders, they were largely free of customary authority. Those who stayed for longer periods became part of the lower end of the Queensland or Fijian working classes.[75] They all learnt quickly to speak Queensland Pijin English or the Pijin English used in Fiji (along with Pijin Fijian) and Samoa.[76] Many of the longer-term overseas residents also spoke good English. A few spoke some Hindi, French, German

---

75 Moore and Finnane 1992.
76 Siegel 1982.

or Samoan.⁷⁷ Some labourers had even picked up Pijin languages on Malaita before they departed. Many also became literate through overseas Christian 'Bible schools', although some simply memorised hymns and Bible passages, which they could recite to perfection. Pijin English and Fijian was so widely spoken on the Malaitan coast in 1896 that the first resident commissioner, Charles Woodford, who spoke Fijian, found little problem communicating when visiting since he could always find ex-labourers to communicate with or act as interpreters.⁷⁸

Trade Goods on Malaita

In later chapters I will return to the topic of indentured labour during the protectorate years. Although Malaita was several decades behind some islands in getting access to European goods, we need to consider the consequences of huge quantities of trade goods inundating the island before World War II. There are records of in excess of 51,000 Malaitan indentured labour contracts between 1870 and 1942. Any calculation of wages earned and repatriated home must reckon the number of recruits, the proportion who reengaged, the numbers of men and women (except for first contracts, women earned less), the level of mortality and the extent that wages were spent outside of Malaita. Nevertheless, the value of goods earned by Malaitans under indenture from 1870 through 1942 must have exceeded one million pounds sterling, most of it earned after the 1880s. The modern equivalent is difficult to calculate, but, conservatively, it would have been at least AU$200 million in 2015 values, and probably much more.⁷⁹

Just over 9,000 Malaitans entered contracts to travel to Queensland as indentured labourers from 1871–1904. The majority were first-indenture labourers paid £6 per year on standard three-year contracts, for both males and females. Labourers who reenlisted in the islands had already served one or more contracts in Queensland, Fiji, Samoa or New Caledonia, and received from £6 to £12 per year. The information on beach bonuses is

---

77 Mühlhäusler 1975; 1976; 1981a; 1981b; 1996; 2002; Mühlhäusler and Mühlhäusler 2005; Siegel 1982; Mühlhäusler, Bennett and Tryon 1979; Dutton 1980.
78 Woodford 1896, 20 June, 17; Siegel 1982, 17.
79 www.measuringworth.com/ukcompare/relativevalue.php (accessed 8 Jan 2015). I have used 1900 and 2015 as my two comparative years. Based on the increase in the value of £1, one can use real price (£94.41), labour value (£364.00) or income value (£549.54). If we convert this to dollars then the amounts double. If we take the lowest option (real price) the amount is £94 million ($188 million).

fragmentary, but indicates that in early decades the standard rate varied between 10 shillings and about £2, usually paid in goods.[80] Queensland's time-expired labourers—those who were reindentured in the colony—received between £16 and £25 per year (1884–1901), depending on their skills and the length of the contract. As noted, time-expired females were always paid less, but they too received more pay commensurate to experience. These time-expired labourers dominated Queensland's Islander workforce during the final decades of the century. The last category was an elite but ever-diminishing group, generally called 'ticket-holders'—835 Islanders (including some Malaitans) already in the colony in September 1879. From 1884 on, this group were exempted from all subsequent restrictions, and in effect they became colonists. Some of them owned small farms and boarding houses.[81]

Payment was made annually (1863–76) and then biannually (1876–1907). One of the myths of the contemporary Australian South Sea Islander community is that their ancestors were never paid (and hence slaves). Contrary to this, at Mackay, the main sugar-producing district, the Islanders were using bank accounts as early as 1875 (because officials banked part of their earnings), and 10 years later when the government began compiling annual banking statistics, 61 Islanders had together deposited £251. Between 1888 and 1904, the government published a full record of the total number of accounts and their credit and debit transactions. Mackay had 1,271 individual Islander account holders in 1892. The total amount deposited fluctuated, with £5,985 the highest level in 1893. Transactions also varied, but during an average year £2,900 was deposited and a similar sum withdrawn. In 1892, Islanders in Queensland had £18,641 in the government savings bank. Individual deposits were usually small, most no more than £5 or £6, although there is evidence from Maryborough of Islanders with up to £50 in their accounts.[82] There is no doubt, then, that they were paid, though there clearly could have been some trickery—we know trade goods were often sold at inflated prices, Islanders did not always understand the value of the various coins, preferring large coins to small ones, and to some of them banking would have seemed a mysterious process.

---

80 Shlomowitz 1979a, 20 n 25, 73; 1981; Moore 1985, 72–74.
81 Shlomowitz 1979a, 85, 90–94; 1982.
82 Moore 1985, 179–83; Shlomowitz 1979b, 168–83; 1981, 70–91; 1982, 327–62; *QVP* 1893, 2, 539, 'Summary of Savings Bank Operations of Pacific Islanders for the year 1892'.

The minimum amount to pay 9,187 three-year Malaitan first-indenture contracts and a beach bonus of £1 each is £174,553. There was a high death rate in Queensland: 24 per cent of all contracts and approximately 30 per cent of individuals. After 1885, only 15.6 per cent of the wages of deceased Islanders were returned as trade goods to relatives; between 1871 and 1884, the return rate was even lower. Given that labourers reengaging in the islands and Queensland were better paid, earning £10 to £20 a year, the total amount paid to Malaitans in Queensland before 1908 is likely to have been around £300,000, and if we deduct one-third (for deaths) it is still £200,000. Not all of this made its way back to Malaita, but a large amount did.[83]

The Fiji labour trade with Malaita operated between 1870 and 1914 with over 5,000 indenture contracts.[84] The legislative framework that governed the trade was established in two ordinances in 1877 and 1888, and the evidence from before 1877 suggests that the earlier pattern was similar. Labourers could be engaged on up to five-year contacts, although most were for three years. They were mainly adults (defined as over 14 years of age) and were paid a minimum of £3 per year, although youths as young as 10 (from 1877) or 12 (from 1888) or 16 (from 1908) were legally able to be recruited at £1 per year. Until 1891, experienced male recruits continued to receive £3 per annum, but the average wage increased. It was between £4 and £6 in the mid-1880s, £6 per year 1885–1903 and £8 per year from then until the end of the labour trade in 1914. The £3 legal minimum was observed until 1904, but thereafter most new recruits received £6 per year, in keeping with the competitive market. Most female recruits received £3 per year throughout the period, but after 1883 experienced female labourers reenlisting we paid between £4 and £6 per year. Time-expired labourers were paid around £10 per year.[85] Beach bonuses would have been similar to those of Queensland recruits—around £1 to £2, paid to relatives, or to the recruits themselves if they insisted. If we take the lower £3 figure as the base for our calculations (until 1885, about half of the total), along with the usual beach bonus, up until 1885 Malaitans in Fiji were paid around £27,000. Workers after 1885 often earned more—around £5 a year plus a beach bonus—probably well in excess of £40,000 or £50,000. Given wage variations and deaths while away, the total would have been no less than £50,000 or £60,000.

83 Moore 2015a.
84 Siegel 1985.
85 Shlomowitz 1986.

Figure 2.9: At Mackay, Hugh Hossack owned one of the larger 'Kanaka stores', shops that catered predominantly to Islanders. They bought their trade boxes and their contents there, and were allowed to store their possessions there. The photograph shows how central Islanders were to Hossack's trade, and his relationship with them.
Source: Clive Moore Collection.

Within the Solomons between 1913 and 1940, Malaitans undertook 36,596 indenture contracts (see Table 7, Chapter 10). Workers could contract for periods of between one month and two years, and in 1908 and 1909 three-year contracts were permitted. Ralph Shlomowitz and Richard Bedford found that data on the distribution of the lengths of contracts was available only for 1913, 1914 and 1919, but in these years there was a clear preference for two-year contracts, a pattern that is also indicated by more fragmentary and anecdotal evidence. Initially (up to 1922), labourers were paid £6 per year and a beach bonus of several pounds, paid in tobacco, axes, knives and cloth, not cash. The bonus varied between £1 and £12 and Malaitans on two-year contracts received the highest bonus: £1 to £3 (1909–13); £3 to £5 (1915–16); and £8 to £12 (1921–23). In 1922 the Advisory Council recommended that the bonus be limited to £7. The bonus system was abandoned altogether in 1923 when the wage was increased to £12 per year. In 1935, during the Great Depression, the minimum labourer's wage was halved from £1 to 10 shillings a month, with a decrease in the beach bonus from £6 to £3. Between 1915 and 1919, 7 per cent of the labourers reengaged, and between 1935 and 1940 17 per cent did so.[86] Mortality was high, probably in excess of 10 to 15 per cent, and we have no clear idea of how often contracts of deceased labourers were paid out. A conservative estimate would suggest that Malaitan labourers should have been paid in excess of £700,000 between 1913 and 1940, mainly in the form of manufactured goods, although once taxation was introduced in the early 1920s (5/-, later reduced to 1/- per adult male) wages were paid partly in cash. Once more, this translates into huge quantities of manufactured items (including enormous amounts of stick tobacco) and cash reaching Malaita. The extent of the beach bonus was considerable, as was the amount of goods paid to passage masters around Malaita.

Mortality robbed thousands of Malaitans of a chance to return home from Queensland and Fiji. My calculations suggest that about 2,170 Malaitans died in Queensland during the labour trade.[87] Death rates on Fiji plantations were also high—23 per cent—an indication that around 1,840 Malaitans may have died there. Death rates on protectorate plantations were lower, but still high.[88] Others deliberately chose not to return, or lost contact with their families and were presumed dead. Even so, they may still have remitted goods home with other Malaitans, or relatives may have received government recompense through the government agents. Based on Queensland calculations, less than 16 per cent of the wages of deceased Islanders were returned to their next-of-kin.[89]

86 *Planters' Gazette*, 8 Dec 1922, 1; Shlomowitz and Bedford 1988, 67.
87 Graves 1993, 248–49; Moore 2015a.
88 Shlomowitz 1986, 112–13; Bennett 1993, 140, 143–44.
89 Moore 2015a.

Even accepting that many of the trade goods were overpriced and of poor quality, this substantial influx of foreign manufactured items into Malaita (and other islands) before the Second World War has never been properly considered. The beach bonus paid to the relatives was the initial recompense. In one 1880s example, this consisted of '400 sticks of trade tobacco (twenty-six to the pound), three axes, two dozen assorted fishhooks, a fishing line, four knives, a belt, a sheath knife, a pair of scissors, a heap of clay pipes, and a dozen boxes of matches, the whole estimated in value at between 30s, and £2'.[90] Interpreters received the same types of items in larger quantities. The passage masters amassed the most foreign items and lived in semi-European style. Kwaisulia of Lau Lagoon collected a vast array of European goods at his `Adagege home. In 1892, Sam, a bigman at Maanakwai and at `Aioo Island off of east Kwaio, had a copy of a whaleboat—actually a clinker-built boat painted red, with sail and oars—given to him by the captain of the *Lochiel*. He worked for several ships as interpreter: on the *Helena* in 1892; and on the *Para* in 1894 between Port Adam and Fokanakafo, for which he was paid 300 pounds (136 kilograms) of tobacco and another boat. James Goodrich, commander of HMS *Royalist*, described him as having 'been a long time in Queensland, and talks English fairly well', and as 'the most intelligent Solomon Island native I have met'.[91]

Returning labourers brought the most foreign possessions to Malaita. Some of these were clothes that soon perished or were discarded. Malaitans arrived back resplendent in the new clothes, such as this group at Waisisi, west `Are`are in 1887:

> I had taken a boatload of natives to a beach with their boxes and other personal belongings. They had dressed themselves in all their finery for the occasion of their homecoming, wearing coloured shirts and ties, trousers and coats, and hats too if they had them. None of the head-gear fitted, and being merely perched on the tops of their fuzzy mops of hair, they were no protection whatever from the sun.[92]

When the *Helena* returned labourers from Queensland in 1892, the 64 returnees had spent approximately £300 to fill their trade boxes, each weighing around 100 kilograms.

---

90 Melvin 1977, 33–34.
91 *Ibid.*, 35; Wawn, private log, *Para*, 2 Aug 1894; WPHC, C 8 III, 23, 1894, RNAS Case 63, Commander James E. Goodrich to CC, 29 Aug 1894.
92 Cromar 1935, 239.

The goods were not particularly remarkable for their variety. In value, and sometimes in bulk, tobacco was the most important item. There were cases of the 'weed' weighing over thirty pounds, for which £5 sterling each was said to have been paid. Parcels of pipes, from the common clay to the stylish briars, and a gross or two of matches were natural corollaries. Assortments of axes, hatchets, cutlery, calico, and coloured hand-kerchiefs were common to all. Saucepans and billycans were also in evidence. Amongst the uncommon articles were musical boxes, a bundle of score music, bathing pants, ginghams, pomatum [perfumed ointment used to groom the hair], fancy soap, and some shells being taken back to where they had been gathered.[93]

Guns and ammunition were the most sought-after items. After 1884, importing firearms from Queensland and Fiji was outlawed, limiting but not stopping the arms trade. False bottoms were added to trade boxes and dynamite and cartridges were often found wrapped inside innocent items.[94] Control tightened after 1898 when Resident Commissioner Woodford insisted that all recruiting ships call at Tulagi, pay an annual £100 licence fee, complete a medical check on all passengers and crew and allow a search for contraband.[95] Guns still reached Malaita nonetheless, such as a Winchester repeater rifle smuggled on the *Sydney Belle* in 1906.[96] It was also still possible to get firearms locally through traders in the Solomons, such as Oscar Svensen at Marau Sound, Guadalcanal, and from French and German labour traders.[97]

Tens of thousands of firearms reached Malaita in all, although their numbers must have become more limited after the mid-1880s and even more in the early twentieth century. In the 1920s, the district officer attempted a census of firearms on Malaita: 1,070 were identified from one district in the north, an indication perhaps of around 10,000 guns

---

93   Melvin 1977, 7, see also 7–9. The reference to the shells is tantalising, but nothing further is known.
94   Graves 1983 provides the best summary of the nature of the trade goods brought back from Queensland.
95   Smith 1898, diary from the *Sybil II*, 7 Feb.
96   QSA POL/J29, In-Letter 01574 of 1906, Brisbane Commander of Police to Inspector-General of Police, Sydney; *BC*, 2 Jan 1906.
97   Bennett 1981a, 174–76; QSA GOV/A33, IG to US, CSD, 8 Sept 1898. A good example of weapons seized is from the *Sybil II* in 1897, before the ship left Queensland: 14 Snider rifles, 2 revolvers, 370 cartridges, 1 bayonet, and 2 pounds of gunpowder. A less thorough search would have meant these ended up in the islands. For instance, *Sydney Belle* was searched twice before it left Queensland, but Woodford still found gunpowder and cartridges on board when the ship reached Tulagi. QSA POL/J29, 2719 of 1897; GOV/A39, GA A.H.K. Ussher to IA, 29 Oct 1903.

on the island at the time.[98] In the Western Solomons, trade goods, particularly guns and axes, exacerbated internecine fighting and led to potent, marauding indigenous head-hunters and slavers who roamed the nearby islands. The effect of the influx of foreign goods on Malaita was internal, not external as it was with the people from the northwest. The influx of European material items quickly changed Malaita. Guns became necessary extensions of male weaponry and prestige. Missionary Walter Ivens described the consequence of the spread of firearms on Malaita as a 'thirty years' war'[99] that decimated the island.

> The possession of rifles set up a state of war and lawlessness among a community that hitherto had been more or less at peace, and whereas homicide had been confined before mainly to the killing of those accused of black magic or of adultery, or had followed the infraction of some tabu or the wounding of some man's pride, men now killed either for the sake of killing or in order to get for themselves some desirable object owned by another. Big Mala, through the introduction of firearms, became a place of high-handed dealing by sets of bravoes, a place where fighting-parties made life insupportable to the ordinary peaceably disposed individual. It was the ambition of every young Mala man to own a rifle, and there were very few among them whose ambition in this respect was not gratified.[100]

Not all of the returnees brought back large quantities of goods. Woodford reported in 1886 on one man from west Malaita who returned from Fiji aboard the *Christine*. He had worked there for four years, the first three at £6 a year and the final year at £12. Earlier he had worked in Queensland. He had a trade box, but its main contents was a small cash box containing £40 in gold sovereigns. He had brought back sugar, and purchased tea and tobacco from the ship's captain. The man was planning to work in Samoa after a short stay. In his negotiation over the tobacco he complained at the price, and when told it was cheaper than he could buy it in Suva, he replied 'yes, but you pay no duty', showing an understanding of European finances.[101]

While the external labour trade progressed, more permanent traders settled in the Solomons, at Tulagi, Gizo, New Georgia's lagoons, Savo, Uki, Makira, Santa Ana and Guadalcanal, but not Malaita. As Judith Bennett observes, their presence was important, not only for providing

---

98   Ivens 1930, 43.
99   *Ibid.*, 45.
100 *Ibid.*, 43–44.
101 Woodford 1886.

a regular supply of foreign goods but also in demonstrating the usefulness of the items.¹⁰² From the 1890s onward, the supplies gained via the labour trade were supplemented in west `Are`are and Langalanga by trade goods received from European traders based at Marau Sound.¹⁰³ As early as the 1900s, Rev. Hopkins, familiar with north Malaita, wrote that the standard of manufacture of day-to-day artefacts was becoming cruder. Bows and arrows, spears and clubs, bowls for food, nets, combs, shell breast plates, armlets and nose ornaments had all become less well constructed and harder to obtain.

> The more they get the use of tools from outside, the less skilful gets their own work. Guns of all sorts replace the old weapons, and kettles, saucepans, etc., exempt them from making the old native bowls. What they do make is made anyhow, and not with the old patience and toil.¹⁰⁴

The new items, particularly steel tools and rifles, also entered established customary networks; they were hired out in exchange for shell currency, and could even acquire a sacred status.¹⁰⁵

Kwaisulia and His Family

The labour trade created a new group of important Solomon Islanders: the passage masters and interpreters. There were many on Malaita: Bobi Ledi from Rakwane, at Fokanakafo, east Fataleka; Peter Waimaku and Tom Miuldo at `Ataa in the south of Lau Lagoon; Fo`alanga and his son Peter Sua from Walade on Small Malaita; and Kwaisulia from `Adagege in Lau Lagoon.¹⁰⁶ The key points of contact for all foreigners, they were the translators and negotiators, the middle-men who enabled the labour trade to operate reasonably safely. Their support could aid or negate missionary endeavours, and the protectorate government also tapped into their powers. They achieved a status different from the *aofia*, *fataabu* and *ramo* triumvirate, although they drew on elements from the old leadership system and were able to negotiate with the new.

---

102 Bennett 1987, 45–102.
103 Bennett 1981a.
104 Hopkins, 'Mala and Its People', *SCL*, June 1908, 11.
105 Akin 1999a, 250 n 12.
106 Moore 1985, 45, 52–53, 90–93.

'Adagege islet is next to Sulufou. It had been built by refugees from further south and taken over by Sulufou as a women's birthing island, then subsequently ritually cleansed and used for a village. Kwaisulia's father was from an inland descent group on the mainland opposite the lagoon and had married into a Sulufou chiefly family, providing him with good connections. Born in the 1850s on 'Adagege, Kwaisulia had been a friend of Jack Renton, the Scottish castaway who lived on Sulufou from 1868 to 1875 under the care of chief Kabbou. After his rescue from Malaita, Renton visited Lau again as an interpreter and recruiter in 1875, on the brigantine *Bobtail Nag*, which led Kwaisulia and others to enlist for Queensland. He stayed in Queensland for six years and returned home fluent in Pijin English. There is no clear evidence on where he worked: we know he visited Brisbane and was mightily impressed, and he may have worked around Rockhampton, a prosperous, mainly pastoral district. Kwaisulia must have worked on one three-year contract at £6 per year, with the addition of board and lodgings, minimal health care and a passage home. He would then have negotiated a new, more lucrative contract, probably for another three years.

After his return home in 1881, Kwaisulia soon became the major Lau passage master, and consequently, between the 1880s and his death in 1909, the most powerful bigman in north Malaita. He had the language skills and enough savvy of European ways to negotiate with the recruiters. Described as about 177 centimetres high, and a strong, dark-skinned man with a powerful build, his manner evinced authority and his words held sway.[107] He was never a Christian and opposed Peter Abu'ofa's plans to begin QKM missionary work in Lau in 1894 (see Chapter 5). He was initially antagonistic to the Melanesian Mission's encroachment on his power base in the lagoon when they wanted to establish a base at 'Ataa in 1898. However, he welcomed the presence of that mission's Rev. Arthur Hopkins, sent to live at Ngorefou in the lagoon in 1902 (see Chapter 4). Presumably he felt that the prestige of having his own white man outweighed the disadvantages.

Kwaisulia managed to build up his importance to a degree that Europeans sought him out before dealing with anyone else from Lau, or indeed in most of north Malaita. He managed to amass great wealth from the labour trade and usurped the legitimate chiefly line of Sulufou. Once Kabbou

---

107 Corris 1973b, 255, 260.

died in the mid-1880s, Kwaisulia was able to take over the leadership of ʻAdagege and Sulufou. He lived in style on fortified ʻAdagege, with European furniture given to him by labour trade captains, and his own whaleboat. His wealth in rifles, ammunition, dynamite and other trade goods, plus barbed wire, clothes, clocks and music boxes, was part of his power.[108] Explosives were his undoing when he died while dynamiting fish in 1909. Hopkins described Kwaisulia as on one occasion wearing 'a white drill suit, spotlessly clean, sun helmet, sash and a broad smile',[109] but he was just as capable of holding court wearing pyjama pants.

Kwaisulia's oldest son, Jackson Kaiviti (Kaiʻfigi), was baptised while working in Fiji, then on his arrival back home returned to his ancestral religion. He succeeded his father as the next leading Lau passage master and bigman. They befriended recruiters, naval captains and finally Resident Commissioner Woodford, to whom Kwaisulia rather imperiously sent greetings when he first took up residence at Tulagi in 1897. The short-staffed protectorate was also capable of using the family's authority. In 1902, Woodford's deputy, Arthur Mahaffy, asked Jackson Kaiʻfigi to arrest two murderers from just south of ʻAtaa. Another son, Timothy (or Tom) Kakaluʻae, flourished once government was established on Malaita. Kakaluʻae joined the constabulary in 1921, rising to the rank of corporal in 1927. He also played a role in the 1927 punitive expedition to avenge the deaths of District Officer William Bell and his tax-collecting team in Kwaio (see Chapter 10).[110] He was appointed government headman for Lau in the late 1920s and remained in this role until 1941. By the 1930s, Kakaluʻae's power in Lau was as great as his father's had been, and like his father he refused to become a Christian. The government backed him, although it was clear that as the 1930s progressed Kakaluʻae became more corrupt, failing to untangle his own interests from those of the protectorate. This led to his dismissal in 1941.[111] For a short time Kakaluʻae was Maasina Rule Head Chief for Lau, but he soon found this incompatible with his loyalty to the British and became a bitter enemy of the movement.[112]

---

108 *Ibid.*, 259–60.
109 *Ibid.*, 263; Hopkins 1928, 155.
110 *SCL*, June 1900, 1; *SCL*, Nov 1910, 89; Hopkins 1949; Keesing 1992b, 180.
111 Keesing and Corris 1980; Akin 2013a, 59, 159.
112 Akin 2013a, 250, 269–72.

For almost 30 years, Kwaisulia managed to use the power and authority of the colonial economy and state to his advantage, and his sons inherited his power. From the next generation a grandson, Christopher Igilana (England) Kwaisulia, was involved in the Christian Remnant Church from the 1950s until the 1980s.[113] Igilana Kwaisulia also led a Lau delegation to `Are`are in 1945 to find out about Maasina Rule, and returned as a strong supporter. Kwaisulia and Kakalu`ae, pagan father and son, permanently transformed the authority structure in Lau Lagoon between the 1880s and the 1940s, while Kwaisulia's grandson attempted to reform Malaitan Christianity to his own political ends.

Their close relative Jack Taloifulia, born on Sulufou Island in the 1870s, was around 16 years old when he was taken to Mackay on a labour trade schooner; he remained for some 16 years and became the star pupil at the Anglican Selwyn Mission. In the 1900s, once the announcement of deportation of the Islanders was made, he asked to be sent to the Melanesian Mission's college on Norfolk Island to be trained as a missionary before returning to Malaita. He reached Norfolk via Brisbane, Sydney and Auckland, providing him with knowledge of large cities. Because he was much older than the rest of the students, Taloifulia did not learn easily, and he preferred the farm and chapel life outside of the classroom. After two years, he returned to Malaita and in 1904 began a mission school on land at Fouia on the mainland opposite Sulufou, despite the opposition of his uncle Kwaisulia. In recognition of his devotion, he was taken to Siota to study to be a deacon and in 1919 returned to Siota to study for the priesthood.[114] Taloifulia became an Anglican priest, a different path from that of his other Sulufou relatives, but he was just as important among the Lau.[115] These generations of Lau men covered the roles of passage master, warrior, chief and Christian leader, and show just how much change took place in the lagoon over the decades.

The Trope of Violence: Real or Imagined?

The Introduction raised the trope of violence as one of the markers of modern Malaitans. The labour trade provided guns, exacerbating Malaitans' abilities to fight each other. Malaitans were not more violent

---

113 Maeliau 1976; 1985; Keesing 1992b.
114 Moore 2013c, Taloifulia entry.
115 Tippett 1967, 163–70.

than their neighbours; indeed, the head-hunters and marauding slavers of New Georgia were clearly more fearsome.[116] However, on plantations and back on Malaita, the increased fighting enabled by new technologies enhanced their reputation for ferocity, unequalled by any other island group who worked as labourers in Queensland or Fiji, except perhaps the Tannese from the New Hebrides. The labour trade vessels and their whaleboats were also easy targets for attacks. This is quite a claim to fame, considering that all Pacific Islanders sometimes used violence to solve disputes, and while we must be wary of creating false tropes, the evidence of attacks on ships at Malaita is substantial (see Chapter 7).[117]

Bishop Cecil Wilson, for instance, described Malaitans in Queensland in the mid-1890s as 'mostly as wild as hawks' and excessively proud of 'their nationality'.[118] Many Europeans in Queensland were murdered by Islanders in the 1890s, particularly by Malaitans. Folk memory at Mackay records that Europeans believed that it was easy to know the origin of a murder: if the victims' head was smashed or missing then the culprit was sure to be Malaitan. Iron bars and lumps of lead on ropes, whirled around to add momentum before making contact, were favourite methods of despatch, as were the ubiquitous axes, cane knives, clubs, bows and arrows. 'Swaggies'[119] (tramps) and other isolated men were favourite targets. Often swaggies were not missed and as solitary travellers they were easy to kill. Similarly, on Malaita, warrior bounty-hunters often chose to kill isolated women and children alone in gardens rather than pick a fair fight. The compensatory death was all that was necessary.[120]

In Mackay in 1894, after the murder of a European woman, the local paper railed against the Malaitan perpetrators, who had been sentenced to death:

> The first blow is struck in the district to free it from the terrorism of the Malaytan Islanders. The attitude of these Kanakas deserves something more than passing notice. At the present time fifty per cent of the Polynesians in the district are natives of Malayta, while ten years ago the proportion was only about 15 per cent. The habits of the Malayta boys are of particular interest. Their thirst for blood is notorious …

---

116 McKinnon 1975.
117 Bennett 1987, 390–96; Moore 1985, 347–56.
118 Wilson, *OPMM*, Nov 1895, 153.
119 'Swaggies' is an Australian term for itinerant workers who carried a 'swag', usually a folded blanket enclosing their possessions.
120 Moore 1993.

> Of recent years the aggressiveness of these boys in the district has become unbearable. Apart from any graver offences of which Malaytan Islanders may be suspected, it is notorious that they boast of the impunity with which they can defy their employers and commit crime. White men who have lived in the district for years, now sleep with revolvers near to hand, and admit the terrorism inspired by this class of boys … [It] is the boast of the Islanders that the white man dare not hang them. It is argued also that, if we hang Kanakas, reprisals will follow in the Island trade, and to this we reply that, hanging or no hanging, the Malayta boys would cut off the first ship they could, and would murder any whiteman they could get a show at.[121]

In Pacific cultures, the physical and spiritual worlds intermingled; medicine, magic and religion were inextricably mixed. Illness and death were often not seen as the natural results of diseases, epidemics or old age, sickness and death. Even what were clearly accidents could be explained as having supernatural causes. Sickness was a direct punishment for misconduct, inflicted by ancestors who had to be appeased if the ailing individual was to survive. Malaitans believed that disease epidemics were caused by antagonistic spirits, ever circulating in the sky, waiting for a chance to commit a malevolent act. Murders and often other deaths, either from sorcery or by physical violence, had to be avenged to maintain social equilibrium.[122] Melanesians in Queensland and Fiji were exposed to new diseases, and death rates were extremely high, which exacerbated the problem.

The major killers were 'droplet' and virus infections. 'Droplet' infections (where droplets of saliva are passed on through sneezes and coughs or from singing or projecting the voice loudly) spread easily in confined spaces; they could be from virus or bacterial diseases. Measles, influenza, whooping cough and diphtheria are in this category. Pneumonia, bronchitis, pleurisy, and respiratory tract infections such as tuberculosis (then called 'consumption', and widespread amongst nineteenth-century Europeans) were an extension. Infectious diseases, particularly measles, Rubella, smallpox and chickenpox, also killed people, although a single attack could provide lifelong immunity for survivors. Colds and influenza, which could be particularly fatal in a community with no immunity, are both caused by viruses; they do produce immunity, but of a shorter duration. Other diseases came from contaminated food or water,

---

121 *MM*, 22 Nov 1894.
122 Moore 1993, 195; Oliver 1989, 1,748–85, esp. 768–69; Stephen 1987; Coppet 1981a; 1981b.

or drinking vessels or food utensils. Diseases of this type, such as bacillary dysentery (gastroenteritis), affected the gastro-intestinal tract, and little immunity was acquired from an attack.[123]

The three-year circular migrations continuously exposed fresh supplies of labourers to the new disease environment. Ralph Shlomowitz calculated that the crude death rate of Melanesians in Queensland in the first year of their indentures was 81 per 1,000, more than three times that of the long-term Melanesian immigrant population. Evidence suggests that those who survived the first three years in the colony had every chance of living to old age, remembering of course that, statistically, people died much younger in the nineteenth century than today. The deaths from diseases were of young men in their prime, aged 16 to 35 and judged medically fit when they first arrived. The death rate of Europeans in Queensland over the same period, of all ages, was 15 per 1,000. The death rate for European males in the colony of similar age to the Melanesians was around nine or 10 per 1,000. The Islanders, including Malaitans, responded to the high mortality with retaliations.[124] Malaitan responses were multifaceted, varying from outright revenge by murders and other forms of physical violence, to the sabotage of crops, farm animals and machinery, to intertribal fights and reactions targeted inward such as suicide and sorcery. Sorcery is an immeasurable dimension in a historical context such as this, invisible but devastatingly potent for those who believe in its power.[125]

Knowing exactly how to analyse behaviour overseas is difficult given that we have only fragments of evidence and the complexity and dynamism of the scene. The violence was always noted in Queensland, but how does it relate to other cultural practices? We need to be careful in portraying overt practices—dance, dress and even performing rituals—as an indication that 'culture' is or is not being maintained overseas in any simplistic sense. Oral evidence indicates that during the lifetimes of the original immigrant Islanders, religious and magical practices figured prominently in the Queensland community.[126] Presumably the same was true for Fiji, Samoa and New Caledonia. From photographs, we know that *sango* dancing was performed in Fiji. This dance and accompanying panpipe music were part of *maoma* (mortuary) rituals and exchange cycles performed

---

123 McArthur 1981, 3, provides a clear summary.
124 Shlomowitz 1987; 1989; Moore 2015a.
125 Moore 1993.
126 Mercer and Moore 1976.

throughout north Malaita and imported south into Kwaio in the mid- to late nineteenth century. In Kwaio, it was performed into the 1910s or early 1920s as part of bounty collections and associated rituals. Soon after, the government eradicated bounty-hunting, and *sango* rituals, at least in Kwaio, were modified solely into mortuary events. They continued to be performed regularly, in Kwaio approximately every two years, for the associated ancestors. Akin explains that *sango* rituals include strong fertility symbolism and that women play a role (though not in dancing or panpiping). It is important to note that *sango* dancing can sometimes be performed for entertainment, meaning that the Fiji photographs are not on their own evidence that *sango*'s ritual aspects were maintained there. *Mao*, another dance found all over Malaita, was performed and perhaps invented among plantation communities in Queensland. The lyrics for the Kwaio *mao* songs include Lau language and archaic Pijin English, presumably Kanaka Pijin English from Queensland.[127]

Slit-drums and body ornamentation, augmented with trade store beads, were all part of plantation culture overseas. But was this secular practice, and what changes or continuities occurred in people's thinking? Akin stresses:

> the extension of taboos and ancestral practices abroad was (a) highly varied from person to person or group to group, and no doubt varied over time, and (b) this was all part of a long-term process of extending the areas exempt from taboo practices from home to abroad and then back again to ever-growing areas of the Solomons.[128]

The participation of Malaitans in the colonial labour community continued over several decades, increasing in the final decades of the nineteenth century. Although there were always long-staying Malaitans, large numbers recruited for only one three-year contract. Each individual had their own form of relationship with their ancestors, and we know from modern Kwaio examples that some Malaitans can place ancestral relationships into abeyance, to be restored at more suitable times. And not all rituals have to be performed at central shrines by priests. The short-term labourers suffered most from the unfamiliar disease environment and presumably they (and their families at home) reacted most strongly in terms of seeking compensation. Malaitan males poured off their island and on to Queensland and Fijian plantations and farms in the 1890s,

---

127 I am indebted to David Akin for discussing these points with me, Nov 2015.
128 *Ibid.*, and see Akin 2013a, 23–24.

even more so in the 1900s, at a rate of over 1,000 each year, in far greater numbers than from any other island. An even larger number left Malaita each year during the first three decades of the twentieth century to work elsewhere in the protectorate. Mixed with Malaitan beliefs and behaviours, this was a potent cocktail and may well partly account for their reputation for violence. On the plantations they faced new situations equipped with strategies both new and old. As I have stressed, we cannot presume inflexibility, or that the situation in 1901 was the same as in 1871. On Malaita, imported diseases significantly increased mortality and the excess of guns certainly made internecine fighting easier and more deadly there.[129]

Conclusion

Malaitans exhibited complex responses to 'plantation culture' and to adopting Christianity and other foreign influences. They returned home much changed and in turn changed Malaitan society. Our knowledge of Malaitan ways of dealing with travel to foreign places, whether within the Solomons and therefore within their 'eight isles' world view, or overseas, is partly based on historical information but also on contemporary observations. In the 1970s, Judith Bennett interviewed 27 Malaitan ex-labourers: although she noted the 'spiritual vulnerability' among the predominantly traditional believers, it was also clear that they carried with them relics of shell valuables associated with ancestral shrines that they used to keep themselves safe.[130] David Akin's interpretation, based largely on his knowledge of the Kwaio, is similar:

> People negotiated with their ancestors new ground rules for proper behaviour abroad: to follow taboos where possible but waive them as necessary. Like so many other things, taboo observation, and taboos themselves, changed over time and varied from person to person, and those who stayed in Queensland and Fiji longer were less likely to observe taboos, among other reasons because more of them became Christians. Models developed for religious practices abroad extended older principles for adjusting, mitigating, or waiving ancestral taboos at home, in ways that allowed men to live a normal life while away. Many of these models are still applied by non-Christian Malaitans on plantations or in towns.[131]

---

129 Moore 1993, and Mercer and Moore 1976, extend the argument presented here.
130 Bennett 1993, 137, 175, 186; 1981a, esp. 143.
131 Akin 2013a, 23.

This assessment is also supported by the observations and writings from other anthropologists of Malaita, such as Roger Keesing and Ben Burt.[132]

There are well-established mechanisms used by followers of ancestors while away from their island. My own oral testimony work in Queensland in the 1970s, and my 40 years of observation of Malaitans on their own island, elsewhere in the Solomons and in Australia, plus the research and writing of Noel Fatnowna, a well-known Malaitan in Australia, confirms the ability of Malaitans to adapt to foreign circumstances.[133] As Akin says, our knowledge is made easier to ascertain because some Malaitans still practise their pre-Christian beliefs, allowing observation of similar contemporary behaviour.

David Akin's research makes clear that followers of ancestors had (and still have) the capacity to participate in travel without undue disruption to their religious rituals:

> Malaitans quickly developed new strategies for managing religious rules in places where they had little control. The chief difficulty was interactions with foreigners, both European and Melanesian, who did not know, let alone observe, the behavioural rules or taboos that ancestral spirits enforced among descendants. At home, even Malaitans from the same language group followed different taboos enforced by their specific ancestors, and rules that a person observed at home and abroad were key identity markers. In recruiting, taboos could become problematic as soon as a man entered a ship's hold if women were known to have trodden the deck above, since men could not be underneath women or places they had walked.[134]

When away from their home territories, Malaitans were unable to make full sacrifices to their ancestors through their priests. Before they left home they took precautions to ensure that they were protected while abroad and promised to fulfil all obligations once they returned home. Priests had responsibility to carry out sacrifices to protect labourers abroad and to give thanks and compensation when they returned. Labour recruits also carried 'small magic' with them in the form of ritual objects and substances when they travelled. They used these items in small shrines within their homes when overseas. For some Malaitans, travel to plantations was fully protected by priests who placated their ancestors and enabled an

---

132 Keesing 1986b; Burt 1994.
133 Mercer and Moore 1976; Moore 1985; Fatnowna 1989.
134 Akin 2013a, 22–23.

easy transition back into the cultural system when they returned home. However, there were always others who lost or had less protection when they departed from Malaita, because they had been kidnapped or ran away or were escaping some crime or offence. These Malaitans were more vulnerable and susceptible to conversion to Christianity, as were those who reengaged on second or multiple contracts—the 'time-expired' men and women or 'ticket-holders'. Such 'alienated' Malaitans found membership in a Christian congregation reassuring and if they eventually returned to Malaita they were more likely to return to mission stations than their home villages.

Figure 2.10: This photograph, of a Malaitan canoe in Fiji, presumably manufactured and decorated there, is one of the most remarkable from the overseas plantations. The image, from a collection by A.M. Brodziack & Co., was probably taken in the 1880s. The canoe is in Walu Bay, an old local shipping area and Solomon Islander settlement.
Source: Max Quanchi Collection.

Travel to plantations became a rite of passage for young men, and continues today as Malaitans move in and out of Honiara and other urban and plantation areas. They have been able to do this continuously and successfully for over 140 years, confirming that they have a flexible ability to deal with the spiritual and other cultural consequences. From the 1870s until the 1930s and 1940s, the majority of these Malaitan labourers were traditional believers, not Christians, although as I argue in the next few chapters there were also large numbers of Christians, even though they retained many ancestral beliefs. Despite the desire for the financial and material rewards of wage labour, they were able to participate in the labour trade because they possessed cultural mechanisms to smooth the transition from Malaita to the plantations and their return. However, one consequence was probably increased Malaitan violence at home and abroad.

Figure 2.11: Malaitans at Innisfail in north Queensland early in the 1900s. The slit-drum and the bows and arrows would have been made in Queensland.
Source: Clive Moore Collection.

The next four chapters discuss the spread of Christianity on Malaita. After participation in indentured labour, Christianity was the most important force for change on the island before the formal arrival of government. Chapter 3 looks at Malaitan Christianity overseas as a necessary precursor to the spread of Christianity on Malaita. These chapters deliberately separate the different missions because they had quite different motivations and beliefs. They also detail the names of the people involved, with the aim of returning individuals to the historical record. This will also facilitate future studies of the development of Malaita's colonial and postcolonial elites.

3
Malaitan Christians Overseas, 1880s–1910s

It is easy to understand why labourers in Queensland should have become Christians. They were cut off from all home influences, separated from their relatives, and in some cases entirely alone, and it was only natural that in such circumstances they listened to the urgings of the only Europeans who appeared to take an active interest in their welfare—perhaps the only Europeans who went out of their way to be kind. Christianity, moreover, was a religion of the white men who in all material achievements were so superior to their own people.

—Ian Hogbin, Experiments in Civilization (1939)[1]

The previous chapter discussed changes that occurred through labour migration: these were considerable and involved all communities, even those isolated in the central mountains. Men in particular became used to wage labour away from home. This altered the established social order when they returned to their small-scale societies. They brought back new material possessions in heavily laden trade boxes, but also carried invisible baggage from their exposure to European diseases and colonial society. One of the major underpinnings was Christianity, conversion to which became integral to methods of control used in the colonies where they laboured and also to British political control in the British Solomon Islands Protectorate. Those who worked in Queensland also returned with Pijin English, the new *lingua franca* of Solomon Islands. Wage labour, Christianity and Pijin English

---

1 Hogbin 1939, 179.

(and to a lesser extent Pijin Fijian)[2] altered Malaitan society long before the new government of the BSIP was proclaimed in 1893 and an administrative base was established at 'Aoke in 1909. As this chapter explains, around 2,000 Malaitans living on Malaita in 1909 had become Christians while overseas. As outlined in this and the following chapters, if we tally also those who became Christians on Malaita, there were at least 4,000 to 5,000 Christians on Malaita that year, many of whom had achieved basic literacy. Although Malaita is usually depicted as a non-Christian island in the 1900s, this was far from true, and the Christian presence greatly affected how change occurred in the century's first half.

Malaitan communities usually did not welcome early Christian missions or returning Malaitan Christians. Leaders soon recognised that the new spiritual regime would undermine the indigenous religion and could displease their ancestral spirits, which would in turn disrupt social equilibrium and incite ancestral retribution. Early Christians often built stockades for protection and when times were tense armed guards were needed to safeguard church services and even ordinary activities. Nonetheless, Christianity began to be established on Malaita onwards from the 1870s, starting on Small Malaita. This chapter examines the outreach of Christian missions in colonies in which Melanesians worked as indentured labour, the precursor for the establishment of Christianity on Malaita before the government arrived. The major overseas Christian training ground was in Queensland.

Malaitans and Christianity in Queensland

Pacific Islander labour migrants first entered New South Wales in 1847 and Queensland in 1860, although the regular flow of labour to Queensland did not begin until 1863. While there were Christians amongst the early labourers, particularly those from the Loyalty Islands and the New Hebrides,[3] there was no attempt to establish organised missions until the 1880s. Once they began, those most active with Islanders were run by the QKM and the Anglicans—the Church of England—with lesser operations mounted by the Presbyterians, Churches of Christ, Lutherans, the Salvation Army, Baptists and the Brisbane City Mission. Despite its Pacific presence, the Catholic Church never competed for Melanesian souls in Queensland.

---

2   Siegel 1982.
3   Moore 2015c.

3. MALAITAN CHRISTIANS OVERSEAS, 1880s–1910s

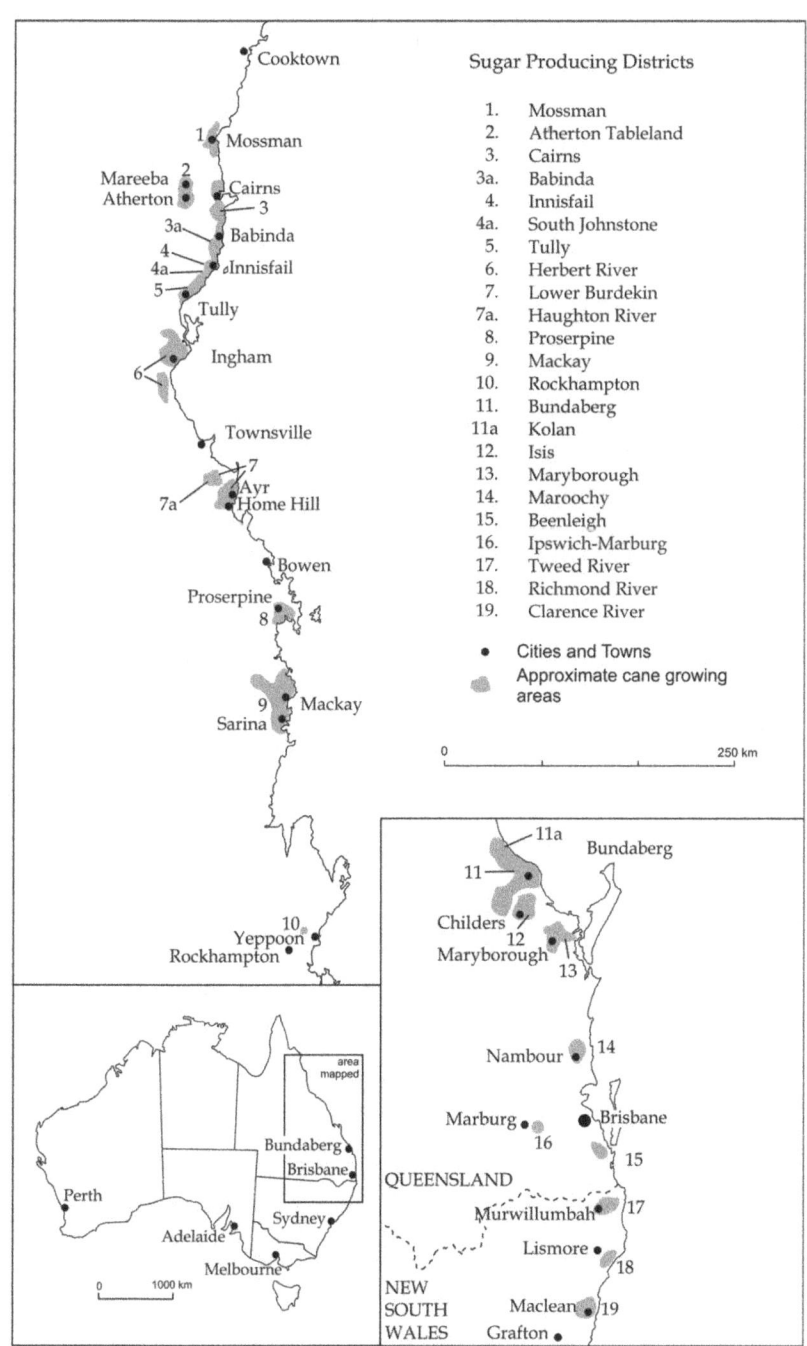

Map 11: Sugarcane growing areas in Queensland and New South Wales.
Source: Peter Griggs, first published by Peter Lang AG in 2011, reprinted by permission.

Studies of Christian missions in the Pacific have usually been based within indigenous communities, not on plantations overseas.[4] The plantation context is very different: the people are outside their usual cultural environment and primarily engaged in wage labour. However, using the Islander labourers on Queensland and Fiji plantations and farms as the base for Christian Pacific networks was highly successful and served to transfer Christianity back into the islands. The first Queensland Christian outreach to the Islanders was through the Anglican Selwyn Mission at Mackay in 1882. The Young family's mission at Bundaberg, also started in 1882, formalised as the Queensland Kanaka Mission in 1886. Both of these missions developed strong connections with the Solomons and particularly with Malaita. Estimates from the early 1890s suggest that by then around 75 per cent of the Islanders in Queensland had some degree of contact with Christian missions, and 10 years on the extent of contact was even higher.[5] These male (and some female) labourers were transported to Queensland at their employers' expense and thus provided a cheap way to access potential converts. They were separated from their extended kin, usually for the first time, in a strict work environment and initially many were bewildered by the experience, leaving them more open to ministrations and friendship from the missionaries.

As Ian Hogbin says in this chapter's epigraph, the missionaries were probably the first Europeans who treated the Islanders with kindness. The missions provided an educational venue on evenings and weekends that reduced the chance of the Islanders getting involved in less wholesome activities. Beginning in the 1880s, Queensland-based missions began to teach literacy through the Bible, provided a path to Christian conversion, and encouraged abstinence from alcohol.[6] In its first issue in June 1895 the Anglican mission journal, the *Southern Cross Log*, reported on their Queensland success:

> Some boys walk six and seven miles to school after the day's work is finished. Night after night, Mrs. Robinson's school at Mackay is crowded with a class of 100 boys. At Bundaberg, the Rev. E. Clayton has a small system of schools and on the Herbert River the Rev. F. Pratt has been teaching the boys around him. There are schools also belonging to the Presbyterians in the Mackay district, and to Mrs. and Miss Young at Bundaberg.[7]

---

4   Barker 1990; 1992.
5   Corris 1973b, 96.
6   Moore 1991.
7   This refers to Ellen Young, the wife of Horace Young, and Florence Young. *SCL*, June 1895, 12.

Although many Malaitan labourers remained resolute worshipers of their ancestral spirits, the Malaitan converts were among the most fervent of those baptised and took easily to the new cultural milieu. Malaitans also taught in evening and Sunday schools.[8] When the labour trade ended in 1906, the largest Malaitan community in Queensland was in the Pioneer Valley at Mackay, with other substantial groups around Bundaberg and Maryborough and a scattering up and down the coast. The Bundaberg-Isis district rivalled Mackay in the numbers of Malaitans there, with close to equal numbers in the early 1900s.

Table 2: Estimate of major Pacific Islander populations in Queensland, 1891 and 1901.

District	1891	1901
Torres Strait	219?	672
Cairns and Mossman	100	500
Johnstone River (Innisfail)	800	530
Herbert River (Ingham)	800	1,233
Burdekin (Ayr & Homehill)	400	500
Bowen & Proserpine	624	298
Mackay	2,277	1,475
Rockhampton	111	150?
Bundaberg	2,000	1,912
Isis	700	500
Maryborough	170?	900
Brisbane & Logan	335	500
Other	266?	367?
TOTAL	8,802	9,537

It is difficult to estimate from the census districts, because boundaries changed between the two census years. The question marks indicate a degree of uncertainty. Bishop Cecil Wilson gave the following estimate in 1895, presumably based on figures provided by Church sources: Brisbane 1,000, Bundaberg 2,500, Isis 800, Rockhampton 70, Mackay 2,240, Burdekin River 500, Herbert River 800 and Johnstone River 800. *OPMM*, Nov 1895, 155. The Wilson figures differ from my calculations.

Source: Based on the author's files and accumulated personal knowledge, and *Census of Queensland* 1891, 459; *QVP* 1892, 3, 1391; 1901, 2, 956.

---

8   Wetherell 1977, 100.

One interesting feature of the census records (used in Table 2) is the large number of minors among the Islander population. The legal adult age began at 21 years, and many labour recruits were only youths, but the statistics also included large numbers of children born in Australia. Almost all of the children were Christians and some returned home in the 1900s, such as Timothy George Mahratta.[9] What follows outlines the involvement of the major denominational missions to Islanders in Queensland (including Torres Strait) and northern New South Wales. Along the way, I will pay particular attention to calculating how many Malaitans became Christian.

Queensland Kanaka Mission

The QKM developed into the largest Christian mission to Islanders in Queensland, eclipsing its major competitor, the Church of England. The QKM became the SSEM in 1907, and today its successor church, the SSEC, is the third-largest Christian denomination in Solomon Islands and the largest on Malaita. The QKM was founded by New Zealand-born 28-year-old Florence S.H. Young on her brothers' Fairymead sugar plantation near Bundaberg in 1886.[10] The Young family, from England via India and New Zealand, arrived in Bundaberg in 1880. From a wealthy family, they were steeped in the beliefs of the Open Plymouth Brethren and influenced by the English Keswick Convention.[11] Florence's father, Henry Young, was born in Machilipatnam in India in 1803 and worked for the East India Company, becoming the youngest judge in India. He retired and moved to Invercargill, New Zealand, where he began a farm. His wife Catherine died in 1875, the farm was not a success and a few years later Henry moved his family to Bundaberg to a new sugar plantation.[12] Florence settled at Fairymead plantation in 1882 and became interested in spreading the Christian message to the Islanders. Her family offered

---

9   Moore 2013c entry.
10   Henry Cathcart Arthur Young (known as Arthur) and Horace Edward Broughton Young purchased Fairymead's 5 square miles (12,950 hectares) on river flats on 23 March 1880. They had previously had a sheep property in New Zealand, which had been devastated by a rabbit plague, and were looking for new challenges. Their brother Charles Earnest (known as Ernest) also joined the partnership. Braga 2005; Griffin 1990; Young 1925.
11   The Plymouth Brethren, formed in Ireland and England in the late 1820s, rejected hierarchical church government, special priestly orders and rituals beyond those of the Bible, and close involvement with the state. They called each other 'brother' (hence Brethren). The English Keswick Convention was an interdenominational evangelical group founded in England in 1875 with Anglican and Baptist roots.
12   Hamlin with Little 2001, 11–12.

her the use of an old house, a 'deserted tumble-down old building with its shingle roof, the first dwelling on Fairymead, built long before it became a sugar plantation'. As she recounted:

> There were the ten stalwart men from the New Hebrides … and little La-as-si, who formed my first class … I knew nothing then of missionary work, but the Master had said, 'Preach the Gospel to every creature', and these people had never heard the good news.[13]

By 1885 the classes were attracting 80 Islanders on Sundays with 40 every evening. The QKM was formally constituted in 1886 as a nondenominational evangelical mission based on the models of the China Inland Mission and the Livingstone Inland Mission. The pattern in these missions was to have a founder or a small nucleus of founders and a focus on a particular region of the world where the pagan inhabitants were beyond existing missionary activities. Theologically, they maintained an uncompromising evangelical stance with doctrines centred on a literal interpretation of scripture, and were organised by a voluntary union of lay members of various denominations who agreed to come together for the specific purpose. These missions were dependent on gifts from individual sympathisers and usually did not appeal directly for funds, believing that God would provide, often based on Christ's teachings on Providence in St Matthew's sixth chapter.[14] The QKM-SSEM was dogmatic and uncompromising. Based on SSEM sources, Hilliard describes the mission's theology:

> Missionary candidates were required to give assurance of 'soundness in the faith', especially with regard to those doctrines assailed by 'modernism': the divine inspiration and supreme authority of the whole canonical Scriptures, the Trinity, the moral depravity of man, Substitutionary Atonement, Justification by Faith, the resurrection of the body, the everlasting life of the saved and the eternal punishment of the lost.[15]

The mission's governing structure was congregational, its leadership constituted in elected elders. There was no clergy, although in the early decades the real authority resided with the European missionaries. The Christian message centred on personal salvation as a gift from God through faith in Jesus Christ. There were only two ordinances to observe:

---

13   Young 1925, 178.
14   Hilliard 1969, 42–43.
15   *Ibid.*, 59.

full emersion adult baptism and Holy Communion. Confessions were in front of an entire congregation and the words of the Bible were the final arbiter and authority.

Figure 3.1: Queensland Kanaka Mission baptism by full emersion, Johnstone River, Geraldton (Innisfail), 1906.
Source: State Library of Queensland, neg. 18063.

Initially, Young relied on help from her sister-in-law Ellen Young, and she was encouraged long-distance by Mrs Ben Dowling, who had been a missionary in India. Once the QKM was formalised in 1886, Florence Young became superintendent, supported by the Young, Deck and Grant families, and assisted by Mr C.F. Johnston, who had previously worked on the Lower Congo as part of the Livingstone Inland Mission.[16] The QKM stress was on salvation before education or civilisation. Their outreach was well received by the Islanders, and since it was the first Bundaberg mission, the other planters also supported the development. In January 1887, Florence and her brother Ernest wrote to the Bundaberg district plantation owners asking for classroom space and assistance to get their Islander employees to attend evening and Sunday classes.[17] Florence Young was in England and India during 1888–89 and spent six years between 1891 and 1900 as a missionary in China, and she suffered a nervous breakdown due to the tensions there. She finally returned to Bundaberg after the Boxer Rebellion and swung her full energies over to the QKM. Later, between 1904 and 1926, she devoted herself to the SSEM, making lengthy annual visits to Solomon Islands from her bases in Sydney and Katoomba. During her absences in the 1890s, the QKM was run by Rev. Alfred E. Eustace and his wife L.D. Eustace, who joined the mission from Victoria, Rev. James Coles, Mr and Mrs C.F. Johnston, Mr and Mrs McKenzie, assisted by Florence Buchanan and Ellen Young. The QKM message was spread by open-air hymn singing, long prayer sessions and mass baptisms in local rivers.

The mission attracted large numbers of adherents, with 2,461 Islanders baptised in Queensland between 1886 and 1906. During 1900–01, 4,776 classes were held, and efforts were increased as the final deportation loomed. In 1906, 589 Malaitans were amongst a total of 734 Solomon Islanders baptised. Overall, Malaitans made up 23 per cent of the QKM converts.[18]

One Malaitan, Martin Supone, who had arrived in Queensland in 1885, was amongst the initial eight male baptisms in April 1886. Progress with Malaitans was slower than one might assume, given that the QKM eventually shifted to Malaita and became the SSEM. Of the 322 Islanders baptised between 1886 and 1889, only four were Malaitans.[19] During 1892, 1,620 Islanders, more than half the district's Islander

---

16 Young 1925, 133.
17 Letter by H.E.B. Young and F.S.H. Young, Jan 1887, in Griffiths 1977, 19–20.
18 *NIV*, 1906–07, 8. The breakdown of converts is Malaita 589, Guadalcanal 104, Makira 16, Gela 12, Savo 3, Ulawa 3 and Isabel 2.
19 PMB 1201, Reel 1, 'South Sea Evangelical Mission, formerly Queensland Kanaka Mission, Register of Baptisms'. The name is spelt 'Suepone' in the baptismal register and 'Soeypona' in the government records.

population, attended Sunday schools around Bundaberg. A single feast at Bundaberg in 1890 attracted 1,000 participants. Dr Harry Guinness of the Livingstone Inland Mission in the Congo observed one session of baptisms at Bundaberg in October 1901:

> On Sunday morning, in sight of a very large gathering that crowded the river bank, the shore, and one of the wharves of the Burnett River, these thirty-seven coloured Christians were buried with Jesus, by baptism into death, that 'Like as Christ was raised up from the dead by the glory of the Father', even so they also 'should walk in newness of life'. The service was simple and beautiful, and the reverence of these men was most impressive. With clasped hands they entered the river, one by one, and were immersed in its flowing tide by Mr. Fricke. With hands still clasped, and lost in prayer, not seeing any of the crowd around them they slowly came out of the water, having received the new name by which henceforth they will be known.[20]

By 1904, the QKM had 1,881 baptised converts. Seventeen paid European missionaries and 101 unpaid Islander teachers worked in 11 different centres, along the Queensland coast as far north as Mossman and into the Tweed district in northern New South Wales.[21] Activities intensified during the years leading up to the forced deportation of the Islanders that began in 1906: two more European missionaries joined the QKM staff and another 603 Islanders were baptised. Fourteen thousand classes were held during 1906, attended by 6,000 to 7,000 Islanders. The QKM grew to operate from 13 centres: the headquarters were always in Bundaberg, where there were 2,000 to 3,000 Islanders, with five local regions (Fairymead, North Bundaberg, Bingera, Kalkie and Avondale), and branches nearby in the Hapsberg area (Isis) and at Gin Gin. The QKM then spread to Ayr, Ingham, Geraldton (Innisfail after 1910), Cairns and Mossman, and to Cudgen in New South Wales. This 1900s expansion eclipsed the more steady progress by the Anglicans.

There were around 900 Islanders in the Isis-Gin Gin district inland from Bundaberg, mainly around present-day Childers. This QKM branch took root in the early 1900s, with Mr and Mrs Douglas and Mr Lancaster living in the mission house on Hapsberg plantation.[22] When Florence Young visited Hapsberg in 1905 she was impressed by the fervour of the

---

20 Young 1925, 133.
21 Kerr 1993, 57–58.
22 Young 1925, 130–31.

new adherents. Prayer was central to the message. Long periods were spent in direct communication with the Holy Spirit and some Islanders prayed on their knees for hours. Young's believed the fervour was being driven by divine intervention:

> It was Sunday evening; a full and happy day had been spent in the mission hall. In the evening the workers went to different classes, and now we stood at the door of a large grass house … Within, a bright light lit the faces of twenty-five men, gathered for the evening meeting. Mats on the earthen floor, and a neat cloth and a bunch of flowers on the table gave an air of comfort; but these were hardly noticed, for a strange sense of the presence of the Holy Spirit laid hold of us. As we entered the room we were conscious of an atmosphere literally charged with divine power.[23]

There can be no doubt that the Christian message was strong and well received. Young mentions six Malaitans from Bingera plantation who were going home to their island:

> Only one thing I take with me to my country—Jesus! I know Jesus died for me. My country, heathen country—When we go speak to them, they mock us, but praise God, we take Jesus there …[24]

Another Malaitan, on the Herbert River in 1905, was probably typical. He had accepted Christianity a year earlier and was full of praise, but said, 'I cannot read much, but Jesus He been light His fire in my heart …'.[25] However, there were always other Malaitans, like those at Fairymead plantation in 1906, who taunted their Christian kin and called on rain to wash out rejoicing after a baptism.[26]

In 1899, John Southey and Frederick Fricke visited north Queensland and realised that there was scope for expansion there. They installed Charlie Tarasol-Aurora (from Pentecost Island) at Port Douglas (near Mossman), Jack Aoba (from Aoba Island) at Nelson (near Cairns) and Thomas Tavangtang-Sandwich (from Efate Island) on the Johnstone River (Geraldton). Both Tarasol-Aurora and Tavangtang-Sandwich later became teachers on Malaita. In mid-1900, Fricke went north again to take F.J. Purdy to Nelson and Mr and Mrs O.C. Thomas (from Western Australia)

---

23   *Ibid.*, 161.
24   *Ibid.*, 162.
25   *Ibid.*, 165.
26   *Ibid.*, 177.

to Innisfail.[27] In 1901, Norman Lumsden took over from Tarasol-Aurora at Mossman, replaced the next year by Richard Ruddell and his wife, while Lumsden moved to the Herbert River (Ingham and Halifax). In 1902, Mr Rendall began work at Ayr in the Burdekin district.[28] Florence Young toured the northern missions in 1905. At Green Hill outside Cairns she and her niece Catherine Deck visited a Chinese-owned plantation (presumably Hap Wah)[29] where 42 Islanders were in classes. At Geraldton she went out to Macknade plantation to visit 80 Islanders at the QKM's mission there. At Mackay, Young visited Rev. McIntyre's Presbyterian Mission, which had been operating for 17 years, although she makes no mention of contact with Mary Robinson's Anglican Selwyn Mission a few kilometres away.[30]

Between 1898 and early 1904, some 3,500 Malaitans arrived in Queensland (38 per cent of the total who enlisted, 1871–1904), almost 1,000 a year between 1900 and 1903. It was during this period that the QKM and the other missions made their major progress with Malaitans.[31]

Beginning in 1903, Florence's brother Ernest and his wife Margaret began an annual 'Convention for the Deepening of the Spiritual Life' at their holiday home at Katoomba in the Blue Mountains west of Sydney. The next year Florence took eight Islanders to the convention. Photographs show them in the midst of a large gathering of fashionably dressed Europeans, the cream of Sydney's evangelical elite. Florence was determined to put into practice the motto Ernest and Margaret had borrowed from the English Keswick Convention, 'All One in Christ Jesus'.[32] During the 1904 convention a decision was made to form a Solomon Islands branch of the QKM, with a separate council based in Sydney and Melbourne. Florence decided to lead the first official QKM expedition to Solomon Islands in the mid-year, despite fears that the environment was too severe for a middle-aged, upper middle-class European woman.[33]

---

27 Presumably this was Thomas Tavangtang-Sandwich, who later moved to Malaita. *Ibid.*, 127. Purdy later joined the Churches of Christ and became a missionary and trader in the New Hebrides. Crocombe 1987, 291.
28 Young 1925, 135–38.
29 Bottoms 2015, 84, 85, 86.
30 Young 1925, 164–65.
31 Advisory Boards were also established in Sydney and Melbourne. QKM 18th Annual Report, *NIV*, 1903–04, 22; *NIV*, 1906–07, 5–8. Kerr 1996, 43–45.
32 Braga 2003, 46, 110.
33 Young 1925, 142–43.

The Anglicans and the Melanesian Mission

The Church of England began the first formal mission to Islanders in Queensland and slowly developed links with the Melanesian Mission (the Diocese of Melanesia), but even so they never achieved the success of the QKM. One reason may have been the church's unwieldy structure. By 1900, there were four Church of England dioceses in Queensland, each controlling its own mission activities. Not until 1894 did the Melanesian Mission begin to work cooperatively with them to develop missions along the same lines as their St Barnabas College on Norfolk Island. Queensland's Anglican dioceses evolved in a convoluted way as the colony grew. The Brisbane area was included in the Newcastle diocese after 1847 (when the area was still part of New South Wales), while the Sydney diocese still controlled the more northerly areas of what became Queensland in 1859. Once the new colony was formed, Brisbane became a separate diocese reaching north to the 21st parallel south (including the area that in 1860 became Mackay). The first Islanders arrived in Torres Strait in 1860, around Brisbane in 1863, and at Mackay in 1867. The first Malaitans reached Queensland at Mackay in October 1871.[34]

Brisbane was an early major Pacific port and the Melanesian Mission always had contacts with the Brisbane diocese. The Melanesian Mission was interested in establishing links with the Queensland plantations as an extension of the net cast first from New Zealand and then Norfolk Island. Queensland, however, had its own Anglican ecclesiastical organisations separate from the Diocese of Melanesia. Several heads of the Melanesian Mission are known to have visited Queensland. Bishop John Coleridge Patteson preached in Brisbane in 1864 and returned the next year to consider Curtis Island, off the coast near Gladstone, as a replacement headquarters for St Andrew's at Kohimarama, Auckland.[35] In 1872, Rev. Robert Codrington from the Melanesian Mission's St Barnabas College on Norfolk Island (and temporary head of the Melanesian Mission after Bishop Patteson was murdered) visited Queensland, and spoke with Islanders in Maryborough. Bishop Edward Tufnell in Brisbane promised to try to get the priest at Mackay to begin a mission to the Islanders, although the challenge was not taken up for another six years, by which time Mackay was in a different diocese. Tuffnell's successor,

---

34 Moore 1985, 26.
35 *Moreton Bay Courier*, 9 Apr 1864; Ross 1983, 41.

Bishop Mathew Hale, said that he felt frustrated by the colonists' prejudice against any attempts to spread Christianity to non-Europeans, whether Aborigines, Asians or Pacific Islanders.[36] The next substantial Melanesian Mission link came two decades later, in 1895, when Bishop Cecil Wilson toured coastal Queensland trying to foster connections with the Queensland dioceses. While he was in the colony several Islanders asked his permission for them to join St Barnabas College.[37]

In 1878, a North Queensland diocese was formed, cut loose from Sydney, with a new boundary between the Brisbane and North Queensland dioceses at the 22nd parallel south (roughly at Broadsound), which placed Mackay into the northern diocese. The next change came in 1892, when Rockhampton diocese was excised from the north of the Brisbane diocese, leaving the boundary between the two at just north of Bundaberg. In that same year the Australian Board of Missions took responsibility for British New Guinea. The last of the colonial changes came in 1900 when the Carpentaria diocese was formed, cutting through Queensland's east coast just above Cairns (placing Mossman's sugarcane fields into the new diocese) and including Cape York and Torres Strait, the Gulf of Carpentaria and all of the Northern Territory. These divisions are important because the Church of England missions to the Islanders were usually diocesan initiatives.

The earliest and always the most substantial Anglican mission to the Islanders was begun at Mackay by Mary Goodwin Robinson in 1882. This may have been an initiative of the newly installed Bishop George H. Stanton in Townsville, or it may have been an independent move by Rev. Albert Maclaren. Maclaren was priest at Mackay from 1878 until 1891, the same years that Stanton was bishop, after which he left to found the Anglican mission in British New Guinea.[38] When he arrived in the sugar town Maclaren faced opposition from some of his parishioners, with attitudes that were probably typical in other cane-growing districts.

> The white people are against me doing anything in the way of teaching them [the Islanders], their argument being that they pay me not to look after the souls of black but of white people.[39]

---

36 Information provided by Alan Davidson at St John's Theological College, Auckland/University of Auckland, from letters held in the Rhodes House Library, 11 May 2006.
37 Wetherell 1977, 101; Hilliard 1978, 105–06.
38 Wetherell 1977; Diocese of Brisbane 1872, 10.
39 Moore 1985, 310.

Given the racist nature of Queensland colonial society, this attitude changed very little over the decades. Late in 1906, one of Malaita's earliest Anglican missionaries, Arthur Hopkins, found much the same attitude:

> In some places it was lamentable to see how Church people themselves hindered the work. They turn a cold shoulder on boys coming to the Holy Communion, and grudge the use of Sunday Schools for classes. The battle that S. Paul had to fight against race-prejudice is not even fully won.[40]

However, Maclaren was able to interest two prominent parishioners in beginning mission schools. Mary Robinson, the wife of a plantation manager, began the Selwyn Mission at Te Kowai plantation in 1882, followed soon after by a smaller venture undertaken by Elizabeth Watt Martin, the wife of a pastoralist at Mandurama on the north side of the Pioneer River. Initially, Robinson conducted the classes in her home, and then shifted to land donated by Meadowlands plantation closer to Mackay, before moving the base to Marian further down the Pioneer Valley when her husband became mill manager there in the early 1890s. One 1896 report describes the unusual degree of access that she allowed the Islanders to her home:

> Before school begins they wander into her private house, of which they have the run, and sit about in her parlour as if it was their own. She has always allowed this, and says they have never abused the privilege on any occasion. Few ladies would have the power and influence necessary for the allowing of such liberties. She is not only pastor and instructor, but doctor and sick nurse to the boys, and her house is their hospital. While there, we saw one of her patients, a sick boy about 18, lying in a little room adjoining her house.[41]

When Rev. A. Brittain visited the Selwyn Mission's Marian base on behalf of the Melanesian Mission in 1894, he described the mission as 'worked on a system of her own, and gradually evolved' and 'undoubtedly the best school in Queensland'.[42] Mrs Robinson gave instruction in Pijin English, which she found a better medium than English, and worked 'single-handed, and without any intermission as a rule even for an evening from year to year, and without any fund from which to supply the ordinary school materials'.[43] She taught reading, writing and arithmetic and prepared

---

40   Hopkins, 'A Letter from Queensland', *SCL*, Mar 1907, 114.
41   Buxton, 'Impressions of Plantation Life', *OPMM*, Mar 1897, 276.
42   Report of Rev. A. Brittain, *OPMM*, Christmas 1894, 98–99.
43   *Ibid.* Also see M.G. Robinson to A. Brittain, 16 Aug 1894, *OPMM*, Christmas 1894, 100–01.

men for baptism and confirmation. Men walked 9 or 20 kilometres every evening to school, in some cases foregoing their evening meal, and even in the cold of July, 70 to 80 attended. The only island group Brittain mentions were the Malaitans:

> The Malayta men have generally an unenviable reputation, and yet they show themselves very willing recipients of Christianity and all civilizing influences when properly brought to bear upon them.[44]

After her husband died in the mid-1890s, the mission shifted back to Meadowlands, where she continued to operate under reduced circumstances. In 1903, Robinson finally left the district to retire to Adelaide and then to England, replaced by Charles Sage, who had previously worked in the New Guinea Anglican Mission. Robinson's Melanesian assistants, supervised by Sage, were able to carry on the mission's work after she left, based at Meadowlands and Te Kowai, and then at St Marys Church at Pioneer on the north side of the river on land donated by the Coakley family.

Figure 3.2: Students at Mary Robinson's Anglican Selwyn Mission when it operated from Marian in the Pioneer Valley west of Mackay. The photograph dates from the 1890s when William Wawn visited.
Source: Wawn 1893, 447.

---

44 Report of Rev. A. Brittain, *OPMM*, Christmas 1894, 99.

3. MALAITAN CHRISTIANS OVERSEAS, 1880s–1910s

Labour trade captain William Wawn visited the Selwyn Mission in the early 1890s at about the same time as Rev. Brittain did. He found over 80 pupils and described a 'fine commodious school-house with excellent fittings, prettily decorated walls, and a harmonium'. Another visitor in 1896 described Robinson hard at work, teaching children in the mornings and men and women after they finished work at night. In her quest for converts, Robinson also visited the hospitals on plantations, the government hospital at Mackay, sick Islanders working for farmers and the jail. Between 9:30 and 11:30 am she held a school for Islander children, then arranged materials for the adult evening school before visiting the sick, some of whom she took into her home to nurse. On Saturdays and Sundays the school was a centre for Islanders who came from as far away as 30 kilometres to attend. Sunday service began at 10:00 am, followed by a class for confirmation candidates, then lunch. Baptism candidates were taught at 2:00 pm, followed by Sunday school at 3:00 pm. Sunday evenings were reserved 'for going after the wild Malayta, and recruiting them for School'.[45]

The Selwyn Mission also established branches on plantations and farms throughout the valley: at Te Kowai, Palms, Marian, Nindaroo, Meadowlands, Pioneer, Mandurama and The Leap.[46] Both the Selwyn Mission at Mackay and Florence Young's QKM managed to interest large numbers of Malaitans, but there was always antagonism from those who still followed their ancestral religion. For instance, three Malaitans baptised by Rev. W.A. Turner at Mackay in September 1896 faced ostracism from other Malaitans, and one found himself locked out of the house he shared. Many others were under instruction and Robinson had high hopes in training teachers to go back in the islands.[47] Her best Malaitan pupil, Jack Taloifulia from Sulufou Island in Lau Lagoon, became the first indigenous Anglican priest on Malaita.[48]

In 1905, the main Selwyn Mission school was furnished with desks, and every night between 7:30 and 9:30 pm Islander men could be seen bent over their copy books, reading aloud, or leaning scripture.

---

45 M.G. Robinson to Bishop J.R. Selwyn, 26 Oct 1896, *OPMM*, Christmas 1896, 260–61.
46 'Selwyn Mission, Queensland', *SCL*, July 1901, 72; 'Selwyn Mission (Mackay)', *SCL*, Feb 1905, 7; 'Selwyn Mission, Mackay', *SCL*, Aug 1905, 6; 'Selwyn Mission, Mackay', *SCL*, Dec 1905, 4.
47 Wawn 1973, 439; *SCL*, Apr 1896, 10; *SCL*, Nov 1896, 3; 'The Melanesian Mission in Queensland', *SCL*, Mar 1897, 7–8.
48 Hopkins 1949; Brown 2006.

The children of the District have their teaching in the mornings. Every Sunday there is a grand assembly from all parts of the District: some arrive on horseback, some on bicycles, some driving the wife and children in a sulky. Long before the time of the service the brown faces may be seen everywhere, and the service itself is hearty and reverent. Once a month those who are communicants tramp into Mackay for the 8 a.m. celebration, a few of them going in the night before: there are about 60 on the communicants' roll. Besides the main school there are small branch schools at plantations too far out for the 'boys' to reach the Selwyn Mission, and these are conducted by Islanders under Mr. Sage's supervision.[49]

Figure 3.3: Many mission photographs are of groups of men, though women and children also attended services and classes. This group is at the Selwyn Mission in 1905.
Source: *SCL*, 9 May 1905.

We have details of the Islander baptisms. The first at Selwyn Mission, in 1885, included one Solomon Islander. The first identifiable Malaitan baptism was of Benjamin Torkon in October 1890. Joseph Baramula, after 1905 one of the teachers at Fiu, Malaita, was another of Robinson's early students. Remaining records do not show enough detail of island

---

49   R.M.F.D., 'Sugar Plantations in Queensland', *SCL*, Sept 1905, 11.

origins to be certain about the extent of Malaitan baptisms, although, just as occurred with the QKM, we can presume that Malaitans dominated the 1900s.[50] My 1970s computer sorting of these records included adults and children and indicated 512 Malaitan Anglican baptisms at Mackay between 1890 and 1906.[51]

Figure 3.4: The congregation at St Marys Church at Pioneer, outside Mackay, in the early 1900s.
The man seated in the centre front is probably Malaitan Alex Sayven, a lay preacher from 1905 to 1913. Most of the congregation was from Malaita or Guadalcanal.
Source: State Library of Queensland, neg. 24462.

The labourers lived mainly in the North Queensland and Brisbane dioceses. Although some of the early arrivals worked in the pastoral and maritime industries, most worked in the coastal cane fields. The other cane-growing areas in the North Queensland Diocese were on the Burdekin River at the twin towns of Ayr and Homehill, at Ingham and Geraldton, around Cairns, and at Proserpine and Mossman. Rev. Francis Drinkall Pritt ministered to the Islanders, based in the

---

50 Anglican Church of Australia, Holy Trinity Church, Mackay, Baptism Registers.
51 This quantitative research was carried out for my PhD thesis (1981a), which was published as Kanaka in 1985. The printouts are available at James Cook University and the Mackay City Council Library.

north Rockhampton parish from 1889 until 1894. He transferred to the Herbert River at Ingham from 1895 to 1898, termed 'missionary to alien races', and operated what predominantly was a mission to Islanders.[52] Pritt's replacement, Rev. F.V. Drake, showed little interest and during his years Ingham district Islanders were left to organise their own services. They built a thatched-roof church at Cordelia Mount, where an Islander held a service every Sunday, and at nearby Halifax there was a church on Anderson's farm where Islanders held regular services. At Geraldton on the Johnstone River was a thatched-roof church run by Motlav Islanders and visited every Sunday by Rev. C. Warren Tomkins. By 1901, there were around 500 Islanders in the Cairns district, but no formal Anglican presence, although one Anglican Islander, Billy Mallicolo, joined his church's mission to Aborigines at Mt Bellenden Ker in 1892.[53] The only early 1890s mission in the Cairns district seems to have been Presbyterian, through a teacher and a church for Islanders at Mulgrave.[54]

Figure 3.5: One of the Islanders' grass-roofed churches in north Queensland, possibly the one at Cordelia Mount.
Source: Clive Moore Collection.

52 Blain's Biographical Directory 2017.
53 'Bellenden Ker Missionaries', *BC*, 20 May 1892.
54 R.M.F.D., 'Sugar Plantations of Queensland', *SCL*, Sept 1905, 11.

Mossman mill, a farmers' cooperative begun in the mid-1890s, housed the most northerly mainland mission in the new Diocese of Carpentaria. A large group of 'old chum' Anglican Islanders transferred from Bundaberg to Mossman in the mid-1890s, spreading the denomination further north, and many Islanders, including Malaitans, lived within the diocese in Torres Strait. Torres Strait came under the London Missionary Society from the 1870s until 1914, when the area became an Anglican preserve. There were also Malaitan families living in pastoral districts, such as the Kulijeri (Reid) family at Charters Towers, although they were isolated and blended into Aboriginal communities.[55]

The Brisbane diocese stretched north to Bundaberg, and included three major ports through which Islanders entered Queensland: Brisbane, Maryborough and Bundaberg. There were substantial numbers of Islanders around Brisbane, most of them long-term residents of the colony. Brisbane and the neighbouring Logan, Caboolture and Redlands districts had an Islander population right from the 1860s.[56] The Anglicans initiated outreach to Islanders around Brisbane in 1886.[57] More 'time-expired' (multiple-contract) Islanders began to drift south from Bundaberg and Maryborough, particularly during the economic recession in the early 1890s, gravitating to Brisbane and Tweed Heads over the border in New South Wales. In 1892, Canon John Stone-Wigg began classes for them at St John's Pro-Cathedral, and a house ('Roslyn') in South Brisbane was acquired as a base for Anglican Islanders in the city. About the same time, Archdeacon Arthur Rivers was given oversight of all missionary activities in the Brisbane Diocese. Early in 1897, J.D. Anderson, who was reading for holy orders and was attached to the Cathedral parish, took over leadership of work with local Islanders.[58] About 20 attended the cathedral on Sundays and had a clubroom in a street close by where they met every night, with formal classes on Tuesdays, Saturdays and Sundays run by Mrs Birkbeck, Mr Gardiner, Archdeacon David and Rev. C.A. Hutchinson.[59]

---

55 'Notes', *SCL*, July 1897, 4–5; Anne Allingham, 'Generations Revealed in Photographs', *Northern Miner*, 10 July 2015, 10; Kerr 1979.
56 Moore 2015c.
57 'Bellenden-Ker Missionaries', *BC*, 20 May 1892.
58 Wetherell 1977, 101.
59 Percy T. Williams, 'Notes from Queensland', *OPMM*, Mar 1897, 270–72.

The Melanesian Mission sent Rev. A. Brittain to Queensland in August 1894 to reconnoitre the scene, in expectation that he would start missionary work there. He was well received by the bishop of North Queensland, who wanted to bolster the work already underway at Mackay and advocated that outreach begin at Cairns, the Johnstone and Herbert rivers, and around Ayr and Homehill on the Burdekin River. Good responses were also received from the bishops of Brisbane and Rockhampton. At the time, the plan was for Brittain to begin Melanesian Mission work at Bundaberg, although this never eventuated.[60] Bishop Cecil Wilson of the Diocese of Melanesia, aware that the Colonial Sugar Refining Company and some planters had promised financial support, kept faith with them by visiting Queensland in mid-1895. In Brisbane, he visited two Malaitans about to be hanged for the murder of a European at Bundaberg. One, Maraskima, had been in Queensland for six years but did not understand English. The other, Miori, had been in the colony a similar length of time and had three months of schooling, although his Pijin English was poor. Six Malaitans had been charged and four pardoned. The executions were difficult to explain to the other Malaitans, particularly since Wilson felt that the clemency given to four was incomprehensible to their ideas of guilt and justice.[61]

While in Brisbane, Wilson held discussions with Premier Hugh Nelson, Colonial Secretary Horace Tozer and other government officials before proceeding north to Bundaberg, Rockhampton, Mackay and Townsville. He counselled the government against closing Malaita to recruiting, one possible solution for dealing with the many years of violence against recruiters. Wilson stressed to his Brisbane listeners that Christianity was the only good thing that the labour trade had brought to Malaita and to cut access would be a retrograde step.[62] He had been told that there were 1,200 Malaitans in Queensland and that only 2,000 of the Islander population of 8,700 Islanders in Queensland were receiving religious instruction.[63] Wilson advocated establishing small training colleges, the graduates of which would then be available to staff mission schools in Queensland and at St Barnabas College on Norfolk Island.

---

60 Brittain felt no particular call to the ministry there and was already well-established in the New Hebrides. Reports by Bishop Wilson, 6 Sept 1894, and by Rev. A. Brittain, *OPMM*, Christmas 1894, 95–100; Wilson, 17 June 1895, *OPMM*, Nov 1895, 154–55.
61 Wilson, 20 May 1895, *OPMM*, Aug 1895, 122–23; Wilson, 6 June 1895, *OPMM*, 153.
62 Wilson, 20 May 1895, *OPMM*, Aug 1895, 123.
63 Compared to census figures this calculation is too high. Census of Queensland, 1891, 459, *QVP* 1892, 3, 1391; 1901, 2, 956.

At this stage, of the 400 indigenous teachers in the Melanesian Mission's network, only two were ex-Queensland labourers.[64] One college site was identified on Mon Repos plantation and a mission church site was suggested for The Grange, both near Bundaberg. Wilson also announced plans for colleges (equivalent to St Barnabas College) at the Burdekin and Mackay districts. The concept was for the Queensland Anglican missions to become self-supporting branches of the Melanesian Mission, although nothing further eventuated.[65] The expense would have been great, and the Presbyterians broke the Anglican monopoly in the Mackay district when they established a mission at Walkerston in 1886. Then the Queensland Government agreed to subsidise payment of staff at mission schools in the colony, using the Pacific Islanders' Fund, which took away some of the urgency.[66]

The trip was also part-motivated by rumours that 200 Queensland Malaitans were about to accompany a lay missionary back to Malaita to form a Christian colony.[67] Wilson raised a storm in the media over some of his comments. He was alarmist and ignored the work of other denominations. The bishop was put in his place by representatives of the Presbyterian Church and QKM.[68]

Details remain of Wilson's time in Bundaberg, where he visited several plantations, including Fairymead, the QKM headquarters. The bishop was accompanied by Rev. Percy T. Williams, who returned in November 1896 to take charge of the Anglican Bundaberg mission as the first full-time 'organising priest in charge of Melanesians' in Queensland, under the auspices of the bishop of Brisbane. His charge was renamed as the 'Melanesian Mission in Queensland'. A Bundaberg Kanaka Mission to South Sea Islanders Committee already existed, although it was not responsible to the Diocesan Board of Missions.[69] Between 1892 and his death in December 1895, J.E. Clayton, a deacon, operated a small mission school for Islanders at Bundaberg, his £200 stipend raised locally. After his death, his wife and daughter and Mr Thornburn took over

---

64 'Bishop Wilson on the Labour Trade', *BC*, 23 Apr 1895.
65 'Church of England Kanaka Mission', *BC*, 5 Dec 1896.
66 Wilson to Bishop J.R. Selwyn, 5 Feb 1896, *OPMM*, Aug 1896, 207–08; *Church Chronicle*, May 1895, 3; and June 1895, 11–13; Wetherell 1977, 101–02; Wilson, *OPMM*, Aug 1895, 122; Moore 2015a.
67 Brittain, quoted in *OPMM*, Aug 1894, 69; Wilson, 6 June 1895, *OPMM*, Nov 1895, 153.
68 Alex O. Smith, letter to the editor, *BC*, 24 Apr 1895; 'Kanaka Missions. The Work in Queensland. Reply to the Bishop of Melanesia. A Voice from Bundaberg', *BC*, 16 May 1895.
69 Brittain, *OPMM*, Christmas 1894, 97–100.

until Williams arrived.[70] New Zealand-born and Cambridge University-educated, Williams set to work in the Bundaberg and Isis districts. His count of the Islander population, which differs slightly from that of Bishop Wilson, is probably more accurate. The number of Islanders around Bundaberg never outnumbered those in the Mackay district, although Bundaberg and Isis combined was similar in size. Williams said there were slightly less than 2,000 Islanders at Bundaberg and another 1,000 working in the Isis. His figures suggest that there were 540 Guadalcanal and Malaita labourers in the Bundaberg district and a further 410 in the Isis district from the same islands. Calculated on the overall numbers from each island that worked in Queensland (9,186 Malaitans and 4,188 from Guadalcanal),[71] there must have been at least 500 Malaitans in the area.

The planters were behind with their pledges, which Williams had to extract to pay wage arrears owed to Mrs Clayton. When he first preached, Williams's Islander congregation numbered 87. Reports from 1896–97 suggest that 20 Islander men took Holy Communion in Williams's Anglican church at Bundaberg and 160 came to Matins. About 90 men, predominantly from Gela and led by John Lamosi who had been a pupil at Norfolk Island, attended Christmas services in a church hall that year. Between services they amused themselves with games of cricket and football, and at the end of the day prayers were said in Mota (the Anglican *lingua franca*) and the Gela language. School classes were held every Tuesday, Thursday and Saturday with an average of 37 Islanders in attendance, with another 24 attending evening classes on plantations.[72] Williams wrote most unflatteringly about the mission room:

> It is simply an old disused barn, attached to a stable and cowshed. It is low and narrow, with an iron roof, and absolutely devoid of paint. There are no windows, merely holes cut in the walls. It is rotten in places, letting in wind, rain, and sun. There are planks for seats, and when there are, say 150 boys in there on a hot Sunday morning, one melts and needs something very good to smell.[73]

Around Bundaberg he was assisted by Rev. William Morris and Miss Brands. Williams regularly visited plantations and farms around Bundaberg to conduct school classes and raised £100 to pay for a resident

---

70 'Notes', *SCL*, July 1897, 4.
71 Price with Baker 1976, 115.
72 Williams, 'The Melanesian Mission in Queensland', *OPMM*, Mar 1897, 269.
73 Williams, 'Notes from Queensland', *OPMM*, Mar 1897, 270–72.

teacher at nearby Childers in the Isis district, £50 of it provided by the Colonial Sugar Refining Company, proprietors of the large plantation mill there, and with extensive commercial interests in Fiji and other Queensland and New South Wales mills and refineries. There was no church building for the Isis Islanders and funds were harder to raise there because the sugarcane came mainly from small-scale farmers rather than the large plantations that dominated around Bundaberg. Williams took the train to the Isis every Monday and remained there until Wednesday. When he was unable to make the trip, local clergyman Rev. Ashburner took the service. Around 30 Islanders came to the services and another 40 attended the school.[74]

Williams left in 1897 and reappeared in the Diocese of Melanesia in 1900, based on Guadalcanal from 1902 to 1905.[75] He was replaced in Bundaberg by the aforementioned J.D. Anderson and in the Isis by G.E. Layton. European missionaries took the weekend services and Islander teachers ran classes during the week on various plantations. In 1899, an observer on one Bundaberg plantation noted that 75 Islanders attended the afternoon Sunday school. Moody and Sankey's hymns were sung perfectly to tune and lessons and preaching were in Pijin English.[76]

The educational, pastoral and religious programs at Bundaberg continued. During 1903, classes were attended by 3,075 Islanders and 891 Chinese (cumulatively, not individuals). Miss McIntyre, who had begun to teach the Islanders in the mid-1890s, held five classes each week, three for Islanders only and two for Islanders and Chinese, assisted by the rector, Rev. R.S. Hay. About 80 Islanders regularly attended church services, of whom 26 had been baptised and 18 were confirmed by the bishop of Rockhampton. The Islanders attended the early service at the parish church and they also had their own church on the north side of the river that operated in much the same way as the Selwyn Mission.[77]

---

74 Williams, 'The Melanesian Mission in Queensland', *OPMM*, Mar 1897, 269–70; and, 'Notes from Queensland', *OPMM*, Mar 1897, 270–72; 'With "Our Boys" in Bundaberg', *OPMM*, Sept 1897, 289–90; 'Report of Queensland Branch of the Melanesian Mission', *OPMM*, Christmas 1897, 323–24.
75 Blain's Biographical Directory 2017.
76 'Melanesia in Queensland', *SCL*, 15 Sept 1899, 4.
77 'Mission Notes', *SCL*, July 1904, 7.

The Brisbane Diocese seems to have made little progress at Maryborough, another major cane-growing area, although as early as 1871 there were Christian Islanders there from Lifou, one of the Loyalty Islands. In 1876, attempts were made to establish an Anglican Maryborough mission, and several Islanders contributed to a fund to build the parish church in the late 1870s.[78] Richard Eva, rural dean at Maryborough from the early 1880s into the 1890s, is said to have made attempts to minister to the Islanders, although nothing further is known. The report notes that these Islanders were colonists, not circular migrants. In 1890, the Lutheran Church started a Sunday school, with good results,[79] and six years later a similar Anglican mission presence began when ailing Mrs Clayton shifted from Bundaberg to Maryborough.[80]

The diocese to the north was based at Rockhampton, the only Queensland district that retains a substantial Anglican Islander population today and one that provided pastoral and sugarcane occupations.[81] The new diocese was created in 1892. In 1889, while the region was still part of the Brisbane Diocese, Francis Drinkall Pritt became the new minister in north Rockhampton. He had previously visited the islands and observed Melanesian Mission activities[82] and was keen to begin work with the Islanders both in north Rockhampton and at Yeppoon on the coast. When Pritt arrived, there were 200 Islanders in his parish, 78 at Yeppoon sugar plantation and the remainder scattered about. Rockhampton Islanders were mainly from the New Hebrides and the Loyalty Islands and had arrived to work in the pastoral industry in the 1860s and 1870s. By 1889, many of them were long-term immigrants with certificates of exemption from the labour restrictions that controlled Islanders who arrived after 1879. As mentioned earlier, in 1894 Pritt transferred to the Herbert River district (Ingham) and was replaced by Canon Alfred H. Julius, who stayed until 1904 and also fostered the Islanders within his congregation.[83]

---

78   Kerr 1987, 68–69.
79   Rev. C. Christenson, letter to the editor, *BC*, 6 Apr 1892.
80   'The Melanesian Mission in Queensland', *SCL*, Apr 1890, 10–11; 'A Melanesian Christmas at Bundaberg', *SCL*, June 1897, 4; R.P.W., 'With "Our Sons" at Bundaberg', *SCL*, July 1897, 8–9; 'The Melanesian Mission in Queensland', *SCL*, 14 May 1898, 8.
81   There were very few, if any Malaitans at Rockhampton during the nineteenth century. Moore 1985, 311; Gistitin 1989; 1995; Kerr 1993, 58; 1996, 43–46.
82   He may have been related to Rev. Lonsdale Pritt, who served with the Melanesian Mission from 1861–67 in New Zealand.
83   Julius had links to the Melanesian Mission through his cousin Ellen Julius (daughter of the bishop of Christchurch, New Zealand), who in 1899 married Bishop of Melanesia Cecil Wilson.

Up until 1897, most of the costs of running the Queensland missions were met by plantation owners and the Islanders themselves, plus small subsidies from the Melanesian Mission. In 1894, Mary Robinson at Mackay received £50 annually, half each from the Melanesian Mission and the Diocese of North Queensland, and the Melanesian Mission was considering paying Rev. Pritt at Bundaberg.[84] Robinson received £70 from Melanesian Mission funds during 1895, with another £50 raised locally, intended to cover her keep and all of the school's expenses. By 1896, however, the bishop had defaulted due to a shortage of funds and was 'anxious to incur the responsibility no longer'.[85] Widowed Mary Robinson could not support herself and her daughter on the money while also paying all expenses, and she contemplated closing the Selwyn Mission. A 'Robinson Fund' was established with £109 collected up until 1897 to subsidise her work.[86]

Anglican and Presbyterian parishioners also supported the various missions by subsidising missionary salaries. Plantation owners and farmers appreciated the quieting effect Christianity had on their often volatile workforce, although they were not keen on Islanders regularly attending evening classes since that left them tired at work the next day.

The Queensland Government had £30,000 in its Pacific Islanders' Fund, made up of the compulsory return fares, unclaimed wages from Islanders who had died, and savings from Islanders who had deposited money in the government Savings Bank and subsequently died. The government agreed to Wilson's proposal that interest from this fund be used to subsidise mission schools for Islanders in Queensland; in the 1880s, the interest had been used to subsidise Kanaka hospitals.[87] After his 1895 visit, Bishop Wilson announced ambitious plans to take Clayton at Bundaberg on to his staff (his £200 per annum salary guaranteed by the local congregation), to pay Pritt (then on the Hebert River) £100 a year to work with Mrs Robinson at Mackay (with another £100 and a house guaranteed by local planters). The final part of the deal was to pay Robinson £150 per annum, and to replace Pritt with a part-time appointment paid £50 a year to work with Islanders at the Herbert River.[88] Although Bishop Wilson's grand plan never eventuated, in 1897 the Queensland Government approved

---

84 Wilson to J.R. Selwyn, 6 Sept 1894, *OPMM*, Christmas 1894, 95–97.
85 Robinson to J.R. Selwyn, 26 Oct 1896, *OPMM*, Dec 1896, 28.
86 'Robinson Fund', *OPMM*, Christmas 1897, 326.
87 Moore 2015b.
88 Wilson, *OPMM*, Aug 1895, 122; Saunders 1976.

£600 per year in subsidies from its Pacific Islanders' Fund (which must have been more than just the interest). That year the Bundaberg and Isis branches of the Melanesian Mission benefited to the extent of £97 10s, enabling the employment of J.D. Anderson. Similar sums were doled out to the Selwyn Mission at Mackay (which, like Bundaberg, also received £70 directly from the Melanesian Mission, subject to its reporting to the North Queensland Board of Missions) and to the QKM and the Churches of Christ Isis mission.[89] The Queensland Islanders also supported the Melanesian Mission: in 1900 Islanders at the Selwyn Mission at Mackay donated £21 17s to the New Ship Fund (to replace the Melanesian Mission's *Southern Cross*), the equivalent of a year's pay for an experienced labourer.[90]

Although it is impossible to untangle Malaitans from this larger picture, in the 1890s and 1900s they were the majority Islander group in Queensland and the Queensland missions fed into the Melanesian Mission on Malaita.

Other Christian Missions

Another substantial but lesser mission to the Islanders was established by the Churches of Christ, which developed out of Presbyterianism in the United States early in the nineteenth century as a restoration of New Testament Christianity. The Churches of Christ was made up of autonomous nondenominational congregational church organisations that advocated a return to Christ's teachings as described in the Bible, as well as youth or adult baptism, which suited the conversion of Islanders. In 1892, it began a mission in the Isis, inland from Bundaberg, and in 1895 expanded to cover Knockroe, Doolbi and Gregory near Goodwood. John Thompson was in charge of what was called the Kanaka Mission, inspired by the work of the QKM. From 1893 he received a wage from the church's Foreign Mission Committee, which also paid to have a mission house and chapel constructed. He managed to convert around 200 Islanders and had a Melanesian assistant named Tabimancon. In 1903, Thompson tried to establish a mission in the New Hebrides but returned home after several months, sick with malaria, to continue his work in the Isis.[91]

---

89   'Notes', *SCL*, July 1897, 4.
90   *SCL*, Oct 1900, 1.
91   Chapman 2004.

Figure 3.6: The Churches of Christ Mission Hall in the Isis,
with John Thompson's house alongside.
Source: Peter O'Sullivan Collection.

A Churches of Christ mission was established at Maryborough, although this may not have been the first Islander mission there, since an early history of Maryborough describes another established by Rev. C. Christenson. The Churches of Christ mission first met in the Protestant Hall and held a special baptismal service for Islanders on 5 July 1896. The hall was filled with Islanders and F.W. Turley conducted the service. Charley Erromango is the only Islander attendee named in the account.[92]

Christian outreach at Mackay, already home to the Anglican's Selwyn Mission, was joined by the Presbyterians in 1888. Their ministers began to visit Mackay in 1872 and a Kirk Session was formed there in 1876. The Presbyterian mission began at Walkerston, a planation dormitory town just outside Mackay, run between 1888 and 1907 by a full-time missionary, Rev. J. McLean McIntyre. Two-thirds of the indentured Islanders who came to work in Queensland were from the New Hebrides, a Presbyterian mission enclave of longer standing than the Solomons' missions. (The Melanesian Mission, the London Missionary Society and the Catholics also operated in the New Hebrides.) Depending on which island they came from, some of the labourers from the New Hebrides were already Christian or had some earlier contact with missions. Twenty years before the Walkerston Mission was established, the Presbyterian General Assembly had instructed its Committee on Foreign Missions to raise funds for a mission to the Islanders in Queensland, although nothing eventuated. The Walkerston Mission was the only one the Presbyterians ever developed in Queensland.

---

92 Loyau 1897, 316.

Figure 3.7: Rev. McIntyre with his Sunday school class, Presbyterian Mission at Walkerston.
Source: Clive Moore Collection.

Rev. McIntyre was supported by two leading Presbyterians: Elizabeth Donaldson from 1890 to 1896 at Sandiford near Oakenden and then later at Homebush, and Frank J. Stevens at Cotton Vale near Homebush.[93] The Islanders contributed funds to the mission, and in 1894 paid £70 to have a new mission hall built at Sandiford.[94] The initial activities were on the south side of the Pioneer River, but spread to the north side in 1895 when John Walker was given oversight of that area, based at Miclere until 1903.[95] The main mission hall, erected at Walkerston in 1895, was badly damaged in a cyclone early the next year, and its Islander parishioners donated £33 to restore it.[96] In 1899, Alfred E. Eustace, who had worked with the QKM while Florence Young was in China, transferred to work with McIntyre at Walkerston and then moved to the Presbyterian mission in the Lower Burdekin.[97] Eustace was back at Walkerston in 1900–01 while McIntyre took six months leave due to ill health. The mission operated quite separately from the main Kirk Session, and when it closed at the end of 1906 the remaining Presbyterian Islanders were not welcome among the European congregation. The Walkerston Kirk's main concern

---

93 'Report of the Northern Territory Commission', *South Australian Proceedings of Parliament*, 1895, 2, 145: information from Elizabeth Donaldson; Elizabeth Donaldson to Sir Samuel W. Griffith, *BC*, 21 Nov 1892.
94 *BC*, 7 Dec 1894, 4.
95 'Kanaka Missions. A Visit to Mackay. Letter from the Rev. A. C. Smith', *BC*, 26 June 1895.
96 Bardon 1949, 47; *MM*, 31 Oct 1895.
97 *BC*, 13 Sept 1899, 6.

was that they were losing an excellent tenant (McIntyre) from the manse. The Islanders continued to meet in the mission hall into the 1910s, although they received communion separately.[98]

One Presbyterian development was 'Tea Meetings' attended annually by up to 500 Islanders at the Walkerston mission hall at Christmas. This was a Christian revival meeting augmented by food and foot races. Aside from the obvious Christian intent of the mission work, the Presbyterians encouraged the Islanders to sign pledges to abstain from alcohol. By 1892, 1,800 Islanders in the district had donned the Presbyterian blue ribbon of the total abstainer. In the early twentieth century, 'Tea Meetings' were also an Anglican event.[99] The other Presbyterian outreach to the Islanders was much smaller, at Mulgrave near Cairns and in the Tweed district in northern New South Wales.[100]

The Baptists established some outreach to Islanders around Brisbane in 1896.[101] The other 1890s Christian denomination working with Islanders was the Salvation Army, which spread its teachings into the Maroochy district north of Brisbane. Sergeant John Potts settled on Buderim Mountain and by 1893 had begun to convert Islanders working for nearby farmers. Assisting him was an early Islander convert, Sergeant Bob Libe from Maré, one of the Loyalty Islands, who was married to a European woman. The Buderim meetings were held on Sunday afternoons and Monday evenings, with a 'Bible school' on Wednesday evenings attended by around 20 Islanders from near Woombye, the rail siding for Buderim's farms. Three Islanders living with Aboriginal women were married by Brigadier Charles H. Jeffries and Major Graham in August 1895, and eight more couples were married before the century's end. By 1896, the mainly Islander congregation at Buderim was flourishing, and in the late 1890s a school house for the Islanders was built at Buderim near Potts's house, with a salary for Potts partly provided out of the government's Pacific Islanders' Fund. In 1896, a group of Buderim Islanders took part in a Salvation Army meeting at Gympie and others travelled to Brisbane to

---

98 Moore 1985, 312–15; Uniting Church in Australia, 'Minute Book', of the Kirk Session, Presbyterian Church, Walkerston, 14 Mar 1907, and 'Report for 1916'. There are no extant baptismal records until 1898 and no Islander baptisms are mentioned until 1911. The Presbyterian records from 1911 to 1939 contain Islander baptisms but the emphasis is on those of New Hebridean descent. Walkerston Baptismal Records, 1889–1939.
99 *MM*, 31 Oct 1895; 24 Dec 1896; 7 Jan 1907; Mercer 1995, 229, 230, 269, 276, 281.
100 R.M.F.D., 'Sugar Plantations in Queensland', *SCL*, Sept 1905, 11.
101 *BC*, 12 Oct 1896.

meet Commandant Herbert Booth and his wife Cornelie. The same year saw the first of what became an annual holiday encampment at Maroochy Heads, with some 200 people taking part. Initially established for the Islanders living around Buderim, this Christian camp became so popular that by the 1910s over 1,000 Salvationists were attending. This was the beginning of tourism at Maroochy. After Libe died in 1897, the Islander group remained with the Salvation Army. In the 1900s, 34 Islander and Aboriginal couples and their children were part of the Salvationist group at Buderim.[102]

New South Wales

An area of Islander settlement that is often forgotten is northern New South Wales. There were about 200 Islanders there in 1897. Some had fled from Queensland in the late 1880s to live under a more benign regime, and others drifted south to try to cope with the 1890s depression years. They grew cane, which they sold to the Colonial Sugar Refining Company's mills, and worked on the district's sugarcane and banana farms.[103] Exempt from Queensland regulations (but not from the Commonwealth's 1901 deportation order), most of them were from the New Hebrides and lived around Cudgen and Tumbulgum.[104] The Islanders built two small Anglican churches: St John's at Cudgen, where Jonah Woqas from Mota Island and Ravu from the Gela Islands conducted services for a few dozen Islanders, and St Barnabas at Tumbulgum, where John Tala from Mota and Jimmy from another New Hebridean island were the preachers. Rev. Frederick C.T. Reynolds, the Anglican priest at Murwillumbah, and the local Presbyterian minister, visited both groups regularly. The QKM also established a base at Cudgen. Malaitans, though, were never a substantial part of this southern Islander community.[105]

---

102 *War Cry*, 9 Mar, 15 June, and 2 Aug 1895; 28 Mar, 23 May, and 5 Dec 1896; Gittins 1994, 5–16; *Full Salvation*, 1 June 1896, 166–67.
103 Smith 1991.
104 The area was within the Anglican Diocese of Grafton and Armidale. Faith Bandler, of Tanna Island and Anglo-Indian ancestry, is the best known of Islander descendants from this region. She wrote several books based on her father's life at Mackay and Tumbulgum. Bandler 1977; 1984; Bandler and Fox 1980; see also Lake 2002.
105 'The Melanesians on the Tweed River', *SCL*, May 1897, 2–3.

Torres Strait

Although peripheral to this account, for the sake of completeness I need to mention Pacific Islander immigrants in the Torres Strait Islands, between Australia's Cape York and the New Guinea mainland, within Queensland territorial waters. Pacific Islanders first arrived to work in Torres Strait maritime industries in 1860. They were mainly from the Loyalty Islands and the southern New Hebrides, but also included some Solomon Islanders. By 1870 around 150 were working on seven vessels, and two years later, after the discovery of commercial quantities of pearlshell, there were 500. The London Missionary Society set up in Torres Strait in 1871, as a stepping-stone to evangelising on the New Guinea mainland. They relied on Pacific Islander mission workers, mainly Loyalty Islanders and Samoans. By the 1880s there was what historian Steve Mullins called a Pacific Islander ascendancy. The Anglican Diocese of Carpentaria included Torres Strait, and when the London Missionary Society withdrew in 1914 the Anglicans took over, establishing St Paul's Mission on Mua Island, which became home to many Torres Strait Islanders of Pacific Islander descent. There were Malaitans in Torres Strait, but none ever returned to their home island.[106]

Malaitans and Christianity in Fiji

There has been little research into missionary outreach to Islanders on Fiji plantations. Malaitans were just as important to the Fijian labour force as they were in Queensland. Fiji Government records show 2,727 Malaitans indentured there between 1870 and 1887 and another 2,422 between 1888 and 1911, with the latter years more likely to be the peak conversion period.[107] Several hundred Malaitans must have had significant levels of contact with Christianity while in Fiji, and the fragments of information available suggest that there were significant attempts to reach out to the Islander labourers there. For instance, Malaitan Peter Otoa, kidnapped by the *Sea Breeze* and taken to Fiji in 1880, reported that he joined his friends at mission classes run by Rev. J. Francis Jones and Mr Horne in Suva in the mid-1880s. Otoa told of other classes run by Rev. William

---

106 Mullins 1995, 70; 1990; David, Manas and Quinnell 2008.
107 Siegel 1985.

Floyd at Levuka, and recounted a time when 400 Islanders attended the Suva Anglican church. The local European congregation objected to them taking up so many seats and, ashamed, they left.[108]

Floyd, a high church Irishman, arrived from Melbourne in 1870 at age 32. He became Fiji's first Anglican clergyman and vicar of rumbustious Levuka, although his appointment was irregular and he was isolated from episcopal support for many years, and later placed under the supervision of the bishop of London.[109] Anglicanism in Fiji had a peculiar status: it was not within the jurisdiction of any established regional diocese, which precluded any equivalent Anglican mission development such as had occurred within the Diocese of Melanesia or the four Queensland dioceses. As we have seen for Queensland, the Anglican diocese divisions were always an impediment. During the 1870s, Floyd became interested in the labourers from the Solomons and New Hebrides. He was assisted for three years by Edward Wogale, sent by the Melanesian Mission from Mota Island in 1875. In 1880, Bishop of Melanesia John Selwyn visited for three weeks to conduct baptisms and an ordination. Selwyn encouraged work among the immigrant Islanders and stationed Rev. A. Poole at Rewa, although he decided it was impractical to place teachers on the Fiji plantations. However, land was purchased at Onivero, where some of the Islanders settled and built a crude church, followed by a second more substantial building nearby—the Church of the Epiphany.[110] Soon after, they were also given land for a school.

In 1884, the capital was moved to Suva, where Holy Trinity Church was constructed, and Fiji Anglicanism received an endowment of land at Natoavatu and Savusavu, the intention being to fund the appointment of a bishop of Fiji.[111] Rev. Jones, who arrived in 1886, supervised the building of a church for the Islanders at Suva, and in 1890 managed to collect £382, including £252 provided by Islanders themselves. Construction of St John the Baptist Church (called the 'Polynesian church') took place over 1892–94. It was opened by the Melanesian Mission's Rev. R.B. Comins,

---

108 'Melanesians in Queensland and Fiji', *SCL*, 15 Feb 1900, 8; Anglican Church of the Province of Melanesia 1894, 30; 'The First Voyage', *SCL*, Jan 1901, 110.
109 Floyd was appointed through the Bishop of Melbourne and Metropolitan of Victoria Charles Perry, with lukewarm support from the Bishop of Melanesia. Perry clearly exceeded his authority, which he based only on Victoria being the major sponsor of Fiji colonisation. Bishop Patteson signed the licence. Whonsbon-Aston 1964, 31–32, 41, 43–45.
110 Hilliard 1978, 106.
111 Whonsbon-Aston 1964, 48–51.

assisted by Luke Masuraa, in front of an Islander congregation of 460 (out of a total Melanesian labour force in the area of around 2,000). Comins gave his address in English and the Malaitan languages used at Walade and Sa`a, as well as a little Mota for the sake of the Banks Islanders present. Malaitans from four or five different language areas attended.[112]

Four years after Floyd shifted to Suva, the Lambeth Conference suggested that Fiji be attached to the New Zealand diocese, but the congregation rejected the proposal. Floyd retired in 1898, replaced by Rev. Horace Packe, who continued to run the mission to Islanders in Suva. Eventually, Fiji was incorporated into the Diocese of Polynesia, which included the previously unattached Diocese of Hawaii, created after the American annexation of the Hawaiian Islands. Thomas Clayton Twitchell became the first bishop of Polynesia in 1908. Discontent over the failure to recognise Fiji as an independent diocese led to Floyd's return that year as archdeacon of Fiji, where he died in October 1909.[113]

Fijian Christian's attitudes to foreign labourers varied, but some offered encouragement. Though there were sometimes open conflicts between Fijians and Malaitans in particular, Solomon Islanders generally felt comfortable amongst Fijians and learnt a pijin version of the Fijian language. This pijin was still used by many Malaitans after they returned to the Solomons,[114] and some of them also adopted aspects of a Fijian lifestyle.

---

112 Commis, *OPMM*, Aug 1894, 69.
113 'Melanesians in Queensland and Fiji', *SCL*, 15 Feb 1900, 8; Anglican Church of the Province of Melanesia 1894, 30; 'The First Voyage', *SCL*, Jan 1901, 110; Whonsbon-Aston 1964, 52–63.
114 Siegel 1982.

Figure 3.8: This photograph is thought to be of the Methodist mission to Islanders in Fiji.

The house front is ornamented in a style used in central Malaita. Many Solomon Islanders returning from Fiji were said to have been introduced to Christianity by the 'Wesleyans'.

Source: British Museum OcA2–21.

3. MALAITAN CHRISTIANS OVERSEAS, 1880s–1910s

Comins received permission from Governor Sir John Thurston to take six of the men from Fiji to school at Norfolk Island for two years. All were Malaitans, two each from Alite Harbour and Fiu, Su`u and Maana`oba, and the coast near Cape Arascides in east Fataleka. All six were already confirmed and literate.[115] Three of these men were amongst 30 Christians, several of them already confirmed, landed at `Ataa and Fiu in September 1898 from the Fiji schooner *Rotuma*.[116] In 1902, Rev. Packe reported that he had eight Islander teachers operating evening and Sunday schools. St John the Baptist Church was free of debt and had just been repainted outside and refurbished inside. Thirty of the Islander congregation were confirmed.[117] Also in Fiji were a few Malaitans schooled there by the Wesleyans and Catholics: Rev. Packe was at pains to stress the spirit of cooperation between the Anglicans and Methodists. One of these Wesleyan adherents, Amasia, returned home in the late 1890s after almost 30 years away and started schools on Ngongosila and then in Lau Lagoon. Bennett mentions Catholic converts from Fiji who helped the church purchase land at Bina Harbour, and Lange refers to Venasio, a Malaitan converted to Catholicism while working in Fiji.[118]

During the 1900s, three large colonies of around 100 former Fiji men returned to Malaita to settle at Fiu on the northwest coast, Ferasubua in Lau Lagoon, and Pululahu in the west of Small Malaita. Other such groups settled around Malaita alongside the dominant communities of former Queensland labourers, although often they chose to be separate since their *lingua franca* was usually Pijin Fijian rather than Pijin English. The Pululahu community was quite typical of other early Christian settlements on Malaita. Seventeen former Fiji labourers, two with wives, arrived in 1903, led by William Maetabu from north Malaita, who had trained for two years on Norfolk Island. Many of this group had attended mission classes in Fiji during the 1890s. Another Fiji return had preceded them by a year and they used his large house as their first base. Rehe, the Pululahu chief, was married to a Sa`a woman, and supported the Melanesian Mission, largely because his son Lilimae had visited Ulawa on the *Southern Cross*. Rehe died soon after the group arrived, almost

---

115 One of the six died in mysterious circumstances on 25 May 1895. Comins, 15 June 1894, *OPMM*, Aug 1894, 70 Palmer, *OPMM*, Nov 1895, 179.
116 Wilson, 'The Second Island Voyage, 1899', *SCL*, 15 Nov 1899, 5.
117 Packe, 'The Melanesian Mission in Fiji', *SCL*, May 1902, 195–96.
118 Ivens, 'Ulawa and Mala', *SCL*, Apr 1904, 18; 'Ulawa and Mala', *SCL*, Mar 1902, 45; and 'Kalilana Mala (The Rounding of Mala)', *SCL*, June 1900, 19–20; Bennett 1987, 145; Lange 2005, 289.

ending the whole endeavour because they were blamed for his death. The group had to stay secure until another man was killed in retaliation, and in the intervening months their taro gardens died. Reduced to eating sago (emergency food on Malaita), one of their number rerecruited and another left to join his ancestor-worshiping family. Lilimae continued to support the school and eventually the situation improved.[119] The Melanesian Mission established a school there in 1904, its first on the lee side of Small Malaita. Rev. Ivens noted that they 'can all read English well, and some twelve of them are confirmed'.[120] The community was given permission to build a village on the coast and two boys were allowed to leave for study on Norfolk Island.[121]

The reports suggest that Fijian-trained Christians, although fewer in number than those from Queensland, were influential in the decade before the protectorate government reached Malaitan shores. They all spoke Pijin Fijian as their *lingua franca*, although they seem to have also learnt English in their schools in Fiji.[122]

Malaitans Baptised Overseas before 1910

The over 9,000 Malaitan labour recruits to Queensland made up a large proportion of the Christian converts, particularly late in the labour trade. Exact statistics on Malaitan Christians in Queensland have been preserved in QKM records throughout the colony/state, and from Mackay, where the Anglican and Presbyterian missions baptised around 1,000 Melanesians over the 20 years before deportations began in the mid-1900s. All three missions combined teaching the rudiments of Christianity, literacy and temperance, and were responsible for producing some well-educated Christian Melanesians, many of them Malaitans. There were 512 Selwyn Mission Anglican baptisms of Malaitans between 1890 and 1906, and, based on their proportion in the local Islander population, Malaitans probably made up reasonable numbers of the Presbyterian converts, although Mackay district Solomon Islanders seem always to have preferred the Selwyn Mission.[123] Allowing for deaths and single-contract labourers

---

119 'In Afflictions', *SCL*, May 1904, 18–19.
120 'The First Voyage, 1900', *SCL*, Jan 1910, 111.
121 Ivens, 'Ulawa and S.E. Mala', *SCL*, Apr 1905, 21.
122 *SCL*, Feb 1901, 137; J.R. Selwyn, *OPMM*, Dec 1894, 102.
123 Moore 1985, 312–15.

returning home after three years, these statistics suggests that at least 600 Christian Malaitans lived in the Mackay district in the early 1900s, and most of them had returned home by 1908.[124]

Table 3: Malaitans baptised overseas before 1910.

Malaitan contracts in Queensland, 1871–1906	9,298
Anglican Selwyn Mission, Mackay, 1890–1906	512
Other Anglican Missions (Cairns, Mossman, Cudgen)	100?
Presbyterian Mission, Mackay	100?
Other Presbyterian Missions (Mulgrave, Tweed)	50?
Queensland Kanaka Mission, 1886–1906	589
Churches of Christ, 1892–1906	100?
Brisbane Baptist City Tabernacle	?
Brisbane City Mission	?
Queensland Total Baptisms	1,451?
Malaitan contracts in Fiji, 1870–1914	5,149
Fiji Total Baptisms	800?
New Caledonia and Samoa Total Baptisms	30?
Malaitans on Norfolk Island Total Baptisms	500?
TOTAL BAPTISMS	2,781?

There were another 589 Malaitan baptisms (23 per cent) amongst a total 2,484 QKM Queensland baptisms. The QKM claimed particular success among Malaitans, which was the main reason that the mission established its new SSEM headquarters on their island. However, the QKM attracted very few Malaitan students during the 1880s, the main progress being achieved in the 1890s and 1900s at a rate far beyond Malaitans' prominence in Queensland.

Bishop Wilson estimated that there were 1,200 Malaitans in Queensland in 1894,[125] and we know that Malaitans made up around 25 per cent of the total number of Islanders in Queensland and northern New South Wales during the final decade of the labour trade. If we add the QKM and Selwyn Mission Malaitan baptism statistics (1,101) to estimates from smaller Anglican and other denominational missions, the total must have exceeded 1,400. Although some would already have returned home, or died, there were at least 1,000 baptised Christian Malaitans in Queensland

---

124 *Ibid.*, 306–09.
125 Wilson, *OPMM*, Nov 1895, 153.

in the 1900s and many of them had also been confirmed as full members of their churches. Most probably as many as 2,700 Malaitans returned home during the deportation years (1901–08), when Malaita had a total population of around 50,000.[126] The majority had been exposed to some Christian teaching: let us presume 1,450, the conservative calculation in Table 3.[127] Five thousand Malaitans also recruited to Fiji, almost 1,600 of them between 1900 and 1911; at least half of this late batch must have been exposed to Christian teaching. There were also a number of Solomon Islanders (including Malaitans) among the 10,000 Melanesians who worked in German Samoa. A lesser number (hundreds) laboured in New Caledonia. It is clear from numerous references to Malaitans able to speak Pijin English from Samoa, and Pijin Fijian, that some of the Christians on the island had worked in these Pacific plantation areas.[128] We also need to add in some hundreds of Malaitans who became Christians at St Barnabas College on Norfolk Island. It is reasonable to estimate that around 2,700 Malaitans living on Malaita in 1909 had become Christians while overseas. This estimate, alongside the conversions on Malaita, suggests that there were thousands of practising Christians on Malaita and many of them had achieved basic literacy. The conclusion (outlined in chapters 4 through 6) is that there cannot have been less than 4,000 to 5,000 Christians on Malaita in 1909. These numbers were substantial, and the difference from better known Christian islands such as Isabel and the Gela Group is that Malaitan converts remained a minority in the much larger population.

The most famous example is Timothy George Mahratta, who was born in the Burnett district near Bundaberg in 1892, and died on Malaita in 1969. His father, Tolimcane (Thomas), was recruited from Langalanga Lagoon by the *Fearless* to work in the sugar industry in the mid-1880s, served three years in Queensland and returned to Malaita on the same vessel. The woman to whom he was betrothed had married another man and he rerecruited for Queensland, where he married Makeni (Maggie) from Small Malaita. Tolimcane became a teacher for the QKM and Timothy was encouraged to gain a European education. As the family moved about for seasonal labour and mission work, he attended three government primary schools around Bundaberg and three in the nearby Isis district.

---

126 Moore 1985, 306–20; Corris 1973b, 95.
127 PMB 1381, Woodford Papers, 8/17, Reel 4, Bundle 23, 'BSIP Statistics to 31 Mar 1909'.
128 Munro 1990, liv, xlvii; Meleisea 1980; Shineberg 1999, 27, 28, 60, 64, 80, 106, 232; Siegel 1985; Corris 1973b; Halapua 2001, 47.

3. MALAITAN CHRISTIANS OVERSEAS, 1880s–1910s

Although eligible to stay in Australia, Tolimcane, who by the early 1900s had a small cane farm near Bundaberg where he ran a few head of stock and employed several of his countrymen, chose to return home with his family in 1906 or 1907. The couple became SSEM missionaries on Small Malaita, and Timothy attended the SSEM school at Onepusu on the west coast. He left the school after six months because his Queensland level of literacy and numeracy meant he was expected to be a teacher rather than a student. He was the best European-educated Malaitan of his day, and went on to become a government headman in the 1920s (and again briefly in 1944) and Small Malaita's 'head chief' during the Maasina Rule movement from 1945 until his arrest and imprisonment in 1947.[129]

The Malaitan Christian Experience Overseas

Modern Malaita, particularly in Kwaio and to a lesser extent elsewhere, still contains pockets of people who remain steadfast adherents to their ancestral religions. In Queensland and Fiji this was presumably the situation for the majority, with the first Christian conversions occurring in the late 1880s. There has been no previous detailed research completed into Christianity on overseas plantations. The main surviving records are QKM and Anglican baptism registers, newsletters and correspondence. Conversion to Christianity began a decade earlier on Queensland and Fiji plantations than it did on Malaita and the two sources fed in together back on Malaita. We know that Christians often asked to be landed at mission stations in the Solomons rather than on their own islands or the districts from which they enlisted. As will become clear in subsequent chapters, overseas-trained Malaitans and mission workers from other islands in Melanesia were at the core of the missionary endeavour on Malaita.

Peter Corris, who conducted interviews in the late 1960s with some of the last surviving Queensland and Fiji labourers, both on Malaita and in Queensland, concluded that 'traditional religious practices and customary observances seem, nevertheless, to have fallen temporarily into abeyance' and that there was no evidence 'of sorcery and other forms of magic being practiced among the Melanesians in Queensland'.[130] Corris attributed this to the absence of the priests and sorcerers and the inhibitions caused by

129 *Pacific Islands Monthly*, Oct 1973; Akin 2013a, 176–77.
130 Corris 1970, 63.

living in a Western society. He was told that 'Queensland was a white man's country ... and the spirits weren't there'.[131] However, oral testimony gathered in Queensland in the 1970s by me and Patricia Mercer, from the first Australian-born generation of Islanders, showed clearly that important religious beliefs were transferred to Queensland.[132]

In his 2013 book on Maasina Rule, David Akin provides a neat summary of the ways in which Malaitans maintained or discarded religious practices while overseas. As discussed in the conclusion to Chapter 2, Malaitans on recruiting ships and abroad were able to negotiate with their ancestors for new ground rules for acceptable behaviour.[133]

Although there is no doubting that Christian conversions occurred, just as on Malaita, some of the Queensland and Fiji Malaitan participation in Christian rituals and social events must have been similar to spectators at a theatre. These were nonthreatening breaks from the daily grind of working on plantations and farms—odd behaviour to be discussed late at night around fires. We can only guess at how they reacted to some situations, for instance Mary Robinson's invitations into her parlour at Mackay. And there are some strange anomalies in the records that leave us wondering. When John Kwailiu Abelfai Fatnowna died in March 1906, his Christian funeral procession was the largest ever seen for an Islander in the Mackay district and he was buried in the Anglican section of the Mackay cemetery. There was even a hearse and European attendants, unheard of for an early Islander funeral. Oral testimony from his family leaves no doubt that Kwailiu (as he is known) was an important Malaitan leader in the district and that he never became Christian. It appears that his family adopted the trappings of a Christian funeral, creating an impressive display that straddled Malaitan and Christian ways of dealing with death. Kwailiu was an in-between man who exemplifies the nature of Islander Christianity in Queensland and Fiji in the 1900s. There must have been many like him who straddled the customary and Christian worlds, in external colonies and back on Malaita, the subject of the next chapter.[134]

---

131 *Ibid.*, 63.
132 Mercer and Moore 1976.
133 Akin 2013a, 22–24.
134 Moore 2013c entry; 1981b; Mackay Regional Council, Mackay Cemetery Trust Register of Burials, Grave 2917, burial on 26 Mar 1906; *MM*, 28 Mar 1906.

3. MALAITAN CHRISTIANS OVERSEAS, 1880s–1910s

Figure 3.9: Kwailiu Fatnowna and his wife Orrani and family at Mackay in 1906, not long before his death.
Back row (L to R): Cecily, Joy, Lucy and Harry. Front row (L to R): Eva, Orrani and Kwailiu.
Source: Clive Moore Collection.

4

The Melanesian Mission, 1877–1909

> The heathen are always threatening us; they come with their bows and arrows again and again, and say they will kill us all and bury the school, but it is mostly words; they say they want three lives, Johnson's, mine, and John's (these are the three teachers). We do not go to meet them with arms, Mr. Comins has told us to seek peace with them, so we give them food and goods, and we try not to get angry with them.
>
> —Luke Masuraa, Aulu, 1896[1]

Introduction

Christianity, labour and government are three of the major influences that shaped modern Malaita before the 1940s. The fourth is an ability to be practical and incorporate change. There is nothing unique in the combination of the first three elements, which were major causes of change in many Pacific Islands societies. Yet virtually no other island experienced the same intensity of labour recruiting or had the strong link with Christian missions in Queensland. As we have seen, many early Malaitan Christians adopted their new spiritual beliefs while working on overseas plantations and attending denominational missions, the strongest links being with the QKM-SSEM and the Anglicans. This chapter further develops themes raised in the last, with a concentration

---

1   Quoted in the Ballarat *Churchman* and reproduced in *OPMM*, Mar 1896, 200.

on the Anglican's Melanesian Mission. David Lawrence, writing about the BSIP's first resident commissioner, Charles Woodford, provides a neat summary of the interactions between the different European groups and local people:

> Missionaries saw themselves as pursuing a political agenda that filled the gap between fervent British colonialism and neutrality. The local people, however, saw the missionaries, the traders, the labour recruiters and later the government officials as representing one group: foreigners with power, technology and unlimited resources. Missionaries certainly saw themselves as a social and moral group much superior to traders and labour recruiters.[2]

The previous two chapters discussed changes that occurred through labour migration. These were considerable and involved all communities. Between 1870 and the early 1940s, Malaitans entered into 50,000 indenture contracts. Youths and men became used to wage labour away from home, and when they returned they disrupted established social orders in their small-scale societies. They brought with them new languages, Christianity, new material possessions, and invisible baggage in the form of exposure to new diseases. Pijin English became the new *lingua franca* of Solomon Islands, and limited literacy was also introduced. Wage labour, Christianity and Pijin English (and to a lesser extent Pijin Fijian) had already altered Malaitan society long before the new BSIP government was proclaimed in 1893. One thread that holds Chapter 4 through Chapter 6 together is influences from outside Malaita, since early Christianity was largely spread and sustained by Malaitans and other Pacific Islanders who had been converted in Queensland, Fiji and Norfolk Island. The second thread is the flexibility of Malaitan ancestral religion, which was arguably more pragmatic and less dogmatic than Christianity, and its ability to continue alongside the new religion.

The main sources drawn upon in the next few chapters are the published records of the Christian missions, particularly the Melanesian Mission and the QKM-SSEM, supplemented by government documents. The documentary evidence is both magnificently detailed and frustrating. As with any source from a century ago, there are gaps that make it hard to follow events and statistics, and one must be careful not to absorb dated interpretations that are now invalid. Most missionaries and government

---

2   Lawrence 2014, 145–46.

officers held strongly Eurocentric views that shaped their descriptions of what they saw. Their explanations of what they were trying to do often appear foolish to us today, and they were certainly overconfident regarding their ability to socially engineer Malaitan societies.

Several techniques have been used to re-create the scenes of more than a century ago. First, the chapters were written keeping an eye on estimating the extent of mission contact with Malaitans, both while they worked overseas as labourers and as they lived on Malaita before 1910. Chapter 3 provided a wider history of Christian missions in Queensland and Fiji, and these missions were crucial to the changes that took place on Malaita. The present chapter and the two that follow chart the development of early Christian settlements on Malaita. This is accomplished by building information about the beginnings of the main mission bases and by following the voyages of mission ships. Ships—the various iterations of the *Southern Cross* and the *Evangel*, smaller vessels such as the cutter *Daphne* and whaleboats—were the lifelines of the Christian communities. As they circled the island, their crews and passengers observed change and development. Though they were always limited to the coast and often misunderstood what they saw, their reports are valuable nonetheless. With the benefit of hindsight, we can use the descriptions to help us piece together the lives and customs of Malaitans at that time. Missionaries began to provide detailed accounts of Malaita two decades before the protectorate established its headquarters at 'Aoke. We owe much of our early knowledge to missionary linguists such as Walter G. Ivens, who provided the first substantial word-window into coastal Malaitan society in the 1890s. Ian Hogbin, the first anthropologist to spend time on the island, did not arrive until 1933, by which time Malaita had already undergone 60 years of substantial change.

The following chapters show the extent that Malaita had already altered before government officers arrived and the complexity of the cultures that were slowly drawn into the British protectorate. Life on Malaita, particularly around the coast, emerges through these explorations of Christianity: the tensions between the inland-dwelling majority and the coastal, initially lagoon-dwelling minority, the extent of violence as a social mechanism and the nature of gender and spatial relationships. The history of Malaita as preserved in mission records is quite different from that found in early government archives. Just as missionaries had their own agendas, so too did government officers, who always lamented their lack of resources and relied on the police force and weapons to achieve their objectives. As is clear in Luke Masuraa's comment at the beginning of this chapter, missionaries were armed mainly with their faith in their Lord. That said, they were also helped by an ample supply of European goods, a small fleet of coastal boats and the support of existing Malaitan Christians.

Rapid changes occurred during the final three decades of the nineteenth century, not the least of which was the introduction of new diseases. Evidence is presented in later chapters of the epidemics that devastated population levels on some other Pacific Islands and also on Malaita.[3] The size of Malaita's population in the 1890s and 1900s is unknown: estimates put the number at between 50,000 and 100,000, with the truth probably closer to 50,000, since there may have been a significant decline in the second half of the nineteenth century. Calculations based on the analysis in Chapter 2 through Chapter 6 suggest that by 1910 around 4,000 to 5,000 baptised Christians and several hundred confirmed Christians lived on Malaita. Many of them spoke Pijin English, learnt on Queensland, Fijian and Samoan plantations and farms; an unknown number could read and write. The level of early literacy was far higher than the government ever gave credit for, and a few individuals, such as Timothy George Mahratta, later of Maasina Rule fame, had been educated in Queensland primary schools.[4]

Drawing on the mission literature helps to restore agency to Malaitans and creates a less European missionary-centred picture than do the mission texts. It also allows us to see how power and agency was refocused on Malaita before formal government arrived, first by the labour trade and then by the Christian missions. This new, 1890s–1900s focus was concentrated on Sa`a, Walade, Fauaabu, Fiu, Bita`ama, Malu`u, Ngorefou, `Ataa, Kwai-Ngongosila, Onepusu and Baunani, and not on `Aoke, the new government headquarters from 1909 (see Map 12 in this chapter, Map 13 in Chapter 6, and Map 14 in Chapter 7). Once the Marist Catholics arrived in the early 1910s, the European presence expanded to include Tarapaina in Maramasike Passage, Rohinari in `Are`are Lagoon and Buma further north. Previous to the missionary incursion, the Malaitan focus had been on language areas and foundational shrines of ancestors, which were mainly inland. The new European bases were concentrated

---

3   For instance, we know that 25–30 per cent of all the Melanesians who laboured in Queensland died there and never returned home. Moore 2015b.
4   Moore 2013c entry.

around the coast in the north, south and the west, although gaps were filled by many smaller Christian schools established along the Kwaio, `Are`are and Small Malaita coasts. Many coastal areas had no residents before this, which made the Christian settlements all the more striking.

Only two other Solomon Islands had significant Christian populations in 1909. The population of the Gela Islands was around 5,000, and by 1894 the Melanesian Mission had baptised some 3,000, a number that increased during the 1900s, leading to claims that Gela was the protectorate's largest Christian community. Isabel Island's population in the 1890s was estimated at just 4,000, of whom roughly one-quarter had been baptised by 1900, extended to most of the population by 1910. At the end of the century's first decade, then, more Christians lived on Malaita than in the Gela Islands or on Isabel.[5]

Christianity was established on Malaita through formal mission stations and schools started by mainstream denominations, and informally by Christian converts who had worked overseas. Significant numbers of indentured labourers became Christians, then returned and built their own small schools. Anglican Bishop Cecil Wilson described these schools as 'beacons all along the shores'.[6] Supplementing the more formal mission bases, the 'light' that spread from these indigenous beginnings was the ongoing, major force behind early Christianity in the islands. For congregation sizes I have not relied on the claims of missionaries, which are often inflated, and I have limited my counts to people who were baptised or confirmed as full members of their churches. Thus it is likely that the statistics I present significantly undercount those who, in some way, became followers of the various denominations.

Just how many Christians there were on Malaita before the Second World War has been a contentious issue. Some sources suggest that by 1930 almost half the population was Christian,[7] while others, referencing protectorate officers, give this same proportion after the war.[8] An increase of 15,000

---

5   Hilliard 1978, 115; White 1991, 105; Jackson 1975.
6   Wilson 1932, 207.
7   Bennett 1993, 145, quoting Hogbin 1939, 173 and Hilliard 1978, 274–75.
8   The 1945 Malaita annual report records that there were 42,000 people on Malaita and that half of them were Christian. Conversion had slowed during the war years, although it sped up in the 1950s. BSIP 27/VI/10, 'Malaita District Annual Report, 1945', 11; Akin 2013a, 402 n 94. Hugh Laracy (1976, 126) suggests that the majority were SSEM (9,000), followed by Anglicans (5,000) and Catholics (4,000), with fewer than 1,000 SDAs. This is not half of 42,000 but both official and mission statistics are notoriously rubbery, particularly in their estimates for inland settlements.

or 16,000 since 1909 (300 per cent) seems large, but is much slower than on neighbouring islands. The impetus from missions in Queensland and Fijian was not continued on the BSIP plantations, and we also need to take deaths into account given that the average life expectancy was probably less than 50 years and the overseas Christian component on Malaita was ageing. Alan Tippett makes the point that what occurred was what he called 'modified paganism', with the Christians and ancestral worshipers partly observing each other's 'rules' and coexisting. Some missionaries attempted to ensure total separation. This seldom occurred, although it may have been more successful when a European missionary resided in the vicinity. No generalisation is possible: the SSEM forbad its followers from observing birth and menstrual rules, which made SSEM villages unsafe for non-Christians. Nevertheless, the lack of progress of conversion is surprising and raises larger questions regarding the many other early estimates of Christian conversion in the Pacific. Also, Christian Malaitans obviously swapped denominations with great ease, and conversion to Christianity from the ancestral belief systems did not mean abandoning the power of ancestors. Non-Christians could see that Christians maintained parts of their old belief systems, and yet they could also break their pacts with ancestors and violate taboos without the usual dire consequences. Perhaps we will never know the answer, but given that officials could not accurately estimate the overall population, why should we trust their estimates of Christian numbers? We certainly cannot trust the missions, which all exaggerated their levels of success.

How much did the early Christians really understand their choice to take on a new religion? Was their conversion more opportunistic than sincere, and how did they combine Christianity with ancestral beliefs? Ben Burt's *Tradition and Christianity* provides the best answer: it was a totally syncretic process.[9] The argument presented in *Making Mala* is that Christianity had more influence on Malaita between the 1890s and 1930s than is often presumed. Even so, adaptation to foreign cultures and understandings of the strengths and weaknesses of European and other mission workers was only slowly and partially adopted by Malaitans. The discrete cultural expectations on both sides go to the heart of differences in attitudes and behaviours.

---

9   Also see Guo 2009, and Keesing 1967.

Concepts of religion, at both philosophical and practical levels, are at the core of these epistemological adaptations and changes. Missionaries usually presented Christianity as an opposing force to Malaitan religion, ignoring, or often just failing to understand, points of similarity and not comprehending that altering religious beliefs meant total societal change. Malaitans, despite variations in different regions of the island, already had one central all-embracing religion based on veneration of ancestors and other spirits, interlinked with languages, philosophy and other aspects of culture. By way of comparison, when the hold of medieval Catholicism began to break down in Europe, the process was accompanied by an alternative—Protestantism, a variation on the same religious tradition— and by new philosophical, scientific and authority structures that eventually challenged and then displaced religion as society's *raison d'être*. European states became more secular and increasingly controlled the lives of their people. On Malaita, the secular state cannot be said to have been even minimally 'in control' until the late 1920s or even the early 1930s. This meant that there were several prior decades when the Christian missions were the dominant foreign influences, and they continued to operate fairly autonomously right into the 1930s. Second, because of the centrality of religion to Malaitan culture, the transfer to Christianity often appeared to be deep, meaningful and immediate. It was deliberately presented this way by the missionaries, ever-conscious of the propaganda value of success stories for their overseas audiences and fundraising.

Much of what was accepted as quick conversion by foreign missionaries was initially fairly shallow adoption of an introduced alien cultural form. This is not to say it was merely a veneer, but the process of incorporating Christianity into existing religious systems was never fast. Some Malaitans converted to flee from angry ancestors. Others appreciated medical assistance given by missionaries, which was enough to win them over to Christianity for practical rather than spiritual reasons. Solomon Islanders readily accepted the theatrical aspects of the new religion and the material benefits adherence to it brought. Church rituals such as baptism and holy sacraments, hymns and prayers, processions and vestments were all interesting markers of the new religion and of the strange behaviour of foreigners. Francis Bugotu from Tasimboko Village on Guadalcanal was one of the first Solomon Islanders to intellectualise the place of Christianity in Solomon Islands society. In his 1968 Waigani Seminar paper, he said that the shift from indigenous religions to Christianity was easy because of the level of transfer was only at 'the conditional "faith and belief" level, not necessarily for its intellectual or common-sense content'.[10] Bugotu touched on the theatre and the illogic of the new religion, based as it was on concepts that were alien and could not be justified in terms of the needs of Solomon Islanders:

> Otherwise, we would want to know, or would want to know more clearly the meaning of the genuflecting, prostrating and crossing oneself in church. We would want to know the meaning of hymns and psalms instead of merely getting emotionally involved in their beauty or rhythm and tunes. We would question the use of foreign languages in our prayers. We would question why we shouldn't eat meat on Fridays; why we shouldn't eat pork and crab for example, when pigs and crabs provide the only source of meat-protein in certain areas. We would question the demand by some Churches that women wear European-style dresses reaching below the knees, in this hot climate, and when money is so scarce, they are not allowed to wear simple skirts and expose their breasts. This is unhealthy for the Church and for our women. Ironically, the purpose of such measures is to encourage health habits. Instead of the required healthy standards, however, our women folk would end up with more skin diseases such as Bakua, that apparently were never present in a pure island society. As for modesty, it is one thing that the Western culture cannot teach my culture, however scantily dressed we may appear to be.[11]

The introduction of Christianity was both theological and practical. Missionaries were also traders, and they often gave generous gifts to likely adherents. They traded for local produce and for control of land on which to build mission stations; in the case of the SSEM, the related Malayta Company acquired large parcels of agricultural land around Baunani. Eventually, missions were appreciated for the peace, tranquillity and love that came with true Christianity, in stark contrast to the sometimes brutal pre-Christian and pregovernment society. In 1990, John Barker argued correctly:

> Through schooling and the application of imported practical arts, missionaries began to familiarize islanders with the orientations and organization of the hegemonic colonial system the Europeans were then building. And, through the provision of the Bible and church liturgies and traditions, they introduced islanders to a language within which Christians could speak about their enlarged social and spiritual community.[12]

---

10   Bugotu 1968, 550.
11   *Ibid.*
12   Barker 1990, 16.

Even so, Malaitans seldom thought of the new religion as totally superior and worthy to replace deeply understood traditional belief systems. Deep and true conversion could take a generation or more, not just years, and aspects of ancestral beliefs survive so strongly today, even among Christians, that in many areas they continue to impede modern economic development and still govern clan discourse and activities. Malaitans still sometimes swap back and forth between, or combine, Christianity and non-Christian belief systems, much to the consternation of churches. Christians have joined the Bahá'í Faith and several thousand Malaitans, particularly men, have left their churches for newly introduced Islam in recent decades, although few fully follow Islamic beliefs and their wives usually remain Christian. They too manage an amalgam of beliefs.[13]

For many Malaitans in the 1890s and 1900s, the missions were a main site of interaction with Europeans, along with labour recruitment for overseas plantations. The Christian missions never claimed to assert control over Malaita in the way that the government did, although they were just as potent a force for change as were the labour trade and the protectorate government. Two more missions arrived after the government base was established at 'Aoke: the Catholics in 1910 and the Seventh-day Adventists in 1924. I have woven assessments of these newer Christian missions into the later chapters, which focus on the government sphere, for the reason that the 'package' of new influences became more homogenous after 1909.

Ben Burt's analysis of the feminine nature of Malaitan Christianity is worthy of note and will be picked up again later in the book. In brief, Burt suggests that, in Kwara'ae, Christianity was incorporated similarly to a new traditional cult. Christianity was a new potent spirit and accepting the new religion did not negate the power of the *akalo*; indeed, the two religions operated side-by-side, a common pattern throughout Pacific Christianity.

> In treating conversion to Christianity as a change of allegiance, the substitution of new spiritual relationships for old, Kwara'ae have inevitably brought the theology of the old religion into the new.[14]

---

13   Moore 2007.
14   Burt 1994, 255.

Did European missionaries realise that there were similarities between Christianity and indigenous religious beliefs? As Burt suggests, God the father, with his power mediated by his son who acts through the Holy Spirit, must have brought a sense of *déjà vu* to Malaitans who sacrificed to their ancestors.[15]

The Melanesian Mission

The Melanesian Mission had a monopoly over proselytising in Solomon Islands until the late 1890s, when they began to face competition from the Catholics, Methodists and QKM. The Anglicans were overstretched, although this eased a little when they established a local headquarters on Gela in 1895. Written almost 50 years ago, Alan Tippett's *Solomon Islands Christianity* still provides an interesting analysis of the shortcomings of the Melanesian Mission. He suggests four major failings: lack of direct identification because 'God's gentlemen' stayed off the front line of the 'battle'; remote control, through training mission workers on Norfolk Island, robbed the mission of continuity; the system was culturally defective because it extracted youths from their own societies and trained them on Norfolk, but then expected them to be able to convert their own people when they returned; and the approach implied an expectation of slow growth, which is what occurred.[16] The Melanesian Mission never developed a systematic missionary philosophy, but did establish a distinctive intellectual tradition based on an understanding of Melanesia through several key members of the mission. The mission always used the English word 'God' and did not try to translate it into local languages:

> At the centre of the teaching of the Anglican missionaries was the idea of God the Creator, 'the Eternal and Universal Father'. This God was an all-powerful spirit. He was present everywhere and made everything in the world, and He was greater than the creator gods and culture heroes who were common in traditional Melanesian religions.[17]

David Hilliard, this quotation's author, describes the Melanesian Mission theological foundations that were laid by bishops George Selwyn and John Patteson between the 1850s and the early 1870s, and then reinforced particularly by three scholarly priests: Robert H. Codrington, Walter G.

---

15 *Ibid.*
16 Tippett 1967, 39–42.
17 Hilliard 2005, 202. This 1866 quotation is from Bishop Patteson.

Ivens (who served on Small Malaita, 1895–1909) and Charles E. Fox (who served on neighbouring Makira from the 1900s and was remarkable for his longevity). All three published their linguistic, anthropological and historical research and were respected far beyond their church.[18] All European members of the Melanesian Mission studied their works, as well as writings by their colleague Arthur Hopkins, who worked in northern Malaita from 1902 to 1914. Anglican staff absorbed the general principles, either while at the headquarters on Norfolk Island or at the larger schools and theological institutes such as Maka or Siota within the Solomons. As the Melanesian Mission matured, scholars developed supporting materials for new staff to use. One manual was *Melanesia To-Day: A Study Circle Book*, compiled by Hopkins in 1927, which explained all facets of mission work.[19] Liberal Anglo-Catholicism pervaded the Melanesian Mission. Selwyn began an offshore 'native agency' policy that slowly created an indigenous ministry by lifting Islanders out of localities and taking them for extended periods to schools first in Auckland (until 1867) and then on Norfolk Island (until 1919). Patteson believed that sincere adoption of Christianity should have a social expression in all human activities, and that Christianity could be adapted to the circumstances of adherents. As Hilliard notes, Patteson though that missionaries should 'distinguish between the "fundamentals" of Christian doctrine and practice—"all men receive that"—and secondary matters reflecting a particular cultural context, which should be adapted to the circumstances of their hearers …'.[20]

Codrington, the greatest of the Melanesian Mission's ethnographers, joined its ranks in 1863, was head of the mission for several years (1871–77) and served as headmaster of St Barnabas College on Norfolk Island until 1887. His influence was profound and he believed that elements present in Melanesian religions made it relatively easy to prepare the way for Christianity, utilising beliefs in greater agency beyond humans, and prayers. Like other areas of Melanesia, Malaitan religion is theistic—based on belief in superior spiritual beings of some kind— and Malaitans have complex dogmas, places of worship and rituals. Missionaries were able to utilise Malaitans' sense of the limitations of human powers in relation to greater powers that were not controllable but could be beseeched on behalf of the living. There was an existing

18 Moore 2013c entries for all three.
19 Hopkins 1927.
20 Hilliard 2005, 199.

Malaitan sense of limitation of human power in relation to a greater power 'above'. But Malaitans had no belief in a single God—a supreme creator. The Malaitan religious system is integrated into all aspects of life and is acephalous—it has no head or centralised authority. There are myriad variations, with different taboos laid down by different ancestors.[21]

Malaitan religious beliefs did incorporate concepts such as *mamana* or *nanama* (sacred power, known elsewhere in the Pacific as *mana*) and *abu* (forbidden, known elsewhere as *tabu*), as well as prayer and sacrifice to ancestral spirits both to placate them and ensure their support for prosperity. One question in missionary minds, once they discovered the importance of ancestral spirits on Malaita, was whether Malaitans worshiped ancestors or just venerated them? That is, did Malaitans worship idols, or were the shrines simply places to respect and venerate ancestors, really no different from Christian churches and cemeteries? Did Malaitans regard ancestors as gods, which Christianity would have to displace from supremacy, or could a singular God concept be added while maintaining deference to the dead?

Codrington's main contribution to anthropology was developing an understanding of *mana* as an invisible power that can act for good or evil and can reside in individuals or a community. He wrote that the effect of *mana* lay in the efficacy of people's prayers, offerings and rituals used to acquire it. He never explored how far Christianity was accepted as a new source of *mana*, nor the relationship between Christianity and the new material possessions that usually came with adoption of the faith. Allan Davidson supports Darrell Whiteman's suggestion that Western observers probably exaggerated the centrality of *mana* to Pacific cosmology and theology, although there is no denying its importance.[22]

Some modern anthropologists have been critical of aspects of Codrington's interpretation. Ben Burt suggests that Kwara`ae ancestral ghosts do not just have power, they are *mamana*. Kwara`ae translate *mamana* as 'true'. Burt comments that *mamana* is best regarded as 'an idiom for describing the action of this power which represents it less in terms of the goals and objectives which it serves … than the relationship through which it is brought into effect'.[23] Despite its possible shortcomings, Codrington's

---

21   I am indebted to David Akin for explaning this issue.
22   Davidson 2003; Whiteman 1983.
23   Burt 1994, 55.

work on *mana* allowed Western missionaries to comprehend a higher intent amongst their congregations and to acknowledge an indigenous level of philosophy and understanding beyond earlier analyses of Melanesian belief systems, including those of Malaitans.

Missionary scholars such as Codrington and Ivens also tried to explain another basic concept, *tabu*, which they glossed as meaning 'forbidden', usually an expression of an opposition between spiritual powers between men and women, expressed through religious sanctions. The term also governs the relationship between humans and the spirit world as a single social system, and extends to political power and law (*taki*). Burt suggests that 'sacrosanct' is the best translation of the Malaitan *abu*, and that the meaning does not always have to relate to religion. Roger Keesing felt that Burt's informants had been overly influenced by Christianity, which had altered the meaning, though Keesing often depicted the mountain Kwaio as unchanging and somehow 'purer' than other Malaitans, when they too had been influenced by change. All of this points to the amount of change that has occurred over the last century, but nonetheless shows that missionaries were struggling to understand Malaitan cosmology, albeit for the purpose of religious conversion.[24]

Codrington also stressed the existing power of prayer. Prayer was nothing new to Malaitans. Prayers took particular forms, and at higher levels they were the province of *fataabu* (priests) and fixed in their recitation of ancestral names. Priests were usually the last to convert and often remained deliberately antagonistic to Christianity, which they saw as harmful, as undermining the powers of the spirits, and as a threat to their own personal power in their communities. There are early examples of Malaitan ancestral priests becoming leaders of Christian communities. For example, two Kwaio ancestral priests who worked in Queensland, Sam Farulate and Diakafu, returned home and introduced Christianity and schools in the 1900s. A later example shows that such conversions could be dangerous and cause mental problems. The British documented a classic case concerning my adopted father, Ishmael Itea in Fataleka in the late 1940s, who left the SSEM to be *fataabu* of his Rakwane descent group and ensure that sacrifices did not lapse. The British interpreted his distress at the time as mental instability, whereas his family's testimony is that he was

---

24 Burt 1988; 1990; 1994, 64–66; Keesing 1984; 1990b.

undergoing a traumatic experience by changing one religion for another.[25] This must have been a common occurrence in earlier conversions. Anyone could communicate with ancestors at a more quotidian level, including women and children, and this provided a broader foundation for grafting on Christian wording into prayers.

Codrington believed that Melanesians shared a universal sense of moral values of right and wrong, and a belief in an afterlife, which could be incorporated into the idea of judgement.[26] The Melanesian Mission was fairly flexible in its syncretism: they allowed separation of sexes during worship and maintained a respect for gender taboos, although people were encouraged to migrate from their inland hamlets to big coastal villages, and nuclear family concepts were advocated. The mission's priests prayed for the success of traditional activities in the same ways that *fataabu* did. Ivens, who knew Small Malaita well in the 1890s, was willing to bless porpoise drives and canoe houses and created new prayers to replace the ancestral versions, although he was generally condescending about Melanesians' thought processes and did not display the respect that Codrington did. Charles Fox, the greatest outsider/insider of them all, respected Solomon Islands religions. He spent an incredible 1902 to 1973 as a member of the Diocese of Melanesia, 11 of these years (1933–44) as a member of an indigenous religious order, the Melanesian Brotherhood (Ira Retatasiu).[27] Fox was enormously respected by other members of the mission for his intellect and writings. He was never based on Malaita, although he often visited there and spent many years on neighbouring Makira.[28] He seems to have achieved an immersion in and understanding of Pacific Islander cultures that can only be achieved after several decades. As with Codrington and Ivens, some of his understanding was gained through access to students on Norfolk Island, including some from Malaita. South Malaitans also had kinship links with Makira and often visited there.

---

25 BSIP 10/I/34/9 W.J. Marquand tour report, 21 Feb 1948; DC Michael James Forster report on Fataleka, Baegu, Kwara`ae, Aug 1948, with cover letter from J.D.A. Germond to D. Trench, 5 Sept 1948; 4/SF108, DC Forster tour reports, Dec 1948, Lau, Fataleka. Later, Itea closed the ancestral altar and returned to Christianity, this time to Seventh-day Adventism.
26 Hilliard 2005, 207–08.
27 Moore 2013c entry. Ivens' attitudes changed considerably over the years, and by the time he returned to Malaita to carry out research in the 1920s he showed more respect for Malaitans and their ways.
28 *Ibid.*

A Black Net with White Corks

The Melanesian Mission used a conversion concept initiated by Bishop George Selwyn: they persuaded adolescent males and some young women (most often wives) to leave their islands to be trained at mission schools, initially in New Zealand and then on Norfolk Island. Selwyn wanted to create a black net (the Islander teachers) supported by white corks (European mission staff), spread throughout the Pacific Islands. The edges of this net extended to the missions in Queensland and Fiji, which were incorporated into Anglican outreach and were in part subsidised by the Melanesian Mission during the 1890s.[29] Teaching combined evangelism, education and industrial skills, with the aim of returning young men to their villages to establish their own schools. This became a rite of passage, much like enlistment in the indentured labour trade, in which youths combined adventure with social betterment on their return home, alongside the added spiritual element. After two years, the students were returned to their homes for six months, and for their return trip to school they were allowed to bring the women to whom they were betrothed and to undergo baptism. If all went well, students remained for around eight years before returning home to plant Anglicanism in their own districts, assisted by visiting or resident European clergy. Tippett's criticism is correct: if there had been more direct involvement of resident European missionaries, the conversion process would have been quicker.

Although its clergy were dubbed 'God's gentlemen' because of their upper- or middle-class British origins, Melanesian Mission policy was that the students should never be asked to perform tasks that the European staff did not do also. While it was appreciated that the bishop and senior staff had other important tasks to perform, they, too, did their share of menial chores, which was intended to develop a spirit of equality.

---

29 'Report of the Melanesian Mission', *SCL*, Dec 1896, 11; 'The Melanesian Mission in Queensland', *SCL*, Mar 1897, 8.

Figure 4.1: St Andrew's College, Kohimarama, Auckland, New Zealand.
A small number of Malaitan students were there between 1862 and 1867.
Source: Courtesy of John Kinder Theological Library.

Bishop Patteson, consecrated as the foundational Anglican bishop of Melanesia in 1861, made his first visit to Malaita at Olaha on Small Malaita as a priest in 1856, although he made little contact with the people. In 1862, Patteson 'picked up two [Malaitan] lads out of a party of 36 in a grand war-canoe', although nothing more is known of them.[30] A year later, on another visit, Patteson is supposed to have persuaded a Malaitan bigman to accompany him to the Melanesian Mission's headquarters at St Andrew's College in Kohimarama, New Zealand.[31] The first converts for whom we have names were Joseph Wate`ae`pule (or Wate), Watehou and Sapibuana, all from Small Malaita, who joined Patteson in mid-1866 in similar circumstances and became part of Anglican history on Malaita.[32] During the Melanesian Mission's first 30 years on Malaita it concentrated its initial efforts on Small Malaita, and onwards from the 1900s in the north at Fiu on the west coast and Ngorefou in Lau Lagoon in the northeast. Outlying schools were established, first around Sa`a and then similarly around the other two centres, until schools were scattered along most of the coast. The *Southern Cross* (a series of ships used the name)[33]

---

30 'Solomon Island Sketches—Introductory', *SCL*, 14 May 1898, 6.
31 Mission Life 1869, 161, 170, records this visit. Also see H. Wallace Mort, letter to *Sydney Morning Herald*, 4 Sept 1900.
32 Fox 1958, 167.
33 Moore 2013c entry.

plied back and forth between Norfolk Island and all of the islands in the mission's net, visiting Malaita on average twice a year. The rest of the sea transport was provided by whaleboats with sails, which as often as not had to be rowed when winds were low or blew from contrary directions. The Melanesian Mission regarded Malaita as 'their island' and grumbled when the QKM and the Catholics began missionary work there as well. While Malu`u, Kwai and Ngongosila and Onepusu eventually became important QKM-SSEM centres, during the late 1890s and early 1900s the Melanesian Mission kept a watching brief over activities at these centres as well, even though Christians based there were trained by the QKM in Queensland. As Bishop Wilson arrogantly explained in 1906:

> Teachers in these schools were not taught in the Church Missions in Queensland, and we cannot complain if they have returned to a form of Christianity which more resembles that of their fathers in Christ than ours does.[34]

Between 1877 and 1909, the Melanesian Mission opened 20 bases on Malaita. Nine were on Small Malaita: at Sa`a, Walade, Alu, Pwaloto, Roas, Pou, Palasu`u, Pululahu and Rokera (Ariel Harbour). Another six operated in northwest Malaita: at Fiu, Foate, Kwarea (Fauaabu in Coleridge Bay), Laulana, Bita`ama and on Maana`oba. There were also three in northeast Malaita, at `Ataa, Ngorefou and Fouia, and one in central east Malaita at Uru.

The missions obviously had a different purpose than the traders, but there were also similarities. As noted in Chapter 2, Malaita had no resident traders to match those already established in other areas of the Solomons. Missions gave away trade goods, or swapped them for services and favours, a form of exchange that would have been recognised by Malaitans. Missions also established small trade stores. The Melanesian Mission's recruiting process had similarities with labour recruiting. For instance, an axe, three boxes of fish hooks, 30 sticks of tobacco and 12 clay pipes was the necessary price to achieve the release of Kwaifunu from Small Malaita in 1900 to join St Barnabas College on Norfolk Island.[35] Participation in the labour trade generated similar beach bonus gifts. Walter Ivens described the method in the same year when six youths left Malaita for Norfolk Island:

---

34 Wilson, 'The Bishop's Visitation, 1905', *SCL*, Mar 1906, 5.
35 'The First Voyage', *SCL*, Jan 1901, 109–10.

None seemed to have the slightest difficulty in leaving their homes, and none of them, as far as I could see, said 'good-bye', or anything like it. Their fathers or their chiefs seemed quite pleased to have an axe in exchange for them. They had no luggage whatever. If they had beads round their necks, such valuables were not allowed to leave the island, the string being untied and appropriated by the boy's father or friends. They came naked enough into their new world, but they had great expectations and were happy in them.[36]

Figure 4.2: The Melanesian Mission school at Uru, east Malaita, 1906.
Source: Beattie Collection, 516.

36 *SCL*, Aug 1900, 41.

The *Southern Cross Log* is full of similar accounts in which boys and youths appear to be given casually to the mission to take to Norfolk Island. The same removal of all ornaments occurred when recruits joined the labour trade. The reason for this is unclear. Most Malaitan ornaments are secular not religious. It may be that the ornaments belonged to their descent groups, not to them personally, and that to take them to a faraway workplace meant they might never be seen again. Europeans at the time noticed the practice and presumed that this temporarily freed them from their religious beliefs, or at least from observing taboos.

Not all became Christians. Some returned home after the two years away (similar to the length of labour contracts), sometimes staying for just a short while before taking the next opportunity to leave again, either on a labour trade schooner or a mission ship. Others seem to have enjoyed their adventure, but then blended back into village life. This method of Christian conversion and training was often a slow process. It took many years to establish a foothold on any island, although in the long run it created a stable indigenous clergy and lay community. The Melanesian Mission was funded by donations gathered in New Zealand, Australia and Britain. In the 1890s, the mission began an 'adopt an island', and 'adopt a scholar' plan, not unlike the 'adopt an African orphan' schemes that operate today. Quaintly, the designated 'chief' of Malaita in 1898 was Mrs Harris of Winton, in Bournemouth, England.[37]

The Anglican *modus operandi* closely resembled that of the QKM-SSEM: both missions radiated out from three major nodes to smaller stations. Both relied on using former labourers who had become Christian in Queensland and Fiji. While some Melanesian Mission leaders, like Joseph Wate at Sa'a, did not have plantation origins, they too relied on ex-labourers for extending Christian outreach.

---

37 'List of "Islands" and their "Chiefs"', *SCL*, 15 June 1898, 31.

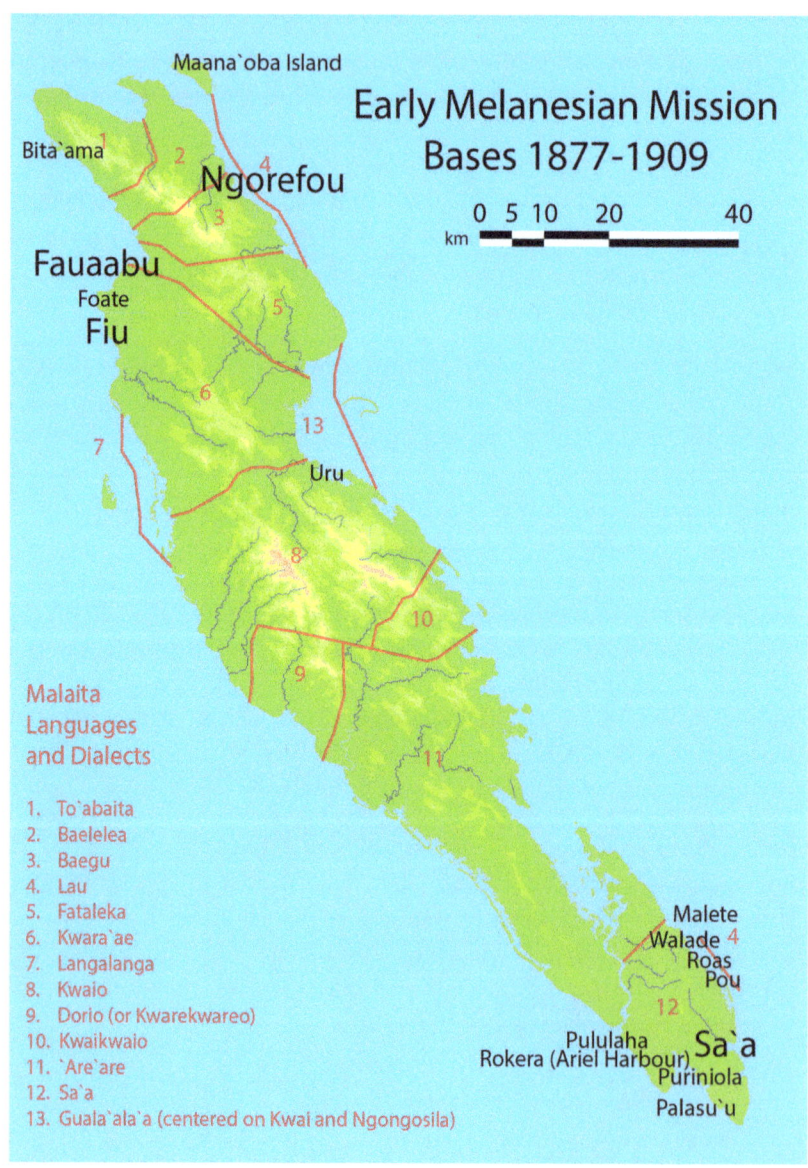

Map 12: Early Melanesian Mission bases, 1877–1909.
Source: Courtesy of Vincent Verheyen.

Sa'a and Small Malaita

Joseph Wate'ae'pule (or Wate), born on Small Malaita around 1854, was the first Christian leader on Malaita. He was 'recruited' by Bishop Patteson from his village on Small Malaita in 1866 to be educated in New Zealand, where he befriended Rev. Joseph Atkin, who became his godfather. Able to return home briefly in 1870, Wate was on the *Southern Cross* when Patteson was killed in 1871 at Nukapu, an atoll in the Reef Islands.[38]

When Bishop George Selwyn visited Malaita in 1857 he was met by a group of 100 Malaitan men. On his next voyage he touched at Oloha on the south coast and persuaded a local man to come back with him to New Zealand. This was a disaster since the man became disturbed; he had to be tied up for the safety of everyone on board and returned quickly to his home.[39] In 1876, Rev. John Still spent a week on Malaita, and Bishop John Selwyn spent time there in 1878, presumably both based at Sa'a.[40] In 1877, Wate and his wife were returned to Sa'a to begin Malaita's first Christian mission. Wate's early years were full of difficulty. His Christian wife died and he took a non-Christian wife, Waikeni, which caused him to be placed under mission discipline, unable to continue to operate the school. In 1881, Rev. Robert Codrington paid Wate a short visit, after which there was no further contact from the mission until 1883 when Wate visited Ulawa. In 1884, he was restored to Christianity by Rev. Richard Comins and began the school again. The school, ritually cursed by Doraweewee, a local leader, struggled on for another two years. Then Wate went back to Norfolk Island, and from there to the Melanesian Mission's base on Ulawa until Doraweewee died in 1890. He did travel back to Malaita during this time; we know he accompanied HMS *Raven* to Maana'oba Island off the northeast coast in 1889 to investigate disturbances related to the labour trade.[41] During his final days, Doraweewee softened his opposition and requested Wate to return to Sa'a, which he did, but Wate faced further trouble when a party of

---

38 The standard interpretation is that Patteson's killing was retaliation for the alleged kidnapping of five Nukapu men by labour traders. However, the most recent interpretation by Kolshus and Hovghaugen 2010 argues that the Melanesian Mission by demanding that men leave to attend their school on Norfolk Island was straining the limited human resources on the atoll.
39 Montgomery 1896, 177.
40 Mort to editor, *Sydney Morning Herald*, 4 Sept 1900.
41 Capt. G.W. Hand, HMS *Royalist* to CC, RNAS, 6 July 1889, 'Australia Station, New Guinea and Solomon Islands', 1889, 6, original copy in author's possession.

Malaitan men from Maramasike Passage killed Uki Island trader Fred Howard in 1893. Britain sent HMS *Royalist* to punish the murderers, and Andrew Dora, Stephen Tara and others from the Sa`a mission helped them. The Malaitan perpetrators of Howard's death retaliated by attacking the school.[42] For several years, Wate and other Christians remained targets for *ramo* assassins.

Comins was worried and conscious that nearby villages could muster 150 to 200 Snider rifles to make an attack. Sensibly, he provided a dozen old rifles and ammunition for the use of mission staff.[43] Then he went to befriend Faka`ia, a powerful young bigman at nearby Walade, whose sister had been away on Norfolk Island for the previous two-and-a-half years and was engaged to Luke Masuraa, Wate's assistant. Faka`ia, although he initially refused to join the mission and would not help it in its early years, was a key person in negotiations to quiet the threats. After Faka`ia made a trip to Norfolk Island, he became more interested and by mid-1896 was under religious instruction. Baptised in 1902, he became a strong supporter, which provided the Anglicans with an entrée to Walade and also Lau Lagoon.[44] When Bishop Cecil Wilson visited Sa`a in late 1894, 120 men, women and children were at the school. The *Southern Cross* picked up two new students at Roas and at Port Adam teachers Oiu and Samo were making good progress, although there was no school building. That year, the Melanesian Mission claimed 78 baptised and five confirmed Christians on Malaita, along with another 240 under instruction by 16 teachers at three schools.[45] By the time Wilson ordained Wate as a deacon in 1897, eight schools had been established in his neighbourhood and 49 people had been baptised during the previous year. Johnson Telegsem from Mota Lava Island in the Banks Group was the teacher at Port Adam. Wate returned to Norfolk Island in 1902 to prepare for his ordination as a priest and to receive treatment for a long-standing cancer on his jaw. He died back at Sa`a in 1904.[46]

---

42 Wate to J.S. Bishop, 17 Oct 1893, *OPMM*, Mar 1894, 56.
43 Wilson, 5 Sept 1896, *OPMM*, Christmas 1896, 237; Ivens, 'Ulawa and Mala', *SCL*, 16 Jan 1899, 31; *OPMM*, Mar 1894, 49.
44 The Ballarat *Churchman*, reproduced in *OPMM*, Mar 1896, 200. Also see Ivens, 'Ulawa and Mala', *SCL*, Mar 1902, 44.
45 Wilson, 'Island Voyage, 1894, First Part: The Bishop's Report', *OPMM*, Aug 1895, 132, 134.
46 Fox 1958, 167–68; 'The First Voyage, 1897', *SCL*, July 1897, 3.

Figure 4.3: Clement Marau and Joseph Wate`ae`pule in about 1890.
Both were taken to Norfolk Island for training in the 1860s. Marau, from Merelava Island in the Banks Group, began work on Ulawa in 1877, at the same time as Wate`ae`pule returned to Sa`a. They were good friends and colleagues.
Source: British Museum, neg. AN00566781002.

New Zealander Walter Ivens was the first Melanesian Mission clergyman to spend a lengthy period on Malaita. He could never have succeeded without the groundwork laid by Wate and other former students of St Barnabas College and teachers trained in Queensland and Fiji. Ivens was the priest in charge of Ulawa and Small Malaita from 1895 to 1909. He translated the New Testament into the Lau, Sa`a and Ulawa languages, and later wrote two famous books, one about the people of Small Malaita and the other about lagoon-dwellers, mainly those of Lau.[47] On 3 August 1896, when he established his base at Sa`a, Ivens was the only European resident on Malaita. His first Sa`a home was a screened-off corner of a men's sacred house. These early missionaries were hardy and capable of feats of endurance. For example, when the *Southern Cross* reached Ulawa in late 1896, Ivens was on Small Malaita; he received a message and set out immediately at night with his staff to row to Ulawa, over 50 kilometres away. During his Ulawa-Small Malaita years he shuttled back and forth, relying on Wate to run the Sa`a mission, which he visited regularly. Nevertheless, despite their early start, the Anglicans made less progress on Malaita than might have been expected.

Sa`a was an excellent regional base because it allowed easy support from the Anglican missions on Ulawa and Makira, and linked to the `Are`are people who lived in the southern part of the main island and along both sides of Maramasike Passage. As well, the Lau of the northeast made regular voyages to visit their kin at Walade, further north on the east coast of Small Malaita.[48] The Lau language was used at Walade and the mission soon realised that Walade was the backdoor entry point to Lau Lagoon, with supportive links to Kwai and Ngongosila on the east Kwara`ae coast, where people spoke Guala`ala`a, which was also widely employed as a trade language.

Six weeks after he arrived, Ivens wrote a report on his Small Malaita district. There were six schools, he said, the most northerly at Kwore in the hills a few kilometres north of Port Adam, the home village of Leo and Farapo, and Lizzie Siakulu (also called Liakulu) from Walade. Siakulu was married to Johnson Telegsem from Mota Lava Island, who was in charge of establishing a school at Roas where there was a commodious bay.

---

47   Ivens, 1927; 1930.
48   Ivens, 'Ulawa and Mala', *SCL*, 16 Jan 1899, 31.

Ivens used interpreters and tried to learn local languages. He planned to spend six months at Roas since he found the passage at Sa`a difficult to enter when the winds were high.[49]

A year after Ivens began working on Malaita the Anglicans claimed to have achieved 300 baptisms and 20 confirmations, with 450 more under instruction. Ivens and Wate were being assisted by 20 teachers at six villages.[50] In 1899, they supplied the following statistics: baptisms (5); marriages (2); celebrations of Holy Communion (3); number of Christians (316); number of confirmed Christians (22); number of teachers (28); under instruction (718); schools (9).[51] The Sa`a mission spread first via a series of schools along the east coast. There was no early church building at Sa`a because the people lived in scattered hamlets, although in 1904 there were 200 Christians there.[52] Some ex-Queensland men were among the teachers sent to Pwalato, to upper and lower Roas and to Pou, up in the hills. Another school had begun on the west coast, the first on that side of Small Malaita, north of Cape Zélée near Palasu`u.[53] The wide spread of the Sa`a mission schools was considered an advantage. Wate was forced to move from Sa`a to Roas for a time because one local bigman was antagonistic, then Wate found himself supported by another bigman who moved his bush village down to the new mission base to protect it. In late 1899 the *Southern Cross* made a visit to drop off Johnson Telegsem, who was returning to Roas with his wife Lizzie Siakulu and their boy Stephen, and they found the whole village was about to convert. The people were awaiting the return of Ivens, when it was expected that 80 people would be baptised. James Iumane, trained at Norfolk Island, was the teacher in charge of Pwalato, where other baptismal candidates were under instruction. Ivens noted that because he could not have personal knowledge of all of the candidates he had to trust the decisions of his teachers and Wate.[54]

---

49 Ivens to E.S. Buchanan, 28 Sept 1896, *OPMM*, Mar 1897, 279.
50 Wilson, 5 Sept 1896, *OPMM*, Christmas 1896, 237; *SCL*, Dec 1896, Supplement; 'The First Voyage, 1897', *SCL*, July 1897, 3–4; Statistics of the Diocese of Melanesia for the Year 1897', *SCL*, 15 June 1898, 9.
51 Ivens, 'Ulawa and Mala', *SCL*, Jan 1899, 30–32.
52 Ivens, 'Ulawa and Mala', *SCL*, Apr 1904, 19.
53 Ivens, 'Ulawa and Mala', *SCL*, Jan 1899, 30–32.
54 Wilson, 'The Second Island Voyage, 1899', *SCL*, 15 Jan 1900, 9; 'Solomon Islands', *SCL*, 15 Feb 1900, 27; 'An Open-air Baptism in Mala', *SCL*, 15 May 1900, 9–10.

Progress on Small Malaita was steady. The policy was to radiate out from Sa`a, confining the mission to the island, although the Walade links with Lau were also fostered. Ivens was away for 15 months in 1899–1900. On his return, he set to with new energy: there were 310 baptisms in 1900 alone, and even some of the old *ramo*, such as Kwaihaodowala, had begun to attend the schools. Progress was being made in inland areas, where there were new schools. Tehena, whose sister was married to Joe Wate, had come down with his family to Sa`a school for a year and then gone back to his inland village high on a mountain spine above the Waloaa River. Ivens visited Tehena's small school there, returning with a boy to take to Norfolk Island for education. By 1902, 650 baptisms had been held on Small Malaita.[55]

Ivens was away in England for 12 months beginning in late 1903.[56] In 1904, a new school was begun at Pululahu on the west coast, and in that year the Sa`a mission decided to try to raise more funds by planting coconut groves at every village school. Coconut palms already grew in small numbers around the coast. Professional photographer John W. Beattie, from Tasmania, who travelled to Malaita on the *Southern Cross* in October 1906, and to whom we owe the best early images from the island, recorded that at Roas Bay and Port Adam the shores were 'fringed very largely with coconut palms'.[57]

In 1905, Bishop Wilson spent some time in charge of the Ulawa and Small Malaita missions while Ivens was on leave. The bishop had to minister to 200 villagers at Sa`a, contend with the usual run of disturbances and balance new customs with old. Trouble occurred after an important leader died and received a Christian burial. His Maramasike Passage kin were enraged, saying that he had been buried 'like a dog' rather than by the traditional method of placing his body in 'some elevated position, on a tree or poles, with all the dead man's shell rings and valuables hung around him'.[58] They destroyed Sa`a's gardens and killed pigs, and threatened to take a human life. Outside of Sa`a, the main mission centre

---

55   'The First Voyage, 1900', *SCL*, Jan 1901, 108; Ivens, 'Ulawa and Mala', *SCL*, June 1901, 54; Ivens, 'Inland in Mala', *SCL*, July 1901, 73–74; *SCL*, Apr 1902, 2; Ivens, 'A Bush School', *SCL*, Dec 1902, 81–85; Awdry 1902, 98.
56   'Norfolk Island Notes', *SCL*, Dec 1904, 1.
57   Beattie 1906, 23–24; Ivens 1930, 21; 'Ulawa and Mala', *SCL*, Apr 1904, 18.
58   Wilson, 'N. E. Mala', *SCL*, Apr 1906, 37; for images of this mortuary practice, see Coppet and Zemp 1978, 28–30.

was at Roas Bay, 18 kilometres away, where there were five schools, and more were being established in inland areas. The inland leader Horou requested a school, as did Sueka, from the small artificial islet of Malete.

By 1907, Small Malaita's mission bases had expanded considerably. More permanent churches were being built, many from coral rock, and schools had been established in the hills at Naoniola, at Tawaniahia in Ariel Harbour in the west, and at Walade. Eighty people were attending the Naoniola school, 40 of them already baptised. At Tawaniahia, 60 attended prayers and 20 were ready for baptism. Although Ivens said the Walade people had a bad name for causing disturbances, they had now become Christians. The Tawaniahia people were part of the `Are`are language group, providing the mission with an entrée into the southern section of the main island and to Maramasike Passage. Their conversion, Ivens hoped, would allow expansion of Anglican activities as far north as Onepusu in the west (by then an SSEM outpost) and `Oloburi (Double Bay) in the east. The Melanesian Mission was aware that the SSEM was also moving into Small Malaita; in December 1907 they had landed two teachers at Pau, with others already at Su`upaina, close to the Melanesian Mission school at Puriniola on the west coast.[59]

Ivens was replaced in 1910 by Walter H. Sage until 1913.[60] Sage left most of the Ulawa work to Solomon Islands teachers Martin Marau and Paul Marita[61] and concentrated his efforts on Small Malaita. The foundations laid by Wate and Ivens bore fruit for the Anglicans. As also occurred in north Malaita, several early mission leaders in the south became clergy. Joe Leo and James Upwe were ordained as priests in 1924, although Leo died soon after. Upwe had been a deacon since 1921 and after Rev. Andrew Thompson (who replaced Sage) left he was able to take over the Small Malaitan ministry. Even while suffering from elephantiasis, he carried on his work until his death in 1934. Two priests in the 1930s also extended the work of the church. Willie Wate, son of Joe Wate, was

---

59 Ivens, 'South-East Mala', *SCL*, Apr 1908, Supplement, 58b-c.
60 Charles Sage, brother of Walter, helped establish the mission in north Malaita in 1907, but was drowned in 1913, at which time Walter left for missionary work in India.
61 Martin Marau was the son of Clement Marau, an early Anglican mission teacher from Melav in the Banks Group and Susie from Ulawa. He was educated at Melanesian Mission's St Barnabas College on Norfolk Island, ordained a deacon in 1920 and a priest in 1924. In 1918 he was put in charge of the Ulawa mission, a position he maintained for the next 24 years. In his youth he was a great teacher, but always in the shadow of his father. His wife Lucy died in 1936, and soon after he suffered declining health, gradually going blind. He died in 1942. Paul Marita was the first Christian on Ulawa. Ordained in 1921, he was trained at Norfolk Island and Siota, Gela, and was in charge of the Makira church in the 1920s. He died at Pawa in 1931. Fox 1958, 161, 166.

ordained in 1934 and John Maesiola was ordained the next year and eventually replaced Upwe. Willie Maruraa, first a Melanesian Brother and then from 1942 a priest, became the most influential representative of the Melanesian Mission in southern Malaita during the 1940s and 1950s.[62]

The southern end of Big Malaita, and Small Malaita, never carried as heavy a population as the central and northern areas where two-thirds of the people lived. Despite these early advances on Small Malaita, the Melanesian Mission was much slower to establish itself in the central and northern areas, where they relied for initial progress on the help of labourers returning from Queensland and Fiji, and were spurred on by the ever-growing QKM-SSEM presence.

Fiu and Northwest Malaita

Fiu, in west Kwara`ae north of `Aoke, was the first Anglican base in north Malaita, and today it is the site of Christ the King Cathedral. Fiu began in much humbler circumstances as a market place. The Anglicans chose this established meeting place as a mission base because it allowed them access to inland and coastal villages along the northwest coast. Anglican progress on the west coast had been slow until late in the 1890s. In 1885, Rev. Alfred Penny had induced Langasia from Alite Island in the Langalanga Lagoon to go to Norfolk Island for training. He spent two years there but, as was the practice, he was not baptised. Langasia returned home in 1902. When missionaries later inquired about him they were told, 'Too much book kill him'.[63] For the next 16 years, although a stream of likely lads left Small Malaita, no more students left Malaita's west coast. When Charles Woodford arrived at Fiu in June 1896 it was 'only a large river mouth with a beach where the saltwater people assemble every six days to hold market with bushmen'.[64] He recognised it, along with `Aoke, as a regular meeting place.

Malaitans returning home from Queensland and Fiji often joined the schools or attempted to begin their own, and they constantly asked the Melanesian Mission to open more.[65] Bishop Wilson credited the opening of north Malaita to the arrival of Anglican Malaitans from Fiji,

---

62 Fox 1958, 170.
63 Comins, 'The Vaukolo of 1902', *SCL*, Oct 1902, 60.
64 Woodford 1896, 16, 17 July.
65 'The First Voyage, 1897', *SCL*, July 1897, 4.

who provided the necessary Christian nucleus. The first 16 Christians at Fiu arrived in 1898 on the Fijian recruiting vessel *Rotuma*. Some had been confirmed while in Fiji.[66] Late the next year Bishop Wilson arrived on the *Southern Cross*, and reported that the group were well settled in a clean, neat village where they grew sugarcane and other plants they had brought from Fiji.

> Some fifteen or more natives dressed in Fiji style, had returned from the labour-field and settled here. The chief was one of them. They were all Christians trained by Mr. Jones, one of the English clergy until lately in Fiji. They were building a church, and they intended, when it was done, to lay out a cricket ground. The only thing they asked for or seemed to want was a cricket-ball, and they wanted that badly.[67]

In 1899, the Melanesian Mission sent Arthur Aka`ako, supported by two Mota Lava Island teachers from the New Hebrides, Joe Gilvete and Barnabas Serbas, to help the ex-Fiji Christians to open a school at Fiu.[68] The next year, when Ivens made his first trip around Malaita in a whaleboat, he found the ex-Fiji men attempting to convert some of the inland villagers. In 1901, two of these men were sent to Norfolk Island for training.[69]

Although Ivens wanted to install a European priest in the community, in 1902 he found a layman instead. Thomas A. Williams lasted a year, living in a small local-style house until he was evacuated ill from fever, his place in the history of Malaita secure because he walked from Fiu across Malaita to visit the `Ataa Christian community, the first European to cross the island.[70] Once Rev. Arthur Hopkins established his base at Ngorefou in Lau Lagoon on the opposite side of the island in 1902, he was able also to supervise the Fiu mission, visiting regularly, often when he was on his way to Siota or Tulagi. By 1903, the Anglicans claimed there were 100 Christians at Fiu and that Pijin English was in widespread use. The main teacher was Charles Turu, a former Fiji labourer who had trained at Norfolk Island. He was assisted by Gilvete and Serbas, whom Hopkins later replaced with two men from Gela.[71]

---

66 *SCL*, July 1900, 26.
67 Wilson, 'The Second Island Voyage, 1899', *SCL*, 15 Nov 1899, 5.
68 'Solomon Islands', *SCL*, 15 Feb 1900, 27; Ivens, 'Ulawa and Mala', *SCL*, 15 Jan 1899, 32.
69 Ivens, 'Kalilana Mala (The Rounding of Mala)', *SCL*, 14 July 1900, 26; Ivens, 'Mala and Ulawa', *SCL*, Feb 1901, 137; Ivens, 'Ulawa and Mala', *SCL*, June 1901, 55.
70 Fox, 1954–56, 10.
71 Hopkins, 'District of N. Mala', *SCL*, Apr 1904, 26; Sinker 1900, 27; Wilson 1915, 52.

From Fiu, the Melanesian Mission made forays south to Langalanga Lagoon. At Kwarea, a Fiu man was trying to begin a school, and when Hopkins visited `Aoke in 1903 he found that Buai, a local bigman who earlier had been against all mission settlements in his area, had mellowed and promised to abandon his opposition. There was a substantial population on `Aoke Island and on the coast nearby, which Hopkins hoped might one day become a mission base. At Laulana, further south in the lagoon, two Fiu Christians were clearing land for a school. Hopkins arranged for support to be sent from Fiu in the form of Joe Noranga. In the far south he met Billy, an important bigman who had been to Queensland and whom Hopkins described as 'a gentleman of very shady repute'.[72]

Figure 4.4: The new church built at Fiu, 1904.
The zig-zag patterned gable is typical of a traditional men's sacred house. Fiu was one of the most successful Christian settlements on Malaita.
Source: Beattie 1906, 549, courtesy of the British Museum.

In 1904, a church had been built and services were being held in the Kwara`ae language. Fiu had now become a centre of refuge for local women and children and for returned labourers. But the close connections

---

72   Hopkins, 'District of N. Mala', *SCL*, Apr 1904, 26.

with the surrounding people also caused problems and inland people had been harassing the station for months. The troubles began after one man attending a school took an inland woman as his wife without paying bridewealth. Her family arrived seeking compensation and caused friction by seizing far more than their due. Then a boy who had been given to the mission for education died, and his descent group demand a death in compensation. The result was that in September Arthur Aka`ako was killed while fishing and James Ivo narrowly escaped, badly wounded. A dozen men from a neighbouring village had come up to the pair in a friendly manner, sharing food, and suddenly shot both men several times. Hopkins was sent for from Ngorefou and by chance the *Southern Cross* arrived soon after and took the witnesses across to Tulagi to report the attack to Woodford, who agreed to supply a Fiu man whom he knew with a rifle and authority as a quasi-policeman. Fiu mission had no firearms, which created difficulties when they were faced by belligerent bush people carrying Snider rifles. However, some of the local men made it their business to protect the mission.[73]

When Florence Young from the QKM visited the Fiu mission in 1904, she counted 32 children in the Sunday school and a large congregation at the service, which was conducted in Kwara`ae, Pijin Fijian and the Gela language, with translations. She was met by George Maitafu (whom she knew from Knockroe plantation in the Isis district, inland from Bundaberg), Thomas Osiskalo (recently returned from Queensland with Maitafu on *Sydney Belle*), Charley Grae, Arthur Aka`ako and others who had become Christians in Queensland. Grae had spent two years at school at Norfolk Island, from where he was sent to Fiu to assist Aka`ako. Young reported that the two Gela men took all of the services. In 1907, when the SSEM's new ship the *Evangel* called at Fiu, the visitors reported only 15 Christians, although this may indicate rivalry more than accuracy.[74]

At Fiu in 1907 there were 28 adult baptisms and eight weddings, and plans were underway to move the settlement across the river to a healthier area. The surrounding bush people were still causing problems: they pilfered from gardens, stole pigs and threatened to raid and kill selected targets. Hopkins had been in Queensland recruiting men to settle at Fiu. He arrived back with 20 men and the promise that Charles Sage (brother of Small Malaita missionary Walter Sage) from the Selwyn

---

73 *Ibid.*; 'The Log of the Second Voyage, 1904', *SCL*, Mar 1905, 8.
74 Young diary, 11 Apr 1904, *NIV*, 1902–03, 6; Deck diary, *NIV*, 1906–07, 22.

Mission at Mackay would join them to begin a new school on the coast near ʻAoke Island at the north of Langalanga Lagoon.[75] Hopkins had toured Queensland's sugar coast, with scant success, he said, due to the wide spread of Malaitans in the colony. In his travels he discovered that the Pioneer Valley at Mackay had the highest proportion of Malaitans, whereas at Geraldton (Innisfail) most the Anglicans were from the Banks and Torres groups and Omba Island. New Hebrideans were the dominant group at Bundaberg, along with men from Gela.[76] Hopkins had hoped to bring more Mackay Malaitans back with him, but at the last minute many of them decided to stay in Queensland.[77] He regarded his trip as a failure and lamented that he had not gone six months or a year earlier, when all of the Malaitans at the Selwyn Mission might have moved *en masse*. Those that did come were ill-prepared. Far from ideal colonists and often difficult, they brought no tools, had few possessions, and lamented that the amenities of Queensland were unavailable on Malaita.[78] Twelve 'returns' refused to enter the church and preferred to meet separately for hymn-singing and extemporary prayer. They were used to services in Pijin English and obviously felt themselves to be above attending services conducted in the Kwaraʻae or Gela languages. Yet Hopkins's trip did have some success since it brought Charles Sage to Malaita in June, the perfect candidate for the post. He had worked previously for the Anglican New Guinea Mission (1898–1904) before his stint at Mackay's Selwyn Mission.[79]

Fiu's first 'daughter' schools were at Kwarea and Laulana, and then another was founded at Foate. Others followed at Gwauʻulu, Manofiu and Airo. Kwarea was on the border between northern Kwaraʻae and Fataleka languages areas, in the centre of a large population. Beginning in 1903, Billy Inimanu from Fiu lived there for 18 months trying to form a school. He closed his first school and had to shelter with Konai, a local bigman, when a friend was murdered and his own life was threatened. For safety, life was lived behind stockades. Both Inimanu and his friend had been trained at Mary Robinson's Selwyn Mission at Mackay. In August 1904, Konai went to Fiu to arrange for another school to begin, and was offered

---

75   Hopkins, 'North Mala District', *SCL*, Apr 1907, 160.
76   Hopkins, 'A Letter from Queensland', *SCL*, Mar 1907, 114; Cecil Wilson, 'General Report of the Melanesian Mission for 1907', *SCL*, Apr 1908, Supplement, 8.
77   Wilson, 'General Report of the Melanesian Mission for 1907', *SCL*, Apr 1908, Supplement, 33; Langmore 1989, 129, 299, 300.
78   Hopkins, 'North Mala', *SCL*, Apr 1908, Supplement, 33.
79   *Ibid.*

land. The next year, once more it was former Selwyn Mission students who took up the challenge when Joseph Baramula and Joe Minata accepted the difficult post. The area had a large population and there was considerable unrest, which enabled the school to become a place of refuge.

> They cannot work their gardens, and sleep at night packed together in one small enclosure. The last attack was in October [1905]: the bush men tried to get to them from the sea with ladders; fired into a house full of people, but hit nobody. A man from Qaqae [Kwakwai] rushed out alone, threw down the ladders, and shot three men in the water …[80]

In 1907, the Kwarea mission moved to nearby Maanaere. Baramula, 'a big, cheery fellow',[81] was doing well because he led by persuasion rather than scolding, the latter being a common fault among mission teachers. He had also ensured his future by becoming betrothed to a daughter of Konai, although she died soon after. When Ellen Wilson visited with her husband on the *Southern Cross* a year or so later, a fine church was under construction, with a plaited, zig-zag patterned gable typical of Malaitan men's houses. Fifty candidates were ready for baptism.[82] Further north, another school opened at Airo, near Bita`ama—an out-movement from a failed Bita`ama school.

When Hopkins returned from Queensland, he was dismayed to learn that a party of 14, led by Tom Basitaloa, had left Fiu to begin a school at Bita`ama at the top of northwest Malaita. They were quickly repulsed from this stronghold of ancestral religion because it was thought that their presence would interfere with the annual porpoise drives.[83] Basitaloa, who hoped that an important local man was about to return from Queensland to support his school, had built a house and planted extensive gardens.[84] The bush people plundered these and threatened the new Christian outpost. Some of the colonists scattered, others moved a few kilometres further north and Basitaloa was soon left with only one assistant. Another expansion, to Kwailabesi, a few kilometres from Fiu, also proved calamitous when inland people burnt down their houses. The group scattered to

---

80 Hopkins, 'North Mala Report, 1905', *SCL*, May 1906, 9.
81 *Ibid*.
82 Wilson 1915, 53.
83 Several decades later, Bishop Leonard Alafurai, himself from Lau Lagoon, harnessed Christian power when he blessed the special stones and the canoes used for the drive. *BSIP News Sheet*, 31 Aug 1968.
84 Hopkins, 'North Mala District', *SCL*, Apr 1907, 159; Hopkins, 'North Mala', *SCL*, Apr 1908, Supplement, 37.

Kwarea and back to their kin groups. The Melanesian Mission also came into direct confrontation with the SSEM, which had a school nearby, enabling them to block the Anglican advance. The other new site was at Dala, north of Fiu (later an agricultural station) and run by Sage. Despite the inauspicious beginnings, within a few years permanent Melanesian Mission schools had been started at Bita`ama and on Maana`oba Island, both well inside territory that the SSEM had claimed as their own.

At Laulana in 1904, two Fiu Christians had begun a school on their own land, with six students.[85] Always feeble, the school collapsed the next year and the remnant moved to Fiu. After failing at Kwarea, Billy Inimanu began a new school at Foate, 8 kilometres from Fiu. Progress was slow since he lacked the support of a trained teacher.[86] Nothing much changed there over several years until, in 1908, the SSEM claimed success at Laulana through three teachers moved in from Malu`u.[87]

Lau Lagoon and Northeast Malaita

When Walter Ivens visited Lau Lagoon in 1900 he described the villages built on the artificial islands and the process of island-building. Coral rock was taken out to shallow areas of the lagoon on bamboo rafts, which were capsised, until a platform was constructed above high water level, then big logs were placed as supports on the outside, soil was brought in and houses built. Sulufou, the largest artificial island, had a population of 300–400 living on about half an acre (0.2 hectare). Except for the very smallest islets, which were usually occupied only by leading men, the islands were divided into three zones: areas for single men that included the sacred house; areas for families; and small isolation areas for women during menstruation and birth, usually built on small adjacent islets. Larger islands had two or three shade trees and 20 or 30 coconut palms. The smallest islets contained only a few palms and two or three houses. People raised log defences around islets to protect themselves from raids by the surrounding coastal people. The refuse from the houses slowly filled the gaps between the rocks, firming the structure. Fishing was the main

---

85 Hopkins, 'District of North Mala', *SCL*, Apr 1905, 28; Hopkins, 'Round Mala', *SCL*, Dec 1905, 3.
86 Hopkins, 'North Mala District', *SCL*, Apr 1907, 159.
87 Young, 'An Itinerary of a Journey Round Malaita', *NIV*, 1907–08, 17.

occupation, and nets were prized possessions protected and augmented by magic spells. Fish were also bartered to inland people. Ivens described a market scene:

> The people are fishermen, and though they have gardens up on the hills, yet they live mostly by netting fish inside the reefs and by bartering the fish for yams and taro with the bush people. Regular market days are held—one market that I saw was well worth seeing. Four canoes containing forty women and two men came with loads of fish. As they came ashore, the bush women flocked out, carrying yams, taro, and areca nuts, to barter for the cooked fish. There must have been nearly three hundred women and only about ten men.[88]

In 1894, Bishop Wilson tried to establish a mission base in Lau Lagoon and sought the support of Kwaisulia, the most powerful bigman in the lagoon (described in Chapter 2). The wily passage master said that he would wait until a European missionary was available. He said the same thing that year to Peter Abu`ofa, who had wanted to begin a QKM base in Lau Lagoon (see Chapter 5).[89] Five years later, Bishop Wilson described a scene in Lau Lagoon:

> In the front hall, as it were, of each house, was a pen of pigs; beyond them was the family. A crowd followed us. Every man I met said he was a chief, and wanted presents of hooks, etc. They took me all over their island, showing me the net-work of stone walls, which would be useful in case of attack; the men's quarter; the women's lying-in island, at a little distance off; the canoe-building shed, and everything else. We made friends, and came away as we had arrived, amidst the yells of the women. This strange little island was swept a year ago by a 'tidal-wave', which washed it clean, the people having previously escaped to the mainland.[90]

There were a few ex-Fiji Christians living at Ferasubua, and Ramofolo, the chief at Fuaga, was loud in his demands for a teacher. Ivens promised to do what he could, thinking to get a Norfolk Island-trained man from Port Adam or Sa`a.[91] In the late 1890s and early 1900s, several youths left Lau Lagoon to train on Norfolk Island: one left Uguka in 1898 and returned in 1900, and the same year Aniuli and Iroi left Fuaga, and Burinali left from Ferasubua.[92]

---

88 Ivens, 'A Visit to Mwala Paine', *SCL*, Dec 1902, 78–79.
89 Moore 2013a.
90 Wilson, 'The Second Island Voyage, 1899', *SCL*, 15 Nov 1899, 7.
91 Ivens, 'Kalilana Mala (The Rounding of Mala)', *SCL*, 15 June 1900, 20.
92 *SCL*, Aug 1900, 40–41.

The Anglicans were aware that the Walade people of east Small Malaita were one key to their future success in the northeastern lagoon. Walter Ivens wrote in 1901:

> The Port Adam [Walade] people occupy a very important position, since they really are natives of Surauna [Suraina], one of the little 'made-up' islets inside the reef at ʽAtaa, and the conversion of the two villages will have a salutary effect on the Apai Haha people—i.e., Westerners—who are constantly making visits to Port Adam in canoes.[93]

The Walade people still took their primary sacrifices back to the customary priests at ʽAtaa in the south of Lau Lagoon, which meant regular canoe traffic up and down the east coast.[94]

The first Anglican progress in Lau came at ʽAtaa Cove, where there were several fortified artificial islands: Waimasi, Suraina, Farere, Talioto, Lolowai and Bio. Suraina was the biggest at about half an acre (0.2 hectare) in extent with 250 inhabitants under chief Erringa.[95] When 15 of the ex-Fiji men from the *Rotuma* landed at ʽAtaa in 1898 (others having landed at Fiu), Kwaisulia came south and confiscated most of their belongings and threw their books and writing materials into the sea. His spurious reason was that they had not brought a letter of recommendation with them from any established mission. However, Rev. Comins knew this was Kwaisulia's common practice and had warned them to leave their books with him at the Siota mission at Gela.[96] One of them, James Dausuke, had been a student on Norfolk Island. He settled at Mangonia near ʽAtaa, where his chief, Ramofolo, allowed him to begin two schools. Another two former labourers, Frank Tamaia and Levi Lanaa, succeeded in establishing a short-lived school on the shore of ʽAtaa Cove, despite initial opposition from their chief and Kwaisulia. A year or so later, Tamaia was shot accidentally and suffered a lingering death. Lanaa decamped to the bush for safety. When Ivens visited Dausuke in 1901 he, rather unfairly, expressed disappointment that the teacher was not spending much time at his school.[97]

---

93 Ivens, 'Mala and Ulawa', *SCL*, Feb 1901, 136.
94 Wilson, 'S. E. Mala', *SCL*, Apr 1906, 37.
95 'The First Voyage', *SCL*, Jan 1901, 109.
96 'Peter Otoa', *SCL*, Oct 1895, 8–11; 'The Second Island Voyage, 1898: Return Journey', *SCL*, 15 Nov 1898, 3; *SCL*, 15 Dec 1898, 1; Comins, 'Siota', *SCL*, 16 Jan 1899, 5; Ivens, 'Ulawa and Mala', *SCL*, 16 Jan 1899, 32; Ivens, 'Kalilana Mala (The Rounding of Mala)', *SCL*, 14 Apr 1900, 1.
97 Wilson, 'The Second Island Voyage, 1899', *SCL*, 15 Nov 1899, 5; Ivens, 'Kalilana Mala (The Rounding of Mala)', *SCL*, 14 July 1900, 25.

In 1901, once Australia declared its intention to return home all Islander labourers, Woodford applied pressure to the Melanesian Mission to create a permanent base in north Malaita. While in Sydney, Woodford made his intentions clear:

> If the Melanesian Mission is not immediately prepared to put an experienced white man in charge of this part of Mala, I beg that you will inform me by first opportunity, because, in case of your refusal, the Wesleyan Mission will, I know, be prepared at once to undertake the duty.[98]

The Melanesian Mission knew that Abu`ofa's QKM base at Malu`u was growing in strength, and now faced the threat of the entry of the Wesleyan Methodist Mission, which was looking for a base in Solomon Islands. The answer came in 1902 when the Melanesian Mission sent Rev. Arthur Hopkins from Norfolk Island to Ngorefou. Hopkins secured a stronghold for the Anglicans in Lau, where he remained until 1914. Arguably, he became more powerful there than any influence from the government based in `Aoke. Hopkins's arrival deflected the Methodists to New Georgia, but did not slow the QKM. Thirty-three years old, Hopkins arrived in April on the *Southern Cross*, which anchored at `Ataa. Kai, a friendly local leader whose son had just returned from Norfolk Island, came aboard for the trip up to Ferasubua and then Ngorefou. They learnt that Amasia (mentioned in Chapter 2 as kidnapped in the 1870s) had begun a mission at Ngongosila Island, but then shifted to Lau where he was killed. Initially, Hopkins settled in Amasia's house at Ngorefou on the mainland near Ferasubua, welcomed by 10 returned labourers from Fiji and others from Queensland.[99] Soon after arrival, Hopkins and Ivens went to visit Kwaisulia at `Adagege. Hopkins, unable to comprehend Kwaisulia's place in Lau society, was condescending:

> We went to see one old humbug and ruffian named Qaisulia. He is a clever old rogue, who has made himself feared all round. In reality he has no more authority than any other chief; he owns just his own little island, but he had gained a great name, and poses as a 'King'. We were ushered into his canoe-house, and were bidden to wait … He appeared clad in a helmet, trousers, shirt (inside out), and a dirty blazer. Some labour-trade captain had given him these clothes.[100]

---

98 'Prospects', *SCL*, Apr 1902, 10.
99 Comins, 'First Voyage, 1902', *SCL*, Aug 1902, 33; Burt 2002.
100 Ivens, 'A Visit to Mwala Paine', *SCL*, Dec 1902, 79; Corris 1973a.

A few years later photographer John Beattie described 'Adagege:

> This island is about a ¼ acre in size, and has a population of 150 more or less. It is just crammed full of houses and people, reeking with smoke, pigs, dogs and filth. The alleys, were, as can be imagined, narrow, and few. Canoes seemed to be stuck all over the place.[101]

Figure 4.5: A food storage house at 'Adagege Island, Kwaisulia's stronghold in Lau Lagoon, 1906.
Source: Beattie 1906, 530.

Although relations with Kwaisulia were difficult, he was generally supportive and in 1903 used his powerful oratory to help Hopkins crush a resurgence of fighting among the Ferasubua people.[102] The missionaries formed better opinions of some of the other Lau bigmen:

> The Ferasubua chiefs constantly visited us, and kindly, courteous gentlemen they were! Their clothing was of the scantiest description. One old chap wore only a big straw hat, and a string of human teeth (his ancestors') round his neck. But I shall never forget their grace and courtesy of manner.[103]

---

101 Beattie 1906, 43.
102 Hopkins, 'District of N. Mala', *SCL*, Apr 1904, 27–28.
103 Ivens, 'A Visit to Mwala Paine', *SCL*, Dec 1902, 80.

A frail, thin man, weakened by illness in childhood, Hopkins weighed only 43 kilograms.[104] He had amazing stamina though, and exhibited bravery when faced with Malaitan aggression and knavery against the mission, which Malaitans interpreted as Christian spiritual power. Hopkins's first house was built up on logs with a stepladder that could be pulled up after him, for safety. In the early years, any mission settlement on Malaita was in danger and armed guards were necessary even to bathe in a nearby stream. Initially, Hopkins was guarded day and night and never allowed to walk about alone. He described the demeanour of the Lau people during his first year:

> The general atmosphere was unpleasantly excited and disturbed. There were rumours of attacks and some real attempts were made. A war party of the men succeeded in getting into the village at dusk, with the hope of picking someone off, but a strong party came up from the friendly island of Fera Subua and overawed them …[105]

Later in 1902, Woodford ordered Hopkins to evacuate to Siota because a British Navy ship was due to punish previous attacks on labour trade vessels. The naval visit took so long to eventuate that Hopkins went back to Norfolk Island until April 1903. The people built a school house in expectation of his return.[106]

Progress was quicker once a permanent presence was established. The *Southern Cross* delivered assistants for Hopkins: Johnson and Lizzie Telegsem transferred from Small Malaita. Johnson Tome and James Ivo from Gela, and Brian Mentela from Makira, were posted there direct from Norfolk Island.[107] The Anglican base in Lau was able to be extended in 1904 when Jack Taloifulia (Kwaisulia's cousin mentioned in Chapter 2) returned from Queensland and established a school at Fouia. Taloifulia was literate, fluent in Pijin English and well versed in Christianity.[108]

---

104 Fox 1958, 171.
105 *Ibid.*, 172.
106 Hopkins, 'N. W. Mala', *SCL*, Mar 1903, 1.
107 Hopkins, 'District of N. Mala', *SCL*, Apr 1903, 25.
108 This may be Tallasfeelar, baptised on 31 July 1898, who gave his parents as Sissea and Kokobay. Anglican 'Baptismal Register', Mackay; Fox 1958, 172; 'The Log of the Second Voyage, 1904', *SCL*, Mar 1905, 8.

Figure 4.6: Rev. Arthur Hopkins's mission house at Ngorefou, Lau Lagoon, 1906.
Source: Beattie Collection, 520.

Figures 4.7–8: Outside and inside the mission palisade at Ngorefou, 1906.
Source: Beattie Collection, 518 and 519.

In October 1903, Lau Lagoon was disturbed by the threat of attack from inland descent groups. A murder had occurred and the victim's family wanted a death in revenge, to save face and mollify ancestors.

> The bush people got up two or three war parties who sat in the bush hard by watching for a chance to snatch a life, or make an attack. However we had good information from our watchers of their movements, nor were they

themselves backward in sending threatening messages and guard was kept up day and night … Meantime the Fera saboa people were busy building a stockade of tree-trunks right around our village, a long and laborious job.[109]

Marauding parties were seen regularly on the outskirts of Ngorefou, and often a counter group from Ferasubua had to be sent for to keep them away. Visits from naval vessels, such as HMS *Pylades* in June 1904, also quieted the situation in Lau.[110] Even when peace was restored, there was still the possibility of lone assassins. The inland groups seldom attacked in large parties, choosing instead to infiltrate, posing as friends.

While historians a century later must be wary of missionary exaggerations and their desire to depict non-Christians as deficient and barbaric, Hopkins's detailed reports allow us some insight into daily life in Lau Lagoon in the 1900s. There was an amazing amalgam of influences. After church on Sundays, a game of cricket was held on the pitch just outside of the mission stockade. Then, after dark, the Ferasubuans used the area for dances and singing, mainly of Fijian songs, with the singers decked out in greenery and feathers, the necessary light provided from torches set in bamboo.

Indigenous activities continued, such as a feast arranged by Ramofolo of Fuaga, where it was rumoured that a bush boy had been captured to be killed. Hopkins set out to investigate but was assured by Kailafa, a bigman from Ferasubua, that nothing would happen since he had forbidden the killing.

> This practice of boy-snatching or attempted boy-snatching, has been terribly prevalent lately. Qaisalea [Kwaisulia], the man of most influence in these parts, has taken a prominent part in it. Two months ago he went to Foeda and got a boy there, handed him to the Funafou people for ten pigs and much native money, to be done to death with arrows by the Funafou boys. This was to 'make square' between these two islets and end a long standing quarrel and was followed by a great exchange of presents and making of peace. Qaisalea is accused of having two more transactions of the same kind in hand. One I heard of at Taga on my way to Malu. I turned back with a very frightened and sulky boat's-crew to enquire. Qaisalea we found quietly at his village and not as they said on his way south to Qai [Kwai] with the boy. He admitted buying a boy from near Malu, but only he decided to keep him to work for him and

---

109 Hopkins, 'Some Experiences on a New Station in the Solomons', *SCL*, June 1904, 6.
110 Hopkins, 'District of North Mala', *SCL*, Apr 1905, 23.

> live at Adegege. His son Jackson told me exactly the same story. I doubt them, but I could only warn him that I should report the matter to the authorities, and that it would be a very serious matter for him if he was lying.[111]

During 1904, six new Lau schools were begun and existing schools increased their attendance numbers.[112] Hopkins also regularly visited Malu'u, Fiu and Langalanga Lagoon. In September 1905, he circumnavigated Malaita in a whaleboat for the first time—over 320 kilometres—visiting the new QKM head station established at Onepusu on the Kwaio west coast.[113] The next year, Hopkins reported matter-of-factly that the QKM had now taken over at Malu'u and Bina. The Melanesian Mission had three new schools on the east coast: at Uru in east Kwaio, at Foate, with another being developed at Vuru. Uru had 11 students in 1906, but lacked a dynamic teacher. One of the other schools was at Taba near Malu'u, where five men were continuing to clear land.

Beattie described Ferasubua as like 'a dirty, smellsome Scotch fishing village' squeezed onto a small island with 'narrow streets, the hordes of children, pigs and dogs, and the women—shouting just like a Bedlam … They are fisherfolk one can see and smell'.[114] However, the proximity of Ferasubua had kept the mission safe in its initial years, although it also meant that the lures were close and strong when it came to non-Christian feasts and dances.

Conditions at Ngorefou had improved to the extent that the stockade had been allowed to decay, but in October 1906 Beattie found it restored and the settlement in 'practically a state of war', since two men had just been shot by bushmen:

> The whole place is surrounded by a huge palisade of strong logs, stuck into the ground with a doorway just wide enough to allow one to squeeze through, and standing by it was a determined looking old man carrying a rifle, wearing a cartridge pouch.[115]

---

111 Hopkins, 'Some Experiences on a New Station in the Solomons', *SCL*, June 1904, 7–8; see also Hopkins, 'District of North Mala', *SCL*, Apr 1905, 24.
112 Hopkins, 'District of North Mala', *SCL*, Apr 1905, 22.
113 Hopkins, 'Round Mala', *SCL*, Nov 1905, 10–11; *SCL*, Dec 1905, 2.
114 Beattie 1906, 26.
115 *Ibid.*

In February 1907, the Ngorefou school house was dumped off its piles by a cyclone and had to be rebuilt. The primitive protectorate justice system failed in the same month when the three convicted murderers of Amasia and Arthur Aka`ako managed to escape from Gizo in a stolen boat, equipped with rifles and ammunition. They returned to terrorise Lau Lagoon. In August, when HMS *Torch* anchored overnight at `Ataa, the local people thought the ship had come to seek out the escaped prisoners, but in fact the crew knew nothing of their presence. The escapees killed the son of Ramofolo, a bigman at Fuaga, which Europeans interpreted as because of the *Torch* visit. Not long after this, Kwaliasi, a bushman, after friendly bartering over a belt, shot dead Gela man James Ivo at point-blank range. The reason seems to have been that Kwaliasi's wife had cursed at him that morning, which Hopkins thought had caused him to take his revenge on the innocent man. This was enough to ensure that the stockade was repaired and Ngorefou returned to siege conditions. Hopkins sailed to Tulagi to report the murders to Woodford, who came himself and appointed Kwaisulia as a temporary policeman to try to keep order.[116]

Hopkins viewed the `Ataa people as the most obstreperous in the lagoon. He recounted how `Ataa men had tried to use a big war canoe to intercept his whaleboat on the way back from Uru in March. Although warned that there might be an attack, he still travelled unarmed. In the end there was no confrontation, which Hopkins interpreted as his calling their bluff. Of course, there may have been other reasons involved.

When HMS *Cambrian* bombarded the artificial islands and the mainland at `Ataa in July 1907, the people had been expecting the visit. The ship's commander warned the people to go to the mainland before he shelled three of the islands, breaking down walls and destroying coconut palms, and then turned his guns on the shore villages. The people were more impressed by the noise than the damage, although one child was accidentally killed when a piece of shell burst in a village.[117]

Ngorefou progressed, slowly drawing converts from the surrounding inland areas and further along the coast. This brought its own problems since Ferasubuans were feuding with inland neighbours. Several incidents occurred, such as when John Daomai from Ferasubua took a pot-shot at the bushman Silo while he visited the mission. Hopkins went to Ferasubua, confronted Daomai and demanded 10 strings of shell wealth

---

116 Hopkins, 'North Mala District', *SCL*, Apr 1907, 158.
117 *NIV*, 1906–07, 19–20; Hopkins, 'North Mala', *SCL*, Apr 1908, Supplement, 34.

as a guarantee of good behaviour. When Hopkins left for Queensland he had been expected to return with a man-of-war, and when he did not harassment increased. The visits by HMS *Cambridge*, and HMS *Torch* to Fiu in September, when another bombardment took place, suppressed violence around Malaita's north until late in the year.[118] The problems with incursions by inland descent groups continued. In 1910, a group of 20 hid near Ngorefou, sending two men into the mission to reconnoitre, hoping to kill someone. Lainan, a bushman friend of the mission realised what was happening and threatened them with repercussions unless they withdrew.[119]

Jack Taloifulia's school at Fouia had a dozen students.[120] Kwaisulia on nearby 'Adagege continually undermined Taloifulia. There had been trouble over some of his students who joined Sulufou people in raids, which had led to the killing of a child. Progress was slow as Taloifulia negotiated his relationship with his non-Christian kinfolk, and his assistant Joe Ongamon was unwell. Another Christian, James Damiki, was also living at Fouia, but because of his non-Christian wife and the liability of a diseased arm he was of little use to Taloifulia. When Damiki's wife was murdered some kilometres inland he insisted on walking there armed only with a spade to bury her mutilated body.[121]

The most southerly outreach from the Lau Lagoon Anglicans was into Kwaio on the central east coast. Uru, an artificial island in the Kwaio harbour of the same name, was the most isolated of Malaita's early Melanesian Mission outposts. One of the early Christians there was Isaac Lau'a, who had been kidnapped along with his brother and taken to Fiji in the early 1870s, probably by the *Nukulau* in 1871. He returned to open a school in 1905. During their Fiji years both had become Christians and married Fijian women. Isaac had arrived back at Ngorefou and set out in a canoe for Uru, capsized, was robbed, returned to Ngorefou and tried again. His brother joined him but the Uru people killed the brother and both of their wives in retaliation for an old wrong. Isaac fled back to Ngorefou, but returned to Uru in 1905. He was illiterate, and after clearing land for a school on the mainland opposite Uru Island he asked for teachers. Hopkins visited Uru in March and the Melanesian Mission

---

118 *Ibid.*, 36.
119 Hopkins, 'Diary of the Rev. A. I. Hopkins', *SCL*, Nov 1910, 89–90.
120 Tippett 1967, 163–70.
121 Hopkins, 'North Mala Report, 1905', *SCL*, May 1906, 7; Hopkins, 'North Mala District', *SCL*, Apr 1907, 158–59; Hopkins, 'North Mala', *SCL*, Apr 1908, Supplement, 37.

provided teachers late in 1905. There had been minimal progress and when Isaac died soon after most of the families withdrew, which left the teachers Raymond Kelen and his wife with little to do. In May 1905, Hopkins visited again and removed Kelen and his family, thereby abandoning Uru to the SSEM. Hopkins subsequently concentrated on setting up schools along the east coast in southern Kwaio and `Are`are.[122]

Norfolk Island Christians

The number of Melanesian Mission converts on Malaita before formal government reached the island is difficult to calculate. Until there is further research into Anglican records, the exact number of Malaitans trained at Norfolk Island remains unknown. The Anglican mission base shifted from Kohimarama, Auckland, to Norfolk Island in 1867. As early as 1871, there were seven males and one female from Malaita there,[123] and over the four decades before 1909, an average of 20 to 30 Malaitans were based there at any one time. Several hundred Malaitans must have passed through the Norfolk Island college during these decades.

Figure 4.9: St Barnabas College staff and students, Norfolk Island, 1906.
Source: Beattie Collection, 209.

---

122 In 1906, Beattie described the 1870s incident. As with the history concerning Alfred Amasia from Ngongosila Island, this probably also relates to the 1871 voyages of the *Nukulau* and the *Peri*. Lau`a claimed to have spent 21 years in prison after the event, which is unlikely. Beattie 1906, 4; Hopkins, 'North Mala', *SCL*, Apr 1908, Supplement, 35; Hopkins, 'Round Mala', *SCL*, Nov 1905, 11; Wilson, 'The Bishop's Visitation, 1905', *SCL*, Jan 1906, 11; Burt 2002.
123 Brooke 1872, 223.

Figure 4.10: Interior of the St Barnabas College dining room, Norfolk Island.
Source: Beattie Collection, 221.

Although the majority were male, young Malaitans of both sexes trained at Norfolk Island, with more emphasis given to training women onwards from the 1900s.[124] Some of them have already been mentioned. Amina Laki from Sa`a was the first Malaitan woman confirmed, in 1880 in the newly opened Bishop Patteson Memorial Chapel. She returned to Ulawa where she had a married sister, uncertain of her welcome at Sa`a while bigman Wariehu, who had placed a curse on her when she left, remained powerful. Never strong, she was shunned and died prematurely.[125] Another Small Malaita woman, Lizzie Siakulu, referred to earlier, left Walade with her brother Joseph Leo. At Norfolk in 1895 she was betrothed to Johnson Telegsem, who had been teaching at Port Adam when he met Siakulu. It was a modern marriage in that no bridewealth changed hands. Circumstances altered when bigman Faka`ia forbade the match and after threats from Faka`ia a school at Siakulu's village was evacuated. Eventually the situation improved and the marriage took place.[126] Another Walade

---

124 'A New Year's Letter from the Bishop of Melanesia', *SCL*, Jan 1901, 98.
125 'Amina Kali, the Mala Christian Maiden', *SCL*, 15 Apr 1899, 4–6.
126 Extract from the Ballarat *Churchman*, *OPMM*, Mar 1896, 200–01.

woman, Alice Alite, was also based on Norfolk Island before returning to help the school at Port Adam, where she married, also with no bridewealth payment, to Luke Masuraa. Lizzie Siakulu had been orphaned at a young age, it was said due to sorcery. She described Alice Alite's mother as a 'very good and very beautiful' woman who cared for many widows and orphans and the sick. Although she sent her children to the mission she never attended herself, and she gave Alice to Luke as a wife without asking for bridewealth.[127] In partnership with her husband, Lizzie was credited with keeping the Port Adam school operating. Following the sexist traditions of the time, mission records are inclined to give sole credit to male teachers and missionaries, when a closer reading of the sources suggests that women were also influential.

Conclusion

This chapter has woven a web of Christian people and places on Malaita in the 1890s and 1900s. The Melanesian Mission, which had Malaita to itself until the 1900s, failed to capitalise on the monopoly. I agree with Tippett's assessment:

> In the years of harvesting the Anglicans never could provide a pastorate to keep pace with the evangelical spearhead. They demanded high standards and experience from a Melanesian before ordaining him to the priesthood and were unable to supply an adequate number of European priests.[128]

Their only substantial indigenous advance was when the Melanesian Brotherhood was established in 1925.[129]

I have concentrated on thick description to show the impressive depth of contact. This is not a picture of the 'heathen' Malaita that is usually depicted in histories. In 1905, the Melanesian Mission claimed that out of the presumed 50,000 inhabitants of Malaita there were 1,791 school students attending 23 village and mission schools, and there had been 1,300 baptisms.[130] The exact number of baptisms in 1909 when the `Aoke government base was established is unknown, but given the

---

127 Quotation from 'Women's Work in the Melanesian Mission', *OPMM*, Mar 1896, 203; 'Peter Otoa', *SCL*, Oct 1895, 9.
128 Tippett 1967, 46.
129 Moore 2013c entry.
130 *SCL*, Apr 1904, 5; Wilson, 'Annual Report of the Melanesian Mission for 1905', *SCL*, Apr 1906, 9.

speed of progress once the Malaitans returned from Queensland, the total number must have been well in excess of 2,000. This, combined with the estimate of around 2,700 Malaitan baptisms while overseas, gives us a total of 4,700, before even considering the QKM-SSEM work on Malaita onwards from 1894. There were always 'backsliders' who did not retain their Christian beliefs, and with an average age of death at around 50 years, not all survived. Nevertheless, the number of Christians is considerable.

Solomon Islanders must have been puzzled by the relationship between the mission stations and the government, with the latter operating from Tulagi and claiming rights to control the entire geographic universe of the average Solomon Islander, and also based at 'Aoke from 1909. Tulagi was far away and the 'Aoke settlement was small. The QKM headquarters at Onepusu and the Malayta Company plantation at Baunani (onwards from 1908) were much more impressive and better equipped with marine transport. The main early foreign presence on Malaita was at the various mission bases and at Baunani. Many of the European missionaries behaved imperiously, and their mission stations were alternative power bases to that of the government. The government introduced new laws, and was willing to adopt and adapt some but certainly not all customary laws. During the first half of the twentieth century, the missions clashed with the British administration in two main practical areas—marriage and morality. They also created education and health systems, for which the government was thankful. From a Malaitan viewpoint, the Christian missions were much more involved with their day-to-day lives than was the early government. It must have appeared to Malaitans that the main government activities were policing and, starting in the 1920s, collecting taxes.

The next chapter extends the web of Christian people and places, tracing the early years of the QKM-SSEM, which developed a Christian network separate from that of the Anglicans. Whether Malaitans understood that the QKM-SSEM was different and separate is a matter for conjecture. However, the inescapable conclusion is that there was a strong Christian presence around coastal Malaita before the government arrived in 1909. The puzzle is, given this early Christian presence, why was Malaita still only half Christian in the 1930s and 1940s, by which time Gela, Isabel and parts of the Western Solomons had made a total conversion?

5
Abu`ofa and the Exodus from Queensland, 1894–1908

They were so difficult to reach. They were fierce and warlike people … of strong character … Although nominally under the Melanesian Mission, no missionary had succeeded in obtaining a foothold on the main island of Malaita. Hundreds of these men have been won for Christ in Queensland & are staunch & splendid Christians, & whereas in the early days it was a triumph to get one Malaita man to School, now we have many hundreds in our classes & for years they have besought us to send missionaries to their Island.

—Florence Young, Queensland Kanaka Mission, October 1903[1]

The Anglican Melanesian Mission had two early rivals on Malaita, the QKM, which became the SSEM in the 1907, and the Marist Catholics after 1910. Seventh-day Adventism was a relatively latecomer in 1924. The literature from the various missions often gives the appearance that each operated alone. Even though all denominational missions underplayed connections with each other (largely for consumption by fund donors), the reality was that each knew exactly what the other mission was doing and where they had their bases. They were rivals, greedy for Malaitan souls, but on the ground they often cooperated when it came to sharing transport or maintaining health. What is difficult to work out is what Malaitans thought of it all, and how they distinguished between the quite different Christian messages of the different denominations.

---

1 Florence Young, private note, Oct 1903, *NIV*, 1902–03; Young 1925, 43.

Peter Abu'ofa and the QKM at Malu'u

The origins of the QKM were outlined in Chapter 3. The tradition of the modern SSEC is that the QKM began operations in Solomon Islands in 1894 at Malu'u, north Malaita, and that this should be viewed as a 'church planting'—the SSEC's beginning.[2] In fact, it was 1895, after a faltering beginning in 1894, and we need to debate the intentions of the QKM and Peter Abu'ofa. Many QKM converts returned to the Solomons during the 1890s and 1900s, among them Abu'ofa, from Gwai'au Village in the mountains of To'aba'ita, situated between Talafaina (Fo'odo) and Malu'u.[3] One of seven children, Abu'ofa had enlisted to work on plantations around Bundaberg. He was baptised there on 28 August 1892.

Two years later, in April, he and two other men, Robert and Daniel, also known as Try (Tri) and Kobey (Kobi), left Queensland to establish a QKM school on Malaita. This fits with a general QKM desire to evangelise in Melanesia, although at that time Florence Young, the founder, was recuperating from a mental breakdown and the QKM was struggling to maintain even its outreach in the Bundaberg area. By comparison, the Melanesian Mission was training teachers at Norfolk Island with the express purpose of creating Christian enclaves in the islands and was busy trying to link the Queensland Anglican missions into the island network. Abu'ofa's efforts were not formally connected to the QKM, although the mission, particularly through Rev. Arthur Eustace, gave him full support. Abu'ofa was loyal to the QKM and used their activities and materials as his model. He succeeded in beginning a major indigenous church, although he could easily have failed. The details of his return to Malaita remain because of two protracted legal trials—known as the *William Manson* case—that ensued after Abu'ofa reported a labour trade captain for kidnapping.[4] The voluminous proceedings of the investigation and subsequent trials were published daily in the *Brisbane Courier* between 18 October 1894 (the date the *William Manson* returned to Brisbane) and the final verdicts on 29 March 1895. Comments on the trial continued to be published until June. The evidence includes substantial testimony recorded from Abu'ofa, Kobey and many others who had been aboard the ship, as the multiple charges were played out in the two courts.

---

2   Moore 2013c entry.
3   *NIV*, 1907–08, 10.
4   QSA CT/CC116.

5. ABU'OFA AND THE EXODUS FROM QUEENSLAND, 1894–1908

Figure 5.1: Peter Abu`ofa in middle age.
Source: Deck Collection, Black and White Photographs, 135dw.

The case is remarkable. Peter Abu'ofa was the first and only Pacific Islander directly to challenge the legality of the Queensland labour trade, generating protracted court cases that involved the governor and the attorney-general. Malaitan cultures were assertive and adaptable, but Abu'ofa was notable as the first Malaitan leader to assert himself in a modern way, not surpassed until the Maasina Rule movement's actions decades later. As we will see in Chapter 9, Abu'ofa also stood up for himself against the protectorate administration in the 1900s and 1910s. Although he probably had the backing of the QKM during the 1894–95 trials, to confront Europeans despite his vulnerable position aboard the *William Manson* off the coast of Malaita took great strength of character and presumably Christian belief.

Abu'ofa had worked in Queensland for six years. Try, from Iwi Harbour, had been there for eight: at Mackay for three years, Rockhampton for two one-year contracts and Bundaberg for three years, where he came into contact with the QKM.[5] Kobey, too, had spent eight years in Queensland, and all three spoke good Pijin English. The *Bundaberg Mail* recorded that the trio, known by their Christian names, Peter, Robert and Daniel, were returning to Malaita on the barque *William Manson*, owned by William Vos and Edward Elsworth, with Vos as captain and G.T. Olver as government agent. The ship left Brisbane on 27 April with 181 male, and 10 female returning labourers, and four children. The ship arrived back in Brisbane with 86 male and seven female indentured labourers.[6] At 366 tons, it was the largest vessel in the labour trade, three times as big as the smallest schooners operating in 1894. The ship had been built in Aberdeen in 1872. Based around Australia since 1875, the *William Manson* sailed regularly in the China tea trade, and undertook occasional voyages to Japan and Mauritius.[7] She was purchased by Vos and Elsworth and refitted in Sydney for the labour trade in 1893; descriptions show the renovations to have been technically advanced and expensive.[8] The steerage (the cargo hold) was well equipped with bunks, similar to those on the European immigrant ships. Vos had an Edison phonograph on board that could record voices: on the ship's first labour trade voyage he used it to

---

5   'Serious Charges against Recruiting Vessel', *BC*, 28 Nov 1894.
6   *Bundaberg Mail*, 13 Apr 1894; *Statistics of Queensland*, Population, Immigration and Emigration, 1894.
7   For instance, see the voyages mentioned in *BC*, 8 Oct 1879, 4; *Mercury* (Hobart), 25 Oct 1879, 2; *Argus*, 4 Jan 1882, 7 and 30 Mar 1891, 4.
8   *Sydney Morning Herald*, 10 Aug 1893; *BC*, 22 Nov 1893.

make recordings of Mackay Islanders to replay to their families in the islands, and in the islands to carry messages back to Queensland. He also took photographs and presented Magic Lantern shows. There was a large clock with moving figures, which would have fascinated the Islanders, and a steam cutter for ship-to-shore work.⁹ The *William Manson* was by far the best equipped vessel in the fleet and Vos's use of technology to attract recruits was unique.

Figure 5.2: Men and youths of `Adagege, Kwaisulia's island, Lau Lagoon, 1906.
Source: Beattie Collection, 532.

The voyage was eventful. It was the *William Manson*'s second voyage in the labour trade, and Vos as part-owner had a large financial interest in the trip. During the voyage, Abu`ofa and his two companions complained about the food and protested to Vos after he slapped a woman. Vos counteraccused Abu`ofa of sleeping in the married couples' quarters (when he had no wife) and there is a suggestion that Vos threatened to put Abu`ofa into irons for his effrontery.¹⁰ At Lau Lagoon, Malaita,

---

9   'An "Up-to-Date" Labour Ship', *BC*, 9 Dec 1893; 'A Queensland Labour Vessel. News of the William Manson', *BC*, 22 Nov 1893; 'Serious Charges against a Recruiting Vessel', *BC*, 27 Nov 1894.
10 'Supreme Court', *BC*, 13 Mar 1895, 2–3; Alfred Dowsett evidence, 'Supreme Court', *BC*, 22 Mar 1895, 7.

Vos offered Kwaisulia, the major passage master, a small boat and a box of goods in return for 10 recruits. However, aware that Abu`ofa and his companions wanted to begin missionary work in the lagoon, Kwaisulia refused permission for them to land, and according to their own accounts they were forced to rerecruit by Vos. Several other labour recruits were also taken against their wills, coerced by Kwaisulia, and there were other problems on the voyage involving nonindentured females on board. The voyage's irregularities were the most extreme since the mid-1880s and never equalled again.

Abu`ofa testified that at Urasi he took a box of his school materials ashore and then returned to the ship, by which time Vos had realised that Kwaisulia would never let the three missionaries land, and insisted that they rerecruit without returning to shore. According to Vos, Kwaisulia said:

> I don't want those—black missionaries here. By-and-by they will be bigger than I am … I am Quisoolia, and I am boss here.[11]

Vos told the court that Kwaisulia was willing to allow the missionaries to land, but denied them permission to begin a school, and that after hearing this Abu`ofa had decided to return to Queensland. Joseph Keld, the second mate, who claimed to have overheard Abu`ofa's conversation with Vos, said that after being rejected by Kwaisulia, Abu`ofa decided that they would 'return to Queensland and work for three years more, and would then return with a white missionary'.[12]

Once it was clear that he would not be allowed to land, Abu`ofa wrote a letter to Rev. Eustace, to be taken back on a nearby labour vessel, the *Roderick Dhu*, which reached Bundaberg on 22 September. Eustace contacted Immigration Agent John O'Neil Brenan in Brisbane.[13] The letter accused Vos of kidnapping and ensured that Brenan was waiting to board the ship when it docked. Abu`ofa repeated his allegations to Brenan, leading to charges of kidnapping under the *Pacific Island Labourers Act 1880*. Vos, Olver, the mate, the recruiter and three seamen were arrested on 17 November 1894 and charged with kidnapping. Two protracted legal trials ensued, the first in the Court of Petty Sessions of the City Police

---

11 William Vos evidence, 'Supreme Court', *BC*, 19 Mar 1895, 2.
12 'Supreme Court', *BC*, 19 Mar 1895, 2.
13 'Kanaka Labour Trade: Charges against a Recruiting Steamer', *Mercury*, 2 Nov 1894; Harrison 2005.

Court in front of Magistrate Philip Pinnock from 19 November until 28 December 1894, and the second in the Supreme Court from 11–23 March 1895 in front of Judge George Harding.[14] The case was dismissed, even though the judge said in his summation that at least two of the recruits, Erringa and Sooquow, had been kidnapped. Despite the irregularities, the jury decided that the evidence was not substantial enough to carry convictions.[15] There is an indication that the jury may have thought the charges were 'trumped-up' by the principal witnesses for the prosecution, including Abu`ofa.[16] The Queensland Government made its opinion on the guilt of the accused parties clear when it banned all of the crew from further participation in the labour trade. The *William Manson* never again sailed to the islands.[17]

The press followed the trials in great detail and the general public must have read the daily newspaper reports rather like a serial story published over several months. Not only was it the first and only time that a Pacific Islander used the full legal system to challenge the legality of the Queensland labour trade, but the Supreme Court case involved Governor Sir Henry Norman, who supplied a brief on the legal jurisdiction of Malaita, after suggestions were made at the trial that it might be within the area annexed by Germany, or that British law did not extend there. The attorney-general was also called to give an opinion.[18] Their advice was that under the Imperial 1872 and 1875 Acts, although Orders-in-Council did not endow the monarch with the right of sovereignty, there was a right to create a protected area, and after 1893 Malaita was under Britain control. Judge Harding also ruled that the 1875 revision of the *Pacific Islanders Protection Act 1872* was sufficient authority for the trials.[19]

The 10 men at the centre of the kidnapping allegations, including Abu`ofa, Try and Kobey, were returned to Malaita on the *Para*, chartered by the Queensland Government. Each was equipped with a liberal allowance of manufactured items at the expense of the owners of the *William Manson*.[20]

---

14 QSA SCT/CC116.
15 QSA COL A.795, In-letter 4471, IA to Permanent Under-Secretary, 16 Apr 1895.
16 'The Kanaka Labour Traffic', *BC*, 26 Mar 1895, 4.
17 Saunders 1974, 85; 'William Manson Cases', *BC*, 27 Mar 1895, 4–5.
18 'The William Manson Cases', *BC*, 16 Mar 1895, 6.
19 *Ibid*.
20 QSA COL A.795, In-letter 447, IA to Permanent Under-Secretary, 16 Apr 1895; 'Queensland', *Argus*, 4 Apr 1895, 5.

The *Para*, also a large ship at 252 tons, had J.C. O'Brien as captain and John Mackay as government agent. The voyage departed Brisbane on 14 August with 116 male and five female returning labourers.[21]

The standard SSEC version of the Abu`ofa story is that he and his companions' initial plan was to establish a base at Urasi in Lau Lagoon, but when landed they faced fierce opposition from Kwaisulia. Vos then tried to persuade them to reenlist for another contract in Queensland.[22] Kwaisulia was undoubtedly just as unfriendly to their endeavours on the voyage of the *Para* as on the *William Manson* voyage. They were received unwillingly and told to sleep beneath the houses with the pigs. Death threats followed, and Abu`ofa thought it wiser to accompany Lau canoes to the beach market at Malu`u on the north coast near the lands of his own inland descent group. He settled at Malu`u, and during the first four years there Abu`ofa made little progress, suffered regular bouts of malaria and survived several attempts on his life.[23]

Presumably this version of events is true, although the voyages of the *William Manson* and the *Para* have been collapsed into a single voyage in folk memory, and Abu`ofa's efforts to invoke the full wrath of legal system on suspect behaviour on board a recruiting vessel have been forgotten. Exactly what motivated Abu`ofa will always be conjecture. He understood Pijin English but had only a rudimentary grasp of English; he could not have comprehended the complexities of the laws involved. Presumably, the QKM staff had schooled him in the rights of recruits, and his Christian faith gave him the tenacity to proceed. Eustace may have told him to report any irregularities he observed. His use of another ship—the *Roderick Dhu*—to carry his complaint back to Queensland was a masterstroke.

Abu`ofa eventually succeeded at Malu`u. He built a school on the pattern of the QKM school at Kalkie, Bundaberg, where he had been baptised, and local people were impressed when his garden was the only one to flourish during a drought. Abu`ofa sent many messages back to the QKM via labour trade ships requesting further help. Eustace considered joining a group of Christian Malaitans returning from Bundaberg in 1896,

---

21 *Statistics of Queensland*, 'Population, Immigration and Emigration, 1894–95'; Arthur E. Eustace, 'Kanaka Missions. The Work in Queensland. Reply to the Bishop of Melanesia. A Voice from Bundaberg', *BC*, 16 May 1895.
22 *Ibid.*
23 *NIV*, 1908–09, 18.

but his doctor dissuaded him from undertaking the trip.²⁴ S.M. Smith, government agent on the *Roderick Dhu*, carried one of Abu`ofa's messages back and in 1899 took several Christian Malaitans to Malu`u. Although not included in the QKM ministry list,²⁵ in February 1900 the South African evangelist Charles B. Pillans, who had worked for the QKM in its Sydney office and at Bundaberg, accompanied Smith back to Malu`u on *Sydney Belle*. The ship circled Malaita (see Map 10, Chapter 2), dropped off returning labourers and recruited 17 more. It landed Pillans at Malu`u on 25 March.²⁶ The SSEC story is that he arrived totally unexpected, but Smith's diary entry contradicts this:

> Mr Pillans was expected, welcomed, and a house built for him so he is all right I am happy to say so and a load is off my mind.²⁷

A few days after his arrival, Pillans wrote back to QKM staff and described the scene. Peter Abu`ofa lived with his wife and young daughter Ruby in a well-established hilltop house, with large gardens and plentiful fruit trees, on a stream about a kilometre inland. He taught from a school next to his house and preached at the local market every three days when the inland people came down to barter with coastal residents. Pillans reported that Didi and Loisa had established a new base several kilometres away. Busy planting gardens and building a house at the new site, they still lived close to the Abu`ofa family. Also nearby was Pillans's house, made from round logs with a thatched roof. The church was there also, with a graveyard next to it. When the Melanesian Mission's *Southern Cross* visited Malu`u a few months later, Pillans was sick with fever and short of food. The Anglicans evacuated him to their headquarters at Siota for a month's rest to restore his health. Pillans had written to Richard Ruddell, then based with the QKM in Bundaberg, asking that he join him. Ruddell set out with Thomas Nguna, a New Hebridean, but by the time they arrived, Pillans, back at Malu`u, had died from fever and Ruddell decided it wiser that they join the Anglicans at Siota for a few months. The intrepid pair visited Malu`u for a week in December 1900 in a whaleboat borrowed from the Melanesian Mission. First they went to Pillans's grave, then to

---

24 'The Melanesian Mission in Queensland', *SCL*, Mar 1897, 7; *Queensland Baptist*, 'Obituary, Rev. Arthur Edwin Eustace', May 1903, 66.
25 The Queensland Kanaka Mission Baptismal Register, 1902–05, contains a short history of the dates of arrival of European staff, 1903–11. PMB 1201, Reel 1, 'South Sea Evangelical Mission, formerly Queensland Kanaka Mission, Register of Baptisms'.
26 Moore 1985, 88, Map 8.
27 Smith 1900, diary from the *Sydney Belle*, 25 Mar.

the little church with its walls hung with the same texts and hymn sheets used in Bundaberg. Friday was market day and Abu`ofa preached to the assembled crowd. Sunday was a full day of church activities, beginning at 8:00 am. Ruddell and Nguna left for Fiu, the Melanesian Mission station on the northwest coast, and then sailed back to Siota and eventually returned to Australia. Two years later, Ruddell became a full-time staff member of the QKM and he eventually spent many years on Malaita.[28]

In 1902, two more Europeans tried to settle at Malu`u. Frederick Schwieger and Joseph Watkinson had studied at Martin's Missionary Training Home in Sydney and then sought missionary work in Noumea. When there were no openings they went to Port Vila, New Hebrides, where they earned enough money to buy a small boat to sail to Malaita, intending to join Abu`ofa at Malu`u. On 26 January 1903, Schwieger, suffering from malaria, met the same fate as Pillans.[29] Resident Commissioner Woodford removed Watkinson and forbade any more European missionaries to settle on Malaita unless they were part of an established church.[30] Other QKM converts at Malu`u also died of malaria and other fevers. Two Malaitan assistants, Fred and Zaccheus from the Geraldton branch of the QKM, both succumbed to fever on the same day that February. When Florence Young first visited Malu`u in 1904, the graveyard, overgrown with crotons, held several recent graves.[31]

When Anglican missionaries Hopkins and Ivens visited the Malu`u station late in 1902, Abu`ofa had four helpers, 100 followers at Malu`u and another 30 in a nearby village. The Anglicans aspired to include Malu`u in their mission outreach, and a year later Hopkins spent a month there helping Abu`ofa and provided copies of his Lau language prayer book, which met with little welcome given the difference in languages. Abu`ofa's mission is included in *Southern Cross Log* reports as if it was the beginnings of an Anglican settlement. Anthropologist Ian Hogbin, resident in the north in 1933, wrote that in the 1900s the Melanesian Mission settled two indigenous teachers on the other side of Malu`u harbour from the QKM mission at Irombule, although within a few

---

28 Young 1925, 140–41.
29 *BSIP AR*, 1902–03, 6.
30 *Ibid.*, 141.
31 Pillans to F. Fricke, 27 Mar 1900, *NIV*, 1899–1900, 10–11; *NIV*, 1900–01, 11; 'Diary of Florence Young', 11 Apr 1904, *NIV*, 1902–03, 6.

years they were withdrawn and the area surrendered to the SSEM.[32] Descriptions of Abu'ofa's services suggest an average congregation of 100 to 160 out of a flock approaching 200. Preaching in a mixture of the To'aba'ita language and Pijin English, he had no formal training as a mission worker and used his own methods. Hopkins observed:

> Peter reads aloud the hymn, the first verse at any rate, the rest repeat after him. A long word Peter discreetly jumps boldly over, others he takes gallant shots at, but you can generally tell what hymn he is aiming at. Then they sing; the well-disposed stand, the idle lounge, but if the tune is familiar, the hymn goes with great force and vigour, though of the meaning of the words the mass of the congregation can have no idea.[33]

By 1905 Malu'u had four branch schools in the surrounding area, all run by ex-Queensland Christians: at Sutoti, Tekinana and Manofiu, all inland, and at Gamour further along the coast.[34] Accompanied by Rev. Percy T. Williams, who had spent from 1895 to 1898 in Queensland working as an Anglican missionary with the Islanders, Hopkins had earlier trekked inland about 16 kilometres to Manofiu Village, where John and Dick, two returned Queensland labourers, had established a school under the aegis of Abu'ofa at Malu'u. They found a crude school building and several houses, with 49 students, who faced antagonism from the surrounding non-Christians. About 10 of the inhabitants had been in Queensland.

> We were taken first to their 'gamal' [village central area], which was surrounded by an enormous stockade of amazing strength. It was made of two circles of big tree trunks, 10 to 15 feet in height, about 3 feet apart. The space between the trunks was filled in with logs, stones and earth, etc., jammed into a solid mass; the whole great wall thus formed was thickly overgrown with vegetation. Here they had lived in safety till the early storms blew over.[35]

The stockade was entered through a small, well-barricaded archway. Opposition from the surrounding people had declined after a few years and the stockade was no longer so crucial to their survival. They were contemplating shifting to the coast and had started clearing a site about 16 kilometres from Malu'u.[36]

---

32   Hopkins, 'N. W. Mala', *SCL*, Mar 1903, 1; *SCL*, Apr 1904, 5; A.I. Hopkins, 'District of N. Mala', *SCL*, Apr 1904, 28.
33   E.A., 'A Service at Mala', *SCL*, May 1904, 12–13.
34   Hopkins, 'District of North Mala', *SCL*, Apr 1905, 25.
35   Hopkins, 'District of N. Mala', *SCL*, Apr 1904, 2.
36   Hopkins, 'A Bush Village', *SCL*, May 1903, 20–21.

The existence of the British protectorate, with a small physical presence onwards from 1896, was beginning to have an effect. Several murders occurred around Malu`u in 1904, and that September Woodford arrived on his 33-ton ketch-rigged *Lahloo* to arrest one of the culprits, who was taken to Tulagi, tried, and served a one-year prison sentence.[37]

Abu`ofa tried hard to get his own immediate family to become Christians. He won over his parents and brothers Tommy, Aufil, Maito and one other, but failed to convert his brothers Gosila or Raatalo, who fiercely resisted to the extent that they killed Charlie Loisa at Malu`u in 1907. However, in 1909, a dispute arose between Gosila and Raatalo when some relatives who had sought refuge in the village were betrayed and one was killed. Abu`ofa went to see if he could help, and Gosila, angry with Raatalo, finally agreed to move to Malu`u and brought his family and several others with him. Christians took Gosila's decision to join Abu`ofa as a sign that the old ways were fading. The QKM interpretation was that the remaining ancestor-worshipers felt that the arriving Christians were destroying the spiritual power of their ancestors.[38]

Labour trade ships regularly brought letters back to Queensland from other ex-QKM converts who were working to establish mission bases in their own areas of Malaita:

> Not only in Maluu, but in other parts of Malayta, Christian Boys from Queensland are building schools, and bravely preaching Christ to the heathen. Their appeals to us for help have been most pathetic, and during the past year we have been constrained to undertake work in the islands as well as in Queensland.[39]

Florence Young Reconnoitres Malaita, 1904

At Bundaberg, Florence Young was conscious that all of the Christians in the islands needed support, and aware after the Commonwealth passed the 1901 Acts that established the White Australia Policy, the Islanders' days in Australia were numbered. She had received entreaties from Peter Abu`ofa for the QKM to follow him to Malaita, but felt inadequate for the task. She would also have known of the deaths of Pillans, Schwieger,

---

37   Hopkins, 'District of North Mala', *SCL*, Apr 1905, 25–26.
38   *NIV*, 1908–09, 17–20.
39   *NIV*, 1903–04, 7.

5. ABU'OFA AND THE EXODUS FROM QUEENSLAND, 1894–1908

Fred and Zaccheus at Malu'u. By the 1900s, there had been European missionaries in several of the New Hebridean and Solomon Islands for decades. Young maintained a correspondence with the Rev. John G. Paton, one of the leading Presbyterian missionaries connected to the New Hebrides, who was by then based in Australia. She had suggested to Paton that the Presbyterians extend their mission work into the Solomons, but Paton responded that his mission was already fully committed. Approaches were also supposedly made to the Anglican Church Missionary Society, which gave a similar response.[40] After Schwieger died at Malu'u, QKM missionaries Mr and Mrs O.C. Thomas from Geraldton offered to replace him. Mr Thomas reached the Solomons alone, but fell ill and never reached Malaita. With knowledge of what was happening at Malu'u, knowing that the Presbyterians were unable to begin work on Malaita, and not satisfied to leave evangelism to the 'Catholic' Anglicans, Florence Young, after a great deal of prayer, decided to embrace the challenge of moving the QKM's sphere of operation to the Solomons.[41]

Ever determined and never short of finances or faith, on 26 March 1904 Florence Young arrived on Burns Philp & Co.'s SS *Moresby* at Gavutu opposite Tulagi. Not a woman to travel light, on this first trip she brought with her a prefabricated house, the *Daphne* (a 12-ton lugger) and supplies for six months. She was accompanied by several missionaries. One was O.C. Thomas, who had survived his earlier Solomons adventure and returned to the QKM's Geraldton branch. Another was George Caulfeild, son of Henry St George Caulfeild, Queensland's government inspector of Pacific Islands labour (1887–1906) at Bundaberg, who had a reputation for supporting Islanders when their employers tried to shortcut the indenture system. Also in the party were A. Hedley Abbott, a carpenter and missionary candidate from Ballarat, Victoria, Miss L. Ruddell, presumably a relative and possibly a daughter of the Ruddell couple, and Miss C.S. Dring. Margaret Fricke, whose sister Alice Henry had worked with Florence in China, accompanied her to the Solomons as a companion. The mother of five children, she was married to Frederick Fricke, a Ballarat stock-and-station agent who moved with his family to Bundaberg in 1886

---

40   It is unclear why the Church Missionary Society was approached in relation to territory within the Anglican Diocese of Melanesia. Perhaps it was because, as an evangelical movement, its beliefs were more in line with QKM's. Griffiths 1977, 34.
41   QKM, Solomon Island Branch, address by W.H. Dibley, Honorary Secretary and Treasurer, Sydney, 1 Feb 1904, *NIV*, 1902–03. Dates of QKM-SSEM events in PMB 1201, Reel 1, 'Solomons Baptismal Register', 1902–05.

as a self-funded member of the QKM staff.[42] At Tulagi, Woodford had gone cold on the idea of allowing the QKM party to travel to Malaita, although he had previously given Young permission when she met him in Sydney. Florence could be formidable, and that the expedition was well-equipped alleviated some of Woodford's fears. One can only imagine the conversation that took place up in the residency—no other woman had ever arrived in Solomon Islands with such determination, and eventually he yielded to her insistence.[43]

Figure 5.3: The final decision to close the Queensland Kanaka Mission and reestablish it as the South Sea Evangelical Mission was made at this religious convention at Katoomba, New South Wales, in 1904.
Source: Deck Collection, Black and White Photographs, unnumbered.

The missionaries on board the *Daphne* arrived at Langalanga Lagoon on 7 April. They visited 'Aoke Island, hosted by George and 'Big Charlie', whom they knew from Queensland.

> Our little vessel is thronged with natives, all clamouring for 'toback' [tobacco]. Clothing is conspicuous by its absence, with the exception of one Boy from Tulagi. We look in vain for signs of civilization. Some of these men have been in Queensland for years, but—there are no Christians amongst them.[44]

---

42 *NIV*, 1903–04, 8–9; Penington 2010, 6.
43 Young 1925, 146.
44 *Ibid.*, 147.

Figure 5.4: The 12-ton lugger-style *Daphne*, which Florence Young brought with her in 1904. The ship served as the main means of transport for the QKM until the *Evangel* arrived in 1907.
Source: Deck Collection, Black and White Photographs, 142.

A local bigman offered to sell the QKM land opposite on the mainland, although he showed no interest in Christianity and suggested that they would be better served converting the inland people. Leaving Langalanga, they sailed north to Rarata Islet, where Henry Rambootan (from the Melanesian Mission's Fiu mission) had established a small school at Laulana on the mainland opposite. The next stop was Fiu, where they took part in the Melanesian Mission's Sunday service, then on Monday sailed for north Malaita. As the lugger approached Basakana Strait, the QKM party was passed by a large canoe containing 18 men, all wearing European clothes. They were bound for Koa Bay, carrying rations for the teachers there, an outstation of the Malu`u mission. They reached Malu`u on the afternoon of 12 April, and Peter Abu`ofa, quiet and unassuming, was obviously delighted.

Figure 5.5: Florence Young, superintendent of the Queensland Kanaka Mission and the driving force of the South Sea Evangelical Mission until the mid-1920s.
Source: Young 1925, frontispiece.

The party remained at Malu'u for eight days before returning to Gavutu. Their original intention was to travel to Cape Astrolabe at Malaita's northwest tip, where Christian converts from Queensland had established a base, and then down the east coast to Sinalagu in Kwaio, where men in Queensland had told them there was an excellent harbour, but bad weather and constant fevers prevented the expedition going any further.[45] On the way back to Tulagi the *Daphne* was becalmed near Basakana

---

45 *Ibid.*, 153.

Island, which allowed the visitors to call in at Fo`odo on the northwest coast, where Abu`ofa and his Malu`u adherents had been visiting for some years, and to Bena Islet. Both places were judged unsuitable for a permanent base, although nearby Bita`ama was thought to be a possibility. The party, stricken with fevers, only just managed to get back to Gavutu. When Young and Fricke returned to Sydney, Thomas had to go with them to recuperate. Caulfeild and Abbott returned to Malaita to try to found a base at Bita`ama, where the leaders were willing to negotiate the sale of land. Florence Young lost 12 kilograms in weight during the 10-week trip.[46]

The QKM purchased land in various auspicious coastal areas. Just after Christmas 1904, the mission paid money for land at Irobule on a ridge in Malu`u Harbour. Work commenced on clearing the land and by early February the two-room prefabricated house with a corrugated iron roof had been erected on the edge of the cliff. Both local people and the Melanesian Mission's missionaries were reluctant to accept the QKM presence, though for different reasons. Rev. Hopkins was unimpressed, and complained that since 'they belong to no denomination it seems a grievous pity they should come to ground already occupied by the [Anglican] Church'.[47] Malu`u villagers who had allowed Abu`ofa's presence were now wary about Europeans settling on their land. In May 1905, the mission was visited by a large party from inland descent groups who inspected everything thoroughly. Their leader, Toibeu, showed interest in attending the school, at which his people scoffed, telling him it was 'school all same women'.[48] Converts had a variety of problems: Boudoko, an elderly Malu`u bigman with two wives, had begun to convert in 1903, but was faced with how to choose one wife if he was baptised. Menace was always near. Early in January 1905, a local man attending the mission was shot dead by a bush man who accused him of sorcery, and on several occasions the mission store was broken into.[49]

When the *Daphne* returned to Malu`u in late February, Abbott and Caulfeild battled against squalls for four days to sail down the east coast to visit `Aioo Island, near the border of the modern Kwaio and `Are`are language districts. That April, Caulfeild returned to Sydney for the annual QKM conference at Katoomba in the Blue Mountains, replaced in May by

---

46   QKM, 1903–04, *NIV*, 1903–04, 5–10; Young 1925, 155.
47   Hopkins, 'District of North Mala', *SCL*, Apr 1905, 25.
48   *NIV*, 1903–04, 9.
49   *NIV*, 1904–05, 5–8.

a rejuvenated Joseph Watkinson who had first ventured to the Solomons in 1902 when Woodford ordered him to leave until there was a larger group of missionaries. Abbott remained at his post and on 27 May left again for `Aioo on the *Daphne*. The winds were so strong that they gave up at Maana`oba and instead circumnavigated Malaita via the west coast, stopping at Fiu, Kwai, Su`u, Onepusu, Aineo and Waidala before passing through Maramasike Passage and then north to `Aioo. The `Aioo land was purchased on 7 June and the next day they set off north. The return trip to Malu`u took only one day, which gives readers some idea of the strength of the winds that often rake along the east coast.[50] The rough weather prevented their visiting one isolated Christian, Sam Pilate at Uru.[51] Meanwhile, Watkinson was busy at Bita`ama and Fo`odo. A school house had already been constructed by Jonah Tonabasia at Bena, 3 kilometres from Bita`ama, and Arfiliu and others had given the mission land at Fo`odo, where a house was being built. They preached to a large group of people from the inland while on the beach at Fo`odo, and at nearby coastal Walow Village they visited Herafoon, an old chief whose brother Heelacoon had converted at Malu`u.[52] Since there was no consultation with the government, their land purchases were all provisional.

The Exodus from Queensland to Malaita, 1901–08

Florence Young had reacted to two Australian 1901 parliamentary acts—the *Immigration Restriction Act* and the *Pacific Island Labourers Act*—that together ensured the end of the labour trade and the eventual deportation of the majority of the Islanders. There were then around 9,500 Pacific Islanders in Queensland, but much of the desired decline was achieved by attrition when contracts were not renewed. The intention was to taper back immigration during 1902 and 1903 and to halt it entirely after 31 March 1904, with the deportation of as many Islanders as possible when the last of the three-year contracts expired by the close of 1906 or early in 1907. In the end, the process took until 1908. After a royal commission, 2,500 Islanders remained in Australia, some 1,000 of them illegally. In March 1904, Woodford estimated that there were 6,000

---

50   *Ibid.*, 8–9.
51   Hopkins, 'Round Mala', *SCL*, Nov 1905, 11; Wilson, 'The Bishop's Visitation, 1905', *SCL*, Jan 1906, 11.
52   *NIV*, 1904–05, 10.

Solomon Islanders still in Australia, around 3,600 of them Malaitans. By late in 1905 there were 5,380 still to leave. There was a temporary reprieve in 1907 for 427 of Queensland's Islanders, about half of them Malaitans, who were rehired by Colonial Sugar Refining Company to work on its Fiji plantations. This transfer would have increased the number of Christian Solomon Islands labourers in Fiji.[53]

Woodford attempted to supervise the return process, and in 1901 made representations to the governor of Queensland to introduce more stringent searches of labour vessels leaving the colony. Starting in 1898, all labour ships from overseas had to call first at Tulagi, and a special officer was appointed to supervise the emigration starting early in 1905. This enabled medical checks, gave returning Islanders a chance to decide their final destination, and enabled a check on illegal shipments of arms and ammunition. Woodford believed that 'not a single labour vessel leaves Queensland without a quantity of arms, ammunition, and dynamite concealed on board'.[54] Some returnees preferred to land at mission stations rather than at their home passages, or to take work on the new plantations within the protectorate. Woodford encouraged denominations to establish more outstations to accommodate the Christian converts. The Melanesian Mission and the QKM, already established on Malaita, responded to his plea. The Anglicans, with their island network already in place, wound back their Queensland missions in 1906. The QKM also closed its Queensland operation, in late 1906, shifting its headquarters from Bundaberg to Onepusu on Malaita's west coast.[55] Malaitans continued to be indentured to work in Fiji until 1911, the last contracts there ending in 1914. During the early 1910s, the return of Fiji labourers followed much the same pattern seen at the close of the Queensland labour trade, although with smaller numbers, as the returns established new Christian settlements around the coast.

Once the end of the Queensland labour trade was announced there was a last flurry of recruiting, at a rate of almost 1,000 a year during the 1900s. This late Malaitan rush to Queensland secured their place as the dominant

---

53   Mercer 1995; Moore and Mercer 1993; Corris 1973b, 132–33; *BSIP AR*, 1904–05, 24.
54   *BSIP AR*, 1902–03, 15. In September 1903, Woodford took the extreme measure of suspending the labour trade in the protectorate, aware that the captains and government agents were flouting his wishes. High Commissioner Sir Henry Jackson visited on HMS *Pylades* from 19–21 October, and as a result Queensland passed new regulations to allow Woodford's authority to override the government agents. *BSIP AR*, 1903–05, 27; Corris 1972; Moore 2000.
55   Moore 1985, 274–331; Moore 2000.

group there in the trade's final years. Some of these men had already been to Queensland and Fiji and were now making a second or third tour, and there were Christians amongst them. The number of labour vessels visiting the protectorate increased, with some ships making three trips in a year. There was still some violence, including attacks on recruiting vessels, and occasional calamities, such as when the *Sybil II* was lost in April 1902. The ship left the Solomons but never reached Queensland, and 100 people perished. The wreck is suspected to have occurred on Indispensable Reef near Rennell and Bellona islands.[56]

In 1905, Woodford was expecting 4,500 to 5,000 Solomon Islanders to be deported from Australia after 1 January 1907, with perhaps 500 remaining as long-term immigrants, including several legally married to white or Aboriginal women.[57] When the Australian Government partly relented in 1906 and allowed large numbers to remain, the main exemption category was long-term residence, which did not apply to the 1900s recruits. Furthermore, some of the long-term Malaitan residents chose to return home. In 1909, once the situation stabilised, Woodford reported that around 1,000 Solomon Islanders had returned home between 1901 and 1904, and 3,438 between 1905 and 1908.[58]

In 1906, the regular stream of returns became a human flood. Queensland mission classes continued up until the end of 1906 with a last run of students.[59] Florence Young said that many Islanders between the end of their contracts and their repatriation 'were almost desperate for extra teaching' and would stay at the schools all day, keeping teachers busy. Then, while waiting in Bundaberg to go home, they were 'unsettled and distressed'.[60] Many left through Brisbane, where Mrs L.D. Eustace (ex-QKM and wife of Alfred E. Eustace) from the Brisbane City Mission held twice-daily classes at Yungaba, the Immigration Depot at Kangaroo Point, for as many as 300 to 400 Islanders over the 12 months while the deportation was at its peak.[61]

---

56   *BSIP AR*, 1902–03, 13; QSA GOV/A38, CS to G, 8 Sept 1902; *MM*, 7 Mar 1905. Interestingly, these deaths do not appear in the Queensland Statistics. *Statistics of Queensland*, 1902, 'Population', Table VI, 5.
57   *BSIP AR*, 1903–04; 1904–05, 24.
58   PMB 1290, Woodford Papers, Reel 4, Bundle 23, 8/17, BSIP Statistics to 31 Mar 1909.
59   Price with Baker 1976; Moore 2000.
60   Young 1925, 183.
61   QKM 'Report', 1906–07, and L.D. Eustace letter, *NIV*, 1905–06, 5–10; L.D. Eustace letter, *NIV*, 1906–07, 9–10.

5. ABU'OFA AND THE EXODUS FROM QUEENSLAND, 1894–1908

Figure 5.6: Mrs L.D. Eustace, holding classes at 'Yungaba', the Immigration Depot at Kangaroo Point, Brisbane, 1906.
Source: *NIV*, 1906–07, 14.

Eleven Malaitans were interviewed by the 1906 Queensland Royal Commission into Sugar Industry Labour. On average they had lived in Queensland for 11.9 years: Maluni and Harry Delamo had each been in the colony for 22 years. Maluni was interviewed at Bundaberg, where he had travelled from Mackay. He had a Malaitan wife and three surviving children (the fourth had recently died). He had not been home since he arrived in 1884 and was not Christian. Maluni was bitter about the money he had been forced to spend for transport to get to Bundaberg.[62] The other long-stayer was Harry Delamo from Cairns, who had also arrived in 1884. He had been back to Malaita once many years before and then reenlisted. Delamo had an Aboriginal wife but no children and did not want to be deported; he was worried that his wife would be killed on Malaita. Keeserere, also from Cairns and also married to an Aboriginal woman, had been in Queensland for 13 years; he likewise feared for her life if she returned with him to Malaita.[63] Quiramoo (Kwairamo) from Fiu in west Kwara`ae had spent five years in Queensland, gone home for a year, and then returned for another five years. He had finished work, had spent all of his money on food, and was unwilling to go home without a box of goods. Another, Tommy, had only been in Queensland

---

62 *Royal Commission into Sugar Industry Labour* (Queensland), 1906, 60–61.
63 Ibid., 314.

for three-and-a-half years, although he had also worked in Fiji. He spoke good Pijin English but had gambled all of his money away. He was willing to leave if he was provided with a box of goods.[64]

The main point that emerged from these interviews was that these men had been forced to pay their own maintenance once their contracts had ended, and also their passages on ships to the collection points (Brisbane, Bundaberg and Cairns) where the return to the islands was organised. The passage alone was as much as £10, usually close to their entire savings. They had no money left to buy goods to fill a box to take home and were unwilling to leave without this cargo. The Pacific Islanders' Fund contained the deposited return fares for all Islanders, but only £5 per individual, and current employers had no obligation to pay the difference. Each Islander had supposedly been informed of this by the inspector or magistrate when he or she had signed their first indenture contract. While legal, that could have been 20 years earlier and they may not have understood the English used.[65] The other element that emerged was the risk to spouses who were not from the labourer's island. Under the more lenient changes later in 1906, those with more than 20 years residence or with wives not from their own island were allowed to remain in Australia.

The trips back from Australia were similar to the hundreds of other voyages in the labour trade, although after early 1904 it meant a one-way passage on large steamers, and being closely examined for contraband guns, cartridges and explosives. The returnees and their belongings were searched before they left Queensland, several times while at sea and once more at Tulagi. Even so, arms managed to get through; cartridges were sewn into petticoats and guns were hidden in chimneys, air vents and pump wells. In March 1903, when the *Ivanhoe* became stranded in the Solomons, police helping to discharge ballast were alarmed when they discovered dynamite cartridges already fitted with fuses and detonators among the stone ballast under the women's quarters.[66] Jack McLaren was working on one of the returning ships in the 1900s:

> Any roll of cloth was liable to contain a short-barrelled Martini-Henry in its centre. Umbrellas hid dismantled shotguns in their folds. A woman who walked with a certain queer stiffness was found to have a Snider rifle strapped to her leg beneath her dress. A man carried an antiquated

---

64 *Ibid.*, 315.
65 QSA, PRE/84, IA to UC, CSD, 12 Feb 1906.
66 *BSIP AR*, 1902–03, 15.

revolver slung under his armpit, beneath his shirt, and in a pair of boots he never wore were cardboard boxes of cartridges to fit it. In hollowed interiors of caddies of tobacco we found modern .303 ammunition, and powder flasks and bags of bullets for old-fashioned muzzle-loaders. In the timber of the forepeak and in spare cable in the chain locker were half a dozen new Winchesters, and jambed [sic] in about the cargo of the hold we found some more.[67]

The Malaitans, in particular, pleaded to be able to keep their weapons, offering bribes of all sorts, from goods, to alcohol to sex with young women on board. The crews recognised the sense of their arguments and entreaties—that they faced real danger on their return—but had no choice other than to search for and confiscate all contraband. After being checked at Tulagi, the ships sailed for Malaita and the other islands. Each steamer carried hundreds of Islanders away from Queensland. The lessening numbers in each district led to the closing before Easter 1907 of all of the missions to Islanders.

Islanders had few alternatives regarding deportation. As mentioned, 427 men managed to transfer to Fiji, and between 1895 and 1906, 16 men from the Selwyn Mission at Mackay, along with eight from Bundaberg, went to New Guinea to join the Anglican Mission there.[68] Another option was for those who returned to Malaita to settle at mission schools and offer themselves as teachers. Woodford had arranged for returning Malaitans to go directly to mission settlements if they wished. This gave Christians a better chance to maintain their new beliefs. It also strengthened the main mission bases and provided a trained group of teachers to place on new outstations.

There was a sense of sad closure in Queensland, while immense new opportunities were opening in the islands. Presbyterians from Queensland were able to make links with the church's missions in the New Hebrides. The Churches of Christ mission had tried to widen their operations to the New Hebrides early in the 1900s, but only succeeded later. The QKM established three major mission stations on Malaita: the headquarters at Onepusu, the north coast branch at Malu'u, and the east coast branch

---

67   McLaren 1923, 160.
68   Mackay had strong connections with the New Guinea Mission. Rev. Albert McLaren, founder of the New Guinea Mission, had been the local parish priest at Mackay from 1878 to 1891. In 1901, Mackay Malaitans took around the collection box for the New Guinea Mission. Wetherell 1977, 99–106, 116–17.

at Kwai-Ngongosila. O.H. Abbott skippered the *Daphne*, and there were 13 outstations staffed by Solomon Islanders and a few New Hebrideans.[69] For the QKM, the refocus away from Queensland also brought a change in name, to the South Sea Evangelical Mission.[70]

The Melanesian Mission was strongest on Small Malaita, and had established other major stations in Lau Lagoon and at Fiu on the northwest coast. Anglican missionaries Charles Fox and Walter Ivens described the scene in 1906 and 1907:

> Everywhere in that year were seen Melanesian men and women in European clothes, men with thick black boots, black hats and blue serge clothes, speaking pidgin English, asking what price white men had given for native land, so much a foot in Queensland, most of them very indignant that they had been turned out of Australia. Most of them, if they were Christians, were accustomed to prayers in English and did not want them in island languages … For a time the *kanakas* were very important people in the islands to which they returned.[71]

> Sewing-machines and gramophones might have been bought up cheaply a week or two after the returns had landed. In some cases sewing-machines were actually abandoned on the beach, for no one cared to carry them slung on a pole into the interior over razor-backed ridges and up the bed of swollen mountain torrents. Brown boots and bowler hats and starched shirts and collars and ties were seen adorning the persons of all and sundry in the neighbourhood when the trade boxes of the returns had been opened.[72]

Rather like the goods sold by Chinese stores in modern Solomon Islands, known for their cheapness rather than their quality, many returning Islanders had made dubious purchases. Jack McLaren described them:

> dressed in cheap finery and loaded with 20-pound caddies of tobacco and boxes filled with flimsy cloth, bead necklaces, reels of imitation silk, coloured paper, and other rubbish on which they had squandered their savings in Chinese stores.[73]

---

69 'San Christoval', *NIV*, 1906–07, 34–35.
70 'List of Stations and Workers in Malayta', *NIV*, 1905–06; *NIV*, 1906–07, 11.
71 Fox 1958, 44.
72 Ivens 1918, 232.
73 McLaren 1923, 158.

Anglican missionary Hopkins, stationed in northeast Malaita, could see the good and the bad in the exodus:

> On the one hand, to these men is due the starting of new schools, and in doing this they have to face the resentment of their heathen neighbours and the jealousy of local chiefs at the formation of new villages outside their control. Or, if they go back to their own villages, the distribution of the contents of their boxes, often done by force, is a fruitful cause of quarrels. Then there are the worthless ones who are 'wanted' for old offences, or who return only more able for mischief than before … No doubt it will be easier to judge when they have all returned. The next two years will be anxious ones.[74]

Figure 5.7: Malaitans on the beach just after returned labourers have been landed with their boxes of trade goods, northwest Malaita, 1907. Similar scenes occurred thousands of times between the 1870s and the 1930s.
Source: British Museum, Photograph by George Rose, Rose Stereographs, neg. 1257, in Thomas Edge-Partington Collection.

---

74 Hopkins quoted in *BSIP AR*, 1903–05, 25.

McLaren, who had worked as an overseer in Queensland's sugar industry before moving to Solomon Islands, also noted the splendid physiques of the returning males, built up with 'regular food and regular hours'.[75] They were obvious in comparison with Malaitan men who had not travelled away, even when they had in other ways blended back into the crowd. Their Pijin English was quite sophisticated but peppered with swear words.

The return of such large numbers of people brought advantages and disadvantages to Malaita. There must have been an increase in diseases; although the Queensland men had developed immunities, they would have passed various ailments onto their families at home. Even a common cold could be lethal to those without immunity. Most of the returning men and women brought possessions with them that circulated in the economy, which caused an overabundance of foreign goods for a few years. They returned with so much cash that one of the main exports from the protectorate in 1908–09 was gold coins worth £2,500.[76] The many Christians among them founded and taught in mission schools. Another downside was that there were linguistic confrontations between the Queensland-trained Pijin English speakers, the speakers of Pijin Fijian and the Norfolk Island-trained Mota- and English-speakers. As Hopkins delicately put it: 'Their attitude if not unfriendly is critical'.[77] The men returned with large boxes of manufactured goods, which were usually distributed among their relatives, often a little unwillingly, and this sparked quarrels. Those who had left to escape the repercussions of some offence returned to find that Malaitan memories are very long and compensation was demanded or murders occurred. There were also a good number of colonial sophisticates (much like Malaitans today returning from Honiara or overseas) who showed off of their 'superior' ways and annoyed those with established authority.[78] Bishop Wilson welcomed the end of the Queensland trade, which he claimed had been responsible for much of the unrest on Malaita.

75   McLaren 1923, 158.
76   Bennett 1987, 118.
77   Hopkins, 'District of North Mala', *SCL*, Apr 1905, 24.
78   *Ibid.*, 22.

Great numbers of 'boys' died in Queensland, and the life of a white recruiting agent was often taken as a forfeit. After that no one could go near the place where the murder had been done. Besides which these ships shed tobacco plentifully, and many of them bullets too. There was little or no chance for a mission ship when the counter attractions of the labour-vessels were ever at hand. People who doubt my theory will find it hard to account for the fact that as soon as the 'labour trade' has been ended, every village on the coast is asking for schools.[79]

What the bishop failed to acknowledge was that the task of the missions was made much easier by the returning labourers. Many of them were Christians, they assisted the missions to purchase land and added their voices to the need to establish schools. The missions may genuinely have feared that disturbances would follow the return of the Queensland recruits, but the spate of murders that some Europeans had predicted did not occur.

Contrary to oral testimony from Australian South Sea Islanders today that the 'returns' were literally dropped off anywhere and died on foreign beaches, they were landed at the exact passages they requested. If they were in any way uncertain of their safety, the ships had to take them back to Tulagi or to mission stations. The same thing occurred in the New Hebrides.

There were three categories of returning Malaitans: active Christians, adherents to the ancestral religion who had fully resisted mission influences while in Queensland, and the much larger group who slid in between. All arrived decked out in the latest Queensland fashions. A day later, the missionaries reported, they were indistinguishable from their kin, except that they were more worldly wise. This was wishful thinking: it was an instance where 'clothes don't make the man'. Those who followed their ancestors tried to blend back into their families. The Christians tried to live near a school and many encouraged their families to come down to the missions, while often those same kin urged them to return to their ancestors. Both groups were hugely changed by their plantation experiences and were at the forefront of negotiations with the colonial government in the proceeding decades.

---

79 Wilson. 'The Bishop's Visitation, 1905', *SCL*, Jan 1906, 12.

Figure 5.8: A scene of labourers returning to east Kwaio, probably at the site of the present-day SSEC Gounaabusu Village at the southern end of Sinalagu Harbour.

The man wading ashore has his belongings slung over his shoulder in a classic long Kwaio *wa'i* bag, its top edge decorated with white *sona* beads made from cone shell. He is unlikely to have been a returning labourer, and probably walked out to the boat that brought others home.

Source: *NIV*, 1914, 39; Young 1925, facing 46; Deck Collection Colour Slides 42b; bag description and site identification, David Akin, 3 Dec 2015.

As the Queensland exodus continued, it caused accommodation problems at the SSEM stations and trauma for Queensland-born children who were 'very frightened of the unclothed crowds'.[80] The *Malekula* arrived at Onepusu on Friday 12 July carrying 22 adults and 13 children, including some families from the Young family plantation of Fairymead. They were billeted around in the mission house and with Christian families. At the same time, Onepusu took in three refugees from Uru, a young woman, her husband and his father. The couple's teenage daughter had been murdered and the rest of the family had been promised the same fate. They escaped on a ship to Tulagi, before ending up at Onepusu.[81]

---

80 Deck diary, *NIV*, 1906–07, 16.
81 *Ibid.*

Sometimes the mere presence of the returning labourers opened up old feuds. A large proportion of them had maintained their ancestral religious affiliations and were quickly absorbed back into family feuds, while others boasted, swaggered and otherwise caused trouble by lording it over their 'country cousins'. It has been suggested that the returned labourers were responsible for selling a good deal of land to the missions, often unbeknownst to the other customary owners.[82] Many of the Christians were easily absorbed into the Malaita missions, but even they had trouble since they had learnt about Christianity through English or Pijin English and remained aloof from instruction in local languages.[83] There was also a number who stayed for only a short time, choosing to extend their wage-labouring experience in Fiji, Samoa or on the plantations that were beginning in the protectorate.[84]

A similar process occurred after Fiji was closed to recruiting from Solomon Islands in 1911 and people were returned from there in 1914, although their numbers were smaller. That period is described in Chapter 7.

---

82   Bennett 1987, 118.
83   Ivens 1918, 232.
84   Ivens, 'South-East Mala', *SCL*, Apr 1908, Supplement, 58c.

6

From QKM to SSEM, 1904–09

> Barnabas brought a big chief to see us this evening—such a fine-looking man, with upright carriage and springly walk; he wore a scrap of calico and a cartridge belt, and had a keen, intelligent face. He is feared for miles around up and down the coast, and protects the school people, but knows nothing yet of God's love. Poor Harasimai!
>
> —Catherine Deck, SSEM missionary, Onepusu, 6 July 1907[1]

South Sea Evangelical Mission

The South Sea Evangelical Church is today the largest Christian denomination on Malaita and the third-largest church in Solomon Islands. The QKM, SSEM and now SSEC philosophy clearly appeals to many Solomon Islanders.

David Hilliard's assessment of the Anglican Melanesian Mission was that it 'taught of a God who was fulfilment rather than a denial of existing Melanesian beliefs', which differed significantly from denominations like the Presbyterians in the New Hebrides and the SSEM, which were always much more hostile to indigenous Melanesian religions and cultures generally. The Melanesian Mission never relegated all nonbelievers to hell; the QKM-SSEM certainly did. As outlined in Chapter 3 and Chapter 5, the QKM began in the 1880s as a nondenominational evangelical mission to Islanders on Queensland sugar plantations and

---

1   Deck diary, *NIV*, 1906–07, 16.

Map 13: Major SSEM and Malayta Company plantation bases on Malaita.
Source: Courtesy of Vincent Verheyen.

farms, founded by Florence Young, in the style of the China Inland Mission. The QKM closed at the end of 1906, moved its headquarters to Malaita and became the SSEM. The QKM-SSEM followed what Hilliard described as 'an uncompromising Evangelical position, its doctrines centred upon the plenary and literal inspiration of Scripture'.[2] The Christian gospel was always the mission's primary inspiration, overshadowing educational, medical or social aspects.

Figure 6.1: SSEM mission staff and children in the 1910s.

In the back row (L to R): Miss Searle, Mr McBride, Jessie Deck (wife of Northcote Deck) and an unknown man. In the front (L to R): Miss Mitchell, Northcote Deck, his sister Kathy (Catherine) and Miss C.S. Dring.

Source: Deck Collection Black and White Photographs, 26, identification from the back of the photograph and Burt 2015, 38.

---

2 Hilliard 1969, 43.

Figure 6.2: Senior teachers at Baunani in the 1910s.
Norman Deck named them as (back row, L to R): 'Loi, Stephen Sipollo [*sic*]; (middle row): Firosia [?], Joshua my cook, Torialli [?], Shadrach [Amasia?]; (front row): Tehara, Timothy Anilafa'. Stephen Sipolo became a police sergeant-major, a leader during Maasina Rule, a Malaita Council member and a teacher at King George VI School. Timothy Anilafa became a leading figure in the SSEM.
Source: *NIV* 1910, 9; also Deck Collection, Black and White Photographs, 26; see Burt and Kwa'ioloa 2001, 93; 2015, 39, 78.

Some of the terminology associated with the SSEM was unfortunate and gives an indication of the church's lack of sympathy with prior religions. Malaitan ancestors were glossed as 'evil spirits' and customary priests were 'witch doctors'.[3] This is contrary to Malaitan views, in which ancestors remain as much part of a descent group as the living people and are custodians and guardians of land and cultural norms. The QKM-SSEM demanded change 'rather than adaptation or assimilation',[4] which was usually the Anglican and the Catholic style. QKM-SSEM beliefs were strong and clear: like the Seventh-day Adventists who made a late entry to Malaita in 1924, the QKM-SSEM did not compromise and expected

---

3   Griffiths 1977, Glossary. The Melanesian Mission cannot be totally excused from this style of thinking; refer to Hopkins 1927, 19–20, on the subject of magic and magicians.
4   Hilliard 1969, 51.

adherents to take their doctrine seriously. This is in conflict with religious pluralism typified by much of Pacific Christianity.[5] The missions were imposed institutions and the foreign missionaries operated within their own cultural frameworks, intent on conversion. Missionaries liked to present themselves as in control of the situation and of Malaitans. The Melanesian Mission was clearly more 'friendly' to Pacific cultures than was the QKM-SSEM, but even their clergy seldom fully realised the complexity of the processes in which they were involved. The early QKM-SSEM had a reputation for dogmatism, yet even they must have recognised that there was syncretism at work. From the perspective of a century later they must be judged as very successful missionaries, although they were completely surprised by Maasina Rule in the 1940s and 1950s, when they were ostracised by most of the movement's adherents. The question is why they were so successful in the early decades.

The QKM on Malaita, 1904–06

Chapters 4 through 6 provide a complex picture of the Christian missions and their projects on Malaita between the 1870s and the 1900s. I have chosen to forefront the missions in these early years because they were the only important foreign element sited on the island. One ongoing theme is circulation—no one seems to have stayed in one place for long. The missions operated through circulation of personnel and by tapping into existing networks of men and women returned from Queensland and Fiji. Although Pijin Fijian was not as widely spoken as Pijin English, the missions used both for communication. The picture that emerges is of constant activity and energetic networking, all before the government held much sway on Malaita. There is also much competition as the Melanesian Mission and the QKM-SSEM battled for supremacy.

Although Florence Young wrote an autobiography and there are many extant QKM publications and papers, I have found no clearly stated operational plan for the outreach to Malaita. Certain elements are clear. First, the QKM was inspired by similar missions in China, Africa and India, and Florence Young had extensive experience from her participation

---

5   Tippett 1967, 281. Burridge 1969 is one of the most interesting equivalent studies of an Island Melanesian people, showing the degree of syncretic mixing. Also see Trompf 1977; 1991; Loeliger and Trompf 1985; Steinbauer 1979; Lawrence and Meggitt 1965; Habel 1983. Three recent Solomon Islands studies are McDougall 2013; Scott 2013; and White 2013.

in the China Inland Mission in the 1890s. She had survived China in the years leading up to the Boxer Rebellion, and although her six years there took a toll on her health, Young was extremely knowledgeable about the problems of maintaining a mission in new and difficult circumstances. Second, many of the staff, both European and Islander, had already served with the QKM in Queensland, making the extension easier. Established protocols that had worked to expand the QKM in Australia were applied on Malaita. There were also many Malaitans on the island who were either baptised by or knew of the QKM or had had contact with one of the other Christian missions in Queensland or Fiji. They formed the core of the QKM's congregations and support base, and a network of Christians into which the QKM tapped right around the island. The direct connection to Fairymead plantation is a third steady theme in the contacts made on Malaita in the early years. The big difference from Australia was the lack of any supportive infrastructure, the danger to health and the possibility of violence.

Aside from some assistance, however grudging, from the Melanesian Mission, the QKM staff were provisioned to cope by themselves, sometimes for lengthy periods in a hostile environment. The early deaths at Malu`u and knowledge of the travails faced by Abu`ofa and his supporters would have left little doubt of the difficulties. The QKM adopted several strategies to cope: the two most important were constructing a transport network and establishing a central base from which to operate. The mission operated a small fleet of ships and smaller boats that enabled communication between their outposts. The *Daphne* and other small vessels, and later the motorised schooner *Evangel*, became the lifelines. The decision to create a headquarters at Onepusu, with sub-bases at Malu`u in the north and Kwai-Ngongosila in the middle of the east coast, and later another on Small Malaita, created a stable central web from which to construct outer strands (see Map 13 above). This matched the Melanesian Mission's Sa`a-Walade, Lau and Fiu focus (see Map 12, Chapter 4) and created a second successful Christian network around the island.

The final part of the plan was to create a substantial coconut plantation on the west coast of Malaita north of the SSEM Onepusu headquarters. Although not officially part of the SSEM, the Malayta Company (described in chapters 8, 9 and 10) provided a commercial presence and ensured there was always sufficient logistic support. Just as Florence's brothers had created an entrepreneurial base at Fairymead plantation outside of Bundaberg, from which the QKM spread, the growth of the Malayta Company beginning in 1908 gave the SSEM the backing it needed for success, exploiting an industrial Christianity concept and mixing commerce and God. The protectorate's government allowed the company to purchase a 24-kilometre strip of coastal land centred on Baunani and covering 4,000 hectares. This massive land alienation (the only one on Malaita at the time and still the largest-ever foreign-controlled land alienation there) was begun before the government established a base on the island. Resident Commissioner Woodford was trying to build up the copra industry and welcomed the Malayta Company's investment. He allowed the land sales with no prior government survey. (There were no government surveyors until the 1910s.) The company began with a nominal capital of £30,000, one of the largest investments in Solomon Islands to that date. The Young brothers were the directors and held two-thirds of the shares, with the rest distributed amongst members of their extended family and other SSEM supporters. Although this company was established after the SSEM was formed, there is every reason to suppose that it was part of the initial plan to close the QKM and begin the SSEM.

Florence Young was back on Malaita in mid-1905. Enough details remain to piece together the complexity of movements between the QKM's bases and to comment on their relationship with the Melanesian Mission. Much as Chapter 4 did for the Melanesian Mission, what follows shows the complex logistics of the Christian web that preceded government, and its links to former Queensland labourers. On this second visit in 1905, Young called at Aineo Island at Rohinari, the home of Samson Maenuta, who was based at Onepusu. The *Daphne* then sailed on through Maramasike Passage up to Takataka on the east coast where they met ex-labourers who enquired after their friends still in Queensland and asked that a mission base be established there. The Takataka men had already written to some of the Malaitan QKM teachers in Queensland asking for their help.[6] Proceeding to Maanawai on the `Are`are–Kwaio border, the QKM party discussed the possibility of a school with a local bigman who had spent three years working at Fairymead, although they failed to make contact with two other ex-QKM men, Abraham Taria and Moses Sutou, whose villages were in the mountains nearby. At `Aioo Island they met Thomas Sipolo, who had returned from Queensland on the *Lady Norman* a month earlier. The *Daphne* party examined the land the QKM had already purchased on the island, concerned that it was too unhealthy

---

6   *NIV*, 1904–05, 12; Young 1925, 169.

for a mission station. Former Queensland labourers came to meet them at ʻAioo, and at ʻOloburi they met four young men whose father was still working at Fairymead.

Figure 6.3: The SSEM church and school at ʻOloburi, east Malaita.
Source: Deck Collection, Black and White Photographs, 38.

Figure 6.4: *Evangel*, the first of many SSEM ships of this name. It was built for the mission in Sydney in 1906 and arrived in the Solomons the next year.
Source: Deck Collection, Black and White Photographs, 18.

The QKM's *Daphne* and later their *Evangel* became a constant presence around Malaita, rivalling the Melanesian Mission's larger *Southern Cross* and Queensland and Fiji labour vessels in the degree of contact they had with Malaitans. The *Evangel*, donated by supporters in 1906, was a purpose-built 16.7-metre ketch-rigged vessel with a 20-horsepower Gardner engine. The new ship, with comfortable accommodation and capable of sailing at 8 knots, arrived at Malaita in late June 1907.

Malaitans could identify the different European vessels and knew the purpose of each. In the still air of the islands, the different noises from ship's engines are easily identifiable long before they are close enough to see. Bishop Wilson, who visited 'Oloburi in October 1904 on the *Southern Cross*, provided a word picture of what the *Daphne* party must have experienced half a year later:

> A canoe with four bushmen came out to meet us, but they could not manage the craft, and wobbled so badly that we had to help them ashore again. People [were] quite naked and shameless. The men had nose shields, made up of two of three plates of mother-of-pearl. There were plenty of rifles, all full-cocked and loaded. The chief when he sat down to talk quietly unloaded one or two, saying after some time: 'these bullets are not meant for these people, but for those up the coast'. A man named Taraia, baptised in Queensland, has begun a school here, and has ten children going to it.[7]

Early in 1903, ex-Fairymead Christian labourers had settled at the next harbour north in east Kwaio, Sinalagu. When Florence Young reached there in 1905 she searched for Sam Pilate, who was from an inland village, and with the help of another ex-Fairymead man he was located further around the bay. For two years Pilate had tried to establish his own school, always meeting with opposition. The local people destroyed his canoe and other possessions. Defeated, he took the opportunity to join the *Daphne* and went to Malu'u and then on to Onepusu.[8]

---

7 'The Log of the Second Voyage, 1904', *SCL*, May 1905, 9. A year later, on their next visit, Taraia was not doing well. His clothes had disintegrated and he was naked. The bishop gave him a new loin cloth and tried to reteach him the letters of the alphabet, which he had forgotten. Wilson, 'The Bishop's Visitation, 1905', *SCL*, Jan 1906, 12.
8 Ivens, 'Mala and Ulawa', *SCL*, Mar 1903, 21; *NIV*, 1904–05, 13.

Table 4: Major QKM and SSEM bases and schools, Malaita Island, 1895–1906.

North Malaita	East Malaita	West Malaita
Malu'u, 1895	Sinalagu, 1903–05	Onepusu, 1902–05
Talafaina (Fo'odo)	Kwai-Ngongosila	Laulana, 1906
Sutoti	Wunfor, 1906	Asimana, 1906
Tekinana	Forti, 1906	Kwari'ekwa, 1906
Manofiu	'Aioo, 1906	Hauhui
Gamour		Boronasu'u, 1906
Asimani		Araora
Sio, 1905		Baunani
Maana'oba		

Figure 6.5: Northcote Deck at a river baptism at Maanakwai in north Malaita.
Source: Deck Collection, Black and White Photographs, 46.

On Young's visit she was accompanied by Caulfeild, Miss Foster (who had been a missionary in Tibet) and Annie Taylor. Abbott met the SS *Moresby* at Aola and travelled with the trio to Gavutu where the *Daphne*, crewed by Charlie Lofeah (Lofea) from Malu'u and Sam Tu'wu, Malachi and three others, waited to take them to Malaita. The government was in disarray: Woodford was away on leave, his deputy had been called to Sydney and the next down the line was ill and was being assisted by a young lieutenant from a passing British naval vessel.[9] This time no one

---

9   Young 1925, 166.

questioned their departure to Malaita. Their first stop was Onepusu, after which Young and her party departed on a 12-day trip around most of Malaita.[10] On 3 August they reached Malu`u, where good progress had been made. Caulfeild had been to Fo`odo to prepare candidates for baptism and on Sunday 29 July; 25 men and women were baptised in the river, watched by a crowd of 200. A few days later, the visiting QKM party set out in the *Daphne* for nearby Sio Harbour, the home of Sam Tu`wu, where people had requested a teacher. Johnny Forsai was left there to begin a school until Tu`wu was available. Two weeks later, the *Daphne* set out for Onepusu with 11 helpers, stopping off at Bita`ama to meet with the three teachers and 60 locals at the site of the new church. At Fiu, John Senale and John Aliwane joined the party to transfer down to Onepusu; and at `Aoke, the local bigman Tom `Aoke came out in his canoe to hitch a ride to Gavutu. They arrived in time for the visitors to catch the steamer before it left for Aola. The *Daphne* then sailed to Onepusu.[11]

Young made her third visit to the protectorate in mid-1906, accompanied by Mr and Mrs Ruddell and five Islander teachers. By this time large numbers of Christian Malaitans had returned home, swelling the QKM's flock. Mission-trained men were still moving out further around Malaita, travelling in small canoes and QKM vessels. Some of their ventures were less successful than others. While Young was at Onepusu, Barnabas set out by canoe north to Hauhui and Kwari`ekwa in Su`u Harbour. He had previously visited the Kwari`ekwa people on many occasions, but this time they pleaded for a teacher, and soon after they received Thomas Ambiasim on a preliminary visit. These processes were always accompanied by prayer; Ambiasim said that the Lord had guided him to make the move.

Samson Maenuta made a similar trip south from Onepusu, paddling to Aineo and Uhu. Florence Young set out on the *Daphne* with Louisa (the part-Australian Aboriginal wife of Charlie Tarasol-Aurora) and several teachers, stopping first at Uhu where Samson and Barnabas had begun a school. The weather was squally and very wet, which slowed the small vessel as they travelled through Maramasike Passage and north to Takataka, where Sam Kon Kon had established a new school. They delivered a box of goods sent to Sam by his QKM Islander friends in Queensland. Young began negotiations to purchase land near Ia`ura (South Sister) Island from Homar, and then sailed north in dangerous seas, which prevented

---

10   *NIV*, 1904–05, 14.
11   *Ibid*, 14–15.

their calling at Maanawai and carried them on to `Aioo Island. Thomas Tavangtang-Sandwich was on board, ready to establish a mission base at `Aioo, but they carried him north to Kwai-Ngongosila where Thomas Sipolo, who was from the `Aioo area and was to be the initial interpreter, was helping Watkinson. Tavangtang-Sandwich returned to `Aioo at the end of June. At Sinalagu Harbour they found a group of `Aioo Christians waiting for better weather before travelling home. Simeon was in charge, with Sam and Peter Fito (Fiito`o) at an outstation. They had opened schools at Wunfor and Forti just south of Sinalagu. Young noted:

> Returned Boys from Queensland are found in various places who can sing hymns, etc. At one big gathering for a feast about fifty Boys were able to join in the singing![12]

Caulfeild sailed south from Malu`u to Kwai-Ngongosila in a whaleboat, which the *Daphne* towed back. At `Ataa they saw the *Ivanhoe*, a Queensland labour vessel wrecked on a reef in May 1906. The crew had escaped to Gavutu and Rev. Arthur Hopkins from the Melanesian Mission's Ngorefou base further up Lau Lagoon had taken charge of 11 returning labourers aboard who had lost all of their possessions. The wreck had been stripped and provided a great bonus of metals and other materials for the Lau people.[13] Caulfeild visited one of the islands in `Ataa Cove, probably either Talito or Suraina, before proceeding through the lagoon to Maana`oba Island to visit Daniel Farkyer, who had started a school there. (There is no mention of Hopkins at Ngorefou, which Caulfeild sailed past.) Reaching Malu`u on 3 July 1906, they discovered a despondent Peter Abu`ofa. His brother Aufili had died at Fo`odo three weeks earlier and Abu`ofa's baby girl had died the week before.

Abbott helped construct a new church at Malu`u. Preaching on market days continued, as did church services, Sunday school and general school. The *Daphne* set out again, down the west coast. Seventy-five people gathered at Fo`odo for the Sunday service in a decorative church next to a pleasant mission house. Florence Young decided to establish Charlie and Louisa Tarasol-Aurora at Fo`odo, with Matthew Matai, Luke and Job as interpreters until the couple learnt the local language. The *Daphne* also took aboard three women with their children. All were in fear of their lives, and one had hidden in the bush since her husband and child had

---

12 Young diary, *NIV*, 1905–06, 14.
13 Stevens 1950, 361–403, 387; Young diary, *NIV*, 1905–06, 15; Hopkins, 'North Mala District', *SCL*, Apr 1907, 157; 'Schooner Wrecked in the South Seas', *Advertiser*, 7 June 1906, 8.

been killed in January. Becalmed at Bita'ama, they managed to row the overloaded small cutter a few kilometres to Welieke and Gamu Island. Caulfeild and Young then took the whaleboat down to Subongi (Coleridge Bay) in west Fataleka to visit Henry Bu'ai before sailing back to Fo'odo, where they found that Baalmoli, one of their baptismal candidates, had been shot while working in his garden. Tommy came down from Gwai'au in the mountains and helped bury the man, who left behind a wife and five children.[14]

The *Daphne* now sailed south once more, heading for Fiu where Young, herself stricken with fever, meet with Caleb and other former Queensland labourers. Then they crept on to 'Aoke Island, where she described the chief:

> I saw the old chief—a veritable heathen savage. He would not appear for some time, and then came out with a rush and a yell, shaking a spear—such an ugly looking, wicked man![15]

They continued south to Langalanga Lagoon and on as far as Onepusu, calling at Biakwa, Su'u and Paulin on the way. A few days later, Young was taken to Aola on Guadalcanal to catch the steamer back to Australia on 9 July. Miss C.S. Dring, who had made an earlier trip to Malaita, arrived on the same steamer and took up residence at Onepusu.[16]

Florence Young returned to Australia via British New Guinea. She visited Samarai and the Abels at Kwato Mission in China Strait and also took the opportunity to call in at the QKM's North Queensland missions and Rev. Macintyre's Presbyterian Mission at Walkerston outside Mackay. Historian David Wetherell credits Charles Abel's contact with Horace and Ernest Young in 1909 as instrumental in Abel's desire to begin an industrial mission at Kwato. But it may have been this earlier, 1906 Florence Young visit to Abel at Kwato, and resulting discussions on the value of industry-based Christianity, which gave the Young brothers the final assurance they needed to invest heavily in land on Malaita to establish the Malayta Company coconut plantation and also led to Abel's similar plans for Kwato.[17]

---

14 Young diary, *NIV*, 1905–06, 16.
15 *Ibid.*, 16.
16 *Ibid.*, 17.
17 Wetherell 1996, 102–03; Young 1925, 177. The Youngs considered taking up land in Milne Bay to begin plantations, but chose instead to begin the Malayta Company, directly aiding the SSEM's Malaita work.

Figure 6.6: Much of the religious teaching employed a roll of illustrated Bible stories. Here Northcote Deck and his staff carry a roll as they go ashore to preach at Fouia in Lau Lagoon.
Source: Deck Collection, Black and White Photographs, 36.

After Young's third visit to Solomon Islands, the *Daphne* was soon off again, delivering teachers to their stations around Malaita: Thomas Ambiasim to Kwari`ekwa (Su`u Harbour, west `Are`are) and Isaac to Subongi (west Fataleka). Thomas Moona, Jimmy Philip and Charlie and Louisa Tarasol-Aurora travelled with them. At Kwari`ekwa, Samson Forlesikwa met the boat and Ambiasin landed, then they continued to Kwaria Bay, near Fo`odo, where Isaac was landed and much welcomed by Henry Bu`ai. At Fo`odo, Caulfeild was absent and the men on the station were 'away hunting bushmen, who were found lying in wait to kill someone'.[18] The men at the outstation insisted that they remain under constant guard while the Tarasol-Aurora's possessions were unloaded, including a water tank.

---

18   Abbott diary, *NIV*, 1905–06, 17.

At the end of July 1906, Watkinson and a party from the Kwai-Ngongosila station sailed off to Sinalagu again, after which they moved on to `Aioo Island where they remained for 23 days, living in an abandoned house and inhibited by incessant rain. Enoch Jack Lio was from Afilikwoi on the mainland and Daniel Mosman came from Maanawai, where he had built a small house. They gained permission for Lio to build on land at the river market at Afilikwoi, thought to be the best base from which to contact the scattered population. In the short time available, a school was erected at `Aioo as was the frame of a three-room house for Thomas Tavangtang-Sandwich.[19]

In August, on another trip to Sinalagu, Watkinson and his crew climbed the steep mountains at the back and found a tiny new school high up at Nuu`ina and a larger one at Wunfor.[20] Another ex-Queensland man, David Barata, had tried to settle on his father's land opposite `Aioo Island, but found it too difficult to carry on a Christian life in isolation. He boarded the *Daphne* to travel to Kwai-Ngongosila, where the mission house was complete and the teaching activities were progressing well. Joseph Wilkinson had visited Sinalagu several times and made a trip down to Walade and Port Adam on Small Malaita to visit the several ex-Queensland QKM men there, and a family, Maggie and Tom and their children. He made no mention in *Not in Vain* that this was a Melanesian Mission base and also near a major Melanesian Mission settlement (Sa`a), another sign of the rivalry between the two missions.[21]

Onepusu: QKM Headquarters

As QKM-SSEM plans developed during the mid-1900s, Onepusu became the headquarters, with Malu`u and Kwai-Ngongosila providing the main north and east bases and servicing many outstations. Substantial houses were built at Malu`u and Fo`odo during 1905, but Onepusu in west `Are`are had the natural advantages to become the main headquarters. Two ex-Queensland men and one woman had settled at Onepusu in about 1902, built a tiny school and three houses and began to clear the land. The Melanesian Mission's Walter Ivens visited them in 1903 hoping to establish a base there. In the end, the QKM followed the lead and

---

19 Watkinson diary, *NIV*, 1905–06, 22–23.
20 *Ibid.*, 23.
21 Young diary, *NIV*, 1905–06, 15.

purchased land at Onepusu in June–July 1905.[22] Onepusu is on a narrow neck of land formed from a raised coral reef that encloses a safe bay, close to the large bay at Waisisi (Royalist Harbour), and soil along the coast opposite is fertile. It had the further advantages of being a regular stopping point for canoes travelling up and down the coast, close to Aola, Guadalcanal, where the steamer called, and an easy sail from the main port and capital at Tulagi and its neighbouring commercial satellite islands of Gavutu and Makambo. Onepusu also sat away from the mangroves and swamps that were the main source of mosquitoes and the dreaded malaria.

Figure 6.7: The newly constructed SSEM mission house at Onepusu, west Malaita, probably in 1905.
Source: Deck Collection, Black and White Photographs, 54.

By mid-1905 Onepusu was progressing well. The mission had purchased around 24 hectares on the 400-metre-wide peninsula. This was being cleared and planted with coconuts by 40 workers. The main house was substantial and comfortable, with four bedrooms, a dining room and a kitchen, with verandas on three sides. Built on 3-metre stumps with only one set of stairs, it caught the breezes and was secure. Abbott was

---

22 'An Itinerary of a Journey around Malaita', *NIV*, 1907–08, 8.

busy building a boatshed, a women's house and kitchen, and a wharf and harbour beacon, and repairing the whaleboat. They had taken two or three orphaned children into the house. Mrs Ruddell described the scene at Onepusu:

> The weather has been beautiful, we get lovely cool breezes; you would enjoy the view from the high veranda, of glittering sea on one side, and beautiful wooded mountains across the harbour … The heathen come to work, and some get calico for wages in advance, as they have nothing to wear while they work, and any that come near the Mission House put a little covering of some sort on … The heathen come and look about; they wear a lava-lava of all shades and colours, the women the same, and their teeth are blackened through lime and betel nut, which they chew; some have nice faces and well formed bodies, but others are covered with skin diseases.[23]

Once Miss C.S. Dring arrived at Onepusu in 1906, she and Mrs Ruddell began school and medical work while Richard Ruddell supervised land clearing and the planting of 20 hectares of coconuts. The aim was to begin a commercial plantation to support the mission's work.[24]

Expanding the Northern Base: Bita'ama and Talafaina (Fo'odo)

In September 1904, Caulfeild travelled from Gavutu to Bita'ama to see Jackson Kaiviti (Kai'figi), son of Lau bigman Kwaisulia. Kwaisulia, who was related to the people of Bita'ama and nearby Basakana Island, spent several months of each year at Bita'ama, which was one of several centres for porpoise hunting.[25] Perhaps they reasoned that since Bita'ama was a centre of activity the site would facilitate the expansion of Christianity. What the missionaries failed to realise was that the hunts involved spells and rituals that their presence disturbed.

---

23 Mrs Ruddell Letter, *NIV*, 1905–06, 19. The teeth-blackening is intentionally applied and is not, as has often been supposed, from chewing betel nut.
24 Young 1925, 176.
25 Information from Leonard Kakalu'ae, grandson of Kwaisulia, Honiara, 25 July 2006.

Figure 6.8: Malu'u mission house, north Malaita, probably in the 1910s.
Source: Deck Collection, Black and White Photographs, 119.

The QKM wanted to purchase land at Bita'ama and had asked Kwaisulia to arrange the deal. Jackson, at Bita'ama for market day, reneged on his offer to transport Caulfeild, who was forced to set off in a dinghy as far as Malu'u, accompanied by Hopkins from the Melanesian Mission. When they met Jackson at Gwaru he apologised and said that his canoe had been too overloaded to take Caulfeild. Hopkins then offered to lend Caulfeild his dinghy if he could find a crew at Malu'u, which he did. They set off immediately, travelling all night.

Kwaisulia met with Caulfeild but refused to arrange a land sale at Bita'ama, and suggest that Welieke, a couple of kilometres from there, would suffice. He promised to come to show them the site. Caulfeild and his sleep-deprived crew kept sailing down the lagoon to Ngorefou, Hopkins's base, and the next day returned to Maana'oba Island accompanied by Kwaisulia. Winds from the north forced them to row all the way back to Malu'u. Kwaisulia and Abu'ofa negotiated over the Bita'ama site, but neither yielded, and then all set out for Bita'ama and Welieke. The QKM staff later judged Welieke unsuitable and negotiations continued over another area nearby. In the end, Talafaina (Fo'odo), not Bita'ama, became a major Malu'u outstation.

The whole mission phenomena must have worried Malaitan leaders such as Kwaisulia, even though they appreciated the European goods brought by the new presence. They may not have understood that the missions wanted to permanently alienate the land they had 'purchased', since the permanent transfer of land ownership was rare in Malaitan land tenure systems. The QKM party met Jackson near Bita'ama, and Kwaisulia was nearby at Basakana on his way to Gela. Wearing a pandanus leaf hat and little else, he was still trying to negotiate a high price for the land at Welieke and appeared concerned at the QKM success at Malu'u and Bita'ama. There were now 20 ex-Queensland Christians at the Bita'ama and Fo'odo bases. Large groups of adults and children showed their interest by helping to clear roads and cut timber for buildings.[26]

Caulfeild recorded in his journal his experiences on Malaita from July 1906 to the following April, and it carries us through the transition from the QKM to the SSEM. The only real change was the name. Caulfeild was at Fo'odo when the *Daphne* left on a trip. Charlie and Louisa Tarasol-Aurora were doing well; Charlie's knowledge of Pijin Fijian enabled him to communicate easily with labourers returning from Fiji who preferred to settle at mission stations rather than their former communities. Caulfeild walked back to Malu'u through the mountains, spending a night high up at Gwai'au on the way, which was the home of Peter Abu'ofa's parents and brothers. Back at Irobuli (Malu'u), John Kwa'ala had received death threats, and sometime later, after the chief of his people had been killed, he sought safety at the school at 'Ainiuke begun by John Aliwane.[27] Caulfeild went around to Maana'oba in late September with Daniel Fukia, who had built his house a kilometre or so along the outer beach from the main village, being yet another stopping place on the way to and from Malu'u. Back in Malu'u in mid-October, a seven-year-old boy, the son of Job, was murdered as he walked along a track with his mother as they were returning from a dance at Gwai'au. Caulfeild had seen a canoe with about 17 men aboard paddling fast below the cliffs that morning, but thought nothing of it. Clearly, the canoe had contained the execution party seeking Job, who was unwell and had stayed home.

---

26 *NIV*, 1904–05, 10.
27 Caulfeild diary, *NIV*, 1906–07, 29–30.

Men rushed to the Kalkie *beu abu* (sacred house) when their big slit-drum announce the death, but they were divided as to whether they should retaliate. Job's brother Moses had been killed in similar fashion at Suama 10 months earlier.[28]

The next day, Caulfeild left with Abbott on *Daphne* to visit Fo`odo. He returned a week later over the mountains via Gwai`au, where he was told large fighting parties were moving through the district. At Malu`u, nearly all of the people had gathered at Kwaidiu, about 3 kilometres from Kalkie. Three large canoes had been found hidden in the harbour, supposedly sent by a bigman at Gwass, Isabel Island. Fearing attack, the people had taken to the bush, sleeping rough. The Kalkie houses were almost deserted, and only Peter Abu`ofa, Sam Tu`wu and about six others remained. A guard was mounted for the Sunday service, but when the attack came it was on a village nearer to Gwai`au. Afterward, one of Abu`ofa's brothers found the attackers sleeping in a cave and shot one, which turned their anger back on the Gwass bigman who had hired them.[29]

By the time Caulfeild returned to Malu`u late in December, after a month at Onepusu, the new church was complete. It had a broken-coral floor, a corrugated iron roof and a bell. The first service was held on New Year's Day of 1907, attended by 150, followed by a celebratory tea party for mission staff Caulfeild, Charlie Tarasol-Aurora, Abu`ofa, Emma, Meshach, Charlie Lofeah, Daisy and Ruth. Job also came along; he could speak little English, but Tarasol-Aurora had a long talk with him in Pijin Fijian.[30]

The euphoria was short-lived since murders always remained a factor. On 8 January, two women and a girl were murdered near Malu`u, butchered terribly in retaliation for the death of another girl. The killers had been guided by a spirit divination light called *unu* in north Malaita. Barnabas Alebiu and others who went to investigate were sickened by the 'terrible way the bodies were cut about'.[31] One week later, news came from Fo`odo that Peter Suto's brother had been shot at Thathangi and his students there had all fled to Fo`odo. Caulfeild went to help and was there on the evening of Tuesday the 26th when a woman gave the alarm that something was wrong down at the landing place. Two young girls had

---

28   Ibid., 30.
29   Ibid., 31.
30   Ibid., 31–32.
31   Ibid., 32.

been attacked. One was dead and the other, recently arrived at the school, had a deep axe wound to the back of her head and died soon afterward. Sometime later Tarasol-Aurora met the murderer, a youth too young to grow a beard. The Christian Malaitans placed their trust in their Lord and were not overtly perturbed by such events, but non-Christians lived in fear behind fortifications. Caulfeild visited one of Abu`ofa's 'heathen brothers' who lived only 3 kilometres from the school atop of a rocky hill, his hamlet surrounded by a thick wall over 4 metres high.[32]

The QKM's work spread slowly and faced ongoing retaliation. At `Ainiuke, John Kwa`ala's wife and sister were ready for baptism, but a few days later some Gwass people destroyed his yam and *pana* garden on which he depended for food for the coming months. Former plantation workers often came to the mission seeking help. Mark Ngalafoo, son of an ex-Queensland man and now the leader at Usulangi, wanted the QKM to begin a school in the village. Occasionally individuals, some quite young, came to the mission from non-Christian communities. In early April, nine-year-old Akalofenda came down and asked to stay at the mission and to be protected from his family if they tried to reclaim him, which they soon did.[33]

Kwai and Ngongosila

Kwai and Ngongosila are small contiguous islands just off the east Kwara`ae coast, each of 10 to 12 hectares and each with a 1900s population of around 150. A sandbar allowed walking between the two at low tide. This pair of islands was at the core of the Guala`ala`a language, which was also used as the trading dialect along parts of the east coast. When Walter Ivens and his crew rounded Malaita in a whaleboat early in 1900 they had called at Ngongosila. The Melanesian Mission hoped to include Kwai and Ngongosila in their outreach, and Amasia arranged for a youth named Kwaifunu to go to Norfolk Island. In 1905, when QKM missionaries began work at the two islands, they made no mention of the ex-Fijian labourer Amasia's earlier work there, although they must have known of it. They focused instead on Enoch Sori and his son Charlie. In mid-1905 Enoch had established a school attended by women and

32   *Ibid.*, 33.
33   *Ibid.*

children. The QKM purchased 0.8 hectare of land at Feriasi on the mainland opposite Kwai, which they hoped to make the centre of their east coast operation.[34]

Figure 6.9: Feriasi SSEM mission station on the mainland opposite Kwai and Ngongosila, east Malaita.
Source: Deck Collection, Black and White Photographs, 49.

In 1905, Caulfeild was in charge of Malu`u. Ruddell, the missionary who had spent a short time with Abu`ofa at Malu`u in 1900 and had since been stationed at the QKM's Mossman branch, returned with his wife to work alongside Watkinson at Onepusu, now fully functioning as the mission's headquarters. Abbott was based at Kwai on the east coast. They often swapped around, depending on health, abilities, leave periods and other duties. By February 1906, Caulfeild was in charge of Onepusu and Watkinson and Abbott were building the mission house at Ngongosila. Several QKM-trained New Hebrideans had also joined the mission's forces on Malaita: Thomas Nguna, who had visited Malaita and Siota with Ruddell in 1900, was back again. Tavangtang-Sandwich (the New Hebridean prayer leader from the QKM Isis branch) and

---

34   *NIV*, 1904–05, 13.

Tarasol-Aurora and his wife Louisa have already been mentioned.[35] The *Daphne* continuously plied between the Malaitan stations, Aola on Guadalcanal, Tulagi, Makambo and Gavutu carrying supplies and mission personnel. In November, the substantial Onepusu mission house was almost complete and Watkinson took the *Daphne* around Malaita once more, out of Onepusu to the east via Maramasike Passage and on to Takataka, with which they had had no contact since July. There they renewed acquaintance with John Lofana and an old man, Hoaredoa, before heading for 'Aioo Island where Thomas Sipolo was waiting, but they were unable to meet Peter Suto, another ex-Queensland man. At Sinalagu, Sam Pilate was still operating his school, assisted by Simeon. Watkinson was able to meet with 'Arumae, an ageing bigman from Tetefou just inland from Sinalagu, who had organised a failed 1886 attack on the Queensland labour trade ship the *Young Dick*.[36] 'Arumae admitted that his people had tried to thwart Pilate, but he seemed impressed at the QKM's perseverance and promised to cooperate.

The Ngongosila station was prosperous. When Watkinson visited in November 1905, Enoch, who had been despondent during the missionary's last visit, was in good spirits and had built a substantial school. The Ngongosila chief expressed regret that he had been away when Young had purchased land on Kwai, since he would have preferred the base to be on Ngongosila, and he offered land for a second mission house.[37] His offer was accepted, and during the following February and March Watkinson helped Abbott complete a house on Kwai. The coming of the mission allowed a reciprocal relationship to develop. Taiboo, the leading Kwai bigman, was pleased to have the mission base on his island as a sign of his power, and the QKM used the occasion of a wedding feast, when Taiboo's son was married to an 'Ataa woman, to preach to the assembled crowd. Maifou gave Watkinson the name Kala (small), which he said had been his father's name. In the meantime, villagers inland from the coast opposite killed a person from Kwai in March and sent messages that they intended to kill one of the missionaries as well.[38]

---

35   *NIV*, 1905–06, 6.
36   *Ibid.*, 7. 'Arumae (sometimes improperly written Arumai) organised the May 1886 attack, in which four Europeans and one recruit from the ship died, along with about 14 Kwaio men. 'Arumae afterward posted a bounty for a European death to avenge the Kwaio ones. Information from David Akin, 15 Aug 2009. Also see Fowler 1969; Keesing 1986a; Keesing 1986c.
37   *NIV*, 1905–16, 8.
38   Watkinson diary, *NIV*, 1905–06, 9.

Figure 6.10: The SSEM mission station on Ngongosila Island, east Malaita.
Source: Deck Collection, Black and White Photographs, 57.

As already mentioned, the QKM also negotiated to purchase land on ʻAioo Island near the border between east Kwaio and ʻAreʻare. The plan was to reach ex-Queensland Malaitans in that area, and the mission encouraged returned labourers to settle at the new Christian communities. The *Ivanhoe*, out of Queensland, landed one group in May 1905 and six others trained by the Anglicans on Norfolk Island soon joined them.[39] The QKM (and the SSEM) operated through unceasing circulation around the island. Their ships, cutters and whaleboats made it all possible, providing a degree of mobility that outmanoeuvred the Anglicans, and after 1909, the government.

New Gender Patterns

Ben Burt suggests that Malaitans interpreted Christianity as the arrival of a female ancestor or spirit. This may have made the new religion easier to absorb without damaging the male spiritual hierarchy. Christianity broke and abolished women's taboos. In the 1910s and 1920 this led to *bulu* cults, an intermediate alternative way to proceed, drawing neither on the power of the *akalo* (ancestral spirits) or Christianity.[40] These cults may have aided the QKM-SSEM in another way, since many of their missionaries were women. In precontact Malaita, men achieved gender

---

39 *NIV*, 1903–04, 5–6, 8.
40 Burt 1994, 256; Akin 1996.

and social identity through warfare and rituals, whereas women matured biologically into femininity, although they were severely restricted during menstruation and birth. Men provided protection, did the heaviest garden clearing, hunting and deep-sea fishing, and waged war against enemies. They also controlled formal power structures. The labour trade provided access to metal tools, which freed men from about one-third of the time once spent in heavy garden work, canoe-building and artefact production. Women's work seems to have increased.[41]

Although there were a good proportion of women among the foreign mission workers, the Malaitans heavily involved in missions were almost always males. Often these men had Christian wives who were the unsung partners in their endeavours, but the women were never the spokespeople for the new religion. The labour trade and Christianity predominantly benefited males, heightened their place in the existing social system and provided new occupations beyond old social structures. Although the state limited some previous social mechanisms that ensured male control (warfare, for instance), *kastom* has incorporated other changes that exacerbate women's indebtedness to men. Patriarchal masculinities have survived well in the new Melanesia and *kastom* works largely to benefit males.

Pacific people, as Marilyn Strathern suggests, are gendered 'masculine' or 'feminine' through social activities, the concept not immediately related to their anatomy.[42] In recent centuries, Western concepts of gender relate to individuals, whereas in the Pacific personal relationships are created through exchange with others, both male and female. Pacific gender is contextual and can be applied to nonhuman things. The norm, as far as European missionaries were concerned, was nuclear families in which the husband slept with his wife and couples brought up their children under one roof. On Malaita, differences between males and females were exhibited as residential separation and male (and in some contexts female) fear of pollution from inappropriate contact with menstrual blood and childbirth. The most *abu* priests usually slept in their men's house, and Malaitan couples usually (but not always) slept in separate houses.

---

41 Bennett 1987, 34; Akin 2013a, 18.
42 Jolly 2000b; M. Strathern 1972; 1987, 279–302; 1988.

Adoption for shorter and longer periods was very common, and children were, and still are, often brought up for shorter or longer periods by uncles, aunts, grandparents and older siblings or cousins. The nuclear family concept remains foreign to Malaitans—the differences between a cousin and a brother are still largely irrelevant, even in modern urban settings. Mimicking European family structures brought praise from missionaries steeped in European middle-class notions of normality, but Malaitans have never abandoned extended family concepts.

Malaitans still observe gender taboos: a female will never allow a postpubescent male to step over her legs because it violates sexual propriety and can be seen as a sexual proposition. Ancestral taboos are violated if a woman steps over a man. The protection of positive values is advanced by a prohibition of negatives. Once gender spheres are breached, transgressions are more likely and compensation payments may result. Other forms of new behaviour were adopted as well. Clothes became *de rigueur*, although Europeans also thought that they harboured disease and that wet clothes caused illness, and across Melanesia both males and females were discouraged from wearing European clothes above the waist. Missionaries advocated building houses off the ground on short stumps, which had some health benefits. However, higher mountain areas were much colder than coastal zones and, despite the smoky environment that resulted, building houses there on the ground made sense because such dwellings are much warmer. There were also implications in allowing access under houses. Even today, many Christian Malaitan men and even women will not walk under clotheslines where women's garments are ever hung, or under houses when women or their belongings are known to be above. Honiara has two under-street walkways that have been closed for years, mainly because Malaitans will not use them.

Transgressing gender taboos was once, and in some places still is, believed to cause sickness and death unless purificatory sacrifices were offered to ancestral spirits through customary priests. Sometimes compensation was also demanded from the offending party. These residual beliefs remain strong. It was an enormous leap of faith to put one's life in the hands of an untried Christian God and ignore the possible consequences. Trust in the power of a Christian God did not occur quickly. Discussions with David Akin, an anthropologist with long connections with the Kwaio, and my own observations back to 1976, suggest that there were often various stages. The first converts must have been watched carefully to see if ancestral punishments occurred when they breached taboos. Once these did not occur, others would have joined them with more confidence. One common reason given for conversion to Christianity has long been to gain protection from ancestors angry at violations of taboos. But this did not mean an entire change in belief systems. Total conversion from one system of religious faith to another was a slow process taking many years.

Figure 6.11: Street scene in the women's quarters on Ferasubua Island, Lau Lagoon, 1906.
Source: Beattie Collection, 526.

Missionaries were universally sorry for Malaitan women, whom they viewed as downtrodden and degraded by their menfolk. Writing in the 1900s about the Lau artificial islands, Ellen Wilson, wife of the Anglican bishop, asked, 'Could women find a much lower level?' She described the 'low hovels' down a 'narrow dirty alley' and the 'darkness and stifling atmosphere' in the women's quarters.[43] Missionaries usually wanted to liberate women from drudgery and separation during menstruation and birth, and complained about the way women were regarded on Malaita, often concluding that they were treated like slaves. SSEM missionary

---

43   Wilson 1915, 54.

Catherine (Kathy) Deck described women at Kwai Island off east Malaita in 1908 and, through lack of knowledge, may have invented and certainly exaggerated customs related to infanticide:

> The maternity customs here are very cruel. The mother had to live in a tiny dog-kennel of a hut by herself, and a young girl is set apart to bring her food, which may not come to the island in the ordinary canoes, but must be brought on a rough bamboo raft to a special beach and conveyed by the women's path to the hut.
>
> If the baby cries much on the first night, or becomes sickly, it is buried alive! This is done to break the spell. It is supposed that otherwise all succeeding children will die.
>
> This had happened twice during our stay here, but we have only just heard of the custom.
>
> The last case was a little boy, a first child, and its mother buried it three times. Twice it writhed and cried; her heart failed her, and she took it out. But superstition gained the day, and the third time she completed the dreadful work by actually standing upon the little mound.[44]

Enraged by their understandings of what they saw, Misses Deck and Dring went to see the mother and could not understand the angry response from the other women when they tried to comfort her. The two were frustrated by taboos stopping them touching the mother or providing food and medicine. Miss Dring stormed off to find Maifou, the chief, who wisely had retreated to the *beu abu* and would not come out. The next day, Maifou placated the missionaries and allowed them to visit the woman, as long as they did not touch her.[45] Deck was not alone in her belief that infanticide was customary in some circumstances, as Ellen Wilson repeats this in the 1910s. However, much of her writing is recounting mission stories and is not drawn from her own experience. She quotes Lizzie Telegsem from Port Adam as her direct source:

> Many are the tales that Lizzie tells of the heathen customs among the women, and of the infanticide which takes place to such a frightening extent. Many and many a time has Johnson [Telegsem] interfered and rescued an infant from its living grave, attracted by its cries.[46]

---

44 Catherine M.A. Deck, 'Life at Kwai', *NIV*, 1907–08, 34–35.
45 *Ibid.*
46 Wilson 1915, 50.

This missionary interpretation needs to be considered in relation to wider missionary reactions to the ancestral life of Malaitans and other Pacific peoples. The denigration is common in other contexts. Margaret Jolly takes up the issue for Vanuatu and Fiji where maternal practices were condemned.[47] David Akin, writing on Malaita, notes that Europeans blamed women for not being maternal and that mothers and infants were portrayed as 'helpless victims of cruel ancestral birth taboos'.[48] Nevertheless, even taking deliberate creation of tropes into account, the frequency of the references to infanticide is puzzling.

Roger Keesing's articles on the Kwaio area suggest that Malaitan women never challenge the dominant ideology in a countercultural way.[49] Keesing said that whereas men 'depict themselves as active agents in maintaining relations with the ancestors (through sacrifice, prayer, and ritual), Kwaio women often depict themselves as custodians of virtue, the moral keystones of their tiny settlements'.[50] He suggested that women see their bodies in terms of purity, not pollution. More recently, David Akin has brought into question status and age differences among the same group of women, which affect male and female perceptions of women's roles and temper some of Keesing's conclusions.[51] Ben Burt rather confounds this picture by mention of *fataabu keni* (women priest) in Kwara'ae. Admittedly rare, they add complexity to the interpretation.[52] In support of this, Akin describes Kwaio women as sometimes having access to significant ancestral powers in the past. Some women had great knowledge and powers, often granted by ancestresses. These women had their own shrines and were respected by men, and sometimes feared.[53] Malaitan women also interpreted separation during menstruation and at birth very differently than did the missionaries who wanted to end such practices. Malaitan women viewed their network as providing support, not alienation. Akin's research suggests that the meaning of menstruation and other women's taboos has changed greatly, particularly since the 1940s, and these changes have had implications for the forms of taboos and the status of women. Changes occurred partly due to inroads made by Christianity and the challenge of taboos being discarded by Christians and their communities,

---

47 Jolly 1988.
48 Akin 2013a, 117, 376 n 77.
49 Keesing 1985b; 1987.
50 Keesing 1987, 38.
51 Akin 2003.
52 Burt 1994, 58.
53 Akin 2003.

which have also influenced changes in the ancestral system. This is an important reason for the decline in the power of ancestrally connected women. Burt and Akin's work has retrieved gender patterns that have been submerged during the twentieth century, which has led to a more male-centric Malaitan depiction of power.[54]

Francis Bugotu, who possessed more Western education than any other Solomon Islander in the 1960s, tried to explain the role of women:

> Whatever the man acquires, becomes the woman's. How could she be a slave? She fulfils at her own wish, at her family's wish and at her husband's wish, all the functions as dictated by society-codes to the fullest of her abilities. She doesn't have to be told to work hard as she does, to carry as much as she does, and to look after her children as well as she does. Society is the judge and she knows it.
>
> She knows also that she is the most respected by the society in which she belongs. Her smile does not show any stings or restrictions of slavery. She knows and feels she belongs, and most important of all, the society and people belong to her.[55]

Women who moved to Christian villages lost statuses that they would have had if they stayed in ancestral villages. As mentioned earlier, women's workloads also grew as metal tools allowed the clearing of more gardens, which in turn allowed more pigs to be raised, their food provided mostly through women's labours.

Conclusion

Although the Anglicans and the SSEM had different *modi operandi*, the final result was still always religious pluralism rather than any simple replacement of indigenous religions by outside forms. Malaitans expressed agency in the labour trade and also in their approach to Christianity. It can be argued that Malaitans were responsible for the arrival of the QKM in the Solomons and for the formation of the SSEM. Peter Abu`ofa brought the QKM with him in 1894–95 and the decision to found the SSEM was based on the ongoing, extensive QKM work on Malaita. No doubt Florence Young saw it as the Lord's doing, but the

---

54 Akin 2004; 2005. I am indebted here to David Akin for his patient and insightful assistance.
55 Bugotu 1968, 551.

decisions she made, along with the QKM board and her staff, including the move to transform the QKM into the SSEM in 1904, were also based on practical considerations. Malaitans were the dominant group from the Solomons and the largest single island group in the Queensland labour trade (though the Solomons made up only one-third of the overall Islander community in Queensland). Another point favouring Malaita and the Solomons was that there was less established missionary work there (only the Anglicans) since the Catholics and Methodists were new arrivals in the archipelago. Furthermore, a British protectorate had been established in the Solomons whereas in the New Hebrides the government situation was less clear cut. Perhaps most important, Malaitans, both individuals and communities, had encouraged the QKM to set up on Malaita. Although Young paints a picture of difficult but willing souls ready to be saved for Christ, Malaitans' motivations, as this chapter suggests, were complex, and there was never a wholesale conversion of the sort Young envisioned or portrayed.

While outsiders tend to perceive ancestor-worshiping Malaitans as conservative, they have been in many ways less fixed in their views and more open to experimentation and innovation than have Christians in denominations with set doctrines. Religion on Malaita was in some respects a very personal thing and its specific practice depended on taboos laid down by one's particular ancestors. Neighbours could react differently to a specific circumstance because of their specific ancestors. Malaitans can experiment, and if the experiment works, change can be rapid. They were (and many still are) in regular contact with their ancestors and can seek guidance in novel situations and monitor change. This flexibility in religious behaviour can extend to change in general, and Akin suggests that this 'mindset' contributes to Malaitan adaptability. It may explain why they have remained so successful in the modern Solomon Islands. Malaitans did not abandon bridewealth or compensation payments. Malaitans sometimes changed from one church to another, or descended to coastal Christian villages only to return later to their ancestral villages to suit their circumstances. They accentuated and modified some Christian rules in ways similar to their management of ancestral taboos, and they gave greater emphasis than some missionaries wished to confession, which is also important in the ancestral religions. In other words, Malaitans were crucial agents in the processes through which Christianity developed on their island, and even in other parts of the Solomons, particularly where the SSEM spread.[56]

The QKM made fast progress in its early decades, not so much through quick conversions, since they came slowly, but rather in establishing a network of major bases and outstations that laid the foundation for later growth, and through creating an efficient, small seagoing fleet. From Abu`ofa's tentative start in 1894, and with the support of other ex-QKM students who had returned home, the QKM in the space of a few years was able to become a clear rival to the Melanesian Mission, which had taken 30 years to gain a foothold and still had achieved nothing like the spread of the QKM. Both churches were positioned to deal with the coming exodus from Queensland as the deportation process moved into final gear in the mid-1900s. Missions built villages specifically to accommodate the returning Malaitans.

The QKM proved that dedication, finances and vigorous, determined leadership could speed the growth of Christianity on Malaita. They were assisted by having available both European and Pacific Islander staff freed up by the closure of the QKM in Queensland and by the mass exodus of literate Christian Malaitans from there during the new century's first decade. While Florence Young would no doubt have cited the powers of prayer and the blessings of the Holy Spirit as enabling the QKM's successful move to Malaita, temporal factors were clearly key to how the process unfolded.

To answer my earlier question, Malaitans in the 1890s–1900s did indeed distinguish doctrinal differences between the Anglicans and the QKM. There were similarities: both were Protestant faiths and used mainly Pijin English in day-to-day communications, although Melanesian Mission official policy advocated use of Mota, the Anglican's chosen *lingua franca*. Both faiths rigidly separated their followers from the surrounding non-Christians, which was not the norm in Queensland or Fiji. The practice of separation began for the QKM on Malaita through Abu`ofa at Malu`u, developed from the need to ensure safety from attack. Both the QKM-SSEM and the Melanesian Mission found it easier if their adherents made a total break from their previous lives, and this usually meant shifting their residence closer to a mission station or at least to the coast.

---

56 For processes of religious innovation, see Akin 2003; 2004; 2005.

Non-Christian Malaitans, for their part, also wanted and even demanded such separation because it set apart Christians who violated taboos, for example by refusing to separate women at menstruation and birth or observe the sanctity of ancestral shrines. To force ancestral communities to live in close contact with people so openly flouting taboos would have ensured violent confrontation. All that said, *pace* Alan Tippett's analysis of 'modified paganism', there was also accommodation alongside separation.[57]

On some occasions, the Melanesian Mission and QKM staff tried to convince nascent Christian communities to join their faiths, with one triumphant and the other withdrawing. There was a constant jockeying for dominance during the 1900s. The rival Christian groups (including the Catholics and, later, the Seventh-day Adventists) sometimes displayed a palpable, mutual dislike, although their personnel could be counted on to support each other during emergencies. Once a particular denomination was established in a settlement, the differences became more obvious. Modern SSEC members would probably point to significant differences such as that between baptisms of young children (Anglican) and mature-age baptism (SSEC). Anthropologist Ian Hogbin, who spent some months living near Malu`u in 1933, provided the first independent published assessment of the way the two Christian denominations operated in To`aba`ita. Hogbin found the Anglican approach at least superficially similar to High Anglican Christianity outside the Solomons: there was a church providing Matins and Evensong services, celebrated partly in the two languages of To`aba`ita and Lau.[58]

It is hard from the distance of a century to discern exactly what the differences were on the ground in the 1900s, but another was the Open Brethren thinking that permeated the QKM-SSEM, leavened with equality in front of God and openness and acceptance, as well as less ornate physical trappings in line with Baptist simplicity. In this church rules and formality were minimal, and if one believed in holiness and sanctification then it followed that there was equality for everyone who had achieved this state. There are indications that the QKM-SSEM did not stand on ceremony, and that there was acceptance of all in front of

---

57 Tippett 1967, 319–29.
58 Hogbin 1939, 176.

God. In the 1930s, the Malu'u SSEM church was not ornamented and adherents placed no store on the treasures of earth, preferring the future treasures of heaven. As Hogbin wrote:

> Holy Communion, in which the mission has substituted taro and coconut fluid for bread and wine, is celebrated from time to time, and adult baptism by complete immersion is also carried out, though only after candidates have passed an oral examination. Confession is also practiced, but the penitent, instead of telling his sins in private to a teacher, has to humble himself before a full congregation. Public prayers are then offered for his forgiveness, though if the offence is a serious one he may be temporarily suspended from church membership.[59]

Many Solomon Islanders found the simplicity and directness of the QKM-SSEM message fulfilling. It contained a rejection of bishops and priests, tradition, altars, and accommodation with sinful society, with a powerful focus on salvation of the individual soul and on prayer. Liturgical worship was also rejected as 'formalistic' and limiting to the power of the Holy Spirit. Prayer, both individual and collective, was paramount and often lengthy.

Although 'God's Gentlemen' (the Melanesian Mission's European priests) liked to believe that they were one in Christ with their indigenous students, catechists, deacons and priests, one takes the impression that they were actually far more separate from them than were the QKM-SSEM staff. Nonetheless, as already noted, the Melanesian Mission was more 'friendly' to Pacific cultures in that it was not as condemnatory of nonscriptural practices and was willing to accommodate mass conversions led by bigmen. QKM-SSEM conversion was always at an individual level.

Did any 1880s–1890s Malaitans have a depth of Christian knowledge sufficient to be able to debate and to compare the two approaches? By the 1900s, some who had worked in Queensland of Fiji had had 25 years of experience of Christianity, and a few were highly trained in the affairs of their mission churches. Unfortunately, we know little of the views of men like Joseph Wate from Small Malaita or Jack Taloifulia from Lau. Peter Abu'ofa, the most prominent early QKM Malaitan, seems to have had fervour and spiritual commitment, but, because of his limited literacy, no deep understanding of the tenets of QKM Christianity. While we must be cautious in introducing contemporary Malaitans into our equation,

---

59 *Ibid.*, 77.

today there is no shortage of village-level debate about the differences between Christian faiths, and between Christianity and the Bahá'í Faith, as well as newly introduced Islamic beliefs. We can make an informed guess that Malaitans a century ago, too, probably studied the different denominations and formed conclusions as to their values and benefits. A modern Christian response to our question would probably be that spiritual awareness cannot be measured by knowledge of doctrine and texts alone, and that by any Christian standards many of the early Malaitan Christians became devout and worthy.

This and the last two chapters show how important coastal communications were in an age when these mission enclaves could otherwise be isolated for months at a time, and just how many dozens of small Christian settlement there were. The network of ex-Queensland and ex-Fiji men and women was what made Christian expansion possible. If Australia's White Australia Policy had not forced so many Malaitans to return home, Christianity would have grown much more slowly on the island. In the 1900s, the bulk of Malaitans still lived inland, but what is evident from the 1900s descriptions is the beginning of dense coastal communities that grew continuously over the next century. Even so, not until the 1930s and 1940s was fully half of Malaita's population Christian, a much slower rate of growth than on any other of the Solomon Islands, and one must ask why.

Just as tantalising is the question of how aware the Melanesian Mission and the QKM-SEEM hierarchy were of linguistic boundaries and population concentrations on Malaita, and whether they used this knowledge to choose sites for their major bases? The documents I have consulted give no clear answer. Missionaries had only vague notions of how linguistic areas divided, and certainly little idea of where boundaries lay beyond the coast. Geography and history was probably at least as important in their decisions; wind systems that prevailed at different times of the year made it very difficult to move around the coasts until motorised vessels became more common.

The Melanesian Mission initially concentrated its efforts on Small Malaita mainly because it was close to Ulawa Island, an existing Anglican base. Only much later did they target the northeast and northwest coasts. This was a stepping-stone approach that made logistical sense but left a large proportion of the population unexposed to Christianity. The QKM-SSEM took the north coast because of Abu`ofa at Malu`u;

the choice was based on it being near his place of birth and not on any QKM-focused logistic decision. However, Malu'u is within huge Suu'aba Bay, which was a definite advantage. The mission then set up in the central east and west of the main island, with an emphasis on Onepusu, Baunani (the Malayta Company headquarters) and Kwai-Ngongosila. Later, when they expanded to Small Malaita, the new outreach seems to have been run from Onepusu. The Malu'u district in the To'aba'ita-language area was not heavily populated, but it was easy to reach from Tulagi and Gela, as were Onepusu and Baunani. To today's SSEC congregations, Abu'ofa was just as much the founder of the SSEC as was Florence Young. In SSEM history, the year 1894 when Abu'ofa returned remains as significant as 1886, the year the QKM was founded. The next expansion of the QKM strategy gave them control of the Kwara'ae east coast and west Kwaio and west Kwara'ae. Their Kwai-Ngongosila base was the nucleus of the Guala'ala'a language and its trading offshoots, which linked to the Lau in their northern lagoon and the Lau at Walade on south Malaita. The SSEM Kwara'ae and Kwaio bases enabled the SSEC to become the dominant denomination in the most populous central areas of Malaita. Did the QKM-SSEM realise the linguistic advantage of Kwai and Ngongosila, or were they simply attracted to the small twin islands on the central east coast? Certainly, the Melanesian Mission knew that the Walade people on Small Malaita spoke the Lau language, which enabled it to place its next European-staffed base in Lau Lagoon.

When one considers the relentless Christian circumnavigations of Malaita during the century's first decade, there is a sense of missionaries being drawn into ex-Queensland and ex-Fiji networks as their entryways into fortress Malaita. This was more important than any calculated strategic positioning of bases, although Onepusu was well-placed to sustain communications with Aola and Tulagi, just as Fiu was ideally located in the northwest. Early missions were always around the coast, at places easy to access via ships.

What Malaitans thought of the missionary incursions can never be totally clear. Wider analysis of early cross-cultural contacts, particularly research from the New Guinea Highlands, suggests that while Europeans thought they controlled contact situations, in fact local initiatives were just as important, and in fact Europeans and other foreigners were often manipulated to suit local agendas.⁶⁰ How Christianity was perceived—using Burt's Kwara`ae-based analysis of it as a female spirit—was a strong factor in its adoption. And Europeans were always outsiders, 'floating coconuts' in the parlance of modern Malaita, who arrived at the shores, to be picked up and used or ignored by the local people. The missionaries were an intrepid, interloping foreign group to be incorporated, deceived or avoided. Alliances were made, and broken, based primarily on local epistemologies, not on the introduced and partially understood concepts brought by a particular Christian denomination.⁶¹

Crucial also were what personnel were available and their personalities. The QKM was founded by a woman and incorporated European women into its ministry, although the Melanesian Mission male hierarchy seemingly fitted better with the traditional Malaitan emphasis on male power. What Malaitans thought of Florence Young, Kathy Deck and their female colleagues is unclear. These women sometimes broke taboos, unknowingly and knowingly, and were authority figures in a way that Malaitan women seldom could be. Because they were outsiders, with substantial resources, they were able to ignore customary ways of behaving in a manner that even today many Malaitans would find unacceptable. In Malaitan religion, women can be symbolically powerful, and can drive away spirits in a way that men cannot, and some female spirits can push out other ancestral spirits. There may actually have been an advantage to European female missionaries far beyond anything the missionaries themselves ever realised.

These outsiders were supported by returned Malaitan Christians and QKM-SSEM staff from other Solomon and New Hebridean islands. In the early years, Charlie and Louisa Tarasol-Aurora, Thomas Tavangtang-Sandwich, Thomas Nguna and Sam Pilate were just as crucial to the success of the QKM-SSEM as was Peter Abu`ofa. We know very little of their roles, although they were on the mission's front line and capable of living in local conditions, learning new languages, and travelling without complex logistical support.

---

60   In particular, refer to Moore 2003, 154–78; Gammage 1998; Kituai 1998; Schieffelin and Crittenden, with Allen 1991.
61   Gegeo and Watson-Gegeo 1996; 2002; Gegeo 2001.

As was the case with the labour trade, where Malaitan passage masters became key arbiters of access to certain coastal areas, personal relationships linking the outsiders with local leaders were crucial and support from local leaders made all the difference to the success of missions. Lau passage master Kwaisulia and his son Jackson Kaiviti loom large in all government and mission accounts of north Malaita early in the century. They were powerful, often regarded by outsiders as a nuisance and accused of behaving inappropriately, but they were important negotiators and cross-cultural brokers. Clearly, the Christian returning labourers were also important since they negotiated the purchase of land for outstations and were the linguistic links between Christian missions and the local people. Malaitans could benefit from Christian bases, but also feared them because they eroded local autonomy. Missions altered the balance of power and provided a local supply of European manufactured goods that had largely eluded Malaitans who could only access them through the labour trade.[62] The missions also brought a movement of people from inland areas to the coast. This coastal concentration was one reason for Christianity's success and eventually allowed the government easier contact with large numbers of people who had once been inaccessible.

Florence Young had good reason to be pleased with QKM's success on Malaita between 1904 and 1906, enough to make Malaita the centre for the new SSEM after 1907. Her life from 1882 until 1906 was, in retrospect, all preparation for the birth of the SSEM out of the QKM. She was undaunted by Malaita and Malaitans, at a time when even the fledgling administration of the British protectorate had not ventured to establish an administrative base on the island. Her Christian dedication and the wealth of her family and other supporters created a strong, vibrant church in Solomon Islands.

Just as with the Melanesian Mission, the pace of SSEM work on Malaita picked up in a frantic attempt to absorb the new arrivals, with 20 new outstations opened during 1907 alone, and the mission's work extended to Small Malaita, Guadalcanal and Makira. The mission's budget for the year was £1,170, all of it covered by donations. One-third was spent on stores and allowances for missionaries, one-third on purchasing and clearing land and on trade goods. The other third was absorbed by two large expenses: passage fares for the European missionaries and the upkeep and crews of the mission's ships and smaller vessels.

---

62   Moore 2007.

Malaitans who still followed their ancestral religion visited the mission stations, some timidly and others boldly, obviously assessing the Christian enclaves and their future. At Onepusu in 1907, Doromae, an elderly local chief, came to greet the SSEM staff, and for several days inland people came down to tour the new *Evangel*. One young man, Kausimae, whom Kathy Deck described as 'a handsome young heathen', crept up onto the mission house veranda eager to communicate despite the language barrier. Although they may not have known it, their most important visitor was Arisimae (Harisimae), the best-known *ramo* in southern Malaita. His wife had died 10 days earlier, and assuming she was a victim of sorcery he had retaliated by killing two men and a woman just north of Onepusu. Through Barnabas as interpreter, he told the staff that his father, who lived at Ainee, desired to come to the mission to learn about Christianity, but Arisimae wanted the old man to remain with his ancestors. These changes in allegiance were seldom blunt shifts in beliefs, and Arisimae's attitude to his father is typical. These visits were all signs of the rapid changes about to begin when a government base was established at 'Aoke in 1909. But even with Arisimae, we have only the partial missionary version of the conversation, and we do not necessarily know Arisimae's real reasoning.

People chose different missions based on different assessments of their specific qualities. For some, they stayed with what they knew in Queensland or Fiji: this applied to Anglicanism and the QKM-SSEM, although if they had been Presbyterian they needed to change denominations. For certain individuals, like Peter Abu'ofa or Jack Taloifulia, their mission 'brand' became a career path. Some preferred the SSEM emphasis on rules and the personal access individuals had to God, without an intermediary as Catholicism required. Individuals had personal access to their ancestors, and there was good reason to desire the same type of access to the Christian God. There could even be advantages in having to adhere to difficult rules (such as the SDA prohibitions of types of food and tobacco). Some assumed a religion with onerous rules was obviously more potent and worthwhile. Others, by contrast, were attracted to Anglicanism and Catholicism because in them one had to give up the least, often only prayer and sacrifice to ancestors. Others may also have been attracted to the theatre of Latin services, Anglican and Catholic clerical garments, and different types of music, singing and processions. Other Malaitans had only one mission in their area, or perhaps one that was particularly generous in dispensing European goods. In other cases a person's relatives had already joined a particular mission and so it was logical for them to join it as well, and the existing support network. Reading through the surviving literature, and considering what motivates Malaitans today to become Christian, or change from one Christian denomination to another, or even to the Baháʾí Faith or Islam, it becomes clear that their choices have long entailed complex reasoning, including considerations of material advantage. Malaitans were likely 'shopping around' as far back as the 1890s and 1900s.[63]

---

63 Acknowledgement is due to David Akin for his assistance with these conclusions.

7
Qaibala: Establishing `Aoke Station, 1909–14

Every white man on Malaita knows the risk he runs and must take his chances, if he is not prepared to do this it were better to go elsewhere for safety. It is not to be expected that because white men settle in a wild part of the group for their own ends, that the Government will be able to assist and protect them.
—Acting Resident Commissioner Frederic J. Barnett, 30 June 1915[1]

PS. We have told the heathen that you are coming, but they only laugh.
—Louisa Tarasol-Eurora (Mrs Charlie), Fo`odo, 7 March 1910[2]

British Authority before the Protectorate

The third aspect of change that engulfed Malaita, after the labour trade and Christianity, and unified the island was the establishment of a government base. The Western Pacific High Commission (WPHC) extended its reach into the protectorate in the 1890s, but had no presence on Malaita until 1909. Once `Aoke was opened, British authority could slowly be extended and enforced, although until the 1920s and 1930s there remained no substantial protectorate authority on the island. Until 1909, the Queensland and Fiji labour trades and Christian missions

---
1   SINA, BSIP 14/10, A/RC FJB to A/DO Ralph B. Hill, 30 June 1915.
2   SINA, BSIP 14/82, Louisa Tarasol-Aurora to RM TWE-P, 7 Mar 1910.

operated around Malaita almost unencumbered. Analysis of Malaita after 1909 must expand its focus to concentrate on the slow institution government control. Whereas early chapters dealt with labour and missions as independent entities, from 1909 they were subservient to government processes emanating from 'Aoke and Tulagi, at least in theory.

Chapter 2 outlined the beginnings of British authority in the Pacific through the Royal Navy Australia Station (RNAS) and the WPHC, with the governor of Fiji in the role of high commissioner, exercising extraterritorial authority over British subjects in the Solomon Islands. In 1884, Britain declared a protectorate over southeast New Guinea and the Germans established a *Schutzgebiet* (mercantile territory) over northeast New Guinea. After further negotiations, the German territory was confirmed in 1886 as extending south to include the north of the Solomon Archipelago: Buka, Bougainville, the Shortlands (except Mono or Treasury Island),[3] Choiseul, Isabel and outlying Ontong Java Atoll. The southern German boundary passed between Isabel and Malaita.[4] The central and southern Solomons were acknowledged to be under British influence through the WPHC and RNAS. However, Britain had only tenuous authority there until the protectorate was declared in 1893 and the first resident commissioner arrived in 1896.[5] Attempts to control the labour trade were part of these territorial manipulations.

After a royal commission into New Guinea recruiting in 1885, the Queensland Government announced that the labour trade was to cease and no more recruiting licences would be issued after the end of 1890.[6] This closure was revoked in February 1892 when Premier Griffith, faced with large-scale discontent in the sugar industry and wider economic downturns in the colony, reversed his 1885 decision and reintroduced recruiting licences. The only area remaining closed to Queensland recruiters was around eastern New Guinea, by then formally within British and German jurisdictions. Recruiting to Fiji, Samoa and New Caledonia had continued during these years of uncertainty. The British

---

3   In 1885, HMS *Lark* had left a few bags of coal at Mono while surveying Bougainville Strait. This led to its designation as a British coaling station. *BSIP Handbook* 1911, 19.
4   Lawrence 2014, 84–85; Sack 2005, 344.
5   Lawrence 2014, 84–89; Moore 2003, 133–34, 149–52. The legality was based on Western Pacific Orders-in-Council, 1877, 1879, 1880 and 1893, the *British Settlements Act 1887* and the *Foreign Jurisdiction Act 1890*.
6   Jamison 1990.

Government realised that there had to be better supervision of the Pacific end of the labour trade. The WPHC and the Admiralty began to discuss creating a Solomon Islands protectorate with its own permanent deputy commissioner, to match the joint (but limited) French-British naval presence in the New Hebrides from 1888, and the British New Guinea and German New Guinea administrations.

The declaration of a formal British protectorate over the Solomon Archipelago south of German New Guinea and down to Makira occurred in March 1893, partly motivated by Queensland's 1892 decision to recontinue the labour trade. The Santa Cruz Group, Rennell and Bellona, Sikaiana and Tikopia were added between 1897 and 1899. The 1893 Order-in-Council gave the high commissioner the power to control prisons, immigration, imports and exports, to fulfil the terms of treaties, and to legislate for peace, order and good government. The Colonial Office allowed the protectorate to be proclaimed on the understanding that the islands would have to 'pay their own way', and as a measure to control the labour trade.[7] Malaita became part of this formal British protectorate.

Declaring the British Solomon Islands Protectorate

After Queen Victoria signed the necessary documents, establishing the legality of a protectorate under international law required a physical visit and some show of compliance by the inhabitants of any newly acquired area. In May 1893, HMS *Curaçoa* under Captain Gibson and HMS *Goldfinch* under Lieutenant-Commander Floyd departed from Australia

---

7   *QVP* 1894, 2, 925–73, Pacific Order-in-Council, 1893. The Order-in-Council included several island groups: the Friendly, Navigators, Union, Phoenix, Ellice, and Gilbert islands, Solomon Islands as far north as the border with German territory, and the Santa Cruz Islands. CO 225/39, Western Pacific Queensland, no. 222 (microfilm 2316), top-numbered 5 Jan 1893, 622. Extract from minute by Lord Ripon (23853), and J.B. Thurston, WPHC, to SSC Marquis of Ripon, 21 Nov 1892; *BSIP AR*, 1898–99, 16.

with orders to visit the Solomon Islands and land on all of the main islands to assert British authority.[8] An officer from HMS *Curaçoa* recorded his view of the visit to Malaita:

> The natives have a reputation of being more quarrelsome and dangerous than those of any other island. They came in large numbers to the beach, and were mostly armed with Sniders, though some carried spears, clubs, and axes. They were complete savages. We all landed with revolvers, and did not venture off the beach or out of sight of the ship. Men, women, and children were entirely unclothed, but they struck us as being larger and finer in physique than the inhabitants of most of the other islands …[9]

Anglican missionary Rev. Richard Comins, who joined HMS *Curaçoa* at Siota in the Gela Group, also described the scene. At each stop they landed, hoisted the Union Jack, fired a *feu de joie*, read a proclamation and gave out presents. In most cases, copies of these proclamations were either handed to chiefs or buried in bottles, and small presents of hatchets, knives, cloth and tobacco were given to local leaders. The ceremony was enacted at several areas on Malaita. In most places the people would not take the flag or touch the copy of the proclamation. This was better than what happened at Roviana Lagoon, New Georgia, where the people immediately ripped up the flag for loin cloths.

The only Malaitan opposition was at Laulasi in Langalanga Lagoon, where the people seem to have feared that alignment with the British would make the inland descent groups think the lagoon people were preparing for war and cease trade.[10] At Port Adam, a 21-gun salute was fired and the Union Jack was duly hoisted, left under the care of local leader Faka`ia and Melanesian Mission teacher Luke Masuraa. There was a similar ceremony at Sa`a, where the situation was still volatile from the mission staff having earlier aided the crew of HMS *Royalist* to punish the murderers of Uki

---

8 Although the 1893 Order-in-Council included the Santa Cruz Islands, the proclamation was not formally made in these islands until 1898. In June 1897, when HMS *Wallaroo* visited Rennell and Bellona and the Stewart Group, including Sikaiana, these were proclaimed by Captain G.N. Pollard to be under British protection. During 1898, the commanding officers of HMS *Mohawk* and HMS *Goldfinch* extended British protection to the Santa Cruz Islands, the Reef Islands and Duff Islands, plus Vanikolo and Tikopia, and helped with general policing duties. The islands of the Shortland Group, Isabel, Choiseul, and Ontong Java Atoll were transferred to Great Britain by a convention with Germany dated 14 November 1899. *Pacific Islands Monthly*, Sept 1952; *BSIP News Sheet*, Oct 1961, Apr 1966.
9 Naval Officer 1893, 450.
10 WPHC 8 III 22 (1), Australian Station, Solomon Islands, 1893, H.W.S. Gibson, HMS *Curaçoa*, to CC, 13 July 1893.

Island trader Fred Howard.[11] Other nearby villages expressed sorrow for the Walade, Port Adam and Sa`a people, thinking that they had been shelled by the naval vessel.[12] This was typical of the experience of floating European government for all Solomon Islanders. British, French and sometimes German naval ships had patrolled around the coasts for decades, and contact most often took the form of a bombardment in retaliation for some offence. The British Navy usually only patrolled between May and October each year, a pattern that villagers would have noted, allowing them the rest of the year with no naval threat.[13] The only other British presence probably escaped local notice, although labour recruits would have realised their importance on the ships: government agents. Since the early 1870s, these agents on Queensland and Fiji recruiting vessels had provided reports (some of dubious quality) on each voyage, and they had ultimate power on board each ship. They provided information to the Queensland and Fijian governments, usually in the form of diaries, or if an incident occurred then in lengthy reports.

Between 1870 and 1896, the government agents and the RNAS were the sole British representatives in the Solomons. Permanent resident authority came with Charles Morris Woodford, initially appointed as deputy commissioner from April 1896. He toured around, then travelled back to Sydney and Fiji, and then in March 1897 returned as resident commissioner and set up his headquarters on Tulagi. Woodford had visited the Solomons previously on three trips as a naturalist (1886–88). During his first visit, on the Fijian recruiting ship *Christine*, he spent some time collecting specimens on Malaita.[14] He had lobbied High Commissioner Thurston for the position in the Solomons and spent a short term as consul and deputy commissioner in Apia, Samoa (1894–96), as a form of apprenticeship for the Solomons position.[15]

A haphazard pattern of foreign bases had emerged since whalers had arrived in the archipelago in substantial numbers in the 1820s, mainly in the New Georgia Group and at Kolombangara, Simbo, Ontong Java and Makira. These were also Christian missions, often sited on small but secure offshore islands. Woodford's first official report listed almost 50 foreign residents, only one of whom, Rev. Walter Ivens, lived part-time

---

11   Golden 1993, 274, 278, 434.
12   Comins and Welchman reports of the proclamation, *OPMM*, Mar 1894, 49–50.
13   Lawrence 2014, 149–58.
14   Woodford 1890; Lawrence 2014, 63–137.
15   Lawrence 2014; Heath 1974.

at Sa'a on Malaita. There were 21 cutters, ketches and schooners trading within the protectorate, plus the visiting labour trade and naval vessels. Although Woodford's initial plan was to place the government base on Uki Island, he instead chose small Tulagi Island in the Gela Group and used nearby Gavutu, a trader's station, as his headquarters until buildings were constructed on Tulagi just across the passage.[16] He had also considered Guadalcanal, where he had spent several months in the 1880s, but decided it was unhealthy. Woodford seems not to have considered Malaita as a possible base, presumably because of the reputation of Malaitans and because the island was not geographically central to the protectorate. He visited Malaita in November 1899 when he recruited some men for his police, although he would have been in regular contact with Malaitans on recruiting vessels, which by law (after 1898) had to call first at Tulagi. Woodford was aware that weapons and ammunition were still being smuggled from Queensland and Fiji to Malaita and other islands, even though labour vessels were thoroughly searched when they left these colonies and again at Tulagi. The main weapon sellers seem to have been European and Islander crew members. Ships from New Caledonia and German Samoa were also supplying arms and ammunition to Malaitans.

Governing Malaita, 1880s–1908

No one knew the true size of the Solomons Islands population, although all estimates suggest that Malaita was the most populous island in the protectorate. Estimates of the population in the early twentieth century usually varied between 100,000 and 150,000, with 50,000 to 100,000 people on Malaita.[17] Protectorate officials could only count Malaitans who lived around the coast and had no idea how many lived inland. In 1910, Arthur Mahaffy described most Malaitans as living 'perched upon the sides of precipitous mountains or hidden in the recesses of the virgin forest', impossible to count.[18] Even 1930s and 1940s estimates were likely inaccurate.

---

16   CO 225/39 (1892) (microfilm 2316), 'Solomon Islands: Resumption of Labour Traffic; Submits Observations on the Conduct of this Traffic and Recommends the Annexation of the Solomon Islands'.
17   Bennett 1987, 151.
18   CO 225/91 (1910), 286 (microfilm 2915), Arthur Mahaffy, assistant to HC Sir Everard im Thurn, report of visit to Solomon Islands, 8 Apr 1910.

7. QAIBALA: ESTABLISHING 'AOKE STATION, 1909–14

As mentioned in Chapter 1, precontact numbers could have been much higher, given the degree of depopulation thought to have occurred throughout Near Oceania in recent centuries. Declaration of the protectorate in 1893 meant nothing on Malaita, though Woodford slowly began to assert his authority starting in 1896–97. His initial 'equipment' consisted of an 8.2-metre whaleboat, eight police and a £1,200 grant-in-aid. He used the RNAS ships to deal with any 'incidents', although because the fleet was based in Sydney and only sailed through the islands for half the year, and acted in consultation with the high commissioner in Fiji, response time was usually very slow. Woodford instituted a stringent three-week quarantine regulation, especially for any ship coming out of German New Guinea, where people were dying of smallpox and influenza on New Britain. He insisted that all ships entering the protectorate had to call first at Tulagi, and he began to tighten regulation of the labour trade and land purchases.[19] His main tasks were regulating the external and internal labour trades and instituting colonial law and order (called 'pacification') to a level that would enable plantations to be established in the BSIP. Even when he was notified of incidents needing investigation, Woodford often had insufficient time or capacity to respond effectively. While Malaita was close to Tulagi, there was little he could do to govern the island. His main contacts were the mission stations' European and local teacher staffs with whom he exchanged correspondence. He occasionally did manage to make his presence felt, such as when he ordered Rev. Hopkins to evacuate Lau Lagoon for an upcoming naval bombardment in 1902, or when he arrived at Malu'u in 1904 on the government vessel *Lahloo* and arrested a man for murder. Woodford's first resident magistrate, Arthur Mahaffy, visited Malaita on HMS *Sparrow* in 1902 to investigate several deaths.[20]

As part of my research from the 1970s into the 1990s, I collected details of violent incidents between indigenous inhabitants of New Guinea and Island Melanesia and foreigners over hundreds of years. These statistics cover 584 violent incidents, accounting for more than 1,400 foreign deaths and untold numbers of indigenous deaths—the true number was probably twice that. There are two other relevant lists of incidents, one by Bennett and another in my book *Kanaka*: both of these sources are

---

19 Comins, *OPMM*, Sept 1897, 309–10; CO 225/50 (microfilm 2329), 'Regulations 6 and 7 of 1897', Woodford, 'Report on the British Solomon Islands', Mar 1997; CO 19055 (1897) (microfilm 2331), 'Bills of Sale Registration'; 'Solomons Labour Recruitment', *BSIP AR*, 1897–98.
20 Hopkins, 'N. W. Mala', *SCL*, Mar 1903, 1; Lawrence 2014, 198–206.

included in my main list.[21] My Island Melanesia statistics accounted for 318 incidents with in excess of 684 foreign deaths (Europeans and their crews).[22] The numbers would be higher if Queensland and Fiji plantation incidents were included. During the second half of the nineteenth century, naval investigations and consequent retaliation often followed indigenous attacks. Investigations could take from six months to two years to complete and almost always ended in bombardment or with shore parties destroying villages, fruit trees, canoes and pigs. The research located 35 substantial attacks around Malaita before there was a government base on the island. On Malaita, the first known attack against European ships occurred in 1827,[23] then none are recorded until 1872,[24] followed by a spate of serious attacks in the 1880s involving attempts to take control of and loot ships and kill their crews. Damaging attacks were made on the *Borealis* (1880),[25] *Janet Stewart* (1882),[26] *Young Dick* (1886)[27] and *Minota* (1907).[28] Unsuccessful attempts were made on the *Helena* (1884),[29] *Savo* (1888),[30] *Fearless* (1890),[31] *Marie* (1890),[32] *Meg Merrillies* (1890),[33] and *Para* (1895).[34] The *Borealis*, *Janet Stewart* and *Young Dick* were all attacked along a few kilometres of the east coast between Uru Harbour and Leli Atoll. There were around 44 deaths and eight serious

---

21   Bennett 1987, 390–96; Moore 1985, 347–56.
22   Moore 2003, 161–67.
23   Forster 1975, 97; Bennett 1987, 30–31, 350; Rhodes 1937, 253 (Rhodes provides no source).
24   Scarr 1967a, 38.
25   Keesing 1986a; Keesing 1986c; Akin 2012; *MM*, 6 Nov 1880; *Fiji Times*, 13 Oct 1880 in RNAS 15: Wellington, Lieutenant Commander J. Bowen, HMS *Sandfly* to Commander Wilson, 5 Oct 1880; Wawn 1973, 219.
26   *MM*, 3 May 1882; *Queenslander*, 25 Nov 1882; Wawn 1973, 244; Rannie 1912, 70–72; Mitchell Library, RNAS FM4/1665, 23, 'Australia Station, New Guinea, Solomons and New Hebrides, Correspondence Respecting Outrages', 20; QSA COL/A783, In-Letter 1,572 of 1892, GA Rannie to IA, 19 Dec 1892.
27   Keesing 1986a; Keesing 1986c; Akin 2012; Fowler 1969; Cromar 1935, 234–36, 265–66; Wawn 1973, 418–21; Scarr 1967b, 14; Woodford 1890, 15; Rannie 1912, 195, 197, 199; Mitchell Library, RNAS FM4/1678, 38, 'Australian Station, New Guinea and Solomons, 1886, Correspondence Respecting Outrages', Case 14, 28–42.
28   Mitchell Library, RNAS FM4/1683, Australia Station, 44, Enclosure 18, Captain Lewes of HMS *Cambrian* to CC, 11 Aug 1908; NAA CRS A1/ 08/6443, clipping from the *Age*, 9 Sept 1908; London 1911, 262–65, 267, 271.
29   QSA COL/A411, In-Letter 169 of 1885, 'Evidence of Inquiry'.
30   Mitchell Library, RNAS FM4/1665, 'Correspondence Respecting Outrages, New Guinea and Solomons, 1889', J. Tucker, HMS *Albatross*, to Messrs Kelly and Williams, 13 July 1889; Wawn 1973, 424; Woodford 1890, 16; WPHC 8 III, 18 (2), W.H. Hand, HMS *Royalist*, to CC, 5 Nov 1889.
31   Wawn 1973, 424–25.
32   W.T. Wawn, private log, *Para*, 10 July 1894; Wawn 1973, 425.
33   *Ibid.*, 434.
34   QSA COL/A795, In-Letter 10323 of 1895, IA to US CSD, 28 Aug 1895, Appendix B: extract from GA log; QSA GOV/A28, IA to US CSD, 18 Feb 1895.

woundings of foreign crews, a recorded 21 Malaitans killed (a number that can probably be doubled or tripled), seven Malaitans were taken to Australia for trials and four, including a woman and child, were taken to Fiji, and perhaps 40 or 50 recruits from the ships were also killed. During the 1890s and early 1900s, when Malaitan recruiting was at its peak, there were many smaller attempts to capture labour trade ships or kill crews, some of which involved fatalities. Recruiting boats away from the main vessel were easy targets, particularly if they were in rivers and creeks that could be blocked by felled trees.[35]

Malaita certainly had its fair share of incidents, although when considering the statistics we need to keep in mind Malaitan centrality to the labour trade: they made up 58 per cent of Solomon Islanders recruited to Queensland and Fiji, 1870–1911. Consequently, one would expect around half of all labour trade violent incidents in the Solomons to have occurred around Malaita. Using Queensland statistics to gain a wider perspective, in comparison with the number of recruits recorded from the next most important islands (Epi, 5,084; Tanna, 4,241; Guadalcanal, 4,188, Ambrym, 3,464), we see that more labourers were from Malaita (9,187 indenture contracts) than any other island.[36] Analysis of my labour trade voyage files suggests that equally serious attacks also took place on Tanna, Epi, Aoba and Malekula; although no other island's peoples tried to seize as many vessels as did Malaitans, or were as successful. There was an element of luck in the effective attacks since success would not

---

35   *Lady Darling* (1875): *MM*, 11 Dec 1875; *Queenslander*, 1 Jan 1876; *Ariel* (1888): Wawn 1973, 415; Wawn, private log, *Ariel*, 22, 26 Oct 1888, 51–64, map, 64; *Upolu* and *Fearless* (1890): Wawn 1973, 269–72, 424, 434; *Sybil II* (1891): Mitchell Library, RNAS FM4/1665, 23, 'Correspondence Respecting Outrages', 37, Case 51, Captain E.H.M. Davis, HMS *Royalist* to CC, 6 Oct 1891; *Helena* (1893): GA S.M. Smith, private log, *Helena*, 3 Apr 1893; *Sybil II* (1893): QSA GOV/A25, Officer in Charge, Pacific Islands Labour Bureau to US CSD, 1 June 1893; *MM*, 27 May 1893; *Para* (1894): Wawn, private log, *Para*, 8 Aug 1894; QSA GOV/A26, IA to US CSD, 8 Mar 1894; *Sybil II* (1894): Wawn, private log, *Para*, 19 July 1894; QSA GOV/A27, IA to US CSD, 1 Oct 1894; GOV/A27, 841, Appendix A, 2, IA Brennan to Permanent Under-Secretary CSD, 1 Oct 1894; WPHC 8 III, 23, 1894, 'Australian Station, Solomon Islands, 1894', Case 63, James Goodrich, Commander, to CC, 29 Aug 1894; *Lochiel* (1895): QSA GOV/A29, Chief Secretary to Governor, 20 Dec 1895; *Rio Lodge* (1896): QSA GOV/A30 IA to Permanent Under-Secretary CSD, 18 Mar 1896; *QVP* 1897, 2, 1,086, 'Annual Report of the Department of Pacific Islands Immigration'; WPHC 8 III, 25, 'Australian Station, Solomon Islands, 1896', Case 73; QSA GOV/A30 IA to Permanent Under-Secretary, CSD, 13 Mar 1896; *Sybil II* (1896): Smith, private log, *Sybil II*, 20 Dec 1896; *Rio Lodge* (1897): QSA GOV/A32, IA to Secretary to Prime Minister of Queensland, 26 Aug 1897; *Fearless* (1901): 'Annual Report of the Department of Pacific Islanders, 1902', 2; QSA GOV/A36, IA to UC CSD, 27 May 1901; and GA S. M. Smith to IA, 24 Apr 1901; *Rio Lodge* (1902): QSA GOV/A38, IA to US CSD, 9 June 1902; *Roderick Dhu* (1902): QSA GOV/A38 IA to US CSD, 19 Mar 1902.
36   Moore 1985, 26.

have been a foregone conclusion. The list of failed attacks is also long. These attacks and the truculent behaviours of Malaitans working on overseas and local plantations were the main reasons they gained a bad reputation, which fed into the trope of Malaitan violence. It is also clear from the testimony of men such as Saelasi Lounga from east Kwaio, and the documentary evidence, that attacks on ships usually occurred within existing cultural frameworks.[37] What emerges from the oral testimony concerning the related attacks on the *Borealis*, *Janette Stewart* and *Young Dick*, remembered through sung chants about ancestral deeds, is that in each case, and as with any planned Malaitan military attack, religious observances were involved to gain ancestral support, including sacrifices of pigs and the following of special ritual taboos. The beheading of the *Ariel*'s government agent, Thomas Seymour Armstrong, at Maana`oba Island on 6 December 1888 is part of this same sequence.[38]

There were also many smaller incidents involving labour trade vessels at Malaita in which the recruiters managed to escape.[39] The range of incidents outlined above, and others in the 1900s, were typical of what occurred during the late 1870s, 1880s and 1890s and what was to follow over the next few decades. The attacks were usually in retaliation for deaths away from the island, or 'blood money' bounties posted for various offences on Malaita. Armstrong's death is in this latter category—dead relatives had to be avenged to placate ancestors and keep descent groups free from spiritual threat. When *ramo* accepted shell valuables as bounty payments for having taken a life, their actions were not always condoned by leaders of descent groups. However, as Shankar Aswani argues, based on Daniel de Coppet's research in `Are`are (where there was considerably more hierarchy than elsewhere on Malaita):

> A leader extracted dual social benefit from murderous acts: on the one hand he elevated his political stature by the exploits of his warriors/assassins and on the other he emerged as a benefactor who restored peace and socio-cosmic stability via the formation of exchange relations.[40]

---

37 Transcript of account by Saelasi Lounga from Uru, east Kwaio, 4 Aug 1982, courtesy David Akin; Lawrence 2014, 78–79.
38 Keesing 1986c; information from David Akin, 8 Oct 2011; Wawn 1973, 418, 423; Mitchell Library, Wawn, private log, *Helena*, 6 Dec 1888; Melvin 1977, 24; Cromar 1935, 265; *MM*, 22 Jan 1889, report by Captain Norman of *Fearless*, who was then at `Ataa; WPHC 8, 3, 18 (2), 14, evidence of Jackson Ka (Kaiviti), son of Kwaisulia, 22 Aug 1889, Case 29.
39 Moore 1985, Map 6, 62.
40 Aswani 2008, 178–79. See also Coppet 1981a; 1981b; 1995.

The arrival of thousands of guns and axes changed Malaita, as it did other areas of the Solomons. There was an escalation of the violence against outsiders, and *ramo* began to use guns in addition to indigenous weaponry.

For instance, in 1901 the father of a Malaitan who had died in Queensland offered a reward for the retaliatory death of a European. This was extracted twice: on 19 April 1901 when James Arthur, recruiter on the *Fearless*, was shot and killed at `Ataa, and through the death of George McCabe, recruiter on the *Roderick Dhu*, killed by Galla and Jacky Qui (Kwai) at Uru Harbour on 23 December 1901.[41] In response, Mahaffy travelled to Malaita on HMS *Sparrow*, which bombarded a small island near Malu`u. In Lau Lagoon, Mahaffy dealt with another complicated but fairly typical payback killing, mentioned in earlier chapters. Amasia, a man from the Anibiongi descent group, had been kidnapped at Leli Atoll, probably by the Fiji labour trade vessel *Nukulau* in the early 1870s. He learnt about Christianity at a Wesleyan mission and spoke Pijin Fijian rather than Pijin English. Amasia returned home to Ngongosila Island in 1898 or 1899, built a Fijian-style house and was living with his Fijian wife Bauleni (Pauline) and his son Ini`a, Joseph Kwainauri and Waisaki. Against the will of local leaders, Amasia tried to start a Christian school, a task made more difficult by his dogmatic ways and his wife's refusal to follow local customs. Pauline was killed by Avu soon after she defiled an ancestral shrine. After her death, Waisaki moved to Sinalagu, and Amasia and Ini`a left for Kwarande and Ngorefou in Lau Lagoon. Amasia was killed there in 1902 by Waita and Suemai, who were seeking revenge for Amasia's supposed killing of their grandfather three decades earlier.[42] The third set of 1902 deaths that Mahaffy investigated related to Kwairae from Oru opposite Malu`u Harbour, who killed a man in a canoe off `Aoke Island and killed a woman and wounded three men at Foate. Mahaffy demanded that Oru people give up Kwairae, and when they did not, HMS *Sparrow* shelled the island and a shore party burnt down the village and killed their pigs. Lau bigman Kwaisulia was nearby, held hostage on HMS *Sparrow*

---

41 *Fearless*: 'Annual Report of the Department of Pacific Islanders, 1902', 2 (original copy); QSA GOV/A36, IA to UC CSD, 27 May 1901; and S. M. Smith to IA, 24 Apr 1901; *Roderick Dhu*: QSA GOV/A38 IA to US CSD, 19 Mar 1902.
42 Ben Burt, British Museum, identifies Amasia as one of the Malaitans kidnapped by the *Nukulau*. Thirteen survived and 11 were returned to Malaita. Ivens said that Amasia was kidnapped by the *Marion Rennie*, although his description of the circumstances also fits the *Nukulau* incident. Burt's 2002 account can be taken as definitive. Amasia remained in Fiji for the next three decades, and claimed to have been in prison for 21 years. He returned home and attempted to set up as a teacher at Ngongosila before he transferred to Lau Lagoon where he was killed. Burt 1994, 112; 2002; Moore 1985, 38–39; Fox 1958, 172; Ivens 1918, 21; Ivens, 'Kalilana Mala (The Rounding of Mala)', *SCL*, 15 June 1900, 9–20; *SCL*, Aug 1900; Comins, 'First Voyage, 1902', *SCL*, Aug 1902, 33.

while his son Jackson Kaiviti arranged the surrender of Waita and Suemai. At Kwai Island, Avu was not surrendered and the village was destroyed, as were 40 or 50 pigs. The killers of McCabe escaped retribution since they came from an inland village.[43]

HMS *Prometheus* bombarded Suiwa Village on the west coast in January 1907 and later that year Waita and Suemai were still being pursued when HMS *Cambrian* shelled three artificial islands and two inland villages at 'Ataa. The ship also bombarded Waisisi and Fiu to punish murders recently committed.[44] C.C. Mackenzie, an inexperienced recruiter on Oscar Svenson's *Minota*, recruiting labourers for Guadalcanal plantations, was killed at Bina in 1908, tomahawked by men from an inland descent group who came down to Alite Island in Langalanga Lagoon. The lagoon people rescued the ship and local crew, then sailed the vessel back to Tulagi and reported the incident. Woodford arrived on HMS *Cambridge* and landed at Bina, then travelled inland to destroy the village implicated in the death. His shore party burnt villages, killed pigs, and a child was accidentally drowned. Just as would occur in the retaliation for the Bell killings in 1927, innocent people were punished, which in this case led to fighting between them and the actual perpetrators.[45]

Europeans used indiscriminate naval bombardments or naval shore parties to punish Solomon Islanders for 80 years, up until 1927 when the crew of HMAS *Adelaide* were involved in retribution against the east Kwaio people, though only a small group had killed District Officer Bell and most of his party (see Chapter 10). What changed in the twentieth century is that, whereas previously the British Navy and the Queensland and Fiji governments were only interested if the violence involved foreigners (which was the way the laws worked), once the protectorate was established, with reform to the British laws governing protectorates, and with a government base on Malaita, policing could also be applied to all local actions that transgressed protectorate laws.

The Gela Group, where Tulagi was situated, was already stable under an Anglican mission theocracy, and this allowed the government to focus initially on the northwest Solomons. This need of 'pacification' was ample

---

43   WPHC IC 7/1903, RM Arthur Mahaffy to RC CMW, 1 Oct 1902.
44   NAA CRS A1 07/9881, Report by Captain Gaunt, HMS *Cambrian*, 23 July 1907; *MM*, 28 Jan 1907.
45   WPHC IC 7/1903, RM Mahaffy to RC CMW, 1 Oct 1902; WPHC IC 98/1908, CMW to HC Sir Everard im Thurn, 13 Apr 1908; Bennett 1987, 109; Akin 1993, 166 n 40.

justification for the next government bases, at Gizo in 1899 and in the Shortland Island District in 1906.⁴⁶ Apart from the mission stations, there had been no attempts to settle on Malaita, although the island continued to be the mainstay of the labour trade to Queensland until 1904 and to Fiji until 1914. We have seen that once the external movement of labour came to an end, thousands of Malaitans returned home between 1902 and 1914. After a long battle with the WPHC, a protectorate decree was passed in 1910 that ended all external employment of labour.⁴⁷ Woodford argued that the future development of the Solomons required an ample supply of local labourers to build up copra plantations. Malaitans were essential to this plan, and just as they had dominated the overseas labour trades they soon made up over 60 per cent of the protectorate's labour. Malaitans still had few other ways to obtain European manufactured items.

Over the previous 30 years, Malaitans had become used to access to foreign goods. And with guns no longer readily available, tobacco was at the top of their list. Woodford estimated that 50 tons of tobacco was imported into the protectorate every year in the early 1900s. Labourers working overseas often brought back 20 to 30 pounds (9 to 14 kilograms) each, which, based on 500 of the 1,000 returning Malaitans each year, is 5 tons. Presuming that they also obtained part of the general imports of tobacco, well in excess of 10 tons (9.07 metric tonnes, or 520,000 sticks of tobacco) reached Malaita every year in the 1900s.⁴⁸ The protectorate's annual report described the Malaitan predicament:

> It will be interesting to view the effect upon the Island of Mala of the cessation of recruiting. Up to the present time, tobacco and other trade has been poured out upon Mala by the labour ships for the purchase of recruits. The Mala natives will not in future be able to do without it, consequently they will either have to go to work locally in the Protectorate or convert their rifles into agricultural implements and produce some saleable commodity on the own account.⁴⁹

If Mahaffy was correct in claiming that 80 per cent of Malaitan males possessed firearms in the 1900s, we have some idea of how much Malaita had changed in three decades. Malaitans were no longer envious of their northern Solomons neighbours who had attracted earlier supplies

---

46 Bennett 1987, 397–404; Rodman 1979.
47 Moore 2000; Corris 1973b, 126–48.
48 Fifty tons is 100,000 pounds or 45,359 kilograms. There were approximately 26 sticks of tobacco to the pound. A serious smoker can smoke a stick in a day or two.
49 *BSIP AR*, 1902–03, 9.

of Western goods. They had entered consumer society, and had also enhanced their reputation as dangerous with the thousands of guns they possessed and sometimes used on each other and outsiders.[50] This was the background of the situation government officers faced after 1909. Most of the guns were confiscated in the mid-1920s, without compensation. How many were functioning weapons, and had ammunition, is difficult to say.

Establishing Malaita District, 1909–10

Establishing a government presence was for the government much overdue, given the return of thousands of Malaitans from overseas colonies during the 1900s and their effect on Malaitan communities, and of course the need to reharness the Malaitan workforce for Solomon Islands plantations. The Malaita Government station was begun in September 1909, at Rarasu on the west coast at the top of Langalanga Lagoon. Early records (even the note paper) called the station Quibala (Kwaibala) after the local river. The government station was only one of several permanent European bases on Malaita, and for some years Malaitans would have viewed it as a minor settlement, albeit with a large number of armed guards (the police). The station soon became known as ʻAoke (Auki), the name of the island opposite in the lagoon.[51]

Woodford first visited ʻAoke in 1886 while on the *Christine*, a Fiji labour vessel:

> The place where we anchored is called I think Auki (Aoke [crossed out]) and there is a good passage with five fathoms of water. When you are inside there is a good harbour. On the starboard side going in there is a small island covered with coconut trees on which is a very populous settlement. A little distance off in the same direction is another smaller one. On this there appears to be only one large house, most probably a canoe house. Further on again on the edge of the reef is a small rock with trees growing upon it. Immediately on anchoring we were surrounded by small canoes, many of them only large enough to carry one child. There were altogether about fifty and the number of people was about eighty.[52]

---

50   Estimated by Arthur Mahaffy on his visit to Malaita on HMS *Sparrow* in 1902, *BSIP AR*, 1902–03, 15.
51   SINA, BSIP 14/40, RM TWE-P to RC CMW, 30 Mar 1911.
52   Woodford 1886, 4 June, 134.

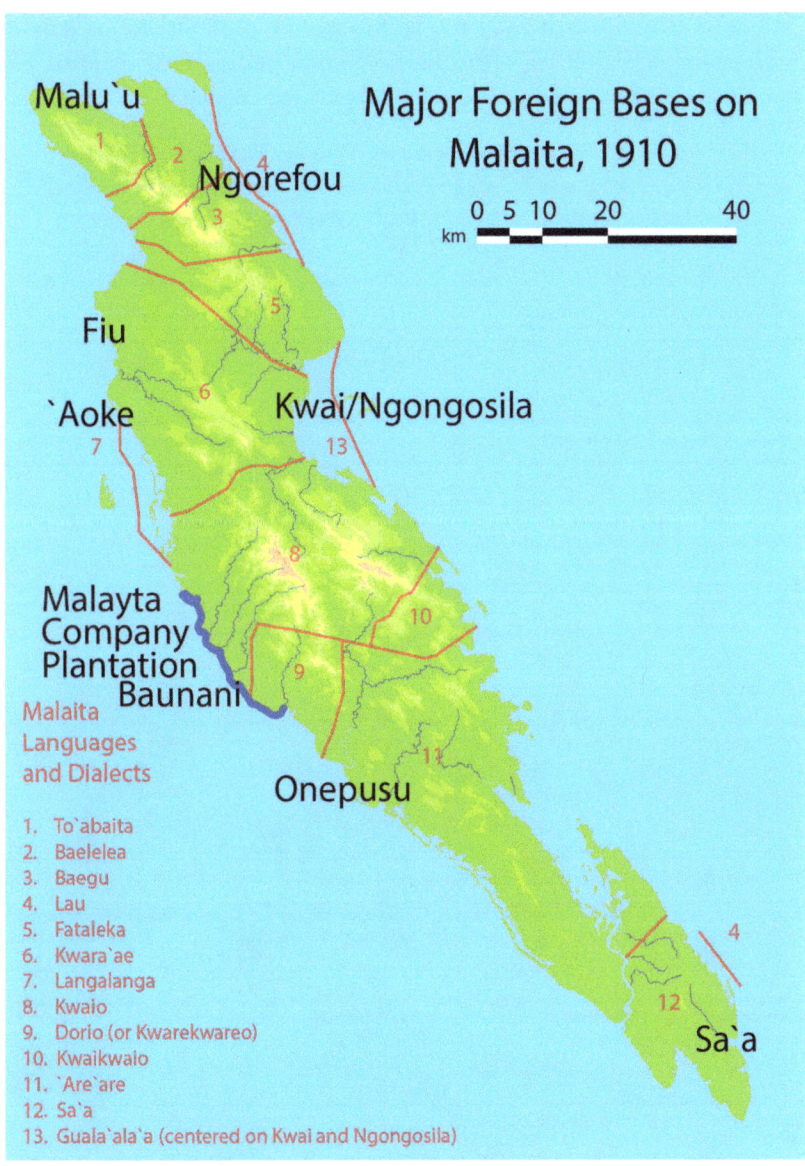

Map 14: Major foreign bases on Malaita, 1910.
Source: Courtesy of Vincent Verheyen.

Ten years later, he estimated the population of 'Aoke Island as around 600, noted its coral rock fortifications and went on to describe the manufacture of shell wealth items in Langalanga Lagoon:

> They get the materials from Gela and Savo. Their canoes go across to Gela for pigs which they buy in exchange for the money. A canoe lately brought back 40 pigs from Boli. Every few days a market is held on a beach on the mainland opposite the island and at Fiu & other places. The island people buy yams & other food & sell the bushmen pigs from Gela & the shell money.[53]

Figure 7.1: The residency, the Malaita resident magistrate's (later the district officer's) house, and the office built for Thomas Edge-Partington in 1910.
Source: British Museum, Edge-Partington Collection, Album 5, Ca44.293.

---

53   Woodford 1896, 15 June, 8–9.

7. QAIBALA: ESTABLISHING 'AOKE STATION, 1909–14

Woodford visited Malaita many times during his term as resident commissioner, using the government ketch or hitching a ride on passing naval ships. In 1908, he visited Bina Harbour in Langalanga Lagoon aboard HMS *Cambrian* to investigate the murder of C.C. Mackenzie.[54] The Kwaibala area was central, had a good harbour and had not been selected as a Christian base. Being situated at the top of lagoon, it provided a sheltered transport route down the west coast, and was close to Aloa, the steamer port on Guadalcanal. Woodford authorised Frank Barnett, then the controller of Customs, to purchase 12.1 hectares immediately west of the Kwaibala River for £10 on 15 July 1909 from Qualagau (Kwalagau), while Woodford paid £10 to purchase an adjoining 18.2 hectares to the west of the first purchase, from Gemite and Malafou.[55] Two months later, Woodford sent Resident Magistrate (RM) Thomas W. Edge-Partington, transferred from Gizo, to establish the 'Aoke headquarters.

Early in 1910, Woodford and Mahaffy both visited 'Aoke, where Edge-Partington was busy supervising construction of the new station and in the process of building his house. 'Aoke was envisaged as the nucleus out of which law and order would emerge, although all three men were well aware of the difficulties faced in incorporating tens of thousands of Malaitans into the protectorate.[56] The nearby Langalanga people, spread out over a series of islands in the lagoon, had an uneasy relationship with their coastal and inland neighbours. In 1896 Woodford observed that the inland people were much better armed, but the lagoon-dwellers had significant advantages in their use of canoes, their control of the production and trade in shell valuables and their control of trade in pigs from Gela to the Malaitan coast.[57]

---

54 No charges were laid and in 1913 Woodford asked Edge-Partington to inform the murderers' village that no action would be taken. Bennett 1987, 109; SINA, BSIP 14/8, RC CMW to RM TWE-P, 4 Dec 1913.
55 SINA, BSIP 14/7, RC CMW to AEW, 11 Mar 1912. Several men were also paid for sago or coconut palms ('more or less imaginary') growing on the land.
56 CO225/91, Western Pacific no. 24619 (microfilm 2915), Arthur Mahaffy to HC Sir Everard im Thurn, 8 Apr 1910.
57 Woodford 1896, 16, 17 June.

The Administration of Malaita, 1909–15

While 'Aoke was being established during the 1910s, Malaita had three Christian denominations operating and a large plantation venture underway—the Malayta Company, exemplifying industrial Christianity. This substantial Christian presence meant that large changes had already occurred on Malaita, extensions of those brought about by the external labour trade since the 1870s.

The administration of Malaita before the Second World War falls neatly into two halves, 1909 to 1927 and 1927 to 1942. David Akin's research shows that 16 European protectorate officials worked on Malaita for some period between 1909 and 1927. These early years were dominated first by Thomas Edge-Partington, and then by William Bell.[58] Edge-Partington, born in 1883 into an English gentry family, joined the colonial service after he failed his lieutenant's examination in the Royal Navy. He served from December 1905 to May 1909 as the first resident magistrate at Gizo, then at aged 26 was transferred to Malaita in the same position between 1 September 1909 and 26 January 1915.[59] These early years were spent establishing 'Aoke and in rudimentary policing operations. Edge-Partington was joined in February 1912 by an Australian, Frederick M. Campbell, commander of the protectorate's police until 1917, when he was transferred to Kirakira as Makira's first district officer (DO).[60] The other important early officer was another Australian, William Bell, who was protectorate inspector of labourers between 1911 and 1915, when he became the DO for Malaita.[61] Before that, Bell had been a Fiji-based labour recruiter, and from 1904 or 1905 to 1911 Bell was a government agent on Fiji labour trade ships that worked mainly around Malaita. Thus when he began at 'Aoke he already had 10 years of extensive contact with Malaitans.

---

58 List of Malaita's colonial officers compiled by David Akin, in Moore's possession.
59 Moore 2013c entry. Except when absent on leave: Edge-Partington took an extended period of leave from February 1912 to February 1913.
60 Moore 2013c entry; Bennett 1987, 401; Boutilier 1983, 44; notes accompanying Edge-Partington's photographic collection, British Museum, www.unithistories.com/officers/RN_officersE.html (accessed 5 Oct 2011). In 1914, the title 'resident magistrate' was replaced by 'district officer' (DO).
61 Moore 2013c entry; Keesing and Corris 1980.

Figure 7.2: The police commander's house at 'Aoke, built for Frederick M. Campbell in 1912.
Source: British Museum, Edge-Partington Collection, Album 5, Dscn1094.

Edge-Partington arrived on Malaita at a time when the Queensland labour trade had ended and thousands of ex-labourers had returned home. The smaller Fiji labour trade was also phased out during his years on Malaita, the external movement of labour replaced by indenture within the Solomons. Malaita's plantation culture, begun in Queensland, Fiji, Samoa and New Caledonia, was now developed further by new generations. The experiences of these men overseas and within the protectorate mitigated the old linguistic and political divisions. Pijin English created a *lingua franca* that had been missing from earlier interactions. Those who had absorbed Christianity no longer held their old leaders in the same awe, and their access to manufactured goods, brought with them from other colonies or earned in the protectorate, altered their status and allegiance to established bigmen. As described in earlier chapters, Christian enclaves all around the coast were beginning to polarise social and political norms. Most of those converted to Christianity overseas were living in coastal Christian villages where the authority of mission teachers had replaced that of indigenous leaders.

Policing continued in the punitive mode of the naval bombardments over the previous 50 years. Edge-Partington was equipped with a whaleboat and a small police squad he had brought with him from Gizo. In their first action, when Joe Sili, a Malaitan man, was murdered on the front veranda of Rev. Hopkins's house at Ngorefou on the mainland of Lau Lagoon in September 1910, they proved ineffective. Visitors from inland descent groups had been sitting on Hopkins's front veranda. Another small group walked up, made friendly banter and then shot Sili dead.[62] Hopkins had been at fault in allowing the second group of men armed with Snider rifles onto his veranda. Sili's death was sponsored by Lainau (Laina`o), a bigman from an inland village, and Simanhu from Ferasubua Island in the lagoon. Irokwato, a famous *ramo*, was also involved.

The event showed just how short-staffed Edge-Partington was. He left only four police to guard `Aoke station and had to ask the `Aoke Island leaders to help protect the settlement. Then he and the remaining 21 police had rowed for three days around north Malaita to Sulufou, calling at Fiu and Maanaere on the way. The police, augmented by eight locals, attacked and burned Lainau's and Irokwato's villages, and also destroyed ancestral shrines, slit-drums and food trees.[63] The inhabitants of Ferasubua were ordered to produce Simanhu within one month or face a large fine in shell valuables and destruction of their village. Edge-Partington was not impressed by his police whom he described as paralysed by fear; his report to Woodford must rate as one of the most honest in the protectorate's records. He told the resident commissioner that he was 'not a fool and to expect a man to go into the bush on this island and fight with a few boys is simply madness'.

> My boys were absolutely useless and if the bushmen had made a stand as they intended to we would never have got out of the bush. This of course may have been because they are absolutely untrained and didn't know which end of the gun goes off …
>
> If I am to quiet Mala I must have the boys to do it. I absolutely refuse to do it with a few creatures called Police that the Mala people are laughing at. What is more I am not living on an Island but on the mainland and after attacking a place I have got to keep a good look out all the time to keep them from coming down and attacking this place for revenge.
>
> I never saw such a hopeless lot to attack a bunch of unfrightened bushmen in my life, and if you want a second opinion about them ask Mr Sage as he was with me and was laughing at them all the time.[64]

---

62   Fox 1958, 172.
63   SINA, BSIP 15 VIII, 134, 1910 'Station Diary', RM TWE-P, 6–12 Sept 1910.
64   SINA, BSIP 14/40, RM TWE-P to RC CMW, 1 Mar, 14, 19 Sept 1910.

7. QAIBALA: ESTABLISHING 'AOKE STATION, 1909–14

For his part, Hopkins began to comprehend the complexity of Malaitan society as each death brought further reprisals.

> It all makes for confusion, treachery and distrust; the atmosphere is horrible. At Fiu a heathen visitor was killed with an axe by an apparently friendly caller—for a murder done some years ago. An old man was killed at Market—shot from behind a tree for an offence his brother committed long ago. A woman of the school was followed by two men and killed to avenge a quarrel in which she had no concern.[65]

Court proceedings were held during patrols and at 'Aoke. There is a photograph from Bell's early years, where a trial is being held on the veranda of the DO's residence, although this may well have been staged since there was also a separate office.[66] The result could be fines in shell or teeth valuables, or custodial sentences. Serious cases, including all murders, were referred to Tulagi. Fines could be collective, to be paid by the occupants of one village or one small island, such as a £50 fine visited on Maana'oba Island off north Malaita in 1912.[67] Local offenders serving short sentences were held at 'Aoke. Government policy was to transfer prisoners with long sentences away from their home areas; thus prisoners from the Western Solomons ended up at 'Aoke or Tulagi and those from Malaita were often transferred to Gizo or the Shortlands. In 1910, 'Aoke had prisoners but no prison and nowhere to detain them, except under Edge-Partington's house during daytime, and in the labourers' quarters at night. Whether prisoners understood the concept behind the punishment is unclear. Edge-Partington warned them that they were confined to the station for a set period of time and would be shot if they ran away; for good measure he added that if they escaped into the bush the local people would kill them.[68] There is an old colonial adage that the prisoners were more interested in the rice, other foods, clothes and tobacco provided than in comprehending the process of being charged, tried, convicted and imprisoned. There was also a sense of stoicism exhibited by not being too concerned by the whiteman's legal system.

Edge-Partington was clearly worried that 'Aoke would be attacked and overrun. There were thousands of rifles on Malaita, mainly Sniders and Winchesters—owning a gun was a badge of manhood—with more still

---

65 Fox 1958, 172.
66 Keesing and Corris 1980, 62.
67 SINA, BSIP 14/41, 1911–13, RM TWE-P to RC CMW, 25 July, 3 Aug 1912; Johnson 1945, 48, plate 2.
68 SINA, BSIP 14/40, RM TWE-P to RC CMW, 2 Oct and 22 Dec 1909; BSIP 14/41 1911–13, RM TWE-P to RC CMW, 19 Dec 1911.

being smuggled in or stolen from recruiting schooners. In 1914, dozens of guns were purchased from Levers Pacific Plantations Ltd's ships at Marau Sound on Guadalcanal and sold to the bush villagers.[69] Plugs of dynamite were sold at one *tafuli`ae* (10 strings of shell wealth) per plug, and cartridges were also available.[70] Trader and later labour recruiter Joseph Dickinson had been in the Solomons since 1908:

> Apart from their own weapons the natives had rifles of old and new pattern, with an abundance of ammunition smuggled in during the Queensland labour trade, or supplied by unscrupulous recruiting ships of that day. This gun-running, like the Malaita man's raiding, was also now [in 1927] a thing of the past. However, the gun-runners had left behind them eight to ten thousand rifles, though the greater number were more dangerous to their owners than to anyone else.[71]

Spies constantly watched the government station and knew where the police rifles were stored. There were also prowlers around the station at night, presumably testing the strength of the garrison. Nearby descent groups were suspected of planning a daytime raid. `Aoke market days were the prime concern, when it was impossible to keep outsiders away and many of them carried guns. Woodford proposed banning guns from the market. Edge-Partington rejected this plan because it would risk the lives of friendly locals on their way to and from the market, placing them at risk from more belligerent types.[72] The inland and lagoon people came to `Aoke market and also recruited from there to the Solomons' plantations.[73] Recruiter and trader J.E. Philp described the scene at `Aoke in August 1912:

> At 9 a.m. we went ashore (or rather to the shore) to a native market where there is always a possibility of getting recruits. It was quite a 'Paddy's Market' as far as noise goes. Dozens of canoes from the islands trafficking with a crowd of bush-folk. The women do most of the business. The bushmen were all armed—most of them with Sniders. Whilst we were interviewing a likely recruit, a boat from the *Sealark* [a naval ship] came close by us taking observations. The officer in charge expressed his surprise at seeing

---

69   SINA, BSIP 14/42, RM TWE-P to Collector of Customs and A/RC FJB, 25 Sept 1914.
70   SINA, BSIP 14/40, RM TWE-P to A/RC FJB, 12 June 1911; RM TWE-P to RC CMW 25 Sept 1911; BSIP 14/41, 1911–13, RM TWE-P to RC CMW, 15 Apr 1913.
71   Dickinson 1927, 51.
72   SINA, BSIP 14/41 1911–13, RM TWE-P to RC CMW, 18 Apr 1913.
73   SINA, BSIP 14/40, RM TWE-P to RC MW, 20 Jan, 8 Mar and 19 May 1910.

so many arms about 'so close to the government station'—and wondered why it was allowed. It would be a problem to stop the natives carrying arms—for no white man has ever gone far into the interior yet.[74]

During 1910, an epidemic of colds and coughs hit the station and surrounding areas and caused deaths on ʻAoke Island and elsewhere. This was common around foreign stations when people were exposed to new diseases brought by labourers returning from Queensland and Fiji.

Edge-Partington attempted to establish his authority in and around Langalanga Lagoon and in May made an expedition into the mountains behind Bina Harbour, arresting Joe Maikali from Laulasi Island for attempting to kill a man. There was also continuing friction between the Kwaraʻae and the Langalanga people and gardens and trees were destroyed. Similar to the mission stations, ʻAoke became a safe haven for refugees from other areas, including six men, six women and three children who lived there in 1911.[75]

The previous 10 years had brought great changes to Malaita. At the end of 1900, no Europeans were living permanently on the island: Charles Pillins at Maluʻu had died and Walter Ivens was commuting between Ulawa and Small Malaita. By 1910, ʻAoke station housed Edge-Partington, 36 police constables and one Fijian police officer. Twenty-eight station labourers from the Western Solomons, Guadalcanal and the Russell Islands on one-year contracts cleared the land and planted crops. These were in addition to the refugees and six prisoners. Beyond ʻAoke, a small foreign population had spread around the island: the Anglican, SSEM and Catholic missions were staffed by 15 European men and five women, one Fijian and several New Hebrideans and Solomon Islanders from other islands. There were also a few Indigenous Australian women who had come with returned-labourer husbands.[76]

---

74 J.E. Philip in Herr and Rood 1978, 166.
75 SINA, BSIP 14/40, RM TWE-P to RC CMW, 5 May 1910, 1 Apr 1911.
76 C.C. Sage and W.H. Sage, two brothers, were based at the Melanesian Mission stations at Fiu and Saʻa. The SSEM had staff at Maluʻu (the Abbots and Caulfeild), Ngongosila (Catherine Deck, Miss Swain and Mr C. Crenan) and Onepusu (Misses Dring and Maclealan, Mr Jacobs, Northcote Deck and Mr Lees). Four European men were at Baunani plantation (Smithers, J. Allen, Every and Stene). The Malayta Company ship the *Royal Endeavour* had two European crew members, Captain W.S. Lane and Mr P. Lane. The crew of the *Evangel* and the *Jubilee* were also often on Malaita. An Australian part-Aboriginal woman named Louisa Tarasol-Aurora lived with her Pentecost husband at Foʻodo, and there may have been more mixed-race people at Onepusu. A small Catholic Marists station had opened at Tarapaina staffed by a Fijian teacher and a Marau man, and visited by priests from Guadalcanal. SINA, BSIP 14/40, RM TWE-P to RC CMW, 28 Feb, 9 June, 1, 12 Nov 1910; RM TWE-P to Collector of Customs FJB, 30 Mar 1911.

Figure 7.3: Malaita's first protectorate official, Resident Magistrate Thomas Edge-Partington, with the Armed Constabulary.
Source: British Museum, Edge-Partington Collection, Album 4, Ca44.293.

The daily business of the RM included supervising movements of labour and dealing with reports of murder or smuggling of guns, dynamite or ammunition, and minor matters relating to payments of money or valuables between individuals, which sometimes involved payments to other islands. A growing part of his work was investigating land purchases made by the missions and the Malayta Company, usually without prior involvement by the government. Edge-Partington faced a difficult problem in June 1911, when on the same day a Malaitan school boy was killed at Maanaere nearby in west Kwara`ae,[77] and Frederick Daniels, an SSEM missionary based on Ngongosila but visiting Uru, was shot just after delivering his Sunday sermon. The multiple reasons given for the murder of Daniels are a window into the complexity of investigations by any RM or DO. The immediate reports suggested two mission-inspired explanations, both of which involved *ramo* claiming 'blood money' offered for the death of a European. The first was that the murderers had wanted to kill Rev. Hopkins, but found him too well protected and chose

---

77   SINA, BSIP 14/40, RM TWE-P to A/RC FJB, 22 June 1911.

Daniels as an easier target. The second version was that Daniels had aided the escape to Onepusu of a couple who had breached sexual codes.[78] Third and fourth explanations were provided by anthropologist Roger Keesing much later, drawing from a conversation Jonathan Fifi`i had in the 1960s with an aged `Alakwale`a, the man who shot Daniels.

Figure 7.4: Men from an inland village around 1910.
Note the number of men smoking pipes and the double- and single-barrel guns augmenting the traditional clubs and bows and arrows.
Source: Deck Collection, Black and White Photographs, 4; see Young 1925, 46.

`Alakwale`a told Fifi`i that two men, Sam Farulate and Diakafu (mentioned in Chapter 4), had been *wane naa ba`e* (*fataabu*, ancestral priests), but when they returned from Queensland they had introduced Christianity and schools, which broke taboos and created grievances. Farulate had fled to Uru from Sinalagu, and Diakafu had been forced to relocate there from a Christian village he had started in the mountains. `Alakwale`a's second reason related to an unfair curse that his mother had made. He and his kinsman Kwa`iga, both from Farisi on the coastal slopes of Uru Harbour, killed Daniels as a means to purify the curse.[79] Edge-Partington wrongly

78 SINA, BSIP 14/40, RM TWE-P to A/RC FJB, 10 Aug 1911.
79 Keesing 1992a, 50–52.

believed a fifth explanation, about involvement by Maeasuaa of Uruilangi (who had organised the 1880s attacks on the *Borealis* and *Janet Stewart*). The Uruilangi settlement was bombarded and destroyed by HMS *Torch* five months after Daniels's death, but Maeasuaa, by then a crippled old man, had by the time of Daniels's murder long since passed on all of his authority to his successors.[80]

There had also been attacks on labourers at the Malayta Company's headquarters at Baunani, mission school boys were killed at various coastal places, and `Aoke itself was still under threat. The attacks were not all one way, nor were they unprovoked: Malaitans living near the Malayta Company land resented the way their land had been taken from them and the manner in which the company had attempted to block their sea access. Their shrines were desecrated and they were attacked if they ventured close to the plantations. The missions also posted guards with guns. Edge-Partington, aware of numerous incidents, requested HMS *Sealark*, then at Tulagi, to proceed to Malaita to help with the investigations. He was rebuffed by Acting Resident Commissioner Burnett, who advised him to formulate a proper scheme for dealing with the 'subjugation of aggressive natives'.[81] Furious and exasperated, Edge-Partington copied his letter to Woodford and Mahaffy. He was insubordinate and sarcastic to Barnett, saying that for all the notice that Tulagi took it was probably not worth reporting 'any further slaughtering of white residents on Malaita'.

> As you know nothing about this island and have hardly set foot on it I fail to see how you could devise tactical schemes for the bringing of the guilty parties to justice as you must be aware it is impossible to go to a village in the bush and arrest one guilty man.[82]

He was summoned to Tulagi to explain the 'general disrespectful and defiant tenor' of his letter, and reprimanded.[83]

Edge-Partington received two taunting message from the Maanaere people from near Dala: that they were looking forward to the visit of the government boat, and would kill and eat the occupants. Hyperbole aside, they were challenging what they knew was a weak government presence. The upshot was that Edge-Partington received a temporary

---

80 *Ibid.*, 52–53.
81 SINA, BSIP 14/40, RM TWE-P to A/RC FJB, 25 June 1911.
82 SINA, BSIP 14/40, 25, 26 June, 15 July 1911.
83 SINA, BSIP 14/40, A/RC JFB to TWE-P, 11 Sept 1911.

assistant, cadet officer L.W. Keppel.[84] To catch the murderers of Daniels, the government reverted to old methods when HMS *Torch* arrived in November 1911 with High Commissioner Sir Francis May aboard. A shore party burned Farisi Village, desecrated ancestral shrines, killed three men, a woman and a child, and badly wounded five others. The murderers escaped. The reprisal was presumably the reason for an east Kwaio threat a few days later to attack Onepusu, on the opposite side of the island.[85]

Edge-Partington felt useless and hamstrung in his attempt to exert control over Malaita by superiors like Barnett and May. In August 1911, with the Daniels murder still not dealt with, he noted that another school boy had been murdered on the mainland opposite Ngongosila, adding to the dozen school murders in the previous fortnight. In an attempt to help them protect themselves, Edge-Partington illegally issued three guns to SSEM teachers, until Woodford found out and ordered their recall.[86] Another European, Otto G. Keller, was murdered at Fo'odo in west To'aba'ita in 1912, and the assassins collected 100 *tafuli'ae* and 10 pigs that had been posted as 'blood money' in retaliation for deaths of Malaitans who had departed in 1902 on the Queensland labour schooner *Sybil II*, which wrecked on its way to Australia. Edge-Partington was on leave and Woodford authorised Acting RM Allen W. Walsh and Police Commander Campbell to investigate.[87]

High Commissioner May issued strict instructions on 15 December 1911 about the manner in which murder investigations were to proceed. This rule reverberated for many years and took away any power for independent action. The RM was to go to the scene of the crime with an interpreter, make enquiries and take statements and attempt to arrest the culprit 'without resorting to an armed expedition into the interior'. If no arrest was made and the resident commissioner was satisfied that arrest was warranted, a demand could be made for the apprehension of the culprit, and if this was ignored, on the decision of the resident commissioner, an armed force of police could be sent to affect the arrest. The police were

---

84 In December 1911, a man from the Western Solomons residing at 'Aoke accused Keppel of raping him. Keppel was charged with assault and left the protectorate. SINA, BSIP 14/41, 1911–13, RM TWE-P to RC CMW, 17 Dec 1911.
85 SINA, BSIP 14/416 Dec 1911; BSIP 14/4, RC CMW to RM TWE-P, 22 Jan 1912.
86 SINA, BSIP 14/40, RM TWE-P to RC CMW, 10 Aug 1911; BSIP 14/7, RC CMW to RM AWW, 1 June 1912.
87 SINA, BSIP 14/40, 1911–13, RM AWW to RC, 4 Jan 1913.

to surround the house an hour before daybreak and if the culprit was not present the occupants and livestock could be seized. Force could be met with force, but no firearms were to be used unless the police were fired on. There was to be no destruction of dwellings until after six months and then only with the permission of the high commissioner.[88] Since there was no judicial commissioner (magistrate) at Tulagi until 1913, it was difficult even to bring murderers to trial. Although Woodford disagreed with the interpretation, Acting High Commissioner Sir Charles Major ruled that under the 1893 Order-in-Council the resident commissioner did have the power to try murders, which Woodford began to do from late 1911. The high commissioner still made the final decision in all capital cases. Woodford directed that May's instructions were to be followed, but that a 'sentence of death must be pronounced in all cases of conviction of murder'.[89]

There are signs that 'Aoke was beginning to fit into normal social patterns. Just before his leave, Edge-Partington organised a large feast for Christmas 1911, one for 500 coastal and inland Malaitans and another for police and labourers.[90] In doing this, he may have been following Mahaffy's example, since he had sponsored similar displays at Gizo, or he may have been influenced by mission stations that also held Christmas feasts. In local eyes, these colonial officials and missionaries were establishing themselves as bigmen of renown.[91] Although whaleboats were still the major form of transport, occasionally the government launch *Belema* was provided to transport Edge-Partington or the several other officers based temporarily on Malaita during these early years. They also used ships of the Malayta Company, the SSEM and the Melanesian Mission, and passed messages via the mission stations. The first sign of indigenous entrepreneurship emerged when Malaitans at Malu'u realised that they, too, could produce copra on their own land, and applied to begin their own coconut plantations.[92] In early 1914, Edge-Partington also managed

---

88   SINA, BSIP 14/4, memorandum of 'Instructions' from the High Commissioner, enclosed in RC CMW to RM TWE-P, 15 Feb 1912.
89   SINA, BSIP 14/41, 1911–13, 3 Jan 1913; Boutilier 1979, 60–61.
90   SINA, BSIP 15 VIII, 136 'Aoke 'Station Diary', 27 Dec 1911. The amount of food prepared for the feasts gives some ideas of their size: on 27 December the guests consumed 14 pigs, 100 fish, 2,640 taro, 2,000 sweet potatoes, 500 coconuts, 10 coconut puddings, 500 nut puddings, and 200 bamboos of nuts. The smaller event, on 29 December, consisted of 3 pigs and 1,000 taro.
91   O'Brien 2011, 202–07.
92   SINA, BSIP 14/7, RC CMW to RM AWW, 17 July 1912.

7. QAIBALA: ESTABLISHING 'AOKE STATION, 1909–14

to make his first visit to Da'i Island between Malaita and Isabel. There were only six hamlets there, and the island had been badly denuded of people by head-hunting raids from Isabel.[93]

After seven years of service, Edge-Partington took leave during most of 1912, his place taken by Allen Walsh. During his absence policing improved, largely because Campbell, appointed commander of police on 23 February 1912, was based in 'Aoke. It was difficult to recruit police and Malaita was considered an unattractive post. Woodford tried to bring in police from Fiji and Hong Kong, and also to get a force of sailors from the RNAS. When this failed, he settled for 21 men from Tanna Island in the New Hebrides, who arrived in January 1912.[94] A Fijian police officer, Ratu Waisele, was brought in to train the police during 1908–09, but within a year he asked to be sent back to Fiji. Edge-Partington reported that 'he was frightened to go out in the sun', missed his wife (who had gone home due to illness), was afraid of getting malaria, thought that he would die and did not 'seem to have the spunk of an ordinary white child'. Without the respect for his being a chief, which he could expect in Fiji, Waisele floundered.[95] Securing adequate police was a perennial problem and some were found in unusual persons, such as former prisoners and refugees at 'Aoke.[96] For a brief period in 1912, Edge-Partington's replacement Walsh was even sent a white prisoner named Hassall to act as his assistant, until Campbell was appointed to take charge of the native police.

Before Campbell's appointment, police training was almost nonexistent and the RM's job became much easier once he arrived. Rather than always being on the back foot, the RM began to be able to enforce protectorate law, at least around the coast. The situation was unusual: the RM had ultimate control over his district but could not interfere in the running of the police, and moreover the police commander was in charge of the police for the whole protectorate.[97] Even then, around 30 police, most of whom were needed to guard 'Aoke, and one whaleboat, were hardly sufficient resources to 'pacify' Malaita. The standards of the police were

---

93   SINA, BSIP 14/41, TWE-P to RS, 4 Jan 1914.
94   Boutilier 1979, 58; SINA, BSIP 14/41, 1911–13, RM to RC CMW, 1 Jan 1912.
95   SINA, BSIP 14/40, RM TWE-P to RC CMW, 18 Dec 1909 and 28 Apr 1910. Waisele left in early May 1910.
96   SINA, BSIP 14/40, RM TWE-P to RC CMW, 16 Sept 1911.
97   SINA, BSIP 14/41 1911–13, minute from HC Sir Henry May on the duties of the police officer, 4 Nov 1911, 17 July 1912.

very different from today. In 1912, Charlie Kwaivania had just completed a two-year sentence for theft, and despite his reputation as a cunning thief while a house servant, and a comment from Woodford that prison did not seem to deter this behaviour, he was so intelligent that Campbell appointed him to the police at a wage of £1 per month.[98]

The BSIP police headquarters was based at 'Aoke from 1912 to 1915, with a detachment of 20 to 25 police on two-year terms. Recruitment was always an issue since the men did not like the mobility necessary for an effective force, and there were no particular qualifications. Most of them were 1st, 2nd or 3rd class privates who earned £12 to £18 a year. Lance-corporals (10) earned £24, corporals (3) £27 and sergeants (2) £36. Many of the men who served their two years refused to reengage, choosing instead to become labourers for much lower pay. Though Campbell found Malaitans to be the best police, few wanted to join, and as a result most came from Guadalcanal or Gela. Police were drilled in a squad using infantry training methods. They were armed with old and unreliable .303 rifles. In 'Aoke they lived in sago palm thatch houses.[99]

Any attack on a European was pursued over the long term, as were other breaches of the peace. The 1908 murder of McKenzie in Langalanga Lagoon was still being followed up in 1913. Some cases involved European property, such as when bush people tried to loot the *Doris* in 1912, a ketch wrecked on Malaita, and killed two of the crew. But Walsh also investigated indigenous disputes, and officers increasingly probed attacks on Malaitans with no connection to Europeans. For instance, at 'Adagege in Lau Lagoon in early February 1912, Kakwari was arrested for murdering his wife Sula, and later that month Walsh arrested Duu from Manalok, close to Fiu, for three murders over the previous three months. However, Walsh was chastised and threatened with dismissal for disobeying High Commissioner May's strict December 1911 code after he burnt villages and destroyed property at Maana'oba. RMs and DOs had to follow cumbersome instructions from Fiji, which undermined local initiative.[100]

---

98   SINA, BSIP 14/7, RC CMW to RM W, 19 Sept 1912.
99   G21141 WPHC MP no. 1814/1916 (1916), 'Report on the Work of the Police in the Protectorate (with Special Reference to Malaita)', 23 June 1916.
100 SINA, BSIP 14/41 1911–13, RM AWW to RC, 5, 21 Feb, 14 June 1913; BSIP 14/7, RC CMW to RM AWW, 11 Nov 1912.

Figure 7.5: Mary Edge-Partington in the living room of the resident magistrate's house, 'Aoke, 1913 or 1914.
Source: British Museum, Edge-Partington Collection, Album 5, Dscn1076.

Edge-Partington returned to Malaita in March 1913 with Mary, his new wife. When based on Gizo he had a mistress from Simbo Island, for which he was forced to apologise to both the resident commissioner and the high commissioner and received an official reprimand from London.[101] It is unlikely that he tried to find a Malaitan replacement. Once his British wife arrived, the couple developed a pleasant lifestyle in the residency high on the hill at 'Aoke, overlooking the bay. His photographs show a comfortable tropical house with wide verandas, a drawing room complete with photographs and a silver service and a tennis court to entertain visitors. Visitors always noted the well-appointed surroundings, rare in the Solomons in the early years, and that Mary Edge-Partington was a genial host.[102] However, in 1914 Edge-Partington still reported that unless more police were provided it was best to abandon 'Aoke. He felt that High Commissioner May's strict instructions for dealing with 'outrages' made it practically impossible to police Malaita properly, and there was still daily

---

101 CO 225/87 170 (microfilm 2915), TWE-P to FJB, 20 Sept 1909; HC Sir Everard im Thurn to CO, 16 Nov 1909; WPHC 4/IV 836/1908, Arthur Mahaffy to HC, 22 Dec 1908; CMW to Major, 30 Sept 1910.
102 Edge-Partington's photographic collection is held by the British Museum. Also see Herr and Rood 1978, 186–87, 195.

fear that the inland people would attack `Aoke.[103] Edge-Partington was frustrated that four years of work had accomplished little, although it is apparent, viewed from a distance of a century, that he had made excellent progress and was exaggerating the direness of the situation.[104]

Figure 7.6: `Aoke police barracks and tennis court, pre-1915.
Source: British Museum, Edge-Partington Collection, Album 5, Dscn1095.

Malaitan people had good reason for disquiet. For one thing, the missions and the Malayta Company had accumulated land without proper authorisation. The largest land purchase was 2,470 hectares by the Malayta Company, but several mission stations sat on land alienated from customary ownership.[105] Arthur Mahaffy, who by 1910 was assistant to the high commissioner, thought that there had been an upsurge in violent incidents in the protectorate over the previous five years because there were fewer European 'old hands' around. With their greater experience they were better able than new arrivals to understand the local people and their expectations. Just as occurred in Australian Papua, the BSIP had become a magnet for adventurous young Australian men who adopted methods that experienced traders and recruiters would never have used.

---

103 SINA, BSIP 14/7, memorandum of instructions by HC Sir Francis May, modified by the SSC, 3 Apr 1912, RC CMW to TWE-P, 15 Feb 1912.
104 SINA, BSIP 14/85, RM TWE-P to RC CMW, 27 Mar 1911; BSIP 14/41, RM TWE-P to RC CMW, 18 Apr 1913, RM AWW to RC CMW, 23 Feb 1912; BSIP 14/42, RM TWE-P to FJB, 12 Oct 1914; BSIP 14/9, FJB to RM TWE-P, 29 Oct 1914.
105 SINA, BSIP 14/40, RM TWE-P to RC CMW, 13 June, 12 and 19 Aug 1911.

Some itinerant labour recruiters took unnecessary risks and displayed grave ignorance of Malaitan ways.[106] Another reason for the increase in violence was that there were now more targets: Malaita's permanent foreign population had increased from zero in 1900 to over 20 in 1910. This rapid growth was largely due to the combined forces of the Malayta Company and the SSEM. In 1912, the former had seven foreign staff at Baunani, Manaba and Hauhui, while the SSEM had five European staff at Baunani, five at Onepusu, one at Fo'odo and two at Malu'u.[107]

Minor incidents of violence were reported almost continuously, sometimes between Malaitans but also involving foreigners, such as the plantation manager and three labourers fired at from the beach while on their way to Baunani in June 1913.[108] The settler community, mainly traders, planters and missionaries, was divided over how to proceed. Missionaries usually advocated peaceful means and lamented violent official reprisals, but most of the other settlers supported the use of full force in the old naval tradition, which punished broadly and often left actual perpetrators unscathed.

Figure 7.7. 'Aoke hospital in about 1914.
Source: British Museum, Edge-Partington Collection, Album 6, neg. Dscn1141.

---

106 CO 225/91 (microfilm 2915), Arthur Mahaffy, Assistant to HC IIT, 'Report of a Visit to the Solomons', 8 Apr 1910, 301.
107 SINA, BSIP 14/41 1911–13, 'List of Whites and Half-Castes Resident on Mala', RM TWE-P to RC CMW, 1 Feb 1912. Part-Australian Aboriginal Louisa Tarasol-Aurora at Fo'odo was the only mixed-race European.
108 SINA, BSIP 14/41 1911–13, RM TWE-P to RC CMW, 16 June 1913.

When the police headquarters shifted back to Tulagi in 1915, a police establishment of 25 remained on Malaita under Sub-Inspector B. Kirke. He and his police were deployed mainly between `Aoke and the north of the island, and around Baunani to the south, where difficulties were ongoing. One police patrol in 1916, accompanied by Kirke and the DO, crossed the centre of the island. The Malaitans they encountered responded violently only once, when the patrol apprehended a murderer. Usually people fled before the patrol, which arrived to find only deserted villages.[109]

After nine years of service in the protectorate, once Edge-Partington returned from leave in 1913 he began to look for a new posting, and asked to be sent to British East Africa or Uganda. On 12 October, he wrote to Acting Resident Commissioner Barnett stating that, without even enough police to protect the station, he considered continued occupation of `Aoke untenable. He resigned two week later, took six weeks leave and left in late January 1915 to work for a plantation company in Ceylon, where he died in 1920.[110]

Conclusion

This chapter began with the beginnings of British naval justice, government agents on recruiting vessels and the early years before `Aoke was created. The main focus has been Edge-Partington's years from 1909 to 1915, when formal government began on the island. Chapter 8 pursues the same years, but from a different perspective, examining the use of Malaitan labour within the BSIP, mainly in the Western Solomons and the Russell Islands, but also on the Malayta Company's plantation at Baunani. We also encounter a new religious element: the arrival of the Catholic mission to compete with the Melanesian Mission and the SSEM. The argument pursued is that once a protectorate presence was established, labour movements and Christianity became subservient to government, although their social effects remained independent and helped to create modern Malaita.

---

109 WPHC G21150, MP no. 500/1917 (1917), Commander F. Campbell, 'Annual Report of the Police and Constabulary for 1916'.
110 SINA, BSIP 14/41, RM TWE-P to RC CMW, 3 May 1913; BSIP 14/42, TWE-P to A/RC FJB, 12, 27 Oct and 5 Dec 1914.

8

Labour, the Malayta Company and Catholicism

> The next day as we were steaming towards Takataka we met Deck in his launch and he came on board and asked if I had got Aliasi and I told him that the boy had run away. Then he asked me if I had got the Marist teachers on board and I said no of course not. He got very nasty and almost ordered me to take them away as they were on his station.
>
> —Resident Magistrate Thomas Edge-Partington, 1910[1]

The Catholic missionaries varied in their class origins, as opposed to the Melanesian Mission clergy, who deserved their moniker of 'God's Gentlemen'. Two brothers, John Northcote Deck and Norman Cathcart Deck, were the mainstays of the SSEM. The Decks were just as much middle-class gentlemen, of impeccable English Quaker heritage with links to the Baring Bank family. Northcote (as he was always known) was a medical doctor and Norman was a dentist. Thomas Edge-Partington, the Resident Magistrate, was of gentry origins as well. Dr Deck, who acted so imperiously to Edge-Partington, could by many accounts be very self-righteous and annoying. It is comical to see the British class system being played out on board ships off the coast of southeast Malaita, with each standing their ground.

---

1   SINA, BSIP 14/40, DM TWE-P to RC CMW, 1 Jan 1911 and 12 Nov 1910.

Once an administrative headquarters had been established at `Aoke, other developments followed. Tens of thousands of male Malaitans were harnessed as labourers on protectorate plantations, adding to the earlier changes that occurred because workers had travelled to overseas plantations and returned with new ways. There was also a local commercial development: the Young family attempted to establish a copra plantation on Malaita, the Malayta Company, which had links to the SSEM. The Christian scene deepened as well, with the arrival of Catholic missionaries who challenged the joint hegemony of the Melanesian Mission and the SSEM. All of these factors brought Malaita more into the mainstream of protectorate life.

Malaitans and Indentured Labour within the Protectorate

Table 5: Internal labour trade in Solomon Islands, 1913–40.

Province	1913–19	1920–29	1930–40	Total 1913–40	Percentage 1913–40
Central	100	350	200	650	1.20
Choiseul	424	319	25	768	1.41
Guadalcanal	1,874	3,831	2,627	8,332	15.3
Isabel	226	284	159	669	1.23
Makira	1,064	1,223	926	3,213	5.93
Malaita	10,476	15,707	10,413	36,596	67.63
Rennell & Bellona	n.d.	n.d.	n.d.	n.d.	n.d.
Temotu	815	1,490	499	2,804	5.18
Western	n.d.	n.d.	n.d.	n.d.	n.d.
Other Islands	268	588	222	1,078	1.99
TOTAL	15,247	23,792	15,071	54,110	

n.d. = no data
Source: Shlomowitz and Bedford 1988, 77.

Woodford knew that there was no way to develop the protectorate and its plantations while most of the available labour supply was being siphoned off to Queensland and Fiji. Although he had no influence over the forced return of thousands of Solomon Islanders from Queensland during the 1900s, it certainly suited his designs. After supervising this repatriation process, he concentrated his efforts on directly achieving the same end for the Fiji labour trade, which in the 1900s was drawing off an average of 250 Solomons labourers a year. After several years of lobbying from Woodford, supported by his old deputy Mahaffy (now assistant to the high commissioner), in May 1910 Sir Everard im Thurn recommended the cessation of the Solomons labour trade to Fiji from the last day of 1911[2]—Indian and New Hebridean labour would suffice for Fiji.[3] Fiji had received 2,623 Solomon Islands labourers between 1890 and 1909. Over those same years, 1,281 were repatriated (an average of 67 a year), 701 died (26.7 per cent) and 223 children were born to labourers. Just over 2,500 Solomon Islanders remained in Fiji at the end of 1909.[4] Malaitans began returning from Fiji in the early 1910s, some with wives and families, in a process similar to but smaller than the exodus from Queensland. Woodford suggested that any Malaitans who so wished should be allowed to settle near 'Aoke station until their future arrangements were made.[5] Just as occurred in Australia, a residual immigrant Melanesian community remains in Fiji.[6]

Fiji contracts were for three years, which meant that the last indentured labourers to work overseas returned in early 1915. German recruiting in the Solomons for Samoa also ceased as soon as the First World War began (it had not stopped under the 1899 Treaty of Samoa). Though Woodford succeeded in holding the labour supply within the protectorate, he failed in another plan: to introduce a capitation tax on adult males. The high commissioner refused this request and the tax did not eventuate until 1921–23.[7]

Just as work in Queensland and Fiji shaped Malaitans and their new plantation culture, so too did work within the protectorate during the first four decades of the twentieth century. Malaitans made up two-thirds of the protectorate's indentured labourers: 36,596 of the 54,110 contracts between 1913 and 1940, or 67.63 per cent.[8] Statistics are inaccurate between 1896 and the early 1910s, although we know indenture

---

2   CO 225/71 (1905) (microfilm 2868), Western Pacific no. 28501, RC CMW to Alfred Lyttleton, SSC, 9 Aug 1905; CO 225/85 (1908), Western Pacific no. 13760, RC CMW to HC Sir Everard im Thurn, 2 Mar 1908; CO 225/91 (microfilm 2915), AM, Assistant to HC IIT, 'Report of a Visit to the Solomons', 8 Apr 1910, 301.
3   Lal 1983; Bedford 1973.
4   CO 225/90 (1910) (microfilm 2914), 'Return of Immigrants Introduced into the Colony of Fiji from Solomon Islands since 1890', with HC Sir Everard im Thurn to SSC Earl of Crew, 19 Jan 1910.
5   SINA, BSIP 14/7, RC MW to DM AWW, 23 Apr 1912.
6   Halapua 2001.
7   CO 225/90 (1910) (microfilm 1814), HC Sir Everard im Thurn to SSC Earl of Crew, 15 Jan 1910; CO 225/91 (microfilm 2914), WPHC HC im Thurn to SCC, comments on Draft Labour Legislation for BSIP, 14 May 1910.
8   Reliable statistics are unavailable from before 1913.

remained at a low level before 1905, when the copra industry began to expand.⁹ There were 10,476 Malaitan contracts between 1913 and 1919, 15,707 from 1920 to 1929 and 10,413 between 1930 and 1940. Ian Frazer calculated that the number of Solomon Islanders recruited actually declined over later years, as did the number of Malaitan recruits: from 1,560 a year from 1913–22 to 890 a year from 1931–40, a decline of 43 per cent. This was due at least partly to the Great Depression.[10] Individuals served multiple contracts and the actual number of Malaitan individuals involved is probably around 27,000, which is nevertheless extraordinary from an island with a population of around 50,000.[11] The only other islands that provided large numbers were Guadalcanal, which provided 8,332 labourers under contract, and Makira with 3,213. The spread of employment in 1911 gives some idea of where Malaitans were working in the early years, although few worked for the Malayta Company except as casual labour.

Table 6: Labour employed in Solomon Islands, 31 March 1911.

Employers	Numbers of Labourers
Levers Pacific Plantations Ltd	1,123
Burns Philp & Co.	642
Burns Philp & Co.	77
Solomon Islands Development Co.	465
Shortland Plantations Ltd	100
Malayta Co. Ltd	649
Svensen & d'Oliveryra	168
Bugotu Rubber Co.	86
Lavare Plantations Ltd	51
William Hamilton	67
J. Oien	82
Gizo Solomon Plantations Ltd	126
Union Planting & Trading Co.	74
Government employment (including police)	141
34 smaller employers	661
TOTAL	3,960

Source: CO 225/96 [1911], [microfilm] 2920, RC CMW, 'Minute of the Supply of Native Labourers for Employment in the British Solomon Islands, for the Information of His Excellency the High Commissioner', 30 June 1911.

---

9   Frazer 1990, 192.
10 *Ibid.*, 193.
11 Shlomowitz and Bedford 1988.

The majority of the contracts (73 per cent in 1914) were for £6 per year for two years, although there was also a tapering, more experienced labour elite (7 per cent) paid over 20/- a month and up to 40/- a month on short contracts, similar to the time-expired labourers in Queensland. As always with indenture agreements, the employers had the upper hand; some cheated new workers of parts of their wages and there was little means to complain or gain recompense. Although there was little direct resistance, aggrieved labourers could resort to covert retaliation, just as their fathers and grandfathers had done in Queensland and Fiji.[12]

Figure 8.1: On board a recruiting vessel in about 1914.
Source: British Museum, photograph by George Rose, Rose Stereographs, Edge-Partington Collection, Album 4, 1037.

---

12   Moore 1993; Bennett 1993.

Judith Bennett divides the regulation of labour into three periods: 1897 to 1913, 1914 to 1920, and 1920 until the outbreak of war in the Pacific. Labour Regulations passed in 1897 set indenture contracts at two years (varied to three years in 1908 until overruled by the Colonial Office in 1911), allowed for government inspections of plantations and required employers to repatriate their labourers. Yet they did not establish average minimum conditions, and despite the new rules the early years were rough and ready and poorly supervised.[13] There were horrific cases of physical abuse. One Yandina overseer used a stockwhip on his men, and at Baunani men were struck with *loia* canes. In some cases, labourers retaliated and deaths occurred.[14]

New Labour Regulations were passed in 1910. They raised the minimum enlistment age from 14 to 16 years of age and included a rations scale, although there is ample evidence that this was not followed and that employers became even more miserly during the 1930s Great Depression. However, two points need to be made, which were equally valid for Queensland and Fiji: labourers cultivated their own gardens, hunted and fished, and traded with local villagers, and in the long run employers had to provide labourers nutritionally adequate rations if they expected them to work hard. Very few copies of the 1910 regulations were printed, which angered the new inspector of labour, William Bell. He complained directly to the secretary of state, which was insubordination of the highest form and indicated both his personality and desperation. Much to Bell's dismay, when an assistant inspector was appointed in 1914 he was immediately seconded into the Customs section of the administration.[15]

The numbers employed could vary by 1,000 between years: at the end of 1913 there were 4,446 indentured labourers in the BSIP; 3,251 at the end of 1914; and 4,111 at the end of 1915. The 1914 downturn was due to dysentery epidemics that killed 101 workers and deterred new recruits. Most new contracts were ratified at Tulagi, and about one-tenth of them at `Aoke. The turnover was huge: of 3,103 labourers in 1914, 2,905 were paid off, 178 died (6 per cent) and 26 deserted. Bell calculated that since 1911 only one-quarter of the labour force had remained stably employed. Even allowing for reengagements, this did not augur well for continuity in skills on plantations, and if workers went home between

---

13 Bennett 1993, 134.
14 Bennett 1987, 154.
15 CO 225/119 (1913) (microfilm 2938), IL WRB to SSC, 10 Apr 1913.

contracts, which they often did, they had to be retrained once they returned.[16] Nor were the overall numbers expected to grow. Woodford believed that the supply could increase to 5,000 or even 6,000 labourers with the incentive of higher wages, but no further, thus placing a cap on the expansion of the copra industry.

How different was the Malaitan plantation experience within the protectorate from that in Queensland or Fiji? The best research is contained in Bennett's *Wealth of the Solomons* and an article and a chapter by her.[17] Parts of the process had not changed since the decades of the external labour trade. The same passage masters or their sons supervised the recruiting (part of the beginning of a colonial elite). Beach bonuses were paid and passed to families, and to bigmen who had an interest in arranging the labourers. Much of the early work involved clearing rainforest, which was strenuous, dangerous work, since *Anopheles* (malarial) mosquitos lurked in the undergrowth. Copra-making was hard work too, but then so also was cutting green cane in Queensland and Fiji. Quite young teenagers were engaged, although some of them worked as domestic servants. All labourers quickly picked up Pijin English, having already been exposed to it on Malaita. Labourers travelled and worked with strangers or enemies from other islands or their own. It was a masculine environment: few women were involved (no single females were recruited after 1909) and if there were women they were married to other labourers. There were no sexual outlets other than the odd clandestine relationship with women in nearby villages or homosexuality, which seems to have flourished.[18] There were no towns to escape to during free time on Saturday afternoons or Sundays. For the most part, labourers were confined to the plantations and close environs. Most first encountered Chinatown and a substantial European settlement when they passed through Tulagi to be paid off.

The plantation regime was harsh: the government's presence was minimal and record-keeping was poor; even six-monthly inspections were spasmodic and rudimentary. Planters maintained their own militias to protect their labourers, particularly on the Malayta Company plantations. The system that developed included compulsion (via a head tax) and coercion, since the government and the planters believed that Solomon

---

16   WPHC MP no. 698/1915 (1915), G21120 WP 12/4 579/15–777/15, IL WMB to RC CMW, 'Report by the Inspector of Labour on the Work of His Department for the Year 1914'.
17   Bennett 1987, chs 7 and 8; 1981; 1993; See also Moore 1993 for a Queensland comparison.
18   Bennett 1993, 147–48.

Islanders were inherently lazy and had to be prodded, forgetting that they had been involved in plantation work elsewhere since the 1870s. Some plantations had reputations as being unsafe or as having harsh overseers (Levers plantations were the worst); passage masters tried to guide 'new chums' to safer plantations, but recruiters sometimes lied, naming safe destinations but then delivering labourers to harsh working conditions. Early on there were many desertions, but these had lessened by the 1910s and 1920s.[19] Overseers were often inexperienced Australians from rural backgrounds; there was a rapid turnover and they proved their authority by physical intimidation, if not outright violence. Bennett describes the scene well:

> New overseers would be provoked by a deliberately disobedient individual, and then a group of his friends and kinsmen would throw themselves at the man. If the overseer acquitted himself well, laborers accepted the odd kick in the backside or hit over the ear he doled out to them—given there was justification.[20]

There is no doubt that order on BSIP plantations was maintained by force and that the government usually turned a blind eye. Labourers were not entirely innocent: some learnt how to operate the system and managed to provoke overseers, then quickly got to the labour inspector before the manager did and lodged a complaint. They also used the 'weapons of the weak', short-weighting sacks of copra, sabotage, setting fires, eating fresh coconuts and killing plantation cattle.[21]

One notable difference from the Queensland and Fiji period is that in the protectorate plantations were not made part of the Christian conversion process. Christian labourers would have teamed up, but there was no outreach from the denominations and plantations were usually isolated from mission settlements. Plantations in the Solomons were mainly secular commercial ventures, except for the Malayta Company plantations at Baunani, Aola and in the Russell Islands, with their SSEM links. Indeed, Malaitan conversion to Christianity seems to have slowed between the 1910s and 1930s, and it may be that without the overseas indenture-Christianity package, which I have argued speeded early conversion on Malaita, there was insufficient outside stimulus to motivate the many non-Christians to convert. In some ways, BSIP plantations

---

19   Ibid., 139.
20   Ibid., 138.
21   Ibid., 141–49.

made it easier to maintain pre-Christian religious concepts, but there were often conflicts, for instance if a menstruating woman cooked food for ancestor-worshiping Malaitans. Labourers preferred to be accommodated in small groups from one island or language area. Plantation owners and managers realised this helped maintain stability, but it is also true that as Christian numbers increased it was often best to separate those who followed ancestral religions so as to lessen disputes and resulting requests for compensation when taboos were broken.[22]

The plantation owners had made a huge land grab and had great expectations, but they worried that the labour supply was insufficient. It was generally believed that the population was declining and that this would impact the numbers of workers available.[23] In 1916, Hubert Murray, lieutenant-governor of Australian Papua, came to the protectorate to report on the alleged labour shortage. He accepted what was a standard calculation in the Solomons—one labourer to maintain 2.47 hectares of coconut palms—but considered this generous and suggested that one labourer to 3.7 to 4.95 hectares was possible by the standards of Papua or the Philippines. He concluded that, based on the 121.7 square kilometres already planted, and with the introduction of cattle to graze down the undergrowth, the available 4,000 labourers were more than enough for maintenance, although there were clearly problems with labour distribution and desires to expand plantations. The issue was more that the planters had taken up an excessive 2,023 square kilometres of land and were calculating a future labour supply based on their acquisition of land rather than on their ability or need to plant more coconut palms. Murray realised that Malaita, with its large population, was the key to future expansion, although officials were still very uncertain of the actual size of the population. Murray estimated 70,000 people, which, if accurate (it was not), he believed was sufficient, along with smaller numbers from the other islands, for future plantation expansion.

The cost of recruiting labour escalated fast: in 1911 recruiters were paid between £6 and £8 a head for labourers; in 1915 this increased on Malaita to £10 to £12 and in 1916 to £14, double similar expenses in Papua. The cost was largely justified by the need on Malaita to use two European recruiters and two boats, one to stand off for safety and cover the other on shore. The recruiting fee reached close to double the average annual

---

22   *Ibid.*, 146.
23   Bennett 2014; Hopkins 1922.

wage. Beach bonuses, the gift given to kin, consisted of trade goods worth about £4 per recruit. If one adds the annual wage to half of the recruiting costs and the beach bonus (for one year), in 1916 Malaitan labourers were costing around £17 a year. The recruiting costs—for the ship and extra crew—were about equal to the wage and bonus costs, an unviable combination. Murray commented further on Malaita:

> The Malaita system strikes one as cumbrous and expensive, and one is inclined to wonder whether, if the island were brought under control, so that recruiters could visit the inland villages, and thus free themselves from the tyranny of the 'salt water men', they could not achieve better results at a less cost.[24]

Murray's advice was to proceed quickly to bring Malaita under government control. Government officials told him this would be accomplished over the next five years, although the planters feared that 'pacification' would result in less recruits being available:

> Very little of the labour from Malaita, it is explained, is voluntary, most of the recruits being sent to work by leading men of their tribe or village; with the advantage of civilisation the power of these leading men will decline, and the young men, being left to choose for themselves, will most decidedly elect to stay at home.[25]

Murray did not take health and mortality issues into account, which affected not only the labourers but all BSIP residents. Dysentery (like malaria) was a major, perennial problem; epidemics during 1913–15 may in some areas have killed as much as 10 per cent of the population. Outbreaks on many plantations caused mortality rates as high as 5–6 per cent in 1914–15, with an average rate of from 2–3 per cent between the mid-1910s and the end of the 1920s. The 1914 death rate was a horrific 10 per cent on Levers plantations, leading to suspension of all recruiting from August to December.[26] In 1928, dysentery broke out in Tulagi jail among the prisoners from Sinalagu, Malaita, imprisoned after the massacre of Bell and his party (see Chapter 10), and 20 per cent died, many innocent of any crime. In 1931, the *BSIP Annual Report* judged dysentery to be endemic. Plantations were ill-equipped to handle

---

24   WPHC MP no. 698/1915 (1915), G21120 WP 12/1 579/15–777/15, J.H.P. Murray, 'Report of Alleged Shortage of Labour in Solomons and Proposal to Recruit Labour from German New Guinea', 29 Apr 1916.
25   *Ibid.*
26   Bennett 1987, 158.

outbreaks of disease: housing was basic, sanitation was poor and hospitals were rudimentary or nonexistent. Bell, then the inspector of labour, said in 1914 that only three plantations had adequate hospitals.[27] If a plantation had less than 50 labourers they were exempt from having any formal hospital.[28]

Malayta Company

While the government was establishing itself on Malaita, the missions continued to expand, although they had already established their patterns of operation. The major change was the arrival of Malayta Company Ltd, registered in Sydney, New South Wales, and begun in 1908–09 by Ernest and Horace Young, brothers of SSEM Superintendent Florence Young, as a commercial trading and copra plantation venture that could help support the mission. Just as the QKM had depended for part of its finances on the Youngs' Fairymead plantation, on Malaita the SSEM worked hand-in-hand with the Malayta Company. While the Youngs claimed the two ventures were separate, they never were—the mission's vessel was used to recruit labourers, the plantation's vessels were used by the mission, and mission head Norman Deck and his brother Northcote purchased land for the company and Norman interfered in the management of its store.[29] Furthermore, the company made applications to purchase land on behalf of the mission and there was a major SSEM boarding school at Baunani, the company's headquarters. Although the decision to shift the QKM's operations to the Solomons was justified as a spiritual challenge, it also involved Florence Young's ambition and some level-headed logistical decisions, including that to establish the Malayta Company on land near the SSEM headquarters at Onepusu. The combined SSEM-Malayta Company operation is the best example of industrial Christianity in the Solomons, and equivalent to Charles Abel's Kwato Mission in Australian Papua.[30]

---

27   Ibid.
28   *BSIP AR*, 1931, 7.
29   CO 225/112 (1908) (microfilm 3096), Walter H. Lucas, Island Manager, Burns Philp to Managing Director, Burns Philp, 'Report of Solomon Islands Properties', 11 Jan 1908.
30   Wetherell 1996.

Figure 8.2: The river mouth at Baunani, showing the young coconut palms on the Malayta Company plantation.
Source: Deck Collection, Black and White Photographs, 28.

There were 500 shares, with two-thirds owned by the two brothers (who were the managing directors) and one-third by various relatives and friends. The company's first base was at Baunani, north of Onepusu. Malaita had no resident traders, who elsewhere in the protectorate facilitated land acquisitions. This left the Youngs and Decks with a difficult task since they had little understanding of indigenous land tenure. Purchases depended on the skills of the Deck brothers, who were both novices at dealing with Solomon Islanders. The Malayta Company land negotiations were motivated by a desire to gain control of a huge block of coastal land, and there was little concern with procedural fairness or establishing good will with the local people. The company's land problems on Malaita were due partly to its staff's inexperience, but also important was that Malaitans and others who had returned from Queensland and Fiji had a greater understanding of land values and were opportunistic in exploiting the company.

8. LABOUR, THE MALAYTA COMPANY AND CATHOLICISM

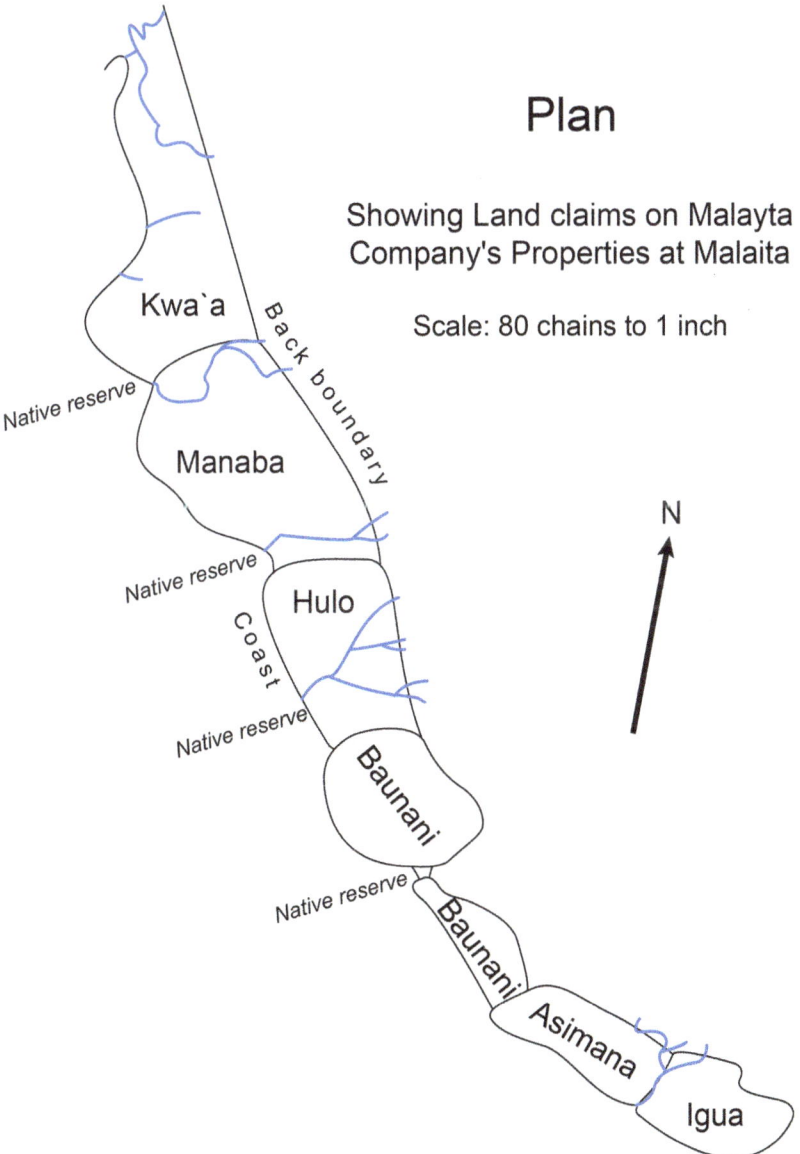

Map 15: The 24 kilometres of Malayta Company land claims along the west coast of Malaita in 1920.
Source: SINA, BSIP 18/II/1, Claims 1–6 and 51, Phillips Land Commission; redrawn by Vincent Verheyen.

In 1908, Malayta Company began to lease land along the coast of central west Malaita. It managed to secure a thin, 24-kilometre coastal strip centred on Baunani and stretching from south of the Kwa`a River to Su`u Harbour (see Map 14, Chapter 7, and Map 15 above).[31] The land was leased in small pieces paid for with a combination of pounds sterling, porpoise teeth, pigs and tobacco, often by Norman Deck or his brother Northcote.[32] The early purchases amounted to 926 hectares, with another 1,469 added in 1911.[33] The company was not skilful at buying land. For instance, Ernest Young purchased 617.5 hectares adjacent to Baunani without accurate knowledge of the ownership, and in another case the company bought land at Baigua Island from the wrong people, land the Catholic Church had already purchased from the correct owners.[34] In later years, particularly during the Phillips Lands Commission of 1919–24, many of these land deals were found suspect. Boundaries were not surveyed, land had been leased from false owners, or payments were improperly distributed amongst the actual land owners.[35] The Malayta Company kept accumulating land: in 1911 Woodford had 14 fresh applications on his desk from the company for provisional land purchases on Malaita and elsewhere.[36] The company also applied to purchase pieces of land on behalf of the SSEM, such as, in 1909, a 19.3-kilometre coastal frontage at `Ataa, and more land at Uru Harbour on the east coast and on Maana`oba Island just off north Malaita.[37]

The Malayta Company accumulated 4,000 ha around Bunani. Their next land acquisition, in 1913 for £35,000, was the most expensive land purchase in the protectorate at that time. This was 12,359 hectares

---

31   The first Malayta Company land was purchased between 24 and 28 October 1908 at Baunani, Kwaifela, Hulo and Ara-Oro. BSIP 18/I/1, certified true copies by S.G.C. Knibbs, 18 Feb 1922; 'Land at Baunani, Malaita Conveyance of 1,500 acres, 28 Oct 1908 between Alick Orunfagaiu and Alexander Mackellar, Bauple, Queensland'.
32   SINA, BSIP 14/40 DM TWE-P to A/RC FJB, 13 June and 12 Aug 1911.
33   SINA, BSIP 18/II/I, 'Land Commission Malayta Company Claims', 1-1-6, map of claims, 23 Sept 1911, 10, and 19 Oct 1911, 168; BSIP 14/10, A/DO WRB to RC, 5 Jan 1920, map of Malayta Company land on Malaita; BSIP 18/II 1, 'Malayta Company Claims, Report of Lands Commissioner Captain G.G. Alexander', 26 Mar 1920.
34   SINA, BSIP 14/40, RM TWE-P to RC CMW, 27 Feb 1911; BSIP 14/6, RC CMW to RM TWE-P, 30 Jan 1911.
35   SINA, BSIP 18/II, 1, evidence relating to the land claims of the Malayta Company, particularly 94–96, evidence of J.N. Deck, 22 Jan 1921. Dickinson 1927, 153–56, describes problems surveying land at Manaba and Su`u in 1914, when, he said, their party narrowly escaped being killed and was rescued by an ex-Queensland Malaitan.
36   SINA, BSIP 18/II/1, 'Claims 1-1-6, Malayta Company', RC CMW to Manager, Malayta Company, Aola, Guadalcanal, 23 Aug 1911, 164–65.
37   SINA, BSIP 14/40, RM TWE-P to RC CMW, 12, 15 Aug 1911.

controlled by trader Billy Pope on Aola Island, northeast Guadalcanal, and Talina and Yandina plantations in the Russell Islands.[38] All up, the Malayta Company accumulated 14,820 hectares, making them the second-largest plantation company during the 1910s and 1920s, after Levers Pacific Plantations Ltd.

Figure 8.3: SSEM teachers at Manaba, part of the Malayta Company plantation.
Source: Deck Collection, Black & White Photographs, 23.

In a pattern rare on Solomons plantations, the Youngs and Decks combined Christian proselytising with commerce. (The only other mission to do this, in a smaller way, was the Methodists.) Just as the Youngs had done in Queensland, the company included evening education and Christian conversion in its activities. In 1911, the SSEM transferred their training school to Baunani, where it remained until the Malayta Company shifted its focus to the Russell Islands in 1918.

In February 1912, the Malayta Company began small trading stations on ʻAoke Island and in Maramasike Passage, along with others near Port Adam. Soon after, the company abandoned trading to concentrate on its plantations, although in the meantime they had annoyed other traders

---

38 Golden 1993, 429; Boutilier 1979, 50.

by paying relatively high prices for locally produced copra. The SSEM encouraged its adherents to recruit for Malayta Company plantations because of the Christian atmosphere, and for a time urged followers to sell copra only to the company. Yet this was as far as Christian sentiment went: the company was mean with labourers' rations, worked them hard and imposed stern discipline, including physical punishments.[39]

Once the strip of land was acquired, during 1910 the company's ship the *Royal Endeavour* regularly recruited batches of 15 to 75 labourers for Baunani plantation and its outstations. They were employed at between £9 and £18 a year on two- and three-year contracts. Most of the labourers were from Makira, Russell Islands and Guadalcanal. As in other areas of the Solomons, labour recruits had to be over 14 years of age and women had to be accompanied by their husbands.[40] In 1911, Malayta Company was employing 649 labourers, just a few more than Burns Philp & Co. (642), but well behind Levers Pacific Plantations Ltd (1,213).[41] During 1910, four Europeans were based at Baunani, but by 1912 there were eight, three employed by the Malayta Company and five by the SSEM. The company also had four overseers at Manaba and Hulo.[42] Until March 1912, all Malayta Company labourers had to be signed on in Tulagi. After that the process became easier since it could be arranged through `Aoke, or onwards from 1914 at Aola on Guadalcanal.[43]

The Malayta Company had continuous troubles with its neighbours—it had failed to honour preservation of sacred sites, which, along with strong feelings that it had misappropriated land, angered Malaitans. The company had to post sentries day and night to guard its plantations from the surrounding people. There are continuous reports of prowlers around at night, although there were suggestions that the watchmen were not being entirely honest and perhaps knew the prowlers better than they admitted.[44] Labour problems began to emerge in September 1911 when,

---

39 SINA, BSIP 14/41, 1911–13, RM TWE-P to RC CMW, 6 Feb 1912.
40 SINA, BSIP 14/40, RM TWE-P to RC CMW, 24 Jan, 4 Mar, 28 Apr, 11 May, 17 May, 4 Oct, and 14 Nov 1910, and 12 Aug and 25 Sept 1911; BSIP 15 VIII, Malaita DO diary, 2 Apr 1910. The early irregular contracts were anomalous since all labourers over age 14 should have received £6 a year.
41 CO 225/96 (1911) (microfilm 2920), RC CMW, 'Minute of the Supply of Native Labourers for Employment in the British Solomon Islands, for the Information of His Excellency the High Commissioner', 30 June 1911.
42 SINA, BSIP 14/41, 1911–13, 'List of Whites and Half-castes Resident on Mala', RM TWE-P to RC CMW, 1 Feb 1912.
43 SINA, BSIP 14/7, RC CMW to RM AWW, 17 Mar 1912.
44 SINA, BSIP 14/41, 1911–13, RM TWE-P to RC CMW, 24 Apr 1912; BSIP 14/10, DO Malaita to A/RC, 17 Nov 1915.

after three months on the plantation, Jackson Tomesulu from Guadalcanal, who had attended a school at one of the Melanesian Mission stations, led a mutiny, during which he attacked the manager and overseer with a hoe and stole items including dynamite and detonators. He was sentenced to three years imprisonment.[45]

We know something about labour conditions on the Malayta Company plantations. When William Bell inspected them during September and November 1913, he counted 112 workers at Baunani, where conditions were good and there were no complaints. At Hulo, the 69 employees were all men from Guadalcanal and Makira, and conditions were 'decidedly bad': they were ill-fed—the rations were mostly sweet potatoes—and many had ulcers and skin diseases that made them unfit for work. The 51 indentured labourers at Manaba were mainly from Guadalcanal, plus 21 local casual labourers, many younger than 16 years, who were paid monthly.[46] When Bell kept his promise to return in November, he found conditions unchanged.

Figure 8.4: The Baunani labour line accommodation sometime before 1914.
Source: British Museum, Edge-Partington Collection, Album 4, Dscn1059.

---

45   SINA, BSIP 14/40, RM TWE-P to RC CMW, 16 Sept 1911.
46   CO 225/118 (microfilm 2936), IL WRB, 'Malayta Company Plantation Report', 6 Sept 1913.

One feature of Baunani was the large SSEM boarding school, the reason given for its presence being that it was cheaper to use the Baunani site than open another major mission base like Onepusu. The Baunani School exposed the falsity of Young and Deck family claims that they separated commercial and missionary activities. Of the 64 male students, 49 were from Malaita, eight from Guadalcanal and seven from Makira. About three-quarters of the boys were under 16 and had attended the school for two years. The teaching pattern was religious instruction combined with reading and a little writing and simple arithmetic. Lessons began at 6:00 am and went for one hour before the boys left to work on the plantation, tending gardens and doing light weeding until 11:00 am. The remainder of the day was spent at school and recreation. The company provided their clothing and food, which consisted of sweet potatoes, vegetables and rice. The few girls who attended the school performed domestic work for the company's and school's European employees. Bell was puzzled, since he could see no benefit to the company from the school, yet one cannot help but wonder if the students were also free labour for Baunani plantation.[47]

In 1915, men from a village about 6 kilometres away from Baunani attempted to murder Rowlands, the assistant manager, who escaped with a shot in his arm. At Manaba outstation, no action was taken to find a man who shot one of the labourers, and DO Ralph Hill reported, 'The bush people in that locality are becoming aggressive and say that as long as the Government does nothing, they will do as they like'.[48] Su`u Harbour plantation was a small outstation with three European staff, four indentured labourers and 18 local casual labourers. There were continuing threats from surrounding descent groups that dated back to an attempted theft in July, when the watchman had shot off part of the ear of one of the thieves and broke his rifle. This made Seiga, who had previously shot a man at Manaba, determined to kill a European or one of the labourers of the Malayta Company plantations.[49]

Just south of the Malayta Company land was another development that would have displeased the SSEM.

---

47   CO 225/119 (1913) (microfilm 2936), William R. Bell, 'Report of Treatment of Native Labour on the Estates of the Malayta Co.', 6 Sept 1913.
48   SINA, BSIP 14/10, A/DO Ralph B. Hill to A/RC, 17, 29 June 1915.
49   SINA, BSIP 14/10, Officer in Charge, Police, `Aoke to A/RC, 7 Aug 1915.

The Catholic Mission

Catholic missionaries, after an unsatisfactory beginning at Tarapaina in Maramasike Passage, had established bases at Rohinari in `Are`are Lagoon and at Buma, then later returned to Tarapaina. The Marist Catholic mission arrived on Malaita at the same time as the government station (see Map 16, Chapter 10).

After the deaths of the first European QKM missionaries at Malu`u in 1902, Arthur Hopkins from the Melanesian Mission's base at Ngorefou visited Peter Abu`ofa, and the Anglicans sent a teacher from Gela to help bolster the Malu`u mission. Presumably they hoped to entice Abu`ofa into the Anglican fold. When interfaith cooperation occurred it was seldom revealed in the published journals of the rivalrous missions, though there were occasional clues.[50] Sea transport was always scarce and, as still occurs in the Solomons, people hitched rides on any passing vessel. In 1904, QKM staff travelled on the Melanesian Mission vessel *Southern Cross* from Malaita to Gavutu, and a year earlier Florence Young had dined aboard the ship at Gela.[51] When Young returned to the Solomons in July 1905, Hopkins had come over to Gavutu in the QKM's *Daphne*, and he offered to take the QKM group back to Malu`u in his whaleboat.[52]

This on-the-ground informal cooperation lessened as new missions became more established. The Melanesian Mission and QKM-SSEM published records convey a studied lack of acknowledgement of the existence of the other denomination on Malaita. Later, the same is true for the Catholics and Seventh-day Adventists. Christian denominations were competitive, not always cooperative, and could be mean-spirited toward each other. The Anglicans regarded Malaita as 'their island', since for decades they had a monopoly on missionary work there. Their slow progress and Malaita's huge population made for too tempting a morsel to be confined to one denomination. When the QKM sent their first European missionary to Malu`u in 1900, the Anglicans lamented that the 'unwritten compact' that had allotted Malaita to them had been breached by an 'undenominational mission'.[53] Throughout the Pacific, the major Protestant missions—the Anglicans, the Methodist Mission, the Presbyterians and the London

---

50 'Report of the Solomon Islands Branch, Queensland Kanaka Mission', *NIV*, 1903–04, 7.
51 Young diary, 12 Apr and 7 May 1904, *NIV*, 1902–03, 10–11.
52 *NIV*, 1904–05, 11.
53 'The First Voyage', *SCL*, Jan 1901, 10.

Missionary Society—managed to coexist in most areas through such unwritten compacts. The latter was an interdenominational church with close ties to the Church of England, and both their and the Methodists' services were based on the Anglican's *Book of Common Prayer*.[54] Relations with the Catholic missions were always more difficult. In his 1910 New Year's message, Melanesian Mission Bishop Wilson recounted how his dioceses had to retreat from Bougainville because the Catholics were already established there. He enunciated what he said was a general principle:

> Whichever Mission, the Anglican or the Roman, first establishes itself in Melanesia, holds the ground against the other, the two not allowed to work in the same neighbourhood.[55]

There was no formal colonial rule about separation of denominations, except in British New Guinea where lieutenant-governors MacGregor and Murray had a policy of containing each denomination in a separate district. Initially, Woodford pursued a similar policy in the protectorate, although he seems to have given up during the 1900s. The separation of denominations there was largely self-imposed and only worked well on the smaller islands. The Methodists, who arrived in 1902, confined their activities to the northwest of the archipelago. The Anglicans already had strongholds on Ulawa, Makira and Isabel and in the Gela Group, where they were too dominant for other denominations to consider trying to break in. Elsewhere, islands with large populations, such as Guadalcanal and Malaita, came to be shared by multiple denominations. The Anglicans and the SSEM learnt to coexist on Malaita, establishing centres that complemented but did not clash with each other, although there were serious tensions at times. However, despite Anglican claims to be a 'true Branch of the Catholic Church',[56] the Melanesian Mission was unhappy when the Catholics arrived and entered into competition. Malaita remained divided between the three mission churches until the Seventh-day Adventists arrived in 1924 as a fourth competitor.

After disastrous attempts to establish a foothold during the 1840s, Catholic missionaries did not return to the Solomons until 1898. Although the Solomons were within the ecclesiastic territory of the Missionaries of the Sacred Heart, because there was no chance of them extending their

---

54 Whonsbon-Aston 1964, 21.
55 Wilson, 'New Year's Letter from the Bishop of Melanesia', *SCL*, Jan 1901, 99.
56 Wilson, 'The Annual Report of the Melanesian Mission for 1902', *SCL*, Mar 1903, 10.

New Guinea-based operation to the archipelago to stop the Protestant advance, Archbishop of Sydney and Apostolic Delegate (papal envoy) Cardinal Patrick Moran persuaded his church that the French Marists should be given the territory.[57]

Woodford, on the grounds that it was too dangerous, advised the Marists against trying to set up a base on Malaita (despite the Melanesian Mission having successfully maintained a minimal presence on Small Malaita since 1895). They chose instead to settle on small Rua Sura Island contiguous with Guadalcanal, and purchased the island from a European trader. This brought them into conflict with the traditional owners, who recognised neither the Marist purchase nor the earlier transaction. Furthermore, Woodford had recently mounted a punitive expedition to the area, which people still resented.[58] Bishop Julien Vidal returned to Fiji and left Father Pierre Rouillac in charge.[59] Then, toward the end of 1899, a canoe from Malaita was wrecked at Rua Sura. The new arrivals begged the mission staff to take them home to Wairaha near Rohinari, which they did on the 19-ton mission schooner *Eclipse*. In gratitude, the people allowed Rouillac to take one of the shipwrecked youths back to his station. Soon after, in April 1901, the *Eclipse*, damaged from hitting a reef, made a memorable 19-day journey to Sydney for repairs. Rouillac made the voyage with four Fijian crew, and four young Solomon Islanders who were baptised there by Cardinal Moran.[60]

Late in 1901, the *Eclipse* visited Langalanga Lagoon to recruit workers. A dozen men returned to Rau Sura, although none showed any interest in Christianity. They did not cope well on Guadalcanal and were repatriated soon after. In 1908, the Prefect Apostolic Father Jean-Ephrem Bertreux used his small schooner the *Verdelais* to travel to west Malaita seeking land for a mission station. The *Verdelais* was difficult to manipulate through the reefs, and just as the *Evangel* had made transport much easier for the SSEM, the arrival of motorised 30-ton *Jeanne d'Arc* in 1909 improved the Catholics' seagoing mobility. In September, the new ship made its first trip to Marau Sound and Malaita. Malaitans travelling with the Marists managed to persuade the Langalanga people to arrange the sale of a piece of coastal land at Buma.

---

57   Laracy 2013, 53–55.
58   Veperdi n.d. This was in relation to the Austrian-Hungarian expedition of SMS *Albatros* in 1895; mateinfo.hu/a-albatros.htm.
59   Laracy 1976, 39–40.
60   Raucaz 1928, 208.

At about the same time, bigman Ara`iasi at Tarapaina in the `Are`are area on Small Malaita had fallen out with the SSEM and sent word that he would like the Catholics to begin operations in his district.[61] Father Bertreux visited, purchased land and left two catechists at Tarapaina.[62] Ara`iasi was the son of a well-known *ramo* and was also the spokesman for Iava`o, the hereditary *araha* (paramount chief) for the area. He had a reputation as a warrior in his own right and supposedly killed more than 80 Malaitans over the years before he became Christian. Historian Hugh Laracy recorded that Ara`iasi was offended by Florence Young in 1909, but that he and Iava`o recognised benefits from having a missionary presence and so invited the Marists to begin a station. Dr Deck was in charge of the SSEM in the islands and had been to Tarapaina before the Catholic presence was established. He purchased land there in October 1910, and also at nearby Orlu Island in June 1911.[63] Deck landed a teacher at Tarapaina. According to Malaita District records, that was when Ara`iasi committed a murder and the teacher was frightened into leaving. Tarapaina was acknowledged to 'belong' to Ara`iasi and Naumauri. Ara`iasi seems to have invited the SSEM first, then taken advantage of the withdrawal of their teacher to invite the Marists to replace them, thereby receiving double payments for land.[64]

The Catholics chose Tarapaina as their first Malaitan base in 1910, purchasing Tarapaina and small Orlu Island from Ara`iasi for £50 that November, although Orlu seems to have been controlled by Homa Hanua, not Ara`iasi.[65] During 1911, the priest at Marau visited his Fijian catechist at Tarapaina several times and decided that the incessant rain and the slippery infertile red clay soils made the site unsuitable. No Catholic expansion into the surrounding area of Small Malaita was possible since the Anglicans had too firm a hold and the SSEM was gaining strength there. This forced the Catholics to search for land along the west coast of the main island. The priest and Ara`iasi set out from Tarapaina in a whaleboat and travelled to Rohinari at the top of `Are`are Lagoon. The local villagers were uncooperative and tried to drive them away. However, Arisimae welcomed the Catholics, being interested more in the

---

61 Petero Ara`iasi was in his eighties when he died on 11 February 1963. *BSIP News Sheet*, 15 Mar 1963.
62 SINA, BSIP 14/40, DM TWE-P to RC CMW, 1 Jan 1911.
63 *Ibid.*, 12 Aug 1911.
64 *Ibid.*, 1 and 2 Nov 1910.
65 *Ibid.*, 12 Aug 1911.

amount of tobacco and matches they could provide than any Christian message. He arranged for them to purchase Rohinari Island and some land on the neighbouring coast.⁶⁶

Figure 8.5: Arisimae, the most feared *ramo* in `Are`are.
This photograph is probably from around 1912. He is wearing a nautilus shell nose ornament called *tare`ereereo*, often worn by men.
Source: *NIV*, Dec 1912.

---

66   Raucaz 1928, 209–13.

Figure 8.6: Two brothers, Donatien and Jean Coicaud, served as Catholic priests on Malaita. This is Donatien and one of his congregation, probably from the late 1910s at Buma.

Source: David Ruthven, courtesy of the British Museum, with extra information from Burt 2015, 48.

The priest returned to Tarapaina, and in February 1912 was back in Rohinari to confirm the land purchase. On 2 July 1912, the *Jeanne d'Arc* brought another priest and eight Guadalcanal men to help clear land. In writing of the Rohinari arrival, Vicar Apostolic Raucaz gave the impression that Father Jean Coicaud was 'alone in this cannibal country',[67] even though the coast was dotted with SSEM and Anglican mission bases and outstations and the government headquarters had been at 'Aoke since late 1909. The nine men, protected by Arisimae, shared one crowded hut with their belongings at one end and an altar at the other. By 1914, Father Coicaud was sure enough of his welcome to leave the island to begin a base on the shore.[68] While Tarapaina was isolated, the Rohinari base was just south of SSEM's Onepusu headquarters, which must have alarmed the evangelicals. He was joined by his brother Donatien, also a Catholic priest.

Catholicism in the early Solomons consisted of station-centred Marist fathers and brothers, with an emphasis on religious education. They worked mainly through French priests, brothers and nuns and, unlike the Anglicans and SSEM, made no effort to introduce an indigenous clergy until the late 1930s. In *Marists and Melanesians*, Hugh Laracy describes Solomon Islanders' views on religion as flexible enough to adapt to new circumstances, whereas Catholicism focused on 'beliefs and behaviour dictated by an authority which transcended circumstance'.[69] Yet the Catholics were also syncretic in their attitudes to Malaitan customs and, like the Melanesian Mission, were not averse to participating in local funeral rites and other ceremonies. One reason for Catholic success was the stability of their missionaries, who often remained at the same stations for decades and grew close to the local people, growing old in their communities and creating a sense of belonging. Father Donatien Coicaud is a good example: posted to Visale in 1913, to Rohinari in 1914, and then to Buma where he remained until his death in 1957.[70] Baptism was the basic measure of good Catholics; anything beyond that could take three generations to accomplish.[71] (The first three Solomon Islanders to become Catholic priests, all Malaitans, were not ordained until 1966 and 1967.)[72]

---

67   *Ibid.*, 214–25.
68   *Ibid.*
69   Laracy 1976, 66.
70   'Obituary for Donatien Coicaud', *Acta Societatis Mariae*, June 1957.
71   *Ibid.*, 70.
72   These were Michael Aiki from Rohinari in 1966, Donasiano Hitee from Tarapaina in 1967, and Timothy Bobongie from Lau Lagoon, also in 1967. Moore 2013c entry for the Catholic Church.

Locals expressed allegiance to the mission by wearing a small Catholic medal strung on a cord on their otherwise naked bodies, although the Marist priests and brothers encouraged them to wear at least minimal clothes. The emphasis was on education of children and the schools served as the main Marist evangelising device; children were thought to be the best candidates for baptism. From the beginning of the twentieth century there were nuns in the Marist mission to the Solomons, although none were based on Malaita until much later. The Marists also had three linguistic peculiarities: their services were in Latin, and they spoke French among themselves, precluding any close understanding by the local people, but they also learnt local languages and did not depend on Pijin English. Marists, like all missionaries, also tried to give medical care, which, even if not always successful, worked often enough to convince Malaitans to accept the faith.

Although most converts came from the surrounding villages, two other Marist devices used to build up the nucleus of a religious community were to 'buy' (give compensation for) orphans and to provide refuge for people cast out of their communities. Father Jean Coicaud did this at Rohinari right from 1912, and Laracy recorded several cases. Petero Kaihione, a 10-year-old boy, covered in sores and near death, was given to Coicaud to care for in January 1913. He recovered and became the first baptism and the priest's mentor for learning the `Are`are language. Petero married Adela Poikana, whom Coicaud also 'purchased' after she fled to the mission to escape the consequences of a curse. The couple became catechists at Takataka in 1924 and Petero's family followed him to Rohinari mission. Another famous case was Senoveva (Genevieve), an orphan baby whom Coicaud saved from a violent death, suckled with goat's milk and put into the care of the nuns at Visale on Guadalcanal.[73]

Conclusion

Missionaries introduced modern spatial systems. They restructured settlement patterns to suit themselves, encouraging people to move into larger coastal villages and construct their houses in orderly lines. Christianity purposefully drew Malaitans to the coast, where they became part of easily supervised, single-denomination communities. Missions also

---

73 Laracy 1976, 76–77.

resettled Malaitans of mixed origins into coastal villages, which in the early years often consisted of large numbers of males without families. These new villages were focused on a school, clinic, church, and mission house, not the ancestral shrines of old. Christian villages were an early stage of the urbanisation still exhibited today in large coastal villages. They were also part of the new economy with new ways to earn incomes. Rudimentary European clothes (often just loin cloths) marked the inhabitants of these villages as different from their families in the surrounding small hamlets, who remained naked.

Although there was ongoing movement between the Christian settlements and neighbouring hamlets, it was like passing between two worlds, one regulated by foreign rules and the other by indigenous beliefs and practices. Shrines were sacred places and Malaitan hamlets were structured to mirror cosmological and gender divisions. The churches were new sacred places, seats of foreign power that mirrored an introduced cosmology and new gender divisions. In mission villages there were different rules of intimacy and new public personas that created new public figures. The same was true in `Aoke and Baunani.

9

Koburu: William Bell, 1915–27

I wish to point out that murders are of constant occurrence in the Malu'u district and the Government have no right to fetter the actions of the relatives of a murdered man while it persists in going no further than the sea beach and will allow nothing to be done either to punish a murderer or prevent a murder. I certainly will not make myself ridiculous by telling natives that the Government wish to be considered their protector when the Government's past and present methods assist murderers and blackmailers.

—William Bell, 'Aoke, 27 November 1915[1]

William Bell

When Roger Keesing and Peter Corris published *Lightening Meets the West Wind: The Malaita Massacre* (1980), they could not have anticipated the storm it would provoke. The book concerned the massacre in east Kwaio of District Officer William Robert Bell and his tax-collecting party in 1927. While it was a brutal act, it paled in significance when compared with the retaliation by the government. The reaction to the book was complex: indirectly it rekindled long-standing Kwaio outrage and their demands for compensation, and brought into play tensions between Kwaio people and the largely north Malaitan police force of 1927. Keesing, an anthropologist, was not allowed to return to Kwaio for several years and sale of the book was for a time banned in the Solomons.[2]

---

1 SINA, BSIP 14/43, A/DO WRB to A/RC, 27 Nov 1915.
2 Akin 1999b. The ban was the doing of the Malaita Province premier, who was a descendant of at least one member of the punitive expedition.

William 'Will' Robert Bell was the most significant official to work on Malaita before the Second World War. His name is remembered by Malaitans because of the manner of his death in 1927, his skull smashed with a rifle barrel. However, Bell also did more than any other early officer to introduce government processes on Malaita. His years coincide with several important changes: the introduction of district and village headmen, the diminution of the role of passage masters, the end of the beach bonus and the introduction of a head tax. His *modus operandi* was to outmanoeuvre the powerful Malaita bigmen: Bell took on the *ramo*— warriors and sometimes bounty-hunters—and attempted to subdue them, cutting deeply into old Malaita. More than any other protectorate officer, Bell was responsible for bringing a degree of peace to Malaita. Much of the final 'making' of modern Malaita occurred during his years. Although consequences of the vengeful retaliation by the government still reverberate today, Bell's death caused the government to take a more mature look at its direction in the late 1920s and 1930s. Although the Great Depression years stymied many of these changes, the post-Bell years were part of a different era.

Figure 9.1: William Bell with his police.
Source: W.M. Mann, courtesy of Roger Keesing.

Born in 1876, Bell was educated in state schools in rural Gippsland, Victoria, Australia. In 1899, he enlisted in the 2nd Victorian Mounted Rifles in the Boer War in South Africa. After the war he was working with

9. KOBURU: WILLIAM BELL, 1915–27

his uncles at harvest time when a pitchfork entered his right hand and a doctor had to remove a portion of his palm and some fingers. He was self-conscious of the injury, and in his early years wore a glove and shook hands with his left hand. He chose to go to Fiji where he began work for a trading company as an accountant. In 1904–05, he began to make labour recruiting voyages for the company and then secured an appointment as government agent on the schooner *Clansman*, which undertook several trips to the Solomons recruiting labour between 1905 and 1911, many of these including Malaita. Two of his shipboard journals have survived, which show him to have been an upholder of regulations.[3] He came to respect the tough and straightforward Malaitans, who were the main labourers recruited. When the Solomons labour trade to Fiji ended in 1911, Bell applied for and received the position of head of the BSIP Department of Labour. Because he was well-known by Malaitans, this caused a few difficulties. Edge-Partington complained:

> There is too much 'Mr Bell' over here, what I mean to infer is that a lot of natives think because Mr Bell was Government Agent of the 'Clansmen' that he is the Resident Commissioner at Tulagi.[4]

The new 1910 Labour Regulations required detailed supervision of the labour trade at a time when plantations were expanding. Recruitment conditions, rations and treatment of labourers on the plantations needed to be strictly inspected and Bell was just the man to do it. However, Bell had no independent transport and felt that he lacked Resident Commissioner Woodford's support. He broke ranks and complained straight to the Colonial Office. Although Woodford was exonerated and Bell castigated, it showed the measure of Bell and that Woodford, about to retire, respected him. Bell was unusual in the Solomons: he did not drink alcohol, was a stickler for what was right and was willing to prosecute the big plantation companies if they transgressed regulations. He also championed the rights of Solomon Islanders.[5] Malaitans nicknamed him 'Koburu' (the stormy, seasonal northwest winds) since his temper could be sharp and furious. His other nickname was 'Buster', a little incongruous for such a tough government officer.

---

3   Keesing and Corris 1980, 45–49; Giles 1968, 121.
4   SINA, BSIP 14/41, 1911–13, RM TWE-P to RC CMW, 4 May 1913.
5   Keesing and Corris 1980, 50–53.

When the First World War began some BSIP officers left to join regiments, but Bell was considered medically unfit because of his hand. He was asked to assume the position of DO on Malaita as a replacement for Edge-Partington. C.G. Norris, Ralph B. Hill and Fred Campbell had all acted in the position earlier in 1915. Bell was reluctant to take on Malaita, but accepted the position in an acting capacity for one year as a trial, beginning in November 1915. He was aware of the enormity of the task—as inspector of labour he had been as much in touch with affairs on Malaita as most of the DOs or the police commanders. The chapter begins with a typical quotation from Bell, from a report to his superior, Acting Resident Commissioner Frank Barnett. After taking a trip to north Malaita he pointed out to Barnett that it was unfair for people of an area like the SSEM stronghold at Malu'u, where killings had largely ceased, to be forbidden to defend themselves against murderous attacks. His advice to the Malu'u people contravened the advice from Tulagi and gained him a reprimand:

> I told them that if the Government were not prepared to protect them that they were justified in taking any necessary steps for the preservation of their own lives. If anyone threatened to kill them and they were sure that the threat was an earnest one, they were entitled to get in first. If a man killed a murderer of his relative I would take no action, but they must only retaliate on the actual active offender. I explained to them that whenever and wherever the Government were able to bring the offender to justice that they would be forbidden to take the law into their own hands.[6]

Just before he took leave to deal with family issues in Australia between January and May 1916, Bell let off another blast at Barnett, providing an analysis of what was needed to bring Malaita under government control. From 1911 until 1914 there had been two European police officers and at times up to 50 police. Then, with the transfer of police headquarters to Tulagi, the Malaita contingent was cut back to one officer and 20 men. There was no suitable jail: prisoners had to be shackled hand and foot and attached to a post in a leaf-house. Bell wanted an adequate number of police and also sufficient maritime transport—he was unwilling to patrol Malaita from a 6-metre whaleboat. He also wanted freedom to do things his way, knowing that Tulagi and the WPHC did not comprehend Malaita. Bell was clearly on a collision course with the administration and was aiming directly at Barnett.[7]

---

6   SINA, BSIP 14/43, A/DO WRB to A/RC FJB, 27 Nov 1915; BSIP 14/10, A/RC FJB to A/DO WRB, 14 Aug 1916.
7   SINA, BSIP 14/44, A/DO WRB to A/RC FJB, 17 Jan 1916.

Figure 9.2: William Bell on patrol by canoe.
Source: W.M. Mann, courtesy of Roger Keesing.

Almost immediately on his return from leave, Bell again crossed swords with Barnett. As in his earlier relationship with Woodford, his behaviour was insubordinate. When Barnett refused to forward his January report to the high commissioner, Bell sent a copy to be forwarded to Fiji. He then wrote to Barnett withdrawing any interest in a permanent appointment on Malaita.[8] Barnett had instructed Bell not to pursue murderers unless they had been involved in European deaths, contrary to Woodford's earlier instructions and to British law. As Bell replied: 'The native looks upon it as a weakness and he is correct'.[9] Barnett believed that killing was endemic on Malaita and involved almost everyone as a way of life, whereas Bell believed that in 90 per cent of the killings the victims were innocent of any crime. Although Bell had a far better understanding of the Malaitan *ramo* system than did Barnett, his insubordination could not be countenanced.

---

8   SINA, BSIP 14/10, A/RC FJB to A/DO WRB, 25 Jan 1916; BSIP 14/44, A/DO WRB to HC Sir Ernest Bickham Sweet-Escott, 19 June 1916; BSIP 14/44, A/DO WRB to A/RC FJB, 7 July 1916.
9   SINA, BSIP 14/44, A/DO WRB to A/RC FJB, 5 Oct 1916.

This was followed in December 1916 by a letter from Bell to the high commissioner, protesting Barnett's decision effectively to demote him to second-in-charge of the Labour Department and not return him to his substantive position. He also belittled Barnett for his timidity and obstruction:

> Under the Mala conditions, I think punitive expeditions for the purpose of punishing natives as a community is as repulsive to the ordinary British mind as is sitting inactive on a Government Station to an ordinary British Officer while innocent men, women and children, are being murdered around him by well known murderers, who in most instances murder for the sake of a reward, and he is being told not to interfere.[10]

Bell's pugnacious and fiery nature required that he explain his thinking at length in writing to justify his complaints, providing us with insights into his views. Here we have an aspect of the trope of the aggressive Malaitan, but Bell knew that a weak response is not an option:

> The administration of Mala is quite a different problem to that of Ysabel, Ngela, and the like places, where the natives have been under Missionary Influence and Government control for many years. The Mala native is quite a different person. He is the most useful when brought under control and given reasonable treatment, but any show of weakness is fatal to that control. He has more force of character than other natives and dominates them wherever he goes. The lack of cohesion among them makes the Mala problem more simple than it otherwise would be. It is to be hoped that no native will arise with criminal tendencies and sufficient personality to bring about any material cohesion.[11]

Although Barnett sacked Bell, he was reinstated and had to beg forgiveness from his superior. Luckily for Bell, Barnett departed and was replaced by a new resident commissioner, Charles Workman in 1918.[12] By this stage, Bell, though he never learnt any Malaitan language, was considered an 'expert' on Malaita and understood the complexities of the island's cultures better than any other European at the time, expect perhaps Anglican missionaries Ivens and Hopkins. Bell, the severe, spartan bachelor officer, became the master of ʽAoke, ensconced in the government residency, working hard to outmanoeuvre any Malaitans who opposed his agenda.[13]

---

10   SINA, BSIP 14/44, A/DO WRB to HC Sir Ernest Bickham Sweet-Escott, 16 Dec 1916.
11   *Ibid.*
12   Moore 2013c entry.
13   Keesing and Corris 1980, 56–65.

Although Bell performed poorly in his promotion exams, Workman valued him highly and had him confirmed as DO in November 1919, commending him for his unswerving honesty. In 1924, he was also confirmed as a deputy commissioner of the WPHC, a venerable and senior position.[14]

Figure 9.3: Three of William Bell's police.
Source: Courtesy of Roger Keesing.

14 SINA, BSIP 14/15, RC CRMW to DO WRB, 30 Nov 1919.

Bell's 1915–27 years were spent pacifying Malaita, using the constabulary as his main weapon. His method was to out-bigman the bigmen. He was like a feudal lord controlling a fiefdom, replete with a small army. Eventually, the resident commissioners decided that he was doing an excellent job and left him alone. Bell was unusual amongst the British career public servants in that he was a self-made Australian. He threw himself into the task and was remarkably successful. He continued to have an aggressive relationship with his superiors, who respected him nonetheless. He also had an uneven relationship with the missionaries, whom he admired, although he decried the more self-seeking zealots (particularly in the SSEM) who wanted to destroy Malaitan customs.[15]

In 1917–18, Malaita provided 1,356 (38 per cent) of the 3,824 labour recruits in the protectorate. The cost of obtaining new recruits had reached the prohibitive price of £18 per head and overall recruiting had slowed, down 10 per cent from the year before. Pacification was slow: 24 murders were reported in the 1917–18 year when Bell arrived, but not one arrest was made.[16]

Malayta Company

Bell inherited the problems that had plagued the Malayta Company plantations since they began in 1908. Baunani and its outstations had a bad reputation, and the company also continued to negotiate for more land. When Bell took over, conditions at Baunani and Su`u were still tense but settling down. There was continued suspicion that the watchmen were somehow in cahoots with the prowlers since the hundreds of retaliatory shots never found their mark. Bell believed that the locals were disputing the boundaries and objected to further clearing of land.[17] As attacks continued on both labourers and livestock, the company tried to capture the offenders and wanted to mount its own punitive expeditions. Bell recommended a more constant police presence and in August 1916 police shot four men at Baunani. Later in the year, Sub-Inspector B. Kirke

---

15   Keesing and Corris 1980, 66–80; SINA, BSIP 14/57, DO WRB to A/RC, 30 May 1924.
16   *BSIP AR*, 1917–18, 2, 3.
17   SINA, BSIP 14/43, A/DO WRB to A/RC FJB, 23 Dec 1915.

camped there with a police party for several weeks, endeavouring to find the cause of the endless troubles the company had with the surrounding descent groups.[18]

The Malayta Company also had a plantation at Aola on Guadalcanal, and established stronger communications with Aola than with `Aoke. Once Aola became a government station in 1914, Baunani's labourers were paid off there rather than at Tulagi. The company had an avaricious attitude toward land acquisition, and although its pursuit of land sales and rights-of-way limited the access of the neighbouring descent groups to the coast, this was not the only reason its plantations were attacked. Bell concluded that the Malayta Company treated boundaries in a caviller manner and had tried to assert control over areas they had not purchased. Some of these problems related to different concepts of land alienation. Bell saw the issue clearly:

> It is also certain that the natives on the small village reserves on the coast never anticipated that they might not be allowed to pass through the land they had sold when they wish to travel to the unalienated land at the back of it. Indeed, under such circumstances the village reserves on the coast would at once become untenable, for the natives must pass over the Company's land to get to land on which they can cultivate their gardens.[19]

Over several years, the Malayta Company was also in conflict with the Catholic mission and the government administration over land at Su`u Harbour on the mid-west coast. Su`u was the safest harbour on that coast and the area was heavily populated. Bell saw through the company's posturing:

> It is endeavouring to obtain a monopoly of the Harbour, which is nature's highway for a large population, so that it can hamper the efforts of labour recruiters and traders and compel the natives to accept its terms in regards to labour and trade.[20]

Earlier, for the same reasons, the company had argued that it needed to control Boronaasu`u Harbour in west Kwaio, and they reused the argument at Su`u. Bell thought that the company's agreements there

---

18   SINA, BSIP 14/55, A/DO WRB to A/RC FJB, 11 June 1916; BSIP 14/10, A/RC FJB to A/DO WRB, 29 July and 15 Aug 1916; BSIP A/DO WRB to A/RC FJB, 9 July 1916; WPHC G21150, MP no. 500/1917 (1917), Commander F. Campbell, 'Annual Report of the Police and Constabulary for 1916'.
19   SINA, BSIP 14/45, DO WRB to A/RC FJB, 11 Nov 1917.
20   SINA, BSIP 14/47, DO WRB to A/RC CRMW, 6 Oct 1919.

were bogus and 'only drawn up with the object of bluffing the natives from negotiating with others'.[21] As well, all along its 24-kilometre coastal claim the Malayta Company had failed to make boundaries clear, boxed in coastal villages, and then foolishly expected there to be no conflict over right-of-ways. The Malayta Company also tried to alienate the riverbanks of the Kwaifela, Hulo and Araora rivers, thus blocking the sea corridor of inland people, and was unhappy when Bell insisted on a 241-metre-wide reserve corridor on both banks of all three rivers. Their argument was that they would have to fence land to stop cattle wandering into local gardens, the 'undeveloped' land would encourage plant pests that would spread to their land, village pigs would uproot young palms and villager-lit fires could devastate the plantations.[22] Bell forecast the future to the resident commissioner:

> The time will come, and very soon, when the Company will object to natives roaming about their plantations. Fires causing serious damage have occurred among the coconuts. I have had to punish several natives for lightening fires in, and on the edge of, the planted area although the fires were only made for cooking purposes …[23]

The full reason for the disturbances did not become clear until 1920. Indigenous activities were clearly being compromised by the Malayta Company's land grab. What emerged was another aspect that would have maximised tension. Following the style of the SSEM, the Malayta Company was not respecting sacred ancestral shrines. At Boronaasu`u, between Bina Harbour and Kwa`a Cove in west Kwaio, one ancestral shrine excluded from land negotiations was wilfully cleared of all timber. Bell was horrified and showed a good appreciation of the nature of Malaitan religious beliefs:

> Such Tabu places exist all over Malaita and are as sacred to the natives as any Christian or other religious place of worship is to the Christian or follower of any other religion. The Malaita native worships the spirit of his dead ancestors who have been great men according to the native ideas. Their sacred place of worship is almost always the place where these men lived or were buried and the people go there to worship their spirits. It is a vital part of their lives. It is very regrettable and reprehensible that such

---

21 SINA, BSIP 14/45, DO WRB to A/RC FJB, 27 Dec 1917; BSIP 14/46, DO WRB to A/RC FJB, 14 Jan 1918.
22 SINA, BSIP 18/II/1, 'Malayta Company Claims', W.J. McGowan, Secretary, Malaita Company Limited to RC CRMW, 6 Sept 1920, 179–87.
23 SINA, BSIP 14/48, DO WRB to RC CRMW, 19 June 1920.

places throughout the Malayta Company's plantations have been violated, and I hope that in future special care will be taken that such places are duly respected.[24]

Bell recommended that a lands commission investigate the situation, which is what came to pass when one operated between 1919 and 1924.

As noted in Chapter 8, in 1913 the Malayta Company purchased 14,820 hectares of Billy Pope's land at Aola, Guadalcanal, and Talina and Yandina plantations in the Russell Islands, which more than doubled their land holdings in the Solomons.[25] In 1918, the name of the Islands Trading Company appears in the records, closely associated with the Malayta Company, with Victor C. Lyndon as manager, purchasing land at Hauhui and Su`u. Having found Malaita too difficult, in 1918 the Malayta Company shifted its focus to the Russell Islands. This extension of their operations caused extra problems when labourers were returned from Yandina to Baunani on the *Royal Endeavour* without the Baunani manager having any legal responsibility for their upkeep or further transport to their homes, still another 72 kilometres away. Resident Commissioner Charles H.R.M. Workman neatly described the company's attitudes:

> The delay in returning the six men whom you met at Baunani amounts to a scandal, inasmuch as the Malayta Company would appear to have taken over three months to convey them 200 miles.[26]

In 1918, there were 107 indentured labourers and 38 casual labourers (including women) working for the company. Work hours were the same as in 1915: from 6:00 to 11:00 am and from 1:00 to 5:00 pm Monday through Friday, and 6:00 to 11:00 am on Saturdays. Reading the reports on the company, one gets the distinct impression that the Malayta Company was skirting the stricter regulations by employing casual or contract labour as they deliberately ran down their Malaita operations. Medical supplies were rudimentary, except at Baunani, although small, substandard hospital buildings existed on all the plantations. Blankets and *lava-lava* (wrap-around cloths as clothing) were of poor quality. Su`u plantation had only one indentured labourer; the other eight were casual employees and exempt from the labour regulations, which benefited the company since conditions were below the specified standard. At Hulo

---

24   *Ibid.*, 24 Oct 1920.
25   Golden 1993, 429; Boutilier 1979, 50.
26   SINA, BSIP 14/46, DO WRB to A/RC FJB, 24 Jan 1918.

plantation 28 indentured labourers lived in local-style leaf houses with dirt floors and bunks made from split palm trunks. At Manaba plantation there were 28 indentured labourers and 10 male casual labourers, and Baunani plantation had 51 indentured labourers, two of whom were married with small families, and 19 male and 11 female casual labourers. The manager admitted that the quarters were substandard but pleaded that shortages of labour and materials were the reason. He said that a hospital to serve all of the Malayta Company plantations was about to be erected. Bell commented that the explanation was weak and simply meant that labourers were deprived of decent accommodation and medical facilities in order to enable more work to be done on the plantations.[27]

In the 1970s, Judith Bennett interviewed one man from coastal south Guadalcanal who had worked at Baunani from about 1915–18. The coconut palms were young and he worked brushing and catching copra beetles (*Necrobia rufipes*). The work hours were as Bell described. Accommodation was in leaf houses, food was biscuits and tea in the morning, with meat was issued twice a week and a few fresh vegetables were provided, although the employees bartered with local villagers for vegetables and betel nut. If labourers complained, after the inspector had left their tobacco ration was stopped as punishment.[28]

The Malayta Company continued to operate its plantations at Su`u, Baunani, Hulo and Manaba, and while it transferred most of its interests to the Russell Islands it was associated with the Islands Trading Company, which held land at Olasuu and Sioru.[29] The Malayta Company's land came under close scrutiny from the 1919–24 Lands Commission,[30] investigated by the its first commissioner, Captain G.G. Alexander, and his deputy, BSIP's Chief Surveyor Stanley G.C. Knibbs. The second commissioner, Judge J. Beaumont Phillips, made some alterations to Alexander's judgements since he had left his initial surveys incomplete. There were 23 land claims, creating a continuous coastal frontage from Kwa`a to Su`u Harbour and inland a kilometre or so to the foothills.

---

27 SINA, BSIP 14/46, 'Malayta Company Plantation Reports, 19, 23 and 30 Apr 1918'.
28 Bennett 1981b, 52–56.
29 SINA, BSIP 14/47, DO WRB to A/RC CRMW, 4 Jan 1919.
30 The Lands Commission, which operated between 1919 and 1924, is known as the Phillips Commission. It only investigated 55 claims out of some 300 European titles. Judge Phillips made it his practice to hold the hearing on the land in question, which revealed numerous discrepancies. Rather than quelling indigenous discontent, the Lands Commission drew attention to the inequity of the land alienation. Moore 2013c entry.

Although some of this land had reached a final settlement stage, much of it was still open to negotiations between the claimants, the Malayta Company, and the protectorate administration. Many of the boundaries had not been properly delineated at the time of the initial purchases. The SSEM's Northcote Deck tried to blame this on an unavoidable lack of examination, with hyperbole (his usual style) in regard to cannibalism:

> There was no possibility of going and marking the back boundary because the place was not safe, and we had not the gang; also no time; it was dangerous; other natives were cannibalistic and would kill us as readily on the land of others as on their own. The natives told us they owned the land as far back as the mountain range.[31]

Phillips made thorough reports: some of the land owners accepted compensation, while others wished to retain part of the land but agreed to accept compensation for the remainder of the claims. Still others refused to reach any agreement. For instance, at Hulo, Alex Kwaifiona was indignant at the claims the company had made over his land. Bell said he had reasonable grounds for anger and should not be pressured to dispose of his land.[32] Phillips disallowed several claims. Alexander met with the Malayta Company directors in Sydney, who agreed to further negotiations, particularly over garden land and rights-of-way. Mr McGown, the Malayta Company secretary, negotiated further 'apparently not without difficulty' over many of the reserves and roadways. The average rate of compensation was 2/- per acre, and Bell ensured that sufficient land was reserved for Malaitan use.[33] One comes away from the record with the distinct impression that the Malayta Company was a greedy commercial concern cloaked in Christian principles.

Bell had a good understanding of Malaitan land tenure systems and inheritance, and used this to safeguard the people when outsiders wanted their land. He knew that Malaitans did not understand the long-term consequences flowing from land alienation.[34] Generally, missions only wanted to control small areas. The Malayta Company was the real problem and its methods and acquisitive tendencies caused instability for

---

31   SINA, BSIP 18/II 1, J.N. Deck, evidence to Lands Commission, 22 Jan 1912, 94.
32   SINA, BSIP 18/II 1, 'Malayta Company Claims', DO WRB, 'Hulo Land Claims', 195–96.
33   SINA, BSIP 18/II 1, 'Report of Lands Commissioner Captain A.A. Alexander, 26 Mar 1920'; Judge J. Beaumont Phillips, 'Memorandum on the Settlement to Date of the Malayta Company Claims', 18 Dec 1920; 'Report of Lands Commissioner J. Beaumont Phillips in Relation to Malayta Company Land Claims', 18 Dec 1920.
34   SINA, BSIP 14/57, DO WRB to RC RRK, 12 Feb 1924.

all of the years it operated. As late as 1925, the company was still buying land, well after they had transferred their main interests to the Russell Islands.[35] The final departure of the company, which never returned after the Second World War, was a blessing for Malaitans because it left their land intact for later generations.

Mala Timber Company at Su`u

There was another commercial venture on Malaita in the 1920s, although it failed to become substantial. Neil MacCrimmon had been manager of the Malayta Company, then set up an independent business.[36] The Mala Timber Company, managed by MacCrimmon, commenced logging operations at Su`u in 1924 and may have had links to his old employer. MacCrimmon wanted to build a wharf and sawmill at Su`u and proposed a deal that would have enabled the company to cut timber for 50 years. Bell said the people would not agree and vetoed the idea. The intention was to export timber via the Burns Philp steamers to Australia every six weeks.[37] Acquiring timber rights proved elusive because they were no areas of unoccupied land and all land had multiple owners. The Mala Timber Company established trading stores in several places around the island and employed some of the better-educated Malaitans such as Timothy George Mahratta from Small Malaita and Stephen Gori`i from Malu`u. Several of the storekeepers were making over £5 monthly and a few as much as £7 a month.[38] In 1926, MacCrimmon once more asked for action on his application for an extra land lease at Su`u, but Bell wisely refused to allow it until the mill was actually in operation.[39]

Malaitan Labour on other Islands

The peak years for indentured labourers were between 1920 and 1930. New Regulations on labour were passed in 1921 and 1923. In 1922, a Labour Commission was appointed, headed by K.J. Allardyce, with

---

35   SINA, BSIP 14/58, DO WRB to RC RRK, 'Land at Bubuitoro', 28 May 1925.
36   'The Solomon Islands', *Queenslander*, 22 Nov 1919, 40.
37   SINA, BSIP 14/57, DO WRB to RC RRK, 12 Feb 1924.
38   SINA, BSIP 14/58, DO WRB to RC RRK, 17 Dec 1925; BSIP 14/59, DO WRB to RS RRK, 'Annual Report, 1925', 20 Jan 1926.
39   SINA, BSIP 14/59, DO WRB to RC RRK, 28 Sept 1926.

a brief to investigate beach payments. A 1923 Regulation forbad payment of passage masters and beach bonuses, but up to one-quarter of the total wage for a two-year contract could be supplied in advance.[40] Indentured labourers should all have been over 16 years of age, although there is evidence that some were as young as 11, and that employers were violating the regulations in other ways. When one boy of 13 (recruited at age 11) was due to return home, rather than being sent back within the regulation 21 days with his transit accommodation paid, he received no proper rations, had to spend his savings to purchase food, and then paid his own passage home since the employer was so slow in making arrangements. He thus arrived home with no recompense for his two years of work. His age was not unusual, and Bell had occasion to complain again in 1926 about underage recruiting.[41] Labourers, ignorant of their rights, were often hoodwinked, even by W.R. Carpenter & Co. or Burns Philp & Co., let alone at isolated plantations. Many reengaged because they were ashamed to return home with nothing. Bell, the former government agent and inspector of labour, was easily angered and never minced words:

> They appear to think that the natives should be treated like cattle, and they do not for one moment consider the people who have suffered pain, and years of worry and toil, in order to provide for them until they reach a state of usefulness. The natives would not continue to propagate their species under cattle conditions and solely for the benefit of the white man.[42]

There were other anomalies in labour contracts when labourers were verbally promised higher wage rates than those actually specified. Bell always defended the labourers, but did not always get his way.[43]

As calculated in Chapters 2 and 8, there were 36,596 Malaitan indenture contracts between 1913 and 1940, with earnings of around £820,000. In any one year, the number of Malaitans working under indenture remained fairly steady at around 3,000. In 1925, there were 1,451 new indenture contracts, mainly on other islands, and a large number were working as casual labourers on Malaita. Most were single youths and men aged between 14 and 35. The vast majority of the protectorate's

---

40   *Planters' Gazette* 6, May 1922, 12–13; *WPHC Gazette*, King's Regulations no. 15 of 1921 and no. 7 of 1923.
41   SINA, BSIP, 14/60, DO WRB to RC RRK, 'Annual Report, 1926', 29 Jan 1927; BSIP, 14/60, DO WRB to RC RRK, 19 Mar 1927.
42   SINA, BSIP 14/55, DO WRB to RC RRK, 16 Nov 1922.
43   SINA, BSIP 14/56, DO WRB to RC RRK, 17 Nov and 11 Dec 1923.

indentured labourers were from Malaita and Guadalcanal.[44] Bell knew which plantations were unpopular and named Levers Pacific Plantations Ltd's many plantations and Malayta Company's Yandina plantation as having bad reputations. At Malayta Company's Su`u plantation, labourers were working more than the regulation number of hours.[45]

The recruiting system in place within the protectorate closely resembled the past one for recruiting Queensland and Fiji labour. Joseph Dickinson was the recruiter on the *Dancing Wave* in the 1920s, and he described returning labourers arriving at Langalanga Lagoon:

> The returning boys are now on deck to a man, admiring their homeland, and arrayed in cheap splendour. Very interesting this dress parade is. New strings of bright beads, white singlets, shirts, hats, long trousers, shorts, umbrellas, belts equipped with three or four pouches, new pipes, whistles, mouth organs. All hands are well perfumed and many gaudy lava-lavas are worn.[46]

Dickson described a recruiting scene near Onepusu, which could have occurred any time onward from the 1880s:

> Bang!!! Crash!!! R-r-r-r-r-r-r!!! Dynamite has been fired on a float from the ship, its terrific report searching the mountains, that all may know a vessel is looking for workers… Many of them answered the ship's signal next day, arriving at the far end of the harbour. A wild-looking lot, who when they surround the shore boat hold it fast, and have its occupants at their mercy, although a covering boat may be in attendance. However, one feels security with this second boat. From it suspicious movements are watched …[47]

> Excitement prevails on shore at Onapusi, as the boat heaves up on the beach. Three men wish to sign, one accompanied by his wife and son. A big crowd are down with the men and women, old and young. All is above board, although the men are fully armed. Having learnt about the ship, and who she is recruiting for, a number get into the boat, leaving their weapons on shore. On board the new chums' names are given by their friends. Seldom do natives give them personally. They are entered up, each man touching the pen as a matter of form. He is not officially indentured until when called before Government labour and medical

---

44 SINA, BSIP 14/59, DO WRB to RC RRK, 9 Aug 1926.
45 SINA, BSIP 14/60, DO WRB to RC RRK, 21 Mar 1927.
46 Dickinson 1927, 149.
47 *Ibid.*, 151.

officers, who verify everything pertaining to each man. If under age, or medically unfit, they have to be returned home. As each boy is accepted on board, after first signing, the Captain hands him one fifteen-pound box of tobacco, one three-quarter axe, a large bush knife, and a parcel of cheap jimnacks; the lot worth £4.[48]

The Bell years coincided with major changes in the labour system. The planters wanted the escalating beach bonus banned. In 1923, the resident commissioner agreed to limit it to a £6 cash advance of the total wage, but stipulated that the wage had to double (it was later decreased) and that recruiting vessels could not sell trade goods. At the same time, between 1921 and 1923, the government introduced an annual head tax of between £1 and 5/- for all able-bodied males between 16 and 60 years of age. The tax maintained the supply of labour (they worked for money to pay tax for themselves and family members), but did not increase the pool of labourers available. Effectively, the government had halved the amount of money that reached Malaita (in the form of goods), and then added taxation.[49]

Figure 9.4: In 1921 the protectorate provided the Malaita administration with its own patrol vessel, the *Auki*.
Source: British Museum, R. Garvey Collection, MM034290_33.

---

48 *Ibid.*, 156.
49 Bennett 1987, 162–64.

Taxation, Beach Bonuses and Trade

Capitalism and government taxation went hand-in-hand. Implementing a capitation (head) tax in the BSIP between 1921 and 1923 had direct consequences on trade and access to manufactured goods. Put crudely, labourers' wages, once clawed back by planters and traders selling them goods at 100 to 200 per cent profit margins, onward from 1923 were diverted straight to the government. The tax was lower on Malaita than in other areas (5/- as opposed to 10/- and £1), and not collected there until 1923. The first official discussions of compulsory taxation began in 1917, with a suggestion for taxation in the form of obligatory labour on road-making projects. Bell opposed this because the large number of Malaitan men away on plantations was the same group who would have done most of the roadwork.[50] The protectorate was edging its way toward direct taxation, against Bell's advice. He believed that there was not enough British currency circulating to pay head taxes, and that the burden would fall onto the inland people, and anyway, there was no way to imprison the number who might be arrested for nonpayment. Bell suggested that one way forward was to compel recruiters to pay all beach bonuses in cash, rather than mostly in tobacco as was the existing practice. A tax of 5/- per head would produce nearly £3,000 in revenue, which would have to be squeezed out by reducing consumer spending.[51]

The Gizo branch of the Solomon Islands Planters' Association proposed making beach bonuses illegal, largely to limit the competition for recruits, which had driven the bonus payment up to between £6 and £10 per recruit.[52] Around 75 per cent of beach bonuses for labourers were paid in tobacco, as much as 30 pounds (13.6 kilograms) weight per recruit. In 1918, Bell calculated that trade goods valued at around £7,000 were being distributed on Malaita each year, mainly in the form of tobacco. In Chapter 8 I calculated, conservatively, that well in excess of 10 tons (9.07 metric tonnes) of tobacco was reaching Malaita each year in the 1900s. Bell's 1918 figures suggest that labourers were returning with about half of their £6 per year wages invested in tobacco. Men, women and children in the Solomons all smoked.[53]

---

50 SINA, BSIP 14/45, DO WRB to A/RC FJB, 12 Dec 1917.
51 SINA, BSIP 14/45, DO WRB to RC CRMW, 19 Feb 1918; BSIP 14/12, RC CRMW to DO WRB, 16 Mar 1918.
52 Dickinson 1927, 157.
53 SINA, BSIP 14/46, DO WRB to RC CRM, 19 Feb 1918.

Let us try another calculation. If 3,000 Malaitan males were away from the island each year on two-year contracts, and 75 per cent of their families received 30 pounds of tobacco for the enlistment of each labourer (2,250 labourers), that is 67,500 pounds or 30,617 kilograms. Plus, if the same 75 per cent invested half of their £6 wage per year in tobacco (let us say 22 pounds, almost 10 kilograms), smoked half and brought half home, then each was responsible for 41 pounds (18.5 kilograms) weight of tobacco reaching Malaita. This is a total weight of 92,250 pounds (41.8 metric tonnes) per year, or about 2 pounds of tobacco for each man, woman and child on the island. The level of addiction would have been high and tobacco must have done inestimable damage to the health of Malaitans (and indeed all Solomon Islanders). The tobacco was in twist or stick form, the leaves wound in tight spirals high in resin, and dipped in humectants or sugars, and sold in boxes weighing 24 pounds (10 kilograms), at around 26 sticks per pound. Smoked in small clay pipes (another trade item) or local bamboo or wooden pipes, it was moist and high in nicotine. Bell knew that the need for tobacco was so great that it would be impossible to pay the head tax and maintain the level of use. Furthermore, prohibiting the beach bonus would drastically reduce the number of labour recruits. The only reform Bell suggested was abolition of per capita payments to passage masters, a system that had been in use since the 1870s. He advocated paying them instead a fixed daily or weekly wage.[54]

In 1920 the imposition of the head tax was looming. Beginning in 1921, the £1 tax was to be applied to most adult males, except on Malaita and Choiseul, with reduced rates on Guadalcanal and Makira. Bell did not oppose taxation, and used it as a bargaining point to have a suitable patrol vessel allocated to Malaita, as well as an assistant DO and more police. It is hard to see how tax collecting could have been accomplished with less. Bell still believed the population to be around 50,000, and a 4,000-person sample census had confirmed his belief. While there was access to the lagoons and the coastal area north of `Aoke, it remained difficult to make an estimate in large areas of coastal Kwara`ae, Kwaio and `Are`are, as well as all through the centre of the island. Bell argued that no tax collection could begin until better facilities were provided. As 1923 began, Bell was warming to allowing the beach bonus to be paid in cash, and felt that, given notice, the majority would be able to pay

---

54 SINA, BSIP 14/46, DO WRB to A/RC, 1 Apr 1918.

the tax, although a larger prison would be needed for defaulters. There was little local produce to sell and the only local copra trading was in the southeast, and there in small quantities. Earlier To`aba`ita plans to plant coconuts for copra had come to little. Even with the large number of labourers leaving the island for plantations, the Langalanga men working as stevedores at Tulagi, Gavutu and Makambo, plus the few working for the Malayta Company as casual labourers, wages would be insufficient to pay the taxes of the entire adult male population. Bell got his way, and the tax was set at only 5/- on Malaita.[55]

The first taxes were collected in October and November 1923 from 5,003 Malaitan men spread through about one-third of the island. There were 402 exemption certificates granted, usually because a man was maintaining four or more children; also excused were 28 mission teachers and 44 men with physical ailments. Pressed for cash to pay the tax, many had to sell shell currency at vastly reduced rates, often to opportunistic police at tax collections. Bell also revised his estimate of the population upward to 60,000 or 70,000 (found wrong in 1931 when the first census enumerated 41,052, closer to his earlier estimates).[56] There was also the question of exactly what Malaitans were getting in return for the £2,700 they now paid each year in head tax, let alone for the indirect taxes on goods, particularly tobacco. The answer, according to Bell, was zero, and in fact services had been reduced because so much effort was going into collecting the head tax; Bell complained that collections consumed much of his time. The expense of collecting the tax was far greater than the revenue generated, but we must remember that it was strongly motivated by the desire to compel indentured labour.[57]

Over the first two tax years, 1923–24 and 1924–25, 23,000 head taxes were collected, netting £5,750. A further 12,536 taxes were collected during 1925–26, with 1,181 exemptions. Most of the cash taken in came from the beach bonuses. Twenty-five tax collection centres had been erected around the coast. During 1924, court was held on 16 days to hear

---

55   SINA, BSIP 14/48, DO WRB to RC CRMW, 14 Oct 1920; BSIP 14/55, DO WRB to RC, 8 Aug 1922; BSIP 14/56, DO WRB to RC RRK, 29 Jan 1923.
56   In some cases 10 strings worth around £2/10s changed hands for as little as 5/- to pay the tax. SINA, BSIP 14/56, DO WB to RC RRK, 2 Dec 1923.
57   SINA, BSIP 14/58, DO WRB to RC RRK, 3 June and 14 Sept 1925; BSIP 14/24, Acting Government Secretary to DO WRB, 17 June 1925.

43 cases, with 34 convictions. In the first quarter of 1925 alone, the court sat for 26 days and tried 161 cases, with 159 convictions, bloated by the many tax default cases. Only five offenders failed to pay their £1 fines.[58]

The Missions

The tripartite division of Malaita between the Anglicans, the SSEM and the Catholics was disturbed by the arrival of the Seventh-day Adventists, who had begun work in the New Georgia Group in 1914, then slowly expanded their area of influence. Adventist beliefs grew out of millenarian Protestant Christianity in the United States in the 1860s. They observe the biblical Sabbath on a Saturday, believe in a six-day creation, and that the 'advent' or the second coming of Christ is imminent. Adventists believe in the doctrine of heavenly sanctuary (a tabernacle or temple) and give special status to the writings of their cofounder Ellen White (1826–1915). They believe that the dead are actually unconscious and that at the time of the second coming the righteous dead and the righteous living will be taken to heaven. The church is in the fundamentalist, revivalist evangelical tradition, with the Bible as the central authority. The key beliefs of the SDA Church are not far away from those of the Plymouth Brethren, and therefore also the SSEM. After White's death and a 1919 Bible Conference in Michigan in the United States, the church was undergoing reform just before it arrived on Malaita. There was a new focus on education, reexamining White's role and authority, the place of prophecies and the interpretation of inspired writings.[59]

The SDA Church is also known for its health care institutions and for following biblical strictures on eating certain foods, particularly proscriptions of pork and crustaceans. Some of these beliefs immediately set the Adventists apart from the other denominations on Malaita. Like the SSEM, they were no respecters of the geopolitical divisions of the earlier Christian missions, and they pursued 'mission-planting' in areas where other missions were already established.[60]

---

58   SINA, BSIP 14/57, DO WRB to RC RRK, 25 Apr, 7 July and 30 Sept 1924; 'List of Malaita Police', 9 July 1924; BSIP 14/58, A/DO A. H. Studd, 'District Report 1st Quarter 1925', 5 Apr 1925; BSIP 14/59, DO WRB to RC RRK, 'Annual Report, 1925', 20 Jan 1926.
59   Campbell 2008.
60   Steley 1983; 1989.

After their initial evangelism in the Western Solomons, the SDAs skipped over the Anglican strongholds of Isabel and the Gela Group and homed in on populous Malaita. They also fairly quickly moved on to the Catholic stronghold of Guadalcanal. SDA records mention a first 'call' for missionaries for Malaita in 1922. Various Malaitans were already working for the SDAs in the Western Solomons, including Mae, a crew member on the *Advent Herald*, and Jackie from Makwano. Jackie assisted the first SDA missionaries and he and his wife were the first SDA baptisms on Malaita, in 1926. In September 1924, Pastor John D. Anderson and his wife Guinevere began missionary work on Malaita. Their first base was at O`io Point, at Wairokai Harbour in west `Are`are, which caused friction because this was only 8 kilometres from the Catholic station at Rohinari. It was a crowded coast with the SSEM at Onepusu and the Catholics and the SDAs nearby. The next SDA base, established by the Andersons, was at Uru Harbour in east Kwaio, close to today's Atoifi Hospital. Next, under Pastor A.F. Parker, the church acquired land at Kwailabesi in the Lau Lagoon as their northern headquarters, unnecessarily close to the Anglican base in the lagoon. This Lau SDA base began through the work of Simi, whose wife had been murdered near Uru Harbour in 1929, where he had been a deacon. He was persuaded to shift to Lau where he worked on the artificial islands and made considerable progress at Makwano on the mainland opposite. By 1932, there were 13 SDA outstations in Makwano. The first few years at Uru were difficult and the site was no longer in use in 1935, when it was leased to the Melanesian Mission for two years. In 1934, Parker was joined by his new wife, Dr Dorothy Mills-Parker, who began a medically oriented approach to missionary work. Converts were few and during the 1930s the main outreach was medical, throughout Makwano, and from the mission and hospital at Kwailabesi. The SDAs resumed activity at their Uru base in Kwaio, but merely plodded along.[61]

Bell believed that all of the Christian missions made an inestimable difference to life on Malaita. One obvious benefit, he thought, was the move to the coast by thousands of inland people and the creation of coastal villages:

---

61   BSIP 14/61, DO JCB to SC, 1 Aug 1930; BSIP 14/64, DO JCB to SG, 2 Aug 1933; BSIP14/66, DO to SG, 17 Oct 1935; Steley 1983, 63–67.

I am afraid they do not get the credit they deserve for the tact they display in handling most difficult situations. One has only to recollect the miles of coast line between here and the North-west point of the island which ten years ago had scarcely a house visible near the beach, but now every few miles there is a settlement of followers of one of the Missions made up of people who have been induced to leave their wild life in the bush. These European men and women, who have sacrificed what most of us cling to, have certainly not failed in the work they have undertaken.[62]

Bell and the missions managed to bring peace to the north by 1916–17 and also encouraged local coconut plantations. Under Peter Abu`ofa's influence, a local cash economy was created at Malu`u. Bell provided the seed nuts and Abu`ofa encouraged his people to begin plantations, thus augmenting the coconut trees Bell had planted to line his newly constructed north road.

Abu`ofa remained a strong force in the north until his death in 1937, although in his later years he was alienated from the SSEM and had fallen out with his younger rival Shem Irofa`alu. In 1908, Abu`ofa claimed to have been deported from Queensland (which was untrue) and petitioned the King of England for a Solomon Islands basic wage of £1 per week. He also added his name to a similar petition in 1912, which asked the resident commissioner to improve work conditions and reopen the Queensland and Fiji labour trades. He was made a district headman during 1914 and 1915.[63] These protests failed, but resentments such as those behind Abu`ofa's 1894–95 kidnapping case, and especially anger at the exploitative indentured labour system, continued to grow over the decades that followed, and would be foundational to the emergence of Maasina Rule in the 1940s.[64]

---

62   SINA, BSIP 14/44, A/DO WRB to HC Sir Ernest Bickham Sweet-Escott, 16 Dec 1916.
63   Bennett 1987, 405–10, reproduces these petitions. BSIP 14/9, CMW to TWE-P, 23 Mar. 1914; 14/42, CMW to TWE-P, 17 Apr. 1914; 14/10, FJB to CGN; 14/43, CGN to FJB.
64   Bennett 1987, 161–62, 405–10; Akin 2013a, 231–37.

Figure 9.5: An elderly Peter Abu`ofa in a SSEM group photograph with his rival Shem Irofa`alu (later a key Maasina Rule leader), among others, probably from the 1920s.

Back row (L to R): Dick Lioiaa, Livae Liufakona, John Kanakwai, Livae Irokula, Isikiel Surioa, Mr Waite, Robert McBride, Northcote Deck, Joel Kanoli, Joseph Naute`e, James Oto`akaloa and Ma`arumae. Middle row (L to R): Peter Abu`ofa, Othanila, Stephen Meke, Mrs McBride and Mrs Northcote Deck. Front row (L to R): Benjamin Kanaa, Nathan Maitofana, Harry Fafanga, Stephen Kumalau, Samuel Laukana, Paul Iro`ota, Dauramo and Shem Irofa`alu. Identification provided by Ian Frazer.

Source: Deck Collection; see also Deck 1928, facing 64.

One should not exaggerate the rate of progress. In 1915, at Rokera (Ariel Harbour), 110 kilometres south of `Aoke on Small Malaita, SSEM missionary Walter Gibbon was targeted by assassins from Waisisi, near the SSEM and Malayta Company headquarters at Onepusu and Baunani. A 'blood money' reward was offered because Oaniasi had recently been shot on Guadalcanal by a white trader named Pritchard. There had been many murders at Onepusu, two in the previous year. Bell believed the latter were paybacks for earlier deaths and not directly related to the victims. He was beginning to come to terms with Malaitan thinking:

> I would like to point out that it is a mistake to think that most of these murders are the result of ordinary vendetta. I find the victims in the majority of cases are women and children who are not alleged to have committed any offences, in some cases it is aimed at the family and in other cases it does not matter what person is killed or to what family the victim belongs.[65]

---

65 SINA, BSIP 14/43, Acting DC WRB to A/RC FJB, 23 Dec 1915.

Edge-Partington and Bell both requested the right to punish adulterers and Bell began jailing male adulterers. Bell had to tread carefully between mission, indigenous and government rules on such matters. On Malaitan, the punishment for adultery, particularly by women, was usually death. Under British law, adultery was an aspect of private morality and not covered under the 1922 Native Administration Regulation. Bell declined to punish women for adultery because 'Aoke's prison facilities were not suitable to detain them. Many non-Christians and some Christians wanted a death sentence imposed, although when the SSEM believers at Malu'u held a meeting they decided that flogging was the most suitable punishment. Bell had to explain that the SSEM could not make its own laws, and advised Tulagi of the issue. Resident Commissioner Workman agreed to imprison men for the offence, but not women. The need for a severe punishment for adultery, with some resemblance to its seriousness in indigenous law, was a persistent theme in Bell's correspondence. Finally, in 1924, the government introduced a fine of £5 or three months in prison for adultery, increased again in 1929. While on some other islands the punishment was thought to be satisfactory or even too heavy, on Malaita the punishment was still thought to be too light.[66]

When Rev. Arthur Hopkins was transferred away from Lau Lagoon in 1914, he was replaced by Rev. Robert Simmons until 1918, by which time the mission had 588 converts in northeast Malaita. Rev. Albert Mason joined the Melanesian Mission's Malaita branch in 1914, based at Fiu together with his new wife Gwendoline (née Child), who had arrived a year earlier and helped to found a girls' school on Gela. The Masons served on Malaita for 30 years, and their perseverance led to the ordination of many of the early Malaitan priests. As occurred on Small Malaita, many of the mission helpers from Hopkins's time at Ngorefou and the Masons' years at Fiu went on to become priests: Charles Turu, Sam Sasai from Tangtalau, Martin Fia from Asiasi, George Kiriau from Aama, Jack Taloifulia, Nat Salaimanu and Henry Maabe, and Andrew Dora from Tae (in Lau), Nat Dolaiasi from Gwau'ulu, Willie Au from Walade, Edward Kasutee from Fiu and Henry Geotee. Taloifulia (mentioned in Chapters 2, 3 and 4), ordained in 1915, was responsible for the conversion of most people on Sulufou, the major artificial island. Turu was long the head of the Fiu mission, where his descent group controlled land surrounding the area that he had donated to the church.

---

66 SINA, BSIP 14/46, DO WRB to RC CRMW, 18 Feb 1918; BSIP RC CRMW to DO WRB, 16 Mar 1918; Bennett 1987, 277–78; Laracy and Laracy 1980; Akin 2013a, 87, 89–90, 367 n 110.

He was ordained in 1916 and died in 1922, and Sasai and Kiriau were ordained in 1934. Salaimanu had been at school at Bungana and then Norfolk Island and was for a time a government headman in Lau Lagoon before he was ordained and took Taloifulia's place. Au, Dolaiasi, Fia and Ma`abe were younger and had trained at All Hallows' School[67] at Pawa on Uki Island. Kasutee was also ordained, but died soon after. Another man, Matthias Finifolota from `Aisaasale in north Malaita, never attended regular schools but was so outstanding that he was ordained in 1943 and served until his death in 1951. Charles Fox noted what a remarkable group they were, and that more men were ordained from north Malaitan during the century's first half than from any other part of the central Solomons.[68] While this creation of indigenous deacons and priests was 30 to 40 years ahead of the Catholics, I agree with Alan Tippett that it was slow progress nonetheless.

Regardless of the Anglican ordinations, the SSEM was the dominant mission, with 11 European staff on Malaita in 1918 compared with two Catholic priests and one Anglican minister. The SSEM and the Malayta Company combined had 17 European representatives. Bell and the Police Sub-Inspector Frederick Taylor were the only European government representatives.[69]

The SSEM had started purchasing land in 1904 (when it was the QKM) and, as mentioned, was still doing so in 1920 even around their head station of Onepusu, where they also rented extra land.[70] The Catholics were slower, but once well-established at Tarapaina and Rohinari, and then Buma, they set out to emulate the SSEM by acquiring choice plots of coastal land near good anchorages. These leases were supposedly for cultivation, but none eventuated, and Bell signalled that he would grant them no more leases except for mission buildings.[71] Bell was always battling one of the Christian denominations or the Malayta Company over their attempts to acquire extra land at the expense of Malaitans.

The missions undertook some educational and health work, but their main object, particularly the SSEM, always remained to convert people to Christianity.

---

67   Moore 2013c entry.
68   Fox 1958, 174.
69   SINA, BSIP 14/46, DO WRB to RC CRMW, census, 1 Jan 1918; BSIP 14/12, RC CRMW to DO WRB, 16 Mar 1918; BSIP 14/56, DO WRB to RC RRK, 18 Feb 1923.
70   SINA, BSIP 14/48, DO WRB to RC CRMW, 29 May 1920.
71   SINA, BSIP 14/59, DO WRB to RC RRK, 29 Apr 1926.

Targeting the Professional Killers

Guns remained readily available on Malaita. In 1908, Woodford thought that there were 4,000 to 5,000 Winchester repeating rifles on the island, and there were many more guns of greater antiquity, most smuggled in by returning labourers.[72] As the years passed, most of the poor-quality and older weapons brought in during the external labour trade deteriorated and became useless. However, the supply continued to be replenished from within the Solomons, sometimes aided and abetted by Europeans but also through theft, such as two Winchester repeating rifles, one Martini rifle and a revolver and dozens of cartridges stolen from Malayta Company's plantation on Guadalcanal in 1916 and brought back to Malaita. Bell pursued these and other firearms that had ended up at Port Adam on Small Malaita.[73] The steady resupply of guns and ammunition made his work far more dangerous. The only Malaitan with a permit to keep a shotgun was Queensland-educated Timothy George Mahratta.[74] Bell was aware that even the Melanesian Mission's *Southern Cross* was a source of contraband weapons and his correspondence is full of reports on illegal firearms. In 1920, he tried to compile a register of firearms on Malaita. Six hundred guns were located in north Malaita as far south as 'Aoke, although Bell believed that there were 1,500 to 2,000 in the area as well as some 3,000 rounds of ammunition. Many people lived in the central and southern areas as well, and if we estimate (conservatively) 2,000 guns in the remainder of the island, the likely number of firearms was around 4,000.[75] One reason Malaitans were angry with Bell in the years before his death was his attempt to confiscate all guns, without compensation. In the 1970s, the oldest of my Fokanakafo Bay informants in east Fataleka remembered a time just before 1927 when Bell came to collect guns and ammunition. He gave the people a chance to shoot off of their remaining ammunition and all day the air was full of explosions.

In 1918, Bell believed that he would bring Malaita under control within a few years; by 1922 he was not so sure and felt that government influence was declining in some areas. Although Bell dealt with all incidents reported to him, his main approach was to target the bounty-hunting

---

72 *Sydney Morning Herald*, 30 June 1908, 7.
73 SINA, BSIP 14/10, A/DO CGN to A/RC JFB, 10 July 1916; BSIP 14/44, A/DO WRB to A/RC FJB, 9 Sept 1916.
74 Moore 2013c entry.
75 SINA, BSIP 14/48, DO WRB to RC CRMW, 27 Mar 1920.

ramo who killed purely for payment and attacked the weak. He wrote of 'the innocent victims of a barbaric custom and of the blood-lust of a few professional murderers. Many of those victims are as law-abiding and as entitled to government protection as much as any European or native in the Protectorate'.[76] Many of the *ramo* had previously worked in Queensland, Fiji and within the protectorate and thus were familiar with many European ways. Bell knew that until he could control them, Malaita would never be pacified.

At Rohinari in 1915, Bell attempted to begin dialogue with Arisimae, the major *ramo* on the southwest coast, responsible for dozens of murders. Arisimae, who was friendly with Catholic Father Jean Coicaud, was not to be found, and seemed to think that the government would not touch him as long as he limited his killings to Malaitans. Other names begin to appear regularly in the records. Bell's attitude was that they were outlaws who should be tracked down and shot on sight, not treated to the niceties of the British justice system. Before he went on leave in early 1916, Bell reiterated that he still advised Malaitans that if they had to kill to protect themselves he would not interfere. Murders of Malaitans occurred so frequently that it was impossible to tally the numbers. Father Jean Coicaud believed that over the previous three years around Rohinari there had been 60 or 70 murders, mainly of women and children. Further north, at Onepusu, the SSEM headquarters just 64 kilometres from ʻAoke, seven people had been murdered during the previous six years, two within the last year. Seventeen more murders occurred along the west coast in the first half of 1916. Several occurred within a few kilometres of ʻAoke, and in most of the cases investigated, no offence against customary ways had occurred.[77]

Ramo Suinaʻo, from around Maluʻu and Bitaʻama, had been under observation for some years. He had stolen firearms and murdered many people to collect bounties. In July 1916, Suinaʻo decided to negotiate with Bell, arriving at ʻAoke with shell valuables to be held as a good behaviour bond to cover himself and his cousin Dalao.[78] Another of the northern bounty-hunters, Alifiu, lived near Bitaʻama and worked for 'blood money' payments with a group of his kinsmen. Police Commander Campbell had previously met with Alifiu to try to get him to cease his killings,

---

76 SINA, BSIP 14/44, A/DO WRB to A/RC FJB, 5 Oct 1916.
77 SINA, BSIP 14/44, 17 Jan, 5 July and 11 Sept 1916.
78 SINA, BSIP 14/44, 29 July 1916.

although since then there had been four more murders thought to be his doing. Bell sent police to arrest him, which ended in several deaths and Alifiu's escape. Alifiu then began to negotiate for a pardon, but Bell was not interested. Bell also begged clemency for men who had murdered in retaliation for murders by Suina`o. In October 1916, Bell travelled with a police patrol to Bita`ama and to an inland village to intimidate some of Suina`o's supporters. Bell also spoke with several other murderers in the north who requested an amnesty and promised that he would not prosecute them for their past misdeeds if they changed their ways.[79]

Irokwato from Baegu was the most powerful *ramo* on the northeast coast. He had been responsible for the killing on Rev. Hopkins's veranda at Ngorefou in Lau Lagoon in 1910, and since then had committed many more murders.[80] His influence extended right through north Malaita as far southwest as Coleridge Bay and `Ataa in the southeast. Bell believed that no bigman had any control over Irokwato and his followers, and in 1917 began planning to visit the *ramo* with a show of police strength to secure a large deposit of shell valuables as surety for his good behaviour. If Irokwato refused, he intended to arrest him and bring him to `Aoke. The confrontation took place in April 1918. Irokwato negotiated for similar treatment to Suina`o: he provided 178 strings of shell wealth and 749 porpoise teeth as a surety of good behaviour.[81] An interesting combination of indigenous compensation payments and British law was developing, with Bell flexible enough to accept that he could negotiate demands, and the bounty-hunters realising that they had to placate him.

Once Charles Workman took charge of the BSIP, much of the timidity that had marked Barnett's years as acting Resident Commissioner receded. For instance, after a double murder at the SSEM's Pou station on Small Malaita in April 1918, Bell was allowed to proceed on the government vessel *Mala* to make arrests, and if necessary to continue inland. Bell utilised contacts he had made as a government agent on the *Clansman* 15 years earlier. He gave the local bigman two days to surrender the murderers, then attacked, although the attack failed due to poor information.[82] In another 1918 case, Bell was able to penetrate the central mountains in

---

79 SINA, BSIP 14/44, 5 Aug and 18 Oct 1916.
80 SINA, BSIP 14/44, 11 Sept 1916.
81 SINA, BSIP 14/44, 9 Jan 1917; BSIP 14/46, DO WRB to A/RC, 1 Apr 1918. It is not clear if these were single strings (*ridi*) or the more usual 10-string *tafuli`ae*; the latter is more likely.
82 SINA, BSIP 14/46, DO WRB to A/RC CRMW, 30 May 1918, 2; BSIP 14/12, A/RC CRMW to DO WRB, 3 May 1918.

search of Arufoofana of Nalaia who had killed Maifonia. Gone were the days of collecting evidence and asking advice from Tulagi or Suva. Once the police party was attacked, they returned fire and killed Arufoofana and his cousin Furingi.[83] The warriors were no longer laughing at the government. Bell was a force to be reckoned with.

Arisimae and Ara'iasi of Tarapaina were the most powerful *ramo* in 'Are'are. Arisimae's power continued for several decades. Joseph Dickinson knew him well in the 1920s.

> Arisimai, with six of his murder-gang, boarded the ship ten minutes after she had fired her first signal. In his canoe were three axes, and as many guns, his own, personal weapon being a short-barrelled snider. Cut into its butt were twenty-six notches. These he no conpunction [*sic*] in telling that this represented his bag of humans, and executed by that weapon alone.
>
> He spoke a little English, and looked to be sixty years old: was tall, sinewy, and powerful, with a cruel mouth, and unpleasant, black, bloodshot eyes, which took in everyone at a glance. It was interesting to watch the crew-boys watching him, in turn, from cover ...[84]
>
> So great was his influence over marked men that did they meet him unexpectedly they became too terror-stricken to move. Never, or seldom, would he strike face-to-face. His method was to stalk them with the cunning of a panther, striking or shooting treacherously at close quarters, and then disappear with a hellish yell. Sometimes he would leave alarmed villagers frozen stiff with fright until daylight, when they would discover the murdered person, with a great hole blown into his back; shot through the lattice-side of the house where the unfortunate man had lain. Often a hand, foot, or even head, of the victim was missing. This had been taken as a token to the instigator of the murder to show that the deed was done.[85]

Petero Ara'iasi was born in the mid-1880s, the son of a *ramo* from Tarapaina. During his life he claimed to have executed 80 Malaitans in return for payment. Like Arisimae, he was a friend of Father Jean Coicaud. In 1916, Ara'iasi was accused of yet another murder and was paroled for four years, to Rohinari, and to Visale on Guadalcanal. This banishment did not last. In September 1918, after a spate of killings, Bell surrounded

---

83   SINA, BSIP 14/46, A/RC CRMW to DO WRB, 30 May and 8 Aug 1918.
84   Dickinson 1927, 160.
85   *Ibid.*, 158.

9. KOBURU: WILLIAM BELL, 1915–27

Ara`iasi's house at Tarapaina before daybreak but failed to locate him. Bell took shell and porpoise teeth valuables and other items from the house, held in pawn to ensure the surrender of Ara`iasi as accessory to murder and his adopted son Kope Pipiala for murder.[86] Ara`iasi then spread rumours that the Catholic bishop had Bell and his police put into prison for their attack on him. Bell demanded a shell wealth deposit as surety, imposed a two-year good behaviour bond and deported him yet again to a Guadalcanal Catholic mission. Based on a reading of government reports, Jean Coicaud was his close ally in an unusual relationship of mutual benefit. Ara`iasi extended his power through access to Catholic medical aid and European goods, and in turn the missionaries received protection that advanced the work of the mission. Ara`iasi was baptised in 1922, and after the death of Bell at Sinalagu in 1927 he was appointed headman of Tarapaina for three years. Thereafter he lived a Christian life, much respected as a hereditary chief. He died on 11 February 1963.[87] Arisimae was never as beholden to the mission, although he was baptised on his deathbed in 1947.[88]

Bell's surety collection of shell valuables must have been larger than any other repository on the island. In one swoop in February 1919, he collected 200 *bata* strings from four men because they had posted 'blood money' for a death.[89] He must have had thousands of strings in his bank. We can only conjecture as to what Malaitans thought of this new centre of power, presumably based in the residency. Nevertheless, in 1922 Bell was despondent about his progress and forecast trouble ahead. He also made clear that the WPHC's instructions on how to deal with murder investigations (attack at dawn, etc.) were unworkable.[90]

`Aoke Station

In 1917, `Aoke was costing around £500 a year to operate, plus the wages for the DO and the police.[91] The settlement slowly expanded, although there were no trade stores. In 1915, C.F. Swanson and R.J. Collins were granted a lease over a site at `Aoke for a store, with which they did

---

86 SINA, BSIP 14/12, A/RC CRMW to DO WRB, 10 Oct 1918.
87 *BSIP News Sheet*, 15 Mar 1963; Laracy 1976, 48–49.
88 Laracy, 1976, 48–49; *BSIP News Sheet*, 15 Mar 1963.
89 SINA, BSIP 14/47, DO WRB to RC CRMW, 14 Feb 1919.
90 SINA, BSIP 14/55, DO WRB to RC RRK, 22 July 1922.
91 SINA, BSIP 14/45, 1917, DO WRB to A/RC FJB, 'Budget Estimate', 23 Sept 1917.

not proceed. In 1917, Leong Tong, on behalf of Man Chong & Co. of Tulagi, applied for land for a store, which was refused. The same Chinese company tried again in 1920 through Ay Choy, representing Kwong Chong & Co., an associated company. They, too, were refused. Finally, in October 1927, Bell recommended that Chinese traders be allowed to establish stores at Su`u and at `Ataa.[92]

A proper lock-up for prisoners was built in 1917 and station gardens were expanded to increase food supplies.[93] The first Solomon Islands clerk, Marcus John Linana`au, formerly a police lance-corporal, was employed in 1920. By 1922 he was considered extremely capable and was earning £48 per year.[94] Bell and his police played cricket in their spare time. `Aoke was becoming like any other government district headquarters.

Figure 9.6: A game of cricket at `Aoke during William Bell's years as district officer.
Source: Courtesy of Roger Keesing.

Edge-Partington had always feared an attack on `Aoke, and 10 years after he opened the station prowlers were found under the DO's house at night and a sentry was shot in the arm. Bell did not think the incident was part of a general uprising, but rather related to his pursuit of Suiasi, a murderer who had escaped from Tulagi prison and was shot by the

---

92 SINA, BSIP 14/48, DO WRB to RC, 22 Mar 1920; 14/14, RC CW to DO WRB, 27 Feb 1920; 14/60, DO WRB to RC, 12 June 1927; 14/25, SG to DO WRB, 5 Oct 1927.
93 SINA, BSIP 14/43, A/RC FJB to A/DO WRB, 9 Nov 1915; BSIP 14/45, DO WRB to A/RC FJB, 26 Aug and 29 Dec 1917.
94 SINA, BSIP 14/48, DO WRB to RC CRMW, 27 Mar 1920; BSIP 14/55, DO WRB to A/RC CRMW, 5 Jan and 18 June 1922; BSIP 14/21, A/RC CRMW to DO WRB, 4 July 1922.

Malaita police.⁹⁵ In 1921, when Bell went to Australia for dental work, he was willing to leave `Aoke in the charge of Sergeant Alick Kongori from Choiseul, an indication of the change over the 12 years since Edge-Partington had arrived in 1909.⁹⁶ In 1920, the government considered shifting its headquarters from `Aoke to Bina, one of the finest harbours in the protectorate, but this never came about.⁹⁷

The days of travel by whaleboat were not over. During the first six months of 1920, Bell estimated that he had travelled over 800 kilometres in the whaleboat and canoes. Only occasionally did he have the use of a small government vessel. However, mail seemed to move between Tulagi and `Aoke very quickly, often within one or two days, and the police were far more mobile than ever before, using the many vessels that travelled around the island.⁹⁸ They had also begun to patrol inland along the many tracks that criss-crossed all parts of the island. The first formal European-style road-making occurred at Malu`u in 1919 using no more than digging sticks and bare hands. Once the head tax was introduced in 1923, travel had to escalate considerably to collect it.

Direct Rule: The District Officer, Police and Patrols

The BSIP's administrative policy was based on direct rule—from the government official direct to the people—until a 1928 report by Sir Harry Moorhouse advocated a change to indirect rule following the Lugard model from British Africa.⁹⁹ In 1922, the government had introduced a Native Administration Regulation, enabling the appointment of district and village headmen and village constables, all selected and supervised by the DOs. Moorhouse's report was in part a critique of this and advocacy for extending the system.¹⁰⁰ Bell was the classic direct ruler, but even he had started to introduce intermediate local officials.

---

95 SINA, BSIP 14/47, DO WRB to A/RC Ralph B. Hill, 16 Sept and 6 Nov 1919.
96 SINA, BSIP 14/20, A/RC Ralph B. Hill to DO WRB, 5 Jan 1912.
97 SINA, BSIP 14/48, DO WRB to RC CRMW, 26 July 1920; BSIP 14/14, RC CRMW to DO WRB, 3 July 1920.
98 SINA, BSIP 14/47, DO WRB to A/RC CRMW, 20 Sept 1919.
99 Akin 2013a, 50–55.
100 Bennett 1987, 210.

Malaitans living on the artificial islands in the lagoons had always been easy to access, and Bell knew that the people there were rapidly conforming to the needs of the protectorate. Those living inland—the bulk of the population—were another matter. The lagoon-dwellers and the coastal Christian villages had become regular targets for inland men killing to collect bounties. Bell began to make extensive patrols through central and north Malaita. He knew that coastal patrols were 'little better than a warship doing likewise, which we know is quite useless' and that until inland people could experience the power of the police and meet the DO they could never feel part of the protectorate.[101] In June 1916 and September 1917, patrols penetrated deep into central Kwara`ae and from Langalanga Lagoon across to Kwai and Ngongosila on the east coast. In November 1916, Bell led a patrol from `Ataa at the southern end of Lau Lagoon and over the mountains of Baegu and Fataleka to Coleridge Bay in the west, and a month later left from the same bay and penetrated Fataleka as far as Abarafi in the central mountains. The following September, a patrol left Kwai and Ngongosila, passed through central Kwara`ae and up into Fataleka, before descending back through Kwara`ae to `Aoke. At `Eri`eri they passed through an area where 'blood money' had been posted for the death of a European. The patrols included police, and in some cases a government medical officer and local guides, and used the established tracks. Bell also prepared a map of the geographic territories of To`aba`ita descent groups, but bristled when Barnett refused him permission to arrest known murderers residing nearby.[102]

A police sub-inspector was posted on Malaita in 1918. Unlike Edge-Partington, Bell did not favour having a senior police officer based at `Aoke. He preferred to travel with the police himself, recognising that from the perspective of the ordinary Malaitan, whoever was in control of the police was seen as the most powerful, and that person had to be Bell. What he wanted instead was extra police and a small ship to travel around the island to speed up administration. But Workman insisted on the separation of police and routine administration, partly so that police patrols under a European officer could regularly be despatched to difficult areas like Baunani, and to deal with offenders such as Irokwato.[103]

---

101 SINA, BSIP 14/44, A/DO WRB to A/RC FJB, 17 Jan 1916.
102 SINA, BSIP 14/45, DO WRB to A/RC FJB, 29 Sept 1917, sketch map; 14/44, DO WRB to A/RC FJB, 2 Nov 1916.
103 SINA, BSIP 14/46, DO WRB to RC CRMW, 30 Jan 1918; RC CRMW to DO WRB, 4 Feb 1918.

Sub-Inspector Frederick Taylor spent several months based at Baunani and Onepusu with a police detachment during mid-1918, but then grew ill and departed.[104] Bell again insisted that he wanted an assistant DO, not a police officer.

Bell also continued normal coastal patrols to hear court cases, investigate murders and arrest culprits. In December 1919, one such trip circumnavigated the main island and cut back to the west via Maramasike Passage.[105] Bell believed that Malaitans made the best police, although he had problems finding recruits. Because transport was easier to the north of the island, it was the first area brought under government control, and most of the police came from there. Compared with plantation labourers, the police were well paid, but their job was dangerous, the discipline was strict and food was poor. Police were flogged for offences and, strangely, Sunday drill parades were held in the nude, which did nothing to encourage recruiting from the well-clothed Christian communities. In addition to floggings, punishment of police offenders included being tied to trees.[106]

Bell would have liked to patrol more and believed that the lack of a police presence had allowed murders to increase. When he could patrol he was thorough and continued to arrest people for murder. He also followed the policy he had announced in 1915 of not arresting Malaitans who confessed to having killed in response to murders of their relatives. He merely advised them that they should seek other means of redress. When innocent people were killed for 'blood money', he pursued the killers with the full force of the law.[107] The size of Malaita's police force varied from 25 to 37, the overall numbers having been allowed to increase from 1923 to 1925 when the head tax was introduced.

---

104 SINA, BSIP 14/46, RC CRMW to DO WRB, 2 May 1918; BSIP 14/48, DO WRB to RC CRMW, 22 Mar 1920.
105 SINA, BSIP 14/47, DO WRB to A/RC CRMW, 1 Dec 1919.
106 SINA, BSIP 14/48, DO WRB to RC CRMW, 12 July 1920.
107 SINA, BSIP 14/49, DO WRB to A/RC CRMW, 20 Jan and 20 Aug 1921.

Indirect Rule: District and Village Headmen and Village Constables

There were experiments with headmen in the mid-1910s,[108] which were never formally instituted until Regulation No. 17 of 1922, known as the Native Administration Regulation. This signalled a change in the style of administration from direct to indirect rule, and a new involvement of indigenous officials. The first official appointments were Joe Uiarai at Su`u and Hauhui in west Kwara`ae, Benjamin Manbili at Kwai in east Kwara`ae, Sirifa at Sinalagu in east Kwaio, and Timothy George Mahratta in Small Malaita.[109] District headmen had the power of arrest, which they began to use, although only Mahratta had the education and ability to perform the duties fully. It was a relatively cheap system: each year district headmen were paid £12, village headmen received £3 and village constables £1 10s annually. Although these were not handsome wages, leading men could now earn money at home and come to understand more about the imposed administrative system. There were falls from grace, such as Uiarai, who was suspended in 1925 and imprisoned for six months.[110] In 1924, Bell expanded the system to include 14 village headmen spread all around the coast. There were already two police posted to outstations, Stephen Gori`i at Malu`u (who had been instrumental in helping the government gain control in the north of the island) and Harry Rafe at `Ataa (ideal, because he had kin connections in Lau, Baegu and Fataleka). Bell suggested that Gori`i and Rafe should be made district headmen.[111]

The year before, new protectorate-wide regulations were introduced for headmen to enforce: abusive language and disorderly conduct received a fine of 5/- or 14 days imprisonment; slander a 10/- fine; and nonperformance of community service a 2/- fine for each day or part of a day missed. Headmen had to report births and deaths within seven days or themselves face a fine of 5/-. Pigs were to be confined more than 15 metres from houses, with breaches bringing a 5/- fine and possible destruction

---

108 SINA, BSIP 14/9, RC CMW to RM TWE-P, 23 Mar 1914; 14/42, RC CMW to RM TWE-P, 17 Apr 1914; 14/10, A/RC FJ to RM CGN, 22 Apr 1915; BSIP 14/43, RM CGN to A/RC FJB, 14 Apr 1915.
109 Akin 2013a, 85.
110 SINA, BSIP 14/58, A/DO A. H. Studd to RC RRK, 5 Mar 1925; 'Report for the 4th Quarter, 1924'.
111 SINA, BSIP 14/56, DO WRB to RC RRK, 1 May and 21 June 1923; BSIP 14/57, DO WRB to RC RRK, 30 Mar 1924; BSIP 14/58, DO WRB to RC RRK, 3 June 1925; BSIP 14/24, Acting SG to DO WRB, 17 June 1925.

of the pigs. This latter rule angered people since it greatly increased the labour needed to raise the animals. The compulsory community labour regulation was also irksome since adequate footpaths had always existed, but simply did not meet the European ideal of a road.[112] The strangest new regulation required everyone to have the DO's written permission to be away from their village for more than two months, except for paid employment or attendance at a school or mission. Had they known of this rule's existence, it is hard to imagine what the people of ʻAtaa would have made of it when they wanted to spend time with their Walade cousins on Small Malaita.[113] It was bureaucracy gone mad, and an insult to the long Malaitan tradition of mobility and freedom of movement. Fortunately, it was also unenforceable in most places, and ignored.

Another proposed regulation for 1926 was similarly ludicrous: the introduction of marriage certificates issued by the DO. For once, Bell was restrained in his comments, saying that the idea might work on Gela, Isabel or the Shortlands, but not on Malaita, where most marriages were customary ones and there were 'thousands of native women … who had never seen a Government Official, either European or Native'.[114] But the package as a whole—the head tax, the abolition of beach payments, headmen, firearms registration, the pursuit of professional murderers, new village health regulations, obligatory registrations of births, deaths and marriages—was evidence that Malaita was rapidly being incorporated into the government system.

By 1925 there were three district headmen, 14 village headmen and four village constables. The next year, subdistrict headmen were introduced: there were three headmen, 22 subdistrict headmen and eight village constables. The government aimed to have one village constable for every 100 adults—impractical on Malaita, which would have required over 400 village constables.[115] For ordinary Malaitans, this was a sign that the *gafamanu* (government) was strengthening, although it meant much more to those living along the coast than those in the interior where officials rarely ventured. Malaitans began to take disputes to the local courts, thereby eroding the power of existing leaders. This was certainly

---

112 Akin 2013a, 86–87.
113 SINA, BSIP 14/22, regulations under Section 19 of the Native Administration Regulations no. 17 of 1922.
114 SINA, BSIP 14/59, DO WRB to RC RRK, 8 Aug 1926.
115 SINA, BSIP 14/59, DO WRB to RC RRK, 'Annual Report, 1925', 20 Jan 1926.

happening by the 1930s, and Ian Hogbin said it had begun in the north as early as the 1910s, though this seems early considering `Aoke station only opened in 1909. Hogbin first arrived in To`aba`ita in 1933 and was reliant on oral accounts.[116]

Health

Bell managed to get his assistant. A.H. Studd was posted at `Aoke between 1923 and 1925, although he suffered recurrent sickness, including a bout of dysentery that landed him in Tulagi Hospital for five weeks in September–October 1923. Bell himself took 10 months of leave from mid-July 1924, some due to him as annual leave but most of it medical leave and leave on half-pay to allow him to recuperate.[117] After 12 years working for the BSIP Government, his health had suffered and he needed a long break. Studd took over in his absence.

Figure 9.7: Waterfront view of Onepusu, the SSEM headquarters, in the late 1920s or 1930s.
Source: Deck Collection, Black and White Photographs, 53.

From the 1910s to 1930s, Malaita was better served by qualified medical personnel that any other island in the protectorate outside of Tulagi. SSEM missionary Norman Deck, a dentist, served on Malaita from

---

116 Akin 2013a, 86.
117 SINA, BSIP 14/56, DO WRB, 14 June, 26 Sept and 16 Nov 1923 to RC RRK; BSIP 14/57, DO WRB to RC RRK, 12 Feb and 7 July 1924.

1913, his brother Northcote Deck, a medical practitioner, resided on Malaita or at Aloa, Guadalcanal, onwards from 1909 and often visited SSEM bases around Malaita. The SSEM headquarters at Onepusu was commodious and had substantial facilities. Dr Lily Holt-MacCrimmon, the wife of Neil MacCrimmon, the manager of Mala Timber Company, lived on Malaita during the second half of the 1920s. Although most of the Deck brothers' services went to maintain SSEM adherents and staff, onwards from 1926 Dr Holt-MacCrimmon was paid a small retainer by the government to provide medical facilities for the wider population in her area, with the hospital building constructed by the government.[118] Dr Nathaniel Crichlow, appointed in 1911 as one of the government medical officers, between 1926 and 1942 served mainly as travelling medical officer, usually on board SS *Hygeia*, which visited Malaita regularly.[119] Dr Dorothy Mills-Parker began work at the SDA Kwailabesi Hospital in Lau Lagoon in 1934, and Dr Lysander Montague Maybury and his wife Florence Edna Johnson-Kaine (a nurse) founded the Melanesian Mission's Hospital of the Epiphany at Fauaabu in Coleridge Bay in late 1928, which included a leper colony onwards from 1929.

The government records contain many references to monitoring outbreaks of diseases. The excessive tobacco smoking must have caused ill health, although government efforts to limit smoking were usually aimed at pregnant women and children. However, nothing matched the global influenza pandemic that reached Malaita in February 1919. Thousands became sick as it spread through the islands, although the death rate was not as high as first feared. Bell estimated the death rate to be six in every 1,000, although one medical officer guessed that around 3 per cent of the Solomons population died.[120] The first effects were felt in northeast and central Malaita. At Baunani between 80 and 100 of the labourers caught the disease. The highest number of deaths recorded was around 'Ataa.[121] In May, Bell reported:

---

118 SINA, BSIP 14/59, DO WRB to RS RRK, 9 July 1926; BSIP 14/24a, Gov Sec to DO WRB, 5 July 1926.
119 *BSIP AR* 1928, 5; WPHC no. 2954 of 1926, RC C.M. Woodford to WPHC, 21 Feb and 3 Apr 1914, S.C.M. Davies to C.M. Woodford, 16 Feb 1914, WPHC no. 800 of 1914; N. Crichlow to Government Secretary, 27 May 1926, WPCH to R.R. Kane, 15 Oct 1926; WPHC 4/IV 222/1934, RC no. 530, 13 Dec 1933; WPHC 259/1934, RC no. 21, 5 Jan 1934; Keesing and Corris 1980, 206–09.
120 Akin 2013a, ch. 3, and 177 n 72.
121 SINA, BSIP 14/47, DO WRB to RC CRMW, 7 Feb, 22 Apr and 14 May 1919.

> I do not know any part on this island where I am prepared to say that a vessel recruiting therefrom would not be likely to recruit natives who are influenza contacts. There are certain villages which have had the influenza and are now clear of it, but I am not aware of any district which is clear of it. The saltwater people may now be about clear of it, but it is still spreading on the mainland everywhere. Recruiting vessels had spread it around the coast before I knew it was in the islands.[122]

Six months later, influenza was still spreading and had reached the south of Malaita where almost everyone contracted the disease at some level. Another, similar epidemic appeared in the north in late 1919 and early 1920, although the cause of death appeared to be pneumonia not influenza, and the death rates were higher.[123] The epidemic ceased after three years, although occasional, less drastic and more localised epidemics continued to appear in different parts of the island.[124] The DO's reports are full of mentions of minor localised outbreaks of influenza and dysentery, and in 1926 dengue fever was reported at Su'u and Onepusu, introduced by a steamer from Australia.[125] Later that year, there were pneumonia and influenza outbreaks around Su'u and Fiu on the west coast.[126] One task of the headmen was to dispense medicines during epidemics. Native Dressers (male medical orderlies) began to be educated at Tulagi in 1922, although as late as 1926 no Malaitans could be found to join the training.[127] Dr Crichlow calculated that dysentery was responsible for the deaths of 10 per cent of the protectorate's population between 1913 and 1915.[128] Bennett calculated the mortality rate at almost 5 per cent following a 1914 dysentery epidemic, and it remained at 2–3 per cent until 1928, after which there was a lower level until rates rose again during 1937–38. Even so, Bennett is right to remind us that for the most part the health of the labourers was better than that of their kin back in the villages.[129]

---

122 SINA, BSIP 14/47, DO WRB to RC CRMW, 14 May 1919.
123 *Ibid.*; BSIP 14/13, Captain Turner to A/RC CRMW, 14 Aug 1919; BSIP 14/48, DO WRB to RC CRMW, 16 Jan 1920.
124 SINA, BSIP 14/55, DO WRB to RC RRK, 4 Nov 1922.
125 SINA, BSIP 14/59, DO WRB to RC RRK, 'Quarterly Report', 14 July 1926.
126 SINA, BSIP 14/59, DO WRB to RC RRK, 5 Oct 1926.
127 SINA, BSIP 14/59, DO WRB to RC RRK, 27 Dec 1926.
128 Crichlow 1929.
129 Bennett 1987, 177.

Figure 9.8: School boys drilling at the SSEM Onepusu School, 1922.
The drilling practice presumably was a transfer from Australia, where 100 hours of military training was introduced between 1912 and 1929 for all boys and youths between 12 and 26 years of age. Secondary schools also had compulsory military cadet training.
Source: Deck Collection, Black and White Photographs, 55.

Conclusion

While it would be wrong to suggest that all Malaitans felt part of the protectorate and accepted modern practices, by the late 1920s there are continual signs of the beginnings of change, such as a will made by Job Maekalai, who died at Onepusu in 1924. He bequeathed his lands and possessions in a formal manner. In the same year, Acting DO Studd suggested that a Malaitan couple with irreconcilable differences be taken to Tulagi to be formally divorced by the judicial commissioner.[130] A photograph of boys drilling at the SSEM's Onepusu School suggests that the days of casual schooling were over, at least for some. In many ways, 'making Mala' was complete in a rudimentary way by the mid-1920s, except for our prescient knowledge of the murder of Bell and Lilley and

---

130 SINA, BSIP 14/57, DO WRB to RC RRK, 12 Feb and 5 Dec 1924.

their tax-collecting party in 1927. Tax-collection was becoming an annual event, although Bell harped on the amount of work involved for the small financial gain, and wondered if Malaitans thought that his main job was 'to extract money from them'.[131] ʻAoke had become a comfortable outpost of empire. The police accompanied the DO to all parts of the island, and two constables were based permanently away from ʻAoke. There was even a young bugler for police parades.[132]

---

131 SINA, BSIP 14/58, DO WRB to RC RRK, 'Annual Report, 1925', 20 Jan 1926.
132 SINA, BSIP 14/57, 25 Apr, 7 July and 30 Sept 1924; 'List of Malaita Police', 9 July 1924; BSIP 14/58, A/DO A. H. Studd, 'District Report 1st Quarter 1925', 5 Apr 1925; BSIP 14/59, DO WRB to RC RRK, 'Annual Report, 1925', 20 Jan 1926.

10
Making Mala into Malaita, 1927–42

> Further progress has been made in the development of Native Administration during the year. This progress, unfortunately, continues to be slow, and must be so until facilities for the setting up of native courts are available. Nevertheless, it has been possible in many parts of the island to lay the foundations of such Courts, and councils of elders, arbitrating in native custom, have proved of great assistance in administration.
>
> —Charles N.F. Bengough, District Officer Malaita, District Annual Report, 1941[1]

Introduction

This chapter covers the years after Bell and until the Second World War reached the Pacific. The argument pursued in this book has been that most of 'Making Mala' occurred between the 1870s and the mid-1920s. Then followed a slow period during the 1930s and until 1942, when, hurried by the war, the protectorate administration introduced a few crucial developments. The Bell massacre in east Kwaio in 1927 was a substantial setback but an aberration, a piece of bad luck that could have occurred at any time between 1909 and 1927. The Pacific War provided a space for the emergence of the Maasina Rule movement between 1944 and 1952, which brought radical changes.

---

1   BSIP 27/VI/6, DO CNFB to SG, 'Annual Report, 1941', 31 Dec 1941, 1.

There was no dramatic decline in the number of labourers leaving Malaita during the 1930s, but Malaitans, like other Solomon Islanders, were less able to pay taxes and there was a concomitant decrease in the revenues available to tax. Inexorably, government and mission services declined and were stretched thin. Some schools ceased operations altogether. At the same time, the administration of the island moved from a pattern of reaction to Malaitan truculence to routine activities and violence declined markedly. Health services improved, roads were constructed and some Malaitans began to be involved in district administration and local courts. Without the war, the economic downturn would eventually have revived. Without the war, the disturbance caused by Maasina Rule might never have occurred, or perhaps would have been more easily controlled by the government.

In the 1930s, Christians were probably about equal in number to followers of ancestral spirits, and certainly were after the 1940s, and a Christian ascendancy followed during the 1950s. Even the most conservative Malaitans were effectively brought under the protectorate administration through taxation and visits from government patrols, although many hamlets in the central mountains were seldom if ever visited by officials and never by Christian missionaries. As will be abundantly clear, the years covered in this chapter were radically different from the period from 1909 to the mid-1920s. Malaita had become a regularised part of the British Solomon Islands Protectorate.

David Akin's 2013 book *Colonialism, Maasina Rule, and the Origins of Malaitan Kastom* provides an excellent introduction to these directly prewar years. Akin's analysis is based on a deep knowledge of Malaitan culture and history, and uses the Malaitan Government archives closely. He concludes that government officials often overestimated their understanding of Malaitans. This chapter will take note of Akin's corrective text and register here what all historians know: that colonial sources have their weaknesses; but then so too does oral testimony. To our advantage, the government's archives provide exact statistics and its officers were often perceptive within their personal limits. As long as their files are used with caution, and always compared against surviving indigenous sources, they, like the mission archives preceding them, provide a crucial outline.

Killing Mista Belo

There is a sense of satisfaction for any historian who knows what is about to occur when the historical actors under consideration do not. The Malaita Government records cease in late 1927 and do not begin again until February 1928. The reason is that William Bell, cadet officer Kenneth C. Lillies and 13 police were murdered on 5 October 1927 during a government tax-collecting patrol at Sinalagu Harbour in the Kwaio area of east Malaita. This was the most notable single event in the prewar British Solomons, both the attack and the vicious official retribution.

Men primarily from three descent groups inland from Sinalagu made the attack. Two Kwaio men were killed as the government party gamely fought back. Most of the dead were police from north Malaita.[2] Two weeks later, a government punitive force consisting of 50 Australian naval personnel, 28 European special constables, and some 50 Malaitan police and volunteers (primarily from the north) arrived at Sinalagu on MV *Ranadi* and HMAS *Adelaide* (an Australian warship called into action), along with the Australian naval collier HMAS *Biloela* as the supply ship. This was the last time the British used a naval ship to attack Solomon Islanders, although there was no bombardment, just an extensive land expedition.

The 1927 reprisals led to simmering resentment and ongoing compensation claims from the Kwaio.[3] In 1977, on the 50th anniversary of the deaths, anthropologist Roger Keesing suggested some form of official ceremony take place, but permission was refused by Chief Minister Peter Kenilorea. A private ceremony was organised at Sinalagu and Ngongosila, attended by Bell's only surviving sister. Then, in 1980, Keesing and Peter Corris published *Lightning Meets the West Wind*. The book is a good combination of Pacific history and anthropology, but in other circumstances it might have gone unnoticed beyond academic circles. Its publication actually had little impact in Kwaio itself, although it disturbed the provincial and national governments.[4] However, in 1984, east Kwaio people boycotted the national election, although they agreed

---

2   Keesing and Corris 1980, 83–147.
3   *Ibid.*, 148–205; Akin 1999b; Keesing 1990a; BSIP 14/28, SG to DO JCB, 9 Sept 1930.
4   Keesing 1990a; information from David Akin, Mar 2016.

to a bye-election in 1985. Kenilorea visited east Kwaio twice while Prime Minister to try to sort out the grievances. His autobiography reveals him to have been quite uncomfortable in dealing with the Kwaio.[5]

How did it all happen? Bell returned from leave in mid-1925, as testy as ever, earning a rebuke from Resident Commissioner Richard Kane.[6] While DO he had been to Sinalagu several times. In July 1925, for instance, he held court at Sinalagu and delivered tax receipts to ex-labourers of the Malayta Company. The party worked on improving the landing place at the leaf tax-house that had been erected for government use. Joe Maeana, the local village headman, reported that he knew that a number of men had not paid their head tax for 1924, and the next day Maeana and another village headman, Kwaiatiboo, brought in a few men who had taxes to pay.[7] Bell was back at Sinalagu in October for a day, while collecting taxes along the east coast.[8] In 1926, taxes were collected there on 7, 12 and 13 February. At the same time, Bell and Lillies investigated a murder from two years before and another committed just a few days before they arrived. Bell recorded no incidents of noncompliance or signs of agitation.[9]

Bell returned to the east coast in May to investigate an alleged conspiracy to kill him.[10] *Ramo* Irokwato in Baegu had suggested that Bell should be assassinated. His reasons were the head tax, the forced building of the tax-collection houses and compulsory road building. Irokwato had not done anything further and the incident was dismissed as minor. Bell commented:

> Irokwato is not a native of high status by birth, but, at one time, he was greatly feared as a professional murderer and thief. His past unscrupulous career and the fact that he has few friends and many enemies renders it unlikely that any advice which he may have given would be favourably received by natives outside his particular community.[11]

---

5   Allan 1990, 157; Kenilorea 2008, 267–71.
6   SINA, BSIP 14/24, Acting SG to DO WRB, 17 Aug 1925.
7   SINA, BSIP 14/58, 'Log of District Vessel Auki', 1 July – 30 Sept 1925, DO WRB to RC RRK, 9 Oct 1925.
8   SINA, BSIP 14/59, 'Log of District Vessel Auki', 18–25 Oct 1925.
9   SINA, BSIP 14/59, 'Log of District Vessel Auki', 1 Jan – 31 Mar 1926, DO WRB to RC RRK, 13 Mar 1926.
10 SINA, BSIP 14/59, DO WRB, 'Report for the Quarter' ending 30 June 1916, 29 May 1926.
11 SINA, BSIP 14/59, DO WRB to RC RRK, 'Quarterly Report', 14 July 1926.

10. MAKING MALA INTO MALAITA, 1927–42

Not easily intimidated, William Bell clearly had no idea what was about to occur.

He was back in east Kwaio in November 1926, reporting a severe influenza epidemic, for which he left medicine with the subdistrict headman at Sinalagu, and he investigated a murder at 'Oloburi.[12] Bell did not visit Sinalagu during the early months of 1927, but did so in May. He collected a few outstanding taxes and inquired into a marital disturbance.[13]

On 30 August 1927, Bell applied for four-and-a-half months leave and was unhappy when the administration replaced him with Francis B. Filose, a married man who would have to share his house during the changeover period. He did not want his bachelor lifestyle disturbed by the presence of strangers, particularly a woman, and the government had been negligent in not providing separate housing.[14] Bell and Lillies then set out on their last fateful tax collecting expedition to the east coast. No single act led to their deaths. It was a matter of personalities, among the Kwaio, and of course Bell's sometimes belligerent attitudes toward administering Malaita.

Figure 10.1: A member of the 'Whiskey Army' expedition, possibly one of the crew from HMS *Adelaide* sent from Australia to support the 1927 government expedition to east Kwaio. The Malaitan man is from Kwaio.
Source: Jeff Willmot Collection, 274.

---

12   SINA, BSIP 14/60, 'Log of MV Auki', 3–4 Nov 1926, DO WRB to RS RRK, 31 Dec 1926.
13   SINA, BSIP 14/60, 'Log of MV Auki', 18 May 1927; DO WRB to RC RRK, 5 July 1927.
14   SINA, BSIP 14/60, DO WRB to RC RRK, 30 Aug 1927.

Similar to what always occurred in labour trade attacks, the Kwaio assailants had made preparations to ensure the support of ancestral spirits. The massacre in Kwaio is still talked about today—it has become a Solomon Islands trope. The manner in which the government reacted to the killings, by inflicting almost indiscriminate retribution, did it no credit.

Although the Europeans were ineffectual in the rugged mountainous terrain, the north Malaitan police and volunteers were efficient and ruthless, avenging the deaths of their own people who had been in Bell's police. Women and girls were gang-raped and many were shot, children were murdered and prisoners were executed and mutilated. The retaliatory raid roamed north to Uru Harbour, into the ʻOloburi area and into west Kwaio, far away from the area where the attack had occurred. Keesing and Corris estimated that around 60 people were shot and others, some children, died from exposure while hiding in the jungle. Ancestral shrines and sacred men's houses were desecrated, which the Kwaio believe caused their angry ancestors to kill more descendants later through illness and mishap.

One hundred and ninety-eight men, most innocent of the crimes charged, were taken to prison in Tulagi. The event played out between October 1927 and February 1928, with an astonishingly high death rate amongst the men imprisoned: 173 were hospitalised for dysentery during their time at Tulagi and 30 died (28 in 1928 and two in 1929). The government tried to explain away some of the deaths as due to old age and senility, but while a few of the prisoners were elderly, the question then becomes why such vulnerable men were in prison, initially uncharged with any offence, and what role they could have played in the attack? Perfunctory trials eventually proceeded. Eleven were charged with murder and six were executed. Seventy-one were tried for offences less than murder, of whom 51 were acquitted. Six were imprisoned for life, eight for 20 years, two for 12 years and one for three years. Their wives and families either fled further inland or took shelter in the SSEM villages along the coast or at the SDA mission base at Uru. There was little food left in their gardens and there were few materials available to rebuild houses.[15] The Kwaio massacre and its aftermath was the most severe random punishment ever meted out by British authorities in the Pacific. The Kwaio people have never forgotten.

---

15 Moorhouse 1929.

The 1928 official investigation into the massacre by Lieutenant-Colonel Sir Harry Moorhouse, the retired lieutenant-governor of Nigeria (1921–25), critiqued the BSIP administration and contributed to moves to change from direct to indirect rule, along the lines of British administration in African colonies.[16] Moorhouse advised against Kane's plan to relocate the Kwaio population to Isabel Island, and recommended that indirect rule be gradually introduced.[17] The next few resident commissioners all had some African background, which aided the policy change. While the social structures of Solomons societies were much smaller in scale than those of most African societies, the argument in favour of indirect rule— the 'dual mandate' Lugard model, based on experience in Nigeria—was lauded as more efficient in terms of cost and commercial outcomes, and best for 'developing' native peoples. Lord Lugard had advocated that all officers learn a local language and understand local cultures. He argued for stationing officers in one place for as long as possible and that they should tour often around their districts. While this was good advice, one can doubt the sincerity and indeed common sense of British imperialism. Lugard's model came from chiefly tribal societies and foundered in Malaita and other places where leadership was sited at lower levels and more fluid.[18]

Figure 10.2: Feeding the labourers and police who accompanied the punitive expedition to east Kwaio, 1927.
Source: Jeff Willmot Collection, 269.

16 *Ibid.*
17 Akin 2013a, 49, 51.
18 *Ibid.*, 50–55.

MAKING MALA

After the Bell massacre government functions were slowly restored, with various officers seconded to fill the gap during 1928–29, until Colin E. J. Wilson took over as DO in May 1929. Wilson had been one of the officers in charge of the punitive expedition in Kwaio.

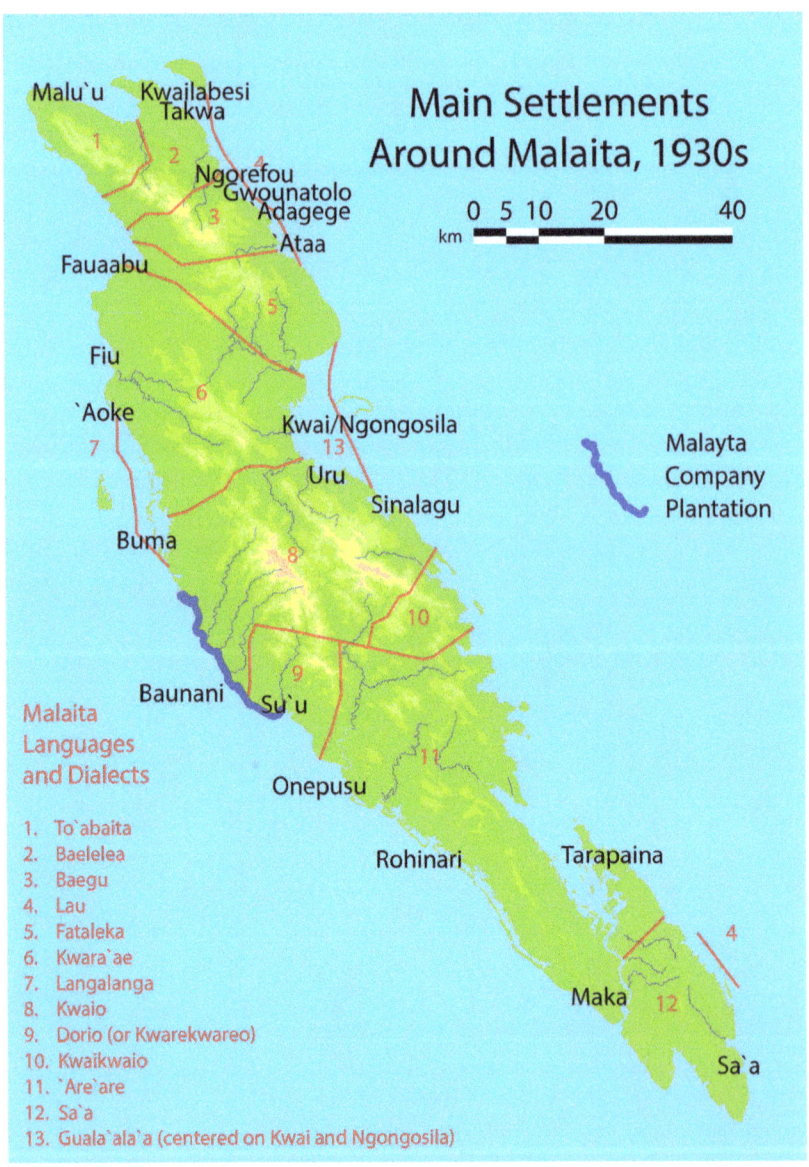

Map 16: Major settlements around Malaita, 1930s.
Source: Courtesy of Vincent Verheyen.

The Economy in the 1930s

In 1909, Malaita was only notionally part of the BSIP. During the second half of the 1910s and up to 1927, Malaita had a stable but aggressive DO in William Bell. During his years, the government process had already slowly begun to change from direct to indirect administration, augmented by reforms in labour recruiting and taxation. By the time Bell died, Malaita was on the way to stronger incorporation into the protectorate, although the final components were not added until just before the Second World War. The population in 1935 was approximately 38,000, excluding those away working in other parts of the protectorate. This figure subdivided into: Bali, from To`aba`ita and south to Fataleka (11,200);[19] Kwara`ae (9,600); Kwaio (6,500); `Are`are (6,200); and Small Malaita (4,870).[20]

The Solomons economy depended on one crop, copra, the profitability of which was often marginal. Copra was produced by smoke-drying the flesh of coconuts. Solomons copra was used only for soap manufacture, the bottom end of the market, and the protectorate produced an insignificant 5 per cent of the world's smoke-dried copra. The choice to build an economy based on copra was sound before the First World War, when prices were high, but the postwar BSIP economy became shaky. Copra prices fluctuated during the war and again in 1922–24. Then, in 1929, the copra price fell back to its 1924 level, and the next year crashed further. Bennett calculated that in 1935 the price was 'less than £1 4s. or £13 below the 1929 price…'.[21] The smaller plantation companies often were financially overextended and were foreclosed on by Burns Philp & Co. or W.R. Carpenter & Co., who cut off their credit and ruined them. The big companies had enough resources to weather the financial storm, but were nevertheless relieved when prices rose again in 1936. The reprieve was short-lived, and prices soon fell again until 1940, by which time there were war-driven shipping shortages.[22]

Malaita still had no substantial export economy other than labour, which remained the main source of cash and goods. The Malayta Company plantations continued to operate, and added cattle to their operations just as the other larger plantation companies had done, although its early

---

19 See Map 4 in Chapter 1. Bali includes To`aba`ita, Baelelea, Lau, Baegu and Fataleka.
20 SINA, BSIP 27/VI/1, DO to SG, 'Annual Report, 1935', 14 Jan 1936.
21 Bennett 1987, 218–20.
22 *Ibid.*, 223–31.

economic promise was never achieved. During the Great Depression years the company almost closed, some of its land leases were cancelled, and its operations continued at such low levels that only a few casual labourers were required. It operated until 1936, when it was sold for £95,000 to Fairymead Sugar Company Ltd (also controlled by the Young family) against the wishes of the minority shareholders. By 1939, the Fairymead company operated only from Baunani and Manaba, each under a European overseer, and employed just 63 labourers. In the final analysis, the Malayta Company was avaricious and its management tactics alienated the local people. It did much better in the Russell Islands until it was ruined by the Pacific War.[23]

The MacCrimmons' 1920s Mala Timber Company discarded its logging ambitions and became a trading business. The Depression closed off Australian markets for hardwood. MacCrimmon shut down his sawmill in July 1930 and sold his equipment to Boldery & Cheetham (timber millers). In September 1930, the couple departed to join the Vanikoro Kauri Timber Company. MacCrimmon became manager and his wife the company's medical officer.[24] Boldery & Cheetham failed and sold out to the Mala Development Company, managed by G.H. Robertson, but in 1931 that company cancelled its leases at Su`u and went into liquidation. They were replaced by a New South Wales company, McLeod, Bolton & Co., which leased the Su`u land and took over the Mala Development Company trade stores around Malaita.[25] However, by 1934 they had closed their stores and sold their leases to Kwong Chong & Co. of Tulagi. The Malayta Company continued to operate one store at Su`u and another at Abu near `Aoke, and financed a few licensed hawkers.[26]

In 1929, the only Malaita District exports were 727 tons of copra, 40 tons of ivory nuts (from sago palms) and 17 tons of trochus shell, mainly collected by Chinese traders. The few local producers were based around Malu`u and Fo`odo in the north and on Small Malaita. Once prices began to fall during the 1930s, most Malaitans stopped preparing copra. The Small Malaita trochus shell harvest also declined as the reefs there

---

23 SINA, BSIP 27/VI/1, DO GEDS to SG, 'Annual Report, 1937', 31 Dec 1937; BSIP 27/VI/4, DO CNFB to SG, 'Annual Report, 1939', 31 Dec 1939.
24 Bennett 2000, 71, 106, 147.
25 SINA, BSIP 14/63, A/DO AFJW to RC FNA, 13 Jan 1932; BSIP 14/64, DO JCB to SG, 8 May 1933.
26 SINA, BSIP 27/VI/1, DO GEDS to Government Secretary, 'Annual Report, 1934', 1 Jan 1935, 35; BSIP 14/32, Leon Ting, Kwong Chong & Co. to RC FNA, 3 Mar 1934; Bennett 2000, 71.

were depleted. The Langalanga people had entered the modern economy more fully than other Malaitans. They continued to supply the wharf labour for Tulagi, Makambo and Gavutu, traded in pigs with Gela and remained the largest manufacturers of shell wealth. As early as the 1910s, a few Langalanga men became local agents for trade stores owned by the Malayta Company. In the 1920s, the Mala Development Company picked leading Malaitans to be its storekeepers. An entrepreneurial few managed to establish limited lines of credit with Burns Philp to purchase cutters, which they used to transport stevedores and trade with Gela. Though, as mentioned, government policy discouraged Chinese traders from establishing permanent stores at 'Aoke, but they traded from vessels that plied the coast buying copra and trochus shell. During the 1930s, a few dozen Malaitans had store or hawker licences.[27] Kwong Chong & Co.'s presence was only made possible by the economic downturn in the 1930s, which caused Australian-owned trading companies to withdraw.

Table 7: BSIP annual labour statistics, 1924–39.

Year	Malaita Labourers Recruited	Malaitans as a Percentage of Total Recruits	Total Labourers Recruited	Total Labourers Employed
1924	1,438	69.73	2,062	5,766
1925	1,439	64.47	2,232	5,741
1926	1,813	68.03	2,665	6,368
1927	1,527	64.70	2,360	6,115
1928	1,459	67.04	2,176	6,016
1929	1,408	70.22	2,005	5,171
1930	1,276	66.84	1,909	5,363
1931	839	75.45	1,112	4,301
1932	1,121	64.94	1,726	3,927
1933	690	62.55	1,103	2,495
1934	759	64.98	1,168	3,578
1935	834	74.33	1,122	2,043
1936	977	85.25	1,146	2,373
1937	1,111	71.77	1,548	2,628
1938	9 68	67.55	1,433	2,471
1939	955	72.45	1,318	2,383

Source: WPHC, BSIP Annual Labour Statistics, 1924–39.

27 SINA, BSIP 14/61, DO JCB to SC, 'Quarterly Report to 30 Sept 1930', 9 Oct 1930; Bennett 1987, 267–69.

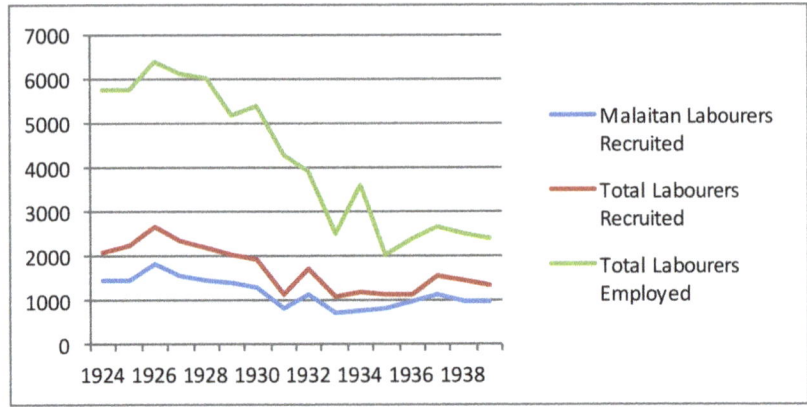

Graph 3: BSIP annual labour statistics, 1924–39.
Source: WPHC, BSIP Annual Labour Statistics, 1924–39.

The Depression affected the movement of labour and returns from taxation, although compared with the total decline in employment of indentured labour after 1930, Malaitans still averaged 69 per cent of the protectorate's labour supply from 1924 to 1939. As shown in Table 7, on average, 917 labourers left Malaita or were reindentured each year between 1931 and 1939. In 1935, the minimum labourer's wage was reduced from £1 to 10/- a month, with a related decrease in the beach bonus from £6 to £3. During the 1920s, labour conditions had improved, but in the 1930s planters cut corners and were more exploitative. The workers were fully conscious of the deteriorating conditions, although recruiters, planters and government officers managed to delude themselves that the labourers did not notice. How could they not notice that their wages had halved? They had no knowledge of the deterioration in the world economy to help them understand the sudden drop in their wages. Many, particularly those from the southern half of Malaita, refused to work for reduced wages. The reduced wages decreased the money available to pay taxes. Recruiters followed the tax-collectors around Malaita because men were easier to recruit when they were being threatened with imprisonment for nonpayment. Inland people, in particular, had nothing to sell except their labour, but even so, most recruits no longer left their beach bonuses with their families. Just as recruits had done when recruiting to Queensland and Fiji, they began to take their beach payments with them, or a large part of the bonus, so as to have some money during their first few months of work and to compensate for the reduced wages.[28]

---

28 Akin 2013a, 94–97.

Figure 10.3: Lining up to pay taxes at Maro'umasike (Takataka or Deep Bay), southeastern 'Are'are, about 1936. A policeman stands on the right.
Source: British Museum, Robert A. Lever Collection, BM Oc.B98.95.

With less cash circulating, taxes had to be reduced to 2s 6d. Recruiting continued in north Malaita and from Kwaio, but ceased in 'Are'are due to fears of depopulation. Half of the 1,200 'Are'are taxpayers were expected to be unable to pay, with similar problems in Kwaio. In 1935, taxes varied by region, with poorer areas paying less: 2s 6d in 'Are'are; 3/- to 5/- in Kwara'ae and 5/- per head in the northern Bali region. This was reduced in 1938 to 1/- for all inland peoples, although the 5/- rate was maintained around the coast.[29] Men could also work off their

---

29   SINA, BSIP 14/66, DO WF to SG, 8 Nov 1935; BSIP 27/VI/1, DO to SG, 'Annual Report, 1935', 14 Jan 1936, 12–14; BSIP 27/VI/4, DO WFMC to SG, 'Annual Report, 1939', 31 Dec 1939, clauses 58–59.

tax debt through communal labour. These reductions, fought for by the DOs, were often opposed by Tulagi. Malaitans never understood why they had to pay tax at all, given the paucity of services they received in return. The inland people suffered the most, unable to either pay taxes or purchase the few European luxuries they used—tobacco, clay pipes, machetes and cloth—and most had no access to government or mission health services on Malaita.

Trade in copra from village plantations ceased entirely between 1933 and 1935, then resumed on Small Malaita and at Malu`u and Fo`odo. By 1937, the government sponsored moves to establish village coconut plantations and all new roads continued to be lined with coconut palms.[30] Several trading stations were also operating, all Chinese-owned except the SSEM store at Onepusu.[31] There were few openings for indigenous entrepreneurs, as Malaita's 1935 annual report noted:

> The lack of productive coconut groves, the growing scarcity of trochus shell, and the tendency of the wage earners of the Tai [Tae in Lau] Lagoon and Langa Langa to spend their wage earnings at Makambo and Tulagi, do not encourage efforts. It is true, too, that the natives who might be expected to open small trading stations in this district are already engaged in such profitable matters as transporting wharf labourers to and from Tulagi, and also in negotiations over the buying and selling of cutters.[32]

The total effect of this economic gloom is hard to calculate, but certainly there was anger and hardship on Malaita, which contributed to the airing of new political ideas like those of the Fallowes movement, which started on Isabel Island.[33] Any possibility of further rebellions was cut short by the Pacific War, although during the war there were labour strikes among Labour Corps men, and economic discontents fuelled the postwar Maasina Rule movement.

---

30 SINA, BSIP 27/VI/1, DO GEDS to SG, 'Annual Report, 1938', 31 Dec 1938, 29–31.
31 SINA, BSIP 27/VI/1, DO to SG, 'Annual Report, 1935', 14 Jan 1936, 32.
32 *Ibid.*, 33.
33 Bennett 1987, 259–63; Akin 2013a, 101–06.

Health

Officials and missionaries were certain that Malaita's population had declined significantly. Rev. Arthur Hopkins, a long-term resident of Lau Lagoon (1902–14), suggested several causes. Overall he thought that there had been a decline in family sizes. He also identified a trend toward men marrying late, which may have related to men leaving the island for several years while participating in the external and internal labour trades. My own research in Queensland suggests that many labourers stayed away for 20 years or spent terms in different colonies, and Judith Bennett's interviews with ex-labourers from BSIP plantations suggest that in the early twentieth century Malaitans spent on average about seven-and-a-half years away, on more than one contract, with a return home in between.[34] Hopkins also thought that polygamy had decreased and that abortions were widespread, as were venereal diseases. Dysentery and other diseases heightened infant mortality.[35] Woodford thought that the labour trade was responsible for the population decrease, and added 'injudicious use of unsuitable clothing' that when worn damp led to pulmonary disease. He also credited the decline to the introduction of new diseases such as dysentery and influenza, and an increase in yaws, notably more prevalent among the coastal peoples.[36] If we extend this introduction of new diseases back to the 1870s, when labour movements began, by the 1930s there had been 60 years of exposure and the deaths rates would have been high over an extended time. The limited amount of medical care available would have done little to offset the decline.

Although epidemics continued to break out, health services had improved in the 1920s and 1930s. A poliomyelitis epidemic in 1928–29 caused many deaths, as did a cerebral-spinal meningitis epidemic in north Malaita during 1936 and an epidemic of German measles (Rubella) in 1939. Tuberculosis remained prevalent. As the economic downturn continued, the protectorate had fewer funds to run the Malaita District vessel, thus limiting the ability of the DOs to collect taxes and supervise health.[37]

---

34   Bennett 1987, 186.
35   Hopkins 1922, 62–66.
36   Woodford 1922, 69. See also Bennett 2014.
37   SINA, BSIP 14/28, DO JCB to SG, 'Annual Report, 1929', 17 Jan 1930; BSIP 14/51, DO WFMC to Manager, Fairymead Sugar Company Ltd, Baunani, 21 Jan 1939.

Once Dr Holt-MacCrimmon departed in 1930, Su'u Hospital was closed and the buildings were moved to 'Aoke, leaving only the Hospital of the Epiphany at Fauaabu in northwest Malaita as a major regional hospital.[38]

Anglican, SDA and government hospitals all began during the 1930s. As mentioned in the previous chapter, the Anglicans opened their hospital at Fauaabu. They had a well-trained medical practitioner in Cambridge-educated Dr L.M. Maybury, who arrived late in 1928. The hospital, designed and built by Maybury, opened on 16 June 1929 with an operating theatre and 40 beds in several concrete-floor buildings. There were three trained nurses—his wife Florence, and M.T. Simson and B. Guyles from New Zealand—and six male orderlies.[39] American doctor Sylvester M. Lambert, part of a yaws and hookworm eradication team that visited Fauaabu in the early 1930s, described the hospital and leprosarium as very well run.[40]

Figure 10.4: Hospital of the Epiphany at Fauaabu, northwest Malaita in the 1930s.
Source: British Museum, Lloyd Francis Collection, 1.

---

38   SINA, BSIP 14/63, DO to RC FNA, 'Quarterly Report to April 1932', 2 Apr 1932; BSIP 27/VI/1, DO GEDS to SG, 'Annual Report, 1937', 31 Dec 1937; BSIP 14/51, DO WF to Medical Officer, Hospital of the Epiphany, Fauaabu, 1 July 1936.
39   Detailed documentation on Fauaabu is held by Helen Barrett, of Brisbane, a copy of which is in the author's possession. The orderlies were John Patterson Nana, Frederick Fafele, Simon Peter Nwasina, Thomas Tosia (short term), Joe Qai (short term) and Ereryn Tharetona (also a teacher).
40   Lambert 1933; 1946, 348–50; Hilliard 1978, 267–69; Boutilier 1974, 22, 31.

In 1933, the number of beds was increased to 80. Dr Maybury also began a leprosarium, which consisted of a small concrete ward surrounded by local-style houses for the patients. There were 79 leprosy (Hansen's disease) patients under treatment in 1930. Despite a government subsidy of £5 to a total cost of around £17 per patient each year, this facility closed in 1933 because of insufficient funds. It reopened on a smaller scale in 1938. Surveys in 1935–36 identified 239 definite and 44 suspected cases of leprosy on Malaita. Further detailed surveys were carried out the next year by Dr James Ross Innes, appointed by the administration.[41]

Figure 10.5: Qaibaita leper colony, the first in Solomon Islands, was established in 1929 as an outstation of the Hospital of the Epiphany at Fauaabu. In the 1930s it was moved closer, to a new site overlooking the hospital.
Source: British Museum, Lloyd Francis Collection, 4.

---

41 SINA, BSIP 27/VI/1, DO to SG, 'Annual Report, 1935', 14 Jan 1936, 28; Akin 2013a, 153; Innes 1938.

Figure 10.6: Patients at the Hospital of the Epiphany at Fauaabu.
Source: British Museum, Lloyd Francis Collection, 2.

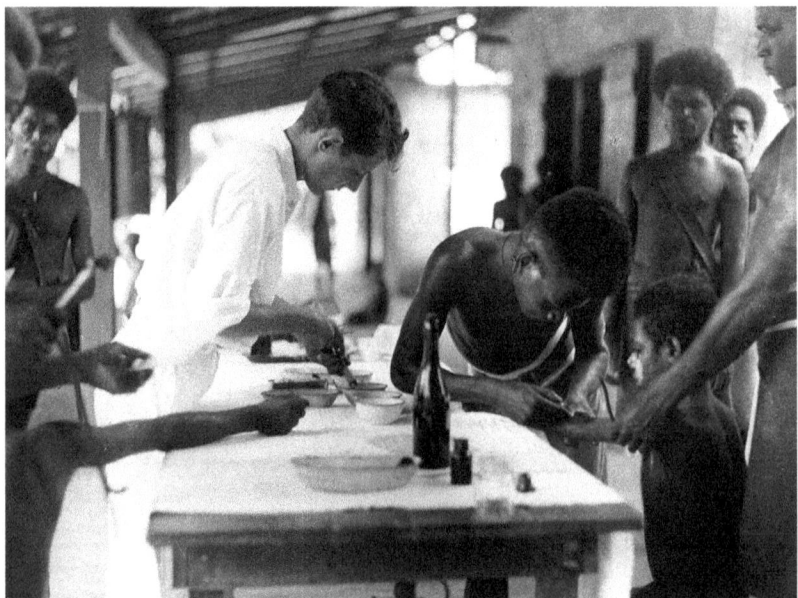

Figure 10.7: Training a young boy as a dresser (an orderly) at the Hospital of the Epiphany at Fauaabu.
Source: British Museum, Lloyd Francis Collection, 3.

Onwards from 1933, the SDAs established a primitive hospital at their Kwailabesi mission near Makwano on the shore of Lau Lagoon, which was run by Dr Dorothy Mills-Parker after she joined her husband A.F. Parker there, in 1934. While their proselyting was only marginally successful, their medical work in Lau and Makwano was a great success, although there were constant issues about infringing on Malaitan custom.[42]

There was no government medical policy for Malaita until 1930, with the only guidance coming from occasional visits from the Tulagi-based touring government medical officer, and DOs trying to deliver basic medical care. Then, in 1931, George Bogese, the first Solomon Islander to graduate from Fiji's Central Medical School as a Native Medical Practitioner (NMP), was based at ʻAoke, replaced in 1932 by NMP Fijian Malakai Ravai.[43] In 1934, Bogese was convicted of adultery and fined £4. He returned to Malaita again in 1936, and faced a number of serious related charges—rape, incest and indecent assault—concerning one of his daughters, but he was acquitted of them all. Laracy examined the evidence and concluded that the charges were missionary-motivated, and that no white medical officer would have faced the same level of scrutiny. That said, one does come away with the view that he was sexually delinquent.[44] He was replaced by Guso Rato Piko from Choiseul.[45] In turn, Piko was replaced by Eroni Leauli (another Fijian), and then by two mixed-race NMPs, first Hugh Wheatley, relieved by Geoffrey Küper (July 1940 – July 1941) while he was on leave. Piko also returned for a few months on relief duty during Küper's time.[46] In 1939, there were two dressers (male orderlies) employed at ʻAoke's leaf-house hospital and three village-based dressers in other parts of Malaita, with plans to place a NMP at Wairokai Harbour in west ʻAreʻare the next year.[47] Dr Nathaniel Critchlow, the BSIP travelling medical officer in the late 1920s and throughout the 1930s, also visited regularly on MV *Hygeia*. The NMPs were responsible for treating leprosy, but did so with varying levels of dedication: Ravai was

---

42 Steley 1983, 66.
43 Moore 2013c entry; Laracy 2013, 229–42.
44 Laracy 2013, 235.
45 Moore 2013c entry. SINA, BSIP 14/65, DO JCB to SG, 'Quarterly Report', 10 July 1933; BSIP 27/VI/1, DO John K. Brownlees to SG, 'Annual Report 1936', 1 Jan 1937.
46 Moore 2013c entry under 'Kuper, Heinrich'; Akin 2013a, 379 n 104.
47 SINA, BSIP 14/54, DO WFMC to Senior Medical Officer, 25 Sept 1939; DO CNFB to Senior Medical Officer, 29 July 1941; 14/54, DO Michael James Forster to Senior Medical Officer, 29 Feb 1940; Akin 2013a, 153.

effective, but Bogese lost the confidence of his patients.[48] A government leprosarium was built near 'Aoke in 1941 and a postnatal clinic was established at 'Aoke that same year.[49]

The one concerted disease eradication effort was the Rockefeller Foundation campaign to end yaws and hookworm. On Malaita in the 1920s, the infection rate of yaws was 60 to 65 per cent, and up to 90 per cent among coastal people. This disfiguring and painful disease produces high sickness and infant mortality rates. Intravenous and intramuscular injections of neo-arsphenamine were begun in the late 1920s, aided substantially by the Rockefeller campaign, which provided thousands of injections. Dr Lambert was the director of the 1928–31 campaign, with Dr Menzies in charge of one unit and Dr Harry B. Hetherington (Tulagi's government medical officer), assisted by Gordon White, was in charge of the other. Each European member of the team had two Islander helpers and a dresser. Native Medical Practitioners, missionaries and members of the foundation's medical team all gave injections throughout the protectorate, and this brought great relief from yaws. The missions also participated in the campaign: in 1929, staff of the Hospital of the Epiphany gave 696 injections. Individuals travelled long distances to get the 'nila' (needle). The Rockefeller visits continued during the 1930s. The drugs used brought a real improvement, although they were not totally effective. Penicillin, available starting in the 1940s, made an enormous difference.[50]

Although the missions had provided basic medical care since the 1890s and 1900s, their finances and abilities were limited. Once government services and overseas agencies like the Rockefeller Foundation began to intervene into medical care and hospitals like that at Fauaabu began, those Malaitans who received their help could see some return for taxation and incorporation into the protectorate.

---

48 SINA, BSIP 27/VI/1, DO GEDS to SG, 'Annual Report, 1936', 23 Dec 1941.
49 SINA, BSIP 14/54, DO WFMC to Senior Medical Officer, 25 Sept 1939.
50 *BSIP AR* 1930, 13–14; 1931, 6; Boutilier 1974, 28; Akin 2013a, 69–70; Moore 2013c entry 'Health: Yaws'.

Missions and Education

Education remained totally a preserve of the missions. The level of mission influence varied considerably. Small Malaita was mainly under Anglican and Catholic mission influence, with the SSEM the third group. The Melanesian Mission established a small theological college at Maka in 1935, which closed in 1939. The only substantial Melanesian Mission school was a 'Bible school' run at Fiu by Gwendoline Mason, wife of the resident missionary Rev. A.E. Mason. There were also many schools run by indigenous teachers.[51]

Figure 10.8: SSEM girls' school at Onepusu, with Mr and Mrs Cronau and son, and Miss Dring.
Source: Deck Collection, Black and White Photographs, 56.

The SSEM trained its own catechists at Onepusu, although the standard was considered to be too low to rate their exemption from taxation.[52] In 1935, the SSEM had 113 students at Afio and Onepusu, mainly from Malaita, along with a few from Guadalcanal and Makira. Onepusu School provided basic instruction in reading, writing, singing and manual training, and religious instruction. The Marist mission combined Christianity with education, and was teaching 93 students at Buma and

---

51 SINA, BSIP 27/VI, 1, DO WF to Government Secretary, 'Annual Report, 1935', 14 Jan 1936, 29–30, 39; BSIP 27/VI/1, DO GEDS to SG, 'Annual Report, 1937', 31 Dec 1937, 48.
52 SINA, BSIP 27/VI/1, DO GEDS to SG, 'Annual Report, 1924', 1 Jan 1935; BSIP 14/32, A/RC to Norman C. Deck, 9 Feb 1934.

Rokera. The SDAs slowly established schools, some run by indigenous teachers; although, as with the other denominations, Christian teachings were allied to literacy. Girls made up around one-third of the students in all schools.

Map 17: By the mid-1920s, the SSEM had spread throughout Malaita and Makira, with other bases on Guadalcanal, the Russell Islands and Rennell and Bellona Islands.
Source: Young 1925, facing 256.

The first major inquiry into education on Malaita occurred in 1939, conducted by William C. Groves, who was seconded from the Victorian Government in Australia. Groves reported that the SSEM operated training centres at Onepusu (for men) and Afio (for women), regional schools and innumerable small village-level schools. The village schools were 'Bible schools' in which the aim was to inculcate Christianity in adults and children through literacy in vernacular texts and the Bible in English. The teachers received help to establish themselves but were unpaid and expected to be self-sustaining. The dozen regional schools included boarding and day schools; the teachers were trained at Onepusu or Afio and standards there were higher than in the 'Bible schools'. There were 136 males and 36 females (mostly wives of male students) enrolled at Onepusu Training Centre. Their ages ranged from 15 to 50 and they were recruited from all areas where the SSEM operated (Malaita, Makira, Guadalcanal and Rennell Island). Afio Girls' Training School, situated at the western end of Maramasike Passage, enrolled 50 to 60 girls. Joan Deck (sister of Norman, Northcote and Kathy) was the principal, assisted by two European women. Students were taught literacy and handicrafts, the intention being to improve their education but not to alienate them from village life.

Even with its early start, the Melanesian Mission had become the minor partner to the SSEM. The only two Melanesian Mission European priests on Malaita were Rev. Mason at Fiu and Rev. Edwards at Maka Theological Training Institution. Gwounatolo, their new station in Lau Lagoon, was occupied by a group of indigenous Melanesian Brothers[53] who were responsible for teaching in the area. There was an indigenous priest at Fouia in Lau: the school there, planned to be staffed by four teachers, was in abeyance. Adjacent to Malu`u (the most advanced of the SSEM regional schools) was a small Melanesian Mission village school at A`ama operated by Rev. George Kiriau and a deacon, Benjamin Akwa, along with one teacher, Daniel Dosata. The latter had been trained at St Mary's School at Pauma on Makira and All Hallows' School at Pawa on Uki Island, the best schools in the protectorate.[54] As already mentioned, Gwendoline Child began teaching on Gela, married Albert Mason and ran schools at Fiu for boys and girls, with teaching in the local Kwara`ae language and in the Anglican *lingua franca* Mota. There were other village schools but all were faltering. During the five years it operated, Maka Theological Training Institution was the peak educational institution on the island, preparing students for the Anglican priesthood.

At Takwa in the Makwano region in the northeast were two Marist Catholic priests, fathers Joseph Halbwachs from France and Scanlon from New Zealand, and two Marist sisters. The boys' school there was closed

---

53 Moore 2013c entry.
54 *Ibid.*, see entries.

and the only students were 12 girls. The mission's ability to maintain students was limited by financial straits. Two more schools were operated at Buma by Father Donatien Coicaud, a lay-brother, two religious sisters and two lay-nursing sisters. Thirty-nine boys and young men attended one and 30 girls the other. Two younger priests and three sisters ran the Rokera station, where 43 boys and 45 girls attended school.

In 1939, the Seventh-day Adventist operation was centred at Kwailabesi in Lau Lagoon, close to the Marist station at Takwa and the Anglican station at Gwounatolo. Because no resident SDA European missionary had replaced the Parkers, the hospital was closed, although the school was proceeding efficiently under the care of a teacher from Marovo Lagoon, New Georgia. Ken Ferris, lately from the New Hebrides, had recently arrived to take over. The enrolment was 25 males aged between 10 and 25, and 10 or 12 girls. The language of instruction was Marovo, the SDA *lingua franca*. Students wore school uniforms, which was unusual for the time. Kwailabesi was the only station on Malaita where females wore clothes above the waist.

Malaitans were being educated in local languages, Mota, Marovo, Pijin English and English, an unsatisfactory mixture that compounded the problem of finding adequate texts. English was only in use on the SSEM stations, and even there the standards were low. Groves advised the government to impose more curriculum uniformity, which was difficult to accomplish when the schools were funded by individual, uncooperative denominations. Schools assisted development by teaching modern agricultural techniques, and they were also an avenue for training young women in modern domestic duties. One of Groves's major recommendations was that a central government school be established, which after the Second World War came to fruition as the 'Aoke Experimental School, later renamed King George VI School.[55]

Although there had been plans to begin government schools before the war started, the provision of 'Aoke Experimental School was in part a response to pressures from Malaitans during Maasina Rule. They were dissatisfied with the standards of the mission schools and felt that, as with medical care, better schooling was a reasonable government *quid pro quo* for taxation.

---

55   WPHC 4/IV MP 2736/1939, W. C. Groves, 'Education Report, Malaita', 21 Oct 1939; Moore 2013c entry.

Administration, Demography and Authority

After William Bell, there were a series of short secondments, then came three DOs who left significant marks on prewar Malaita: Englishman, Oxford-educated Jack Barley (1930–32, 1933); an Australian, George Eustace Sandars (police sub-inspector 1928, 1929–30, 1931–32, 1933–35, DO 1936–38, 1943, 1945–47); and a Londoner, Charles Bengough (acting, assistant and full DO 1934–35, 1936, 1938–40, 1940–43).[56] Others came and went in various assistant capacities, and, given the need to fill gaps in the BSIP administrative team, Barley, Sandars and Bengough were also moved around, a breach of the Lugard maxim for officers to have continuity in any position. Sandars and Bengough were close friends, with Sandars the mentor. Akin shows that despite their expertise, they failed to understand things as simple as Malaitan numerical systems and their phenomenal memory abilities, or the complexity of Malaitan systems of religion, kinship and morality. And like most officers, they stuck to the coast whenever possible and seldom ventured into the mountains. When they did travel inland they rarely socialised with the people there, including most headmen. Significantly for Malaitans, they seldom shared food, the core of reciprocal relations and friendship.[57]

In 1931, the BSIP carried out its first full population census, recording a total of 94,066: 89,568 Melanesians, 3,847 Polynesians, 478 Europeans, 164 Chinese and 9 Others.[58] With the help of the headmen and village constables, the DO calculated that there were 39,830 Malaitans on the island. The main island had an indigenous population of 34,486: 17,451 males and 17,035 females. Small Malaita had a population of 4,870: 2,749 males and 2,121 females. There were another 474 Malaitans in indentured or casual service or attached to mission stations in some capacity, and at least another 5,000 either working on indenture contracts or domiciled in other parts of the protectorate. The total Malaitan population was approximately 40,000, much lower than Bell's 1924 estimate of 60,000 to 70,000. There were also 135 other Solomon Islanders, one Fijian female (George Bogese's wife), the Bogeses' daughter, one man of part-Black American origin, 51 Europeans and three Chinese. Thirty-three

---

56 These details come from David Akin's useful list of the terms served on Malaita by BSIP officials.
57 Akin 2013a, 73–78.
58 McArthur 1961.

of the Europeans were missionaries.[59] There is reason to believe that the count was incomplete for inland areas, although even if it was wrong by several thousand the total population of the island must still have been under 45,000, with another 5,000 to 6,000 Malaitans elsewhere in the protectorate.[60]

Malaita's population had certainly declined during the late nineteenth and early twentieth centuries. We know this from piecing together fragments of information and comparison with neighbouring islands. Malaria remained endemic and debilitating, horrific yaws had been widespread, and tropical ulcers were commonplace. Some of the respiratory diseases were self-inflicted from living in smoky houses where cooking and heating fires were enclosed in the buildings. These diseases had long been part of Malaitan life, however, and the rapid population decline came from newly introduced ones—dysentery, influenza, measles, and presumably lung cancer, given the growing level of tobacco use. These new diseases were either introduced or exacerbated by traders, the labour trade and missionary and government contacts.

One of the most difficult things to estimate in the Pacific in the eighteenth and nineteenth centuries is the extent of population decrease through introduced diseases. In some areas, such as eastern Polynesia, the early postcontact death rate in the first 50 to 100 years has been estimated to have been as high as 90 per cent. Demographers caution, though, against accepting numbers based on random estimates by explorers and missionaries, before reliable census-taking. We are on surer ground with indigenous Fijians: the 1840s population estimate is 200,000 to 300,000, then more reliably 150,000 in 1874, 114,478 in 1881 and 84,470 in 1921. Using safe statistics, from 1874 to 1921, indigenous Fijians declined by at least 43 per cent, and probably more.[61] There is good reason to believe that this rate of decline, or higher, also occurred in Solomon Islands. Chapter 1 raised the possibility that the precontact population for the New Hebrides could have been 700,000 and that there was a rapid postcontact decline. Even if we regard this as an exaggeration, given that the modern Solomon Islands has twice the population of Vanuatu (New Hebrides), 500,000 is a possible precontact population for Solomon Islands (including Bougainville).

---

59   The official count is 41,052. The 45,000 is the composite figure suggested by DO Barley. BSIP 14/62, 'Census, 1931', DO JCB to SG, 6 June 1931.
60   Akin 2013a, 116.
61   Jolly 2000a.

10. MAKING MALA INTO MALAITA, 1927–42

Chapter 2 outlined the types of diseases introduced through missionaries, traders and the labour trade. When considering the size of Malaita's population, it is useful to note the calculation by Michael Scott of the rate of population decline on neighbouring Makira,[62] the number of Malaitans working overseas and within the protectorate, the death rate among labourers in Queensland and Fiji (around 24 to 30 per cent), and the constant importation of diseases. Even if we allow for a lower initial population because of less fertile soils (not renewed by volcanic activity as in Vanuatu, except on Bougainville) and the effects of the higher rainfall and the relative lack of seasonality nearer the equator, we can assume there was a greater than 50 per cent population decrease on Malaita.

There were times, such as during the 1860s and 1870s, when measles epidemics took many lives in Near Oceania. For instance, measles spread through areas of the New Hebrides in the 1860s, and killed about one-quarter of Fiji's population in the mid-1870s. Measles also spread through the Islander community in Queensland and into Torres Strait, and then passed into southern New Guinea.[63] At Mackay and other sugar towns in 1875–76, many hundreds of Islanders became infected with measles and large numbers died.[64] The incubation period of the disease is short—up to two weeks—so it may not have survived a voyage from Queensland to the Solomons; its survival on the shorter voyages out of Fiji is more likely. Measles may have spread through the archipelago in 1875 and 1876, even though Bennett's fine-textured research did not locate evidence of that, nor did I in my study of labour trade sources. Demographer Norma McArthur reports that measles epidemics in the New Hebrides in the 1860s were not universal, probably because of indigenous social and linguistic barriers to close personal contact. Similar patterns may have occurred in the Solomons,[65] but measles epidemics did erupt there in the 1880s and 1890s. The 1919–23 mortality rates during the Spanish influenza pandemic were very high, and mission and government records often refer to localised epidemics. Venereal diseases also spread, even though endemic yaws gave immunity to syphilis. Gonorrhoea and other venereal diseases may have caused sterility among women, although direct

---

62 Scott 2007, 82–88.
63 Mullins 1995, 123, 136–37, 145–46; Stone 1880, 48, 34, 92; 1876, 54.
64 *MM*, 29 Apr, 3; 31 July; 16 Oct, 13; and 20 Nov 1875; and 1 Jan 1876; *Queenslander*, 1, 22 and 28 Jan 1876; Mackay Cemetery Trust Register of Burials, 1875–76.
65 McArthur 1981, 16–18. I have one reference from mid-1875 that suggests measles had not yet reached the Solomons, but was expected soon. *MM*, 31 July 1875, report from Captain Rosengren of the *Lyttona*.

transmission by Europeans (whalers, traders, etc.) was unlikely on Malaita. Mercifully, there were no large outbreaks of smallpox in the Solomons. The disease did spread through northeast New Guinea and its eastern islands, and whalers may have brought the disease south into the Solomon Archipelago. Although smallpox was introduced into Tanna in the New Hebrides in 1853, there is no evidence of major outbreaks anywhere else in Near Oceania.[66]

Epidemics of bacillary dysentery and respiratory diseases such as influenza, pneumonia and whooping cough were common on Malaita and other Solomon Islands during the early twentieth century.[67] Based on the annual medical reports for the 1910s and 1920s, dysentery was almost endemic on plantations and anywhere Solomon Islanders were forced to congregate, such as prisons.[68] As mentioned in Chapter 9, dysentery epidemics in 1913–15 were thought to have killed no less than 5 per cent and possibly 10 per cent of the entire population, and 3 per cent of the population of the Solomons may have died during the first two years of the Spanish influenza pandemic, with much higher death levels recorded in some areas, for instance at Malu`u. These numbers balance well against Walter Ivens's 1924 estimate that the population of Sa`a in Small Malaita had halved since he first visited there in the mid-1890s. He also noted that there were few young children. In 1931, an influenza epidemic brought by the Anglican's *Southern Cross* was estimated to have killed 2.8 per cent of Malaita's population, an indication of what must have happened regularly after mission and labour trade ships started to visit in the 1870s.[69]

There was a survival advantage to living in scattered inland hamlets; this maintained adequate food supplies and could mitigate the spread of diseases. The highest death rates were always in the new Christian villages on or near the coast. Surprisingly, death rates were usually lower among

---

66   Measles killed one-quarter of Fiji's population in 1875, and 13 per cent of Rotuma's in 1911. Cliff and Haggett 1985, 26; Moore 1985, 263; Corris 1973b, 115–16; Saunders 1982, 88; Corney 1883–84, 85; Morens 1981; Shanks, Lee, Howard and Brundage 2011; Graves 1993, 79; Jolly 2000b; Moore 2003, 176–77; Bennett 1993, 38–40; McArthur 1981, 19–20.
67   SNA, BSIP 14/56, DO WRB to RC RRK, 15 Oct and 31 Dec 1923; BSIP 14/57, DO WRB to RC RRK, 8 Jan 1924; A/DO A. H. Studd to RC RRK, 17 Nov 1924.
68   WPHC, BSIP Annual Medical Reports, 1916–27. Photocopy in the possession of the author, courtesy of Ralph Shlomowitz.
69   Akin 2013a, 116; Scott 2007, 82–88. The population decline on Makira and Ulawa is much clearer. DO Barley collected statistics from his post on Makira, where half of the people died in a 1914 influenza epidemic. Walter Ivens believed that Ulawa's population had declined by a quarter between 1909 and 1924.

the lagoon-dwellers, who lived in crowded conditions but remained remarkably healthy. Christian villagers abandoned old sanitary rules that had served their ancestors well in the mountains but were now seen as belonging to a pagan world. And let us not forget endemic malaria, which debilitated most of the population, particularly around the coast and at lower altitudes, and killed unknown numbers. The population shift to the coast can only have increased the toll. Those most in contact with the colonial world also wore clothes, which, it was often said, caused sickness when worn wet and damaged their health.[70] Adding up the death estimates and allowing for smaller disease epidemics, Malaita's population could easily have declined by 40 or 50 per cent between the 1870s and 1930s.

David Akin provides a lengthy analysis of the depopulation phenomenon. Over several decades, Europeans blamed it on the inherent weakness of Melanesian cultures, what they saw as their unhealthy lifestyles and the people's inability to cope with being part of a global community. It is true that they were unable to withstand common European diseases, but they were also sometimes accused of having lost the will to live. This psychological explanation for depopulation permeated the thinking of missionaries and government officers. Their supposed weakness was used to justify government policies, well-meaning perhaps, but often social engineering gone wrong. The `Are`are were presented as a prime case of a demoralised people whose own customs relating to the size and frequency of mortuary feasts were dragging them down. DO Bengough also blamed their expensive courtship practices (*haruna*) and large marriage payments (*toraana*), said to discourage marriages. Officials also condemned the large number of mortuary feasts (*houraa*) for supposedly disrupting gardening, overburdening married men and forcing single men to stay that way, or at least to marry late, thus reducing birth rates.[71] The administration's solution was to limit the number of feasts and when they could occur (with no thought to the centrality of these feasts in Malaitan society).[72] Officials also wanted to cap bridewealth payments, and to limit compulsory road-building projects, which people saw to be essentially useless to them. Sandars suggested persuading the people to limit the timing of their feasts to periods when the *nali* nuts and yams were ripe (September–December

---

70 This could have been a colonial rationale for stopping 'natives' from adopting European ways.
71 Akin 2013a, 119–25; 375 n 73; 376 n 81; 377 n 85.
72 Coppet 1968; 1970a; 1970b; 1973; 1976; Coppet and Zemp 1978.

and April–May) and in plentiful supply. A few years later, this ploy was reported as being well-received, although by 1937 the limits had been rejected.[73]

The Pacific War probably provided the `Are`are a great advantage: it meant the British left them to their own devices for some years. It is no accident that, after the war, the Maasina Rule movement was founded in `Are`are in the same area where the British had concentrated their dubious repopulation efforts. Akin also points out that three of the foundational leaders—Arisimae, Hoasihau and Nono`oohimae—had all attended Fallowes movement meetings in Gela and came from the area where the government's social engineering scheme was concentrated.[74]

Subdistrict Leaders

Malaita in the 1930s had entered a new phase that would carry through until the Pacific War. The largest difference was that these were years of economic depression that stunted plantation growth and limited labour needs, consequently leading to a decline in government revenue. This had an impact on administration throughout the BSIP.

`Aoke had become a comfortable outpost, with a few eccentricities. The DO's house on the hill was described by Martin Clemens, who occupied it in 1938, as 'a pagoda-like structure', the walls added after the main frame. 'The result was that every time the wind blew, the roof rose until it was almost airborne, discharging a host of insects, and, on one occasion, a live rat, which danced a jig on top of my mosquito net.'[75] There was also a radio receiver, vastly improving communications with Tulagi.[76] Increasingly, part of the DO's portfolio was dealing with debts relating to bridewealth payments and other financial transfers between Malaitans on Malaita and elsewhere. Alec Maena, the district clerk since 1929, was capable of running the government station in the DO's absence, and the highly respected Guadalcanal man Sergeant-Major Jacob Vouza ran an

---

73   SINA, BSIP 27/VI/1, DO GEDS to SG, 'Annual Report, 1934', 1 Jan 1935; BSIP 27/VI/1, DO John K. Brownlees to SG, 'Annual Report, 1936', 1 Jan 1937; BSIP 27/VI/1, DO GEDS to SG, 'Annual Report, 1937', 31 Dec 1937, 22.
74   Akin 2013a, 105, 122–25. Two other key leaders of the movement, Stephen Sipolo of Kwai and `Abaeata Anifelo of Sinalagu, also attended Fallowes movement meetings (*ibid.*, 105).
75   Clemens 1962.
76   SINA, BSIP 14/54, DO CNFB to Engineer-in-Charge, Tulagi Radio, 28 Feb 1939.

efficient police force.⁷⁷ The battle for a permanent assistant DO was won for a few years after 1930 when a second government officer was stationed at Maka at the western entrance to Maramasike Passage, with a small ship provided for his use. The Great Depression soon put an end to this, and Maka was acquired by the Diocese of Melanesia as its short-lived training college.⁷⁸

In January 1934, the official correspondence contains a letter noting the transfer of 10 of the 30 police constables on Malaita back to Tulagi, justified because it was no longer necessary to maintain such a large police establishment. This is a clear sign that Malaita of the 1930s was different from Malaita of the 1910s and 1920s. While there was still plenty of police work to do, it was now more routine and the fears of counterattack from irate Malaitans had passed, except in east Kwaio (and even there the threat was imagined rather than real).⁷⁹ In 1934, DO Sandars asked for the force to be increased to 25 men, but his reasoning was very different from that used by earlier DOs:

> Although Malaita is certainly quieter than in those days, the work of the Police in their normal function grows heavier yearly owing to the work of investigation—a greater number of crimes being reported. This is not due to lawlessness but rather to the fact that the Malaitaman now comes to the Government to settle his differences instead of concealing them from the Administration.⁸⁰

Reported homicides, once several dozen a year, during the 1930s averaged only two to four a year. In 1935, offences against the person (35) and against property (26) were average for a district of the size of Malaita. The marked change was in adultery charges, of which there were 50 that year.⁸¹ There were still rumours of planned attacks on the DO,⁸² although all over Malaita authority structures were changing. Earlier Malaitan leaders owed their prominence to their acceptance within a 'line' of descent groups as *aofia*, *fataabu*, or *ramo*. While the new mission and administrative posts did not replace these leadership roles, and sometimes they were occupied by men who were also *aofia* or had been *ramo*, they did provide a new tier of authority. By the 1930s, most of the feared

---

77   Moore 2013c entry.
78   SINA, BSIP 14/61, DO JCB to SG, 27 Apr 1930.
79   SINA, BSIP 14/32, RC FNA to DO GEDS, 23 Jan 1934; Akin 2013a, 69, 362 n 57.
80   SINA, BSIP 14/65, DO GEDS to SG, 'Quarterly Report', 30 June 1934.
81   SINA, BSIP 27/VI/1, DO WF to SG, 'Annual Report, 1935', 14 Jan 1936, 35.
82   *Ibid.*, 16–19.

ramo of pre-1909 fame had died or were elderly: Arisimae and Ara'iasi in 'Are'are and Suina'o of To'aba'ita were the last surviving great *ramo*. In 1937, the only north Malaitan leader singled out as powerful, because he was a leading *fataabu* and *aofia*, was Raitalo (Taloanimae) of Fo'odo, who was respected throughout To'aba'ita.[83]

Malaita's DOs were ambivalent about implementing the Moorhouse report's recommendations on appointing local officials. Nevertheless, they all appreciated having an extra set of eyes and ears in the subdistricts to provide them with local information. Many of Jack Barley's appointments from the early 1930s were still serving up until, and even beyond, the Pacific War; he preferred weaker local officials who owed more to the administration than to their local communities.[84] Akin suggests that many of these local officials held no sway in mountain communities and seldom visited inland areas.[85] Malaita of the 1930s was divided into five administrative zones, contiguous with the main language divisions: Bali; Kwara'ae; Kwaio, 'Are'are; and Small Malaita. Bali in the north had a substantial population and although the people had a reputation as hot-headed, they also solved most disagreements through discussion, not violence. The Kwara'ae and the Langalanga were caricatured as the hardest workers, with the Kwara'ae district also heavily populated, and its language the most difficult to learn.[86] In 1938, the majority of the Kwara'ae were adherents of either the SSEM or the Melanesian Mission. The coastal Christian villages had attracted followers from far away, so reallocation of land resources was required, which caused disputes. The Kwaio district included the island's most rugged mountains and its people were always depicted as taciturn and conservative: dour, abrupt, suspicious of outsiders and apt to resort to their own methods of justice. As mentioned earlier, the 'Are'are were regarded as little better, and depicted as perpetually wandering from one feast to another, neglecting their gardens.[87] The people of Small Malaita were described more favourably since they were industrious producers of copra and trochus shell, early converts to Christianity, and closely related to the inhabitants of Makira and Ulawa, which stood them apart (though many of them

---

83 SINA, BSIP 27/VI/1 1937, DO GEDS to SG, 'Annual Report, 1937', 31 Dec 1937.
84 Akin 2013a, 70.
85 *Ibid.*, 62–63.
86 Deck 1933–34; Ivens 1931.
87 Ivens 1931, 114–28.

were 'Are'are people.) While each of these descriptions was in itself a trope, this is how Europeans saw the various Malaitan groups. Every annual report repeats some variation of the same pattern.

Subdistrict administration had devolved to 47 headmen, subheadmen and village constables, though most of these men had limited practical power and little formal education, the majority being illiterate. They were appointed supposedly because they were respected in their communities, but BSIP officers also kept a weather eye on their likelihood to toe the government line. They were the core of the administration throughout Malaita, with 26 of them stationed north of 'Aoke and 21 to the south. District Officer John White summed them up this way:

> Some were appointed after service under the Government in another capacity—and have no other qualifications—others have some Government service training and are also the Chiefs of 'lines' that form part of their subdistrict, whilst others hold their office by virtue of a tyranny in pregovernment days when their force of character, personality and truculence earned them universal respect.[88]

These men were tasked with keeping birth, marriage and death registers (though their efficiency in doing so depended on their level of literacy) and they had a rudimentary knowledge of what the government was trying to achieve.

There is no one pattern as to how Malaitan men became government headmen. Protectorate officers looked for several things. First, they had to be willing to do the job, and the pay was not much better than could be obtained as a labourer. They needed to have leadership qualities, or at least the possibility of developing them. Already being a community leader was a good thing but not essential. Former policeman had an advantage, and ability in Pijin English was useful. Being too closely tied to a mission was a disadvantage, because they might be easily influenced by the missionaries. And although being an outright scoundrel was not considered a good quality, having a forceful personality was helpful. Literacy was not crucial, so long as they had family members who could help with the recording tasks. The best of them were excellent. Timothy Kakalu'ae, son of Kwaisulia of Lau Lagoon, worked with 'dignity and with complete lack of ostentation', controlling his subdistrict. DO William Fowler went on to describe him as 'very intelligent', 'deeply interested in any new departures and developments' and 'intensely loyal'. Other local officials, while they

---

88 SINA, BSIP 14/63, A/DO A. John F. White to RC FNA, 30 Aug 1932.

were criticised for shortcomings, were also praised: Maekali at Malu`u, Ouasihu at Wairokai, Mamama at Fo`odo, Siru at Kwai and Doraweewee on Small Malaita.[89] Maekali was the most powerful headman, and in the 1930s he was allowed to judge serious cases unaided, although there was always a review by the DO. Maekali was a strong leader, both loved and hated by his people.[90] However, the administrative team also included former *ramo* such as Ara`iasi at Tarapaina, and elderly Arisimae at Wairokai Harbour, who were still feared because of their old positions. Arisimae, who retired from government service in the mid-1930s, was still consulted on matters of custom. Suina`o from Malu`u and Bita`ama, the youngest of the surviving northern *ramo*, was never added to the team, but was an extremely powerful leader and sought out for advice.[91]

Map 5 (Chapter 1) shows the Bina and related descent groups in east Fataleka. The first east Fataleka headman was Harry Rafe from the Kanole descent group cluster, who had worked in Fiji. (The British recorded him as from `Ataa, which was not his primary place of allegiance.) Lotaa from the Rakwane descent group held the deputy headman position from 1925 to 1927. He had worked on plantations in the Western Solomons. Both Lotaa and Rafe spoke Pijin English, Rafe also spoke Pijin Fijian, and they were wise to the ways of Europeans. Rakwane was the most powerful descent group in east Fataleka, with a direct line of descent from Bina, the founding clan. Kanole descent group was likewise important, being a large 'line' among inland descent groups. Both men were appointed by William Bell, but their authority depended on their preeminence within east Fataleka. Lotaa resigned in 1927 when Bell was killed, but Rafe continued in his position until succeeded by Alatala from Farere, a descent group from an artificial island at `Ataa, closely related to Rakwane. Alatala only held the position for about one year before he was sacked for corruption. He was followed by Fono from Kanole for two years, but Fono was dismissed when he objected to collecting the head tax, replaced by Kwaisiisigwa from Gwalekafo Village in Kanole, for another year or so until he too was dismissed, for stealing pigs. Nenemo from Fusai followed, serving for about four years; he died from tuberculosis late in the Pacific War. Ishmael Itea, Lotaa's son, was appointed headman in 1947 and held the position until 1975. Itea, an ex-labourer and policeman, had in 1942 joined the

---

89   SINA, BSIP 27/VI/1, DO WF to SG, 'Annual Report, 1935', 14 Jan 1936, 6–7.
90   Akin 2013a, 84–86.
91   SINA, BSIP 14/63, DO to RS FNA, 'Quarterly Report', 2 Apr 1932; BSIP 27/VI/1, DO GEDS to Government Secretary, 'Annual Report, 1934', 1 Jan 1935, 19.

British Solomon Islands Defence Force assisting the Allies. In 1943 he served as part of the guard for the high commissioner in exile on Malaita. Itea said that he was chosen to be the next headman by the powerful Ilokwao, the last *foakali* (senior *fataabu*) of Bina, and presented to the DO as the most suitable candidate. It may well be that after Bell DOs tried to select compliant leaders, but this was never so in east Fataleka, where local people helped to find the best candidate.[92]

These new-style bigmen remained an alternative power base to the European missionaries, overwhelmingly from the SSEM, and a growing group of indigenous mission teachers, also mainly from the SSEM, although indigenous Anglican priests had also begun to make their mark. Education was entirely in the hands of the missions, run through 'Bible schools', which used access to literacy to win converts for Christianity rather than pursuing a more robust educational process. Whereas once Malaitan men aspiring to transcend their normal lives had left the island to work as labourers, beginning in the 1920s two other paths became available: joining the government or the missions. Literacy, gained through the missions and a path for advancement since the 1880s, became an increasingly important cultural bridge during the early decades of the century.

The subdistrict system and the three levels of Malaitan officials became more settled and organised. Boundaries were delimited and more isolated areas were included in the web of administration.[93] The subdistricts on the east coast were still largely beyond effective administrative contact—the coastal people viewed government officers as primarily tax-collectors and hunters of murderers, while people living inland remained mostly aloof in their isolated small hamlets. DO Barley wrote:

> The District Headmen are, for the most part, trying to do their best under the circumstances, but it must be remembered that they have in the past been taught to regard themselves as men in charge of so many 'Tax-houses' only, that they are quite unaccustomed to acting as agents in bringing their people into personal contact with the Government and are in fact, in many instances, afraid to venture without Police protection into various parts of their sub-Districts which are supposed to be under their administrative control.[94]

---

92 Information collected by the author in east Fataleka in 1976; Laracy and White 1988, 118.
93 SINA, BSIP 14/61, DO JCB to SG, 3 July 1930.
94 SINA, BSIP 14/28, DO JCB to SG, 'Quarterly Report to 30 June', 3 July 1930.

The subdistricts were established along linguistic, tribal and political boundaries, as understood by the DOs. Slowly, they became geographic administrative units, each with a tax-house erected on the coast at a recognised meeting and market place frequented by both coastal and inland people. The subdistricts' boundaries were clear on the coast, but not inland.

The colonial administration's communication was mainly by small government vessels and the decaying coastal road to the north. During the late 1930s, this road—really a 2.7-metre-wide track—was renewed around the north from 'Aoke to Lau Lagoon, and there were plans to extend it south along the east coast to 'Ataa. The main vehicles were envisaged to be bicycles, of which there were already a few on Malaita. DOs in the 1930s also noted that a road was needed across the central mountains from Dala to Fokanakafo (later the route of the first cross-Malaita road, built in the 1970s), and another in 'Are'are from Wairokai in the west to Takataka in the east (not built to this day).[95]

Native Councils and Courts

Extra Native Administration Regulations were passed in 1929, added to the already onerous 1922 Regulations. Villages had to be sanitary and structurally reorganised along lines that officers felt were proper. Violators could end up in the native courts.

Local councils in the Solomons were developed in a very *ad hoc* manner and initially the emphasis was on the codification of custom. Early experiments in local government began with the Melanesian Mission's Vaukolu gathering on Gela from 1887, later taken over by the government, and then sidelined.[96] However, in 1939 the government began trials of local government bodies in north Malaita. Each district was split into a series of territorial divisions known as administrative subdistricts. Establishing native courts to deal with customary offences was discussed as early as 1929, but the high commissioner concluded that customary law needed to be codified first, with differentiation between Christians

---

95   SINA, BSIP 27/VI/1, DO GEDS to SG, 'Annual Report, 1937', 31 Dec 1937; BSIP 27/VI/4, DO WFMC to SG, 'Annual Report, 1939', 31 Dec 1939. Sir Peter Kenilorea gives an amusing account of a trip he made over this proposed route in 1972 (2008, 175–77).
96   Moore 2013c entry; Akin 2013a, 56–58, 358 n 22; Bennett 1987, 92.

and followers of ancestors, particularly on Malaita. This approach was impracticable and native courts slowly evolved without codification. The native court concept was boosted by the support in 1934 of anthropologist H. Ian Hogbin, who had visited Rennell Island briefly, researched his doctorate on Ontong Java in 1927, and then completed more fieldwork on Guadalcanal and north Malaita in 1933. Hogbin, a strong advocate of native administration, suggested reasserting the powers of bigmen to mediate and judge in customary situations. DOs tried to make a deeper study of customary laws and the geographic boundaries of language areas, although they still had little understanding, and these early local courts had no legal standing. By the late 1930s, based on very partial and sometimes erroneous government knowledge of indigenous cultures, native arbitration courts began to operate. The first started in 1939 on Isabel and in To`aba`ita in north Malaita, in 1940 on Small Malaita, and in 1941 in Baelelea and Baegu, also in northern Malaita. These councils began working to codify custom within their particular areas. Kwara`ae operated under a single native court from October 1941.[97] Discussions were underway for similar courts in Kwaio and `Are`are, aimed particularly at limiting the elaborate *houraa* mortuary ceremonies that officers and some local people saw to be problematic.

DO Bengough was dubious about the ability of the courts to judge properly, and since there was no extra money to train headmen, the process was muddled.[98] Similar courts and councils began in other districts between 1940 and the Pacific War. Some of the government headmen were unhappy with the courts because they cut into their authority (forgetting that they in turn had themselves cut across earlier indigenous authority). Solving land disputes through the court system became more common in the 1930s, particularly in Western District and in north Malaita and also around `Aoke. A Native Courts Ordinance was passed in 1942 to create a mechanism for solving local disputes. Hogbin, advisor to the BSIP on the establishment of local courts, prepared a booklet in 1942 on native councils and courts. He was always optimistic, but here proved overly so regarding the level of success the courts had or would have, and the Pacific War derailed any real progress under government auspices, since the government essentially ceased to function on Malaita.[99]

---

97 SINA, BSIP 14/67, DO CNFB to SG, 'Quarterly Report', 30 Oct 1941.
98 Akin 2013a, 128–30.
99 Bennett 1987, 210–12, 397–404, 281–82.

Between 1940 and 1942, various district officers established local court systems on a trial basis. In 1944, High Commissioner Sir Philip Mitchell proposed a system of local councils based on his work while posted in Uganda in the 1930s. When the administration resumed after the war, by 1946 Isabel had 4 separate councils, Choiseul 7, Guadalcanal 13, Gela 3, and Malaita 15.[100] While colonial officials believed Malaitans were inflexible in their customary beliefs, they also worried that codification might make customary beliefs still less flexible. David Akin points out that although Malaitans do have strong beliefs, they are also very political and have proved adept at modifying indigenous codes in changing circumstances; evidence for this reaches back to the Queensland and Fiji labour period. Compensatory payments were a necessity in most customary court negotiation, although BSIP officers often made poorly informed decisions regarding how to allocate awards.[101] DO Barley, who opposed appointing local officials, was also against codification and asserted that Malaitans were incapable of serving impartially on native courts.[102] Akin gives a neat summary of Malaitan attitudes and abilities:

> When Malaitans assess disputes they often draw on deep local knowledge of long-term, complex relationships of the disputants and their groups. Such sophistication comes only from enduring social engagement. I have often heard Kwaio declare their inability to properly evaluate disputes between Kwaio who live far away and whom they do not know well, citing their lack of social and historical knowledge about the case and its principals. In any Malaitan community certain individuals are known for their superior knowledge of social networks and legal and other histories and for having the brains, talent and integrity to effectively apply it to skilfully managing disputes; they are called on when trouble arises.[103]

It was no different in the 1920s and 1930s, and like many colonial officials, the DOs had to rely on knowledgeable Malaitans to advise them when hearing disputes. Listening to and watching the reaction of an audience at a court case was sometimes their best recourse in deciding on their verdicts.[104]

---

100 Hogbin 1944; 1945–46.
101 Akin 2013a, 82–84.
102 *Ibid.*, 65.
103 *Ibid.*, 79–80.
104 *Ibid.*, 81.

10. MAKING MALA INTO MALAITA, 1927–42

Customs and Punishments

Malaita in the 1930s was no longer the old Mala. Malaitans mixing together as labourers in Queensland, Fiji, Samoa, New Caledonia and the BSIP introduced new languages, particularly Pijin English and Pijin Fijian (though the latter soon faded as a viable *lingua franca*). The diversity of languages spoken on Malaita had never been an insurmountable barrier. Malaitans who travel outside of their own language areas say that they can 'hear' the other languages even if they cannot reply fluently in them; although, say, `Are`are in the south would have to strain to communicate with To`aba`ita from the far north. The intermixing of labourers and mission workers only increased their abilities to communicate across languages, and Pijin English developed into a stable common language.[105] One telling indicator of change was a June 1934 request from the Burns Philp manager at Makambo for Langalanga dancers to perform for tourists on visiting Burns Philp ships, in addition to the stevedores who already danced as a sideline.[106] Exactly what they performed is unknown, but one photograph shows dancers at Fauaabu hospital in the 1930s who seem to be combining elements of *mao* and possibly *sango* performances. This may be similar to the dances that were performed for tourists at Tulagi. Malaitans were improvising and changing cultural performances to meet new circumstances.

Also in 1934, for the first time, Malaitans gained access to what an anthropologist had written about them. A copy of Ian Hogbin's *Oceania* article on his fieldwork on Guadalcanal and Malaita (1934) was available at Malu`u and caused annoyance because of erroneous comments he made on the prevalence of incest. DO Sandars, who did not like Hogbin, said that the To`aba`ita had good reason to complain since they were 'the most strictly moral' of all Malaitans.[107] The missions and the government brought about major changes in local activities such as bridewealth exchanges at marriages. Inflation had increased the size of such payments to such an extent that they exceeded the ability of many young men to pay. This meant that some men could no longer marshal enough bridewealth contributions to get married, or remained bachelors so as to avoid the great social debt to contributors that would result. SSEM adherents in

---

105 Keesing 1988a; 1988b.
106 SINA, BSIP 14/32, Manager, Burns Philp (South Sea) Company Ltd to RC FNA, 18 Aug 1934.
107 SINA, BSIP 14/65, DO GEDS to SG, 'Quarterly Report', 1 Oct 1934.

east Kwara'ae had fixed bridewealth at three *tafuli'ae* (10 joined strings of shell wealth a fathom (1.82 metres) long, valued at £3 per *tafuli'ae*) for a single woman and one *tafuli'ae* for a widow. DO White suggested that attempts should be made to establish this as the standard throughout Malaita.[108]

Figure 10.9: This dance was performed at the Hospital of the Epiphany at Fauaabu in the early 1930s.

Close examination shows a wooden structure on poles in the centre, around which singers would have been sitting, and a slit drum. The performance appears to have been staged for visitors and may be a hybrid form of *mao* and *sango* dance performance, or simply a Fauaabu area variation of *mao*.

Source: British Museum, Lloyd Francis Collection, 3; David Akin's analysis 13–14 Dec 2015.

The demographic changes caused by the formation of large Christian villages around the coast had multiple consequences. Except on the crowded artificial islands, most Malaitans had always lived in small hamlets. The new concentrations were foreign and provided a much freer lifestyle, which altered moral standards as men and women mixed more freely, separate accommodation of males and females ceased, and

---

108 SINA, BSIP 14/63, A/DO AFJW to RC FNA, 3 May 1932; BSIP 14/30, RC FNA to A/DO AFJW, 5 Apr 1932. Intra-mission debates over the proper size of bridewealth carried on for decades and continue still.

older authority and behavioural rules faded in import. Adultery, once punishable by death, became more common, even though it went against both Christian and indigenous teachings. In 1924, a new law punished male and female adulterers with a £5 fine or three months in prison, with six months for a second offence.[109] Penalties were increased again in 1929, with an agreement that the full severity of the law would be applied only on Malaita. Akin researched a sample of 225 court cases on Malaita between 1931 and 1935 and found that 20 per cent involved adultery.[110] The court statistics for 1935 reveal that adultery convictions from Christian settlements were twice as high as among the majority of Malaitans who still followed their ancestors. Malaitans, particularly non-Christians, were never happy with what they saw to be the light punishments dished out for adultery. The maximum penalty after 1929 was one year in prison, and two years for a second offence. In some cases the sentence was only four months. Although few Malaitans continued to advocate death as the fitting punishment for adultery, most still thought the offence warranted at least a 10-year sentence.[111]

Another area of difference between the government and Malaitans was sorcery and its punishment. The government wanted to end the power of the *ramo* to punish transgressions, yet it was unwilling to punish sorcery, which most Europeans, with the exception of some missionaries, thought was mere superstition or the work of charlatans. But to Malaitans it was real and an alternative to tangible punishment. By the 1930s, Malaitans were convinced sorcery had increased due to government inaction and officers were at a loss as to how to deal with the issue.[112]

Other changes were beyond government control. A taro blight ruined crops on Malaita during the mid-1920s and caused a switch to the sweet potato as the root crop staple. This had social consequences since many crucial ceremonial rituals were focused on taro and yam gardening.[113] Taro and yam gardens were a source of pride for men, who worked hard in them. Both declined as crops, and as they did many associated rituals and linkages between different regions on Malaita faded away or were

---

109 Akin 2013a, 89–91.
110 *Ibid.*, 89–90.
111 SINA, BSIP 14/66, DO GEDS to SG, 'Quarterly Report', 10 Apr 1935, 21; N. C. Deck to RC FNA, 3 May 1935.
112 Akin 2013a, 91.
113 Packard 1975 reports on a taro blight that struck Bougainville in the 1940s, which was an extension of the same problem that began on Malaita in the 1920s.

greatly simplified. Sweet potato was viewed as a woman's crop, which changed gender dynamics and led to more women's work, just as had the introduction of metal gardening tools. In Kwaio, people believe their taro has never fully recovered from the attacks and shrine desecrations by police patrols following the massacre of William Bell and his party in 1927. The Kwaio way of dealing with the blight was to reintroduce feral taro varieties and breed them with the domestic verities, showing a sophisticated knowledge of horticultural techniques.[114]

The last great divide remaining was between the Christians and those who still followed their ancestral religions. There were many tensions, for example over non-Christian claims of *fa`abua* (compensation) against Christians, for everything from sexual trespass to homicides. Many Christians rejected what they said was a payment to the devil and protested that compensation rules no longer applied to them, but they nevertheless feared the consequences of outright refusal to pay.

Figure 10.10: Peter Abu`ofa in old age working on carving a slit drum. By the time Abu`ofa died in 1937 he had become alienated from the SSEM, which he helped found.
Source: Deck Collection Coloured Glass Slides, 5.

---

114 SINA, BSIP 29/I/4, DO WFMC to SG, 30 June 1939; Akin 1993, 230–34; 2013a, 18, 401 n 81.

Conclusion

The coming war was beginning to affect Malaita. By 1939, there are references in the official correspondence to the war raging in Europe and thoughts about forming a local militia. In east Kwaio, a story circulated that an important ancestress spirit, La`aka, had announced that American warships and troops would soon arrive and destroy Tulagi and the BSIP administration. When the ships did not arrive at Uru Harbour on the predicted day, the organisers were arrested, but not before many people had killed pigs or, in a few areas, left their homes and resettled within two specified, protected villages.[115]

The 1940 and 1941 annual reports provide a snapshot of Malaita just before the Pacific War. Labour recruiting for plantations had steadily decreased. Very few signed on at `Aoke, most being taken to Tulagi where they signed in front of the inspector of labour. Even the regular movement of labour from Langalanga to Tulagi to work as stevedores had dwindled. Taxes had recently been collected from 8,298 Malaitans, 85 per cent of them at only 1/-. Whereas in late 1900 no Europeans lived permanently on Malaita, in 1910 there were 16, along with a Fijian, some Indigenous Australian women, and a few New Hebrideans. In 1941, Malaitans on the island were said to number around 41,100, and 49 Europeans and one Chinese resided there. There were also 300 cattle, five horses and 20 goats.

The four Christian denominations were now well-established and their congregations together were equal to the number of Malaitans who still practised their ancestral religions. Presuming these statistics are correct, the early rates of conversion to Christianity had slowed in the 1920s and 1930s. Health facilities had increased from nil to several small hospitals, leprosariums and a postnatal clinic. Schools of various types were functioning, although their standards were low. Thousands of Malaitan men continued to enlist as indentured labourers, even at the reduced pay rates. From a situation where the DO did not feel safe even in his house at `Aoke, now a team of local administrators was spread throughout the island.

---

115 SINA, BSIP 29/I/4, DO WFMC to SG, 'Quarterly Report', 30 Sept 1939. David Akin has corrected Bengough's and Clemens' much exaggerated reports. Akin 2013a, 106–09.

There were two motorised district vessels, a far cry from Edge-Partington and Bell in their whaleboats. The MV *Auki*, now 44 years old, was about to be retired and replaced by MV *Mala II*. Roads and bridges were under construction: the upgraded northern road was complete and the west coast end of one from 'Aoke to Kwai on the east coast was being cleared. A demonstration farm had been established on the Kwaibala River near 'Aoke in 1941, on the site that later became King George VI School. Paddy rice had been introduced in north Malaita and at Bina and Anoano. Commercial agriculture was now limited to the Fairymead Sugar Company plantations at Baunani and Manaba, where 900 hectares of coconut palms produced 370 tons of copra a year, and 16 hectares was planted with cocoa. To save money, the two plantations were being run as one. Trade was minimal—there were five Chinese trade stores in 1940, and still none at 'Aoke. By 1941, only one remained open, although Chinese trading vessels were still circumnavigating the island.[116]

The rudiments of the new Malaita were in place, supressed by economic depression, but about to experience revolutionary changes due to the Pacific War.

---

116 SINA, BSIP 27/VI/5, DO CNFB to SG, 'Annual Report, 1940', 31 Dec 1940; BSIP 27/VI/6, DO CNFB to SG, 'Annual Report, 1941', 31 Dec 1941.

Conclusion: Tropes, *Kastom* and the Modern Solomon Islands

> Maleita, unknown as yet, dark with records of savagery and cannibalism, stretches as far as the eye can see backwards and forwards… I have seen some of them on Maleita who seemed not only savage, but wild…
>
> —Bishop Henry H. Montgomery, *The Light of Melanesia* (1896)[1]

> Malaitans are fierce. Malaitans are warlike. Malaitans are mysterious. There are points on which all people in the Solomon Islands agreed, especially the Malaitans themselves. It was Malaitans who made the last great stand against colonialism in 1927, when they smashed the skull of a British tax collector and murdered his fourteen assistants. It was Malaitans who controlled the police, who had outwitted and humiliated the Guadalcanal militants, who had the government under their thumb. It was Malaitans who still offered blood sacrifice to the sharks and octopuses that prowled their lagoons. It was Malaitans, or at least a few thousand villagers in the island's Kwaio highlands, who still refused the Church and the authority of the government.
>
> —Charles Montgomery, *The Last Heathen* (2004)[2]

This concluding chapter briefly describes the direct effect of the Pacific War on Malaita and attempts to consider the tropes that still dominate discourses on the island. Outsiders and other Solomon Islanders have developed some fixed views on how Malaitans behave that have no anchor in reality. Yet, there are intriguing aspects about Malaita that are a challenge to explain. One, of course, is that there are so many individuals of Malaitan descent in Solomon Islands that they cannot fail to dominate the nation. We can unravel the tropes but no one can doubt their dominance. There are also peculiarities about Malaitan Christianity,

---

1   Montgomery 1896, 175, 176.
2   Montgomery 2004, 178.

particularly recent beliefs that some hold about their descent from the Lost Tribes of Israel. These beliefs are more pronounced in north Malaita, though they have also spread to some central areas. This idea probably dates back to the origins of the SSEC in the QKM. My conclusion is that historical circumstances have made Malaita different from other Solomon Islands.

The Pacific War

Evacuation of Tulagi, other administrative centres, plantations and missions began in late December 1941, first the women and children, followed by government and commercial companies' staff and equipment. On 22 January 1942, Japanese aircraft bombed Gavutu, next to Tulagi, and the first retaliatory shot was fired. The last European civilians were evacuated from Tulagi on SS *Morinda* on 8 February, which although bombed on its voyage managed to escape damage. The Japanese occupied Bougainville in March and landed in the Shortland Islands on 10 April. From January to May 1942, a small Australian force based at Tulagi watched and attempted to harass the Japanese, and the Royal Australian Navy employed local government officers and planters to form a chain of Coastwatchers, who remained behind to monitor the Japanese presence.[3] Tulagi was first strafed on 29 January, then Tulagi, Gavutu-Tanambogo and Makambo were bombed intermittently during March and April. After heavy air raids on 1 and 2 May, Tulagi fell on 3 May, and then, starting on 20 June, the Japanese occupied Guadalcanal. In late July they began building an airfield at Lunga and a camp at nearby Kukum, from which they intended to harass Allied shipping in the Pacific and operations in nearby New Guinea.[4]

In late January, Resident Commissioner William Marchant began to move the government headquarters to `Aoke, taking with him crucial government documents, particularly Secretariat, Lands and Treasury files, which were later sent via Port Vila to Sydney. Marchant travelled back

---

3   Horton 1970; Lord 1977.
4   There is a huge literature on the Second World War in Solomon Islands. Some of it is written purely from an American point of view, and most does not relate to Malaita. The best work including Solomon Islanders is Laracy and White 1988; White, Gegeo, Akin and Watson-Gegeo 1988; White and Lindstrom 1989; Akin 2013a, ch. 4; Lindstrom and White 1990; and Bennett 2009.

and forth to Tulagi and was in constant contact with the Coastwatchers.[5] The Tulagi Masonic Lodge's paraphernalia was shifted to a village near 'Aoke. The Anglican bishop packed up the altar silver and relics at Siota and hid them in another Malaitan village. District Officer Charles Bengough was despatched to north Malaita to begin coastwatching duties on 4 April, but was often back in 'Aoke. Refugees from Gizo, Choiseul and the Shortlands travelled to 'Aoke in small boats, from where they joined SS *Morinda*, which left for Sydney on 8 February.

Marchant moved his headquarters to Furi'isango (also written as Fulisango) in the hills behind 'Aoke on 4 May. His core group included DO Bengough, the Tulagi wireless officer T.W. Sexton, H.W. Bullen of the Melanesian Mission who acted as a cypher officer, and the Anglican bishop, followed later by the Catholic bishop. Others came and went with regularity, such as the Coastwatchers and Dr Thomson. This secret government in Malaitan leaf houses lasted for a few months. Bishop Walter Baddeley continued to visit the Anglican hospital at Fauaabu, which was still open, although there were plans to evacuate it to a safe inland village where a secondary dispensary had been prepared. Also with Marchant, but forgotten in war histories, were a group of police and other Malaitans that included Jasper Irofiala of Fo'odo, Salana Ga'a of Areo near 'Aoke, Ishmael Itea and Eban Funusau (aka Sau) from Fataleka, and Tome Toloasi Teoboo of east Kwaio. They were to become important postwar leaders, all but Itea within the Maasina Rule movement. There was also the 'Aoke clerk Alec Maena, from the Western Solomons.[6]

In late July, a troop of Japanese soldiers landed on Malaita at Afufu, which moved on to loot the Hospital of the Epiphany's operating theatre on 28 July, and then on 30 July arrived at the government headquarters at 'Aoke where they took small items. They also seized some of the Anglicans' boats. The Japanese maintained a small base 32 kilometres north of Fauaabu until about November. Their arrival caused consternation among the local people and Marchant reported some collaboration.[7] The war did

---

5   The Coastwatchers were prewar planters, officials and missionaries, mainly from Australia and New Zealand, and New Guinean and Solomon Islander scouts, who went into hiding after the Japanese invasion in 1942 and formed a secret communication system to monitor enemy shipping and planes for the Allies. They also rescued Allied personnel who were stranded. There were around 100 Coastwatchers in the South Pacific. Many were stationed in Papua New Guinea and 24 in the Solomon Islands, including two in Bougainville. Their activities were crucial to alerting the Allied forces of approaching Japanese bombing raids.
6   Marchant 1942–43; Trench 1956; Baddeley 1942.
7   Marchant 1942–43, 31 July 1942; Baddeley 1942, 5–6.

affect Malaita physically, although only lightly compared with surrounding islands. Malaitans watched hundreds of planes flying overhead, a few sites on Malaita were bombed and warships neared the coast. Fo'odo mission station was bombed by the Japanese on 6 August, killing six people. The only permanent Japanese installation was a lookout and radio post at Cape Astrolabe in the far north, which Americans destroyed on 4 November, guided there by people from Malu'u and Fo'odo. The Americans contemplated the possibility that the Japanese might invade Malaita and briefly sent a seaplane tender to the west mouth of Maramasike Passage on 7 August, but only for two days. That same day, a Catalina seaplane that was anchored in the entrance to Maramasike Passage accidentally hit a reef and remains there still. Another Catalina crashed off 'Are'are Lagoon in November 1943, killing six of the 10 crew.

The worst damage was done on Malaita by the Americans. Probably because of a navigational error, on 7 July 1942 American planes bombed Laulasi Island in Langalanga Lagoon, killing 18 people and wounding several others, the war's worst mistaken Allied bombing in the Solomons. The Americans also inexplicably bombed Gamu in To'aba'ita, a canoe in Uru Harbour in east Kwaio, Fousaari'i and Hauhari'i (Sail Rock) at Small Malaita, Anutu Island and Takataka in 'Are'are.[8]

Several planes ditched around Malaita. One Japanese bomber crashed on Da'i Island after bombing Lunga Point on Guadalcanal. After a fight with American planes, another Japanese plane ditched near the river at 'Ataa, and the 'Aoke police, led by Corporal Beni Ramo'alafa, were sent over to capture the four survivors.[9] A third Japanese plane went down at Malu'u, there is an unidentified plane site at Afoa Village on the east coast of north Malaita, and another American plane lies close to the west coast. One American plane ditched into Sinalagu Harbour in east Kwaio. Once the Americans were in control they erected a beacon on Alite Reef, but not in time to stop a landing barge being wrecked there. There is rumoured to be a Japanese ship sunk in Fokanakafo Bay on the central east coast. One American aviator, George W. Polk, was rescued by Shemuele and taken to Kwai Island in east Kwara'ae. Polk may have been from the plane that ditched at Sinalagu, but Kwaio remember only one survivor, named Allen (or Allan). Another American plane ditched on Small Malaita. SSEM and Malayta Company sites were part of the action.

8   See Fifi'i 1991, 44.
9   Marchant 1942–43, 30 Aug 1942; Fifi'i 1991, 38.

CONCLUSION

There was a New Zealand camp at Baunani and the most permanent substantial installation on Malaita was a Royal New Zealand Air Force (RNZAF) radar unit at Cape Astrolabe. One RNZAF plane came down in the mountains near Onepusu on the west coast. The SSEM launch *Arosi* was bombed and sunk in error by the Americans on 7 August 1942.[10]

In October 1942, a group of boys from the Melanesian Mission's Maravovo School in northwest Guadalcanal landed at north Malaita with Mr Rowley. They made their way overland to ʻAoke, dodging Japanese troops. Another, larger group followed and the Maravovo School was reestablished at Fiu on the west coast under the charge of a deacon, Henry Maabe.[11] While Malaita itself was only on the edge of the war, thousands of Malaitan men were recruited into the Solomon Islands Labour Corps or the Solomon Islands Defence Force.[12] The cycle that had begun in 1909 had been broken, although once again Malaitans were asked to travel to other islands as labourers. This time the consequences of their experiences abroad would be very different.[13]

Malaitan Tropes, Custom and *Kastom*

This book's Introduction began with a discussion of Malaitan tropes and how foreigners have often depicted Malaitans as evil, fierce and unpredictable, and even as cannibal head-hunters. Almost always they are described as culturally conservative, holding on to outdated customs. It is fitting to end this conclusion with a nod to modern-day continuations of the same tropes. One example is provided by Charles Montgomery, who toured the Solomons in the early 2000s to retrace the footsteps of his great-grandfather Anglican Bishop of Tasmania Henry Montgomery. The bishop arrived in Solomon Islands on the mission steamer *Southern Cross* in 1892, and later authored the book *The Light of Melanesia*. Charles's book, as indicated in this chapter's epigraphs, shows that, despite the passing of more than a century, little seems to have altered in the Montgomery family attitudes towards Malaitans. However, it is

---

10   Moore 2013c entry on Second World War. The wreckage citations are gleaned from *Archaehistoria*, www.archaehistoria.org (accessed 22 Sept 2013); and Laracy 1988a, 18; Laracy and White 1988; Fifiʻi 1991, 38, 44–45; and Kenilorea 2008, 24.
11   Baddeley 1942, 6.
12   Laracy 1988b.
13   Chapter 4 in Akin 2013a, 132–63, provides an excellent assessment of the Malaitan war experience and further information about the military events that did take place on Malaita (380–81).

not as if Charles Montgomery was alone in maintaining the trope. Roger Webber, a medical doctor in the BSIP administration, in his 2011 book *Solomoni: Times and Tales from Solomon Islands*, singled out Malaitans as having a 'reputation for a ferocious and traditional people'. 'The independence and ferocity of the Malaitan people', he wrote, 'is not far below the surface and never more so than when a land dispute occurs'.[14] In the same vein, a 2000 history of Solomon Islands, Ian MacNeill's *Sweet Horizons*, describes Malaita this way:

> The history of Malaita is bloody and its reputation amongst Europeans was fearsome. The world knew it as the most dangerous corner of the British Empire … Parts of it are still thought of as potentially dangerous or at least unfriendly.[15]

Reading such statements is like stepping back into the 1870s and 1880s—the Malaita tropes are disturbingly alive and well.

Learning about Malaita between the 1870s and the 1930s is of direct relevance to understanding Malaita today. Chains of transmission and interpretations of knowledge stretch across the now more than 140 years since outsiders first began to venture there in significant numbers. Iconic religious figures such as Joseph Wate, who brought Anglicanism to Small Malaita, and Peter Abu`ofa, the founder the QKM in north Malaita, are the stuff of legends. The Bible and particularly Old Testament theology, introduced in the nineteenth century, still pervade religion in modern Malaita, to the extent that the myth of descent from the Lost Tribes of Israel seems real to many. Explanations of Malaitan origins often involve connections to the Lost Tribes and the laws and covenants of the Old Testament are applied. These connections, also made in other Pacific societies, are particularly strong in central and north Malaita.[16]

The centrality of Peter Abu`ofa, who returned from Queensland in 1894 and died in 1937, still resonates among many SSEC members and in the Remnant Church. The connection with Israel may date back to the time of Abu`ofa. Some QKM-SSEM members fostered the Lost Tribes interpretation. The Remnant Church, established in the 1950s as a breakaway movement from the SSEC, which involved Anglican teaching as well, incorporated aspects of Lost Tribes of Israel beliefs and has

---

14   Webber 2011, 111, 126.
15   MacNeill 2000, 123.
16   Newland and Brown 2015.

remained strong. In To'aba'ita, the rightful society as envisaged in the book of Isaiah remains a major source of beliefs, and there are claims that an ancient stone temple linked to the Lost Tribes remains in the mountains. The flag of modern Israel hangs in some To'aba'ita churches and in recent years there was a march down to 'Aoke by Lost Tribes believers. Ancestral forms of worship, because they are often depicted to have their origins in Israel, are also seen as connected to these ancient forms of Christianity.[17] Some Kwara'ae maintain similar beliefs and claim primogeniture over other Malaitans based on a grand combination of customary and biblical justifications. This is one-upmanship, claiming a biblical pedigree through descent from the founding inhabitants of Malaita.[18] As Jaap Timmer concludes:

> The reason why some Malaitans adhere to old Jewish rules is that they consider themselves to be a covenant people with an ancestry going back to the biblical kings. Proof of this link with God's chosen people and an earlier movement of people from the Mediterranean to the Pacific stems from the belief that the Ark of the Covenant lies buried in the mountains of Malaita. When telling the story, people talk in similitudes. Thus, original Malaitan *kastom* (tradition) is viewed as the same as old Jewish forms of worship and specific proscriptions regulating social life.[19]

As outlined in the Introduction, Maasina Rule (1944–52), which shook British control of the protectorate, could not have occurred without the developments that altered Malaita over the preceding decades. The movement was not directly responsible for independence in 1978, which emerged from a long-term desire by the British to rid themselves of their Pacific Island territories, and international pressures for decolonisation. That said, Maasina Rule did give Malaitans and other Solomon Islanders the confidence that they could stand alone.[20] There were echoes of Maasina Rule in the Malaita Eagle Force of the late 1990s and 2000s.[21] Ma'asina Forum, a continuing and successful Malaitan-based political forum and pressure group, also maintains the link.

---

17 Burt 1983; Timmer 2008; 2011; 2012; 2015; Brown 2010a; 2010b; 2015; Daefa 2004; Maggio 2015.
18 Burt and Kwa'ioloa 2001, 10–21.
19 Timmer 2008, 204.
20 Moore 2013b; Akin 2013a.
21 Moore 2004a, 123–36.

Since the 1940s, Malaitans have also created a unified *kastom*, a Solomons Pijin term that can refer to shared traditions, but also to contemporary ideas and institutions perceived to be grounded in indigenous concepts and principles. Thus *kastom* is not, as is often supposed, synonymous with the English 'custom'. It is not a version of 'Melanesian ways' from before Europeans arrived in the islands. In addition to its usage in everyday language, anthropologists have analysed and debated *kastom*'s meanings. Particularly in its political uses, *kastom* is often closely tied to indigenous means of dispute resolution, or *kastom loa* (law), set in opposition to state or 'government law'. The word has developed different meanings in different Pacific countries and cultures. In Solomon Islands, relative to Vanuatu and Papua New Guinea, the state has made little attempt to harness *kastom* as an ideological tool. David Akin suggests that this is partly because several leading Christian churches have long opposed retention of what they see as 'customary ways' (though this is slowly changing), and, more importantly, because on Malaita—the most *kastom*-conscious island—*kastom* has, since the Pacific War, been at the centre of various antigovernment ideologies and movements. *Kastom* is a fluid concept that is used selectively and creatively, and is for many Solomon Islanders a key mechanism for adapting to and channelling modernisation and change.[22]

Akin concludes that the development of *kastom* as an organised political ideology on Malaita is largely a postwar phenomenon. *Kastom* is often inextricably linked with Christianity and modern politics. While *kastom* is most often presented as authentic and traditional, it underpins local circumstances and rights and interpretations and shifts over time. What, then, were the ingredients that brought Malaitans together, and when and how did that coalescence occur? My answer would be that collective *kastom* began to emerge in the nineteenth and early twentieth centuries. Outsiders often give an impression that Malaitans have immutable rules in their religions and secular societies. However, since nineteenth-century labour trade days, Malaitans have been malleable in how they deal with travel and confronting circumstances not found at home. After all, tens of thousands left their island to work overseas and within the protectorate between the 1870s and 1940s. This would not have been possible if they

---

22   Akin 2004; 2005; 2013a; Keesing and Tonkinson 1982; Keesing 1982a; 1982b; 1993; Babadzan 1988, 2004; Gegeo 1996.

were incapable of creative cultural experiments. They managed to build a proud and politically shared identity and developed an ability to overcome regional differences.

Since the 1970s, I have been trying to decide in my own mind if Malaita was home to a unique Pacific society or if Malaitans are actually fairly similar to the inhabitants of neighbouring islands. Although there were a dozen language and dialect divisions, they are all cognate and there is an overarching cosmology and way of behaving. This must have aided communications, as did Solomons Pijin. Chapter 1 attempted to describe what Malaita might have been like before any substantial outside influences. The chapters that followed steered forward to the early 1940s. My conclusion is that Malaita is not unique and that Malaitan dominance is a product of historical circumstances.

Another factor has been Malaita's large population. Evidence suggests that the island has long carried a larger population (for its size) than any of the neighbouring islands, including Bougainville. This has put different pressures on land and sea resources than are found on other less populous islands. Perhaps this has produced a more competitive society. It is probably a matter of luck that the Malaitan population has stayed large for at least 500 years, although I have argued here that numbers likely decreased in the nineteenth century.

On many other Pacific Islands, introduced disease decimated populations and reduced political and economic importance. Malaita was excluded from the early whaling and trading ventures, an advantage to its people since they also avoided early large-scale population declines from introduced diseases. In the mid-to-late nineteenth century, warfare, raiding, and probably new diseases depopulated large areas in the western and central Solomons. The effect was particularly marked in the New Georgia Group and on Choiseul and Isabel, but raids also affected the Russell Islands, Savo and parts of Guadalcanal. By the second half of the century, decades of head-hunting raids from New Georgia, intertribal fighting and introduced diseases had reduced Isabel's population to just a few thousand. Head-hunting raids from the north never affected Malaita's population numbers to any significant extent.

Malaitans were the major labour force in Queensland and Fiji (1870–1914) and also internally in the Solomons from early in the twentieth century. The external circular labour trade, and also the Anglican Melanesian

Mission's transportation of students on its ships, constantly introduced new diseases, which must have killed many Solomon Islanders. Epidemics of measles brought in the mid-1870s reduced population in some areas of the Pacific by as much as one-quarter to one-third. Whether measles had the same early affect in the Solomons is unclear. The BSIP archives record many epidemics on Malaita, yet the island maintained the largest population in the protectorate. The only conclusion can be that increases in numbers over time exceeded the declines. The 2009 Census recorded 515,870 Solomon Islanders, 137,596 of whom lived on Malaita, and Honiara had a population of 64,609, half of whom would have been Malaitans, a total of around 170,000 or 32 per cent. The 2016 national population is estimated to be around 620,000 and Honiara is thought to be home to around 100,000. The estimate for the population of Malaita Province has not been revised.[23] If the 2009 proportion is correct, then there must be approaching 200,000 individuals who at least part identify as Malaitan in origin, even if married into other island groups.

Malaitan males steadily engaged in wage labour onwards from the 1870s, to an extent unequalled anywhere else in similar societies in Solomon Islands or Vanuatu. In a 2007 article I argued that the misappropriation of Malaitan labour was one of the historical origins for what Solomon Islanders call the 'Tension Years', 1998–2003.[24] My argument is that the root cause of the disturbances during those years was economic not ethnic, related to infrastructural underdevelopment, use of labour, changes exacerbated by the influences of Christianity and government, and shifting power relations. Historically, the main areas of alienated land in Solomon Islands are in Western and Guadalcanal Provinces. The only move to alienate land on Malaita—by the Malayta Company and Fairymead Sugar Company Ltd of the 1900s to the 1930s—was, mercifully, a failure, leaving Malaitans with their customary lands intact. Malaita's land is just as suitable for development as that of any of the other islands. During the 1950s and 1960s, the BSIP Government surveyed the geology and land use potential of all islands and initiated development plans. The Malaita District Land Use Survey, published in 1974, left no doubt that the island has potential similar to other islands in the nation.[25] The 2001 Provincial Development Profile for Malaita shows similar

---

23   Solomon Islands Government 2015, 81.
24   Moore 2007.
25   Great Britain Government 1974b.

potential.²⁶ A key factor is the large population, which leaves no areas empty or lightly populated other than in the mountains of the 'middle bush'. If all Malaitans were to return to Malaita (as 20,000 did during the Tension Years), there would be even more strain on land resources. The future for the many Malaitans who have become urban citizens of Honiara and the other towns is as wage earners, continuing the century-and-a-half trend. The skills that Malaita males have learnt from working away from home have made them different.

One of the Malaita tropes is that they remained a non-Christian and nonliterate people for longer than other Solomon Islanders. The argument put forward in this book in chapters 3 to 6 is a substantial repudiation of this. Malaitan literacy began in Queensland and Fiji in the 1880s and, along with Christianity, progressed fast, continuing on Malaita once missions were established there, starting in the 1890s and 1900s. Although early conversion was much more complete on islands such as the Gela Group and Isabel, these islands had much smaller populations. It did take a long time for the majority of Malaitans to convert to Christianity and adopt literacy, but these two cultural changes were at the base of the success of communications during Maasina Rule. Many Maasina Rule leaders were members of the SSEM. Timothy George Mahratta, a Maasina Rule leader, had been educated in Queensland and was one of the most Western-educated Solomon Islanders of his day. Literacy enabled Malaitans to circulate a flow of letters all around the island, providing information for Maasina Rule followers.

There was another great change, no different than on other Solomon Islands, although it was harder to achieve on Malaita, was the introduction of the protectorate government. By comparison, the pacification of the feared head-hunters and slavers of the Western Solomons took only five years. On Malaita it took from 1909 into the 1930s to achieve a similar level of control, and even then it remained tenuous. The government's resources were stretched thin as more areas were opened up, and the 1930s Depression years further limited resources. As well, there was little alienated land and only a small, mainly missionary foreign presence, whereas in the Western Solomons there were many plantations and foreigners. Although not obvious to Malaitans, it was inevitable that the government would eventually win and Malaita's *ramo* would have to bow to British authority.

---

26   Solomon Islands Government 2001b.

While my conclusion is that Malaitans are at core much like other Solomon Islanders and other inhabitants of Near Oceania, there are circumstantial historical differences that explain the unique success of Malaitans. Chapters 2 to 10 charted and analysed the changes that took place between the 1870s and the 1930s. The Introduction and Conclusion serve to remind readers that the discourses around work, religion and the state are fluid and ever-changing. Malaitans are not conservative; they are extremely innovative and flexible, and this strength is a key explanation for their success.

In the Introduction, I noted that *Making Mala* owed much to other scholars, and does not answer all of my questions about Malaitan societies and how they have changed over the many decades covered here. No work by an outsider will ever manage to do this, particularly not one as linguistically ill-equipped as me. However, I am also sceptical that writings by insiders—Malaitans—will be able to provide a full answer.

I am conscious that the colonisation process has been closely linked to the way Western knowledge is depicted as dominant and rational. Although we have come to see perceptions of knowledge as part and parcel of the ways in which we construct history, empiricism and critical analysis are still vital to providing perspectives on change. Regardless of questions that arise about my own scholarship, which is healthy and necessary, I also maintain a faith in my intellectual training and use of analytical skills. Nevertheless, let us hope that the efforts of outsider historians and anthropologists will inspire Malaitans and other Solomon Islanders to take up the challenge to correct our faults. Thankfully, some are beginning to do so even now.

Bibliography

Institutional and Government Documents and Publications

Anglican Church of Australia

Diocese of Brisbane

1872   *Report of the Proceedings of the First Session of the Third Synod of the Branch of the Church of England in the Diocese of Brisbane in the Colony of Queensland.*

Diocese of North Queensland

1867–1946   Holy Trinity Church, Mackay, Baptism Registers.

1867–1900   Holy Trinity Church, Mackay, Marriage Registers.

Anglican Church of the Province of Melanesia

1894   *Occasional Papers of the Melanesian Mission (OPMM).* J.R. Selwyn and D.D. Ludlow (eds). Guildford: Melanesian Mission.

1895–1942   *The Southern Cross Log*, journal of the Melanesian Mission (two editions were published: England and Auckland, New Zealand).

Great Britain Government

British Solomon Islands Protectorate

1911   *British Solomon Islands Protectorate Handbook, with Returns up to 31st March 1911.* Tulagi.

Ministry of Overseas Development, Land Resources

1974a *The British Solomon Islands Protectorate*, vol. 2, Guadalcanal and the Florida Islands. Division (J.R.F. Hansell and J.R.D. Wall). Surbiton, Surrey: Land Resources Division, Ministry of Overseas Development.

1974b *The British Solomon Islands Protectorate*, vol. 3, Malaita and Ulawa. Division (J.R.F. Hansell and J.R.D. Wall). Surbiton, Surrey: Land Resources Division, Ministry of Overseas Development.

Western Pacific High Commission

1921 *WPHC Gazette.*

1923 *WPHC Gazette.*

1955–75 *British Solomon Islands, News Sheet.*

Mackay Regional Council

1873–1925 Mackay Cemetery Trust Register of Burials, vols 1–3.

Queensland Government

Queensland State Archives

Statistics of Queensland.

Votes and Proceedings of the Parliament.

1906 *Royal Commission into Sugar Industry Labour.* Brisbane: Government Printer.

Royal Navy Australia Station Records

South Sea Evangelical Church

Queensland Kanaka Mission

1895–1906 Baptismal Registers.

1904–06 *'Not In Vain': What God Hath Wrought amongst the Kanakas. Queensland. Report of the Queensland Kanaka Mission.*

South Sea Evangelical Mission

1907–42 *'Not In Vain': What God Hath Wrought amongst South Sea Islanders. Report of the South Sea Evangelical Mission.*

Solomon Islands Government

National Statistics Office

2015 *Household Income and Expenditure Survey: National Analytical Report*, vol. 1. Honiara.

Ministry of Provincial Government and Rural Development

2001a *Guadalcanal Province Development Profile, 2001.* Honiara: Ministry of Provincial Government and Rural Development.

2001b *Malaita Province Development Profile.* Honiara: Ministry of Provincial Government and Rural Development.

South Australian Government

1895 Report of the Northern Territory Commission. *South Australian Proceedings of Parliament.*

Uniting Church in Australia

1889–1939 Presbyterian Church, Walkerston, Baptismal Records.

1907–16 Presbyterian Church, Walkerston, Minute Book, of the Kirk Session.

Newspapers and Magazines

Acta Societatis Mariae

The *Advertiser* (Adelaide)

The *Age* (Melbourne)

The *Argus* (Melbourne)

The *Australasian Sketcher* (Melbourne)

The *Brisbane Courier*

The *Bundaberg Mail*

The *Church Chronicle* (Brisbane)

The *Churchman* (Ballarat)

Fiji Times (Suva)

Full Salvation: A Monthly Record of Salvation Army Warfare among the Nations

Illustrated Monthly Herald (Melbourne)

The *Mackay Mercury and South Kennedy Advertiser* (Mackay)

The *Mercury* (Hobart)

The *Moreton Bay Courier* (Brisbane)

Northern Miner (Charters Towers)

The *Planters' Gazette* (Gizo)

The *Queensland Baptist*

The *Queenslander*

The *Sydney Morning Herald*

Vanuatu Daily Post (Port Vila)

The *War Cry* (Salvation Army)

Other Sources

Akimichi, Tomoya
1978 The Ecological Aspect of Lau (Solomon Islands) Ethnoichthyology. *Journal of the Polynesian Society* 87 (4): 301–26.

Akin, David
1993 Negotiating Culture in East Kwaio, Malaita, Solomon Islands. PhD thesis, University of Hawai`i.

1996 Local and Foreign Spirits in Kwaio, Solomon Islands. In *Spirits in Culture, History, and Mind*, edited by Jeannette Marie Mageo and Alan Howard, 147–71. New York and London: Routledge.

1999a	Cash and Shell Money in Kwaio, Solomon Island. In *Money and Modernity: State and Local Currencies in Melanesia*, edited by David Akin and Joel Robbins, 103–30, 249–51. Pittsburgh: University of Pittsburgh Press.
1999b	Compensation and the Melanesian State: Why the Kwaio Keep Claiming. *Contemporary Pacific* 11 (1): 35–67.
2003	Concealment, Confession, and Innovation in Kwaio Women's Taboos. *American Ethnologist* 3 (3): 381–400. doi.org/10.1525/ae.2003.30.3.381.
2004	Ancestral Vigilance and the Corrective Conscience: *Kastom* as Culture in a Melanesian Society. *Anthropological Theory* 4 (3): 299–324. doi.org/10.1177/1463499604045566.
2005	*Kastom* as Hegemony? A Response to Babadzan. *Anthropological Theory* 5 (1): 75–83. doi.org/10.1177/1463499605050871.
2012	Kwaio Piracy as Moral Instruction: Lessons from Archival and Oral History. Talk for Melanesian Anthropology: Archival Perspectives, a symposium in honour of the newly renamed Tuzin Archive for Melanesian Anthropology, Geisel Library, University of California, San Diego, 9 May.
2013a	*Colonialism, Maasina Rule, and the Origins of Malaitan Kastom*. Honolulu: University of Hawai'i Press. doi.org/10.21313/hawaii/9780824838140.001.0001.
2013b	Malaitan Clubs. In *Melanesia: Arts and Encounter*, edited by Lissant Bolton, Nicholas Thomas, Elizabeth Bonshek, Julie Adams and Ben Burt, 228–33. London: British Museum Press.
2015	Sentence de Mort, Meurtre et Prestige. In *L'éclat des Ombres: L'art en Noir et Blanc des Iles Salomon*. Paris: Musée du quai Branly.

Allain, Jean and Kevin Bales

2012	Slavery and Its Definition. *Global Dialogue: Queen's University Belfast Law Research Paper* no. 12–06, 14 (2), papers.ssrn.com/sol3/papers.cfm?abstract_id=2123155.

Allan, Colin Hamilton
1990 — *Solomons Safari, 1953–58 (Part II)*. Christchurch: Nag's Head Press.

Amherst, W.A. and Basil Thomson (eds)
1967 [1901] — *The Discovery of the Solomon Islands by Alvaro de Mendaña in 1568*. Nendeln, Liechtenstein: Ashgate/Hakluyt Society.

Anderson, Athol and Sue O'Connor
2008 — Indo-Pacific Migration and Colonization—Introduction. *Asian Perspectives* 47 (1): 2–11. doi.org/10.1353/asi.2008.0010.

Aswani, Shankar
2000 — (guest ed.) 'Essays on Head-Hunting in the Western Solomon Islands'. Special issue of *Journal of the Polynesian Society* 109 (1).

2008 — Forms of Leadership and Violence in Malaita and in the New Georgia Group, Solomon Islands. In *Forms of Leadership and Violence in Malaita and in the New Georgia Group, Solomon Islands*, edited by Pamela J. Stewart and Andrew Strathern, 171–94. Durham, NC: Carolina Academic Press.

Awdry, Frances
1902 — *In the Isles of the Sea: The Story of Fifty Years in Melanesia*. London: Bemrose & Sons.

Babadzan, Alain
1988 — *Kastom* and Nation-Building in the South Pacific. In *Ethnicities and Nations: Processes and Interethnic Relations in Latin America, Southeast Asia, and the Pacific*, edited by Remo Guidieri, Francesco Pellizzi and Stanley J. Tambiah, 199–228. Austin: University of Texas Press.

2004   Commentary: *Kastom* as Culture. *Anthropological Theory* 4 (3): 325–28. doi.org/10.1177/1463499604045567.

Bach, John
1983   The Royal Navy in the South West Pacific: The Australia Station 1859–1913. *Great Circle* 5 (2): 116–32.

1986   *The Australia Station: A History of the Royal Navy in the South West Pacific, 1821–1913*. Kensington: New South Wales University Press.

Baddeley, Walter Herbert
1942   'Behind It All Is God': The Melanesian Mission in War-Time. *The Bishop's Report for 1942*. Sydney: Australian Board of Missions.

Bandler, Faith
1977   *Wacvie*. Adelaide: Rigby.

1984   *Welou, My Brother*. Sydney: Wild and Woolley and Aboriginal Artists Agency.

Bandler, Faith and Len Fox
1980   *Marani in Australia*. Adelaide: Rigby.

Banivanua-Mar, Tracey
2007   *Violence and Colonial Dialogue: The Australian-Pacific Indentured Labor Trade*. Honolulu: University of Hawai`i Press.

2010   Cannibalism and Colonialism: Charting Colonies and Frontiers in Nineteenth-Century Fiji. *Comparative Studies in Society and History* 52 (2): 255–81. doi.org/10.1017/S0010417510000046.

Bardon, Richard
1949   *The Centenary History of the Presbyterian Church of Queensland, 1849–1949*. Brisbane: Smith & Patterson.

Bargatsky, Thomas
1980	Beachcombers and Castaways as Innovators. *Journal of Pacific History* 15 (2): 93–102. doi.org/ 10.1080/00223348008572391.

Barker, John
1990	Introduction: Ethnographic Perspectives on Christianity in Oceanic Societies. In *Christianity in Oceania: Ethnographic Perspectives*, edited by John Barker, 1–24. Lanham, MD: University Press of America. doi.org/10.1017/cbo9780511585753.001.

1992	Christianity in Western Melanesian Ethnography. In *History and Tradition in Melanesia*, edited by James Carrier, 144–73. Berkeley: University of California Press.

Bartle, J.F.
1952	The Shell Money of Auki Island. *Corona* 4: 379–83.

Bathgate, Murray A.
1993	*Fight for the Dollar: Economic and Social Change in Western Guadalcanal, Solomon Islands*. Wellington, New Zealand: Alexander Enterprise.

Beattie, J.W.
1906	Journal of a Voyage to the Western Pacific in the Melanesian Mission Yacht Southern Cross. Hobart: Royal Society of Tasmania MSS RS. 29/3.

Beaver, Dan
2002	Flesh or Fantasy: Cannibalism and the Meanings of Violence. *Ethnography* 49 (3): 671–85. doi.org/ 10.1215/00141801-49-3-671.

Beck, Stephen
2009   Maritime Mechanisms of Contact and Change: Archaeological Perspectives on the History and Conduct of the Queensland Labour Trade. PhD thesis, James Cook University.

Bedford, Richard D.
1973   *New Hebridean Mobility: A Study of Circular Migration*. Department of Human Geography Publication HG/9. Canberra: The Australian National University.

Bedford, Stuart and Christophe Sand
2007   Lapita and Western Pacific Settlement: Progress, Prospects and Persistent Problems. In *Oceanic Explorations: Lapita and Western Pacific Settlement*, edited by Stuart Bedford, Christophe Sand and Sean P. Connaughton, 1–15. Canberra: ANU E Press.

Bedford, Stuart and Matthew Spriggs
2008   Northern Vanuatu as a Pacific Crossroads: The Archaeology of Discovery, Interaction, and the Emergence of the 'Ethnographic Present'. *Asian Perspectives* 47 (1): 95–120. doi.org/10.1353/asi.2008.0003.

Bennett, Judith A.
1974   Cross-Cultural Influences on Village Relocation on the Weather Coast of Guadalcanal, Solomon Islands, c. 1870–1953. MA thesis, University of Hawai`i.
1981a   Oscar Svensen: A Solomons Trader among 'the Few'. *Journal of Pacific History* 16 (4): 170–89.
1981b   Personal Work Histories of Solomon Islands Plantation Labourers—Methodology and Uses. *Pacific Studies* 5 (1): 34–56.
1987   *Wealth of the Solomons: A History of a Pacific Archipelago, 1800–1978*. Honolulu: University of Hawai`i Press.

1993	'We Do Not Come Here to Be Beaten': Resistance and the Plantation System in the Solomon Islands to World War II. In *Plantation Workers: Resistance and Accommodation*, edited by Brij V. Lal, Doug Munro and Edward D. Beechert, 129–85. Honolulu: University of Hawai'i Press.
2000	*Pacific Forest: A History of Resource Control and Contest in Solomon Islands, c. 1800–1997*. Leiden and Cambridge: Brill, and White Horse Press.
2009	*Natives and Exotics: World War II and Environment in the Southern Pacific*. Honolulu: University of Hawai'i Press. doi.org/10.21313/hawaii/9780824832650.001.0001.
2014	A Vanishing People or a Vanishing Discourse? W.H.R. Rivers' 'Psychological Factor' and Depopulation in the Solomon Islands and the New Hebrides. In *The Ethnographic Experiment: A.M. Hocart and W.H.R. Rivers in Island Melanesia, 1908*, edited by Edvard Hviding and Cato Berg, 214–51. New York: Berghahn.

Blain, Rev. Michael

2017	*Blain Biographical Directory of Anglican Clergy in the South Pacific*, anglicanhistory.org/nz/blain_directory/directory.pdf.

Bottoms, Timothy

2015	*Cairns: City of the South Pacific, a History, 1770–1995*. Cairns: Bunu Bunu Press.

Boutilier, James A.

1974	The Role of the Administration and the Missions in the Provision of Medical and Educational Services in the British Solomon Islands Protectorate, 1893–1942. Annual Meeting of the Association for Social Anthropology in Oceania, at Asilomar, Pacific Grove, California, March. Copy held by Anglican Church of Canada, Church House Library.

1979 Killing the Government: Imperial Policy and the Pacification of Malaita. In *The Pacification of Melanesia*, edited by Margaret Rodman and Matthew Cooper, 43–87. Ann Arbor: University of Michigan Press.

1983 The Government is the District Officer: An Historical Analysis of District Officers as Middlemen in the British Solomon Islands Protectorate, 1893–1943. In *Middlemen and Brokers in Oceania*, edited by William L. Rodman and Dorothy Ayers Counts, 35–67. Ann Arbor: University of Michigan Press.

Braga, Patricia

2005 *Henry and Catherine Young: Life Goes on, Seven Generations to 2005*. Beecroft, NSW: Patricia Braga.

Braga, Stuart

2003 *A Century of Preaching Christ: Katoomba Christian Convention, 1903–2003*. Sydney: Katoomba Christian Convention.

Braithwaite, John, Sinclair Dinnen, Matthew Allen, Valerie Braithwaite and Hilary Charlesworth

2010 *Pillars and Shadows: Statebuilding as Peacebuilding in Solomon Islands*. Peacebuilding Compared Project Working Paper 7. Canberra: ANU E Press.

Brewster, A.B.

1937 *King of the Cannibal Isles*. London: Robert Hale & Co.

Brooke, C.H.

1872 The Melanesian Mission. In *Mission Life: An Illustrated Magazine of Home and Foreign Church Work*, vol. III, part 1, edited by J.J. Halcombe, 223–26. London: W. Wells Gardner.

Brown, Terry

2006 Sermon, All Saints Church, Brisbane, 9 July.

2010a Heaven Descends: Jonathan Ilala and the Malaita Anglican Visionaries, 1976–2000. European Society for Oceanists Conference Paper. St Andrews, Scotland: St Andrews University.

2010b Jerusalem the Golden: Cargoistic Thinking and Current Malaitan Expectations of Wealth. Conference Paper. London: British Museum.

2015 Jerusalem and Malaita: The Visions and Prophecies of George Umai of West Kwara`ae, Malaita, Solomon Islands. In 'Descent from Israel and Jewish Identities in the Pacific, Past and Present', Lynda Newland and Terry M. Brown (guest eds). Special issue of *Oceania* 85 (3): 283–98.

Bruny, D'Entrecasteaux, J-A. R.

2001 *Voyage to Australia and the Pacific, 1791–1793*. Translated and edited by Edward Duyker and Maryse Duyker. Melbourne: Miegunya Press.

Bugotu, Francis

1968 The Impact of Western Culture on Solomon Islands Society. Paper presented at the Second Waigani Seminar, Port Moresby and Canberra: UPNG and RSPS, The Australian National University, 549–56; republished in *BSIP News Sheet* no. 10, 31 May 1968: 8–11.

Burridge, Kenelm

1969 *Tangu Traditions: A Study of the Way of Life, Mythology and Developing Experience of a New Guinea People*. Oxford: Clarendon Press.

Burt, Ben

1983 The Remnant Church: A Christian Sect of the Solomon Islands. *Oceania* 53 (4): 334–46.

1988   Ābu`a `i Kwara`ae: The Meaning of Tabu in a Solomon Islands Society. *Mankind* 18 (2): 74–89.

1990   Kwara`ae Conceptions of Abu: A Reply to Roger Keesing. *Australian Journal of Anthropology* 1 (1): 48–49.

1994   *Tradition and Christianity: The Colonial Transformation of a Solomon Islands Society*. Chur, Switzerland: Harwood Academic Publishers.

2002   The Story of Alfred Amasia: Whose History and Whose Epistemology? *Journal of Pacific History* 37 (2): 187–204.

2015   *Malaita: A Pictorial History from Solomon Islands*. London: British Museum Press.

Burt, Ben and Lissant Bolton (eds)

2014   *The Things We Value: Culture and History in Solomon Islands*. Canon Pyon, UK: Sean Kingston Publishing.

Burt, Ben and Michael Kwa`ioloa (eds)

2001   *A Solomon Islands Chronicle, as Told by Samuel Alasa`a*. London: British Museum Press.

Campbell, Ian C.

1998   *'Gone Native' in Polynesia: Captivity Narratives and Experiences from the South Pacific*. Westport, CT: Greenwood Press.

Campbell, Michael W.

2008   The 1919 Bible Conference and its Significance for Seventh-day Adventist History and Theology. PhD thesis, Seventh-day Adventist Seminary, Andrews University.

Carter, Jennifer M.T.

1999   *Painting the Islands Vermillion: Archibald Watson and the Brig Carl*. Melbourne: Melbourne University Press.

Chapman, Graeme

2004 Thompson, John (1858–1945), *Australian Dictionary of Evangelical Biography*, webjournals.ac.edu.au/ojs/index.php/ADEB/article/view/769.

Chapman, Murray and Peter Pirie

1974 *Tasi Mauri: A Report on Population and Resources of the Guadalcanal Weather Coast*. Honolulu: East-West Population Institute, East-West Center and University of Hawai`i.

Chowning, Ann

1968 The Real Melanesia: An Appraisal of Parsonson's Theories. *Mankind* 6 (12): 641–52. doi.org/10.1111/j.1835-9310.1968.tb00757.x.

Clemens, Martin

1962 Two Decades Have Brought Big Changes to Malaita, BSIP. *Pacific Islands Monthly* 33 (10): 79–81.

Cliff, Andrew D. and Peter Haggett

1985 *The Spread of Measles in Fiji and the Pacific: Spatial Components in the Transmission of Epidemic Waves through Island Communities*. Department of Human Geography Publication HG/18. Canberra:, Research School of Pacific Studies, The Australian National University.

Codrington, R.H.

1891 *The Melanesians: Studies in Their Anthropology and Folk-Lore*. Oxford: Clarendon Press.

Connell, John

1977 The Bougainville Connection: Changes in the Economic Context of Shell Money Production in Malaita. *Oceania* 48 (2): 81–101. doi.org/10.1002/j.1834-4461.1977.tb01326.x.

Coombe, Florence

1911   *Islands of Enchantment: Many-Sided Melanesia Seen Through Many Eyes, and Recorded.* London: Macmillan & Co. Ltd.

Cooper, Matthew

1970   Langa Langa Ethics. PhD thesis, Yale University.

1971   Economic Context of Shell Money Production in Malaita. *Oceania* 41 (4): 266–76. doi.org/10.1002/j.1834-4461.1971.tb01167.x.

1972   Langalanga Religion. *Oceania* 43 (2): 113–22. doi.org/10.1002/j.1834-4461.1972.tb00322.x.

Coppet, Daniel de

1965   Land Tenure in `Are`are and on Small Malaita. Manuscript in author's possession.

1968   Pour Une Étude Des Échanges Cérémoniee Mélanésia. *L'Homme* 8 (4): 45–57. doi.org/10.3406/hom.1968.366991.

1970a   1, 4, 8, 9, 7. La Monnaie: Présence Des Morts et Mesure Du Temps. *L'Homme* 10 (1): 17–39. doi.org/10.3406/hom.1970.367102.

1970b   Cycles de Meurtres et Cycles Funéraires Esquisse de Deux Structures D`Échange. In *Échanges et Communications: Mélanges Offerts Á Claude Lévi-Strauss*, edited by P. Pouillon and P. Maranda, 759–81. The Hague: Mouton.

1973   Premier Troc, Double Illusion. *L'Homme* 13 (1/2): 10–22. doi.org/10.3406/hom.1973.367325.

1976   Jardins De Vie, Jardins De Mort En Melanesie. *Traverses* 5/6: 166–77.

1977   First Exchange, Double Illusion. *Journal of the Cultural Association of the Solomon Islands* 5: 23–39.

1981a   Gardens of Life, Gardens of Death in Melanesia. *Kabar Seberang* 8/9: 22–31.

1981b	The Life-Giving Death. In *Mortality and Immortality: The Anthropology and Archaeology of Death*, edited by S.C. Humphreys and Helen King, 175–204. London: Academic Press.

1985	'… Land Owns People: In Honour of the Late Aliki Nono`ohimae Erehau. In *Contexts and Levels: Anthropological Essays on Hierarchy*, edited by R.H. Barnes, Daniel de Coppet and R.J. Parkin, 78–90. Oxford: Journal of the Anthropological Society of Oxford.

1995	`Are`Are Society: A Melanesian Socio-Cosmic Point of View: How Are Bigmen the Servants of Society and Cosmos? In *Cosmos and Society in Oceania*, edited by Daniel de Coppet and André Iteanu, 235–74. Oxford: Berg.

Coppet, Daniel de and Hugo Zemp

1978	`Aré`aré: Un Peuple Mélanésien et sa Musique*. Paris: Editions du Seuil.

Corney, Bolton G.

1883–84	The Behaviour of Certain Epidemic Diseases in Natives of Polynesia, with Special Reference to the Fiji Islands. *Transactions of the Epidemiological Society of London, New Series* 3: 76–94.

Corris, Peter

1970	Pacific Island Labour Migrants in Queensland. *Journal of Pacific History* 5: 43–61. doi.org/10.1080/00223347008572164.

1972	'White Australia' in Action: The Repatriation of Pacific Islanders from Queensland. *Historical Studies* 15 (58): 237–50. doi.org/10.1080/10314617208595469.

1973a	Kwaisulia of Ada Gege: A Strongman in the Solomon Islands. In *Pacific Islands Portraits*, edited by J.W. Davidson and Deryck Scarr, 253–65, 328–31. Canberra: Australian National University Press.

1973b   *Passage, Port and Plantation: A History of Solomon Islands Labour Migration, 1870–1914*. Melbourne: Melbourne University Press.

Crichlow, Nathaniel
1929   The Prevalent Diseases of the British Solomon Islands. *Transactions of the Royal Society of Tropical Medicine and Hygiene* 23 (2): 179–84. doi.org/10.1016/S0035-9203(29)90568-X.

Crocombe, Ron (ed.)
1987   *Land Tenure in the Pacific*. Suva: Institute of Pacific Studies, University of the South Pacific.

Cromar, John
1935   *Jock of the Islands: Early Days in the South Seas, Being the Adventures of John Cromar*. London: Faber and Faber.

Daefa, Frank
2004   *The Lost Temple*. Honiara: Liberty Productions (video).

David, Bruno, Louise Manas and Michael Quinnell (eds)
2008   Gelam's Homeland: Cultural and Natural History on the Island of Mua, Torres Strait. *Memoirs of the Queensland Museum Cultural Heritage* 4 (2).

Davidson, Allan K.
2003   The Legacy of Robert Henry Codrington. *International Bulletin of Missionary Research* 27 (4): 171–76. doi.org/10.1177/239693930302700407.

Dawbin, W.H.
1966   Porpoises and Porpoise Hunting in Malaita. *Australian Natural History* 15 (7): 207–11.

Deck, John Northcote
1928   *Seeing Greater Things: Some of the Far Horizons of Faith.* London: Pickering and Inglis.

Deck, Norman C.
1933–34   Grammar of the Language Spoken by the Kwara`ae People of Mala, British Solomon Islands. *Journal of the Polynesian Society* 42: 33–48, 133–44, 241–56; 43: 1–16, 85–100, 63–79, 246–57.

1934   Letter to the Editor. *Oceania* 5 (2): 242–45. doi.org/10.1002/j.1834-4461.1934.tb00146.x.

Dickinson, Joseph H.C.
1927   *A Trader in the Savage Solomons: A Record of Romance and Adventure.* London: Witherby.

Dinnen, Sinclair and Stewart Firth (eds)
2008   *Politics and State Building in Solomon Islands.* Canberra: Asia Pacific Press.

Douglas, Bronwen
1979   Rank, Power, Authority: A Reassessment of Traditional Leadership in South Pacific Societies. *Journal of Pacific History* 14 (1): 2–27. doi.org/10.1080/00223347908572362.

2014   *Science, Voyages and Encounters in Oceania, 1511–1850.* Basingstoke, UK: Palgrave Macmillan. doi.org/10.1057/9781137305893.

Dureau, Christine M.
1994   Christianity and History in Women's Lives on Simbo, Western Solomon Islands. PhD thesis, Macquarie University.

Dutton, Tom

1980   *Queensland Canefields English of the Late Nineteenth Century: A Record of Interview with Two of the Last Surviving Kanakas in North Queensland, 1964.* Canberra: Pacific Linguistics, The Australian National University.

Duyker, Edward

2014   *Dumont d'Urville: Explorer and Polymath.* Dunedin: University of Otago Press.

Edridge, Sally

1985   *Solomon Islands Bibliography to 1980.* Suva, Wellington and Honiara: Institute of Pacific Studies, University of the South Pacific; Alexander Turnbull Library; Solomon Islands National Library.

Fatnowna, Noel

1989   *Fragments of a Lost Heritage.* Edited by Roger Keesing. Sydney: Angus & Robertson.

Fifi`i, Jonathan

1991   Remembering the War in the Solomons. Translated and edited by David Akin. In *Remembering the Pacific War*, edited by Geoffrey M. White, 37–46. Occasional Paper 36. Honolulu: University of Hawai`i Center for Pacific Islands Studies.

Forster, Honore

1975   A Sydney Whaler 1829–32: The Reminiscences of James Heberley. *Journal of Pacific History* 10 (2): 90–104. doi.org/10.1080/00223347508572269.

Fowler, Wilfred

1969   The Young Dick. *Queensland Heritage* 2 (1): 23–35.

Fox, Charles E.

1954–56   The Solomons Fifty Years Ago and How They Have Changed. Paper presented at the British Solomon Islands Society for the Advancement of Science and Industry, 20 Jan.

1958   *Lord of the Southern Isles: Being the Story of the Anglican Mission in Melanesia, 1849–1949.* London: A.R. Mowbray & Co.

Fraenkel, Jon

2004   *The Manipulation of Custom: From Uprising to Intervention in the Solomon Islands.* Wellington, New Zealand: Victoria University Press.

Frazer, Ian L.

1990   Solomon Islands Labour History and Maasina Rule. In *Labour in the South Pacific*, edited by Clive Moore, Jacqueline Leckie and Doug Munro, 191–203. Townsville: Department of History and Politics and the Centre for Melanesian Studies, James Cook University.

Friedlaender, Jonathan Scott (ed.)

1987   *The Solomon Islands Project: A Long-Term Study of Health, Human Biology, and Culture Change.* Oxford: Oxford University Press.

Froehlich, J.W.

1987   Fingerprints as Phylogenetic Markers in the Solomon Islands. In *The Solomon Islands Project: A Long-Term Study of Health, Human Biology, and Culture Change*, edited by Jonathan Scott Friedlaender, 175–214. Oxford: Oxford University Press.

Gaggin, John

1900   *Among the Man-Eaters.* London: T. Fisher Unwin.

Gammage, Bill

1998 *The Sky Travellers: Journeys in New Guinea, 1938–1939*. Melbourne: Miegunyah Press at Melbourne University Press.

Gege, Jackson

2014 Clan Valuables on Guadalcanal. In *The Things We Value: Culture and History in Solomon Islands*, edited by Ben Burt and Lissant Bolton, 63–65. Canon Pyon, UK: Sean Kingston Publishing.

Gegeo, David Welchman

1998 History, Empowerment and Social Responsibility: Views of a Pacific Island Indigenous Scholar. *History Teacher* 36 (3): 24–33.

2000 Indigenous Knowledge and Empowerment: Rural Development Examined from Within. In *Voyaging through the Contemporary Pacific*, edited by David Hanlon and Geoffrey M. White, 64–90. London: Rowman and Littlefield.

2001 Cultural Rupture and Indigeneity: The Challenge of (Re)Visioning 'Place' in the Pacific. *Contemporary Pacific* 13 (2): 491–507. doi.org/10.1353/cp.2001.0052.

Gegeo, David Welchman and Karen Ann Watson-Gegeo

1996 Priest and Prince: Integrating *Kastom*, Christianity, and Modernization in Kwara`ae Leadership. In *Leadership and Change in the Western Pacific: Essays Presented to Sir Raymond Firth on the Occasion of His Ninetieth Birthday*, edited by Richard Feinberg and Karen Ann Watson-Gegeo, 298–342. London and Atlantic Highlands, NJ: Athlone Press.

2002 Whose Knowledge? Epistemological Collisions in Solomon Islands Community Development. *Contemporary Pacific* 14 (2): 377–409. doi.org/10.1353/cp.2002.0046.

Gesner, Peter
1991 A Maritime Archaeological Approach to the Queensland Labour Trade. *Bulletin of the Australian Institute for Maritime Archaeology* 15 (2): 15–20.

Giles, W.E.
1968 *A Cruize in a Queensland Labour Vessel to the South Seas*. Edited by Deryck Scarr. Pacific History Series, no. 1. Canberra: Australian National University Press.

Gistitin, Carol
1989 *Kanakas: Labour of Love*. Rockhampton: Carol Gistitin.

1995 *Quite a Colony: South Sea Islanders in Central Queensland 1867 to 1993*. Brisbane: Aebis.

Gittins, Kay
1994 *The Salvation Army Nambour Corps: 100 Years of Service on the Sunshine Coast*. Nambour: Salvation Army Nambour Corps Centenary Committee.

Godelier, Maurice
1986 *The Making of Great Men: Male Domination and Power among the New Guinea Baruya*. Translated by Rupert Swyer. Cambridge: Cambridge University Press.

Golden, Graeme A.
1993 *The Early European Settlers of the Solomon Islands*. Melbourne: Graeme A. Golden.

Graves, Adrian
1983 Truck and Gifts: Melanesian Immigrants and the Trade Box System in Colonial Queensland. *Past and Present* 101: 87–124. doi.org/10.1093/past/101.1.87.

1993   *Cane and Labour: The Political Economy of the Queensland Sugar Industry 1862–1906*. Edinburgh: Edinburgh University Press.

Gray, Alastair C.

1999   Trading Contacts in the Bismarck Archipelago during the Whaling Era, 1799–1884. *Journal of Pacific History* 34 (1): 23–43. doi.org/10.1080/00223349908572889.

Green, Roger C.

1976   An Introduction to the Southeast Solomon Islands Culture History Programme. In *Southeast Solomon Islands Cultural History: A Preliminary Survey*, edited by R.C. Green and M.N. Cresswell, 9–17. Wellington: Royal Society of New Zealand.

1991   Near and Remote Oceania—Disestablishing Melanesia in Cultural History. In *Man and a Half: Essays in Pacific Anthropology and Ethnobiology in Honour of Ralph Bulmer*, edited by Andrew Pawley, 491–502. Auckland: Polynesian Society.

Green, Roger C. and M.M. Cresswell (eds)

1976   *Southeast Solomon Islands Cultural History: A Preliminary Survey*. Bulletin 11. Wellington: Royal Society of New Zealand.

Griffin, Helga M.

1990   Young, Florence Selina Harriet (1856–1940). In *Australian Dictionary of Biography*, vol. 12, 597–99. Melbourne: Melbourne University Press.

Griffiths, Alison

1977   *Fire in the Islands: The Acts of the Holy Spirit in the Solomons*. Wheaton, IL: Harold Shaw Publishers.

Groube, Les
1993 Contradictions and Malaria in Melanesia and Australian Prehistory. In *A Community of Culture: The People and Prehistory of the Pacific*, edited by M. Spriggs, D.E. Yen, W. Ambrose, R. Jones, A. Thorne and A. Andrews, 164–86. Canberra: Department of Prehistory, Research School of Pacific Studies, The Australian National University.

Guidieri, Remo
1972 Fathers and Sons: Ritual Cannibalism in Malaita. *Nouvelle Revue de Psychanalyse* 6: 85–109.

1975a Enclos et Clotures: Remarques sur les Discontinuites Et Les Segmentations Oceaniennes. *Journal de la Société des Océanistes* 31 (47): 123–41. doi.org/10.3406/jso.1975.2698.

1975b Note sur le Rapport Male/Femelle en Melanesie. *L'Homme, Revue Francaise D'Anthropologie* 15 (2): 103–19.

1976 Fataa, Fa`a, Fo`o`a: 'Dire', 'Faire', 'Parfaire': Conceptualisation et Effectuation de Pratiques Rituelles Melanesiennes (Fataleka, Salomon Orientales). *Annales* 31: 218–36. doi.org/10.3406/ahess.1976.293706.

1980 *La Route Des Morts*. Paris: Seuil.

Guo, Pei-yi
2003 Island Builders: Landscape and Historicity among the Langalanga, Solomon Islands. In *Landscape, Memory and History: Anthropological Perspectives*, edited by Pamela J. Stewart and Andrew J. Strathern, 189–209. London: Pluto Press.

2004 Performing 'Manufacture': Notion of Things and Performing 'Shell Money Making' among the Langalanga, Solomon Islands (in Chinese). *Museology Quarterly* 18 (2): 7–24.

2006 From Currency to Agency: Shell Money in Contemporary Langalanga, Solomon Islands. *Asia-Pacific Forum* 31: 17–38.

2009   Separate Space, Negotiating Power: Dynamics of Ancestral Spirits and Christian God in Langalanga. In *Religious and Ritual Change: Cosmologies and Histories*, edited by Pamela J. Stewart and Andrew J. Strathern, 69–108. Durham, NC: Carolina Academic Press.

2014   *Bata*: The Adaptable Shell-Money of Langalanga, Malaita. In *The Things We Value: Culture and History in Solomon Islands*, edited by Ben Burt and Lissant Bolton, 55–61. London: Sean Kingston Publishing.

Habel, Norman C. (ed.)

1983   *Powers, Plumes and Piglets: Phenomena of Melanesian Religion*, Bedford Park, SA: Australian Association for the Study of Religions.

Halapua, Winston

2001   *Living on the Fringe: Melanesians of Fiji*. Suva: Institute of Pacific Studies, University of the South Pacific.

Hamlin, Catherine, with John Little

2001   *The Hospital by the River: A Story of Hope*. Sydney: Pan McMillan Australia.

Harrison, Jennifer

2005   Brenan, John O'Neill (1856–1940). In *Australian Dictionary of Biography, Supplementary Volume*, 44–45. Melbourne: Melbourne University Press.

Heath, Ian

1974   Charles Morris Woodford of the Solomon Islands: A Biographical Note, 1852–1927. Masters qualifying thesis, The Australian National University.

Herr, R.A. and E.A. Rood (eds)
1978 *A Solomons Sojourn: J. E. Philp's Log of the Makira 1912–1913*. Hobart: Tasmanian Historical Research Association.

Hilliard, David
1969 The South Sea Evangelical Mission in the Solomon Islands: The Foundation Years. *Journal of Pacific History* 4: 41–64. doi.org/10.1080/00223346908572145.

1978 *God's Gentlemen: A History of the Melanesian Mission, 1849–1942*. St Lucia, Qld: University of Queensland Press.

2005 The God of the Melanesian Mission. In *Vision and Reality in Pacific Religion: Essays in Honour of Niel Gunson*, edited by Michael Reilly, David Hilliard and Phyllis Herda, 195–215. Christchurch and Canberra: Macmillan Brown Centre for Pacific Studies, University of Canterbury, and Pandanus Books.

Hogbin, H. Ian.
1934 Culture Change in the Solomon Islands: Report of Field Work in Guadalcanal and Malaita. *Oceania* 9 (3): 233–67. doi.org/10.1002/j.1834-4461.1934.tb00110.x.

1939 *Experiments in Civilization: The Effects of European Culture on a Native Community of the Solomon Islands*. London: George Routledge and Sons.

1944 Native Councils and Native Courts in the Solomon Islands. *Oceania* 14 (4): 257–83. doi.org/10.1002/j.1834-4461.1944.tb00404.x.

1945–46 Notes and Instructions to Native Administrations in the British Solomon Islands. *Oceania* 16 (1): 61–69. doi.org/10.1002/j.1834-4461.1945.tb00430.x.

Holthouse, Hector

1988 *White Headhunter: The Extraordinary True Story of a White Man's Life among the Headhunters of the Solomon Islands*. North Ryde, NSW: Angus and Robertson.

Hopkins, Arthur I.

1904 (Compiler) The Reef Dwellers of the Solomons. *Southern Cross Log*, Dec: 6–10.

1922 Depopulation in the Solomon Islands. In *Essays on the Depopulation of Melanesia*, edited by W.H.R. Rivers, 62–66. London: Cambridge University Press.

1927 *Melanesia To-Day: A Study Circle Book*. London: Society for Promoting Christian Knowledge.

1928 *In the Isles of King Solomon: An Account of Twenty-Five Years Spent amongst the Primitive Solomon Islanders*. London: Seeley, Service and Company.

1949 *From Heathen Boy to Christian Priest*. St Christopher Books, no. 33. London: Society for Promoting Christian Knowledge.

Horton, Dick Crofton

1970 *Fire over the Islands: Coast Watchers of the Solomons*. Sydney: A.H. and A.W. Reed.

Huffman, Kirk

2012 Making Land Work? *Explorer* 34 (3): 30–32.

Hviding, Edvard

2014 Across the New Georgia Group: A.M. Hocart's Fieldwork as Inter-Island Practice. In *The Ethnographic Experiment: A.M. Hocart and W.H.R. Rivers in Island Melanesia, 1908*, edited by Edvard Hviding and Cato Berg, 71–107. New York: Berghahn.

Innes, James Ross
1938   *Report of Leprosy Survey in the British Solomon Islands Protectorate*. Suva: Government Printer.

Ivens, Walter G.
1918   *Dictionary and Grammar of the Language of Sa`a and Ulawa, Solomon Islands*. Washington, DC: Carnegie Institution.

1927   *Melanesians of the South-East Solomon Islands*. London: Kegan Paul, Trench, Trubner.

1930   *The Island Builders of the Pacific*. London: Seeley, Service and Company.

1931   A Grammar of the Language of Kwara`ae, North Mala, Solomon Islands. *School of Oriental Studies Bulletin* 6: 679–700. doi.org/10.1017/S0041977X00093186.

Jackson, K.B.
1975   Head-Hunting in the Christianization of Bugotu 1861–1900. *Journal of Pacific History* 10 (1): 65–78. doi.org/10.1080/00223347508572266.

Jamison, Bryan
1990   Blackbirding in New Guinea Waters: The 1884 Voyage of the *Hopeful* and the Queensland Labour Trade. BA honours thesis, University of Queensland.

Johnson, Osa
1945   *Bride in the Solomons*. London: George G. Harrap and Company.

Jolly, Margaret

1988 Other Mothers: Maternal 'Insouciance' and the Depopulation Debate in Fiji and Vanuatu, 1890–1930. In *Maternities and Modernities: Colonial and Postcolonial Experiences in Asia and the Pacific*, edited by Kalpann Ram and Margaret Jolly, 177–212. Cambridge: Cambridge University Press.

2000a Demography. In *The Pacific Islands: An Encyclopedia*, edited by Brij V. Lal and Kate Fortune, 84–85. Honolulu: University of Hawai`i Press.

2000b Gender. In *The Pacific Islands: An Encyclopedia*, edited by Brij V. Lal and Kate Fortune, 415–16. Honolulu: University of Hawai`i Press.

Jourdan, Christine

1995 Stepping-Stones to National Consciousness: The Solomon Islands Case. In *Nation Making: Emergent Identities in Postcolonial Melanesia*, edited by Robert J. Foster, 127–49. Ann Arbor: University of Michigan Press.

Kabutaulaka, Tarcisius

2015 Re-Presenting Melanesia: Ignoble Savages and Melanesian Alter-Natives. *Contemporary Pacific* 27 (1): 110–45. doi.org/10.1353/cp.2015.0027.

Keesing, Roger M.

1967 Christians and Pagans in Kwaio, Malaita. *Journal of Polynesian Society* 76 (1): 82–100.

1968 Chiefs in a Chiefless Society: The Ideology of Modern Kwaio Politics. *Oceania* 38 (4): 276–80. doi.org/10.1002/j.1834-4461.1968.tb00973.x.

1973 Kwara`ae Ethnoglottochronology: Procedures Used by Malaita Cannibals for Determining Percentages of Shared Cognates. *American Anthropologist* 75 (5): 1,282–89. doi.org/10.1525/aa.1973.75.5.02a00060.

1975   *Kin Groups and Social Structure*. New York: Holt, Rinehart & Winston.

1978a   `Elota's Story: The Life and Times of a Solomon Islands Big Man*. St Lucia: University of Queensland Press.

1978b   Politico-Religious Movements and Anticolonialism on Malaita: Maasina Rule in Historical Perspective, Part I. *Oceania* 48 (4): 241–61. doi.org/10.1002/j.1834-4461.1978.tb01350.x; Part II. *Oceania* 49 (1): 46–73. doi.org/10.1002/j.1834-4461.1978.tb01374.x.

1982a   *Kastom* and Anticolonialism on Malaita: 'Culture' as Political Symbol. In 'Reinventing Traditional Culture: The Politics of *Kastom* in Island Melanesia', Roger Keesing and Robert Tonkinson (guest eds). Special issue of *Mankind* 13 (4): 357–73.

1982b   *Kastom* in Melanesia: An Overview. In 'Reinventing Traditional Culture: The Politics of *Kastom* in Island Melanesia', Roger Keesing and Robert Tonkinson (guest eds). Special issue of *Mankind* 13 (4): 297–301.

1982c   Keeping to Themselves. *Hemisphere* 26 (4): 248–50.

1982d   *Kwaio Religion: The Living and the Dead in a Solomon Islands Society*. New York: Columbia University Press.

1984   Rethinking *Mana*. *Journal of Anthropological Research* 40 (1): 137–56. doi.org/10.1086/jar.40.1.3629696.

1985a   Killers, Big Men, and Priests on Malaita: Reflections on a Melanesian Troika System. *Ethnology* 24 (4): 237–52. doi.org/10.2307/3773736.

1985b   Kwaio Women Speak: The Micropolitics of Autobiography in a Solomon Island Society. *American Anthropologist* 87 (1): 27–39. doi.org/10.1525/aa.1985.87.1.02a00040.

1986a   The *Young Dick* Attack: Oral and Documentary History on the Colonial Frontier. *Ethnohistory* 33 (3): 268-92.

1986b   Plantation Networks, Plantation Culture: The Hidden Side of Colonial Melanesia. *Journal de la Société des Océanistes* 42 (82–83): 163–70. doi.org/10.3406/jso.1986.2830.

1986c	The *Young Dick* Attack: Oral and Documentary History on the Colonial Frontier. *Ethnohistory* 33 (3): 268–92. doi.org/10.2307/481815.
1987	*Ta`a Geni*: Women's Perspectives on Kwaio Society. In *Dealing with Inequality: Analysing Gender Relations in Melanesia and Beyond*, edited by Marilyn Strathern, 33–62. Cambridge: Cambridge University Press.
1988a	*Melanesian Pidgin and the Oceanic Substrate*. Stanford: Stanford University Press.
1988b	Solomon Pidgin Pronouns: A Further Look. *English World-Wide* 9 (2): 271–92. doi.org/10.1075/eww.9.2.08kee.
1989	Sins of a Mission: Christian Life as Kwaio Traditionalist Ideology. In *Family and Gender in the Pacific: Domestic Contradictions and the Colonial Impact*, edited by Margaret Jolly and Martha Macintyre, 193–212. Cambridge: Cambridge University Press. doi.org/10.1017/CBO9781139084864.011.
1990a	Colonial History as Contested Ground: The Bell Massacre in the Solomons. *History and Anthropology* 4 (2): 279–301. doi.org/10.1080/02757206.1990.9960801.
1990b	Kwara`ae Conceptions of Abu: A Further Note. *Australian Journal of Anthropology* 1 (1): 44–47. doi.org/10.1111/j.1835-9310.1990.tb00006.x.
1992a	*Custom and Confrontation: The Kwaio Struggle for Cultural Autonomy*. Chicago: University of Chicago Press.
1992b	Kwaisulia as Culture Hero. In *History and Tradition in Melanesian Anthropology*, edited by James G. Carrier, 174–92. Berkeley: University of California Press.
1993	*Kastom* Re-Examined. *Anthropological Forum* 6 (4): 587–96. doi.org/10.1080/00664677.1993.9967434.
1997	Tuesday's Chiefs Revisited. In *Chiefs Today: Traditional Pacific Leadership and the Postcolonial State*, edited by Geoffrey M. White and Lamont Lindstrom, 253–309. East-West Center Series on Contemporary Issues in Asia and the Pacific. Stanford: Stanford University Press.

Keesing, Roger M. and Peter Corris
1980   *Lightning Meets the West Wind: The Malaita Massacre.* Melbourne: Oxford University Press.

Keesing, Roger M. and Jonathan Fifi`i
1969   Kwaio Word Tabooing in Its Cultural Context. *Journal of the Polynesian Society* 78 (2): 154–77.

Keesing, Roger M. and Robert Tonkinson (guest eds)
1982   'Reinventing Traditional Culture: The Politics of *Kastom* in Island Melanesia'. Special issue of *Mankind* 13 (4).

Kenilorea, Peter
2008   *Tell It as It Is: Autobiography of Rt. Hon. Sir Peter Kenilorea, KBE, PC, Solomon Islands' First Prime Minister*, edited by Clive Moore. Taipei: Centre for Asia-Pacific Area Studies, Academia Sinica.

Kerr, John
1979   *Northern Outpost.* Mossman: Mossman Central Mill Company Limited.

1987   *Sugar at Maryborough: 120 Years of Challenge.* Maryborough: Maryborough Sugar Factory Limited.

1993   *Southern Sugar Saga: Bundaberg Sugar Company Limited.* Bundaberg: Bundaberg Sugar Company Limited.

1996   *Only Room for One: Isis Central Sugar Mill.* Childers: Isis Central Sugar Mill Co. Ltd.

Kirch, Patrick
1984   The Polynesian Outliers. *Journal of Pacific History* 19 (4): 224–38. doi.org/10.1080/00223348408572496.

Kituai, August Inbrum
1998   *My Gun, My Brother: The World of the Papua New Guinean Colonial Police, 1920–1960.* Honolulu: University of Hawai`i Press.

Knibbs, S.G.C.
1929 *The Savage Solomons, as They Were and Are: A Record of a Head-Hunting People Gradually Emerging from a Life of Savage Cruelty and Bloody Customs, with a Description of Their Manners and Ways and of the Beauties and Potentialities of the Islands.* London: Seeley, Service & Co.

Kolshus, Thorgeir and Evan Hovdhaugen
2010 Reassessing the Death of Bishop John Coleridge Patteson. *Journal of Pacific History* 45 (3): 331–55. doi.org/10.1080 /00223344.2010.530813.

Kwa`ioloa, Michael
2014 Traditional Money and Artefacts in Malaita. In *The Things We Value: Culture and History in Solomon Islands*, edited by Ben Burt and Lissant Bolton, 47–53. Canon Pyon, UK: Sean Kingston Publishing.

Lake, Marilyn
2002 *Faith: Faith Bandler, Gentle Activist.* Crows Nest, NSW: Allen & Unwin.

Lal, Brij V.
1983 *Girmitiyas: The Origins of the Fiji Indians.* Canberra: Journal of Pacific History.

Lambert, S.M.
1933 Diary, May–June. Geisel Library Special Collections, University of California, San Diego, MSS 682, folder 22 (as noted by David Akin).
1946 *A Doctor in Paradise.* London and Melbourne: J.M. Dent and Sons Ltd and Georgian House.

Lange, Raeburn

2005   *Island Ministers: Indigenous Leadership in Nineteenth Century Pacific Islands Christianity*. Christchurch and Canberra: Macmillan Brown Centre for Pacific Studies, University of Canterbury, and Pandanus Books, The Australian National University.

Langmore, Diane

1989   *Missionary Lives: Papua, 1874–1914*. Honolulu: University of Hawai`i Press.

Laracy, Hugh M.

1974   Unwelcome Guests: The Solomons' Chinese. *New Guinea* 8 (4): 27–37.

1976   *Marists and Melanesians: A History of the Catholic Missions in the Solomon Islands*. Canberra: The Australian National University.

1983   *Pacific Protest: The Maasina Rule Movement, Solomon Islands, 1944–1952*. Suva: Institute of Pacific Studies, University of the South Pacific.

1988a   War Comes to the Solomons. In 'Taem Blong Faet: World War II in Melanesia', Hugh M. Laracy and Geoffrey White (guest eds). Special issue of *O`O: A Journal of Solomon Islands Studies* 4: 17–26.

1988b   Appendix 1: Those Who Served. In 'Taem Blong Faet: World War II in Melanesia', Hugh M. Laracy and Geoffrey White (guest eds). Special issue of *O`O: A Journal of Solomon Islands Studies* 4: 117–37.

2013   *Watriama and Co: Further Pacific Islands Portraits*. Canberra: ANU E Press.

Laracy, Hugh, and Eugenie Laracy

1980   Custom, Conjugality and Colonial Rule in the Solomon Islands. *Oceania* 51 (2): 133–47. doi.org/10.1002/j.1834-4461.1980.tb01963.x.

Laracy, Hugh M. and Geoffrey White (guest eds)
1988 'Taem Blong Faet: World War II in Melanesia'. Special issue of `O`O: A Journal of Solomon Islands Studies 4.

Lawrence, David R.
2014 *The Naturalist and His 'Beautiful Islands': Charles Morris Woodford in the Western Pacific.* Canberra: ANU Press.

Lawrence, Peter and M. J. Meggitt (eds)
1965 *Gods, Ghosts and Men in Melanesia: Some Religions of Australian New Guinea and the New Hebrides*, Melbourne: Oxford University Press.

Lindstrom, Lamont and Geoffrey M. White
1990 *Island Encounters: Black and White Memories of the Pacific War.* Washington, DC, and London: Smithsonian Institution Press.

Loeliger, Carl and Garry Trompf (eds)
1985 *New Religious Movements in Melanesia.* Suva and Port Moresby: University of the South Pacific and University of Papua New Guinea.

London, Jack
1911 *The Cruise of the Snark.* London and New York: Mills & Boon Ltd and Macmillan.

Lord, Walter
1977 *Lonely Vigil: Coastwatchers of the Solomons.* Annapolis, MD: Blue Jacket Books, Naval Institute Press.

Loyau, George E.
1897 *The History of Maryborough and Wide Bay and Burnett Districts from the Year 1850 to 1895.* Brisbane: Poole, Outridge & Co.

McArthur, Norma

1961   Report on the Population Census of 1959. *Western Pacific High Commission, British Solomon Islands Protectorate*. Honiara: British Solomon Islands Protectorate.

1981   *New Hebrides Population, 1840–1967: A Re-Interpretation*. Occasional Paper no. 18. Noumea: South Pacific Commission.

McDougall, Debra

2004   The Shifting Ground of Moral Community: Christianity, Property, and Place in Ranongga, Solomon Islands. PhD thesis, University of Chicago.

2013   Evangelical Public Culture: Making Stranger-Citizens in Solomon Islands. In *Christian Politics in Oceania*, edited by Matt Tomlinson and Debra McDougall, 122–45. New York and Oxford: Berghahn Books.

McKinnon, J.M.

1975   Tomahawks, Turtles and Traders: A Reconstruction in the Circular Causation of Warfare in the New Georgia Group. *Oceania* 45 (4): 290–307. doi.org/10.1002/j.1834-4461.1975.tb01872.x.

McLaren, Jack

1923   *My Odyssey*. London: Ernest Benn Ltd.

MacNeill, Ian

2000   *Sweet Horizons: A History of the Solomon Islands*. Melbourne and Sydney: Acland Press and Mieli Press.

Maeliau, Michael

1976   The Remnant Church: A Separatist Church. Long Essay written at Christian Leaders Training College, Banz, Papua New Guinea.

1985 The Remnant Church: Two Studies. In *New Religious Movements in Melanesia*, edited by Carl Loeliger and Garry Trompf, 120–48. Suva and Port Moresby: University of the South Pacific and University of Papua New Guinea.

Maggio, Rodolfo

2015 *Kingdom Tok*: Legends and Prophecies in Honiara, Solomon Islands. In 'Descent from Israel and Jewish Identities in the Pacific, Past and Present', Lynda Newland and Terry M. Brown (guest eds). Special issue of *Oceania* 85 (3): 327–41.

Marchant, William S.

1942–43 Diary, 2 January 1942 to 6 May 1943, transcribed by J. French, aide-de-camp to the High Commissioner, 29 Dec 1962, SINA, BSIP 5/IV/1.

Maranda, Elli Kongas

1970 Les Femmes Lau—Malaita, Iles Salomon—dans L'espace Socialise; Notes de Topographie Sociale. *Journal de la Société des Océanistes* 26: 155–62. doi.org/10.3406/jso.1970.2152.

1974 Lau, Malaita: 'A woman is an alien spirit'. In *Many Sisters: Women in Cross-cultural Perspective*, edited by Carolyn J. Matthiassen, 177–202. New York: Free Press.

Maranda, Pierre

2001 Mapping Cultural Transformation through the Canonical Formula: The Pagan versus Christian Ontological Status of Women among the Lau People of Malaita, Solomon Islands. In *The Double Twist: From Ethnography to Morphodynamics*, edited by Pierre Maranda, 97–120. Toronto: University of Toronto Press. doi.org/10.3138/9781442681125-007.

2008 *Voyage Au Pays Des Lau (Îles Salomon, Début Du Xxi Siècle) Le Déclin D'une Gynécocratie*. Paris: Éditions cartouche.

Maranda, Pierre and Elli Kongas Maranda
1970   Le Crâne et l'Utérus: Deux Théorèmes Nord-Malaitans. In *Échanges et Comminications: Mélanges offerts à Claude Lévi-Strauss à l'occasion de son 60 ème Anniversaire*, edited by Pierre Maranda and Jean Pouillon, 829–61. The Hague: Mouton.

Marwick, J.G. (ed.)
1935   *The Adventures of John Renton*. Kirkwall: Mackintosh.

Maude, H.E.
1968   *Of Islands & Men: Studies in Pacific History*. Melbourne: Oxford University Press.

Mayr, Ernst
1931   Birds Collected during the Whitney South Sea Expedition XVII: The Birds of Malaita Island (British Solomon Islands). *American Museum Novitates* 504 (1): 1–26.

Meleisea, Malama
1980   *O Tama Uli: Melanesians in Samoa*. Suva: Institute of Pacific Studies, University of the South Pacific.

Melvin, D.J.
1977   *The Cruise of the Helena: A Labour-Recruiting Voyage to the Solomon Islands*, edited by Peter Corris. Melbourne: Hawthorn Press.

Mercer, Patricia Mary
1995   *White Australia Defied: Pacific Islander Settlement in North Queensland*. Studies in North Queensland History, no. 21. Townsville: Department of History and Politics, James Cook University.

Mercer, Patricia and Clive Moore

1976 Melanesians in North Queensland: The Retention of Indigenous Religious and Magical Practices. *Journal of Pacific History* 11 (1–2): 66–88. doi.org/10.1080/00223347608572291.

Mission Life

1869 *The Island Mission: Being a History of the Melanesian Mission, Reprinted from Mission Life*. London: William MacIntosh.

Montgomery, Charles

2004 *The Last Heathen: Encounters with Ghosts and Ancestors in Melanesia*. Vancouver and Toronto: Douglas & McIntyre.

Montgomery, Henry Hutchinson

1986 *The Light of Melanesia: A Record of Thirty-Five Years Mission Work in the South Seas, Written after a Personal Visitation Made by Request of the Right Rev. John Selwyn, D.D., Late Bishop of Melanesia*. London: Society for Promoting Christian Knowledge.

Moore, Charles

1850 Extracts from a Journal Kept by Charles Moore (1820–1905), Formerly Director of the Botanic Gardens, Sydney, N.S. Wales, of a Voyage to New Caledonia, New Hebrides, Vanikoro and Solomon Islands, in H.M.S. 'Havannah' Captain (afterwards Commodore) Erskine, Extending from 14th July to November. The journal is in manuscript and was in the possession of Moore's family in Sydney. In PMB 1290, C. M. Woodford Papers, Reel 4, Bundle 24, 12/2.

Moore, Clive

1979 (ed.) *The Forgotten People: A History of the Australian South Sea Island Community*. Sydney: Australian Broadcasting Commission.

1981a   Kanaka Maratta: A History of Melanesian Mackay. PhD thesis, James Cook University of North Queensland.

1981b   Fatnowna, John Kwailiu Abelfai (1866?–1906). In *Australian Dictionary of Biography*, 8 (1901–1939), 473–74. Melbourne: Melbourne University Press.

1985   *Kanaka: A History of Melanesian Mackay*. Port Moresby: Institute of Papua New Guinea Studies and the University of Papua and New Guinea Press.

1991   'Me Blind Drunk': Alcohol and Melanesians in the Mackay District, Queensland, 1867–1907. In *Health and Healing in Tropical Australia and Papua New Guinea*, edited by Roy McLeod and Donald Denoon, 103–22. Townsville: Department of History and Politics, James Cook University of North Queensland.

1992   Revising the Revisionists: The Historiography of Immigrant Melanesians in Australia. *Pacific Studies* 15 (2): 61–86.

1993   The Counterculture of Survival: Melanesians in the Mackay District of Queensland, 1865–1906. In *Plantation Workers: Resistance and Accommodation*, edited by Brij V. Lal, Doug Munro and Edward D. Beechert, 69–99. Honolulu: University of Hawai`i Press.

1994–95   Noel Fatnowna and His Book: The Making of *Fragments of a Lost Heritage*. *Journal of Pacific Studies* 18: 137–50.

1997   Queensland and Its Coral Sea: Implications of Historical Links between Australia and Melanesia', *Northern Exposures*. Occasional Paper 19, papers from the 1996 Symposium of The Australian Academy of the Humanities, edited by Malcolm Gillies, 17–44. Canberra: Australian Academy of the Humanities.

2000   'Good-bye, Queensland, Good-bye, White Australia; Good-bye Christians': Australia's South Sea Islander Community and Deportation, 1901–1908. *New Federalist* 4: 22–29.

2003   *New Guinea: Crossing Boundaries and History*. Honolulu: University of Hawai`i Press.

2004a   *Happy Isles in Crisis: The Historical Causes for a Failing State in Solomon Islands, 1998–2004*. Canberra: Asia Pacific Press.

2004b   Rakwane. In *Pacific Places, Histories: Essays in Honour of Robert C. Kiste*, edited by Brij V. Lal, 242–66. Honolulu: University of Hawai`i Press.

2007   The Misappropriation of Malaitan Labour: Historical Origins of the Recent Solomon Islands Crisis. *Journal of Pacific History* 42 (2): 211–32. doi.org/10.1080/00223340701461668.

2008a   No More Walkabout Long Chinatown: Asian Involvement in the Solomon Islands Economic and Political Processes. In *Politics and State Building in Solomon Islands*, edited by Sinclair Dinnen and Stewart Firth, 64–95. Canberra: Asia Pacific Press.

2008b   The Kanaka Generation: The Visual Heritage of Melanesians in Australia. In *Les Cahiers Du Ciéra: La Restitution Du Patrimoine Matériel Et Immatériel: Regards Croisés Canada/Mélanésie*, edited by Frédéric Laugrand, Pierre Maranda and Florence Dupré, 79–113. Québec: Centre interuniversitaire d'études et des researches autochtones, Université Laval.

2010–12 Changes in Melanesian Masculinity: An Historical Approach. *South Pacific: Journal of Philosophy and Culture* 11: 28–41.

2013a   Peter Abu`ofa and the Founding of the South Sea Evangelical Mission in the Solomon Islands, 1894–1904. *Journal of Pacific History* 48 (1): 23–42. doi.org/10.1080/00223344.2012.756162.

2013b   Indigenous Participation in Constitutional Development: Case Study of the Solomon Islands Constitutional Review Committees of the 1960s and 1970s. *Journal of Pacific History* 48 (2): 162–76. doi.org/10.1080/00223344.2013.776784.

2013c   *Solomon Islands Historical Encyclopaedia, 1893–1978*, www.solomonencyclopaedia.net/.

2014 (ed.) *Looking beyond RAMSI: Solomon Islander's Perspectives on Their Future*. Honiara: Regional Assistance Mission to Solomon Islands.

2015a The Pacific Islanders' Fund and the Misappropriation of the Wages of Deceased Pacific Islanders by the Queensland Government. *Australian Journal of Politics and History* 61 (1): 1–19. doi.org/10.1111/ajph.12083.

2015b Australian South Sea Islanders' Narratives of Belonging. In *Narrative Practices and Identity Constructions in the Pacific Islands*, edited by Farzana Gounder, 153–74. Amsterdam: John Benjamins Studies in Narrative series.

2015c The Don Juan and Townsvale: Queensland and Indentured Pacific Islanders in the 1860s. In *Quintessentially Ross*, edited by W. Ross Johnston (and Margaret Kowland and Di Perkins), 41–75. Brisbane: Boolarong Press, catalogue.nla.gov.au/Record/7084519.

Moore, Clive and Mark Finnane

1992 Kanaka Slaves or Willing Workers? Time-Expired Melanesian Workers and the Queensland Criminal Justice System in the 1890s. *Criminal Justice History: An International Journal* 13: 141–60.

Moore, Clive and Patricia Mercer

1993 The Forgotten Immigrants: Australia's South Sea Islanders, 1906–1991. In *Race Relations in North Queensland*, edited by Henry Reynolds, 208–42. Townsville: Department of History and Politics, James Cook University of North Queensland.

Moorhouse, H.C.

1929   British Solomon Islands Protectorate. Report of Commissioner Appointed by the Secretary of State for the Colonies to Inquire into the Circumstances in which Murderous Attacks Took Place in 1927 on Government Officials on Guadalcanal and Malaita. Presented by the Secretary of State for the Colonies to Parliament by Command of His Majesty. London: H.M. Stationary Office.

Morens, David M.

1981   Measles in Fiji, 1875: Thoughts on the History of Emerging Infectious Diseases. *Pacific Health Dialogue* 5 (1): 119–28.

Mühlhäusler, Peter

1975   The Influence of the German Administration on New Guinea Pidgin. *Journal of Pacific History* 10 (4): 94–111. doi.org/10.1080/00223347508572283.

1976   Samoan Plantation Pidgin English and the Origins of New Guinea Pidgin: An Introduction. *Journal of Pacific History* 11 (2): 122–25. doi.org/10.1080/00223347608572295.

1981a   Foreigner Talk: *Tok Masta* in New Guinea. *International Journal of Sociology of Language* 28: 93–113. doi.org/10.1515/ijsl.1981.28.93.

1981b   Melanesian Pidgin English (Kanaka English) in Australia. *Kabar Seberang* 8–9: 93–105.

1996   Pidgins and Creoles of Queensland. In *Atlas of Languages of Intercultural Communication in the Pacific, Asia, and the Americas*, edited by Stephen A. Wurm, Peter Mühlhäusler and Darrell T. Tryon, 69–82. Berlin: Walter de Gruyter. doi.org/10.1515/9783110819724.2.69.

2002   Pidgin English and the Melanesian Mission. *Journal of Pidgin and Creole Languages* 17 (2): 237–63. doi.org/10.1075/jpcl.17.2.04muh.

Mühlhäusler, Peter, J.A. Bennett and D.T. Tryon

1979 Some English-Based Pidgins in the Southwest Pacific. In *New Guinea and Neighbouring Areas: A Socio-Linguistic Laboratory*, edited by Stephan A. Wurm, 53–78. The Hague: Mouton.

Mühlhäusler, Beverley S. and Peter Mühlhäusler

2005 Simple English in the South Sea Evangelical Mission: Social Context and Linguistic Attributes. *Language Problems and Language Planning* 29 (1): 1–30. doi.org/10.1075/lplp.29.1.02muh.

Mullins, Steve

1990 'Heathen Polynee' and 'Nigger Teachers': Torres Strait and the Pacific Islander Ascendancy. *Aboriginal History* 14 (2): 152–67.

1995 *Torres Strait: A History of Colonial Occupation and Culture Contact, 1864–1897*. Rockhampton: Central Queensland University Press.

Munro, Doug

1990 The Origins of Labourers in the South Pacific: Commentary and Statistics. In *Labour in the South Pacific*, edited by Clive Moore, Jacqueline Lecki and Doug Munro, xxxix–li. Townsville: Department of History and Politics, and Centre for Melanesian Studies, James Cook University.

Nagaoka, Takuya

2011 Late Prehistoric–Early Historic Houses and Settlement Space on Nusa Roviana, New Georgia Group, Solomon Islands. PhD thesis, University of Auckland.

Naitoro, John Houainamo

1993 The Politics of Development in `Are`are, Malaita. MA thesis, University of Otago.

Nanau, Gordon Leua

2014   Local Experiences with Mining Royalties, Company and the State in the Solomon Islands. *Journal de la Société des Océanistes* 138–39: 77–92. doi.org/10.4000/jso.7089.

Naval Officer

1893   Hoisting the Flag in the Solomon Islands. *Mission Field* 38 (1): 447–52.

Newland, Lynda and Terry M. Brown

2015   Introduction: Descent from Israel and Jewish Identities in the Pacific, Past and Present. In 'Descent from Israel and Jewish Identities in the Pacific, Past and Present', Lynda Newland and Terry M. Brown (guest eds). Special issue of *Oceania* 85 (3): 251–55.

Nunn, Patrick D.

2007   *Climate, Environment and Society in the Pacific during the Last Millennium.* Developments in Earth and Environmental Sciences, vol. 6. Amsterdam; Oxford: Elsevier. doi.org/10.1016/s1571-9197(07)06001-6.

Nunn, Patrick D., Rosalind Hunter-Anderson, Mike T. Carson, Frank Thomas, Sean Ulm and Michael J. Rowland

2007   Times of Plenty, Times of Less: Last-Millennium Societal Disruption in the Pacific Basin. *Human Ecology* 35 (4): 385–401. doi.org/10.1007/s10745-006-9090-5.

O'Brien, Aoife

2011   Collecting the Solomon Islands: Colonial Encounters and Indigenous Experiences in the Solomon Island Collections of Charles Morris Woodford and Arthur Mahaffy (1886–1915). PhD thesis, University of East Anglia.

O'Brien, Claire
1995   *A Greater than Solomon Here: A Story of Catholic Church in Solomon Islands*. Honiara: Catholic Church Solomon Islands Inc.

O'Callaghan, Mary Louise (ed.)
2013   *Rebuilding a Nation: Ten Years of the Solomon Islands-RAMSI Partnership*. Honiara: Regional Assistance Mission to Solomon Islands.

Oliver, Douglas L.
1989   *Oceania: The Native Cultures of Australia and the Pacific Islands*, vol. 1. Honolulu: University of Hawai`i Press.

Ouou, Emulio-Ree
1980   *History of South Malaita, Origins of Livings, Centre and Diameter of the Universe*. Honiara: Emulio-Ree Ouou.

Packard, Jerry C.
1975   *The Bougainville Taro Blight*. Miscellaneous Working Paper 1975–1. Honolulu: Pacific Islands Studies Program, University of Hawai`i.

Parsonson, G.S.
1966   Artificial Islands in Melanesia: The Role of Malaria in the Settlement of the Southwest Pacific. *New Zealand Geographer* 22 (1): 1–21. doi.org/10.1111/j.1745-7939.1966.tb00001.x.
1968   Artificial Islands Re-Examined. *New Zealand Geographer* 24 (2): 189–94.

Penington, David
2010   *Making Waves: Medicine, Public Hospitals, Universities and Beyond*. Carlton, Vic: Miegunyah Press.

Premdas, Ralph R., Jeffrey S. Steeves and Peter Larmour
1984   The Western Breakaway Movement in the Solomon Islands. *Pacific Studies* 7 (2): 34–67.

Price, Charles A., with Elizabeth Baker
1976   Origins of Pacific Island Labourers in Queensland, 1863–1904: A Research Note. *Journal of Pacific History* 11 (2): 106–21.

Randell, Nigel
2003   *The White Headhunter.* London: Constable.

Rannie, Douglas
1912   *My Adventures among South Sea Cannibals.* London: Seeley, Service and Company Ltd.

Raucaz, L.M.
1928   *In the Savage South Solomons: The Story of a Mission.* Boston: Society for the Propagation of the Faith.

Rhodes, F.
1937   *Pageant of the Pacific: Being a Maritime History of Australia.* Sydney: F.J. Thwaites.

Richards, Rhys
2012   *Head Hunters Black and White: Three Collectors in the Western Solomon Islands 1893 to 1914, and the Diary of Graham Officer, Collector of Museum Objects in the Solomon Islands in 1901 for Museum Victoria in Melbourne.* Wellington: Paremata Press.

Rodman, Margaret
1979   Introduction. In *The Pacification of Melanesia*, edited by Margaret Rodman and Matthew Cooper, 1–23. Ann Arbor: University of Michigan Press.

Roe, David
1992   Investigations into the Prehistory of the Central Solomons: Some Old and Some New Data from Northwest Guadalcanal. In *Poterie Lapita et Peuplement: Actes du Colloque Lapita*, edited by Jean Christophe Galipaud, 91–101. Noumea: ORSTOM.

Romilly, Hugh H.
1893   *Letters from the Western Pacific and Mashonaland, 1878–1891*. Edited by S.H. Romilly. London: David Nutt.

Ross, Harold M.
1970   Stone Adzes from Malaita, Solomon Islands: An Ethnographic Contribution to Melanesian Archaeology. *Journal of the Polynesian Society* 79 (4): 411–20.

1973   *Baegu: Social and Ecological Organization in Malaita, Solomon Islands*, Chicago: University of Illinois Press.

1976   Bush Fallow Farming, Diet and Nutrition: A Melanesian Example of Successful Adaptation. In *The Measure of Man: Methodologies in Biological Anthropology*, edited by E. Giles and J. Friedlaender, 550–615. Cambridge, MA: Peabody Museum Press.

1977   The Sweet Potato in the South-Eastern Solomons. *Journal of the Polynesian Society* 86 (4): 521–30.

1978a   Competition for Baegu Souls: Mission Rivalry on Malaita, Solomon Islands. In *Mission, Church, and Sect in Oceania*, edited by James A. Boutilier, Daniel T. Hughes and Sharon W. Tiffany, 163–200. Ann Arbor: University of Michigan Press.

1978b   Leadership Styles and Strategies in a Traditional Melanesian Society. In *Rank and Status in Polynesia and Melanesia: Essays in Honor of Professor Douglas Oliver*, 11–22. Publications de la Société des Océanistes, vol. 39. Paris: Musée de l'homme. doi.org/10.4000/books.sdo.947.

1978c   Baegu Markets, Areal Integration, and Economic Efficiency in Malaita, Solomon Islands. *Ethnology* 17 (2): 119–38. doi.org/10.2307/3773139.

Ross, R.M.

1983   *Melanesians at Mission Bay: A History of the Melanesian Mission in Auckland*. Wellington: Historic Places Trust.

Russell, Tom

1950   The Fataleka of Malaita. *Oceania* 21 (1): 1–13. doi.org/10.1002/j.1834-4461.1950.tb00169.x

Sack, Peter

2005   Who Wants to Know What 'Really' Happened? 'King' Gorai and the Population Decline in the Shortland Islands. *Journal of Pacific History* 40 (3): 339–51. doi.org/10.1080/00223340500312070.

Salisbury, Richard F.

1962a   *From Stone to Steel: Economic Consequences of a Technological Change in New Guinea*. Melbourne: Melbourne University Press.

1962b   Early Stages of Economic Development in New Guinea. *Journal of the Polynesian Society* 71 (3): 328–39.

Saunders, Kay

1974   *Uncertain Bondage: An Analysis of Indentured Labour in Queensland to 1907, with Particular Reference to the Melanesian Servants*. Brisbane: University of Queensland Press.

1976   The Pacific Islander Hospitals in Colonial Queensland: The Failure of Liberal Principles. *Journal of Pacific History* 11 (1): 28–50. doi.org/10.1080/00223347608572289.

1982   *Workers in Bondage: The Origins and Bases of Unfree Labour in Queensland 1824–1916*. St Lucia: University of Queensland Press.

Scarr, Deryck

1967a   *Fragments of Empire: A History of the Western Pacific High Commission, 1877–1914.* Canberra: Australian National University Press.

1967b   Recruits and Recruiters: A Portrait of the Pacific Islands Labour Trade. *Journal of Pacific History* 2: 5–24. doi.org/10.1080/00223346708572099.

Schieffelin, Edward L. and Robert Crittenden, with Bryant Allen et al.

1991   *Like People You See in a Dream: First Contact in Six Papuan Societies.* Stanford: Stanford University Press.

Schreiner, Shelly R.

1977   *The Kwaio Pagan Women of Malaita: The Life Stories of Gwaalau and Lamana.* Honiara: Solomon Islands Women's Association.

Schwartz, Theodore

1962   *The Paliau Movement in the Admiralty Islands, 1946–1954.* Anthropological Papers of the American Museum of Natural History, 49 (2). New York: The American Museum of Natural History.

Scott, Michael W.

2007   *The Severed Snake: Matrilineages, Making Place, and a Melanesian Christianity in Southeast Solomon Islands.* Durham, NC: Carolina Academic Press.

2012   The Matter of Makira: Colonialism, Competition, and the Production of Gendered Peoples in Contemporary Solomon Islands and Medieval Britain. *History and Anthropology* 23 (1): 115–48. doi.org/10.1080/02757206.2012.649276.

2013 Satan's 'Base' in the Pacific? Internal Christian Politics in the Dialogic Construction of the Makiran Underground Army. In *Christian Politics in Oceania*, edited by Matt Tomlinson and Debra McDougall, 49–77. New York: Berghahn Books.

Shanks, G. Dennis, Seung-Eun Lee, Alan Howard and John F. Brundage

2011 Extreme Mortality after First Introduction of Measles Virus to the Polynesian Island of Rotuma, 1911. *American Journal of Epidemiology* 173 (10): 1211–22. doi.org/10.1093/aje/kwq504.

Shineberg, Dorothy

1984 French Labour Recruiting in the Pacific Islands: An Early Episode. *Journal de la Société des Océanistes* 78 (40): 45–50. doi.org/10.3406/jso.1984.2530.

1999 *The People Trade: Pacific Island Laborers and New Caledonia, 1865–1930*. Pacific Island Monograph 16. Honolulu: Center for Pacific Islands Studies and University of Hawai`i Press.

Shlomowitz, Ralph

1979a Markets for Melanesian Labor in Queensland, 1863–1906. Adelaide: Flinders University, unpublished paper.

1979b The Search for Institutional Equilibrium in Queensland's Sugar Industry, 1884–1913. *Australian Economic History Review* 9 (2): 168–83.

1981 Markets for Indentured and Time-expired Labourers in Queensland, 1863–1906: An Economic Analysis. *Journal of Pacific History* 16 (2): 70–91. doi.org/10.1080/00223348108572416.

1982 Melanesian Labour and the Development of the Queensland Sugar Industry, 1863–1906. *Research in Economic History* 7: 327–62.

1986 The Fiji Labor Trade in Comparative Perspective, 1864–1914. *Pacific Studies* 9 (3): 107–52.

1987 Mortality and the Pacific Labour Trade. *Journal of Pacific History* 22 (1): 34–55. doi.org/10.1080/00223348708572550.

1989 Epidemiology and the Pacific Labor Trade. *Journal of Interdisciplinary History* 19: 585–610. doi.org/10.2307/203955.

1990a Differential Mortality of Asians and Pacific Islanders in the Pacific Labour Trade. *Journal of the Australian Population Association* 7 (2): 116–27.

1990b Mortality and Workers. In *Labour in the South Pacific*, edited by Clive Moore, Jacqueline Leckie and Doug Munro, 124–27. Townsville: Department of History and Politics, and Centre for Melanesian Studies, James Cook University.

Shlomowitz, Ralph and Richard D. Bedford

1988 The Internal Labour Trade in New Hebrides and Solomon Islands, c. 1900–1941. *Journal de la Société des Océanistes* 86: 61–85. doi.org/10.3406/jso.1988.2844.

Siegel, Jeff

1982 Plantation Pidgin Fijian. *Oceanic Linguistics* 21 (1–2): 1–72. doi.org/10.2307/3623154.

1985 Origins of Pacific Islands Labourers in Fiji. *Journal of Pacific History* 20 (2): 42–54.

Sinker, William

1900 *By Reef and Shoal: Being an Account of a Voyage amongst the Islands in the South-Western Pacific.* London and New York: Society for Promoting Christian Knowledge.

Smith, Graham
1991 *Sweet Beginnings: A History of Cane Growing on the Richmond River of New South Wales Compiled from the Letters, Reports, and People of an Ongoing Industry.* Ballina: Graham Smith.

Smith, Sydney Mercer
1893 Private diary as government agent, the *Helena*, James Cook University Library, Townsville.

1896 Private diary as government agent, the *Sybil II*, James Cook University Library, Townsville.

1898 Private diary as government agent, the *Sybil II*, James Cook University Library, Townsville.

1900 Private diary as government agent, the *Sydney Belle*, James Cook University Library, Townsville.

Smith, Thomas W.
1844 *A Narrative of the Life, Travels and Sufferings of Thomas W. Smith.* New Bedford, MA: Wm. C. Hill.

Spate, O.H.K.
1988 *Paradise Found and Lost: The Pacific since Magellan, Volume III.* Canberra: Australian National University Press.

Spriggs, Matthew
1995 The Lapita Culture and Austronesian Prehistory in Oceania. In *The Austronesians: Historical and Comparative Perspectives*, edited by Peter Bellwood, James J. Fox and Darrell Tryon, 112–33. Canberra: Department of Anthropology, Research School of Pacific and Asian Studies, The Australian National University.

1997 *The Island Melanesians.* Oxford: Blackwell.

Steinbauer, Friedrich
1971   *Melanesian Cargo Cults: New Salvation Movements in the South Pacific*. Translated by Max Wohlwill. St Lucia: University of Queensland Press.

Steley, Dennis
1983   Juapa Rane: The Seventh-day Adventist Mission in the Solomon Islands, 1914–1942. MA thesis, University of Auckland.
1989   Unfinished: The Seventh-day Adventist Mission in the South Pacific, Excluding Papua New Guinea, 1886–1986. PhD thesis, University of Auckland.

Stephen, Michelle (ed.)
1987   *Sorcerer and Witch in Melanesia*. Melbourne: Melbourne University Press.

Stevens, E.V.
1950   Blackbirding: A Brief History of the South Sea Islands Labour Traffic and the Vessels Engaged in It. *Royal Historical Society of Queensland Journal* 4 (3): 361–403.

Stone, Octavius C.
1876   Description of the Country and Natives of Port Moresby and Neighbourhood, New Guinea. *Journal of the Royal Geographic Society* 46: 34–62. doi.org/10.2307/1798668.
1880   *A Few Months in New Guinea*. London: Sampson, Low, Marston, Searle and Rivington.

Strathern, Marilyn
1972   *Women in Between: Female Roles in a Male World: Mount Hagen, New Guinea*. London and New York: Seminar Press.

1987 Conclusion. In *Dealing with Inequality: Analysing Gender Relations in Melanesia and Beyond*, edited by Marilyn Strathern, 279–302. Cambridge: Cambridge University Press.

1988 *The Gender of the Gift: Problems with Women and Problems with Society in Melanesia*. Berkeley: University of California Press. doi.org/10.1525/california/9780520064232.001.0001.

Summerhayes, Glenn R.

2006–07 Lapita Colonisation of the Pacific? *South Pacific: Journal of Philosophy and Culture* 9: 69–82.

Summerhayes, Glenn R. and Ian Scales

2005 New Lapita Pottery Finds from Kolombangara, Western Solomon Islands. *Archaeology in Oceania* 40: 14–20. doi.org/10.1002/j.1834-4453.2005.tb00575.x.

Taylor, John Patrick

2008 *The Other Side: Ways of Being and Place in Vanuatu*. Honolulu: University of Hawai`i Press. doi.org/10.21313/hawaii/9780824833022.001.0001.

Tedder, Margaret M.

1973 Staple Diets in the British Solomon Islands. *South Pacific Bulletin* 23 (3): 15–19.

Thomas, Nicholas

1989 The Force of Ethnology: Origins and Significance of the Melanesia/Polynesia Division. With Replies by A. Abramson, R.C. Green, M. Sahlins, R.A. Stephenson, F. Valjavec and R.G. White, and a Rejoinder by N. Thomas. *Current Anthropology* 30 (1): 27–34, 34–41; 30 (2): 211–13.

Timmer, Jaap

2008   *Kastom* and Theocracy: A Reflection on Governance from the Uttermost Part of the World. In *Politics and State Building in Solomon Islands*, edited by Stuart Firth and Sinclair Dinnen, 194–212. Canberra: ANU E Press and Asia Pacific Press.

2011   Visualising the Lost Temple and Mapping a Straightening World in Solomon Islands: Two Cultural Products of the Deep Sea Canoe Movement. In *Handbook of New Religious and Cultural Production*, edited by Carole M. Cusack and Alec Norman, 737–52. Brill Handbooks on Contemporary Religion. Leiden: Brill.

2012   Straightening the Path from the Ends of the Earth: The Deep Sea Canoe Movement in Solomon Islands. In *Flows of Faith: Religious Reach and Community in Asia and the Pacific*, edited by Lenore Manderson, Wendy Smith and Matt Tomlinson, 201–14. Dordrecht and New York: Springer Publishing Co. doi.org/10.1007/978-94-007-2932-2_12.

2015   Building Jerusalem in North Malaita, Solomon Islands. In 'Descent from Israel and Jewish Identities in the Pacific, Past and Present', Lynda Newland and Terry M. Brown (guest eds). Special issue of *Oceania* 85 (3): 299–314.

Tippett, Alan R.

1967   *Solomon Islands Christianity: A Study in Growth and Obstruction*. London: Lutterworth Press.

Townsend, Charles Haskins

1935   The Distribution of Certain Whales as Shown by Logbook Records of American Whaleships. *Zoologica: Scientific Contributions of the New York Zoological Society* 19 (1–6): 3–52, plus 12 maps.

Townsend, William H.

1969   Stone and Steel Tool Use in a New Guinea Society. *Ethnology* 8 (2): 199–205. doi.org/10.2307/3772981.

Trench, D.C.C.

1956 Marchant on Malaita. *Corona* 8 (5–7): 5: 106–08; 6: 230–33; 7: 58–61.

Trompf, Garry

1977 (ed.) *Prophets of Melanesia: Six Essays*. Port Moresby: Institute of Papua New Guinea Studies.

1991 *Melanesian Religion*. Cambridge: Cambridge University Press. doi.org/10.1017/CBO9780511518140.

Veperdi, András

n.d. The Journey of SMS 'Albatros' in the Solomons, mateinfo. hu/a-albatros.htm.

Vigors, Philip D.

1850 Private Journal of a Four Month Cruise through Some of the 'South Sea Islands', and New Zealand in H.M.S. Havannah. Manuscript in author's possession.

Wawn, William T.

1888 Private log, *Ariel*. Mitchell Library, Sydney.

1888 Private log, *Helena*. Mitchell Library, Sydney.

1890 Private log, *Upolu* and *Fearless*. Mitchell Library, Sydney.

1894 Private log, *Para*. Mitchell Library, Sydney.

1973 [1893] *The South Sea Islanders and the Queensland Labour Trade*. Edited by Peter Corris. Pacific History Series no. 5. Canberra: Australian National University Press.

Webber, Roger

2011 *Solomoni: Times and Tales from Solomon Islands*. Leicester, UK: Matador, Troubador Publishing Ltd.

Wetherell, David

1977   *Reluctant Mission: The Anglican Church in Papua New Guinea, 1891–1942.* St Lucia: University of Queensland Press.

1996   *Charles Abel and the Kwato Mission of Papua New Guinea, 1891–1975.* Melbourne: Melbourne University Press.

White, Geoffrey M.

1991   *Identity through History: Living Stories in a Solomon Islands Society.* Cambridge: Cambridge University Press. doi.org/10.1017/CBO9780511621895.

2013   Chiefs, Church and State in Santa Isabel, Solomon Islands. In *Christian Politics in Oceania*, edited by Matt Tomlinson and Debra McDougall, 171–97. New York: Berghahn Books.

White, Geoffrey M., David Gegeo, David Akin and Karen Ann Watson-Gegeo (eds)

1988   *The Big Death: Solomon Islanders Remember World War II.* Suva: University of the South Pacific.

White, Geoffrey M. and Lamont Lindstrom (eds)

1989   *The Pacific Theatre: Islands Representations of World War II.* Honolulu: Center for Pacific Studies and University of Hawai`i Press.

Whiteman, Darrell L.

1983   *Melanesians and Missionaries: An Ethnohistorical Study of Social and Religious Change in the Southwest Pacific.* Pasadena, CA: William Carey Library.

Whonsbon-Aston, C.W.

1964   *Pacific Irishman: William Floyd Inaugural Memorial Lecture.* Sydney: Australian Board of Missions.

Wilson, Cecil
1932   *The Wake of the Southern Cross: Work and Adventures in the South Seas*. London: John Murray.

Wilson, Ellen
1915   *The Isles that Wait*. London: Society for Promoting Christian Knowledge.

Woodford, Charles M.
1886   Diary, 16 April to 5 July 1886. PMB 1381/022, Reel 3, Bundle 6, 11.

1890   *A Naturalist among the Head-Hunters: Being the Account of Three Visits to the Solomon Islands in the Years 1886, 1887, and 1888*. Melbourne and Sydney: E.A. Petherick & Co.

1896   Diary of Part of Tour of Duty on 'Pylades', 30 May to 10 August. PMB 1381/033, Reel 4, Bundle 25, 1/1, 1/9, Ref. 8/16/3.

1908   Notes on the Manufacture of the Malaita Shell Bead Money of the Solomon Group. *Man* 8: 81–84. doi.org/10.2307/2839489.

1909   Notes on the Atoll of Ontong Java or Lord Howe's Group in the Western Pacific. *Journal of the Royal Geographical Society* 34: 544–49. doi.org/10.2307/1777282.

1922   The Solomon Islands. In *Essays on the Depopulation of Melanesia*, edited by W.H.R. Rivers, 69–77. London: Cambridge University Press.

1926   Notes on the Solomon Islands. *Geographical Journal* 68: 481–87. doi.org/10.2307/1782004.

Young, Florence S.H.
1925   *Pearls from the Pacific*. London: Marshall Brothers Ltd.

Zemp, Hugo

1971 Instruments De Musique De Malaita (I). *Journal de la Société des Océanistes* 30 (27): 31–53. doi.org/10.3406/jso.1971.2311.

1972 Instruments De Musique De Malaita (II). *Journal de la Société des Océanistes* 34 (28): 7–48. doi.org/10.3406/jso.1972.2352.

1981 Melanesian Solo Polyphonic Panpipe Music. *Ethnomusicology* 25 (3): 383–418. doi.org/10.2307/851551.

1996 The/an Ethnomusicologist and the Record Business. *Yearbook for Traditional Music* 28: 36–56. doi.org/10.2307/767806.

Index

Page numbers in **bold** refer to figures and tables.
The glottal stop (`) is ordered as the last letter in the alphabet.

Abbott, A. Hedley, 243, 247, 248, 254, 270, 272, 276, 280, 282, 283
Abel, Charles, 245, 273
Abu`ofa, Peter, 128, 217, 219, **233**, 245, 247, 266, 272, 278, 279, 280, 281, 282, 290, 292, 294, 295, 296, 297, 299, **386**, **446**
    Malu`u, 239–42
    William Manson case, 232–38
Abu`ofa, Ruby, 239
Acts
    Foreign Jurisdiction Act, 96, 302n5
    Masters & Servants Acts, 118
    Pacific Island Labourers Act, 236, 248
    Pacific Islanders' Protection Act, 97
    Polynesian Labourers Act, 97
adultery laws, 126, 387, 423, 435, 445
Advisory Council, 18, 123
Afilikwoi, 275
Afio, 425, 426, 427
Afoa, 452
Aiki, Fr Michael, 359n72
Aineo, 248, 267, 271
Airo, 214, 215
akalo, 63, 191, 284
akalo keni, 67
Akalofenda, 281
Aka`ako, Arthur, 211, 213, 225

Akin, David, 7, 7n14, 10, 11, 16, 34, 67, 69, 80, 86, 106
Akwa, Benjamin, 427
Alafurai, Bishop Leonard, 215n83
Alatala, 438
Alebiu, Barnabas, 280
Alebua, Ezekiel, 24, 25
Alexander, Capt. G.G., 374, 375
Alifiu, 390, 391
Aligegeo Experimental Primary School, 20
Alite, Alice, 229
Alite Harbour, 175
Aliwane, John, 271, 279
All Hallows' School, Pawa, Uki, 388, 427
Amasia, 105, 175, 219, 225, 227n122, 281, 311, 311n42
Amasia (Shadrach), **264**
Ambiasim, Thomas, 271, 274
American Samoa, 103
Americans, 15, 16, 93, 94, 111
Amina Laki, 228
ancestral religion, 10, 13, 21, 28, 31, 41, 43, 51, 59, 60, 62–66, 77, 79, 80, 81, 82, 129, 134, 135, 136, 138, 140, 143, 179, 184, 188, 191, 194, 195, 196, 196n25, 215, 257, 259, 284, 286, 289, 290, 291, 293, 297, 299, 310, 311, 320, 325, 327, 343, 361, 372, 406, 410, 446, 447, 455

flexibility in, 14–15, 184
in Queensland, 155, 195, 257, 390
Anderson, Guinevere, 384
Anderson, Pastor John D., 384
Anglican Church, 34, 312
   Australian Board of Missions, 152
   Bishop of London, 172
   Bishop Patteson Memorial Chapel, 228
   Christ the King Cathedral, Fiu, 210
   Church Missionary Society, 243, 243n40
   Church of the Epiphany, Fiji, 172
   Diocese of Brisbane, 151
   Diocese of Carpentaria, 152
   Diocese of Hawaii, 173
   Diocese of Melanesia *see* Melanesian Mission
   Diocese of Newcastle, 151
   Diocese of New Zealand, 173
   Diocese of North Queensland, 152, 157, 160
   Diocese of Polynesia, 173
   Diocese of Rockhampton, 152, 160, 163, 164
   Diocese of Sydney, 151
   Holy Trinity Church, Fiji, 172
   Hospital of the Epiphany, Fauaabu, 401, 420, **420**, **421**, **422**, 424, **444**, 451
   Melanesian Brotherhood (Ira Retatasiu), 196, 229
   New Guinea Anglican Mission, 154
   Southern Cross Log, 83, 100, 142, 201, 240
   St Andrew's College, New Zealand, 198, **198**
   St Barnabas Church, Tumbulgum, NSW, 170
   St Barnabas College, Norfolk Island, 1130, 151, 152, 160, 161, 178, 193, 199, 206, 209n61, 227, **227**, **228**
   St John the Baptist Church, Fiji, 172, 175
   St John's Church, Cudgen, NSW, 178
   St John's Pro-Cathedral, Brisbane, Qld, 159
   St Mary's Church, Pioneer, Qld, **157**
   Torres Strait, Qld, 152, 159
   See also Melanesian Mission; Selwyn Mission; ships—*Southern Cross*
Angofia, Rex Ringi, **30**, 32
Anilafa, Timothy, **254**
Aniuli, 217
Anoano, 448
anthropology, 33–34, 185, 194–95, 293, 407, 443
   See also Akin; Burt; Codrington; Coppet; Hogbin; Keesing
Anuta Baita Island, 48
Aoba Island, Vanuatu, 94n25, 309
Aoba, Jack, 149
aofia, 32, 67, 67n48, 127, 435, 436
Aola, Guadalcanal, 270, 271, 273, 276, 283, 296, 342, 349, 350, 371, 373
Apia, Samoa, 305
Araora River, 372
Ara`iasi, 356, 392, 393, 436, 438
Areo, 451
Arfiliu, 248
Ariel Harbour *see* Rokera
Arisimae, 299, 356, **357**, 359, 390, 392, 393, 434, 436, 438
Armed Constabulary *see* police
Armstrong, Thomas Seymour, 310
Arthur, James, 311
artificial islands, 14, 21, 42, 46, 48, **50**, 51, 52, 60, **61**, 64, 68, 70, 81, 94, 209, 216, 218, 225, 226, 287, 312, 384, 387, 396, 438, 444

Asiasi, 387
Asimani, **270**
Aswani, Shankar, 310
Atkin, Rev. Joseph, 203
Atoifi Hospital, 384
Atori, 39
Au, Rev. Willie, 287
Auckland, New Zealand, 101, 130, 151, 193, **198**, 227
Auki *see* `Aoke
Aulu, 183
Australia, 28, 29, 33, 60, 82, 84, 88 Map 7, 97, 136, 144, 171, 179, 219, 234, 240, 266, 273, 303, 309, 318, 327, 364, 366, 376, 395, 402, **403**, 407, **409**, 414, 415, 426, 450
    deportation of Solomon Islanders, 219, 242, 243, 248–59
    White Australia Policy, 29, 219, 242, 248, 295
    See also New South Wales; Queensland; Tasmania; Western Australia
Australian Papua, 332, 343, 345
Australian South Sea Islanders, 12, 29, 32, 99, 105, 120, 170n104, 180, **181**, 201, 257, 337
    oral history, 29
    Queensland Commissioner for Pacific Islanders, 31
Australians, 15, 22, 29, 318, 342, 370, 429, 450, 451
    Indigenous, 106, 111, 117, 271, 323, 323n76, 333n107, 447
Austronesian *see* languages
Avondale, Qld, 48
Avu, 311, 312
Ay Choy, 394
Ayr, Qld, 148, 150, 157, 160
A`ama, 427

Baalmoli, 273
Baddeley, Bishop Walter, 451
Baegu, 50, 59, 62, 391, 396, 398, 408, 441
Baelelea, 59, 441
Bahá'í Faith, 191, 295, 300
Bali region, 413, 417, 436
Ball, Lieut., 89
Ballarat, Victoria, 243
Bandler, Faith, 170n104
Banivanua-Mar, Tracey, 5, 6–7
Banks Islands, Vanuatu, 56, 173, 204, **205**, 209n61, 214
Baptist, 140, 169
Baramula, Joseph, 156, 215
Barata, David, 275
Barker, John, 190
Barley, Jack, 429, 436, 442
Barnett, Frederic (Frank), 301, 317, 326, 327, 334, 366, 367, 368, 391, 396
Basakana Island, 42, 59, 246, 277, 279
Basakana Strait, 245
Basitaloa, Tom, 215
bata (shell wealth) 7, 55–59, 61, 393
Baunani, 186, 190, 230, 267, 296, 323n76, 326, 333, 340, 342, **346**
    labour barracks, 351
    school, **264**, 326, 333, 345, 349, 352
Beattie John W., 208, 220, 224
Bedford, Richard, 86, 122
Bell, William R., 10, 18, 29, 129, 312, 318, 321, 340, 344, 351, 352, 363–404, **364**, **367**, **369**, 405, 407, 408, 409, 410, 412, 413, 429, 438, 439, 446, 448
Bellona Island, 4, 44, 103, 250, 303, 304n8
Bena Islet, 247, 248
Bengough, Charles N.F., 405, 429, 433, 441, 451

Bennett, Judith, 9, 12, 82, 86, 87, 91–92, 93, 126, 135, 175, 307, 340, 341, 342, 374, 402, 413, 419, 431
Bertreux, Fr Jean-Ephrem, 355, 356
betel palms, 53
Bina, 65 Map 5, 438, 439
Bina Harbour, 6, 175, 224, 312, 317, 323, 372, 395, 448
Bingera, Qld, 148, 149
Bio, 218
Birkbeck, Mrs, 159
bisi see women
Bismarck Archipelago, 4, 43, 44
Bita`ama, 59, **60**, 186, 199, 215, 216, 247, 248, 271, 273, 277–81, 390, 391, 438
Bobongie, Fr Timothy, 359n72
Bogese, George, 423, 424, 429
Boldery & Cheetham, 414
Boli Passage, Gela, 56, 316
Booth, Commandant Herbert, 170
Booth, Cornelie, 170
Boudoko, 247
Bougainville Island, 4, 54, 56, 90, 302, 340, 354, 431, 450, 451n5, 457
bounty-hunters, 7, 22, 66, 67, 68, 69, 131, 364, 390, 391
Brands, Miss, 162
Brenan, John O'Neil, 236
Brisbane, Qld, 29, 128, 130, 140, 151, 152, 157, 159, 160, 161, 164, 169, 234, 236, 238
Brisbane City Mission, 140, 250
Brisbane Courier, 232
Britain, 16, 29, 82, 96, 97, 111, 201, 204, 237, 302
British Admiralty, 98, 303
British New Guinea, 152, 273, 303, 354
British Solomon Islands Protectorate, 11, 15, 28, 110, 139, 303–06, 406

Brittain, Rev. A., 153, 154, 155, 160
Brodziack & Co., A.M., **137**
Bruny, D'Entrecasteaux, Joseph-Antoine Raymond, 89
Buai, 212
Bubuileli Council House, **31**
Buchanan, Florence, 147
Buderim, Qld, 169, 170
Bugotu, Francis, 189, 190, 290
Bugotu, Isabel, 10, 91
Buka Island, 4, 44, 302
Bullen, H.W., 451
bulu cults, 284
Buma, 186, 353, 355, 359, 388, 425, 428
Bundaberg, Qld, **114**, 142, 143, 144, 147, 148, 152, 159, 160, 161, 162, 163, 164, 165, 166, 178, 179, 213, 214, 232, 234, 236, 238, 239, 240, 242, 243, 249, 250, 251, 252, 253, 267
Bundaberg Mail, 234
Bungana, Gela, 388
Burdekin district, Qld, 29, 150, 157, 160, 161, 168
Burinali, 217
Burns Philp & Co., 29, 243, 350, 376, 377, 413, 415, 443
Burt, Ben, 34, 67, 80, 86, 105, 106, 111, 136, 188, 191, 192, 194, 195, 284, 289, 290, 297, 297n42
Bu`ai, Henry, 273, 274

Caboolture, Qld, 159
Cairns, Qld, 148, 149, 150, 152, 157, 158, 160, 169, 251, 252
Campbell, Frederick M., 318, 327, 329, 330, 366, 390
cannibals, 5–6, 359, 375, 449, 453
canoes, 8, 10, 29, 43, 45, 49–50, **49**, **50**, 70, 71 Plan 1, 73, 74, 76, 85, 87, 88, 89, 92, 96, 97, 104, 105, 106, **137**, 196, 198, 215n83, 217, 218, 219, 220, 225, 226, 228, 245, 269, 271, 276, 278, 279,

280, 285, 288, 308, 311, 314, 316, 317, 322, 355, **367**, 392, 395, 452
Cape Arascides, 175
Cape Astrolabe, 89, 246, 452, 453
Cape Marsh *see* Russell Islands
Cape York, Qld, 152, 171
Cape Zélée, 87, 89, 207
Carpenter, W.R. *see* W.R. Carpenter & Co.
Carteret, Philip, 88
castaways, 8n16, 48, 85, 92, 93–95, 128
Catalina seaplane, 452
Catholic Church, 34, 140, 167, 175, 187n8, 189, 192, 199, 231, 264, 291, 293, 299, 323, 323n76, 334, 335–36, 348, 353–60, **358**, 371, 383, 384, 388, 390, 393, 425, 427, 451
  Buma, 186, 353, 355, **358**, 359, 388, 425, 428
  indigenous clergy, 388
  land purchased, 348, 357
  Marist arrival, 186, 191, 231, 291, 334, 355
  Pacific War, 451
  Rohinari, 186, 267, 353, 355, 356, 366, 357, 359, 360, 384, 388, 390, 392
  ships, 355
  Takwa, 427, 428
  Tarapaina, 56, 186, 323n76, 353, 356, 359, 388, 392, 393, 438
  theology, 299, 359
  Visale, 359, 360, 392
Catholic relations
  with Melanesian Mission, 354
  with SDA, 383, 384
  with SSEC, 371
Cattlin, Edwin, 90
Caulfeild, Henry St George, 243, 247, 270, 271, 272, 273, 274, 277, 278, 279, 280, 281, 282, 323n76

census (first), 53–54, 85, 381, 429–34, 430
  See also demography; depopulation
Central Medical School, Fiji, 423
Ceylon, 334
Chair and Rule movement *see* Fallowes movement
Charters Towers, Qld, 159
Childers, Qld, 148, 163
children, 7, 8, 32, 49, **50**, 52n21, 70, 73, 92, 96, 131, 144, 155, 156, **156**, 157, **157**, 170, 196, 204, 212, 213, 224, 229, 232, 234, 243, 251, 258, **263**, 269, 272, 273, 275, 277, 279, 282, 285, 286, 288, 290, 293, 304, 323, 337, 360, 368, 380, 382, 386, 390, 401, 410, 427, 432, 450
China, 4, 43, 147, 168, 234, 243
China Inland Mission, 145, 168, 243, 263, 265, 266
Chinatown, 27, **27**, 341, 150
Chinese, 15, 117, 163, 254, 394, 414, 415, 418, 429, 447, 448
Choiseul, 4, 55n31, 91, 103, 302, 304n8, 381, 395, 423, 442, 451, 457
Choy, Ay, 394
Christenson, Rev. C., 167
Christianity, 6, 10, 16, 21, 22, 28, 31, 34, 35, 62, 65, 80, 81, 82, 85, 105, 130, 135, 137, 138, 139, 140–80, 183–300, 301, 311, 318, 319, 325, 334, 342, 345, 355, 360, 383–88, 425–46, 447, 449, 455, 456, 458, 459
  level of conversion, 180
  See also Anglican Church; Catholic Church; Queensland Kanaka Mission; Seventh-day Adventist; South Sea Evangelical Mission
Churches of Christ, 140, 150n27, 166, 167, **167**, 253

525

Church of England *see* Anglican Church
Clayton, Mrs, 161–62, 164
Clayton, Rev. J.E., 142, 161, 165
Clemens, Martin, 434
climate, 42, 45, 118, 190
clothes, 73, 124, 129, 219, 245, 254, 257, 269n7, 286, 321, 360, 361, 428, 433, 448
Coakley family, 15
Coastwatchers, 29, 450, 451n5
coconut palms, 2, 208, 216, 225, 317n55, 343, **346**, 372, 374, 418
codification of native custom, 440, 441, 442
Codrington, Rev. Robert H., 151, 192, 193, 194, 195, 196, 203
Coicaud, Fr Donatien (Donatiey), 80, **358**, 359, 428
Coicaud, Fr Jean, 80, 359, 360, 390, 392, 393, 366
Coleridge Bay *see* Subongi
Coles, Rev. James, 147
Collins, John, 95
Collins, R.J., 393
colonial knowledge and ignorance, 80
colonial regulations, 109, 170, 249n54, 340, 366, 373, 376, 377, 398, 399, 440
Colonial Sugar Refining Co., 163
Comins, Rev. Richard B., 172, 173, 175, 183, 203, 204, 218, 304
compensation, 5, 6, 6n10, 10, 25, 28, 55, 56, 59, 134, 136, 213, 256, 286, 291, 314, 343, 360, 363, 375, 389, 390, 391, 407, 446
Cooper, Matthew, 56, 80
Coppet, Daniel de, 54, 63, 74, 80, 87, 210
Corris, Peter, 34, 86, 87, 93, 179, 363, 407, 410
cosmology, 35, 55, 72, 74–81, 194, 196, 361, 457

courts, 17, 18, 63, 96, 97, 232, 234, 236, 237, 321, 382, 383, 397, 399, 405, 406, 408, 440–42, 445
Crichlow, Dr Nathaniel, 401, 402
cricket, 394
Cromar, Jock, 8, 9
Cudgen, NSW, 148, 170
cultural flexibility, 14–15, 85
currencies, British, 380, 382
currencies, local, 49, 55, 59, 60, 92, 127, 382.
 See also bata; dogs—teeth as wealth; flying-fox teeth as wealth; porpoise teeth as wealth; tobacco
Curtis Island, Qld, 151

Dala, 216, 326, 440
Dalao, 390
Damiki, James, 226
Daniels, Frederick, 324, 325, 326, 327
Daomai, John, 225
Dauramo, 386
Dausuke, James, 218
Davidson, Allan, 194
Da`i (Gower) Island, 42, 88, 329, 452
Deck, Catherine (Kathy), 261, **263**, 279, 288, 299, 323n76, 427
Deck, Jessie, **263**
Deck, Joan, 427
Deck, John Northcote, 1, 6, **263**, **270**, **274**, 323n76, 335, 345, 348, 375, **386**, 401, 427
Deck, Norman Cathcart, 6, 7, 8, 9, **264**, 335, 345, 348, 400, 427
Deep Bay *see* Takataka
Defence Force, Solomon Islands, 15, 439, 453
Delamo, Harry, 251
demography, 5, 14, 23, 53–54, 54n29, 413, 430, 432, 432n69, 436
 See also census; depopulation

INDEX

depopulation, 54, 86, 91, 307, 417, 433, 430, 431
See also census; demography
Deputy Commissioners *see* government officers
descent groups, 28, 31, 32, 35, 39, 43, 46, 48, 50, 62–69, 76, 93, 128, 195, 201, 213, 222, 226, 228, 247, 264, 304, 310, 311, 312, 320, 322, 352, 371, 387, 396, 407, 435, 438
Diakafu, 195, 325
Dickinson, Joseph, 322, 378, 392
Didi, 239
Diocese of Melanesia *see* Melanesian Mission
diseases, 14, 53, 54, 86, 96n27, 106–07, 117, 139, 184, 186, 190, 351, 401, 419, 431, 432, 433, 457, 458
  causation, 132–33, 135
  colds, 323
  dysentery, 133, 340, 344, 400, 402, 410, 419, 430, 432
  epidemics, 51, 87, 132, 322
  German measles (Rubella), 132, 419
  gonorrhoea, 341
  immunities, 256
  influenza, 132, 307, 401, 402, 409, 419, 430, 431, 432
  leprosy (Hansen's disease), 51, 421, 423
  measles, 430, 431, 432, 458
  meningitis, 419
  pneumonia, 132, 402, 432
  poliomyelitis, 419
  respiratory, 51, 132, 430, 432
  smallpox, 132, 307, 432
  venereal, 419
  whooping cough, 132, 432
  See also depopulation
District Commissioners *see* government officers
District Officers *see* government officers
divination (*unu*), 280
Dodo Creek, Guadalcanal, **26**
dogs, 43, 220
  teeth as wealth, 55, 60
Dolaiasi, Rev. Nat, 387
Donaldson, Elizabeth, 168
Doolbi, Qld, 166
Doorey *see* Matthews, John
Dora, Andrew, 204, 387
Doraweewee, 203, 438
Double Bay *see* 'Oloburi Harbour
Douglas, Mr and Mrs, 148
Drake, Rev. F.V., 158
Dring, Miss C.S., 243, **263**, 273, 277, 288, 323n76, **425**
Duff Islands, 4, 304
Dumont d'Urville, Jules S.C., 4n5, 89
Dureau, Christine, 34
Duu, 330
dysentery *see* diseases

economy, modern, 10, 17, 25, 256, 361, 382, 385, 414, 415, 418, 436
  depression, 17, 413–18
  development, 10, 36
  See also labour trade; taxation
economy, pre-European, 55, 73
  See also currencies, local; markets; trade; wealth items
Edge-Partington, Mary, **331**
Edge-Partington, Thomas, 317, 318, 319, 320, 321, 322, 323, 324, 325, 326, 327, 328, 329, 331, 332, 334, 335, 365, 366, 387, 394, 395, 396, 448
education, modern, 20, 25, 31, 139–81, 197, 208, 230, 425–28, 439
  See also Christianity
education, pre-European, 70
Efate Island, Vanuatu, 149
'eight isles', 55, 74, 75 Map 6, 135
Elsworth, Edward, 234

527

Elu`u, **31**
epistemology, 78–79
Erringa, 237
Erringa, chief of Saurina, 218
Erromango, Charley, 167
Erskine, Capt John, 9, 96
European exploration, 85, 87–89
Eustace, Rev. Alfred E., 147, 168, 232, 236, 238, 239, 250
Eustace, L.D., 147, **251**
Eva, Rev. Richard, 164

Fafanga, Harry, 386
Fairymead plantation, Qld, 144, 144n10, 145, 148, 149, 161, 258, 266, 267, 268, 269, 345
Fairymead Sugar Company Ltd, 414, 448, 458
Faka`ia, 204, 228, 304
Fallowes movement, 11, 418, 434
Farapo, 206
Farere, `Atta Cove, 218
Farisi, 325
Farkyer, Daniel, 272
Farulate, Sam, 325
fataabu, 32, 47, 66–67, 127, 195, 196, 325, 435, 435, 439
fataabu keni, 67, 289
Fataleka, 2, 3, 29, **30**, **31**, 41, 46, 50, 59, 62, 64, 65 Map 5, 66n43, 67, 76, 127, 175, 195, 214, 273, 274, 389, 396, 398, 413, 438, 439, 451
Fatnowna, Cecily, **181**
Fatnowna, Christie, **84**
Fatnowna, Harry, **181**
Fatnowna, Hazel, **84**
Fatnowna, John Abelfai Kwailiu *see* Kwailiu
Fatnowna, Joy, **181**
Fatnowna, Lucy, **181**
Fatnowna, Noel, 2, 6, 29, **30**, 31, 136
Fatnowna, Norman, **84**
Fatnowna, Orrani *see* Orrani

Fauaabu (Kwarea), 59, 186, 199, 401, 420, **420**, **421**, **422**, 424, 443, **444**, 451
Ferasubua Island, Lau, **77**, 175, 217, 219, 220, 223, 224, 225, **287**, 320
Feriasi, 282, **282**
Ferris, Ken, 428
Fia, Rev. Martin, 387
Fifi`i, Jonathan, 325
Fiji, 4, 83, 97, 119, 129, 213, 252, 253, 256, 289, 301, 302, 355, 365, 423
  demography, 430, 432
  ex-Fiji labourers, 105, 106, 126, 129, 133, 175, 176, 184, 185, 188, 197, 201, 206, 210, 211, 217, 218, 219, 226, 249, 265, 279, 281, 292, 295, 296, 311, 438
Fiji labour trade, 8, 12, 83, 85, 86, 93, 94, 98, 101, 102, 112, 114, 249, 250, 269, 313, 314, 326, 327, 337, 339, 341, 365, 385, 457
  beach bonus, 120, 416
  Christianity, 171–76, 179–80, 185, 266, 294, 296, 299, 301, 306, 318, 319
  education, 459
  firearms, 125, 306
  Government Agents, 249, 305, 318, 334, 365, 377, 391
  illegality, 103, 104, 226, 311
  mortality, 132, 133, 323
  plantation culture, 133–35, **137**, 142, 211, 223, 311, 337, 340, 346, 390, 442, 443
  plantations, 33, 109, 110
  Solomon Islands community, 337, 340
  statistics, 102, 110, 121, 178, 337
  violence, 307–09
  wages, 121

See also Anglican Church; Methodist Mission; Pijin English; Pijin Fijian
Fijians in Solomon Islands, 15, 117, 226, 323, 323n76, 327, 329, 355, 356, 423, 429, 447
Filose, Francis B., 409
Finifolota, Rev. Matthias, 388
firearms, 66n43, 107, 125–26, 213, 313, 328, 389, 390, 399
Firosia, **264**
first contact with outsiders, 86–98
first settlement on Malaita, 43–46
First World War, 337, 366, 413
Fito (Fiito`o), Peter, 272
Fiu, 156, 175, 186, 198, 199, 210–16, **212**, 218, 224, 226, 240, 245, 248, 251, 254, 266, 271, 273, 296, 312, 316, 320, 321, 323n76, 330, 387, 402, 425, 427, 453
Florida Islands *see* Gela Group
Floyd, Lieut.-Comm., 303
Floyd, Rev. William, 171–72
flying-fox teeth as wealth, 55, 60
foakali, 439
Foate, 199, 214, 216, 224, 311
Fokanakafo Bay, 46, 65, 65 Map 5, 91, 124, 127, 389, 440, 452
Fono, 438
food, 22, 44, 45, 48–49, 52–53, 55, 56, 66, 73, 90, 92, 106, 127, 132, 133, 169, 176, 183, **220**, 235, 239, 251, 256, 281, 288, 316, 320, 328, 362, 374, 394, 397, 410, 429, 432
  taboos, 66, 73, 299, 343, 383
Forlesikwa, Samson, 274
Forti, 272
Foster, Miss, 270
Fouia, Lau, 130, 199, 221, 226, **274**, **274**, 427
Foulden plantation, Qld, **118**
Fousaari`i, 452
Fowler, William, 437

Fox, Charles E., 196, 254, 388
Fo`odo, 232, 247, 274, 248, 271, 272, 273, 274, 275, 277, 279, 280, 301, 323n76, 327, 333, 333n107, 414, 418, 436, 438, 451, 452
Frazer, Ian, 80
Fricke, Frederick, 148, 149
Fricke, Margaret, 243, 247
Fuaga, 217, 223, 225
Funusau, Eban, 451
Furingi, 392
Furi`isango (Fulisango), 451
Fusai, 438

Gaggin, John, 8, 9
Galla, 311
Gamour, 241
Gamu Island, 273
Gao, Isabel Island, 10, 76, 91
Gaomae (Ramos) Island, 79
gardens, 44, 52–53, 66, 72, 73, 92, 107, 131, 176, 208, 213, 215, 217, 239, 290, 323, 340, 352, 371, 372, 394, 410, 436, 445
  See also food
Gardiner, Mr, 159
Gavutu Island, 243, 246, 247, 270, 271, 272, 276, 277, 283, 306, 353, 382, 415, 450
Ga`a, Salana (Maega`asia), 19, **20**, 451
Gegeo, David, 14, 78–79, 80
Gela Group, 3, 11, 15, 43, 48, 55, 56, 74, 76, 89, 91, 162, 170, 178, 187, 192, 209n61, 211, 213, 214, 218, 221, 225, 230, 279, 296, 304, 306, 312, 316, 317, 330, 353, 354, 368, 384, 387, 399, 415, 427, 434, 440, 442, 459
Gemite, 317
gender, 12, 22, 39, 62, 69–73, 106, 107, 185, 284–90, 361, 446
  femininity, 13

masculinity, 12–13, 36
taboos, 81, 196, 286
See also women
Geotee, Rev. Henry, 387
Geraldton *see* Innisfail
German measles (Rubella) *see* diseases
German New Guinea, 4, 303, 307
German Samoa, 85, 101, 106, 110, 117, 118, 119, 126, 133, 171, 178, 186, 259, 302, 305, 306, 319, 337, 443
Gibbon, Walter, 386
Gibson, Captain, 303
Gilbert Islands *see* Kiribati
Gilvete, Joe, 211
Gin Gin, Qld, 148
Gizo, 34
Gladstone, Qld
Gold Ridge, Guadalcanal, 24
gonorrhoea *see* diseases
Goodrich, Capt. James, 124
Goodwood, Qld, 166
Gori`i, Stephen, 376, 398
Gosila, 242
Gounaabusu Village, Kwaio, **258**
government officers
  Deputy Commissioners, 98, 303, 305, 369
  direct rule, 13, 395–97
  District Commissioners, 17, 18
  District Officers, 10, 13–14, 29, 34, 68, 80, 125, 129, 312, 318, 363, 395–400, 405, 437, 442, 451
  headmen, 18, 31, 129, 179, 385, 388, 393, 408, 409, 438, 439
  High Commissioners, 19, **19**, 97, 98, 249, 302, 303, 305, 307, 327, 328, 330, 331, 332, 337, 367, 368, 439, 440, 442
  indirect rule, 13, 34, 398–400, 411
  Resident Commissioners, 18, 36, 119, 125, 129, 184, 240, 267, 301, 302, 305, 317, 320, 326, 327, 328, 331, 334, 365, 366, 368, 370, 372, 373, 379, 385, 387, 391, 408, 411, 450
  Resident Magistrates, 307, **316**, 317, 318n60, **324**, **331**, 335
  See also Bell; Edge-Partington, Thomas; Fiji labour trade—Government Agents; Queensland labour trade—Government Agents; Woodford
Grae, Charley, 213
Graham, Major, 169
Grange, The, Qld, 161
Great Depression, 17, 123, 338, 340, 364, 414, 435
Green Hill, Cairns, Qld, 150
Gregory, Qld, 166
Groves, William C., 426, 428
Guadalcanal, 3, 13, 15, 24–25, 28, 43, 48, 53, 55, 59, 60, 74, 76, **84**, 87, 89, 90, 91, 101, **118**, 125, 163, 189, 273, 276, 283, 306, 317, 322, 349, 350, 351, 352, 354, 355, 373, 386, 401, 425, 434
  Christianity, 147, **157**, 298, 323, 359, 360, 384, 392, 393, 427, 453
  demography, 53–54
  economic development, 33, 37
  ethnography, 441, 443
  head-hunting, effect on, 457
  irrigation, 53
  Isatabu Freedom Movement, 24–25, 28
  Japanese occupation, 450, 452
  labour, 101, 103, 110n63, 162, 309, 323, 336, 338, 374, 378
  land alienation, 458
  Maasina Rule, 11, 167
  militants, 449
  Native Councils, 442
  plantations, 312, 371, 389
  police, 330

taxation, 381
trade, 55
traders, 126
Weather Coast, 79, 86, 90
Guadalcanal Province, 24, 458
Guidieri, Remo, 80
Guinness, Dr Harry, 148
Guala`ala`a, 3, 47 Map 4, 206, 281, 296
Gulf of Carpentaria, Qld, 109, 152
Guo, Pei-yi, 80
Guyles, B., 420
Gwaelaga Island, Langalanga, **58**
Gwai`au Village, 232, 373, 279, 280
Gwalekafo Village, 438
Gwali Asi, **61**
Gwaru, 278
Gwaunaru`u Airfield, 32
Gwau`ulu, 214, 387
Gwounatolo, 427, 428
Gympie, Qld, 169

Halbwachs, Fr Joseph, 427
Hale, Bishop Mathew, 152
Hansen's disease *see* diseases
Hap Wah plantation, Qld, 150
Hapsberg plantation, Qld, 148
Harding, Judge George, 237
Harwood, Capt., 94
Hauhari`i (Sail Rock), 452
Hauhui, 271, 333, 373, 398
Hay, Rev. R.S., 163
head-hunters, 5, 10, 34, 62, 90–91, 126, 131, 453, 459
Henry, Alice, 243, 384
Herbert River, Qld, 142, 149, 150, 158, 160, 164, 165
High Commissioners *see* government officers
Hill, Ralph B., 352, 366
Hilliard, David, 34, 145, 192, 193, 261, 263
historiography, 13, 16, 33–34
Hitee, Fr Donasiano, 359
Hoaredoa, 283

Hoasihau, 434
Hogbin, H. Ian, 34, 80, 293, 441, 443
Holthouse, Hector, 96
Holt-MacCrimmon, Dr Lily, 401, 420
   See also Neil MacCrimmon
Homebush, Qld, 168
Homehill, Qld, 157, 160
homosexuality, 73, 341
Hong Kong, 329
Honiara, 6, 12, 19, 20, 23, 24, 25, 29, 32, 33, 36, 73, 87, 97n31, 137, 256, 286, 458, 459
Hopkins, Rev. Arthur, 80, 83, 127, 128, 129, 153, 193, 211, 212, 213, 214, 215, 219, 220, 221, **222**, 223, 224, 225, 226, 227, 240, 241, 247, 255, 256, 272, 278, 307, 320, 321, 324, 353, 368, 387, 391, 419
Horne, Mr, 171
Hospital of the Epiphany, Fauaabu, 401, 420, **420**, **421**, **422**, 424, **444**, 451
Hossack, Hugh, **122**
Howard, Fred, 204, 305
Hulo, 348n31, 350, 351, 372, 373, 374, 375
human teeth as ornaments, 60, 97, 220
Hutchinson, Rev. C.A., 159

Ia`ura (South Sister) Island, 48, 271
im Thurn, Sir Everard, 337
India, 93n22, 144, 146, 147, 209, 265
Indian labourers, 110, 117, 337
Indian Ocean, 98
Indispensable Reef, 250
Indispensable Strait, 87, 89, 90
influenza *see* diseases
Ingham, Qld, 148, 150, 157, 158, 164

Inimanu, Billy, 214, 216
Ini`a, 311
Innes, Dr James Ross, 421
Innisfail (Geraldton), Qld, **138**, **146**, 148, 150, 214
Irofa`alu, Shem, 385, **386**
Irofiala, Jasper, 451
Iroi, 217
Irokula, Livae, **386**
Irokwato, 320, 391, 396, 408
Iro`ota, Paul, **386**
Isabel Island, 2, 10, 11, 34, 44, 76, 79, 91, 95
Isatabu Freedom Movement, 24–25
Isis district, Qld, 143, 148, 162, 163, 166, **167**, 178, 213, 282
Islam, 296, 300
Islands Trading Company, 373, 374
Israel, Lost Tribes of, 450, 454, 455
Itea, Ishmael Idumaoma, 29, **30**, **31**, 32, 195, 196n25, 438, 439, 451
Iumane, James, 207
Ivens, Rev. Walter G., 39, 48, **61**, 76, 80, 91, 126, 176, 185, 193, 195, 196, 196n27, 199, 206, 207, 208, 209, 211, 216, 217, 218, 219, 240, 254, 275, 281, 305, 311n42, 323, 368, 432, 432n69
Ivo, James, 213, 221, 225
Iwi Harbour, 234

Jackson, Sir Henry, 249n54
James Cook University, Qld, 29
Japan, 15, 117, 234
  See also Pacific War
Javanese, 110, 117
Jeffries, Brig. Charles H., 169
Johnston, C.F., 147
Johnstone River, Qld, **146**, 149, 158, 160
Jolly, Margaret, 289
Jones, Rev. J. Francis, 171, 172, 211
Julius, Canon Alfred H., 164, 164n83

Kabbou, 94, 128
Kai, 219
Kaihione, Petero, 360
Kailafa, 223
Kaiviti (Kai`figi), Jackson, 129, 277, 298, 312
Kakalu`ae, Timothy, 129, 130, 437
Kakwari, 330
Kalkie, Malu`u, 280
Kalkie, Qld, 148, 238
Kanaa, Benjamin, **386**
Kanakwai, John, **386**
Kane, Richard R., 408
Kangaroo Point, Brisbane, 250, **251**
Kanole, 438
Kanoli, Joel, **386**
kastom, 17, 18, 21, 453, 455, 456
Kasutee, Edward, 387, 388
Katoomba, NSW, 147, 150, **244**, **247**
Keesing, Roger, 6n12, 11, 31, 68, 80, 289, 325, 363, 407, 410
Keld, Joseph, 236
Kelen, Raymond, 227
Keller, Otto G., 327
Kemakeza, Sir Allan, 25
Kenilorea, Sir Peter, 33, 407, 408, 440n95
King George VI School, 20, **264**, 428, 448
Kiriau, Rev. George, 387
Kiribati (Gilbert Islands), 4
Kirke, Sub-Inspector B., 334, 370
Knibbs, Stanley G.C., 374
Knockroe plantation, Qld, 166, 213
Koa Bay, 245
Kobey (Kobi), Daniel, 232, 234, 237
Kohimarama, New Zealand, 151, 198, **198**, 227
Kolombangara, 90, 305
Kon Kon, Sam, 271
Konai, 214
Kongori, Alick, 396
Kope Pipiala, 393
Kukum plantation, Guadalcanal, 450

Kulijeri (Reid) family, 159
Kumalau, Stephen, **386**
Küper, NMP Geoffrey, 423
Kwai Island, 3, 186, 199, 206, 223, 248, 254, 266, 272, 275, 281–84, 288, 296, 312, 396, 398, 434n74, 438, 448, 452
Kwaiatiboo, 408
Kwaibala (Quibala), 314, 317, 448
Kwaidiu, 280
Kwaifela River, 348, 372
Kwaifunu, 281
Kwaihaodowala, 208
Kwailabesi, 215, 384, 401, 423, 428
Kwailabesi Hospital, 215, 384, 401, 423, 428
Kwailiu (John Fatnowna), 2, 180, **181**
Kwainauri, Joseph, 311
Kwaio, 6, 7, 7n14, 9, 10, 11, 39, 50, **58**, 59, **62**, 63, **68**, 79, 81, 435, 436, 451
  ancestral priests in Queensland, 195
  ancestral worship, 62–63, 64, 179, 372, 447
  attack on Bell party (1927), 312, 327, 363, 405, 407–12, **409**, **411**
  bata, 59
  chest ornaments, 60
  Christianity, 187, 224, 226, 227, 246, 247, 269, 286, 296, 384–85
  compensation, 10, 363
  courts, 441, 442
  demography, 413
  descent groups, 67
  foods, introduced, 106
  genetic studies, 43
  labour trade, 112, **258**, 283, 283n36, 417
  labour trade attacks, 9
  labour trade influences, 133–34, 135, 310
  lamo batons, 7
  land purchased, 284
  Malayta Company, 370–76
  maoma (mortuary) rituals, 133–34
  Mt Tolobusu, 4
  naval attacks, 327
  Pacific War, 452
  passage masters, 124
  sango dancing, 133–34
  taro, 446
  taxation, 129
  trophy bags, 71
  women, 67, 289
  See also Akin; Bell; Keesing
Kwaisulia, 8, 94, 124, 127–30, 217, 218, 219, **220**, 221, 223, 225, 226, **235**, 236, 238, 277, 278, 279, 298, 311, 437
Kwaisulia, Christopher England (Igilana), 130
Kwaivania, Charlie, 330
Kwakwai *see* Qaqae
Kwaliasi, 225
Kwara`ae, 6, 46, 50, 59, 62, 66, 67, 79–79, 323, 396, 436
  akalo keni, 67, 297
  ancestral religion, 62, 194
  bata, 56, 59
  bridewealth, 444
  cannibalism, 6
  Christianity, 191, 210, 212, 213, 214, 296, 324, 436, 443–44, 454–55
  demography, 413, 436
  education, 427
  epistemology, 78–79
  ex-Fiji labourers, 106, 106, 213
  ex-Queensland labourers, 251
  fataabu keni, 67, 289
  genealogy, 455
  Guala`ala`a, 206
  headmen, 398
  labour trade, 106, 112

labour trade attacks, 9
labour trade illegality, 105
leadership, 66–67
Native Court, 441
Pacific War, 452
tafuli`ae, 56
taxation, 417
women, 67, 297
Kwarea *see* Fauaabu
Kwaria Bay *see* Fo`odo
Kwari`ekwa, 271, 274
Kwato Mission, PNG, 273
Kwa`a Cove, 372
Kwa`ala, John, 279, 281
Kwa`iga, 325
Kwong Chong & Co., 394, 414, 415
Kwore, Small Malaita, 206

La-as-si, 145
Labour Corps, Solomon Islands, 15, 418, 453
Labour Regulations, 340, 365, 373
labour trade, 3, 8–9, 12, 13, 16, 21, 22, 29, 34, 35, 51, 98–138, **117**, 378
   attacks, 9, 101
   BSIP, 188, 336–52, 378
   cultural kidnapping, 99
   firearms, 66n43, 107, 125–26, 213, 313, 328, 389, 390, 399
   German New Guinea, 103
   German Samoa, 101
   historiography, 86–87
   illegality, 93, 103, 104, 311
   Melanesian Mission recruiting, 203, 204, 210, 211, 213, 217, 218, 219, 227–29, 232, 281, 388
   mortality, 123, 132
   New Caledonia, 101
   New Guinea, 103
   oral testimony, 419
   plantation culture, 109–11, 134, 135–38

   recruiting patterns, 112–19
   slavery allegations, 99–100
   statistics, 83, 86, 101
   violence, 130–32
   voluntarism, 99–100
   working class formation, 118
   See also Fiji; Pijin English; Pijin Fijian; Queensland
lagoons *see* Langalanga; Lau; `Are`are
Lainau (Laina`o), 320
Lambert, Dr Sylvester M., 420, 424
Lamosi, John, 162
Lanaa, Levi, 218
Lancaster, Mr, 148
Langalanga, 3, 8, 41, 48, **49**, 56, **57**, **58**, 68, 91, 212, 273, 317, 323, 330, 436
   Alite Island, 312
   bata manufacture, 56–58, 316
   Bina Harbour, 317
   Christianity, 210, 224, 245
   economy, 415
   gender divisions, 68
   government, 323, 396
   head-hunting, effect on, 91
   labour trade, 8, 112, 127, 178, 355, 378
   Pacific War, 452
   porpoise hunting, 59
   proclamation of BSIP, 304
   Rarasu, 314
   stevedores, 382, 415, 443, 447
   trade, 3
Langasia, 210
languages, xxv–xxvii, 3, 21, 22, 35, 43, 46, 47 Map 4, 77, 94, 106, 184, 189, 443
   Austronesian, 4, 43
   Christianity, 14, 173, 190, 191, 192, 206, 207, 214, 249, 254, 259, 293, 297, 360
   education, 428
   trading, 3
   `Aoke Island, 214, 244

See also Pijin English; Pijin Fijian; `Aoke
Lapit, 43, 44
Laracy, Hugh, 16, 34, 356, 359, 360, 423
Lascars, 93n22
Lau, 8, 39, 41, 48, **50**, 56, 59, **61**, 68, 76, **77**, 80, 90, 96, 98, 112, 124, 127, 128, 129, 130, 155, 175, 198, 204, **220**, **222**, 330, 235, **235**, **274**, **287**, 418, 432, 440
  artificial islands, 287
  Christianity, 175, 206, 208, 211, 212, 215n83, 216–26, 238, 240. 254, 272, 293, 307, 320, 330, 384, 387, 391, 401, 419, 423, 427, 428
  ex-Fiji labourers, 175
  gender, 73
  genealogy, 48
  headmen, 388, 437
  labour trade, 94, 123, 124, 127, 128, 129, 272
  leadership, 67, 94, 277, 388, 437
  naval attacks, 307, 311
  Ontong Java connection, 74
  passage masters, 94, 298
  plantation culture, 134
  Urasi, 238
  Walade links, 3, 50, 95, 204, 208, 266, 296
  `Ataa Cove, 51, 80, 218, 396, 398
  See also Amasia; Kwaisulia; Renton; Taloifulia
Laukana, Samuel, **386**
Laulana, 199
Laulasi Island, 304, 323, 452
Lau`a, Isaac, 105, 226, 227n122
Lawrence, David, 184
Layton, G.E., 163
leadership, 15–23, 31, 39, 62–69, 80–81, 127, 129, 130, 145, 292, 411, 435, 437

Leap, The, Qld, 155
Leauli, NMP Eroni, 423
Ledi, Bobbi, 127
Leli Atoll, 105, 308, 311
Leo, Rev. Joseph, 228
Leong Tong, 394
leprosy *see* diseases
Levers Pacific Plantations Ltd, 322, 342, 344, 349, 350, 378
Levuka, Fiji, 172
Libe, Serg. Bob, 169
Lilimae, 175, 176
Lillies, Kenneth C., 407, 408, 409
Linana`au, Marcus John, 394
Lini, Walter, Hon Rev., 5
Lio, Enoch Jack, 275
Lioiaa, Dick, **386**
literacy, 3, 16, 18, 85, 86, 140, 142, 176, 178, 179, 184, 186, 249, 426, 427, 437, 439, 459
Liufakona, Livae, **386**
Livingstone Inland Mission, 145, 147, 148
Lobotalau, **58**
Lofana, John, 283
Lofeah (Lofia), Charlie, 270, 280
Logan, Qld, 159
Loi, **264**
Lolowai Islet, `Ataa, 218
London Missionary Society, 159, 167, 171
Lost Tribes of Israel, 450, 454, 455
Lotaa, 438
Lounga, Saelasi, 310
Loyalty Islands, 99, 140, 164, 169, 171
Lugard model, 395, 411, 429
Luiramo, Charles, 32
Lumsden, Norman, 150
Lunga, Guadalcanal, 450, 452
Lutheran, 140, 164
Lyndon, Victor C., 373

Maabe, Rev. Henry, 387, 453
Maanaere, 215, 320, 324, 326
Maanakwai, **108**, 124, **270**
Maanawai, 267, 272, 275
Maana`oba (Ngwalulu) Island, 42, 56, 94, 272, 278, 279, 310, 321, 330, 348
Maasina Rule, 3, 4, 6n10, 11, 15–23, 33, 34, 35–36, 37, 80, 111, 129, 130, 179, 180, 186, 234, **264**, 265, 385, **386**, 405, 406, 418, 428, 434, 451, 455, 459
Maasupa, **52**
McArthur, Norma, 431
McBride, Mrs, **386**
McBride, Robert, **263**, **386**
McCabe, George, 311, 312
MacCrimmon, Neil, 401, 414
  See also Holt-MacCrimmon
McDougall, Debra, 34
McGown, Mr, 375
MacGregor, Lieut.-Gov. Sir William, 354
McIntyre, Miss, 163
McIntyre, Rev. J. McLean, 150, 167, 168, **168**, 169
Mackay, John, 238
Mackay, Qld, 29, 32, **84**, 86, **118**, 120, **122**, 130, 131, 142, 143, 150, 151, 152, 153, **154**, **157**, 162, 170n104, **181**, 431
  Christianity in, 156, 157, 160, 161, 165, 166, 167, 176, 177, 180, 214, 234, 253, 253, 273, 431
  deportation from, 251
  Islander hospital, 155
McKenzie, Capt. H., 104
Mackenzie, C.C., 312, 317
McKenzie, Mr and Mrs, 147
Macknade plantation, Qld, 150
Maclaren, Rev. Albert, 152, 153
McLaren, Jack, 252
McLeod, Bolton & Co., 414

MacNeill, Ian, 454
Maeana, Joe, 408
Maeasuaa, 326
Maega`asia *see* Ga`a, Salana
Maekalai, Job, 403
Maekali, 438
Maena, Alec, 434
Maesiola, Rev. John, 210
Maetabu, William, 176
Mahaffey, Arthur, 129, 306, 307, 311, 313, 317, 326, 328, 332, 337
Mahratta, Makeni (Maggie), 178
Mahratta, Timothy George, 144, 459
Mahratta, Tolimcane (Thomas), 178
Maifonia, 392
Maifou, 283
Maikali, Joe, 323
Maitafu, George, 213
Maitofana, Nathan, **386**
Major, Sir Charles, 328
Maka Theological Training Institution, 193, 425, 427, 435
Makambo, 276, 283, 382, 415, 418, 443, 450
Makira (San Cristobal), 2, 3, 11, 12, 16, 34, 43, 55, 55n31, 59, 62, 73, 74, 76, 85, 89, 91, 92, 93, 96, 97, 126, 193, 196, 206, 209n61, 221, 298, 303, 305
  Christianity, 147n17, 193, 196, 206, 209n61, 221, 298, 352, 354, 425, 427, 436
  demography, 431, 432n69
  early European contact with, 85, 90, 91, 92, 93, 126
  'eight isles' concept, 74
  government, 318
  labour, 338, 350, 351
  Maasina Rule, 18
  porpoise hunting, 59
  shell wealth, 55
  St Mary's School, Pamua, 427
  taxation, 381

trade and kin links with Malaita, 48, 55, 62, 76, 89, 92, 97
whaling, 90, 305
Makwano, 384, 423, 427
Mala Development Company, 414
Mala, meaning, 2
Mala Timber Company, 376, 401, 414
Malafou, 317
Malaita Council, 19, **19**, **20**, 31, **264**
Malaita Eagle Force, 24, 25, **26**, 455
Malaita Province, 37, 81, 458
Malapa Island, Marau Sound, Guadalcanal, 79
malaria, 45, 48, 54n29, 166, 238, 240, 276, 329, 341, 344, 430, 433
Malayta Company, 230, 262 Map 13, 273, 273n17, 296, 323n76, 324, 345–52, **346**, 370–76, 378, 382, 386, 388, 408, 413, 452
 Baunani school, 349
 Catholic Mission, relationship with, 371
 communications, 371
 hospital, 374
 industrial Christianity, 318, 350, 375, 414
 labourers, 326, 338, 341, 350, 351, 353, 373, 378, 382, 408
 land acquisition, 326, 323, 334, 342, 346, 348, 349, 372, 373
 law and order problems, 370, 372, 375–76, 389
 Pacific War, 452
 relationship with SSEM, 190, 266–67, 296, 328, 333, 336, 345
 trading stations, 349, 414, 415
 violations of ancestral shrines, 373
 See also Fairymead Sugar Company Ltd
Malekula Island, Vanuatu, 309
Mallicolo, Billy, 158
Maluni, 251

Malu`u, 91, 242, 269, 270, 271, 272, 275, **278**, 279, 282, 292, 295, 296, 307, 323, 363, 395, 438
 anthropology, 185, 250, 293, 443
 government, 307, 311, 395, 438
 headman, 438
 markets, 238
 modern economy of, 328, 376, 385, 414, 418
 murders, 242, 280, 311, 363, 366, 390
 naval attack, 311
 Pacific War, 452
 police, 398
 ramo, 390, 436
 Spanish influenza pandemic, 432
 trade stores, 376
 See also Abu`ofa; Young, Florence
Malu`u Christianity, 186
 Melanesian Mission, 199, 224, 239, 240, 293, 353, 427
 QKM, 219, 224, 232, 238–39, 240, 243, 245, 247, 353
 SSEM, 216, 253, 293, 294, 323n76, 333, 387
mamama, 66, 77, 79
Man Chong & Co., 394
 See also Kwong Chong & Co.
Manaba, 333, 348n35, **349**, 350, 351, 352, 374, 414, 448
Manalok, 330
Manbili, Benjamin, 398
Mandurama, Qld, 153, 155
Mangonia, 218
Manofiu, 241
Manus Island, PNG, 4, 43, 56
Maramasike *see* Small Malaita
Maramasike Passage, 2, 3, 21, 41, 50, 90, 397, 427, 435, 452
Maranda, Pierre, 67, 80
Marau, Clement **205**, 209n61
Marau, Jack, **84**
Marau, Martin, 209, 209n61

Marau Sound, Guadalcanal, 3, 59, 60, 76, 79, **84**, 87, 125, 127, 322, 355
Maravovo School, Guadalcanal, 453
Marchant, William, 450, 451
Maré Island, Loyalty Group, 169
Marian, Qld, 153, **154**, 155
Marist *see* Catholic Church
Marita, Paul, 209, 209n61
markets, 51, 210, 217, 238, 239, 240, 272, 275, 278, 316, 321, 322, 440
Maroochy, Qld, 169, 170
Marovo Lagoon, 55n31, 428
Maro'umasike *see* Takataka
Maryborough, Qld, 120, 142, 151, 159, 164, 167
Mason, Rev. Albert, 387, 425, 427
Mason, Gwendoline, 387, 425
Masonic Lodge, Tulagi, 451
Masuraa, Luke, 173, 183, 186, 204, 229, 304
Matai, Matthew, 272
material culture, 76
   fou'atoleeleo, 7
   hauanoreereo, 7
   wa'ifirua, 7
   See also *bata*; canoes; dogs—teeth as wealth; flying-fox teeth as wealth; porpoise teeth as wealth
Matthews, John (Doorey), 94
Maumolu Naunitu Island, Isabel, 79
Mauritius, 234
Maybury, Florence Edna (née Johnson-Kaine), 401
Maybury, Dr Lysander Montague, 401, 420, 421
Ma'arumae, **386**
Ma'asina Forum, 6n10
Meadowlands plantation, Qld, 153, 154, 155
measles *see* diseases
Meke, Stephen, **386**

Melanesian Brotherhood (Ira Retatasiu), 196, 218, 229, 427
Melanesian Mission (Diocese of Melanesia), 35, 100, 101, 128, 130, 151–53, 160, 161, 163, 164, 164n82, 165, 166, 167, 172, 175, 176, 183–230, 199, **200**, 202 Map 12
   Fiji, 171–76, 177 Table 3
   Fiu, 210–16
   Lau, 128, 216–27
   Malaita, 231, 232, 239, 240, 245, 247, 249, 254, 261, 265, 266, 267, 269, 272, 275, 278, 281, 292, 293, 294, 295, 296, 297, 298, 304, 323n76, 328, 334, 435
   Norfolk Island, 130, 227–29
   Pacific Islanders' Fund, 165–66
   Queensland, 151, 153, 160–64, 166, 176, 177
   recruiting process, 100–01, 199
   Sa'a, 203–10
   Small Malaita, 199, 203–10
   St Barnabas College, 130
   statistics, 229–30
   theology, 190, 192–96
Mendaña expedition, 2, 53, 87
meningitis *see* diseases
Menzies, Dr, 424
Mercer, Patricia, 87
metal tools, 107, 272, 285, 290, 446
   See also technology, new
Methodist (Wesleyan) Mission
   Fiji, **174**, 175
   Solomon Islands, 192, 219, 291, 349, 353, 354
migration, 36, 42, 43–45, 48, 51, 65, 65 Map 5, 74, 113 Graphs 1 & 2
   labour trade, 83, 98–108, 112–19, 133–38, 139, 249–59
Mills-Parker, Dr Dorothy, 384, 401, 423, 428
   See also Parker

INDEX

Minata, Joe, 215
Mitchell, Miss, **263**
Mitchell, Sir Philip, 442
Miuldo, Tom, 127
Mon Repos plantation, Qld, 161
Mono (Treasury) Island, 90, 103, 302, 302n3
Montgomery, Charles, 453, 454
Montgomery, Bishop Henry H., 449
Moona, Thomas, 274
Moorhouse, Lieut. Col. Sir Harry, 395, 411, 436
Moran, Cardinal Patrick, 355
Moro movement, 11
Morris, Rev. William, 162
Mosman, Daniel, 275
Mossman, Qld, 148, 149, 150, 152, 157, 159, 282
Mota Island, Vanuatu, 170, 172
Mota language (Anglican *lingua franca*), 162, 173, 256, 292, 427, 428
Mota Lava Island, Vanuatu, 204, 206, 211
Mt Bellenden Ker, Qld, 158
Mt Tolobusu, Kwaio, 41
Mulgrave, Qld, 158, 169
Musée du quai Branly, France, 7

Naitoro, John, 14, 74, 77, 78, 80
Nalaia, 392
Naoniola, 209
nationalism, 16, 36
Native Administration Regulations, 387, 395, 398
Native Courts, 17, 405, 440, 441, 442
Naumauri, 356
Naute`e, Joseph, **386**
Na`oni`au, **58**
Near Oceania, 4, 5, 6, 13, 86, 307, 431, 432, 460
Nelson, Qld, 149
Nelson, Qld Premier Hugh, 160
Nenemo, 438

New Britain, 43, 56, 91, 107, 307
New Caledonia, 4, 85, 95, 101, 104, 106, 110, 117, 119, 133, 178, 302, 306, 319, 443
New Georgia Group, 4, 10, 44, 55n31, 62, 76, 90, 91, 95, 103, 126, 131, 219, 304, 305, 383, 428, 457
New Guinea, 4, 6, 32, 43, 89, 103, 110, 111, 171, 253, 296, 302, 303, 307, 355, 431, 432, 450, 451
New Guinea Mandated Territory, 29
New Hebrides *see* Vanuatu
New Ireland, 43, 91
New South Wales, 89, 95, 96, 97, 109, 140, 144, 148, 151, 159, 163, 169, 170, 177, 345, 414
New Zealand, 15, 97, 144, 144n10, 161, 162, 164, 173, 197, 198, **198**, 201, 203, 206, 420, 427, 451, 453
Ngongosila, 3, 6, 186, 199, 327
  Bell and Lillies' graves, 407
  government, 396
  Guala`ala`a, 3, **47**, 206, 281, 296
  illegal recruiting, 227
  Melanesian Mission, 219, 281
  QKM, 199, 253–54, 266, 272, 275, 281
  schools, 175
  SSEM, 199, 282, **282**, 283, **284**, 296, 311, 311n42, 323n76, 324
Ngorefou, 128, 186, 198, 199, 211, 213, 219, **222**, 223, 224, 225, 226, 272, 278, 311, 320, 353, 387, 391
Nguna, Thomas, 282, 297, 299
Nguni, Thomas, 239, 240, 282, 297
Nigeria, 411
Nindaroo plantation, Qld, 155
Nono`oohimae Eerehau, Alike, 63
Noranga, Joe, 212

539

Norfolk Island, 101, 130, 151, 160, 162, 175, 176, 178, 184, 192, 193, 196, 197, 199, 201, 203, 203n38, 204, **205**, 207, 208, 209n61, 210, 211, 213, 217, 218, 219, 221, 227, **227**, 228, **228**, 229, 232, 256, 281, 284, 388
Norman, Gov. Sir Henry, 237
Norris, C.G., 366
Northern Territory, 152
Not in Vain, 275

O'Brien, Claire, 34
O'Brien, J.C., 238
Oceania, 443
Oiu, 204
Olaha, Small Malaita, 198
Olver, G.T., 243
Omba Island, Vanuatu, 214
Onepusu, 209, 248, 258, 261, 267, 269, 271, 273, **276**, 277, 296, 299, 325, 327, 346, 378, 384, 397, **400**, 401, 402, 403, **403**, **425**
 church, 280
 Pacific War, 453
 school, 179, 425
 SSEM headquarters, 186, 199, 224, 230, 253, 249, 266, 275–77, 282, 283, 323n76, 333, 345, 352, 359, 386, 388, 390, 401
 store, 418
 Training Centre, 426, 427
Ongamon, Joe, 226
Onivero, Fiji, 172
Ontong Java Atoll, 42, 74, 81, 302, 304n8, 306, 441
Open Plymouth Brethren, 144, 144n11, 293, 383
Order-in-Council, 97, 303, 304n8, 328
Orlu Island, 356
Orrani (Fatnowna), 2, **181**

orthography, xxv–xxvii
Osifelo, Frederick Aubarua, **19**
Osiskalo, Thomas, 213
Othanila, 386
Otoa, Peter, 171
Oto`akaloa, James, **386**
Ouasihu, 438

Pacific Forum, 23
Pacific Islanders' Fund, 161, 165, 166, 169, 252
Pacific Islands, geographic division, 4n5
Pacific War, 3, 15, 35, 36–37, 438, 441, 447, 448, 449, 450–53, 456
Packe, Rev. Horace, 173, 175
Palasu`u, 199, 207
Palms plantation, Qld, 155
Papua New Guinea, 4
Parker, Pastor A.F., 384, 423, 428
 See also Mills-Parker
passage masters, 8, 94, 99, 112, 117, 123, 124, 127, 128, 129, 130, 217, 236, 298, 341, 342, 364, 377, 381
Paton, Rev. John G., 243
Patteson, Bishop John Coleridge, 104, 151, 172n109, 192, 193, 198, 203, 203n38
Pau, 209
Penny, Rev. Alfred, 21
Pentecost Island, Vanuatu, 54n29, 100, 105, 149, 323n76
Philip, Jimmy, 274
Phillips, Judge J. Beaumont, 374, 375
Phillips Lands Commission, 348, 374n30
Philp, J.E., 322
Pijin English
 Fiji, 118
 Queensland, 3, 118, 119, 128, 134, 139, 153, 160, 186, 214, 221, 234, 238, 241, 252, 256, 341
 Samoa, 178

Solomon Islands, 2, 3, 16, 85, 86, 118, 119, 163, 184, 211, 259, 292, 319, 341, 360, 428, 437, 438, 443, 456, 457
Pijin Fijian, 86, 118, 140, 173, 175, 176, 178, 184, 213, 256, 265, 279, 280, 311, 438, 443
Piko, NMP Gusto Rato, 423
Pilate, Sam, 248, 269, 283, 297
Pillans, Charles B., 239, 240, 242
Pinnock, Philip, 237
Pioneer plantation, Qld, 154, 155, **157**
Pioneer River, Qld, 153, 168
Pioneer Valley, Qld, 29, 143, 153, **154**, 214
pneumonia *see* diseases
Poikana, Adela, 360
Point Cruz, Honiara, 87
police, 129, 213, **264**, 320, **324**, 334, **338**, 366, **369**, 371, 394, 395, **411**, **417**, 437, 429, 437, 438, 439, 449, 452
  armoury, 322
  attack on (1927), 407
  barracks, **332**
  Commander, 318, **319**, 327, 329, 390
  corporal, 452
  cricket, 394
  district officer, direct control, 13, 185, 327, 329, **364**, **367**, 391, 395, 396, 404
  feast, 328
  Fijian officers, 323, 329
  firearms, 328
  first, 307
  Kwaisulia, 225
  labour trade, 252
  lance-corporal, 394
  Maasina Rule, 18
  Maka, 435
  outstations, 398, 435
  Pacific War, 451
  patrols, 321, 334, 366, 395, 396, **397**, 381, 391, 395, 396, 397, 406, 446
  RAMSI, 27
  recruitment, 306, 329, 330, 330, 363, 397, 407
  regulations, 331
  retribution for death of Bell and Lillies and police, 410
  sergeant, 396
  sergeant-major, 435
  sub-inspector, 334, 388, 396, 429
  tax-collecting, 381, 382, 407
  'Tension Years', 23, 25
  Tulagi, 334
  Western Solomons, 18, 319
  'Aoke, 314, 320, 323, 330, 331, 370–71, 388, 391, 392, 393, 394–95, 396
poliomyelitis *see* diseases
Polk, George W., 452
Polynesia, 4n5, 173
  demography, 430
Polynesian Outliers, 4, 74, 81, 85, 429
Polynesians, 117
Poole, Rev. A. 172
Pope, Billy, 349, 373
porpoise teeth as wealth, 49, 55, 59, 60, **60**, **61**, 76, 92, 196, 215, 277, 348, 391, 393
Port Adam, 95, 96, **98**, 124, 204, 206, 208, 217, 218, 228, 229, 275, 288, 304, 305, 349, 389
Port Douglas, Qld, 149
Port Moresby, PNG, 29
Potts, Serg. John, 169
Pou, South Malaita, 199, 207
Pratt, Rev. F., 142
Presbyterian
  New Hebrides, 243, 253, 261
  Queensland, 140, 142, 150, 158, 161, 165, 166, 167, 168, **168**, 169, 169n98, 273

Pritt, Rev. Francis Drinkall, 157, 158, 164, 165
Proserpine, Qld, 157
Pululahu, 175, 199, 208
Purdy, F.J., 149
Pym, Lieut., 97

Qaqae (Kakwai), 215
Qualagau (Kwalagau), 317
Queensland, 28, 29, 33, 85, 109
    Ambulance Service, 31
    Commissioner for Pacific Islanders, 31
Queensland Christian missions
    Anglican, 151–52, 157–66, 170
    Baptists, 169
    Churches of Christ, 166
    London Missionary Society, 171
    other missions, 166–70
    Presbyterian, 167–69
    Salvation Army, 169
    See also Queensland Kanaka Mission; Selwyn Mission
Queensland Kanaka Mission, 28, 35, 144–50, **146**, 199, 232–48, **244**, **246**, 261–63
    Malaitan baptisms, 177
    See also South Sea Evangelical Mission
Queensland labour trade, 94, 95, 103, 113 Graphs 1 & 2
    ancestral religion preserved, 196, 325, 390
    Christianity, 139–71, **158**, 179, 183
    culture, 106, 109, 133, 134, 176, 180, 196, 337, 340
    deportation, 248–59, 302, 303, 337
    diseases, 323, 431
    education, 179, 186, 206, 459
    ex-Queensland labourers, 176, 178, 201, 206, 207, 210, 212, 213, 214, 215, 219, 221, 230, 232–59, 258, 265, 266, 267, 268, 269, 272, 273, 275, 279, 281, 283, 284, 292, 294, 295, 296, 319, 346, 454
    farms, 109
    firearms, 125, 125n97, 306, 322
    Government Agents, 94, 123, 234, 238, 239, 249, 305, 310, 334
    illegality, 93, 98, 103, 112
    mortality, 121, 123, 132, 133, 311, 431
    oral testimony, 12, 29, 136, 291, 419
    Pacific Islanders' Fund, 161, 165, 166, 169, 252
    Peri voyage, 103, **104**
    plantations, 2, 33, 118, **118**, **138**, 144, 144n10, 145, 148, 149, 150, 153, 154, 155, 161, 164, 166, 213, 258, 266, 267, 268, 269, 345
    Polynesian Labourers Act, 97
    ramo, 390
    ships, 112
    statistics, 83, 86, 101, **102**, 110, 113 Graphs 1 & 2, 119, **153**, 177, **177**, 309
    time-expired labourers, 339
    trade boxes, 124
    violence, 308–09, 312, 327
    voyages, **115**, **116**
    wages, 112, 120
Queensland Pijin English *see* Pijin English
Qui (Kwai), Jacky, 311
Quibala *see* Kwaibala
Quiramoo (Kwairamo), 251

Raatalo, 242
Rabaul, PNG, 29
racism, 111
Rafe, Harry, 398, 438
Raitalo (Taloanimae), 436
Rakwane, 31, 32, 50, 127, 195, 438
Rambootan, Henry, 245

ramo (*lamo, namo*), 7, 67, 69, 127, 204, 208, 299, 310, 311, 320, 324, 356, **357**, 364, 367, 390, 391, 392, 408, 435, 436, 438, 445, 459
Ramofolo, of Fuaga, 217, 223, 225
Ramofolo, of Mangonia, 218
Ramo`alafa, Corp. Beni, 452
Randell, Nigel, 95
Rarasu, 314
Rarata Islet, 245
Ravai, NMP Malakai, 423
Redlands, Qld, 159
Reef Islands, 6, 44, 104, 203, 304n8
Regional Assistance Mission to Solomon Islands, 23, 27, 29
regionalism, 21–22, 35, 39, 46–54, 74–76, 80
Rehe, 175
Remnant Church, 454
Rennell Island, 4, 103, 250, 303, 304n8, 427, 441
Renton, John (Jack), 94–95, 94n25, **95**, 98, 99, 128
Resident Commissioners *see* government officers
Resident Magistrates *see* government officers
Rewa, Fiji, 172
Reynolds, Rev. Frederick C.T., 170
Rhodes, F., 94
Rini, Snyder, 27
Rivers, Archdeacon Arthur, 159
Roas Bay, South Malaita, **72**, 199, 204, 206, 207, 208, 209
Robertson, G.H., 414
Robinson, Mary Goodwin, 142, 150, 152, 153, 154, **154**, 155, 156, 165, 180, 214
Rockefeller Foundation, 424
Rockhampton, Qld, 128, 152, 158, 160, 163, 164, 234
Rohinari, 186, 267, 353, 355, 356, 357, 359, 360, 384, 388, 390, 392

Rokera (Ariel Harbour), 87, 199, 386, 426, 428
Ross, Harold, 80
Rouillac, Fr Pierre, 355
Roviana, New Georgia, 91, 304
Rowley, Mr, 453
Royal Australian Navy, 450
Royal Navy Australia Station, 91, 96–98, 312
Royal New Zealand Air Force, 453
Royalist Harbour *see* Waisisi
Rua Sura Island, Guadalcanal, 87, 355
Rubella *see* German measles
Ruddell, L., 243
Ruddell, Mrs, 150, 271, 277
Ruddell, Richard, 150, 239, 240, 271, 277, 282
Russell Islands, 43, 55, 323, 334, 342, 349, 350, 373, 374, 375, 414, 457

Sage, Rev. Charles, 154, 156, 209n60, 213, 214, 216, 323n76
Sage, Rev. Walter H., 209, 213, 323n76
sago palms, 53, 414
Salaimanu, Rev. Nat
Salekana, **31**
Salvation Army, 140, 169, 170
Samarai, PNG, 29, 273
Samo, 204
Samoa *see* German Samoa
San Cristobal *see* Makira
Sandars, George Eustace, 429, 433, 435, 443
Sandiford, Qld, 168
Sango, Fataleka, **30**
sango performances, 443, **444**
Santa Catalina, 90
Santa Cruz, 4, 27, 44, 103, 303, 303n7, 304n8
Santa Ana, 90, 125
Santa Ysabel *see* Isabel Island

Sapibuana, 198
Sasai, Rev. Sam, 387
Savo Island, 43, 55, 126, 316, 457
Sayven, Alex, **157**
Sa`a, South Malaita, 2, 91, 104, 112, 173, 175, 186, 198, 199, 201, 203–10, 217, 228, 266, 275, 304, 305, 306, 323n76, 432
Schwieger, Frederick, 240, 242, 243
Scott, Michael, 12, 13, 34, 431
Searle, Miss, 263
Second Word War *see* Pacific War
Seiga, 352
Selwyn, Bishop George, 192
Selwyn, Bishop John, 172
Selwyn Mission, Mackay, 142, 150, 153, **154**, 155, 156, **156**, **163**, 165, 166, 167, 215
    Malaitans at, 130, 176, 177, 214, 253
    See also Robinson; Sage, Charles
Senale, John, 271
Serbas, Barnabas, 211
Seventh-day Adventist, 34, 191, 196n25, 231, 254, 293, 353, 354, 383, 428
Sexton, T.W., 451
sexuality, 73, 92
Shadrach, **264**
shell wealth, 55n31
    See also bata
Shemuele, 452
shipping routes, 88 Map 7, 89
ships
    Advent Herald, 384
    Alfred, 90, 94
    Ariel, 309n35, 310
    Auki, **379**, 448
    Australian, 90
    Belema, 328
    Bobtail Nag, 94, **95**, 128
    Borealis, 308, 310, 326
    Carl, 104
    Christine, 126, 305, 314
    Clansman, 265
    Dancing Wave, 378
    Daphne, 185, 243, 244, **245**, 246, 247, 248, 254, 266, 267, 269, 270, 271, 272, 273, 274, 275, 279, 280, 283, 353
    Doris, 330
    Espérance, 89
    Evangel, 185, 213, **245**, 266, **268**, 269, 299, 323n76, 355
    Fearless, 178, 308, 311, 311n41
    Hallie Jack, 95
    Hashemy, 94
    Helen, 104
    Helena, **114**, 115m, 124, 308, 310n38
    Hygeia, 401, 423
    HMAS *Adelaide*, 312, 407
    HMAS *Biloela*, 407
    HMS *Basilisk*, 103, **104**
    HMS *Cambrian*, 225, 312, 317
    HMS *Curaçoa*, 303, 304
    HMS *Dido*, 96, 97, 98, 103
    HMS *Goldfinch*, 303, 304n8
    HMS *Havannah*, 9, 96, 98 Map 8
    HMS *Prometheus*, 312
    HMS *Renard*, 94
    HMS *Royalist*, 124, 204, 304
    HMS *Sealark*, 322, 326
    HMS *Sparrow*, 307, 311
    HMS *Swallow*, 88
    HMS *Torch*, 225, 226, 326, 327
    Ivanhoe, 262, 272, 284
    Janet Stewart, 308, 310, 326
    Jeanne d'Arc, 355, 359
    Lahloo, 242, 307
    Lochiel, 124
    Madeline, 8
    Mala II, 448
    Malekula, 258
    Marie, 308
    Meg Merrillies, 308
    Minota, 308
    Moresby, 243, 270

Morinda, 450, 451
Nukulau, 96, 103, 104, 226, 227n122, 311, 311n42
Para, 308
Plato, 95, 97
Ranadi, 407
Recherche, 89
Renard, 94, 95
Roderick Dhu, 236
Royal Endeavour, 322n76, 350, 373
Savo, 308
Sea Breeze, 171
Southern Cross, 166, 175, 185, 198, 203, 204, 206, 207, 208, 211, 213, 215, 219, 211, 239, 240, 269, 353, 389, 432, 453
St Jean-Baptiste, 89
Sybil II, 250, 327
Sydney Belle, 125, 125n97, 213, 239
Young Dick, 283, 308, 310
Verdelais, 355
William Manson, 232, 234, 235, 237, 238
Shlomowitz, Ralph, 122, 133
Shortland Islands, 4, 34, 56n33, 103, 302, 304n8, 313, 321, 399, 450, 451
Siakulu (Liakulu), Lizzie *see* Telegsem
Sikaiana Atoll, 42, 74, 81, 90, 303, 304n8
Sili, Joe, 319
Simanhu, 320
Simbo (Eddystone) Island, 90, 305, 331
Simmons, Rev. Robert, 387
Simson, M.T., 420
Sinalagu Harbour, **62**, **68**, **258**, 272, 275, 283, 311, 325, 344, 393, 398, 407, 408, 409, 452
Singhalese (Sri Lankan), 117
Sio Harbour, 271
Siota, 193, 209n61, 211, 218, 221, 239, 240, 282, 304, 451, 130

Sipolo, Stephen, **264**, 434n74
Sipolo, Thomas, 267, 272, 283
Sirifa, 398
Siru, 438
Small Malaita (Maramasike), 2, 3, 41, 48, 67–68, 87, 89, 92, 178, 187, 398
    Anglican, 140, 176, 193, 196, 198, 199, 203–10, 213, 221, 254, 266, 294, 323, 355, 387, 425, 454
    Catholic, 355, 356, 425
    Christianity, 140, 179, 213, 221, 228, 298
    demography, 413, 429, 432
    economy, 414, 418, 436
    ex-Fiji labourer settlements, 175
    government, 389, 391, 436
    headman, 438
    labour trade, 104
    Lau links, 50, 59, 76, 80, 95, 112, 127, 204, 206, 208, 209, 218, 275, 296, 399
    leadership, 67, 294
    Makira links, 76, 92
    native court, 441
    Pacific War, 452
    porpoise hunting, 196
    QKM-SSEM, 178–79, 275, 296, 298
    Ulawa links, 206, 295, 323, 355
    `Are`are links, 76, 92
smallpox *see* diseases
Smith, Sydney Mercer, 239
Sogavare, Manasseh, 25
Solomon Islands Planters' Association, 380
Sooquow, 237
Sori, Charlie, 281
Sori, Enoch, 281
South Africa, 239, 364
Southern Cross Log, 83, 100, 142, 201, 240
Southey, John, 149

South Sea Evangelical Church, 28, 261
South Sea Evangelical Mission, 1, 6, 13 Map 10, 28, 34, 35, 210, 261–300, 261, **263**, **270**, **276**, **282**, **349**, 359, **386**, **400**, 426 Map 11, **446**
  beginnings, 265–74
  Bita`ama, 277–80
  education, 349, 352, 403, **403**, **425**, **426**, 427, 439
  indigenous clergy, 359
  industrial Christianity, 267, 350
  Kwai, 199, 281–84
  land acquisition, 190, 348, 388
  leadership, 265, 267, 284, 293, 323, 323n76, 333
  Maasina Rule, 17, 459
  networks, 201, 230
  Ngongosila, 199, 281–84, **284**, 344
  Onepusu, 177, 275–77, 359, 345, 384
  Pacific War, 453
  relations with
    Catholics, 353
    Melanesian Mission, 213, 216, 227, 265, 353, 354
    SDA, 353
  ships *see Daphne*; *Evangel*
  South Malaita, 178–79, 209, 275, 296, 298, 356
  statistics, 187n8, 388
  Talafaina, 279
  theology, 145–46, 188, 261, 263, 294, 370
  trade stores, 418
  women as leaders, 284–85
  See also Abu`ofa; Deck; labour trade; Malayta Company; Malu`u; Queensland Kanaka Mission; South Sea Evangelical Church; Young; `Oloburi Harbour

Spriggs, Matthew, 54, 54n29
St Barnabas College *see* Anglican Church
Stanley, Sir Robert, 19, **19**
Stanton, Bishop George H., 152
Steley, Dennis, 34
Stevens, Frank J., 168
Still, Rev. John, 203
Stone-Wigg, Canon John, 159
strangers, 66n43
Strathern, Marilyn, 285
Studd, A.H., 400
Sua, Peter, 127
Subongi (Coleridge Bay), 273
Suemai, 311
Suiasi, 394
Suina`o, 390, 391, 436
Suiwa Village, 312
Sula, 320
Sulufou, **61**, 94, 128, 129, 130, 155, 216, 226, 320, 387
Supone, Martin, 147
Suraina, 218, 272
Surioa, Isikiel, **386**
Surville, Jean-François-Marie de, 88–89
Suto, Peter, 280, 283
Sutoti, 241
Sutou, Moses, 267
Suu`aba Bay, 50, 51, 56, 91, 112, 296
Suva, Fiji, 80, 126, 171, 172, 173, 392
Su`u Harbour, 39, 271, 273, 274, 348, 352, 370, 371, 373, 374, 376, 378, 394, 398, 402, 414
  hospital, 420
Su`upaina Bay, 87, 209
Svensen, Oscar, 60, 125
Swanson, C.F., 393
Sydney, NSW, 29, 89, 94, 96, 130, 147, 150, 151, 152, 219, 234, 239, 240, 244, 247, **268**, 270, 305, 307, 345, 355, 375, 450, 451

taboos, 3, 64, 66, **68**, 77, 81, 82, 134, 135, 136, 189, 194, 196, 201, 284, 286, 287, 288, 289, 291, 293, 297, 310, 325, 343
Taga, 223
Taiboo, 283
Taiwan, 4, 43
Takataka (Deep Bay), **52**, 267, 335, 360, **417**, 440, 452
Takwa, 427, 428
Tala, John, 170
Talafaina, 232, 277, 279
  See also Fo`odo
Talina, 349
Talioto, 272
Talo, Fred, 32
Taloifulia, Rev. Jack, 130, 155, 221, 226, 294, 299, 387
Tamaia, Frank, 218
Tanambogo Island, Gela, 450
Tangtalau, 387
Tanna Island, Vanuatu, 170n104, 309, 329, 438
Tara, Stephen, 204
Tarapaina, 56, 150, 186, 323n76, 353, 356, 359, 388, 392, 393, 438
Tarasol-Aurora, Charlie, 149, 271, 272, 274, 279, 280, 281, 283, 297
Tarasol-Aurora, Louisa, 271, 272, 274, 279, 283, 297, 301, 323n76, 333
Taro Blight, 445, 445n113
Tasimboko, Guadalcanal, 189
Tasmania, 96, 208
Tavangtang-Sandwich, Thomas, 149, 150n27, 272, 275, 282, 297
Tawaniahia, 209
taxation, 10, 16, 17, 18, 55, 105, 123, 129, 341, 363, 364, 379, 399, 404, 406, 407, 408–09, 413, 416, 417, **417**, 418, 424, 425, 428, 438, 439, 440, 447, 449

introduction of, 107, 123, 230, 337, 380, 381–83, 395, 397
  See also Bell
Taylor, Annie, 270
Taylor, Frederick, 388, 397, 419
Taylor, John, 100, 101, 105
technology, new, 92, 107, 119–27, 131
  magic lantern shows, 235
  voice recordings, 235
Tehara, **264**
Tehena, 208
Te Kowai plantation, Qld, 153, 154, 155
Tekinana, 241
Telegsem, Johnson, 204, 206, 207, 221, 228, 288
Telegsem, Lizzie (née Siakulu), 206, 207, 221, 288
'Tension Years', 23–28, 29, 32, 33, 36
Teoboo, Tome Toloasi, 451
territory, 62–69
  See also strangers
Tetefou, 283
Thomas, Mrs, 149, 243
Thomas, O.C. 149, 243, 247
Thompson, Rev. Andrew A., 209
Thompson, John, 166, **167**
Three Sisters Islands, 55
Thurston, Sir John, 175, 305
Tikopia, 303, 304n8
Timmer, Jaap, 455
Timor, 4
Tippett, Alan, 188, 192, 197, 229, 293, 388
tobacco, 8, 92, 93, 98, 105, 107, 123, 124, 125, 126, 199, 244, 253, 254, 257, 299, 304, 313, 321, 348, 357, 374, 379, 380, 381, 382, 401, 418, 430
Toibeu, 247
Tome, Johnson, 221
Tomesulu, Jackson, 351
Tomkins, Rev. C. Warren, 158

Tonabasia, Jonah, 248
Tong, Leong, 349
Tonga, 15
topography, 2, 41–42
Torialli, **264**
Torkon, Benjamin, 156
Torres Strait, Qld, 159, 171, 431
tourism, 443
Tozer, Qld Col. Sec. Horace, 160
To`aba`ita, 51, 56, 59, 232, 296, 327, 396, 400, 413, 443, 443
    Anglican, 293
    anthropology, 34, 80, 293, 441, 443
    economy, 382
    Israel, Lost Tribes of, 455
    labour trade, 112
    Native Courts, 441
    Pacific War, 452
    QKM, 241, 293
    ramo, 436
    See also Malu`u
trade, 3, 55, 91
    goods, 91–92
    maritime, 87–93
    See also markets
Treaty of Samoa, 337
tropes, 1, 5–13, 15, 21, 23, 24, 25, 32, 35, 36, 81, 93, 95, 130, 131, 289, 310, 368, 410, 437, 449, 453, 454, 459
Truth and Reconciliation Commission Report, 28
Try (Tri), Robert, 232
Tufnell, Bishop Edward, 151
Tulagi, 80, 211, 213, 225, 230, 242, 243, 244, 246, 249, 252, 253, 257, 258, 276, 283, 296, 302, 305, 306, 307, 312, 321, 326, 328, 334, 340, 341, 344, 350, 365, 366, 371, 382, 387, 392, 394, 395, 400
Tumbulgum, NSW, 170, 170n104
Turley, F.W., 167
Turner, Rev. W.A., 155
Turu, Rev. Charles, 211
Tu`wu, Sam, 270
Tweed Heads, NSW, 148, 159, 169
Twitchell, Bishop Thomas Clayton, 173

Uguka, 217
Uhu Passage, 87, 271
Uiarai, Joe, 398
Uki ni masi (Uki), 55, 74, 76, 126, 204, 304, 306, 388, 427
Ulawa, 3, 55, 89, 91, 104, 175, 203, 206, 208, 209, 209n61, 228, 295, 323, 354, 432n69, 436
Ulufa`alu, Bartholomew, 23, 25
Upwe, Rev. James, 209, 210
urbanisation, 23–28, 33
Uru Harbour, 59, 91, 224, 225, 226, 227, 248, 258, 308, 311, 324, 325, 348, 384, 410, 447, 452
Uruilangi, 326
USA *see* Americans

Vanikoro Kauri Timber Company, 414
Vanuatu (New Hebrides), 4, 56, 83, 101, 289, 430, 431, 456, 458
    demography, 54n29
Venasio, 175
Victoria, Queen, 303
violence, 22, 131, 307–08
Visale, Guadalcanal. 53, 359, 360, 392
Vos, Capt. William, 234, 235, 236, 238
Vouza, Serg.-Maj. Jacob, 434
Vuru, 224

Waidala, 248
Waikeni, 203
Waimaku, Peter, 127
Waimasi, 218
Wairokai Harbour, 384, 423, 438, 440

Waisaki, 311
Waisele, Ratu, 329
Waite, Mr, **386**
Walade, Small Malaita, 3, 50, 59, 76, 80, 96n27, 112, 127, 173, 186, 199, 204, 206, 208, 209, 218, 228, 266, 275, 296, 305, 387, 399
Walker, John, 168
Waloaa River, 208
Walsh, Allen W., 329, 330
Walu River, Fiji, **137**
Wariehu, 228
Wate, Rev. Willie, 209
Watehou, 198
Wate'ae'pule (Wate), Joseph, 198, 203, 201, 203–04, **205**, 206, 207, 208, 209, 210, 294, 454
Watkinson, Joseph, 240, 248, 272, 275, 282, 283
Wawn, Capt. William, **117**, **154**, 155
Webber, Roger, 454
Welieke, 273, 278, 279
Western Australia, 149
Western Pacific High Commission, 18, 19, 97, 301
Western Province, 24n38
Western Solomons, 85, 91, 323
whaling, 89–93
Wheatley, NMP Hugh, 423
White Australia Policy, 29
  See also Queensland labour trade—deportation
White, Geoffrey, 34
White, Gordon, 424
White, John, 437
Whiteman, Darrell, 194
whooping cough see diseases
Williams, Rev. Percy T., 161–62, 163
Williams, Thomas A., 211
Wilson, Bishop Cecil, 22, 217, 256, 269, 354
Wilson, Colin E.J., 412
Wilson, Ellen, 215, 287, 288

wealth items *see bata*; dogs—teeth as wealth; flying-fox teeth as wealth; porpoise teeth as wealth; shell wealth
Wetherell, David, 273
Wogale, Edward, 172
women, 6, 13, 39, 56–58, 63, 69–73, **69**
  Aboriginal Australian, 447
  bisi, 73
  Fijian, 226, 311, 429
  labour trade, 101
  pollution by, 73
  seclusion of, 73
  See also *akalo keni*; *fataabu keni*; gender
Woodford, Charles, 36, 56, 119, 125, 125n97, 126, 129, 184, 210, 213, 219, 221, 225, 240, 242, 244, 248, 249, 249n54, 250, 253, 267, 270, 305, 306, 307, 312, 313, 314, 317, 320, 322, 326, 327, 337, 355, 365, 367
Woqas, Jonah, 170
W.R. Carpenter & Co., 29, 377, 413
Wunfor, 272, 275

Yandina, Russell Islands, 340, 349, 373, 378
yaws, 419, 420, 424, 430, 431
Yeppoon, Qld, 164
Young, Catherine, 144
Young, Ellen, 142n7, 146, 147
Young, Ernest, 273, 345, 348
Young, Florence S.H., 144–50, 155, 168, 213, 231, 232, 240, 242–48, 250, 263, 265, 266, 267, 269, 271, 272, 273, 290, 292, 296, 297, 298, 345, 353, 356
Young, Henry, 144
Young, Horace, 144n10, 160, 273, 345

'Adagege, 124, 127, 128, 129, 219, 220, **220**, 226, **235**, 330
'Aioo Island, 48, 124, 247, 248, 267, 268, 272, 275, 283, 284
'Aisasale, 388
'Ai'eda, east Kwaio. **58**, **68**
'Alakwale'a, 325
'Aluta River, 41, 46, 46
'Aoke, 32, 210, 230, 302, **319**, **331**, **394**
    government headquarters, 140, 185, 186, 191, 219, 229, 230, 299, 300, 314, 317, 318, 320, 321, 323, 326, 328, 332, 336, 337, 359, 363, 371, 393–95
    hospital, **333**, 423, 424
    labour, 340, 350, 447
    Maasina Rule, 17, 19
    market day, 322
    Pacific War, 450–51
    police, 329–30, **332**, 334, 391, 396, 400
    prison, 387
    residency, 331, 368, 434
    stores, 414–15, 448
'Aoke Experimental School, 20, 428
'Aoke Island, 212, 214, 244, 273, 311, 314, 316, 323, 349
'Aoke, Tom, 271
'Ara'iasi, Petero, 356, 392, 393, 436, 438
'Are'are, 7, 15, 17, 33, 39, 48, 59, 62, 63, 67, 74, 76, 77, 92
'Arumae, 283, 283n36
'Ataa Cove, 50, 51, 76, 80, 127, 128, 129, 175, 186, 199, 211, 218, 219, 225, 272, 283, 311, 312, 348, 391, 394, 396, 398, 399, 401, 438, 440, 452
'Eri'eri, 396
'Oloburi (Double Bay) Harbour, 209, 268, **268**, 269, 409, 410

www.ingramcontent.com/pod-product-compliance
Lightning Source LLC
Chambersburg PA
CBHW040319300426
44111CB00023B/2948